The Economist

YEAR BOOK

The Economist

YEAR BOOK

1992 EDITION

1991 IN REVIEW

First published by The Economist Books Ltd, Axe & Bottle Court, 70 Newcomen Street, London SE1 1YT

Distributed in the trade worldwide by Random Century Ltd,
Random Century House, 20 Vauxhall Bridge Road, London SW1V 2SA.

A catalogue record for this book is available from the British Library and the US Library of Congress
ISBN 0-7126-9867-1

Printed in Holland by Royal Smeets Offset B.V., Weert, The Netherlands

The Economist's main editorial office is at:

25 St James's Street, London SW1A 1HG

For inquiries about subscribing to The Economist please contact:

The Economist, Subscription Services Department
PO Box 14, Harold Hill
Romford, Essex RM3 8EQ
United Kingdom
Tel (44) (0)4023 81555 Fax (44) (0)4023 81211

The Economist, Subscription Department
North America, tel 1-800-456-6086
Colorado & Mexico, tel 1-303-447-9330

The Economist Newspaper Ltd
2 Jurong Port Road, Singapore 2261
Republic of Singapore
Tel (65) 264 4891 Fax (65) 264 1545

THIS YEARBOOK is designed to have a triple value. First, it is a book to browse through for an evocation of a momentous year, presented in a style and format that readers of *The Economist* will find familiar. There are essays on 1991 and its legacy, subject by subject, accompanied by articles whose worth (or misguidedness) seems to us to have outlived the week in which they were written.

Second, it is a work of reference. When, precisely, did that coup or bankruptcy happen? At what level was this or that statistic on such and such date? Who was the foreign minister of Utopia before its election last spring? (Or was it summer?) The yearbook's chronologies plot 1991's history, area by area, theme by theme, day by day. *The Economist*'s particular way of presenting the world's statistics is expanded to cover the whole year. And there is an up-to-date list of who was in power at the year's end, where and since when.

Last, this yearbook and its successors should mature as a history of *The Economist*'s view of the world. They will provide a compact solution for all those who have not got the space or desire to collect back-numbers of *The Economist*, but who cannot bring themselves to throw them away until the yellowing pile starts to topple.

The people, events, numbers, attitudes and arguments of 1991 are distilled in this book for years to come.

CONTENTS

CONTENTS

Death of a superpower

THE symbolism was exquisite. In the closing moments of 1991, Moscow time, the red flag was hauled down from the top of the Kremlin. The Union of Soviet Socialist Republics was no more. All that it represented—superpower threat, mischief-maker to the third world, torch-bearer of Marxist dogma—went with it. For decades it had been one of life's defining realities. Its demise was, on its own, enough to make 1991 a momentous year.

Death was hastened by an attempt to prolong life. The three-day putsch in August was the old guard's answer to Mikhail Gorbachev's reforms. But the coup failed because the people refused to lie down; and in the days that followed, they all turned narrowly nationalist. The Baltic states split off, without so much as a by-your-leave. Boris Yeltsin, leader of the resistance to the coup, became a distinctively Russian hero. Ukraine voted for independence. The place simply fell apart.

Out with the old

In dissolving itself, the Soviet Union proved the West's longstanding charge: that it had always been an empire, held in place by force and fear. With hindsight, though, it was not the evil empire of Ronald Reagan's fears; more the weevil empire, so riddled with internal inconsistencies that it was eventually no more than a husk. Many of those inconsistencies have started taking open form, and may thereby seem more threatening. Economic collapse, ethnic tensions, territorial and financial disputes between republics—all these are becoming the stuff of headlines, where once they had been hidden by Kremlin decree. The rest of the world will have to come to terms with this new, open, instability, and do what it can to help. But that is for 1992, and many years beyond.

For other bits of the old empire, 1991 was a year to bid farewell to with relief. In economic terms, Eastern Europe had a difficult time. Depending on which figures you cite (cite, note; you should not believe any of them), real output fell in Poland, Czechoslovakia and Hungary; slumped in Bulgaria and Romania; and collapsed in Yugoslavia. Inflation was, by western standards, awful, though at least it was being slowed. That other reality of a market economy, unemployment, was high, and rising: more invisible boot than invisible hand.

Marx rebuffed

For the time being, most East Europeans see these pains as unavoidable, and necessary. But that stoicism will not last for long, which is why most East European governments have gone for the "big bang" approach to economic reform. In 1991 they completed the freeing of prices, cut public deficits a bit more, and got some grip on monetary expansion. Unfortunately, the area where they made least progress is the one where most is needed: privatisation. Until it is clear who owns the old state industries, basic notions like profit and loss cannot act as a guide to prosperity. The delays over privatisation in 1991 were for apparently plausible reasons: a desire not to be ripped off by buyers (especially former communists), the difficulty of deciding which tier of government should get the money from selling state assets, and so on. Plausible or not, the delays were ominous; in some cases, they may prove fatal.

There was one other kind of notable delay in the dialectical progress towards capitalism. In a few countries in 1991, some old men chose not to see the obvious. Fidel Castro marched on towards socialism, even though his island ran out of petrol and Cubans were queueing for sugar. That great and venerable leader, Kim Il Sung, kept North Korea in thrall; pitiable, were it not for the evidence that his country was close to having a nuclear bomb. And the leaders of a quarter of mankind did not loosen their one-party hold on China. Economically, though, they mattered less and less. Away from Beijing, the Chinese are taking to commercial life as surely as did their compatriots in Taiwan, Hong Kong and Singapore decades earlier. The fastest-growing economy in the world was almost certainly the province of Guangdong, where real output is doubling every five years.

So the biggest waves in 1991 came from the unMarxist tide that began in the 1980s. The beach those waves were heading for is clearly western—free markets and free elections—which would normally be taken as the triumph of western pluralists. Yet the curious thing about 1991 was just how untriumphant the old pluralists were. For most of the year, they were downright glum.

This was doubly odd, considering how 1991 began. In the Gulf, allied forces continued their build-up, while at

Might rebuffed

the UN the Security Council achieved unprecedented unity in authorising the use of force to evict Saddam Hussein from Kuwait. When threats failed to budge that bully, the allies struck. Devastatingly. Six weeks of bombing were followed by just four days of ground war, and then it was all over. The western allies lost fewer than 200 men, Stormin' Norman passed into the language along with Scuds and Patriots, and stockmarkets had some heady days. Dictators, it seemed, had gone ex-growth.

The battle for Kuwait was won. The war, however, was not. This was largely because nobody could agree on what "the war" was for. Iraq was driven from Kuwait, but Mr Hussein survived. Some of those who had been most critical of using any force started saying that too little had been used, that the allies should have gone on to take Baghdad. All the old tangles in Iraq—the Kurds in the north, the Shias in the south—were still there, though the allies did manage to provide some psychological reassurance for the Kurds. As for the even older tangles in the wider Middle East, they too did not suddenly yield before the allies' triumph.

In time, they may. Certainly it is possible to trace a link from the Kuwait battlefields to the polished tables of Madrid, where in November almost all the parties involved in the Arab-Israel dispute gathered to talk about peace. But there were other forces at work, such as America's refusal to guarantee some credits that Israel needed to finance another consequence of the dissolving Soviet Union: the arrival of 120,000 Jews in 1991, on top of the scores of thousands who had already come. And the high hopes in Madrid were quickly lowered by more familiar realities, as the parties bickered over where to meet next and what to talk about. The Middle East is still an unforgiving place, where memories are measured in millennia.

An economist's lag, a politician's catastrophe

Time is what the world felt short of in 1991. The main reason why the mood turned from triumph to gloom was economic: the motor of the world, the 24 rich economies belonging to the Organisation of Economic Co-operation and Development, was more sluggish, and for longer, than people expected it to be. In December 1990 the OECD forecasters thought that real GNPs would grow by 2.0% in 1991; a year later, with six to nine months of data to go on, they had scaled back to 1.1%. They had also turned gloomier about 1992.

This view was shared, increasingly openly, by national politicians. None of them took comfort from it, least of all George Bush and John Major. Both were facing elections in 1992, and both were being told by opinion polls that rising unemployment and squeezed incomes were making them unpopular. Both had expected their economies to recover in mid-1991, and the statistics show that that was indeed what happened. But the pace of growth was so slow that it made little impression on public opinion, whether in the boardroom or in the shops. Whereas previous American recoveries had seen GNP growth averaging 6% at an annual rate, the recovery in 1991 managed an annualised 1½%. Something had gone wrong.

Quite what that something was became a matter of hot debate. Uncertainty, some said, and indeed there was enough of that in 1991. The Gulf saga caused oil prices to yo-yo, and kept people from travelling. The future of world trade was left in doubt as the Uruguay round of GATT talks again failed to meet its deadline for completion. But "the future is highly uncertain" is a perennial cliché; it could not explain all the dashing of economic hopes in 1991.

A better clue lay in the way that governments, companies and individuals had all borrowed heavily in the 1980s. Their burdens of debt changed their priorities. The new concern of companies and households was to save, not spend; to repay debt, not to take on any more. As for governments, some were able to react to a cyclical slowdown in a classically counter-cyclical style, by increasing their borrowing. This happened in most of Western Europe, particularly in Germany and Britain. But it happened hardly at all in the United States, where the Reagan boom-year deficits made it much harder, politically as well as financially, to contemplate any big expansion of borrowing to get out of a slump. And in Japan, which saw a marked slowdown in GDP growth during 1991, the government was reluctant to use the public-sector surplus it took so long to build up after the big deficit years of the 1980s.

So has borrowing binge been replaced by credit crunch? The alliteration alone ensured that this argument attracted attention in 1991. To say that banks will not lend money sounds implausible; that is their job, after all. But there was some truth in the claim, because the banks had lost so much on their earlier lending and were turning cautious.

Too late, said some critics, looking at the list of egregious errors that came to light in 1991. Donald Trump, Asil Nadir (founder of Polly Peck), and Robert Maxwell were hyped-up borrowers who got away with behaviour that creditors and accountants should have spotted much sooner. The same was true of Bank of Credit and Commerce International, which was closed in July, after fraud that may total $20 billion. And in Japan some of the biggest names in broking and banking were caught doing things that ranged from the illegal to the dishonourable. Communism may have had a terminally hard time in 1991, but it was not a good year for capitalism either.

Contents

LEADERS

As we reported then

Don't save this face

JANUARY 12TH   **The time the United Nations had granted Saddam Hussein to negotiate his way out of Kuwait was running out. With some Europeans wavering, we reviewed the powerful case for war**

BENJAMIN FRANKLIN said there never was a good war, or a bad peace. He was half right. Nobody can be glad that, after the failure in Geneva, the stalemate in the Gulf seems this week to be slipping miserably into war. The result of all wars is men killed, maimed or made insane by horror. This time the horrors may include ballistic missiles, chemical weapons, even—if Iraq is foolish enough to lash out at Israel—nuclear ones too. Can any cause be great enough to justify the slaughter?

The answer is Yes. There is no good war, but sometimes a bad peace can be worse than war itself. A peace that left Saddam Hussein unchallenged in Kuwait would be trebly bad. It would mean sacrificing a high principle: no country has the right to overrun and annex another. It would mean abandoning a great interest: secure access to the oil of the Gulf, on which the prosperity of the whole world has come increasingly to depend. And, because of those two things, it would mean accepting a peace that was no peace at all, merely the lull before a bigger explosion.

Until this week the world had assumed that Iraq's dictator would take some sort of step before January 15th to prevent the outbreak of war. After that day, if his army remains in Kuwait, Resolution 678 of the United Nations Security Council allows any nation, at Kuwait's request, to remove him by force. It is still possible, as the last few days trickle away, that he will come up with something: a partial withdrawal, or a firm promise to give up his conquest in return for something else. He may be willing to offer to the secretary-general of the United Nations or some other mediator what pride stopped him from offering the United States. But the meeting in Geneva between James Baker and Tariq Aziz left few grounds for hope. America's secretary of state came from Washington. Iraq's foreign minister acted as if he had come from Krypton.

The representative of a country that decided six months ago to delete another, and steal everything in it, refused to accept a letter from America's president on the ground that its language was impolite. Mr Aziz claimed to stand for peace and justice, then announced that if war started Iraq would attack Israel—regardless of whether Israel was a party to the war or not. He insisted, despite the evidence of geography and everything else, that Iraq had destroyed Kuwait to liberate Palestine. But his master in Baghdad did not even allow him to say out loud that Kuwait could be swapped for the West Bank. Indeed, Mr Aziz refrained from uttering the word Kuwait once during his Geneva press conference. "Linkage" between the West Bank and Kuwait was always a preposterous notion. Now it looks as if it may not be on offer anyway.

Because of the long gap between the crime and its punishment, the world's indignation about the stealing of Kuwait has

given way since August to anxiety about the cost of a war to retrieve it. But it is important to remember the simple principle that would make such a war legal and just. Since August Mr Hussein has minted a treasury of lies designed to show that Kuwait was an artificial country—corrupt, selfish, undemocratic and undeserving of an independent existence. The truth is quite different.

Kuwait was no democracy. But by the standards of the Arab world it was a decent place, tolerantly run, with a freeish press and livelier politics than any Mr Hussein could ever countenance. An artificial state? Tiny, yes, but no more artificial than the other nations of the modern Middle East—Jordan, Lebanon, Syria, Iraq itself—which were given their borders by former colonists. Iraq's claim to Kuwait rests on the argument that the Ottomans ran it as part of the province of Basra. Britain made it independent, which is how Kuwaitis themselves wished it to stay until Mr Hussein turned it violently into a colony again last August.

Foolishly poor, generously rich

Mr Hussein's second great lie is that he invaded Kuwait on behalf of the Arab poor. But Iraq itself is richer in oil than Kuwait was, and would have been prosperous too had Mr Hussein not poured its riches away in eight years of futile war against Iran. Some Kuwaitis made their country unpopular by flaunting their wealth, but their government was a prudent manager of its oil. It kept the price low in order to maximise its share of the market and protect its investments in the world economy—not, as Mr Hussein says, because it was part of a Zionist conspiracy to impoverish Iraq. As for being selfish, Kuwait in its heyday dished out a higher share of its GDP (4% in 1982) in foreign aid than any other country, and gave jobs to many thousands of migrant workers.

Kuwait, though, was a small country. Is it worth fighting a big war, in the name of an abstraction like sovereignty, in order to restore it? The world has come to live with other conquests: China has not been driven from Tibet, Turkey from northern Cyprus, Israel from the West Bank and Gaza. These continued occupations are, and should be, deplored. They do not invalidate the principle that the acquisition of territory by conquest is inadmissible. That principle is no pious abstraction, but a practical rule that helps to keep the world safe.

This is the principle at stake in the Gulf. But there is an interest, too, in which the whole world has a share. It would be nice to believe that Mr Hussein's ambitions would have ended after digesting Kuwait; or that, having seen how badly his invasion had fared, he would learn his lesson and behave better in the future. The evidence suggests otherwise. Mr Hussein's invasion of

Iran in 1980 exposed his taste for *Lebensraum* to the east. The subsequent war went disastrously wrong: it took Iraq eight years of fighting and lavish outside help to save itself from ignominy. And yet, far from learning to behave better, he waited only two years before starting all over again—this time sending his armies south, into Kuwait. The full extent of his other territorial ambitions is uncertain, but the explicit aim of the Baathist ideology on which his regime is founded is to sweep away "artificial" borders (plus, naturally, Israel) and unite the Middle East behind himself. Unlike previous Baathists, Mr Hussein has built a war machine that might, if left unchecked, be able to make this dream come true.

Hard luck Middle East? No: hard luck world. It would be dishonest to pretend that the world can think about the Gulf without thinking about the three-letter word that belongs to it. Ever since Iraq invaded Kuwait, good-natured people have felt queasy about fighting merely for the sake of oil. They should reconsider that "merely".

Oil is not just any commodity, it is the fuel on which almost every country's hopes for growth and prosperity rest, and will continue to rest until they embrace nuclear power or some technology not yet invented. This war is not being fought for the oil companies or to keep oil "cheap"—no war came after the oil shocks of 1973 and 1979—but to keep the hands of a ruthless blackmailer off the windpipe of the world economy. With Kuwait, Mr Hussein already controls 19% of the world's oil; with Saudi Arabia he would have 44%. Mr Hussein says openly that he needed to control Kuwait in order to control the price of oil, in order to pay for his war machine, in order to ... This is an impossible position for the world to accept, and no shame attaches to acknowledging the vital self-interest at stake. It would be shameful to conceal it.

How to define victory

This is the case for war, and the test against which any outcome in the Gulf must be measured. First, Kuwait must be restored, to uphold the principle of sovereignty. Then the threat Mr Hussein poses to the Gulf must be removed. The best way to remove the danger would be to remove Mr Hussein from power; but at the very least he should be made to emerge deflated from his attack on Kuwait. These aims would certainly be achieved by war. It would be far better if they were achieved peacefully—with a last-minute decision by Mr Hussein to comply, to the letter, with the demands of the Security Council.

Because the indictment against Iraq is so clear, the world's response to August's invasion has until now been exemplary. For nearly half a year the Soviet Union and United States have walked in tandem. The Security Council has passed 12 resolutions against Iraq, demanding its full and unconditional departure from Kuwait. Iraq refuses to go, so war is logically the next stop—barring that last-minute failure of Iraqi nerve. Yet there is also another possibility, one even more dismal than the prospect of fighting. It is the possibility of Mr Hussein keeping his nerve and the alliance cracking first.

Given the balance of forces, political and military, it seems extraordinary that Mr Hussein could stare down the powerful coalition massed against him. No fundamental loss of will is evident among the alliance's chief members. George Bush, whose army would shoulder the main burden of fighting, seems grimly ready for war. Most of Iraq's neighbours, who would suffer directly if it happened, believe the price worth paying. The wavering is in Europe, and notably in France. There the conviction has grown that Mr Hussein must be offered some way to escape from Kuwait without embarrassment. Blessed, sometimes, are the peacemakers. Yet it is clearly not possible both to save Mr Hussein's face and to deflate the menace he poses in the Gulf.

If face-saving is bad enough in itself, the means by which the French hint they might achieve it are worse. The idea is to pretend to believe the third of Mr Hussein's great fibs: his claim to have invaded Kuwait for the sake of Palestine. This "linkage" is a more blatant lie than his argument that he invaded Kuwait because it was "artificial", or on behalf of the Arab poor. It only occurred to him to utter it ten days after the invasion, when he understood that his adventure was turning sour. But it is also, alas, a powerful lie.

Ever since the creation of Israel, Arab dictators in trouble have found it expedient to wrap themselves in the flag of Palestine, usually—remember Nasser and 1967—to the detriment of the Palestinians themselves. Yet linkage, if it works at all, works in reverse. Israel's intransigence on the West Bank comes partly from religious motives, mainly from the fear that the Arab world will never accept Israel's presence. By invading Kuwait and threatening daily to douse Tel Aviv in chemical fire, Mr Hussein simply makes that fear stronger.

It is sobering, so soon after the collapse of Eastern Europe's dictatorships and the ending of the cold war, that fighting men are once again strapping on their boots and preparing for battle. Half a year ago, many people in the democratic and newly democratising world had begun to hope that war had become obsolete, a shameful anachronism. That was before August 2nd, when Saddam Hussein's army shot its way into Kuwait. Mr Hussein has a few more days to return peacefully what he stole by force. If he does not, the fighting men can evict him from Kuwait, their consciences clear.

A Lutine peal at Lloyd's

MARCH 9TH   Three dreadful years of losses were shifting Lloyd's bedrock—the unlimited liability of wealthy members. Time to admit that the system's day had passed

WHEN Richard Rogers was hired to design the ultra-modern Lloyd's building in the City of London, his brief was to provide a space easily adaptable to the notorious ups and downs of the insurance industry. Little did those who commissioned the building guess that, within five years of its completion, Lloyd's would be in danger of expiring altogether—and only partly because of bad times in the insurance business. The biggest reason Lloyd's risks extinction is that the 303-year-old market's most honoured tradition—the unlimited liability of its investors—no longer works. The sooner it grasps this, the more of the skills and reputation which Lloyd's has gained over the centuries will survive.

Lloyd's investors are its 26,500 "names"—those rich, mostly

British individuals who pledge their wealth to back the 360-odd underwriting syndicates which carry out their business from booths on the market's floor. During the 1970s, when Britain's top personal-tax rates were as high as 98%, Lloyd's appealed to names as a giant tax haven because underwriting profits were practically tax-free. Now that the top rate is only 40%, a big attraction of Lloyd's has gone. Moreover, Lloyd's is now incurring losses at a life-threatening rate. This matters to more than just the names. Their market's reputation for speed and innovation has rubbed off on London's wider market in international insurance, and it has long been a champion of Britain's invisible exports.

What makes Lloyd's different from the rest of London's, and the world's, insurance industry is its notion of unlimited liability. All other insurers keep a fat cushion of reserves against future claims. Lloyd's proud boast is that every insurance policy which its syndicates sell is backed by the whole wealth of all the market's names—right down to their spats. The market's old guard argues that unlimited liability gives Lloyd's the credibility to win business against normal insurance companies. These same people assume that there will always be enough names to risk everything for profit.

Recent losses imperil that assumption. For a start, Lloyd's is now being hit by liabilities from three extraordinary years, 1988-90, of natural and man-made calamities—the fire on the North Sea's Piper Alpha oil platform, the Alaskan oil spill of the *Exxon Valdez*, the San Francisco earthquake, America's Hurricane Hugo and more. Other liabilities date back further. Asbestos and pollution claims, some maturing after decades, will cost billions. Professional-indemnity insurance taken out by the executives of bankrupt American savings-and-loan institutions may reach £2.5 billion ($4.7 billion). In all, the bill for Lloyd's names in the coming five years could total £15 billion. The Lloyd's market as a whole barely broke even for 1988. For 1989 it will probably make a pre-tax loss of around £1 billion, its first loss since the 1960s. Nor does 1990 look much better.

The steady stream of names leaving the market (6,000 have resigned in the past three years) would turn swiftly into a flood were it not for the fact that nearly half are tied into syndicates with "open years"—that is, those whose liabilities are too big and vague to be settled. Many names suspect that the underwriters they backed acted negligently, or were misled by other syndicates at Lloyd's when writing reinsurance. Nearly one-fifth of all Lloyd's names are in dispute with their syndicates or each other. The mutual trust, once Lloyd's hallmark, has been damaged.

One way or another, the coming losses at Lloyd's are slowly, surreptitiously, being "mutualised", a taboo word that means the entire market will have to pick up tabs unmet by individual names—the opposite of individual unlimited liability. Those names sensible enough to have covered themselves with stop-loss policies—bought in the Lloyd's market—will, as so often at Lloyd's, merely pass their losses on to other syndicates and other names. Within 15 years, death will have claimed half of Lloyd's current names, thinning the ranks of names still further.

With a growing wave of claims about to hit a shrinking base of names, the Lloyd's establishment prays that, by the time the biggest lump of losses is called in 1992-93, today's depressed insurance premiums will have risen enough to dissuade more names from leaving. Such a prayer gambles with Lloyd's very existence. The Lloyd's task force that begins this month to look at the market's future should wake up to immediate reality and call swiftly for the end of unlimited liability for new members. That would open the gates of the market to established insurance companies or any limited company wishing to risk its capital.

Current names would still have to shoulder, and share, the burden of their losses. And the legal borders separating Lloyd's from the rest of London's insurance industry would quickly dissolve. But Lloyd's has a reservoir of skills and a brand that would survive such changes and help keep London a thriving insurance centre. Many big French and German insurers would cherish access to the American insurance market which Lloyd's could offer. Otherwise, ask not for whom the Lutine bell tolls. It tolls for Lloyd's.

Recessions aren't forever

FEBRUARY 9TH **Anxious to avoid panicky recourse to inflation, we took a robust attitude to the world's faltering economic growth in 1991. Our line came under ever greater pressure**

THE word "recession" was hardly used until the late 1930s. Then Americans took to it, as the way to avoid mentioning "depression" again. Now the euphemisms go further. Governments are so loth to own up to recession that the first official admission is a pretty good leading indicator that recovery is on the way. Across the world, that rule of thumb is likely to be true in 1991, provided finance ministries and central banks stay clear about the vital distinction between cyclical changes and structural ones.

Much of what is happening at the moment is cyclical. By early 1990 the OECD economies had been growing for seven years, the longest upswing since the second world war. It would have been extremely odd if they had not started to slow down; and odd, too, if the sharpest slowdowns had not been in America, Britain, Canada and Australia. The Anglophone bits of the OECD mostly be-

gan their 1982-83 recovery sooner than the rest; and their growth, relative to their past performance, was more exuberant. So they ran into supply shortages first, and had to rein back demand.

Thank goodness they did. The worst follies of post-war economic policy came in 1963-79, when governments thought they could stave off recessions at the cost of "only" slightly higher inflation. It took unemployment rates of 8% and double-digit inflation to persuade them that the easy option does not exist. The more that inflation is contained by consistent macroeconomic tightness, the less it needs periodically wrenching back.

Since the Anglophone countries are now being wrenched, their cyclical news is particularly painful. Unemployment is rising steeply, and bankruptcies with it. Industrial production has been falling, a change that has recently hit France, Italy and some of the smaller European economies as well. Yet these are statistics that look backwards and are published late, so they are not a good guide to the future. One index out this week—the Dun & Bradstreet survey of sales expectations—does consciously look ahead, and shows a sharp fall. But even that may be reflecting more the prevailing pessimism, itself born from past statistics, than any genuine sense of what comes next.

In purely cyclical terms, it is hard to see this downturn lasting long. First, because several economies are still growing strongly. They are led by Japan and Germany, which now account for one-fifth of gross world product. Second, because companies now control their stocks (inventories) much better than they did; with less to clear from their warehouses, they will cut their output less. And, third, because falling commodity prices—including the likelihood of a big drop in the oil price once the Gulf war ends—will help to increase the real value of any given amount of nominal demand without the need for a fiscal or monetary boost.

Even though much of this downturn looks cyclically familiar, wise governments will recognise the possibility that some fundamental, longer-term forces are at work, things that could turn cyclical slide into structural slump. One danger today lies in trade, another in finance.

The trading danger is plain. Great structural benefits have come from 45 years of trade liberalisation, but these are now threatened by impasse in the GATT's Uruguay round. While bombs have been blasting the Gulf, trade diplomats have been working quietly to revive that round. They may be succeeding. If they fail, though, the prospect of closed markets, throughout a world now accustomed to exporting for growth, could bring deep cuts in investment.

The structural threat from finance is harder to define, so harder to recognise and quantify. In essence, capital flows more freely around the world than it has done for a century; and, within each country, the institutions and markets that borrow and lend are freer and more accessible than ever before. Desirable though these changes have been, it would have been astonishing if they had happened without fuss: no structural change ever does. In this case the fuss has been all too human. Some borrowers have used the new freedoms to borrow too much, from lenders who lent too much.

Nominal GNP, G7 average
% increase over previous period

That does not damn the whole change. It merely means that its next phase will involve caution, particularly by lenders with burnt fingers (which means just about all of them). This caution goes by several names—credit crunch, debt deflation, credit liquidation; but whatever it is called, it could indeed make the recession worse, because recoveries usually begin with borrowed money.

All that is awkward for governments and central banks. They have grown used to starting recoveries by making borrowing cheaper. This time, they fear, it may not work. That fear, though legitimate, can easily be exaggerated. Provided financial systems really are liberalised, new lenders (and new lending channels) will appear, often absorbing the old ones along with the lessons from their failure.

For governments, therefore, the acid test of macroeconomic policy should remain one that embraces both structural and cyclical factors: the need to keep nominal demand growing at a pace that restricts the scope for both inflation and prolonged recession. That means growth in nominal GNP of 4-6% a year, compared with the 6-10% that actually occurred in the seven largest economies in 1989.

By that 4-6% yardstick, it is clear that America has been slowing too much: in the second half of 1990 its nominal GNP grew at an annual rate of less than 3%. Canada, too, has been undershooting. In both countries, interest rates have been cut—and rightly so. In Germany, by contrast, nominal GNP has been accelerating. In the third quarter of 1990 it was 9.5% up on the same period a year earlier. That is why the Bundesbank has been right to raise its interest rates. Other members of the European Monetary System have also had nominal GNP growth of more than 4-6%, so will benefit from the monetary tightening in Germany. Only if the growth in their demand falls below 4-6% would they be right to cut interest rates (provided their exchange rates can take the strain), or else to give their economies a fiscal boost.

All these judgments can be wrong, of course—which will sound wicked only to those who believe there is such a thing as perfect macroeconomic policy. The trick is not to seek perfection, but to minimise error. The greatest error today is still the one that occurs so often in a recession: to be panicked into believing that downturns go on forever, so concerted reflation is essential. They don't, and it isn't.

America's wasted blacks

MARCH 30TH   **America's greatest challenge is the poverty of its blacks. Both blacks and whites should meet it by focusing less on blackness and more on the causes of poverty**

A GENERATION ago America convulsed its society and changed its laws to free black people from discrimination. Legally and socially, no country on earth tries so hard to be free of racism. Yet no country is so obsessed by race. It infects almost every debate. George Bush makes a campaign television commercial about crime, but it features a black criminal, so he is called racist. The FBI prosecutes a cocaine-using mayor and is accused of racism because he is black. The army that fought in the Gulf was disproportionately black, so there were cries that blacks would die for a white quarrel. Car dealers are found to offer better deals to white

people than black. AIDS kills more blacks than whites. The high blood pressure of black men was blamed by a medical report on discrimination. A film director turned the Jewish judge in "The Bonfire of the Vanities" black, to avoid giving offence. Race is still America's top domestic issue.

No wonder. The average black boy is more likely to go to prison than university. His life expectancy is falling and he is seven times as likely to be murdered as a white boy. In parts of the country, a black man between the ages of 15 and 25 is more likely to be killed than was an American soldier in Vietnam. The chances are almost two-to-one that he was brought up in a father-less household. The median family income of blacks is just 56% of that of whites.

Despite all its efforts, America still has its racists. In January a national poll found that most whites think blacks are lazy, less intelligent and less patriotic than whites are. David Duke, a former Ku Klux Klan grand wizard, won almost two-thirds of the white vote in the Louisiana Senate race last year. And in one poll 29% of blacks were willing to countenance the idea that AIDS was created by whites to eradicate blacks.

Race is genetic, poverty is not

But is racism the cause of black deprivation? Historically, yes. Blacks would have been better off now if, after being shipped to America in chains, they had been allowed the same freedom to prosper as willing immigrants were. But what about today? The progress America has made in dismantling discrimination is extraordinary. A generation ago in the South, blacks could not even go to white lavatories or be buried in white cemeteries—let alone compete for good jobs or live in white suburbs. Since then blacks have got richer at almost the same rate as whites, but they have not caught up at all. In recent years they have fallen back. Is that because discrimination lingers on? Many black-rights groups claim that black deprivation is the result of continuing racism, and that reversing discrimination will rescue blacks from poverty. A growing number of black intellectuals, and white politicians, disagree. Ending what remains of racism is eminently desirable, they say, but it will do little to improve the lot of the poorest blacks.

It suits both white guilt and black anger to sustain the myth that racism is still the main problem. The irony of black power is that just as whites once used skin colour as a source of privilege, so blacks now use it as a source of entitlement. At one university, professors have demanded higher pay for black professors—because they are black. At another, black students (but only blacks) are paid for improving their grades, a Pavlovian training in the mentality of entitlement and a perpetuation of the idea of blacks as victims. Are they?

First, confront the one thing everybody avoids discussing. Deep in their minds some whites have begun to think again what their ancestors thought, that blacks are genetically inferior in the traits that count for economic success, and that this is proven by the fact that blacks have lost ground as discrimination has re-treated. Therefore, think some whites, the plight of blacks is a problem that cannot be solved. That conclusion is utterly unjusti-fied. The underclass is disproportionately black by historical ac-cident, not genetics: blacks migrated to the northern cities at an unlucky moment, just as manufacturing jobs were disappearing to take new form in the suburbs. They are trapped there by crime, drugs, unemployment and poor education.

The cultural variant on this argument holds that black family structure—more single mothers and itinerant fathers—is the source of black disadvantage. Certainly, single-parent families are commoner among blacks, are worse for children and are per-versely rewarded by the welfare system. But they are more symp-tom than cause. Rural blacks in the South stick together more.

Yet would a white child born into the same conditions as the most disadvantaged inner-city black (to a drug-taking, teenage, single mother, say) be more likely to succeed than a black? Quite possibly—but not because of present discrimination. That white can see, by looking at other whites, that he is capable of success in lots of different ways. A black can envisage success most easily as a musician or a footballer. Which is why, in recent years, policy has increasingly turned to "affirmative action" (positive discrimina-tion) in the hope that better black role models will result.

But affirmative action is a two-edged sword. It suggests to the black who gets the job, and the white colleagues he meets, that he did not get there on merit, but because of the colour of his skin. Racial resentment follows. In 1990 Jesse Helms defeated a black opponent in a Senate race in North Carolina after running televi-sion commercials showing imaginary whites being rejected for jobs because affirmative action had given those jobs to blacks. Job preferment stigmatises those who do not need help, starts a back-lash from whites and reinforces the myth of racial inferiority, the most pernicious effect of which is that blacks have believed it as much as whites. Above all, affirmative action assuages white guilt.

For some individuals, affirmative action may still do more good than harm. But the real problem is that it reaches mainly those who need it least. The chief beneficiaries of affir-mative action are university students and black businessmen, who are the blacks most likely to succeed anyway. It does not touch most poor blacks' lives. And yet it dominates the debate. Blacks need to realise that affirma-tive action cannot solve their most serious problems, whites need to remember that affir-mative action does not make it an advantage to be born black.

Two bad ideas clutter the debate. The first is black separatism, in vogue in universities (racially separate degree-ceremonies and fraternities are popular with the people most angry at apartheid) and with extreme black activists. But who can doubt that, if the two races were to "separate", the blacks would be the poorer? They live in a mainly white country, just as South African whites live in a mainly black one. Integration is the best hope for both. Black separatism is like the free East Germans choosing to rebuild the Berlin Wall.

The second bad idea is reparations. A few years ago Japanese-Americans were compensated for being interned during the sec-ond world war, and some (mostly white) people have begun to point out that blacks have yet to be compensated for centuries of slavery. In other words, for a steep sum, whites could buy the right to forget their guilt. In reality that would only increase white rac-ism and try to solve with money a problem that cannot be bribed away.

A better idea is to forget such racially minded solutions alto-gether. If America were to attack the reasons for the underclass's existence, the beneficiaries would be disproportionately black. Whites need to recognise that blacks cannot hope to prosper in any numbers while they are confined to ghettos of crime, poverty and lousy schools, and that it is society's duty to do something about it. That means the same law enforcement in inner cities that the rest of the country expects and receives. Firmness on crime is what most inner-city blacks cry out for: their life is made hell by muggers, pimps and drug dealers. (And four Los Angeles policemen beating a black man 56 times after stopping him for speeding does not count as better law enforcement.)

It means gun control, which urban blacks want, but many whites illogically hate. It means treatment, not just punishment,

16

for drug takers. It means expensive policies to lure better teachers and school managers into the cities, to build transport links to the suburbs where the jobs are, to train young people for jobs. Whites have retreated to the comfortable suburbs, whence they contribute to a city's costs but avoid paying its taxes or providing work for its underclass. Such policies are not cheap or easy, but nor is the waste of black America's talent.

Black leaders in turn need to recognise that such measures will do far more to help poor blacks than any amount of affirmative action, reparation, calls for black separation, or courses designed to teach that Socrates stole his ideas from ancient black Egyptians. Their duty is to tell blacks that although group political activism can stop discrimination, growing rich, wise and safe

is then up to the individual—to hammer home a message of homework, punctuality, saving and self-discipline, the things that helped America's immigrants get off the floor. Some black leaders already say this. Most still prefer the rhetoric of victimisation.

Unless something like this is done, America's blacks will suffer the same collapse of morale that American Indians have. In 1965 Lyndon Johnson told Congress that "If we stand passively by while the centre of each city becomes a hive of deprivation, crime and hopelessness ... if we become two people, the suburban affluent and the urban poor, each filled with mistrust and fear for the other ... then we shall effectively cripple each generation to come." A generation has passed. The crippling goes on.

Poor men at the gate

MARCH 16TH **Immigration from the newly-liberated East and from the teeming South seems set to become Western Europe's greatest problem of the rest of the decade.**

THOSE thousands demonstrating in the shadow of the Kremlin must look threatening to Mikhail Gorbachev, as he thumbs dejectedly through yet another report on the Soviet Union's economic decline. They look increasingly sinister to westerners too. Even before two boatloads of fleeing Albanians arrived on Italy's reluctant shores, it was clear that the crumbling of Europe's communist block would drive many of its citizens to seek their fortunes in the West. Once western governments began worrying about migration from east to west, they noticed that even larger numbers might want to move from south to north. Immigration, with all its uncomfortable baggage of racism and nationalism, is set to become one of the hardest issues for liberals to handle, because the old liberal preference for an open-door welcome is not going to work any more.

Already, developed countries are receiving immigrants from new places, and on an unprecedented scale. America accepted more immigrants in the 1980s than in any previous decade in its history. And immigrants of a quite different kind: in 1965 the proportion of European to non-European immigrants was nine to one; 20 years later that ratio had been reversed. The long-term consequences of the change will be huge. Today more than three-quarters of all Americans are white; by the middle of the next century that proportion may have fallen below half. Among California's schoolchildren, it already has.

The way rich countries react will depend partly on their past. America, a land built by immigrants, has a strong commitment to welcoming newcomers. Europe, by contrast, has traditionally exported people. Its southern countries—Spain, Italy, Portugal, Greece—remained net exporters well into the 1970s. Even when northern Europe began to recruit workers in Turkey, Yugoslavia and the Caribbean, the myth persisted that these were temporary guests, who might one day go back where they came from. Yet several European countries are now home to more foreigners, proportionately, than the United States. More than 8% of Britain's population and 11% of France's are foreign-born, compared with 6% of America's.

More will come. The first rush, from East-

ern Europe and the Soviet Union, has already begun, with roughly 2m people leaving there last year. As unemployment sweeps through Eastern Europe and the Soviet Union disintegrates, the numbers may continue in the low millions in each year of the 1990s. The citizens of Western Europe, already suffering from rising unemployment, are deploying troops to keep out refugees along the old Iron Curtain.

Immigrants from Eastern Europe and the Soviet Union will be easy to absorb, though, compared with what may follow. The communist countries, present and former, are lands of stable or falling populations. Given two decades of economic recovery and (harder to predict) an absence of ethnic strife, Western Europe's eastern neighbours will mostly prefer to stay at home. Even most of those who move will share with their hosts a common inheritance in terms of race, religion, education and culture. They are, after all, Europeans.

Not so most of the potential immigrants from the south. The population of the world's poorer countries is growing twice as fast as Europe's did at its peak in the late 19th century, when its huddled masses crossed the Atlantic. The population of the rich world will probably stabilise well below 2 billion, but in poorer countries the numbers will rise from about 4 billion now to more than 8 billion and maybe, in 40 years or so, to more than 12 billion. Most of those billions may prefer to stay home, but the movement of even a tiny fraction would appear to northerners as an invasion.

The greatest gap, demographic and economic, will yawn between the two shores of the Mediterranean sea. Earnest Spanish civil servants already talk of Europe's "southern flank"; the military overtones, the sense of siege, are unmistakable. For while the growth of population has started to slow down in Latin America and Asia, the lands from which most of America's latest immigrants have come, in much of Africa it is still accelerating. And though real incomes in North America are far higher than in Latin America, the gap between Africa and Europe is almost twice as great.

As Africa grows younger, Europe ages. On

the Mediterranean's southern shore, the average woman has between four and six children; on the northern shore, between one and two. Each year 1m more babies are born in the countries of north Africa than in the European Community. By 2025 a number of African countries that now seem medium-sized will have populations that equal or dwarf those of the larger countries of Europe. Turkey will have 20m more people than united Germany; Sudan as many as France; Egypt as many as Spain and Italy combined. The fastest growth will be among the young, the age group most willing to do a Dick Whittington. To a youngster in Cairo's slums, Italy will seem a land of fabulous wealth. Measured in terms of purchasing power, its living standards are four times those of Egypt's. And Egypt is rich by sub-Saharan standards.

For white liberals, brought up to believe in equal human rights and free movement of labour, the hardest thing is to recognise that the scale of migration changes the way countries react to immigrants. Today, no country in the world allows free immigration: the voters would not stand for it. As the number of aspiring immigrants grows, only tough controls will assure the safety of those black and brown workers who have already arrived. Other-

wise, all will risk persecution as gate-crashers. To minimise racism at home, many countries need to have racist controls on immigration.

Rich countries will bully and bribe poorer ones to hang on to their citizens. Aid programmes will emphasise jobs, not just investment. But trade will help more than aid. If poor countries are to boost the incomes of their spiralling numbers, they need to create jobs. Yet the most labour-intensive industries—textiles, metal manufacturing, engineering, food processing—are all ones where rich countries struggle to protect their own markets. Absurdly, those industries often survive in richer lands partly by employing cheap immigrant labour. Wise governments will let the jobs go to the countries that can do them most efficiently.

As for companies in today's industrialised world, they should stop clamouring to import workers and take their investment abroad instead. Japan has chosen to export capital rather than import labour; western companies must copy it. If, as a result, poor countries grow rich faster than the already-wealthy, all to the good. If foreign trade and investment do not narrow the gap between rich world and poor, then vast movements of humanity will try to do so instead.

From Marx to the market

MAY 11TH **Eastern Europe was transformed into the biggest crash-course in capitalism ever launched. We explained why privatisation was the central challenge**

THE task that confronts the economies of Eastern Europe is only now becoming clear. The region's political transformation, extraordinary though it has been, was just the start. A much bigger challenge lies ahead. It is not merely to build capitalism, but to build it from the wreckage of an existing, and still sort-of-functioning, economic system; to maintain support for policies that are sure to make many, if not most, people worse off, at least for a while; and, hardest of all, to disappoint hopes of a quick recovery without destroying the ambition to succeed in the years to come.

Even in eastern Germany, with all its advantages, the transition to capitalism is proving much tougher than most people expected. Since unification, output has slumped; unemployment, open and disguised, is rising fast. Even the enterprises that were the pride of the old regime, the show-piece earners of hard currency, have turned to dust. In Poland, which has undertaken the boldest reforms in the region, consumer spending fell last year (on admittedly flawed official estimates) by nearly 30% in real terms. Yet the closure of inefficient firms and the surge in unemployment that will go with it have hardly begun. The pace of reform in Hungary and Czechoslovakia has been slower. With economic restructuring there barely under way, output has already shrunk and seems certain to fall further. Except in eastern Germany, with a frowning Bundesbank thrust upon it, inflation in these countries is running at upwards of 40% a year.

The picture is not all black. Small traders have appeared from nowhere and do brisk business (which is often not captured in official figures), belying any lack of entrepreneurship. Best of all,

Eastern Europe's reforming governments, unlike the paralysed leadership of the Soviet Union, seek no illusory "middle way" between communism and capitalism. Their ambition is to create market economies on the western model as quickly as possible. That is why privatisation has become their top priority.

A year ago that could not have been taken for granted. Some western advisers believed that market economies could be created merely by freeing prices, thus abandoning the most visible sign of communist central planning; private enterprise was desirable, of course, and would come, but there was no need to rush. The region's reformers knew better. They saw that you cannot have capitalism without capitalists. Freeing prices replaces the necessary ignorance of central planners with usable information: prices are signals that tell the economy how its resources can best be used. But unless those resources—and, above all, productive assets—are privately owned, the signals will simply be ignored.

Privatisation is essential in other ways, too. When a firm's assets are owned by the state—in effect, by nobody—its managers face no financial discipline. So they borrow even though they have no efficient use for the money. Expanding credit has been a powerful engine of inflation in the region. Privatisation is not a reform that can wait for better times in Eastern Europe. Without it, better times will never come.

The reformers agree; the question is how. Throughout the region governments face a contradiction. To create a market economy, there must first be private ownership. But to create private ownership, there must first be a market—otherwise how are you to value the assets to be privatised?

One answer to this riddle is that the assets of these economies cannot be valued, and must therefore be given away (to a citizenry, mind you, that is already supposed to own them). Poland and Czechoslovakia, though disagreeing strongly over details, have decided to privatise largely by distributing assets free, or at a nominal charge, across wide sections of the population. Arguments over these schemes have caused costly delay, but once agreement is reached privatisation might happen very rapidly: working market economies might be created within months.

Hungary's government has preferred not to wait: it is privatising those assets for which it can find willing buyers. So far, this approach has achieved more, but it would take years to place most of the economy in private hands. Indeed, it may never succeed, because so many of Eastern Europe's enterprises are simply unsellable.

Many of the smallest state-owned enterprises (shops, restaurants and so on) can be—and are being—sold or leased to local buyers; single-family businesses can be sold at knockdown prices to their existing "proprietors". But lack of domestic purchasing-power means that the likeliest buyers for the biggest enterprises are mainly foreigners. Such sales, too, should go ahead, though caution here would be wise. Foreign capital brings new technology and management skills, which are vital. But an over-rapid inflow of hard currency (of which, admittedly, there is no sign yet) could fuel inflation and damage competitiveness, perhaps

causing economic reform to be abandoned before it has properly begun. Chile contracted an almost terminal case of this sickness in the early 1980s; the privatisers of Eastern Europe must take care to avoid it.

The fastest way to privatise some of the biggest and most of the smallest enterprises will be to sell them. But this will still leave the bulk of the economy's capital in the hands of the state. Most companies would continue to be insulated from market pressures and financial discipline. Eastern Europe would undoubtedly be better off than under communism, but it would be plagued by macroeconomic instability and fall short of achieving its great economic potential.

Privatisation schemes of the sort that Poland and Czechoslovakia are discussing are therefore the right way forward. Of the many rival ideas, the simplest would work best. Assign ownership of the enterprises (divided, where necessary, into competitively sized units) to a series of mutual funds, and give an equal number of shares in these funds to each adult. Since everybody would start with the same package of mutual-fund shares, the system would be fair, and seen to be.

This would not make the transition to capitalism easy. Building capitalism is bound to be painful, if only because communism was so good at assigning workers and capital to jobs that made no sense. Rapid privatisation cannot even ensure that the transition will succeed. The most that can be said is this: it is the only approach not guaranteed to fail.

The world order changeth

JUNE 22ND **There was much talk of a post-communist New World Order in 1991. We tried to describe the order and saw quite a lot of that vision survive the second half of the year**

WE SEEK, said George Bush, "new ways of working with other nations to deter aggression, and to achieve stability, prosperity and, above all, peace." He was talking of the New World Order—an epic made possible by Mikhail Gorbachev, realised by Saddam Hussein, starring the United States and shortly to be showing in a conflict near you.

There has always been a touch of show in the idea. Americans prefer to go to war to fight for a great good, rather than just against a thug. So President Bush, not much given to the "vision thing", offered America's Gulf-bound soldiers an ideal beyond curbing Iraq's nastiness. There is, however, much more to the new-order phrase than a warm feeling. The world has been shaken up momentously by the collapse of communism, and its politics have yet to set into their next mould. A New World Order of some sort will come, willy nilly. Should it, can it, be Mr Bush's version?

The new topography of world power supports him. It is dominated by one peak, where only a short while ago it featured two: around one were gathered countries that had espoused democracy and the market economy; around the other the communist command societies. Between them lay the valley of the non-aligned, which lived by playing the peaks off against each other.

The summit that remains is called the G7, the Group of Seven rich pluralist countries. It is surrounded by countries that share the same values and broadly the same approach to running their economies. Of rival peaks they see no sign. The landscape drops away from them past newly industrialised and developing countries to those that are still dirt-poor. The Soviet Union is down on

the slopes now—though Mr Gorbachev is loth to admit it and craves a place on the mountain-top.

On the foot-hills many governments are unhappy, for the game of playing-off has all but ended. Now they have just one mountain to climb. Success is measured by the same yardsticks everywhere—democracy, freedom of economic choice, prosperity and an unspoilt environment. The odd Burma or North Korea still holds out against these criteria, but each will crack in time, Albania-style, and join the mountaineers. Even in China, capitalist shoots poke up through the permafrost. For a blessed moment, world politics is driven by the power of shared values rather than by geopolitical manoeuvring.

In this landscape, the G7 get-together has replaced the superpower summit as the most influential meeting-place in the world—though it has scarcely learnt to use its power. Another gathering, too, has a much-enhanced role: the five permanent members of the Security Council of the United Nations. This is where the haves work to carry the have-littles and have-nots along with them in dealing with international wrongs. The five—America, Britain, France, China and the Soviet Union—in effect determine the decisions of the Security Council, which in turn steers the UN as a whole.

This landscape is an ideal one on which to build a system of more collective leadership—one that would lock in those winning values. To get it, however, America must want it. Mr Bush can fairly claim that those values "have their clearest expression in the US". He can also point to America's military prowess, rediscovered in the Gulf. America now knows that its options are shaped more by self-restraint than by external threat. But, having been financed in the Gulf war to the tune of $37 billion by friendly Arabs and $17 billion by Germany and Japan, it also knows that it no longer has the economic clout for hegemony.

Conceivably, America could now stand aloof from its friends and play a Palmerstonian balance-of-power game, pursuing its own interests independently, as Britain did in the 19th century. But, in peace as in war, America has always needed a loftier view of its world mission: it wants the outward expression of a nationhood founded on shared values rather than on more visceral sorts of kinship. John Kennedy's blank cheque to "pay any price . . . to secure the survival and success of liberty" is no longer on offer. Instead, there is a new readiness to share responsibility in world leadership. Hence the Bush administration's recent invitation to Europeans to get involved in the search for Arab-Israeli peace.

The threats to this Olympian landscape are great. One is that the mountain-top gods will fall out, as gods tend to. Some pundits will predict—in words of grave realism tinged with glee—that the passing of the cold war will allow the nation-state to return to its natural game of jockeying for national advantage. They will also predict that success in this game will now be measured in market share rather than in territory, that trading blocks will replace alliances, that commerce will be the continuation of warfare by other means.

The fraught, fear-dependency relationship between America and Japan certainly points that way. Books claiming that the Japanese are plotting to conquer the world still sell well in America. The French like them too. The rift between Europe and America on farm trade could yet widen nastily. If these triangular tensions get worse, Europe and the emerging North American Free-Trade Area will turn inward. Japan might even overcome Asia's post-second-world-war taboos and champion an Asian block.

So the first big essential for Mr Bush's order lies in the ungripping matter of the GATT—not just its Uruguay round and the improvements in mutual openness this will bring, but commitment by the G7 governments to obey the GATT's rules and adjudication. They will balk at this. But they have no logical excuse for making only selective curtsies to the GATT. Unlike the UN, the GATT cannot undermine the values that the G7 champions; in commerce it surely enshrines them. And what is at stake is not just an economic good—though that is huge—but the prevention of the most obvious, petty bust-up that could divide the leaders of the post-cold-war world.

G7 without oxygen

The GATT helps the New World Order in another way, too. The harder the world's one mountain is to climb, the greater the risk that militant Islam will appeal as a rival set of values and split off as a volcanic peak of its own. And the greater will be the already daunting prospect of economic migration, bringing the developing world into direct conflict with the rich one.

Open trade is, and always was, the best answer—not just so that poor countries can sell to rich ones, but also to allow the rich to help the poor through direct involvement in their economies. The multilateral providers of economic aid—the World Bank, the IMF, the UN agencies—have much to contribute. They and their sponsors have yet to adjust to the post-cold-war era. They no

longer need to give aid on the wrong terms to keep feckless regimes "in the western camp". Equally, they can offer more aid, on the right tough conditions, to countries previously considered untouchable menaces. Multilateral aid should now have a new and more constructive lease of life.

So much for economics. In politics there will be no shortage of threats for any New World Order to cope with. The scope for local conflicts is, if anything, greater in the one-peak world than before. As communism dwindles, mismatches between nations and frontiers on the world map are being violently revealed, often in ways that disturb their neighbours. Local democracy has little truck with cartographers. The cracking-up of the Soviet Union and of Yugoslavia are European examples. Africa, India and the Middle East all suffer from their share of frontier-chafing.

In richer parts of the world, groupings of states can provide an answer of sorts. They give small, released nations—such as the Baltic states will soon be—security, a voice in the world and a framework in which to pay their way. They give small trapped nations, or minorities trapped within larger ones, a court of appeal beyond the unsympathetic capital. Europe has a variety of such clubs, with differing and overlapping memberships and purposes. Many of them are still coming to terms with their new job in the one-peak world. The European Community grudgingly wonders how to adjust its 30-year dream to welcome in the rest of Western Europe, let alone Eastern Europe. NATO wonders how best to embrace or reassure some of the very countries it was set up to fend off.

Pace Margaret Thatcher, who considers all clubs that infringe the sovereignty of nations unnatural and doomed to fail, the creation of such groups does not have to be a repeat of the building of the Soviet empire. It is odd but instructive that some of the proud countries breaking loose from the Soviet system are queueing up to join the tyranny of Jacques Delors in Brussels. Two principles must apply: such groupings should be freely entered into, and open to trade.

Beyond ethnic tension, there is the world's undiminished supply of nastiness, terrorism, weaponry and tyranny. Mr Hussein's recent reminder of that showed up the new potential of the UN to help here. Russia, China and most developing countries held their peace as the UN sanctioned an American-led alliance to eject him from Kuwait and later restrain him from maltreating Iraqi Kurds. After the Saddam experience, would-be wrong-doers will think twice before they defy the UN. Would-be right-doers will be more inclined to seek its blessing. Gradually, case by case, the UN will reach into the affairs of particularly odious regimes.

Next month, in London, the heads of the G7 meet for the first time since the Gulf war showed what was possible in a changed world. They must start to pin those possibilities down. The quest is not for some collective order for its own warm-sounding sake; it is for the best way to prevent the return of petty nationalism among the rich and to establish their values worldwide. The day of American hegemony has gone. That of global democracy has not remotely come. In looking for a middle way, the G7 should remember three imperatives. First, spread wealth through open trade and conditional aid. Second, bow to international disciplines that embrace the right values. Third, seek to achieve consensus among nations, but do not feel bound by the process.

If that sounds painless, it is not. The mountain-top is thick with those who would rather not see trade that is too liberal, aid that is too principled, or arms control that is too self-denying. And America itself needs to remember that a willingness to involve others is not enough to make a collective world order work. There must also be readiness to submit to it. If America really wants such an order, it will have to be ready to take its complaints to the GATT, finance the multilateral aid agencies, submit itself to the International Court, bow to some system to monitor arms exports, and make a habit of consulting the UN. Is it ready to do so? If not, its quest for "new ways of working with other nations" will sound like old-fashioned humbug.

Playing as one?

JUNE 29TH The European Community spent 1991 preparing a new treaty on political union. Just before its mid-year summit, we reflected on the forces needed to bind federations together

LOOK around the world—at Canada, Czechoslovakia, India, Yugoslavia or the Soviet Union—and you will see federations in turmoil. So when the European Community's summiteers meet this weekend to discuss political union, they would do well to ask why some federations, such as the United States and Germany, are flourishing, while so many others are breaking up. They may then understand why a Yugofuture for Europe is the wrong one.

The essential characteristic of a successful federation is a unifying national ethic, an idea or set of values that is common to all the inhabitants of the federation and that pulls them together. For citizens of the United States, this is Americanism—the beliefs enshrined in the Declaration of Independence and the constitution, idealised in the American Dream and acted out in the lives of millions of immigrants over the past two centuries.

Nothing so intellectual binds together the citizens of Germany, one of the few federations that is still gaining recruits rather than losing them. Their bond is a common language and a shared history (excluding 40 unfortunate years), the characteristics that usually tie together the inhabitants of conventional nation-states. Language and history also hold together some other federations, such as Argentina, Australia and Brazil. And a few manage to survive by history alone, maybe reinforced by economic self-interest, despite differences of language, religion or culture; Switzerland is a fine example, though Malaysia shows that polyglot stability can be achieved in less than 700 years.

But not everywhere. Recent history is littered with the wreckage of failed federations, many of them created by the British. In Central Africa and the West Indies, no lasting harm was done by the attempt to impose on the countries concerned a political system the people did not want; but in Nigeria the memory is of a bitter civil war. Canada, apparently so placid and pacific, is in constitutional confusion. Quebec recently decided to hold a referendum on independence for the province.

Quebec will probably draw back from the brink. So perhaps will Slovakia. Croatia and Slovenia will not. They have already declared independence from Yugoslavia. It is probably only a matter of time before the three Baltic republics likewise pull out of the Soviet Union. In India it is far from certain that Jammu and Kashmir, or even Punjab, will not go the same way.

Common to all these disintegrating federations is the absence of a unifying national ethic. In some of them efforts have been made to put one in place: communism in the Soviet Union, Titoism in Yugoslavia, secularism in India, multiculturalism in Canada. But none of these isms has been a match for schism.

Some pretty powerful unifying force is needed to overcome differences of language and culture, especially when the history of the federation has been one of conquest of one group by the other, or of colonial divide-and-rule.

To argue otherwise is to deny the force of tribalism, whose potency has been one of the surprises–and, in its extreme nationalist form, one of the scourges–of the 20th century. However much homogenisers may deplore it, human beings put a value on their differences, whether differences of history, language, culture or religion. Well-intentioned improvers want to minimise the differences between groups, between men and women, young and old, able-bodied and crippled; too often they mistake the need to avoid discrimination based on differences for a need to deny the differences themselves.

When it works, federalism is an excellent way of accommodating differences within a single system, of allowing California to coexist with Rhode Island or Bavaria with Schleswig-Holstein. Different states or groups can then combine to enlarge their markets, to win economies of scale and to maximise their political weight, without sacrificing their distinctiveness. But it works only when the desire to hang on to that distinctiveness is accompanied by a unifying national ethic. It is this that the European Community lacks.

Not so fast, some will say. All over the EC, opinion polls, not to mention politicians, show wide support for a federal Europe; only the British, and maybe just a minority of them, are hostile. Is this not evidence of a unifying national ethic?

The answer is No. It is evidence of a desire to co-operate, a desire that is undoubtedly strong and growing, not just in Europe but elsewhere. The will to co-operate grows out of the recognition that many issues, and not just economic ones, now transcend national boundaries; on environmental matters, on terrorism, on drug trafficking, several countries acting together are plainly more effective than one acting on its own.

In Europe the will to co-operate extends beyond even these areas; there is a widespread readiness to submit to common laws where necessary, to strengthen the institutions that make them, maybe even to create a common currency. But there is no evidence to suggest that a majority of Europeans are yet ready to commit themselves to a federal United States of Europe. The USE, if it were to come into being, would have a common army, a common money, a common foreign policy and—its defining feature as a federation—a central government with ultimate sovereignty.

Such a federation might well be as rich and

powerful and splendid as America. But would it hold together? Would it act as decisively when the next Saddam Hussein gobbled up a small country? Probably not. For the EC was founded upon fear—the fear of another war between France and Germany. That fear never amounted to a national ethic encompassing the whole of Europe and, thanks to the success of the enterprise, is now a diminishing force. In its place has arisen a set of common economic and other interests, which provide a mighty incentive for people to rub along together, but not much more.

Not yet, anyway. At present the EC is a confederation—a grouping in which ultimate sovereignty over most issues, including the right to pull out, still resides in national capitals, not Brussels. It is undoubtedly integrating rather than disintegrating, and already has some federal characteristics, including the supremacy of Community law over national law. In time it may become a full-fledged federation; after all, the United States and Germany both started as confederations. But this weekend's summit in Luxembourg is plainly much too soon.

Yeltsin's army

AUGUST 24TH **The hard-line coup against Mikhail Gorbachev started and failed precisely within the gestation of one week's edition. So we could revel in its failure**

FOR 60 amazing hours the spectre of the cold-war Soviet Union returned to grip the world, before being exorcised as never before. If the coup that deposed Mikhail Gorbachev as Soviet president had not been defeated so swiftly, the West's hopes of Soviet co-operation in a less antagonistic world would have suffered as gravely as perestroika itself. In the event it was bungled, and the coup-makers' flight owed more to the Marx Brothers than to Marx and Lenin. But that bungling does not diminish what was at stake—and what has been won—in the battle for the streets of Moscow.

Nobody doubted that the Soviet Union had changed in many ways over the past six years. Yet, caught in the sights of a gun barrel, nobody—not even Boris Yeltsin or the brave men and women who manned the barricades around the Russian parliament—knew whether those changes had sufficed to wrench the modern Soviet Union out of the grip of fear and apathy. The fact that the coup collapsed so swiftly showed the power of what to many Russians is still a disconcerting idea: that democracy means taking responsibility for your fate into your own hands. For 70 cynical years, and for centuries before that, everything done in the name of the Soviet or Russian peoples had been done without their consent. Now they have given the past six years' changes—which, like all others, had been imposed from above—a manifest seal of approval.

Throughout the hurly-burly of perestroika, the fear of a military blow to bowl over the reforms and restore "order" has constrained Mr Gorbachev. A year ago he was persuaded to abandon plans for radical economic reform by hardliners who claimed to have the guns on their side. Now, with luck, the events of the past few days will strengthen Soviet democracy, just as the attempted coup in Spain ten years ago helped to stiffen that country's democrats against further military manhandling. In future it is likelier that the force of ideas, not the force of arms, will win the day.

Liberal values are not the only winner of the week, nor the junta its only loser. The Soviet Communist Party, unmentioned by the plotters and disregarded by the people, is a casualty with little hope of recovery. Mr Yeltsin, by contrast, is invigorated. It will be increasingly to him that Russians, and maybe other Soviet citizens, will turn.

The first task for the reinstated Mr Gorbachev is to find ways of letting the Soviet empire shrink, peacefully. Among the military men who refused to countenance the overthrow of the Soviet president there will be some who still do not like the idea of letting go those republics that want to leave. Mr Gorbachev, too, has until now wanted to make their leaving as difficult as possible. But this week must have given the remaking of a smaller and more decentralised Soviet Union a powerful shove. Some of the half-dozen republics that had been refusing to sign up for the new union may now be persuaded to do so. The cost of keeping the determined refuseniks in has been shown to be explosively high. A negotiated parting of the ways for the three Baltic republics, at least, ought now to be possible.

The second big task for Mr Gorbachev is the economy. Even before the upheavals in Moscow the economy was in free-fall. Now a swifter end to the war of laws between the republics and the centre should at least help to slow the fall. The defeat of the coup has finally discredited old notions of central planning. It has also, with luck, weakened the arm-lock that the army and the military-industrial complex have had on efforts to redirect resources into the civilian economy. Most of all, in boosting the pro-market Mr Yeltsin at the expense of the more conservative Soviet government, it has helped the cause of market reform and privatisation.

The failure of the coup has shown that the Soviet Union is not congenitally unsuited to democracy. The coup's leaders had expected the crowds to scatter at the first whiff of grapeshot. They did not. Once the tanks on the streets had claimed their first victims without an easy victory, the choice was either to use massive force to quell the growing resistance or to cut and run. The overthrow of Mr Gorbachev had been an act of desperation by a cabal of bureaucrats out of touch with the country they had pretensions to govern. It was not a confident blow struck by men united by a coherent set of ideas for saving the Soviet Union, or by a conviction that unpleasant might could be as right as before.

When the new army of democrats rallied round Mr Yeltsin, and he showed he would not disappoint them, the men of the past quickly returned to the past. Mr Yeltsin played his part with skill and courage. But the huge response to his appeal was a measure of the popular appetite for democracy and reform.

The plotters said they were acting to protect the living standards of ordinary Soviet citizens. Nobody could deny that the failures of perestroika had brought the Soviet economy to its knees. But the damage could not be repaired with rifle butts, still less by a return to the failed policies of the past. As strikes spread from mine to mine, and from mine to factory, in defiance of the coup and in support of Mr Yeltsin, workers were showing that they now had something even more important to lose than their bread: their newly won political freedom.

Economic woe was the excuse for the coup, but the new union treaty was its target. Assuming that it is now signed as planned, it will shift power irretrievably from the centre to the republics. The union treaty has its flaws, but its purpose is to make the bulk of the Soviet Union governable for the first time by consent instead of coercion. Here, again, the coup merely confirmed irreversible change: as one republic after another declared its independence in defiance of the tanks, the attempt to hold the union together at gunpoint promised only to blow it more violently apart.

Just as Mr Yeltsin's position has been enhanced, so Mr Gorbachev's has been diminished. His best hope of regaining popularity is to offer himself for election after a bold series of reforms. But Mr Yeltsin is going to be a tougher opponent than he was before the coup. Unlike Mr Gorbachev, an easier target whose authority had never been put to the test at the polls, Mr

Yeltsin had won popular election as president of Russia barely two months earlier. Behind him this week were gathered the leaders of many other republics, hundreds of thousands of ordinary people who had turned out to defend their legal Russian government, and the leaders of defiant cities and councils across Russia from Leningrad to Sakhalin.

Their defiance might still have ended in bloody defeat but for the deep divisions that quickly emerged in the army and the KGB, supposedly the two chief props of the new regime. Whether officers refused to order their troops to fire on civilians or whether they refused point-blank to support an illegal seizure of power, or both, the sudden collapse of the coup shows just how deeply the democratic idea has penetrated the armour of what was once the world's most fearsome army.

With perestroika restored and the rule of law now strengthened, the reformers must next demolish that other deep-seated suspicion about the Russians: that they are incapable of becoming a nation of entrepreneurs. That could prove even harder than destroying the myth of Russia's indifference to democracy but, if the three-day coup has helped, the plotters really will turn out to be their nation's unwitting saviours.

After Maxwell

NOVEMBER 9TH **The mysterious death at sea of the media baron, Robert Maxwell, opened up a labyrinth of financial wrong-doing. How had so many financiers become trapped in it?**

LOST at sea, off his yacht, before dawn: no script-writer could have done better. Robert Maxwell was indeed straight out of movie-fantasy, and not just in death. His life—penniless refugee, war hero, socialist politician, capitalist tycoon—gained much in the telling, no doubt, but nobody could say he was ordinary. Yet his chief legacy will be his debts. Big debts, naturally; perhaps $4 billion of them. Among those noughts lie some truths for capitalism, the system that gave Mr Maxwell his chance and which whole (and near-penniless) countries are now embracing.

The biggest question is this: are the Maxwells of this world A Good Thing? Keynes talked of "animal spirits" driving economic progress. Schumpeter described a process of "creative destruction", with capitalists laying waste even as they build. Paul Samuelson thought that if entrepreneurs were prevented from pursuing "good clean money" they would become oppressive brutes, intent on "bad dirty power"; happy the society that has billionaires rather than Brezhnevs.

Good, as far as it goes. But that version of the entrepreneur dwells upon success; what about excess and failure? There is little doubt that Mr Maxwell's empire was shaky, and had been for years. It may be salvaged, but it will have to be shrunk. Jobs will be lost, and loans written off. Why was the system that desirably allowed the young Maxwell to launch himself into business then helpless to stop him making a mess?

Mr Maxwell was commonly described as a "newspaper proprietor". The term implies that he could do what he liked with his own property. He did do as he liked, but the property wasn't his. He was chairman of two public companies, in which outside shareholders held large minority stakes. Those companies, plus

his private holding company (based in Liechtenstein), had also borrowed massively from banks and other creditors. The money-lenders made the companies possible, yet they allowed Mr Maxwell to behave as though the firms were an adventure-playground for just one man.

In this, the creditors were, to put it kindly, gullible. They forgot one commonsense rule of capitalism: anybody who needs to base his holding company in Liechtenstein has things to hide. Tax efficiency is the usual claim, but is often only part of the truth. A brass-plate company rarely gives its financiers the information they need to judge its health. By borrowing from dozens of banks, Mr Maxwell managed to avoid giving any of them an overall picture of what he was up to. When the full facts come out, his backers will have ample reason to be ashamed of their naivety.

Not for the first time; Alan Bond and BCCI are just two recent examples of what happens when billions go unsupervised. But the supervision that is needed is less that of the civil servant and the regulator than of the accountant and the bank manager. Once bureaucrats get involved in saving capitalism from its excesses, they tend to kill it off, the good bits as well as the bad. That point is now well understood, in Mr Maxwell's native Czechoslovakia as much as in his adopted Britain.

The lessons from his colourful business life are therefore largely grey. Entrepreneurial capitalism always needs capital, but capital always needs guardians. The swashbuckler is essential to the system's vitality, the bean-counter essential to its survival. The men in dark suits will now have their say. They should have had it sooner.

23

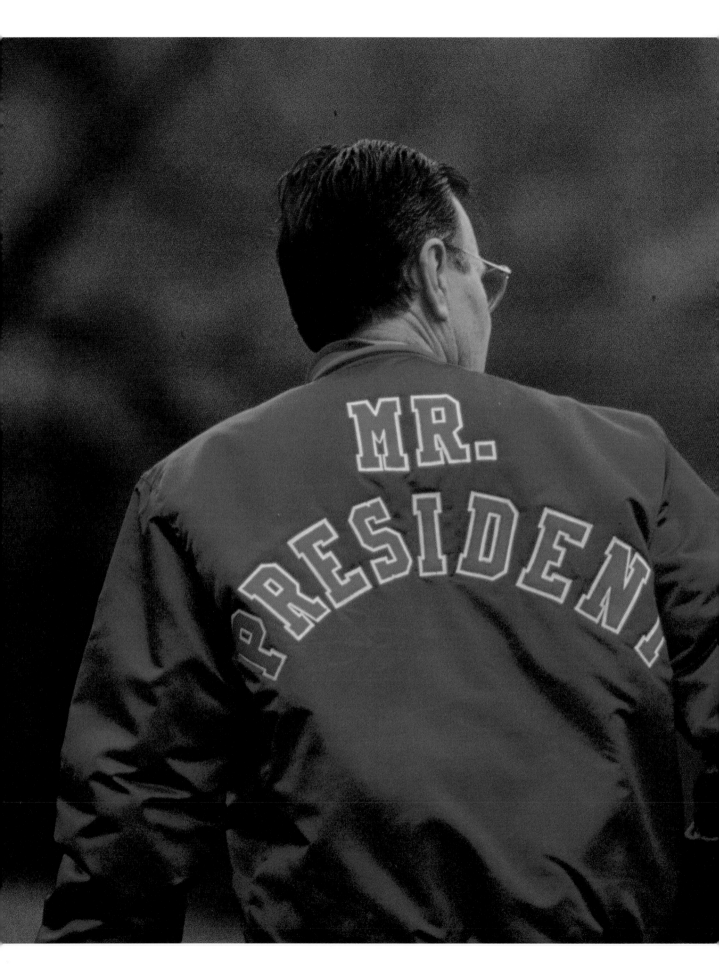

Contents

AMERICA

Foreign glory, home truths

IT WAS, as they say in California, an awesome plummet. If there is one graph that sums up the year in America it is the steady downward slide of George Bush's approval ratings in the opinion polls. From a peak of roughly 90%, just after the end of the Gulf war, the number of those who approved of Mr Bush declined inexorably until it stood below 50% at the end of the year. When asked their opinion of the president, Americans express more than a political view; they also reflect their own degree of optimism. And never had they gone so quickly from euphoria to gloom.

Before the euphoria, there was doubt. It is hard to remember, in the light of subsequent events, just how anguished was the American debate about the impending Gulf war. At the beginning of 1991, the country could think of nothing else. People dreaded the coming slaughter, tied yellow ribbons to almost every porch and tree in memory of the young men and women who were spending new year's day in the Saudi sand and stayed away from ski resorts and casinos lest the frivolity seemed out of place. The relative merit of war and sanctions was earnestly discussed in every public place. There was little trace of jingoism. Congress, catching the mood, held a long debate before narrowly approving the use of force, with most Democrats demanding that sanctions be given more time to work.

And so America found itself in a big war for the first time since Vietnam. One by one, the doubts about the country's resolve and skill were laid to rest. The too-complicated, too-expensive weapons would not work; they did. The public would not stand for heavy casualties; it did not have to. The generals would get bogged down in a war of attrition on the ground; it was all over in 100 hours. The allies would not stand firm; they did. By the end of hostilities in March, America stood amazed at what it had done. It had exorcised the ghost of Vietnam, led a grand coalition of nations to victory, righted wrong and now stood alone in the world, unchallenged as a military and diplomatic power. Mr Bush's words, in his "state of the union" speech of 29th January, no longer seemed like a boast: "Among the nations of the world, only the United States of America has had both the moral standing and the means to back it up." The post-cold-war world was not multi-polar, after all, it was unipolar. The unipower would now forge a "new world order".

The hangover

It was not to last. The very one-sidedness of the victory made it seem less impressive: like shooting fish in a barrel, said one pilot of the slaughter wrought among retreating Iraqi soldiers. And Saddam Hussein did not fall. Instead he began brutally to crush the Kurds. He clung to a remarkably intact nuclear-weapons programme. A job had been left half done. By the end of 1991 it was clear that Mr Bush's undoubted skill in picking and winning a fight with Iraq would not ensure his re-election in 1992.

Hardly had the cheering stopped before the great "domestic gripe" began. Pundits of every stripe demanded that the president give foreign affairs a rest and throw his energies into long overdue chores around the house: reform of health and education; repair of transport infrastructure; reduction of defence spending; renewal of hope for the urban poor. It was a chorus that would not cease, and by the end of the year it had rattled the president severely, provoked a challenge from a conservative isolationist, Pat Buchanan, and given the Democrats their best lines: Senator Tom Harkin ridiculed the "frequent-flier presidency".

In March it seemed to be a matter of Mr Bush risking a little of his immense popularity in a bold reform. He duly produced a package of education reforms, but they did not ignite. He demanded a crime bill from Congress, but could only suggest some eccentric, punitive measures himself, such as new federal death penalties, while resisting more effective measures, such as gun control and community policing. But neither education nor crime was to become the dominant domestic tune: instead, it was health. Eating up 12.4% of GNP, health-care costs were falling ever more heavily on the government, which insures the old, and on employers. But that did not make ordinary people feel secure: for they worried about being only one slip away from being uninsured altogether. By November, Harris Wofford, a Democrat, was able to thrash Dick Thornburgh, the just-retired attorney-general, in a race for the senate in Pennsylvania, largely by banging on about health. Mr Wofford's best line was: "If criminals have a right to a lawyer, working Americans have a right to a doctor."

The valley of darkness

Gradually, though, such long-term worries came to matter less than the immediate recession. Far from proving short and shallow, far from having been exaggerated by the sobriety of war, the recession grew worse. Unemployment rose, banks failed, house prices fell, consumer spending stagnated. Growth resumed in the

Stormin' Norman

third quarter of the year, then seemed to falter again. The dreaded "double-dip" had arrived.

By the autumn the stockmarket was nervous enough to fall at the slightest excuse, the White House was split between those who wanted to "do something" to kick-start growth, and those who felt nothing could be done. This latter group included the treasury secretary, budget director and chief of staff, who knew that the only way to stimulate the economy would be to unpick the carefully knitted budget agreement of 1990 and cut taxes. That seemed crazy at a time when the federal government was living beyond its means to the tune of a third of a trillion dollars a year, when Democrats, in control of Congress, had been stopped, in effect, from spending more on their own pet projects by that very agreement. Any Republican tax cut would be dearly bought in Democratic spending demands. By November this row in the administration had reached such a pitch—encouraged by the president's indecisiveness about which side he was on—that it was ready to claim its first casualty. John Sununu, the abrasive chief of staff, was unceremoniously dropped. The "do-something" brigade seemed to have the upper hand.

Mr Sununu's departure had other causes, too. For alongside the serious questions of recession and domestic needs, the year was a rich one for Washington scandals large and small. Mr Sununu's own scandal was small: he had used a government aeroplane for a family skiing trip and a government limousine for a visit to a stamp auction in New York. This might not have mattered if he had not been so unrepentant. Senator Edward Kennedy found himself embroiled in a deeper scandal. He had taken his nephew and son to a Florida bar in the small hours of Good Friday, where they picked up girls and returned home. The senator's nephew then had sex with one of the girls on the beach and was accused of rape. He was acquitted in December after a trial that was televised live, an unparalleled piece of mass voyeurism thinly disguised by the pretence that the important issue of "date rape" was at stake.

A scandal with more cause to call itself emblematic blew up quite suddenly in September. George Bush had nominated Clarence Thomas, a young, black, conservative judge of humble southern origins to take the seat of Thurgood Marshall on the Supreme Court. Mr Thomas was on the brink of

On the bread line

receiving Senate confirmation (his race had helped deflect Democratic opposition to his views) when somebody leaked the news that he had been accused, by a female former colleague, of sexual harassment, and that the Senate Judiciary Committee had ignored the charge. In the ensuing hearings, the truth could not be found. But the issue loomed ever larger. Feminists denounced widespread male indifference to sexual harassment.

The Thomas affair was entangled in the year's intellectual obsession: "political correctness". America, once famous for its tolerance, had grown oddly dogmatic. The new orthodoxy was especially found in universities, from which came a steady stream of stories of students and teachers silenced, punished or driven

Doughty Thomas

away for no crime greater than holding heterodox views on "political" issues—especially those connected with race and sex.

Of the two, it was race that proved most dangerous. In the autumn, a one-time Nazi and Grand Wizard of the Ku Klux Klan, with no other qualifications, David Duke, got more votes than the governor of Louisiana in the first round of voting. He did so by appealing, often in coded language, to the widespread white belief that blacks are now privileged citizens. No question more torments America than whether it is right to overcompensate for past injustice with present bias. David Duke represented, for the politically incorrect, the long predicted white backlash against a policy that had never helped the blacks who needed help most; for the politically correct, he merely proved once more how much racist prejudice still lurks in the southern soul, and therefore how great is the need for affirmative action to offset it. He had a quick effect on national policy, though. George Bush dropped his opposition to a civil-rights bill before Congress, which he had said would lead to racial employment quotas, the better to retrieve his reputation for racial fairness.

Yet the dropping of his opposition to the civil-rights bill became just another ripple of panic emanating from the president as he sank into unpopularity at the end of the year. Bad election results led him to postpone a trip to Asia; bad economic news led him to call for a cap on credit-card interest rates—which unnerved the stockmarket; the expectation that he would cut taxes to stimulate the recovery, and so increase the budget deficit, hurt the dollar. Mr Bush, the Midas of foreign policy, found that everything domestic he touched turned to dross. Even the fumbling Democrats who were running against him began to gain in stature. A year that began so well for Mr Bush ended in fluster.

Monday 7th
California inaugurated a new governor, **Pete Wilson**. Promising more activism than his predecessor, he inherited a mega-state—the 1990 census found almost 30m Californians, up by a quarter on 1980. To fill his own Senate seat, Mr Wilson appointed John Seymour, known for his fund-raising skill—which he would need for two re-election bids in four years.

Richard Cheney, the defence secretary, did something unprecedented: he **cancelled a big weapons programme** altogether. The A-12, a stealthy attack aircraft, being developed at a cost of $57 billion for the navy by McDonnell Douglas and General Dynamics, was behind schedule, overweight and over budget. Embarrassed that he had earlier lauded the A-12 as a model project, Mr Cheney killed it.

Tuesday 8th
Manuel Lujan, the interior secretary, won his battle to force Matsushita to sell for $49.5m the lucrative monopoly of servicing **Yosemite national park** it had acquired by buying an entertainment company, MCA. Mr Lujan had talked darkly of Japan owning a piece of a national treasure to win his point.

Wednesday 9th
James Baker, the secretary of state, met Tariq Aziz, Iraq's foreign minister, in Geneva to discuss **peace**. Optimism spread as the talks went on. The stockmarket rose. But then Mr Baker announced that nothing had been achieved. Iraq's intransigence was illustrated by Mr Aziz's failure even to accept a letter from President Bush to Saddam Hussein. War now seemed inevitable.

Saturday 12th
Congress voted to support the **use of force in the Gulf** after evading the issue for months. That both houses supported the resolution seemed almost a foregone conclusion after the failure of the talks in Geneva. Nonetheless, the margin in the Senate was close: 52 to 47. The administration, which had earlier suggested that a close vote would undermine its policy, said it was happy with any majority.

Monday 14th
Oregon's legislature began a special session to discuss a **right-to-die** initiative, which had attracted 223,000 signatures. It would allow a person to be prescribed lethal doses of barbiturates so long as two doctors had expressed the opinion that that person would die within six months.

Tuesday 15th
Ann Richards became governor of Texas, the first woman to hold the post since 1935. Facing a $4 billion deficit, she named education as her top priority. A week later the state supreme court greatly complicated her task by unanimously declaring Texas's new law on school finance, laboriously agreed upon after four special sessions of the state legislature, to be unconstitutional.

Wednesday 16th
America went to **war**. The night before he unleashed Operation Desert Storm against Iraq, George Bush had Billy Graham to stay at the White House to discuss the decision to go to war, then took a solitary early-morning walk in the garden with his thoughts. An hour after the bombing of Baghdad started he went on television to explain, and promised "This will not be another Vietnam." Nearly 80% of all Americans watched.

The accuracy and low casualty rate of the air raids on Iraq caused widespread relief and **optimism** that the war would soon be won. CNN, the Atlanta-based cable network that reported the air raids live from Baghdad, quickly changed from hero to villain when it encouraged the early euphoria and then seemed to broadcast what Iraq wanted shown. Psychologists warned people about the "CNN effect": obsession with television news.

Friday 18th
Eastern Airlines stopped flying after 62 years, the last two under the supervision of the **bankruptcy** courts. Pan Am had filed for bankruptcy ten days earlier. The war was the final straw. Fear of terrorism led many Americans to cancel air travel, and wild rumours resulted in a run on gas masks in Los Angeles and multiple bomb scares in New York. Pan Am briefly banned Iraqis from its flights.

Friday 25th
President Bush nominated Representative Edward Madigan as **agriculture secretary**, a hot-seat in the GATT talks. He replaced Clayton Yeutter, who was elected the same day as chairman of the Republican party.

Saturday 26th
The biggest **peace protests** to date, numbering 50,000 in San Francisco and 100,000 in Washington, had little effect on public opinion, which overwhelmingly supported the administration's conduct of the war. Mr Bush's approval ratings in the opinion polls remained above 80%.

Sunday 27th
The Super Bowl played in Tampa, Florida, was the closest and best game for many years, won by one point in the last eight seconds by the **New York Giants** over the Buffalo Bills. Because of the war, security was unprecedented and patriotism uninhibited.

Tuesday 29th
George Bush's "state of the union" address to Congress described a nation **at war and in recession**. Americans, he said, were doing "the hard work of freedom." He sprang no surprises, but endorsed the pet conservative theme of empowering individuals against the bureaucracy, and proposed to shift $15 billion-worth of federal programmes to the states.

Wednesday 30th
The Commerce Department's index of leading indicators **turned upwards**, the first good economic news in six months.

February

Monday 4th
George Bush presented his **budget** proposal for fiscal 1992: total spending $1.45 trillion, or 2.6% more than in 1991. It was more realistic than usual, predicting a deficit of $318 billion, or 5.7% of GNP, but forecasting it would fall below $50 billion by 1995. Congress did not declare it dead on arrival, a good sign.

Tuesday 5th
The administration introduced its plans for **bank reform**, which would abolish the legal barriers that stop country-wide banking and prevent commercial banks from diversifying into other financial services.

Wednesday 6th
Ronald Reagan's **80th birthday** banquet drew 900 select guests to a Los Angeles hotel and raised $2m towards his presidential library. Margaret Thatcher compared notes with the former president on retirement.

The **Central Intelligence Agency** came under renewed scrutiny. The Democratic chairmen of the House and Senate intelligence committees, both Oklahomans, promised tough hearings on the CIA's role in the new world order, questioning its recent competence. Earlier, Senator Daniel Patrick Moynihan had introduced the "End of the Cold War Act" which would put the CIA inside the State Department.

Monday 11th
Detroit's police chief was **charged** with taking $1.3m from the city's "secret service" fund and arranging to get another $1.3m into the hands of a former deputy police chief.

Thursday 14th
Sam Skinner, the transport secretary, unveiled a $105 billion plan for **road-building**. It would boost spending on roads by 39% but shift many programmes to the states. Critics said it showed too much interest in roads and not enough in other forms of transport.

Friday 15th
After the fifth dry winter in a row, California took drastic measures to save **water**. The State Water Project cut off all farmers. The Central Valley Project cut to one-third of normal the amount of water it supplied to farmers. The problem was not supply but price. Farmers got their water for about one-tenth of the cost of delivery—which encouraged profligacy. Cities were paying 20 times as much.

Monday 18th
Bucking the trend, Maryland enacted a permissive **abortion law**, guaranteeing access to abortions while requiring doctors to inform parents if a girl under 18 sought one. Since 1989 in 47 other states abortion laws had been proposed that would restrict access to abortions.

Tuesday 19th
Los Angeles elected a **His-**panic woman, Gloria Molina, to its Board of County Supervisors, making her one of the most powerful Hispanic politicians in America.

Wednesday 20th
James Watkins, the secretary of energy, released his long-awaited **energy strategy** fashioned during 18 months of public debate. It was pre-emptively criticised from all sides as too obsessed with increasing energy supplies through tax breaks for oil drillers and ways to encourage the rebirth of nuclear power, and too little obsessed with energy conservation. Unfair, said Mr Watkins, a former admiral: read the report.

The United States agreed to guarantee a **$400m loan to Israel** for the housing of immigrants, a measure that had been held up by the State Department's worries that the money would be used to support settlements in the West Bank. An apparent reward for Israeli restraint in the Gulf war.

Sunday 24th
Americans woke to the news that the **ground assault on Iraq** had begun.

Monday 25th
George Bush asked Congress for a two-year extension to his "fast-track authority" for **trade negotiations**. This guarantees that trade agreements negotiated by the administration are voted on without amendments. Congress had until June to reject his request, and quickly came under pressure to do so from lobbyists for labour and protected industries, who were anxious about a free-trade deal with Mexico.

Tuesday 26th
Arizona elected **Fife Symington** as governor. He had won an election in November with less than 50% of the vote, so under state law was forced to contest a run-off in February.

Meanwhile, seven of Arizona's legislators were indicted following a sting in which a fake mobster from Las Vegas was videotaped offering them money in exchange for their pressing to legalise gambling in Arizona. "You sure there isn't a camera?" said one, as he stuffed a **$55,000 bribe** into a gym bag.

Wednesday 27th
President Bush decided to **halt the war**. Fighting on the ground had lasted only 100 hours, fighting in the air six weeks. American forces had suffered less than 100 deaths in action. George Bush said: "Seven months ago America and the world drew a line in the sand. We declared that the aggression would not stand. Tonight America and the world have kept their word." A few days later his approval rating in the opinion polls reached an unprecedented 90%.

The same day, while attention was on the Gulf, the Senate ethics committee gave its verdict on the "Keating 5" affair. Five senators had been accused of peddling their influence to stop the regulators closing a bankrupt thrift in return for accepting campaign cash from the thrift's owner, Charles Keating. One, Alan Cranston, was reprimanded, the others exonerated. The ethics committee itself came in for much scorn for this.

Thursday 28th
The House Appropriations Committee estimated that the war had **cost $42.6 billion**, or $10 billion less than had been pledged by America's allies (mainly Saudi Arabia, Kuwait, Japan and Germany). But a profit seemed unlikely: the administration said further costs were on the way.

March

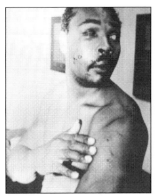

Sunday 3rd
A man who was trying out a video camera in Los Angeles chanced to film four policemen, watched by 20 others, **beating a black motorist** 56 times with clubs and electric stun guns. The incident quickly became a national obsession as the tape was replayed on television news. The Los Angeles police chief, Daryl Gates, apologised "in spite of the fact" that the man turned out to be a paroled robber, but refused to resign.

Monday 4th
Governors and experts were summoned to a two-day summit in Washington on **crime**, which was becoming the domestic preoccupation of 1991. "We are not here to search for the roots of crime," said Dick Thornburgh, the attorney-general, but to "stop the carnage in our own mean streets." President Bush called for a "workable death penalty" and said his crime bill was high on his domestic agenda.

In a blow to tort reformers, the Supreme Court decided that **punitive damages** in tort cases (as opposed to compensation) were legal, despite the fact that civil law is not supposed to punish.

Wednesday 6th
George Bush addressed a joint session of Congress on the end of the war. His speech was interrupted repeatedly by **applause and cheers**. Waving flags and clapping in rhythm, the listening congressmen—Democrat and Republican alike—seemed more like sports fans than politicians.

Friday 8th
Unemployment for February jumped unexpectedly to 6.5%, from 6.2% in January, suggesting the **economy was shrinking** at a 3% annual rate. The Federal Reserve cut interest rates by ¼ point to 6%.

Monday 11th
Buddy Roemer, the governor of Louisiana, left the Democratic Party and **joined the Republicans**, the first state governor to switch parties while in office. His decision owed more to tactics than to principle. Running for re-election in November he faced two formidable opponents in a non-partisan primary: his populist Democratic predecessor, Edwin Edwards, and a former Ku Klux Klan grand wizard, David Duke. So he pre-empted the Republican party by becoming its candidate.

Tuesday 12th
Robert Maxwell agreed to buy New York's *Daily News* from the Chicago-based Tribune Company. The unions agreed to give up 800 of their 2,500 jobs at the *Daily News*. Nonetheless, Mr Maxwell faced an uphill struggle to bring back readers and advertisers to the *Daily News*, whose readership had halved from an already dismal 1.1m during a strike that began in October 1990.

Wednesday 13th
A pregnant woman in a restaurant near Seattle was **refused a daiquiri** by two waiters who thought she should not be drinking while pregnant. The waiters were fired. A week later the Supreme Court ruled that a car-battery maker could not ban fertile women from its factory on the grounds that lead might damage their future children. Two blows struck for a woman's right to make her own decisions, according to feminists.

Wednesday 20th
John Dingell, an investigative congressman, opened hearings into how **Stanford University** contrived routinely to overcharge taxpayers for expenses as part of its research grants. A yacht and furniture for the president's house were among the expenses. The practice of adding high "overheads" to research grants (Stanford's were 74%) was shared with other top universities, but it led eventually to the resignation of the university president, Donald Kennedy.

Wednesday 27th
Norman Schwarzkopf hinted that he had differed with George Bush about when to **stop the fighting in Iraq**. "Frankly my recommendation had been, you know, continue the march. I mean we had them in a rout." The White House gave him a dressing down via leaks.

Douglas Wilder, the governor of Virginia and the first elected black governor, formed a committee to explore whether he should run for president. Yet Iowa remained surprisingly free of would-be Democratic presidents, considering its caucus was only 11 months away. Meanwhile, California's Democratic Party announced that it was considering a party caucus in March 1992, which would radically change the election timetable.

Thursday 28th
Lee Atwater died at the age of 40 after battling a brain tumour for more than a year. Mr Atwater managed George Bush's election campaign with an affection for "negative campaigning" that made him many enemies. In an interview in January, he had apologised to Michael Dukakis for the "naked cruelty" with which the Bush campaign had treated him in 1988.

Ronald Reagan changed his mind on **gun control**. He told a meeting of the doctors who saved his life after John Hinckley's assassination attempt ten years before that he supported the Brady bill, named after his press secretary, who was shot in the head by Hinckley. The bill would impose a waiting period on those buying handguns. Mr Reagan's switch suddenly improved the bill's chances of passage through Congress.

Friday 29th
Pete Wilson, the state's governor, doubled his estimate of **California's budget deficit** for the year from July. He added: "We could close all our state universities; we could open and empty all our prisons; we could eliminate our entire state workforce—and we would still not balance the budget."

Monday 8th
After the war Americans were in a frivolous mood. Kitty Kelley opened a good month for **scandals** with her vicious book on Nancy Reagan, which mentioned her "long lunches" with Frank Sinatra at the White House. Later in the month Senator Charles Robb's "massage" by a beauty queen and John Sununu's too-frequent use of government aeroplanes each briefly dominated the news.

Friday 12th
The defence secretary, Richard Cheney, unveiled a list of 31 big **military bases** and a dozen smaller ones that he planned to close. They included Philadelphia's naval docks, California's Fort Ord and Florida's MacDill air force base, home of General Norman Schwarzkopf. Predictably anguished cries came from Capitol Hill.

Monday 15th
Texas's long struggle to find a way of equalising the money available to **schools** in rich and poor districts that satisfied the state supreme court unexpectedly succeeded. Next problem: finding $5 billion in revenue to pay for it. Ann Richards, the governor, turned to a commission chaired by John Connally. Consider everything, she said: even a state income tax.

The Supreme Court voted to restrict the use of constitutional arguments in habeas corpus writs in federal courts, making it harder for convicts on death row to appeal their sentences. This was part of a series of decisions restricting the rights of **criminal defendants**.

NBC News named the woman who had accused **Edward Kennedy's nephew**, William Smith, of raping her in Palm Beach at Easter, saying the name had already been published by the *Globe*, a Florida tabloid. The next day, the *New York Times* also named her, saying it was following NBC's lead, and wrote an unflattering profile of her. Feminists said this implied she had "asked for it" and broke the long-standing tradition that rape victims be allowed anonymity.

Tuesday 16th
Bowing to public pressure, George Bush ordered American troops into Iraqi Kurdistan to create a **safe enclave** for the Kurds whose plight had been graphically captured by television while the president fished in Florida. Extracting American troops again would not be so easy, said most American commentators.

Wednesday 17th
A national **freight-rail strike** was declared by unions frustrated by management intransigence over wages, manning levels and health benefits. Congress, aware that one-third of America's freight goes by rail, rushed through a bill that George Bush signed immediately. It ordered the unions back to work pending the results of binding arbitration.

Thursday 18th
Lamar Alexander, the new education secretary, unveiled the administration's bold plans for **education reform**. These aimed to change the way schools are run, introduce national tests and try to encourage parents to make their children more interested in learning than watching television. Because most education funding comes from the states, Mr Alexander's plans were largely exhortatory.

Tuesday 23rd
In one of the biggest military orders ever placed, the air force picked the YF-22 from Boeing, Lockheed and General Dynamics, rather than its rival from Northrop and McDonnell Douglas, to be its **next-generation fighter** in use by the end of the century. The aircraft would be stealthy (hard to pick up on radar), fast and economical (able to fly supersonically without using after-burners). The cost? $65 billion-95 billion for 648 of them.

Wednesday 24th
The federal government impounded 24,000 cartons of **orange juice**, escalating its year-long battle to force Procter and Gamble (and others) to take the word "fresh" off the labels of juice made from concentrate. Within days, Procter and Gamble had agreed. "Low-cholesterol" and "good-for-the-heart" claims were next on the Food and Drug Administration list.

Thursday 25th
The Senate approved a **federal budget** for fiscal 1992 similar to the one approved a week earlier by the House. That this had been achieved with little delay or disagreement owed much to the budget agreement of 1990, which set separate ceilings on defence, foreign and domestic spending and required increases in each to be offset by taxes or cuts.

Friday 26th
The Fish and Wildlife Service announced plans that could ban logging in 11.6m acres of western forests, to preserve the **northern spotted owl**, a subspecies recently declared endangered. That figure was far higher than expected. "Biology run amok" said Senator Mark Hatfield of Oregon. The three west-coast states feared they would lose 40,000 jobs if the plan went through.

A 12-day celebration of **"points of light"**, George Bush's phrase for volunteerism, culminated in a party on the White House lawn. The administration's affection for volunteerism seemed to be having an effect. A Gallup poll found that 98m Americans were involved in voluntary work, 23% more than two years before.

Tuesday 30th
Paul Tsongas became the first Democrat to declare he was **running for president**. A Greek liberal from Massachusetts who retired from the Senate in 1984 with cancer, he stood little chance. But he was determined to influence the argument even if he lost. He produced an 85-page tract on America's declining competitiveness and his cure for it: a mixture of economic nationalism and pro-business microeconomics.

Gingerly, Congress began to look into the **"October Surprise"** theory—that in 1980 the Reagan campaign negotiated with Iran to delay the release of the embassy hostages until inauguration day itself, in exchange for weapons via Israel. It had been brought to life by Gary Sick, a member of Jimmy Carter's National Security Council, who said he was now convinced by the circumstantial evidence.

Thursday 2nd
Excavations in New Mexico found evidence of man's presence **36,000 years ago**. Most archaeologists still thought man arrived in the Americas only 11,000 years ago.

Saturday 4th
While he was jogging at Camp David, **George Bush's heart** started beating irregularly. An atrial fibrillation brought on by Grave's disease was diagnosed. Mr Bush had radiation therapy for his thyroid gland and speculation was stirred about the water in the vice-president's house, because his wife also had Grave's disease the year before. Meanwhile America's collective heart fluttered at the thought of President Dan Quayle; there were renewed calls to drop him.

Sunday 5th
In Washington, DC, a young Hispanic was shot in the chest by a policewoman while resisting arrest. This sparked two days of **riots** in which mainly Salvadoran youths burned and looted 31 shops, 19 police cars and a bus. A curfew and a promise by the mayor to examine their grievances brought peace.

Tuesday 7th
The **Democratic Leadership Council**, a group trying to push the Democratic Party rightwards met in Cleveland for what turned into a contest of presidential aspirants. Bill Clinton, the DLC's chairman, had a row with Ron Brown, the party's chairman, but then made an impressive speech. Albert Gore and Douglas Wilder disappointed. Jesse Jackson, pointedly uninvited, made rude noises off.

Wednesday 8th
William Webster announced his retirement as head of the CIA. George Bush nominated **Robert Gates** for the second time—in 1987 he withdrew his candidature after the Senate voiced concerns that he might have known about the Iran-contra scandal.

The House of Representatives at last defied the National Rifle Association and passed the Brady bill, a long-sought goal of **gun-control** enthusiasts, which mandated a seven-day waiting period before a purchaser could pick up a handgun. The bill still faced a big hurdle in the Senate.

The governor of Pennsylvania appointed **Harris Wofford**, a Democrat, to fill the Senate seat emptied by the death in an aeroplane crash of John Heinz.

Thursday 9th
William Kennedy Smith was charged with **rape**, following an incident at the Palm Beach home of the Kennedys at Easter.

Friday 10th
David Dinkins, mayor of New York, presented his **"doomsday budget"** for the cash-strapped city. He threatened to close the zoo, shut shelters for the homeless and suspend the recycling of rubbish. In other words, political scaremongering replaced any realistic attempt to cut the looming deficit of $3.5 billion for the year that would begin in July.

Monday 13th
George Bush announced that he was ready to destroy America's stocks of **chemical weapons** and renounce their use, if others did the same. This was intended to restart the stalled talks on chemical weapons at Geneva.

Tuesday 14th
America greeted **Queen Elizabeth II**. She was hugged by a black great-grandmother in Washington, went to a baseball game in Baltimore and made Norman Schwarzkopf a knight in Florida.

Wednesday 15th
A House subcommittee tried to kill the plan to build a **space station**. The Japanese government reacted by threatening to withdraw its support from the project.

Monday 20th
In a room at Harvard's Kennedy School, Russian and American academics began hammering out a plan known as "**Grand Bargain**", which would swap American money for Soviet economic reform. Grigory Yavlinsky, on the Russian side, was semi-officially backed by Mikhail Gorbachev. The American government kept its distance.

Tuesday 21st
The House of Representatives rejected Mr Bush's **defence budget**, preferring its own, which, though just as costly, put more emphasis on conventional weapons.

As it had done in 1990, the Senate voted to **ban "honoraria"**, or speaking fees, from special interest groups, and set limits on senators' outside income. But the measure was part of a campaign finance bill threatened with a veto by the president.

Thursday 23rd
The House of Representatives voted 231-192 to renew the president's **fast-track authority** to negotiate trade deals. An alliance of textile protectionists in the south, labour unions in the north and environmentalists were worried about the effect of a free-trade pact with Mexico. The Senate voted 59-35 the next day for the fast-track authority.

By five to four, the Supreme Court voted that it was constitutional for the government to stop its family-planning services from discussing **abortion** with their patients. Orwellian, said liberals. He who pays the piper calls the tune, said conservatives.

Monday 27th
George Bush announced that he would extend **most-favoured nation** trading status to China for another year.

Wednesday 29th
George Bush proposed an **arms control initiative** for the Middle East. It would ban ballistic missiles, chemical weapons and material for use in nuclear weapons.

Thursday 30th
Robert Gallo admitted that the AIDS **virus** he discovered in 1984 had been sent to him the year before from the Pasteur Institute, ending a long Franco-American dispute. The week before it became clear that the government had changed its mind and would continue to bar people carrying the AIDS virus from entering the United States.

Neil Bush, the president's son, and the other directors of Silverado, a Denver thrift that failed at a cost to taxpayers of $1 billion, agreed to pay $50m in settlement of a $200m civil suit.

Tuesday 4th
Massachusetts magically solved its budget deficit after a junior state worker found a piece of small print in the law that allowed the state to collect **$489m** from the federal government in matching funds for a programme that taxed hospitals to fill a fund for medical care for the poor.

George Bush picked **Robert Strauss**, a prominent Democrat and a Texan friend, to be ambassador to Moscow.

The attorney-general, **Dick Thornburgh**, announced that he would run for the Senate from Pennsylvania in 1992 to fill the seat vacated by the death of John Heinz in an aeroplane crash.

Thursday 6th
Tears came to his eyes as George Bush told an audience of Southern Baptists about how he relied on prayer during the Gulf war. Electioneering time approached?

Friday 7th
A **bitter feud** between Douglas Wilder, governor of Virginia, and Chuck Robb, a senator from Virginia, broke into the open. Mr Robb said Mr Wilder had described his career as "finished" and urged a reporter to rubbish him. Mr Wilder charged that Mr Robb's allies had tapped his telephone to find that out.

Three Republican senators wrote to the president saying they no longer believed they could save **brilliant pebbles**, the space-based part of the Strategic Defence Initiative.

Tuesday 11th
Mr Bush approved $1.5 billion worth of agricultural credits to provide food aid for the **Soviet Union** over nine months, in response to a request from Mikhail Gorbachev.

Wednesday 12th
George Bush launched a broadside at **Congress** for failing to act on highway and crime bills in 100 days. He had challenged them in March to pass both bills in as long as the Gulf war took.

Sunday 16th
In trouble again, **John Sununu**, the White House chief of staff, defended his use of a government limousine to go to a stamp auction in New York. The president was said to be furious. A third travel scandal then emerged when Mr Sununu was found to have taken corporate jets without proper authorisation.

Tuesday 18th
Buoyed by hopes of economic recovery, the **dollar** surged to a new high, reaching DM1.81, the highest for 19 months. It continued to rise for most of the month.

A judge ruled that the Virginia Military Institute could continue admitting only men and **no women cadets**. To allow in women would destroy 152 years of southern spirit, said some. Meanwhile the four chiefs of staff were split on allowing women soldiers into combat: the army and marines against, the air force and navy for.

Wednesday 19th
Legislators in Louisiana overrode the governor's veto and passed the most restrictive **anti-abortion law** in the country. It banned abortions for all except women whose lives were in danger or who were victims of incest or rape. The law seemed certain to go to the Supreme Court.

The House majority whip, **Bill Gray**, the most senior black in Congress, resigned to run the United Negro College Fund.

Thursday 20th
The Supreme Court reversed a famous **libel** decision. Janet Malcolm had been accused of fabricating quotes from Jeffrey Masson, a controversial Freudian scholar, in an article in the *New Yorker*. The court said words put between quotes were more powerful and potentially libellous than other words, but stopped short of saying fabricated quotes were libellous.

Friday 21st
The Supreme Court ruled that elected judges are "representatives" subject to the 1965 Voting Right Act, which requires **proportional racial representation**. It also said nude dancing was not exactly free speech and was not therefore protected from obscenity laws by the first amendment.

The **Humvee**, a military jeep made famous in the Gulf war, would go on sale to the public from next June, said the manufacturer: priced at $45,000 each. Arnold Schwarzenegger already had a custom-built model.

Wednesday 26th
Tests carried out at the behest of a historian on the corpse of **Zachary Taylor** proved that the old general and president, who died in 1850, was not arsenic-poisoned by southerners. That he caught a bug after eating cherries on the Mall in July seemed more plausible all along.

Thursday 27th
Thurgood Marshall, a black hero of civil rights, resigned from the Supreme Court, citing ill health. President Bush quickly named another black, Clarence Thomas, to replace him, thus raising charges that he was creating a racial quota on the court while arguing against them in business. The switch further emphasised the court's shift to the right. In the term just ended, it overturned five precedents and drastically curtailed the rights of defendants in criminal trials.

Friday 28th
The Senate passed a **gun-control** bill, but reduced the proposed waiting limit for those who would buy handguns from seven to five days. President Bush was therefore certain to receive a crime bill that included some gun control, for which he has an all-American dislike. Would he veto it?

Los Angeles was shaken by an **earthquake** that measured six on the Richter scale, its biggest for 20 years. The damage was light.

At the last minute, the California Assembly approved a record **tax increase**: $4.1 billion from extra sales taxes. A balanced budget for the coming fiscal year remained in doubt.

July

Monday 1st
The fiscal year ended for several states that had passed no **budget** for the next year. Government shut down in Maine and Connecticut. Seven other states, including California, were budgetless for several days.

Iowa outlawed **smoking by those under 18**. The police said they were too busy to enforce such a law.

Tuesday 2nd
A commencement speech lambasting the amorality of contemporary culture by a dean of Boston University, Joachim Maitre (a former East German fighter pilot), was revealed to have been **plagiarised** in large part from an article in an obscure journal. This according to the *Boston Globe*, whose article was then plagiarised by the *New York Times*. Embarrassment all round.

Friday 5th
The **unemployment rate** rose to 7%, a four-year record, after the June figures were calculated. The administration urged another cut in interest rates but was rebuffed by the Federal Reserve.

The closure by the Bank of England of the **Bank of Credit and Commerce International** led to a trickle of serious allegations from the murky world of conspiracy theory. The CIA was said to use the bank, the Justice Department was said to have dragged its feet to stop a Senate committee and a New York prosecutor follow up charges of money laundering and fraud, and politicians were said to have been financed by BCCI.

Tuesday 9th
Alan Fiers, a former chief of the CIA's Central American task force, became the first figure in the **Iran-contra scandal** to reach a plea bargain with the prosecutors, agreeing to tell his story in exchange for leniency. That spelt potential trouble for Robert Gates, the nominee to head the CIA.

Wednesday 10th
George Bush lifted American sanctions against **South Africa**, saying that all conditions had been met. Opponents said the existence of political prisoners meant one condition had not been met.

Bill Bradley, a senator from New Jersey, launched an unusually personal **attack on George Bush**, who, he said, exploited the issue of race for political gain and was not interested in ending racial discrimination.

Thursday 11th
A **total eclipse of the sun** was visible from Hawaii and Mexico. Eclipse fever gripped the nation.

Friday 12th
Stepping up his war of words with Saddam Hussein over a concealed nuclear weapons programme, George Bush approved 20 targets for **aerial attack**.

Saturday 13th
A film about drug gangs called "Boyz N the Hood" opened and spawned copy-cat violence across the country: at least 33 people were wounded and one man died.

Monday 15th
The commerce secretary decided not to revise the **census** to try to take into account the 5m people it overlooked. Since they were disproportionately urban, cities were unhappy and lawsuits were threatened.

Tuesday 16th
At the summit of seven leading industrial economies in London, George Bush breached royal etiquette by **sitting down before the queen**. Anglo-American amity survived.

Wednesday 17th
Mikhail Gorbachev brought to George Bush in London a concession on the last remaining issue holding up a **START treaty** to reduce long-range nuclear weapons. A summit was arranged for Moscow to sign the treaty, which would cut American numbers of weapons from 12,000 to about 8,000-9,000.

Richard Gephardt, House majority leader and squeaky-clean populist, decided not to run for president. He would have been a near-favourite for the Democratic nomination. Instead he became almost certain to succeed Tom Foley as Speaker one day.

New York was horrified by the news that a man had **raped his 3-year old niece** 25 feet from a busy road. He was chased and caught by a truck driver.

Thursday 18th
A photograph purporting to show **three fliers missing in action in Vietnam** alive and holding a sign with a 1990 date, caused their families much hope. The hope was dashed two weeks later by Pentagon workers who found it was taken from a Russian magazine and doctored.

The Senate approved a proposal by Jesse Helms to impose prison terms and fines on **doctors and nurses infected with AIDS** who treat patients without warning them of their infection. A dentist in Illinois who died in 1990 was revealed on July 3rd to have died of AIDS, causing terror in the town where he practised.

Monday 22nd
A **heat wave** that had kept temperatures in the 90s or higher for much of America in July finally broke with welcome cool air from Canada. New York had recorded 102°F, its highest for 14 years.

Tuesday 23rd
Daryl Gates, the embattled chief of the Los Angeles police, announced he would retire next April, a year after the savage beating of a motorist by policemen had plunged him into controversy. A report by a commission headed by Warren Christopher found the Los Angeles police racist and violent.

Friday 26th
A handcuffed and frightened man led police in Milwaukee to the unspeakable horrors of a **serial killer's and cannibal's home**. Jeffrey Dahmer had killed more than 17 people, mainly homosexuals, over several years in Ohio, Germany and Milwaukee. The police had once returned a naked and bleeding intended victim, later killed, to him.

Sunday 28th
Liz Taylor announced her eighth engagement to her seventh fiancé (she married Richard Burton twice). The lucky fellow: Larry Fortensky, a construction worker.

Saturday 3rd
More than 300 people were arrested during an anti-abortion protest in **Wichita, Kansas,** one of the few places where abortion in the last three months of pregnancy was still available. Protests continued for weeks and at times it took 40 policemen to keep the clinic open.

Sunday 4th
Jesse Helms, a Republican senator, leaked a report of the Senate ethics committee that called for **Alan Cranston**, a Democrat, to be censured for reprehensible conduct. His offence: he had lobbied regulators on behalf of a contributor.

Monday 5th
According to a Soviet spokesman, George Bush approved in principle a relaxation of the rules of **Cocom,** the international committee designed to keep high-technology out of Soviet hands.

In search of ideas for saving or raising money, David Dinkins, mayor of New York, opened his doors to all **New Yorkers.** They exposed welfare scams, suggested new parking fees and called for a mosaic festival.

Tuesday 6th
Worried that the recovery seemed to be faltering, the Federal Reserve cut **interest rates** by ¼ point to 5½%. This was prompted by bad unemployment figures.

Wednesday 7th
Jay Rockefeller, a wealthy Democratic senator from West Virginia, decided not to run for president. Oddly, this raised his stature from obscure to someone who was "above the fray".

In New York Mario Cuomo's advisory committee on black affairs dissociated itself from a vicious **attack on Jews** made by a professor from the New York City College, Leonard Jeffreys. He accused Jews of putting together "a financial system of destruction of black people".

Jimmy Carter said he did not believe the **"October Surprise"** story that the Reagan campaign had negotiated to delay the release of hostages from Iran in 1980.

Friday 9th
A book giving practical advice to the terminally ill on how to commit suicide, **"Final Exit",** reached the top of the advice best-seller list.

Sunday 11th
An American hostage, **Edward Tracy,** was released in Lebanon, as part of an effort by the United Nations to end the hostage saga. President Bush hinted that Israel should now release some Arabs.

Tuesday 13th
Vice-President Dan Quayle attacked **lawyers.** Addressing the American Bar Association's annual meeting, he called for limits on personal injury suits, the award of costs to the loser and restrictions on contingency fees. "Does America really need 70% of the world's lawyers?" he asked. The association's president grabbed the microphone to say "yes".

The chairman of First America Bancshares, **Clark Clifford,** a former secretary of defence, resigned in the wake of the revelations that it had been illegally acquired by the corrupt Bank of Credit and Commerce International.

Wednesday 14th
In the wake of the Milwaukee case, serial murderers seemed to be everywhere. A man arrested in Mississippi claimed to have **killed 60 people.**

Friday 16th
President Bush signed a Democratic measure designed to **extend unemployment benefit** for the insured beyond 26 weeks. But he refused to declare an emergency and so trigger the spending of the extra money that would be necessary. The Democrats' attempts to make capital out of the issue of unemployment fizzled out.

Monday 19th
America was shocked by the news that a **coup** had deposed Mikhail Gorbachev. George Bush flew back to Washington from Maine. He said he would suspend aid to the Soviet Union and he condemned the "extra-constitutional" action, but was otherwise cautious in tone and he warned those in the Kremlin that he expected them to honour all treaties.

Democratic governors, meeting in Seattle, tried to focus political heat on President Bush for not doing more about **health care**. Lawton Chiles, governor of Florida, said that the party's draft policy statement, which said that all Americans should have access to affordable health care by 2000, let Mr Bush off the hook. He tried and failed to set a deadline of 1994.

Tuesday 20th
President Bush stepped up the verbal pressure on the **"illegal coup plotters"** in Moscow, as Boris Yeltsin's resistance grew. James Baker set off for Brussels for a NATO meeting.

Hurricane Bob hit Long Island and New England, killing nine people, destroying buildings, leaving yachts on land and cutting the power to millions of homes.

Wednesday 21st
As the **Soviet coup collapsed,** George Bush spoke to Mr Gorbachev by telephone, and predicted a "gigantic leap forward" for democracy in the Soviet Union. The coup's plotters had "underestimated the power of the people."

Despite being the unofficial favourite, **Albert Gore** said he would not seek the Democratic nomination for president in 1992, a job otherwise known as sacrificial lamb. His wife and family, he said, were more important.

Thursday 22nd
Three days of riots between **blacks and Hasidic Jews** tore through Crown Heights in Brooklyn after a Hasidic Jew's car killed a black child. David Dinkins fled from a stone-throwing crowd after visiting the child's family.

Monday 26th
Scores on **scholastic aptitude tests,** used for college entrance, fell to a record low for verbal skills.

Wednesday 28th
A subway train in New York careered **off the rails** at high speed, killing five and injuring 170. Rescuers endured infernal temperatures. Police found crack in the driver's compartment. He admitted to drinking and falling asleep at the controls.

Monday 2nd
President Bush recognised the independence of the **Baltic states**, announcing he would establish diplomatic relations with them.

Tuesday 3rd
A fire at a **chicken-processing plant** in North Carolina killed 25 people behind locked emergency exits, drawing attention to safety problems at such factories.

Wednesday 4th
A woman in Houston, Texas, was found guilty of attempting to have her daughter's **cheerleading rival's mother murdered**. She had asked her former brother-in-law to kill the more successful girl's mother in the hope that it would make the girl unhappy and drop out of the cheerleading team.

Thursday 5th
A **television commercial that slung mud** at three senators in an effort to support the nomination of Clarence Thomas to the Supreme Court was condemned by John Sununu. But the Conservative Victory Committee said it would not drop the commercial, which claimed that Edward Kennedy, Joseph Biden and Alan Cranston were ethically unqualified to judge Mr Thomas.

Friday 6th
Clair George, a former chief of the **CIA's** covert operations, was indicted for failing to tell Congress about the Iran-contra affair.

Sunday 8th
Patrick Buchanan, a conservative pundit, published a stirring call to **isolationism** in the *Washington Post*, thus giving voice to a growing sentiment that America deserved, after the cold war's end, to attend to its domestic affairs, not those of an ungrateful world.

Tuesday 10th
Judge Clarence Thomas began his testimony before the Senate Judiciary Committee and gave little hint of his views. He refused to say if he thought a constitutional right to privacy was also a right to abortion.

Wednesday 11th
The **B-2** bomber proved alarmingly easy to detect by **radar** during a test in California, adding to congressional pressure to deny the Pentagon the money to build more of the bombers.

Thursday 12th
To the fury of the Israeli lobby, President Bush said he would **veto** any congressional attempt in the next 120 days to give Israel $10 billion in loan guarantees to help house Soviet immigrants. It would jeopardise the Middle East peace conference, he said. An Israeli cabinet minister called Mr Bush anti-Semitic.

Sunday 15th
Ending the long hiatus in the Democratic presidential race, **Tom Harkin,** a senator from the early caucus state of Iowa, launched his campaign to be president. His populist rhetoric of economic nationalism and class warfare marked this miner's son out as a left-wing candidate.

Monday 16th
All charges against Oliver North, the former marine at the heart of the **Iran-contra affair,** were dismissed. Meanwhile, confirmation hearings began for President Bush's nominee to be director of central intelligence, Robert Gates. The Senate intelligence committee heard about his inability to recall having known about the Iran-contra affair, and later about charges that he twisted intelligence to fit his world view while deputy head of the CIA.

Wednesday 18th
George Bush, saying he was "**plenty fed up**" with Saddam Hussein's resistance to United Nations inspections, admitted he had put American fighter aircraft on alert and authorised them to escort UN helicopters.

Thursday 19th
The Senate voted to prohibit the National Endowment for the Arts from using its money to support **obscene material.**

Monday 23rd
In a speech to the **United Nations**, George Bush spoke of a world "leavened by the cold war's end," of having no desire to impose pax Americana on the world and said that "we will not retreat and pull back into isolationism".

Wednesday 25th
A proposed survey of Americans' **sexual habits** by the National Institutes of Health was dropped after opposition from the Bush administration.

Thursday 26th
The number of Americans living in **poverty,** that is earning $13,359 or less for a family of four, rose to 33.6m in 1990, or 13.5%, according to the Census Bureau.

Kimberley Bergalis, a young woman who contracted **AIDS** from an infected dentist, testified before a House committee in favour of mandatory AIDS testing for health workers.

Friday 27th
George Bush announced big unilateral **reductions in nuclear weapons** and changes in strategy. He said the United States would no longer keep nuclear bombers and missiles on permanent alert; would destroy all nuclear artillery shells and short-range weapons; would remove cruise missiles from surface ships and attack submarines; would drop the plan for a mobile land-based intercontinental ballistic missile; and would begin talks aimed at eliminating land-based intercontinental missiles altogether. All provided the Soviet Union matched these measures.

The Senate Judiciary Committee **split** 7-7 on whether to recommend Clarence Thomas for the Supreme Court, but sent the nomination to the whole Senate anyway.

Monday 30th
A Vietnam war hero, former governor, ex-boyfriend of Debra Winger and senator from Nebraska, **Bob Kerrey**, joined the race for the Democratic nomination. "I want to lead America's fearless, restless voyage of generational progress," he said in Lincoln.

Wednesday 2nd
The House of Representatives voted to give George Bush the full $2 billion he had requested for NASA's **space station**, which it expected to be working by 1999.

A witness before the Senate intelligence committee accused **Robert Gates**, the president's nominee to head the CIA, of "heavy-handed and under-handed" efforts to distort intelligence to fit political prejudice, while he was deputy head of the agency in the 1980s.

Thursday 3rd
The governor of Arkansas, **Bill Clinton**, joined the race for the Democratic presidential nomination. A moderate only slightly damaged by the jibe that he had been a rising star for three decades (he first became governor in 1978 at the age of 32), Mr Clinton set out to "fight for the forgotten middle class".

Smarting from public ridicule at the discovery that 8,331 cheques drawn on a "bank" for congressmen had bounced, the House voted to close the bank. It then emerged that $300,000-worth of House **restaurant bills remained unpaid**. Cash or credit cards only, from now on, said the Committee on House Administration.

Sunday 6th
Somebody leaked to the press the fact that Anita Hill, a law professor at the University of Oklahoma, had accused Judge Clarence Thomas, soon to face a Senate vote on his confirmation to the Supreme Court, of **sexually harassing** her when they worked together in the Justice Department.

Monday 7th
Within the administration an economic argument began to develop into a steadily more public row. Jack Kemp, Robert Mosbacher and Dan Quayle argued fiercely for the need for a **growth package** of tax cuts to kick-start the economy. John Sununu, Richard Darman and Nicholas Brady opposed anything that would reopen the budget agreement of 1990. George Bush was undecided.

Tuesday 8th
Feminists' fury at the Senate's apparent failure to follow up the **sexual harassment** charges against Clarence Thomas led to a postponement of the vote on his confirmation. At one point, seven congresswomen banged on the door of a Senate hearing room demanding a chance to put their view.

Friday 11th
For two days the Senate hearings on the Clarence Thomas **sexual harassment** affair gripped television audiences all over the country. A furious Mr Thomas said he was being lynched. A pained Anita Hill gave details of the pornographic movies and indecent suggestions she said Mr Thomas had regaled her with. Somebody was lying.

In New Jersey a man dismissed for sexual harassment **killed** four people.

George Bush signed a proclamation to mark the beginning of a year of celebration of the quincentenary of **Christopher Columbus**'s voyage to the Americas. It was more fashionable to accuse Columbus of racism, genocide and ecological terrorism than to praise him. Replicas of Lief Ericsson's ships arrived from Scandinavia to spoil the party.

Sunday 13th
Despite terrible reviews, "**Scarlett**", a sequel to Margaret Mitchell's "Gone with the Wind", quickly reached number one in the *New York Times*'s best-seller lists. The publisher was printing 50,000 copies a day. Alexandra Ripley, the author, chose an ending for the famous story that was "stunningly uneventful", said one reviewer. Frankly, the readers didn't give a damn.

Tuesday 15th
After an anguished debate, the Senate voted by 52 to 48 to confirm **Clarence Thomas** on the Supreme Court. Southern senators, mindful of black votes, swung behind him. A poll revealed that more women believed Judge Thomas than Professor Hill.

Wednesday 16th
A lonely, angry man drove a pick-up truck through the window of a cafeteria in Killeen, Texas, and began **shooting people**. He left 22 dead and 18 injured, then killed himself.

Thursday 17th
The House of Representatives rejected a move to ban **semi-automatic pistols** of the type used at Killeen.

Saturday 19th
In the election for governor of Louisiana, the incumbent, Buddy Roemer, came third and was eliminated from the run-off. His predecessor, the flamboyant Edwin Edwards, got the most votes, closely followed by **David Duke**, a former neo-Nazi and grand wizard of the Ku Klux Klan, who campaigned against affirmative action for blacks. Mr Duke and Mr Edwards then entered the run-off.

Monday 21st
Saying he planned to rid Washington of an "unholy alliance of private greed and corrupt politics", **Jerry Brown**, a former Democratic governor of California, declared himself a candidate for president for the third time.

Wednesday 23rd
An opinion poll gave **George Bush** only 47% of the vote against 37% for an unknown Democratic opponent, underlining a sharp fall in his popularity.

Saturday 26th
After the wounds caused by the Clarence Thomas affair and the success of David Duke, George Bush said he would sign the **civil rights bill** he had opposed as a "quota bill" for two years.

Marion Barry, a former mayor of Washington, started a six-month prison sentence for cocaine use.

Wednesday 30th
After George Bush opened the Middle East peace conference in Madrid, the secretary of state, **James Baker**, said "You have to crawl before you walk and walk before you run. Today we all began to crawl."

Thursday 31st
The trial of William Kennedy Smith for **rape** opened in Palm Beach. Jury selection was to take many weeks.

Saturday 2nd

Saying that "the fire has not gone out", but that "it's just a matter of time" before he runs again, **Jesse Jackson** decided not to run for president in 1992. Sighs of relief from other Democratic candidates, five of whom were in New Hampshire for the first beauty contest of the season.

George Bush flew to **Kennebunkport** to see the wreckage of his home. A fierce storm had sent waves through the ground floor destroying furniture and washing mementoes out to sea. He was not fully insured.

Monday 4th

All five living past and present **presidents** met at the dedication of the Reagan library in California—a record. In 1974 there had been not a single ex-president living.

Tuesday 5th

The voters of **Pennsylvania** elected Harris Wofford to the Senate by a wide margin over the erstwhile favourite, Dick Thornburgh, a former attorney-general. Health care was Mr Wofford's best issue. If criminals had a right to a lawyer, sick people had a right to a doctor, he said.

In other elections **incumbents fared badly**. Ray Mabus, a Democrat, lost the governorship of Mississippi to Kirk Fordice, the first Republican to govern the state in nearly a century. An exception to the trend was Ray Flynn, the mayor of Boston, who was re-elected with 75% of the vote and mused about running for

president in several primaries to bring the plight of cities to national attention.

Reacting to the news from Pennsylvania, George Bush **cancelled** a ten-day trip to Asia, annoying his would-be hosts and causing glee among Democrats.

Thursday 7th

Magic Johnson, one of basketball's greatest players, announced that he had **AIDS** and blamed it on his promiscuous heterosexual lifestyle. The news brought discussion of AIDS among blacks and heterosexuals into sudden prominence.

Friday 8th

In Rome for a NATO meeting, Mr Bush said the organisation should **open its membership** to the countries of Eastern Europe.

Saturday 9th

At a meeting in The Hague, America made a large concession in the negotiations over **farm trade** in the GATT. No longer would it insist on 75% cuts in farm subsidies and 90% cuts in export subsidies: 35% would do. For domestic consumption, the agriculture secretary, Edward Madigan, denied the concession was a big one.

Tuesday 12th

Robert Gates was sworn in as **director of central intelligence**. Mr Bush expressed "deepest trust" in him.

After a poll showed him in a dead heat with an (unnamed) Democrat in an election, the president used the word "**liberal**" more than ten times and the word Democrat only twice in a speech about Congress.

Thursday 14th

Congress and the White House reached a compromise on a bill that would extend **unemployment benefit** beyond the usual six months in many states. The president signed it into law the next day.

Friday 15th

The **Dow Jones index fell 120 points** amid general gloom about the prospect of the economy slipping back into recession. Some people blamed Mr Bush's aside in a speech that credit-card lending rates were too high, which had led to a quickly passed Senate bill capping them: the administration disavowed the measure. Mr Bush thought the stockmarkets were over-reacting: "you see there's some fairly good fundamentals getting out there."

Saturday 16th

To general relief, **David Duke**, an ex-Nazi and former grand wizard of the Ku Klux Klan, failed to become governor of Louisiana. Although he won the votes of most whites, he was easily beaten by Edwin Edwards, a former governor twice acquitted on corruption charges. Mr Duke said he might run in some presidential primaries.

Monday 18th

After more than 2,000 **Haitians** trying to reach Florida in leaky boats had been picked up the Coast Guard, the administration ordered them returned to Haiti. A day later a judge in Miami halted the repatriation pending a hearing.

Tuesday 19th

The largest monthly trade deficit for six months, $6.79 billion in September, triggered a second **fall on Wall Street**: it closed down 41 points.

Wednesday 20th

Anxious about being left to share David Duke's opposition to **racial quotas**, Mr Bush signed the civil-rights bill he had long opposed. The day before, the White House instructed the bureaucracy to cancel racial-preference programmes. Howls of protest, so Mr Bush withdrew the order. Confusion all round.

Sunday 24th

After a week of public disarray, the **arguments within the White House** came to a head, with rows about the flip-flops on civil rights, credit-card rates and above all, the need for a "growth package" to restart the economy. Blame flew in all directions; John Sununu even flung some at the president, saying he had "ad-libbed" the credit-card remarks. Mr Bush's approval rating fell in one poll to 51%, its lowest yet.

Wednesday 27th

Congress broke up for **Thanksgiving** in more than usual chaos. House Republicans tried to call for a special session to pass tax cuts; Mr Bush voiced his support; the Democrats called his bluff and announced a session; the president backed down. Nonetheless, in a flurry of activity, Congress passed a bank bill and transport bill, but balked at passing a crime bill.

Tuesday 3rd
Saying he had ceased to be a "positive element in the administration", **John Sununu** resigned as chief of staff. "I assure you that in pit-bull mode or pussy-cat mode (your choice as always), I am ready to help," he wrote to the president. George Bush chose his transport secretary, Sam Skinner, to replace him. He then announced a team to run his re-election campaign. His approval rating had fallen below 50% in an opinion poll.

Wednesday 4th
After six years in chains in Lebanon, **Terry Anderson**, the longest held of the hostages, was set free. The only other Americans still in captivity, Joseph Cicippio and Alann Steen, had been released in the preceding days.

David Baltimore, a Nobel-winning immunologist and president of Rockefeller University, resigned. Embroiled for years in a scandal over fraudulent data in a paper of which he had been one of the authors, he had subsequently persecuted the whistleblower who discovered the fraud.

Saturday 7th
On the 50th anniversary of the Japanese attack on **Pearl Harbour**, George Bush told 2,000 survivors assembled at the naval base that he had "no rancour in my heart toward Germany or Japan. I hope you have none in yours. This is no time for recrimination." He said the attack had been pro-voked by isolationism, a reference to his modern right-wing opponents.

Sunday 8th
Dallas joined the growing roster of cities with **one newspaper** each. The *Dallas Times Herald* closed its doors and sold its assets to its rival, the *Morning News*.

Monday 9th
San Francisco turfed out its liberal mayor, **Art Agnos**, in a run-off election. He was beaten by a conservative ex-police chief, in a campaign dominated by how to deal with the homeless.

Tuesday 10th
"If we had to take a million Zulus next year, or Englishmen, and put them in Virginia, which group would be easier to assimilate and cause less problem for the people of Virginia?" Thus **Pat Buchanan**, a popular journalist, announcing that he would challenge George Bush for the Republican presidential nomination from the right on a platform of "America First." (Answer, to those who know England: the Zulus, clearly.)

Wednesday 11th
The jury took less than two hours to find **William Kennedy Smith** not guilty of rape after a trial unmatched for its publicity: television had covered every intimate detail of Mr Smith and his accuser's sexual encounter on the beach on Good Friday.

Sunday 15th
The first contest among Democratic candidates for president resulted in a clear victory for the governor of Arkansas. In a straw poll of 1,800 Democratic activists in Florida, **Bill Clinton** won 54% of the vote, easily beating Senator Tom Harkin's 31%. Mr Clinton did less well in the first televised debate of the season in New Hampshire that evening.

Monday 16th
The governor of Arizona, **Fife Symington,** became the first senior elected official to be sued by the government over his role in the collapse of a savings and loan institution.

Tuesday 17th
A federal appeals court overruled a ban on the deportation of 6,000 **Haitian refugees** from an American naval base at Guantanamo Bay, in Cuba. Hours later the district judge in Miami who had imposed the ban issued a new order delaying the deportation until he had heard further arguments.

A chain of restaurants owned by Bob Kerrey, a presidential candidate, was cited by the federal government for 116 **violations of child-labour laws**. The eight "Grandmothers" restaurants were employing 14-15-year-olds for too many hours a week or too late at night.

Wednesday 18th
The worst news yet from the recession: **General Motors** announced that it would close 21 plants and cut 74,000 jobs, or nearly one in five.

An annual survey of drugs found that 18% more people regularly took **cocaine** in 1991 than the year before, the first increase for five years. There was also an increase in the amount of LSD taken, though the total number of people taking all drugs fell.

Friday 20th
After months of teasing the press with hints that he would run for president, and at the last possible moment (the deadline for entering the New Hampshire primary), **Mario Cuomo**, the governor of New York, said he would not run—though he wished he could.

Thursday 26th
George Bush picked **Barbara Franklin** as commerce secretary, to replace Robert Mosbacher, who had resigned to organise the president's re-election campaign. Ms Franklin, a management consultant, had often raised money for the Republican Party.

Friday 27th
Parts of Texas were declared a disaster area as a week of **incessant rain** left people homeless and caused rivers to burst their banks. At least 15 people died. The Colorado River rose 48 feet at Wharton. The president flew over the area on his way to a quail hunt.

Saturday 28th
George Bush decided to take 21 business leaders, including the chairmen of the three big Detroit car makers, on his forthcoming two-week tour of Asia to help argue for more open markets for American exports. This choice was meant to underline to American voters his determination that the purpose of this trip was not world politics, but was threefold: "**jobs, jobs and jobs.**"

As we reported then

The home front

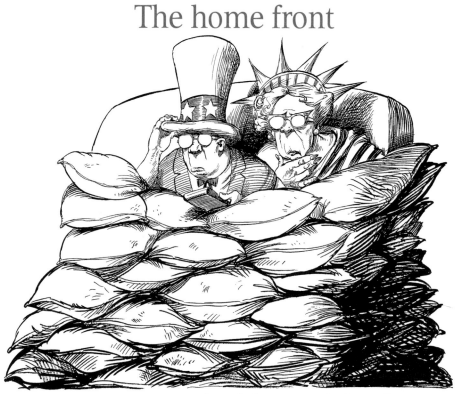

JANUARY 19TH, WASHINGTON, DC *The United States examined its collective conscience in the weeks that led up to the Gulf war. By the time the bombing of Baghdad had begun, the public saw war as inevitable and just; Congress had narrowly voted to support the use of force*

WAR came to America at a little after half past six on the evening of January 16th, when television correspondents reported, live, the sound of an air raid on Baghdad. At eight minutes past seven, Marlin Fitzwater, George Bush's press secretary, announced that the liberation of Kuwait had begun. It was raining in Washington, so there were fewer peace protesters than usual in Lafayette Park, across the street from the White House. Soon, however, 1,000 people had gathered there; not all were calling for peace. As war finally arrived, so did the unmistakable signs of a public rallying around the president. An immediate poll by the *Washington Post* and ABC News found 75% of those asked supporting the president's action. Only 10% said that America should never have attacked Iraq.

The president himself addressed the nation from the Oval Office at nine o'clock. Mr Bush said that the air attacks were aimed at Saddam Hussein's military machine, at his chemical-weapons plants, his tanks and artillery, and at his "nuclear bomb potential". The president said that, while the world waited for Iraq to leave Kuwait,

Saddam had sought to add a nuclear weapon to his arsenal.

It was a speech aimed at an America which had, in the past three months, lost the jingoism with which it first met the Iraqi invasion of Kuwait. It had no new diplomatic message. In an effort to exorcise the demons of the past, Mr Bush said that "this will not be another Vietnam ... Our troops ... will not be asked to fight with one hand tied behind their back". In a now obligatory touch, he read letters from real soldiers, starting with Hollywood Huddlestone, a marine lance-corporal. Normally, when Mr Bush tries this bit of Reaganite hokum, he seems too embarrassed for words. For once, he carried it off with conviction.

The announcement of war relieved a tension that had grown palpable. In Washington, in the days leading up to war, the rumour-mill had been at work. This young man said he had heard that five American subway systems would soon be bombed by terrorists; that young woman said that the Iraqis were going to poison Washington's water. The country as a whole was subdued. In North Carolina (through whose huge

camps many of the troops now in the Gulf have passed), the marine corps sponsored a "Fun and Facts Day" outside Camp Lejeune, with children of servicemen thumbing through their "Daddy's Days Away" activity books. But even in North Carolina the mood was not gung-ho.

Everywhere, the churches were to the fore in protesting against war. In Washington there was a candle-lit march from the Protestant cathedral to the White House; in many cities the Catholic hierarchy led the anti-war movement. The University Baptist Church in Seattle offered sanctuary to members of the armed forces who did not want to serve in the Gulf. And there was, to non-American eyes, an amazing amount of crying: picture someone weeping by candlelight, being comforted by a priest, and you have the perfect image of how much of America looked just before war started.

But not all of America. In the immediate run-up to war, support for the president had grown, though it remains true, as it has from the beginning, that many more men than women support the use of force, and many more whites than blacks. On January 12th, the president won support from Congress for the use of force. He will not, at least for now, have his own hands tied behind his back by the threat of a constitutional crisis.

The votes in Congress—in the House the administration's position triumphed by 250 votes to 183, in the Senate only by 52 votes to 47—showed how cleverly the administration has handled the crisis. Two weeks ago the White House had implied that a majority for force as wafer-thin as that in the Senate would have been unacceptable. When it became clear that bare majorities were the best that could be hoped for, the administration quickly changed the rules. Any majority, it said, would do.

The Republicans lost the votes of two of their own members in the Senate, but gained the support of ten Democrats (seven from southern states). In the House the administration had it easier: 86 Democrats voted for the use of force. The congressional debate did something to retrieve Congress's reputation. For nearly six months its Democratic leaders had prevaricated on the war, wanting neither to vote for the use of force nor to vote to forbid it. But when debate came, it was conducted well, in a tone of high seriousness.

At the State Department, some officials reflected on Saddam Hussein's miscalculations. Had he wanted peace, he could have played for time in all sorts of ways. He could have made a partial withdrawal and said he had won promises that Iraq would not be attacked, that the forces in Saudi Arabia would be removed and that a peace conference on the Middle East would have to be held sooner rather than later. That he made no such move convinced diplomats—and eventually the public—that, whatever concessions were made to him, he had no intention of leaving Kuwait unless forced out.

What happens now? The administration says the war will be short and decisive. Nobody sensible has the faintest idea how American public opinion will react to many deaths. If things go badly, support could wither. In that case, Congress might re-examine its support for the war. A constitutional crisis may have been only postponed.

The majority view is that if the war is successfully prosecuted, and the body count is low, Mr Bush will become a modern hero, and be assured of re-election. A few still

doubt that. Until August 2nd his enormous popularity rested on a never-ending set of foreign-policy successes. The rest of his presidency will be plagued by foreign-policy difficulties far more complicated than the joyous European triumphs of 1989 and 1990. And the old refrain remains true: those difficulties will rankle while the domestic economy is stagnant, and while America's social problems remain as intractable as they were the day Mr Bush became president.

Dark fears

JANUARY 12TH, ATLANTA *In a year that saw a growing obsession with crime, Atlanta tried to force parents to take responsibility for their children*

MOST American parents will have seen a television advertisement which solemnly asks, "Do you know where your children are?" The city of Atlanta has now tacked on an addendum to this familiar question: if you cannot find your children you could face up to 60 days in prison or a fine of $1,000.

This rule followed a couple of nasty blows to the self-image of "the city too busy to hate". Late last year the FBI announced that in 1989 Atlanta had ranked first in reported serious crimes—rape, murder and the like—among large American cities. That and the murders of a four-year-old girl and a 13-year-old boy by teenage gunmen prompted the City Council to act, by imposing a curfew of 11pm on weekdays and midnight at weekends. After these hours those under 17 found on the streets are returned home or detained until their parents pick them up. The parents of frequent offenders are liable to prosecution. After almost two months in operation, Atlanta's curfew appears to be popular with a broad coalition of politicians, parents and policemen.

Curfews have several attractions for municipal governments battling with rising crime rates. They are dramatic, enforceable and cheap. But according to the American Civil Liberties Union, they are also illegal. Later this month the Atlanta branch of the ACLU plans to challenge the constitutionality of the city's curfew law. Michael Hauptman, one of the ACLU's lawyers, says that curfews violate several rights guaranteed under the constitution, including the rights to free assembly and to free speech. The ACLU's longstanding reputation as a defender of unpopular causes is unlikely to be changed by its support for a teenager's right to roam the streets at midnight.

The Atlanta police department

says that it has "interacted with 35 juveniles" since the rule came into force on November 19th. The rate of detentions has declined since the curfew first went into effect: testimony, the police claim, to the increasing rate of voluntary compliance.

The ACLU fears that the curfew will rapidly become an accepted part of Atlanta life. It had aimed to challenge the law almost instantly, but was hampered by a lack of plaintiffs. However, it is still determined to press ahead—with or without plaintiffs—before the curfew becomes set in legal cement.

The civil libertarians worry that once that happens, the curfew will be selectively enforced against blacks and the poor, leaving affluent white teenagers to roam the suburbs unmolested. The curfew's supporters scoff at allegations of racial bias; the law was proposed by a black councilwoman, approved by a black mayor and is being enforced by a largely black police force. White liberals should find other outrages with

which to busy themselves, they say.

The ACLU may find it hard to make charges of racism stick. But it is probably on surer ground in challenging the effectiveness of the law. A pistol-packing, teenage drug-dealer is unlikely to glance at his watch and say "Whoops, it's past 11, I'd better be off home."

In the end, Atlanta's curfew is likely to stand or fall on its legal rather than its social or political merits. Here the record is mixed. In 1989 a curfew imposed on teenagers in Washington, DC, after a similar wave of murders and attendant bad publicity, was struck down by the courts. But other more tightly drafted curfew laws have survived, generally in smaller towns.

The decision of the Georgia courts will be watched around the country. Other cities—Boston is one—are already thinking about imposing their own versions if Atlanta's survives the ACLU's challenge. Overtis Hicks Brantley, one of the Atlanta lawyers who helped draft the curfew, says that she has "received interested calls from literally every part of the United States."

The year of the overdrawn states

FEBRUARY 9TH, WASHINGTON, DC *Just when George Bush's "new federalism", launched in January, has offered the 50 states a new chance to make policy, most of them are struggling to make ends meet*

SIXTY years ago American government had a simple divide. Washington dealt with defence and foreign policy. The states did everything else, from roads to schools. State spending was twice as big as federal spending. Then Franklin Roosevelt changed the rules. By the 1960s the federal government was heavily involved in all domestic policies, and its spending had left that of the states far behind.

Yet the mood at the meeting of the National Governors' Association on February 3rd-5th was not one of gratitude for all this help, but of anger. Anger because, for over a decade, the federal government has been paralysed by its budget deficit while social problems have accumulated. Anger because it has steadily cut most grants to states, so that they account today for 18% of state spending compared with 26% in 1980. Anger because, in place of new thinking about such things as health care, Congress has passed laws telling the states what to do without giving them the cash to do it with. And anger because Washington has pre-empted many sources of state revenue, from alcohol to petrol taxes.

In the absence of federal initiative, policy-making has moved to the state level. The states started worrying about how to improve their schools years before George Bush dreamed up the phrase "education president". While Washington makes empty promises of national strategies, the states have been quietly coping with transport bottlenecks, energy policy, environmental degradation and poverty–sometimes clubbing together in regions to solve their difficulties. This is no longer the old states-as-laboratories idea. It is the states dealing with issues Washington is too timid to address. Europeans who approach 1992 with "subsidiarity" (devolution as far as feasible) as a watchword equivalent to America's federalism would approve of such activism.

One effect has been a reawakening of interest in state government. The eye-catching elections last November were almost all governors' races. No fewer than 14 of the 36 state houses that were contested switched parties. In congressional races, switching has become as rare as rain in California. Of the clutch of new governors, three (in California, Connecticut and Florida) had served in the United States Senate–the first former senators to become governors in over 30 years. In the old days the traffic went the other way: good governors were promoted to the Senate.

The quality of state legislatures and bureaucracies has also improved, even as it has declined in Washington. And people have responded: polls show that voters have more faith in state than in federal government. No wonder the governors have become more assertive.

But the governors also have a negative reason for anger: fiscal troubles. All but one of the 50 states are obliged by their constitutions to balance their budgets. But during the 1980s too many learnt to do this by fiddling the books, storing up trouble for the future. Others took advantage of booming property-tax and other revenues to adopt costly social programmes. Meanwhile Congress was commanding the states to spend more, especially for Medicaid, the federal-state system of health care for the poor.

The recession sent state revenues diving last summer, but in many states elections were approaching. And after the elections there was another pause for new governors to be inaugurated. With the 1991 fiscal year for most states due to end on June 30th, that has left little time to tackle emerging budget deficits that now total over $10 billion. The deficits in some states have reached proportions that are horrendous even by Washington's dreadful standards: Michigan, Rhode Island and Virginia are staring at gaps equivalent to nearly 13% of their spending.

The gaps will be filled, though not at once. In the long run, states may even need a new revenue source (perhaps a consumption tax?). Meanwhile, over half of state legislators said in a recent survey that they expected to raise existing taxes in their current session. Governors like Doug Wilder in Virginia are pushing painful spending cuts through their legislatures. The pressure comes not just from constitutional rules. Even more troubling is the attention of bond-rating agencies that have trimmed the rating of once-proud Massachusetts to BBB, just above junk level. Nobody likes to pay higher interest costs on their debt.

The credit ratings of most states depend on them using borrowing only to finance capital projects, not to support operating expenses in the manner of the federal government. California, for example, has a separately elected treasurer, Kathleen Brown, to insist on just that, and is still rated AAA. But New York, whose rating has now slipped to A, has been carrying operating deficits over from year to year with accounting tricks.

Sununew federalism

All this makes a gloomy background to the renewed push for devolution of spending and decision-making in Mr Bush's 1992 budget. The budget proposes to pick some $15 billion from existing specific grants and turn it over to the states without rules on how the cash should be spent. This would include grants for housing, welfare and environmental administration. Some governors, tired of the old label "new federal-

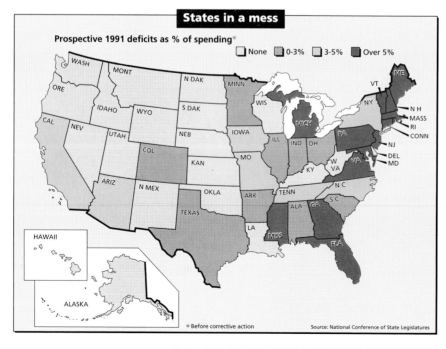

States in a mess

Prospective 1991 deficits as % of spending*

None ☐ 0-3% ☐ 3-5% ☐ Over 5%

WASH, MONT, N DAK, MINN, ME, VT, ORE, WIS, NY, N H, IDAHO, WYO, S DAK, MASS, CAL, NEV, UTAH, NEB, IOWA, ILL, IND, OH, PA, RI, CONN, COL, KAN, MO, W VA, NJ, DEL, MD, KY, VA, ARIZ, N MEX, OKLA, ARK, TENN, N C, TEXAS, ALA, GA, S C, LA, MISS, FLA, HAWAII, ALASKA

* Before corrective action   Source: National Conference of State Legislatures

ism", termed the proposal Sununu federalism, referring to Mr Bush's chief of staff (himself a former governor). After meeting Mr Bush on February 4th, the governors gave a broad welcome to his idea.

Not that they expect it to be enacted. Louisiana's governor, Buddy Roemer, said afterwards that Congress would always tend to be a hindrance, not a help--and he should know, for he served there for eight years. There is also suspicion about promises of "full funding", which might be kept for a few years but then quietly ignored. Transport offers a lesson. Hitherto the federal government has provided 90% of the cash for interstate highways. Under the new plan to be released next week by Sam Skinner, the transport secretary, federal aid for highway building is to be cut to 75%.

Over everything hangs Medicaid, which gets half its money and most of its direction from Washington; the states find themselves ordered to spend more and more on Medicaid to match the federal government. In 1968 the states collectively spent $2 billion on it. By last year that had risen to $33 billion. The governors predict that it could reach $66 billion in 1995 (when the federal share will hit $80 billion).

Two-thirds of the money now goes on long-term nursing-home care, which was not even covered when Medicaid was designed. On Capitol Hill, Henry Waxman, chairman of the House subcommittee on health and the environment, is busily expanding Medicaid into a surrogate national health-insurance system. The governors this week responded by angrily demanding that 1990's mandates to extend coverage to more pregnant women and young children be postponed for two years.

Contrast Medicaid with education policy. The governors are keen to achieve Mr Bush's education goals--the more so now that a former governor, Lamar Alexander, is to be education secretary. They are even prepared to consider heresies such as nationally standardised testing. But none of them pretends that the president (or Congress) is the driving force. It is parents who are pushing for change--even though that often means states also relinquishing power downwards to individual schools.

But even big states cannot solve, on their own, issues like health care, gun control and America's high rate of imprisonment. They need new national policies. If the new push to federalism is just another excuse for Washington to dodge the issues, the states' woes will deepen.

An apology

MARCH 30TH, LOS ANGELES *Our reporting of California's drought had an immediate and dramatic effect. It began to rain, heavily. We took the credit*

ALONG with many other newspapers, we have given the impression that California was suffering from a five-year drought. We may have further suggested that a droplet of rain falling on southern California was as likely as a sincere comment at the Oscars—and that young Californian children would probably never see a cloud in their lifetime.

We now realise that these claims are unfounded. Soon after our article (perhaps as a result of it), it began to rain—and has barely stopped since. San Diego has now had twice as much rain as in the whole of a normal year. We hereby admit that California is, in fact, a lush paradise, where it is sensible to grow crops such as rice and alfalfa with subsidised water. We deeply regret suggesting that farmers, who use around four-fifths of the available water, should be bullied into trading their cheap water with cities.

In our defence we would say that the state's water supplies are still only around half of what is normal at this time of year, and that many Californians, currently refilling their swimming pools and reflooding their orange groves, may live to regret it. In the meantime we offer our apologies to Neptune, Boreas and Thor, and have agreed to pay a substantial sum in damages should they care to collect it.

The Mexican question

APRIL 20TH, DENVER AND WASHINGTON, DC *Protectionists fought a doomed rearguard action against free trade with Mexico*

A POLITICAL issue that may shape the politics of the 1990s more than the Gulf war has gripped Washington. Within the next six weeks Congress must decide whether to extend the "fast-track" authority it grants the administration on trade negotiations. Unless either house of Congress decides to revoke fast-track authority, it will be extended for another two years. If fast-track authority is granted, Congress is limited to voting "yes" or "no" on the results of negotiations; without such authority, Congress can nitpick the outcome of trade talks to death.

In practice, the vote on this piece of congressional arcana will determine whether Capitol Hill supports the administration's desire to negotiate a free-trade agreement with Mexico. Since Mexico and Canada also intend to negotiate such an agreement, and since Canada and the United States already have one, a much-heralded North American Free Trade Area (already called NAFTA) is in sight.

The administration insists at every opportunity that it is not trying to create a regional trading block that would bring an end to its commitment to multilateral free-trade. Any NAFTA, it says, must be conformable to the GATT—there is no plan to create a "fortress America". Mexico's ruling technocrats say much the same thing.

A little more than a year ago, NAFTA was the kind of subject that politicians put in their speeches for padding. It was never going to happen. Mexico, ever protective of its economic independence, was not going to thrust itself into Uncle Sam's arms. Then, last spring, Mexico's president, Carlos Salinas de Gortari, reversed Mexican policy.

His conversion to free trade has placed the Democratic Party in a dilemma. As the Mexican president recently made progress through Texas (before a flying visit to Ottawa), he was greeted rapturously by businessmen and politicians. Simple touches, like Mr Salinas's idiomatic English, allowed some to trumpet his great "leadership". Similar plaudits were offered at a recent conference in Denver on the free-trade pact. This is not how Mexican presidents are usually greeted north of the Rio Bravo (Rio Grande to Yankees).

The western reaction to Mr Salinas gives a clue to one of two ways in which the Democratic Party is now split. The west is gungho for free trade; the east is not. Influential western Democrats like Bruce Babbitt, once governor of Arizona, and Roy Romer, the governor of Colorado, can sound almost messianic about free trade. They—and Californians—know they have no choice but to work closely with Mexico, because (as Mr Salinas never tires of saying) if Mexico cannot export its goods it will export its people. That alone would be enough to convince some westerners of the value of anything

Two-way traffic

that revitalises Mexico's economy.

The 1,900-mile border between Mexico and the United States divides some of the poorest territory of the colossus to the north from some of the richest and most entrepreneurial territory of Mexico. American firms locate plants south of the border, many of them *maquiladora* assembly-lines whose products have, in effect, duty-free entry to United States markets. On some estimates, 500,000 Mexicans now work in the *maquila* industry. Though the boom along the border has unquestionably brought environmental problems, trade between Mexico and the United States has also been an engine of growth—for both countries.

That growth seems far distant if you are a congressman from North Carolina determined to protect your district's small textile factories from the supposed attractions of relocating to Mexico. These eastern Demo-crats are having their case against the free-trade agreement made with vigour by the trade unions in the AFL-CIO. The unions are ferociously lobbying against extending fast-track authority.

This is the second way in which the Democrats are split. Although the share of the American workforce that is unionised continues to decline, unions still have political influence. The AFL-CIO is one of the strongest lobbies in Washington; Mr Babbitt reckons that on the fast-track issue it commands a third of the votes in the House of Representatives (meaning more than half of all Democrats).

The AFL-CIO's case rests on the difference in wage levels between Mexico and the United States. It claims that Mexican production workers are paid rates only 14% of those in the United States (this is not far off: other figures suggest 16%) and that *maquila* workers are paid only 7% of the going rate north of the border. The AFL-CIO hence argues that the principal effect of free trade will be to "export" American jobs to Mexico's cheaper labour.

It is an odd argument. Mr Salinas has already liberalised foreign-investment laws somewhat, *maquiladora* plants already exist, and the American economy is already pretty open to low-cost imports. In those circumstances it is not easy to see how free trade would lead to an export of more jobs than have already gone south (even if trade was a zero-sum game, and even if low wages were the only variable that a company used when deciding where to locate).

Indeed, as Rudiger Dornbusch from MIT points out, the United States' non-oil trade with Mexico swung from a deficit of $1.2 billion in 1986 to a surplus of $2.1 billion in 1989. Using the latest rule of thumb—$1m-worth of net exports equals 30 jobs—that means that the swing in the bilateral-trade balance has already created more than 100,000 jobs in the United States.

But Mexico's average tariff is higher than that of the United States (about 10%, compared with about 4%), and Mexico needs to build up its stock of capital goods, most of which it buys from the United States. So a free-trade agreement could increase the United States' bilateral surplus with Mexico and hence increase American jobs.

These points were made with good effect before the Senate Foreign Relations Committee on April 11th by Robert Zoellick, soon to be under-secretary of state for economic affairs. After that the administration began to be more cheerful. It now feels that the tide is running in its favour.

But a successful vote is not yet in the bag. The AFL-CIO remains powerful and it has been joined in its opposition to the pact both by environmental groups and by those who are bothered about human rights in Mexico. The latter—in an oddly paternalist way—would like to use approval of a free-trade agreement as a stick with which to beat Mexico into political pluralism. The environmentalists are more important. In a letter to George Bush on March 7th, Senator Lloyd Bentsen and Representative Dan Rostenkowski raised the "disparity between the two countries in the adequacy and enforcement of environmental standards" and asked for those issues to be addressed either within the agreement itself or through some "alternative context".

NAFTA buffs now call the latter proposal "parallelism"—the idea that, at the same time as signing a free-trade agreement, the United States and Mexico would commit themselves to co-operate on improving the environment. If parallelism drives a wedge between the environmentalists and the unions, fast-track authority will be extended, and the future of North America will be profoundly altered. If free movement of goods becomes a fact, can free (legal) movement of people be far behind?

A vote in favour of fast-track authority might also, paradoxically, save the Democrats' bacon. They are, at present, perilously close to deciding to snub the government of the developing country that matters most to the United States. They do this not because of some commitment to multilateral free trade or because they have just read what the textbooks say about trade diversion as opposed to trade creation, but because rustbelt industries and unions ask them for protection. As the centre of population moves ever westward, and Spanish-surnamed Americans become ever more numerous, that hardly sounds like good politics.

Congress extended the fast-track authority on May 24th.

Peanut envy

APRIL 13TH, WASHINGTON, DC *An entirely unnecessary peanut shortage developed in April. America restricts both imports and the rights to grow peanuts*

LICENCES to grow peanuts in peanut-hungry America are jealously guarded privileges that pass from father to son. But drought in the south-east, and a nasty peanut disease, have caused the price to rise so sharply that the federal government has had to cut peanut butter from its food-support programmes; children getting subsidised school lunches have been forced to eat cheese sandwiches instead of the peanut-butter ones they traditionally love.

That will not do. So three of the four commissioners on the International Trade Commission have asked the president to lift import restrictions temporarily, to make up for the 13% drop in home production. At present the rules permit only 1.7m lb (771,000 kilos), a tiny fraction of America's peanut consumption of about 3.3 billion lb a year, to be imported from the third-world countries that can grow them more cheaply and would love to sell them. The recommendation is that 300m lb of foreign nuts should be allowed in as a stop-gap measure.

Battle has been joined. Consumer associations are all for the imports, peanut-butter makers are divided, the Department of Agriculture wants to leave things as they are. So, naturally, do the lucky 44,000 farmers in

Georgia, Alabama, Florida, North Carolina and Texas who are licensed to produce peanuts, about one-third of whom are absentee landlords, leasing their production quotas.

Mr Bush will have to make up his mind in the next few days. But there is a precedent for standing up to the peanut farmers by temporarily lifting import restrictions. Jimmy Carter, Georgia's own peanut farmer in the White House, did just that after an even worse peanut crop in 1980.

The dangling vice-president

MAY 11TH, WASHINGTON, DC **When George Bush's heartbeat became irregular on May 4th, America's collective heart fluttered at the thought of Dan Quayle succeeding to the presidency**

DAN QUAYLE'S place on the Republican ticket in 1992 is now secure. It always was fairly safe, because George Bush is a loyal man and because to drop him would be a damaging admission of defeat. But now, after Mr Bush's atrial fibrillation on May 4th, it will be even harder to drop Mr Quayle. No president likes contemplating his own mortality, or suggesting to the electorate that he may die in office.

Nonetheless, the fibrillation was bad news for the vice-president. It made his competence an issue again, but gave him no opportunity to prove himself. For the vice-presidency is a reputation ratchet. A vice-president can get less popular in the job quite easily, but he can do almost nothing to become more popular; that would require doing things that might offend his boss. Mr Quayle, having entered the job with a dismal reputation and made a few gaffes while in it, was waiting for the 1992 campaign: a first chance to surprise his critics.

He has one thing going for him. His reputation is so low that he cannot help but pleasantly surprise people. He was always good at campaigning, and has been successful in glad-handing his way around the country. People like him, blame the media for being horrid about him and, if they are

prospective Republican office-holders, plan to remember his help when 1996 comes along. On policy questions, too, he is taken seriously if only because he has a staff with a reputation for getting things—conservative things—on to the White House agenda.

But this is low-profile stuff. On television, or in front of a microphone, he is as leaden as ever. He rivals Spiro Agnew as the least convincing vice-president of modern times. This week, in a poll by ABC News and the *Washington Post*, 57% of those asked

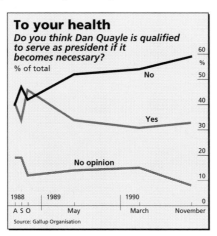

To your health
Do you think Dan Quayle is qualified to serve as president if it becomes necessary?
% of total

Source: Gallup Organisation

thought him unqualified to be president.

According to 16 polls by CBS News and the *New York Times*, George Bush, while vice-president, got a favourable reaction from an average of 35% of people and an unfavourable reaction from 22%. Mr Quayle's average figures from eight polls by the same organisations are 15% favourable and 22% unfavourable. His only consolation is that more people are undecided about him than were about his predecessor.

Democrats are as confused as ever about how to capitalise on the Quayle factor. Some say that Mr Bush should drop Mr Quayle because people have a low opinion of him. Others would prefer Mr Quayle on the ticket, where he might do the president some damage. Still others recognise that they will get few votes next year because of Mr Quayle—people vote for president, not vice-president—so there is little mileage in the issue either way.

The only person who could now remove Mr Quayle from the Republican ticket next year is himself. He is said to find his job frustrating and to wish he could swap places with a cabinet member, to prove himself in a real job. (His preferred switch would be with Richard Cheney, the defence secretary, who, as a former congressman and chief of staff, would make a convincing candidate in 1996, but who has had several heart attacks.) But that might prove a fairly fast track to oblivion, and Mr Quayle knows it.

The cavemen strike back

JULY 13TH, LOS ANGELES **By July California's conservative Republicans could no longer hide their detestation of the Republican governor, Pete Wilson. He found himself under fierce attack within his own party**

WHEN asked to explain why his fellow Republicans were not attending a recent charity roast in Sacramento, Ross Johnson, the minority leader in the California assembly, joked that "they're out hunting spotted owls with AK-47s." He added jovially to the governor, Pete Wilson, that "the owls taste bet-

ter grilled over a redwood fire". Such talk seems out of date. Isn't the new Republican Party made up of kinder, gentler people? Evidence from California, the birthplace of Reaganism and the "cavemen" of Orange county, suggests otherwise.

Mr Wilson is battling to get his $56 bil-

lion budget past California's legislators. He has cut the state's $14.3-billion deficit to $2.3 billion. But on July 3rd the assembly failed to pass it by the necessary two-thirds majority, extending the struggle for 12 more days. The Democrats, whom Mr Wilson had assiduously courted, supported him. The Republican right, furious that the budget includes $8 billion in new taxes, did not. Only nine of the 31 Republicans voted for him.

After a little tweaking, Mr Wilson

should get the last part of his budget through the assembly. Many in Sacramento, including a few on the right, reckon that last week's debacle could have been prevented by Otto Bos, Mr Wilson's widely respected political manager, if he had not died last month. But the vote has cast fresh light on Mr Wilson's conflict with the conservatives.

The animosity dates back to the mid-1970s, when Mr Wilson (then mayor of San Diego) campaigned for Gerald Ford against Ronald Reagan. Mr Reagan remains one of the holy trinity of Orange-county Republicanism. The other two are Howard Jarvis and Paul Gann, who led the Californian middle-class tax revolt which culminated in Proposition 13 in 1978. A dozen of the Republican assemblymen who opposed Mr Wilson will never vote for any new taxes.

Last year the conservatives, a little reluctantly, lined up behind Mr Wilson's campaign for governor. His hawkish record as a senator had pleased some; others held their nose and did not oppose him in the primary because Mr Wilson will now have a big say in how California's congressional and state-legislature seats are redrawn. The last carve-up was under a Democrat, Jerry Brown.

Tom McClintock, one of the hardest conservative assemblymen, now calls supporting Mr Wilson "the biggest political mistake of my career" and accuses the gover-

Cro-magnon Pete

nor of "misrepresenting himself to the people of California." Mr Wilson's sins vary from signing a bill requiring Californians to wear motorcycle helmets to allowing state-financed clinics to recommend abortions. In a speech to adoring Californian Republicans, Pat Robertson, an evangelical, warned Mr Wilson against raising taxes and promoting homosexuality.

Mr Wilson promised to help the nine Republican assemblymen who voted with him on the budget against attacks from the right (an editorial in the *Orange County Register* has already denounced one of them). Some conservatives now talk of running a candidate against Mr Wilson in 1996, though John Seymour and Tom Campbell, moderate Republican candidates for California's two Senate seats next year, look to be certain targets.

Some of this is sabre-rattling. But Mr Wilson's tax increases (which add $1,000 to the average family's tax bill) may give the right the rallying cry it has lacked of late. Some conservatives compare the mood in the suburbs today with that in 1977, just before Proposition 13. The new housing sprawls around Sacramento and San Diego contain voters like those in Orange county.

Reapportionment may give Mr Wilson a few more moderate Republican assemblymen. Many of the current hardliners come from Republican ghettos deliberately created by the Democrats last time round. However, the established wisdom–that moderate Republicans stand the best chance of winning competitive races–is not accepted by the conservatives. Mr Johnson says cheerfully that it is impossible to "create a district where a conservative Republican cannot win the primary." The cavemen, like the spotted owl, will survive.

Out and about

JULY 27TH, NEW YORK AND WASHINGTON, DC **Homosexuals have become more radical in the ten years since AIDS struck. Now they are becoming less united**

"WE'RE here, we're queer, get used to it." So chanted Queer Nation, a noisily radical gay-rights group, during New York's Gay Pride Day parade in June. Confrontational, "in your face" activism is the group's speciality; it also stages all-male "kiss-ins" in heterosexual bars and advocates "outing", the practice of naming well-known Americans who have not admitted to being homosexual. Such tactics are controversial, not least among homosexuals. Ten years after AIDS descended on them like something out of Camus, the solidarity the disease so painfully wrought is starting to crack.

The fissures are many: between younger and older gays; between liberationists and assimilationists; between homosexual men and lesbian women; between those who are infected with HIV, which causes AIDS, and those who are not; between those who defiantly call themselves "queer" and those who do not. Mainstream gay groups, such as the National Gay and Lesbian Task Force (NGLTF), say the divisions are more about tactics than about goals. "The 'isms and schisms' among gays arise naturally from

the community's diversity," says Robert Bray of the NGLTF. "But we all share a common enemy: homophobia."

Maybe. But the differences over tactics are large. The issue of the moment is "outing". On July 17th the Washington chapter of Queer Nation held a press conference to say that a top official at the Department of Defence and a Republican congressman were closet homosexuals. Since then, the name of the congressman has been reported in his home state of Wisconsin and in the *Washington Times*. So far only a dodgy Florida tabloid has carried the name of the Pentagon official.

The silence may not last. The *Advocate*, a respected gay newspaper in Los Angeles, is said to have agreed to publish a story on the Pentagon official by Michelangelo Signorile, a journalist who is the most vocal practitioner of "outing". It was Mr Signorile who set things off last year with posthumous revelations about Malcolm Forbes in *Outweek*, a now-defunct gay magazine. Recently, Outpost, another gay group, began plastering posters around

New York with the faces of Hollywood stars, allegedly secret homosexuals, above the slogan "Absolutely Queer".

The most common argument in favour of such practices is that they expose hypocrites: politicians who pursue anti-homosexual policies but are homosexual in their private lives. That is what Queer Nation said about the Pentagon official; the armed services bar homosexuals. Equally hypocritical, say pro-outers (say a prayer for the English language), is the double standard by which journalists report all sorts of other things about people—their illegitimate children, their drug abuse—but refuse to report their homosexuality.

Most homosexuals—and all of their big organisations—oppose outing. Coming out of the closet, they say, should be a voluntary act of affirmation, of claiming to be what one is. To force anybody's homosexuality into public is rather like the "tool of terror" that anti-homosexuals have used throughout history to blackmail gays. Having a larger number of famous role models would be a good thing, but as Richard Goldstein of the *Village Voice* has written, "no one can force a coward to be a hero."

To radical gays the majority's resistance

is evidence of its cowardice—and symptomatic of why assimilation is doomed to fail. The first gay-rights organisations were formed after the Stonewall riots of 1969, in which homosexuals in a New York bar lashed out at police who had long abused them. Since then, groups such as NGLTF and the Human Rights Campaign Fund have formed the cornerstone of a gay political establishment in Washington, lobbying on homosexual issues and raising money for gay and pro-gay candidates.

They have achieved a great deal. There are now more than 50 openly homosexual elected officials in America, two of them congressmen; in 1980 there were only five. More than 100 cities and counties, and four states, have passed gay-rights laws. A gay civil-rights bill in Congress has 94 sponsors in the House and 13 in the Senate. Last year a bill was passed requiring the police to keep statistics on "hate-crimes", the first law to refer explicitly to homosexuality.

But not everything is going that way. In 25 states and the District of Columbia sodomy in private is illegal—a law upheld by the Supreme Court in 1986. By some measures private employers discriminate against homosexuals more than against any other minority. One chain of family restaurants, called Cracker Barrel, has a policy for its employees prohibiting "lifestyles counter to traditional heterosexual values."

Anti-gay violence appears to be on the rise. Community centres in six cities reported a 42% increase in attacks on gays in 1990 compared with the previous year; the police said the rise was 70%. Nearly 20% of homosexuals say they have been physically abused. On July 24th the police in New York said a series of shootings in Central Park probably had an anti-homosexual cause.

This uneasy mix of progress and setback has splintered gay politics. As in the black and women's move-

ments in the 1960s, a strain of militancy has grown. Articles in *Outweek* proclaimed "we hate straights" and urged gays to "bash back" against heterosexual "oppressors".

Living with death
Nowhere is the splintering more apparent than in the fight against AIDS. When the disease appeared in 1981, the post-Stonewall era of activism was at its zenith. But AIDS transformed America's gays from a burgeoning, increasingly confident and assertive minority into a besieged, panicked—and later, an angry and demanding—one.

Soon the politics of liberation gave way to the politics of survival. As Katherine Boo wrote recently in the *Washington Monthly*,

Proud of it

AIDS brought an educated, middle-class subculture into an unlikely encounter with the welfare state. The subculture did not like what it found and started campaigning for more federal spending on AIDS, safe-sex education and access to AIDS drugs.

Leading the way was ACT-UP (the AIDS Coalition to Unleash Power), which started in 1987. The group's disruptive demonstrations at the Food and Drug Administration and St Patrick's cathedral in New York, and its arresting slogans ("Silence=Death"), earned it publicity and not a little scorn. But by putting pressure on federal bureaucrats and pharmaceutical companies, its Treatment and Data Committee has helped to revolutionise drug-testing procedures and to make AZT, the only effective (if flawed) HIV treatment, available more cheaply.

If ACT-UP was once the unrivalled centre of radical gay politics, it is no longer. A younger generation of activists has arrived in the movement, one not so infected with HIV and more influenced by lesbians. They are not so keen to define their agenda in terms of AIDS. In many cities such as San Francisco, dissension has split ACT-UP in two; some gay people refer to Queer Nation as ACT-UP for HIV-negatives. ACT-UP's democratic structure—and its willingness to put specifically gay issues aside in favour of such goals as national health insurance—makes such instability inevitable.

So does death. As one ACT-UP member says, "It's very hard to run an organisation when your leaders are dying every day." More than 100,000 Americans have died of AIDS; 60% of them were homosexuals. Ten times more will die. Although most heterosexuals have by now known someone with AIDS, they still cannot comprehend that for gays—in the words of Andrew Sullivan of the *New Republic*—"death is less an event than an environment."

The entitlement mentality

SEPTEMBER 28TH, WASHINGTON, DC *It was a year of budget peace. Beneath the calm, though, the deficit swelled alarmingly. The inexorable growth of entitlement programmes was largely to blame*

ON A recent television programme, George Bush's budget director admitted, with little apparent chagrin, that next year's budget is on course for a $345 billion shortfall—a projected 5.8% of GNP. This from Richard Darman, the man who took a bow for cutting last year's "ground-breaking" budget deal with Congress that imposed caps on

various categories of federal spending.

What has gone wrong? Nothing that was not predictable—and predicted—last year. Budget projections invariably suffer from self-deluding bouts of rosiscenariosis. An era of fast-rising revenues always lies just over the horizon. Last year's effort deferred the real deficit-cutting pain until after 1993.

Hints are now being dropped in Congress and by Mr Bush's men that the current budget deal will be junked early in 1993, immediately after the presidential election. That is as good a measure as any of Washington's pitiful resolve.

Yet fully two-thirds of America's $1.5 trillion budget lies outside those "tough" spending caps so agonised over last year. The untouchable things include mandatory "entitlements" for health care and social security (pensions). At least Mr Darman had the courage, which Congress lacks, to suggest that some of these entitlements should now be queried. But he failed to explain what politicians mean by entitlements. It is code for payments to the old. Total entitlement spending accounts for 11.5% of GNP, with the elderly taking two-thirds of that. They have won a huge share of the federal pie over the past two decades.

The cost is hidden. Social-security payments this year will come to about $260 billion—not much less than the defence budget. The social-security trust fund, which will pay the next generation of pensioners, has a fat surplus which is offset against current spending. It should be healthy—the elderly population is growing slowly at present. But a crunch will come in about ten years, when the post-war baby-boomers

start drawing pensions.

If social security is a time-bomb, payments for health care to the elderly are already exploding. Medicare, the principal vehicle, absorbed 1.3% of GNP in 1980, but 2%, or $107 billion, last year. Medicare payments to doctors are forecast to rise indefinitely at a real 13% a year. Political debate about entitlements for the elderly, meanwhile, is taboo. "When I make speeches on the subject," says Rudy Penner, a former director of the Congressional Budget Office, "you wouldn't believe the hate

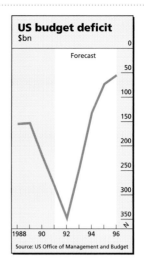

US budget deficit
$bn

Forecast

Source: US Office of Management and Budget

mail I get."

Meanwhile, Congress is finding the will to plug a different kind of deficit. It has emerged that the 435-strong House of Representatives has a $50m bank of its own, the House Bank. Members (salary: $125,000 a year) have gaily been running up overdrafts and still more gaily writing rubber cheques—4,325 bounced in the first half of last year, ten for every congressman. The House speaker, Tom Foley, has now decreed that these bad practices must stop. Economy begins at home—late.

Bob Kerrey's feelings

OCTOBER 5TH *A glamorous war hero turned governor and senator, Bob Kerrey was always going to have to run for president. But is biography sufficient?*

THE first event of Bob Kerrey's presidential campaign was in the Prairie Life Centre, a health club in Lincoln, Nebraska, of which the candidate is a part-owner. In a reversal of usual gladiatorial etiquette, men and women with glistening torsos peered accusingly from a balcony on to a pit heaving with dignitaries.

The next 36 hours were spent more conventionally. An announcement speech in a Lincoln mall; a flight to Denver for a fundraiser and a photo-opportunity at an elementary school; a flight back to Omaha for a rally; a dawn press conference; much hanging around; grumbles from the press corps. At the end of it all, the hitherto murky outline of the Kerrey candidacy was a bit more distinct.

But only a bit. For while everybody in American politics thinks they know Mr Kerrey's personal history—small-town boy, loving family, pharmacist, Vietnam war hero, successful businessman, governor, one-time squire of filmstar Debra Winger, senator—his beliefs are still a mystery. If you tally up the votes, his record in the three years he has spent in the Senate is almost as liberal as that of Tom Harkin, the senator from Iowa who is also a presidential candidate. But while everybody is sure that Mr Harkin is a liberal with a big L, Mr Kerrey is less often tagged with the label. Ev-

erybody is sure that Mr Harkin is a populist. But although he comes from the home state of William Jennings Bryan, that title, too, sits less than easily on Mr Kerrey.

As if to confirm all this, Mr Kerrey's announcement speech was neither classically liberal nor classically populist. In effect it defended the aims of the cold war and (in a passage deleted only because of time) endorsed Ronald Reagan's belief that the Soviet Union had been an evil empire. It was devoid of promises to the poor and hungry. It was polite about George Bush—too polite,

some activists in Denver thought. If it had a theme at all, it was that George Bush was "old" ("a proud man of the cold-war generation") and Mr Kerrey "new". "I want to lead America's fearless, restless voyage of generational progress," was the phrase most quoted later in the day.

Needless to say, this has led to Kennedyesque comparisons. The Democratic Party has been here before. Ever since the assassination of Bobby Kennedy, some party members have been on an uninterrupted search for the combination of youth, glamour and intelligence that the Kennedys were thought to personify.

But the men who were once motivated by the Kennedys are not youngsters any more. JFK was 43 when he was elected president. Gary Hart was 47 in 1984, his best year; Joe Biden (who had his Kennedyesque 15 minutes) was 46 in 1988; and Mr Kerrey will be 49 before next year's election. For all his vaunted sex appeal, he looks his age; when Bruce Springsteen and John Cougar Mellencamp blared out from the loudspeakers at his announcement, his face had the same pained expression that your maiden Aunt Mabel would have if she had to listen to Guns 'n' Roses (Nebraska rumour insists that he is really a jazz fan; this makes sense). Mr Kerrey may appeal to confused parents who are struggling to cope with the fact that their children like sex and drugs as much as they did. But it is not yet clear that he (or any

Democrat) has anything to say to the Republican-leaning under-35s.

More important, it is not clear that Mr Kerrey knows enough to be president. He is a successful businessman, but a small and local one—his partnership has no investments outside eastern Nebraska. He has been in public life for only ten years, and his record as both governor and senator, though competent, is no more impressive than that of many of his peers. JFK had his faults, but lack of intellectual curiosity was not one of them; and he had travelled the world. Mr Hart (whose shadow lies heavy on this year's Democratic field; Mr Kerrey's slick staff is heavy with Hart alumni) certainly had his faults too, but he had prepared for the presidency with great seriousness.

Has Mr Kerrey? Does he really know what he wants to do? If all you did was listen to his thematic speeches you would doubt it, and conclude that he is running on his personality, not on a programme. Somebody who has worked closely with him says that when confronted with a policy choice he says "How do you feel?" not "What do you think?". Feelings are fine (intuition is a great Kerrey word), but presidents need to think too.

Yet not the least of the paradoxes of Mr Kerrey is that in private he has much more command of the detail of policies—on education, trade and tax as well as on health, where he has something of a reputation—than he usually offers in public. Still, he will have to strengthen his ideas and make them more concrete, if only to take on Bill Clinton, the governor of Arkansas, who declared for the nomination on October 3rd and has

eight policies for every two problems.

Mr Kerrey's unwillingness to debate policies suggests that he may not be as self-confident as his boosters claim. There are clues: his Vietnam experience (he lost half a leg there) affected him deeply. He returned an opponent of the war. But the prepared text for his announcement had a perplexing reference to the "cruelties of the communist takeover 16 years ago that are only now beginning to become apparent." It was almost as if he was struggling with the awful possibility that the Vietnam war might have been justified after all; that waging it might have contributed to the containment of a repressive system. In the spring, the line on Mr Kerrey was that he was an interesting man who had not yet worked out what he believed and why. Keep that in mind this winter.

Something awful has happened

OCTOBER 19TH, WASHINGTON, DC *The treatment of Anita Hill's accusations of sexual harassment by Clarence Thomas confirmed people's dislike of Congress*

TOWARDS the end of the Senate's seven-hour debate on the nomination of Clarence Thomas to a vacancy on the Supreme Court, Robert Dole, the leader of the Senate Republicans, rose to speak. Out of the corner of his eye, he noticed that Alan Cranston, a liberal Democrat from California, was anxious to make a point. But the Democrats' time for debate had all but run out. Mr Dole immediately yielded the floor to Mr Cranston. He did so, he said, because tomorrow was another day, and because the Senate had to put two weeks of bitterness behind it.

It will try. Yet everybody is aware that something awful has happened. Mr Dole's gesture was the perfect Senate moment: collegiality in a body that prides itself on that quality more than anything else. Through-

out the day, the chamber had resounded to the sound of senators trying to close ranks. Tributes flowed to Joe Biden, the chairman of the Judiciary Committee. Orrin Hatch, one of the leading Republicans on the committee, apologised unctuously for a slip of the tongue that was offensive to Edward Kennedy, one of its leading liberals. So fulsome was the praise for Jack Danforth, the Republican senator from Missouri who had been Mr Thomas's principal sponsor, that a halo hung around his head.

Outside, on the Capitol steps, a demonstration organised by the National Organisation of Women was rather less polite. "If you like your job", said one banner, aimed at the senators, "vote no". T-shirts carried the face of Anita Hill, the law profes-

sor whose accusations of sexual harassment had plunged Mr Thomas's nomination into turmoil. Betty Friedan, one of the mothers of modern feminism, revealed that she had refused to shake the hand of Alan Simpson, the Republican senator from Wyoming who had been one of Miss Hill's most vicious interrogators.

Yet the threats and the lobbying failed in their objective. At a vote taken with every senator present, Mr Thomas was confirmed by 52 votes to 48, the narrowest margin for any nominee to the Supreme Court this century. Eleven Democrats (seven of them from the old Confederacy) voted for Mr Thomas; two Republicans opposed him.

Six Democrats who before Miss Hill's allegations might have voted for Mr Thomas voted against him. These included Robert Byrd of West Virginia, the king of pork-barrel, who retrieved his reputation with an hour-long tour de force in support of Miss Hill ("I did not see on that face the knotted brow of satanic revenge"), and Joseph Lieberman, the excellent freshman senator from Connecticut, who had earlier publicly supported Mr Thomas. His vote was in doubt until the last minutes.

And so the Senate went home, to return the next day to business as usual: another unsuccessful attempt to override a veto by George Bush, the tedium of roll calls and quorum calls, more overbearing politeness. They would like it to be business as it used to be. But a cloud hangs over Congress. One of the most respected members of the House of Representatives has said that the past few weeks have been the most painful since he took his seat in 1976.

Not just because of the Thomas hearings in the Senate. It is less than a month since *Roll Call*, the Capitol Hill newspaper (with a tiny circulation but the best scoopsheet in town), revealed that members of the House had written 8,331 bad cheques on their own bank in one year. In vain did Tom Foley, the Speaker, rebuke his colleagues; in vain did the House vote overwhelmingly to shut down the bank. The damage was done, and revelation followed revelation: bills in the dining room left unpaid, special perks and expense accounts. Plus the embarrassing re-hashing of an old scandal: the way that Congress routinely excludes its own opera-tions from many employment-protection laws.

The House was in trouble and the Sen-ate relatively smug (forgetting that earlier this year senators had sneaked through a pay rise for themselves at dead of night). But then came Miss Hill's allegations and the mess that Mr Biden's committee made of investigating them when they were first made, followed by the sheer ugliness of the hearings before his committee. Now both bodies are in the firing line.

The criticism, coupled with the frustra-tion that congressmen feel when the two ends of Pennsylvania Avenue are in the con-trol of different parties, has taken its toll. Two good members of the Ohio delegation, one of them barely middle-aged, have just announced that they are fed up with the whole business and will not run again.

Others may find their tenure in Wash-ington cut short by other means. One practi-cal effect of Congress's troubles has been to give a fillip to the movement to limit the terms that its members may serve. George Will, a conservative columnist, is one of sev-eral commentators favouring term limits. The topic is of intense interest to those who are thinking about themes for Mr Bush's re-election campaign. Dan Quayle, the vice-president, has long been committed to the introduction of term limits and is arguing forcefully (and with some apparent success) that the idea should be a central part of the president's platform.

Congressmen worry that popular wrath at their performance will make itself known in next year's elections. Some cooler heads doubt this. They point out that last year, in the wake of the savings-and-loan mess, the Keating Five scandal and what have you, in-cumbency continued to weave its spell. Only one incumbent senator lost his seat, and only 15 members of the House. The elec-torate decided that the rascals trying to get into Congress were no more appetising than the rascals already there.

Cooler heads may be wrong. As Michael Barone of US News & World Report (and of the "Almanac of American Politics") has ar-gued, the 1990 elections carried warning signs for incumbent congressmen. Of those who had opponents in both 1988 and 1990, 65% of House Democrats and 70% of House Republicans saw their share of the vote drop; 53 members of the House won with their lowest margins ever. The fact that this trend was almost equally marked in both parties is the key; it proves that 1990 really did see an anti-incumbent vote, and not (as is usual) a vote against one party or the other.

So look out. If Congress does not pull it-self together soon, quite a few of its mem-bers may be looking for new jobs in 13 months' time.

Thou shalt not fumble

OCTOBER 12TH, DALLAS, TEXAS **The constitution separates church and state—osten-sibly. In practice, Texas seems to be an exception**

IN THE buckle of the Bible Belt, the Lord favours high-school athletics. The 11th commmandment, they say in Texas, is "Thou shalt not fumble". Card-carrying members of the American Civil Liberties Union are as scarce in Texas as ice-storms.

But they can still snarl things up. Two disputes, to do with school and with prayer, have recently gone to court in the Dallas area. In both of them the ACLU brought suit over public religious ceremonies connected with high-school athletics. Both set off acri-monious debates.

The ACLU and the American Jewish Congress filed suit last month on behalf of a Denton high-school student and her parent. This accused the band director, Don Hanna, of promoting Christianity at school games, leading band members in prayer. On October 4th a settlement was reached. The Denton band will continue to play three hymns at its half-time show: "A Mighty Fortress Is Our God", "Precious Lord, Take My Hand" and a Dixieland ver-sion of "Send the Light". But no prayer; and no marching cross.

The hymns were allowed to go on be-cause students had been practising them for a band contest. Discontinuing them, all agreed, would have penalised the students unfairly. "We don't see any need to make the students suffer", said Joe Cook, the exec-utive director of the Dallas ACLU.

Praise the Lord and pass the ball

One girl who did suffer recently was a 14-year-old basketball player in Duncanville. This dormitory town south of Dallas has a remarkable basketball record: its high-school girls won 134 games in 1,156 days, the second longest winning streak in American history. For two decades, after each game, win or lose, the Duncanville girls and their coach would kneel at mid-court and recite the Lord's prayer.

Other Duncanville schools followed suit. But in October 1989 a new student moved into the district and was shocked when her seventh-grade team members joined hands with the coach and began to pray before a physical-education class. She tried to join in, until her father told her she did not have to. Then she stopped. But when the rest of the team knelt in prayer af-ter a game, she heard a spectator scream: "Why isn't she praying? Isn't she Christian?"

School officials, who contend that the prayers are started by the students and are voluntary, refused to stop them when the girl's father complained. And so, last May, to court. The federal judge has yet to rule on the case. In the meantime prayers have been suspended. The girl testified that her history teacher referred to her in class as "the little atheist who didn't want to pray".

The American constitution protects the separation of church and state. But specific cases often bring that principle into conflict with freedom of speech, also guaranteed un-der the constitution. It falls to the Supreme Court to sort out the borderline. In 1989 the court declared school-sponsored prayer un-constitutional. But the court has been trans-formed by the conservative judges ap-pointed recently, and a Rhode Island case coming up soon gives school-prayer advo-cates hope for official sanction.

Texans are not worried, either way. Their schoolchildren will continue to pray, constitutionally or not. Many prayers are piped over school public-address systems. "We've always done it," said a school ad-ministrator. "We just think it's right."

Stirrings from the right

NOVEMBER 23RD, NEW ORLEANS AND WASHINGTON, DC **Two Republicans challenged George Bush for the party's presidential nomination as right-wing dissatisfaction with his moderation boiled over**

THIS is the beginning, not the end", said David Duke on November 16th, as he conceded defeat in the Louisiana governor's race to Edwin Edwards, the erstwhile Democratic governor for whom "colourful" is a wan euphemism. The next day, Republicans lined up on the network television shows to say, with the air of those for whom the wish is father to the fulfilment, that Mr Duke was finished. Mr Duke himself does not think so. He may have failed to beat Mr Edwards, but he won 55% of the white vote in Louisiana and no less than 68% of the votes of whites with just a high-school education or less. On November 18th he announced that he was "not" running for president, but forming an exploratory committee to look at entering some Republican presidential primaries. He wants to stop what he believes is the drift to the left of George Bush's administration.

Whether or not Mr Duke's southern-minted message of racially-tinged populism will play in New Hampshire, the site of the crucial first presidential primary, is a moot point. Many doubt that it will. But however well or badly he now does, Mr Duke's entry into the presidential race has reminded everyone that Mr Bush has always had trouble with the right of his party. In 1980, when he was running for president, he described Ronald Reagan's beliefs as voodoo economics. He was roundly excoriated by the supply-side right for abandoning his pledge not to raise taxes in 1990, attacked by the isolationist right for his obsession with Saddam Hussein, and has never been trusted by what might be called the "cultural right"–those for whom issues like abortion and school prayer are the essence of politics.

It is precisely because there are many mansions on the political right that Mr Bush, if he keeps his nerve, can relax about the right's threat to him. Take Pat Buchanan, a conservative journalist who once worked in the White House under Richard Nixon and Ronald Reagan. Buoyed by a pre-endorsement by the *Manchester Union-Leader*, a conservative newspaper in New Hampshire, Mr Buchanan has said that he is thinking of running for president himself (he thought of it in 1988, too).

Mr Buchanan is an isolationist, an early and consistent opponent of the Gulf war. He is less than friendly to Israel. He has espoused protectionism, seeming to think that it was at the heart of America's 19th century prosperity. (This is an issue on which he has flipped: in a 1988 book he said that to engage in a trade war "because we cannot compete with Korean cars or Japanese computer chips would be an act of almost terminal stupidity for the West.") In short, Mr Buchanan does not represent the Reagan wing of the Republican Party: those who advocate an interventionist foreign policy, love Israel and are for free trade.

It is Mr Bush's good fortune that the only man who could wear the Reaganite mantle with conviction is sitting at his cabinet table. He is Jack Kemp, the housing secretary (Mr Buchanan decided not to run in 1988 so as not to split Mr Kemp's vote). Mr Kemp has made no secret of his impatience with what he believes to be the administration's inactive economic policy. The architects of that policy–Richard Darman, the budget director, Michael Boskin, the chairman of the council of economic advisers, and John Sununu, the chief of staff–have made no secret of their impatience with him. But Mr Kemp's friends maintain that there is no chance of him challenging Mr Bush in 1992. His eyes remain on the prize in 1996.

With Mr Duke removed from his regional base, Mr Buchanan forced to attack Mr Bush's still popular record as a war leader, and Mr Kemp safely indoors, the president should be able to sleep easy, secure in the knowledge that New Hampshire is his. Still, the administration's awful, bickering, panicky autumn has left White House insiders depressed.

The onset of the campaign is anticipated with dread; one who may play a part in it says that it will be full of tears and sackings, as the campaign team and Mr Sununu vie for control of the president. If there is one message that has almost become a cliché, it is the extent to which Mr Bush misses the craft of Lee Atwater, the chairman of Republican Party, who died this year.

....

Mr Sununu resigned on December 3rd.

Squeezed between Duke and Buchanan

Contents

BRITAIN

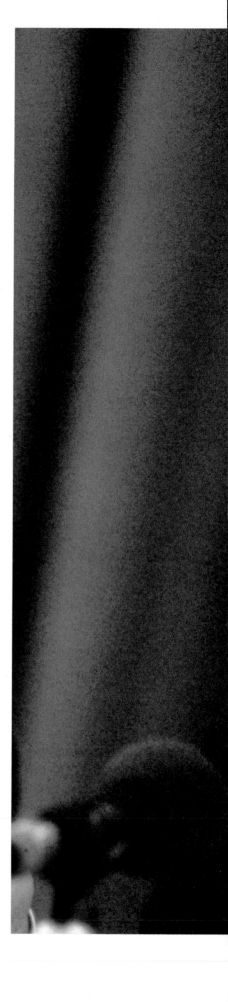

An interlude

A CASE more of out-with-the-old, than in-with-the-new: that must be the verdict on Britain in 1991. While hardly uneventful, it was a year in which events never quite lived up to their billing. Sometimes this came as a relief; the war in the Gulf passed more quickly, and with far less disruption on the home front, than many feared during that night in January when the bombing of Iraq began. Countless other events—including, indeed, the aftermath of the Gulf war—fell flat or simply never happened: anti-climax was 1991's chief hallmark.

There were, inevitably, exceptions. The police and the judiciary had a traumatic time, with several notoriously disputed convictions swept aside—most sensationally, those of the Birmingham Six. Anyone involved in regulating the City, the television industry or the privatised utilities has plenty to remember. It was a bad year for supporting Welsh rugby, owning a pit-bull terrier, espousing a traditional view of priesthood in the Church of England, or being a God-fearing (and law-abiding) small shopkeeper. It was a good one for being a German spectator at Wimbledon, a keen manufacturer of crop circles, or the friend of a Beirut hostage. But in the broader sweep of things, 1991 was, for the British, an interlude between the Thatcher era and the subsequent story of the 1990s.

A thousand political cartoons depicted the Conservative Party at sea and heading for jagged rocks labelled Europe; but as December (and Maastricht) came and passed, the Tory vessel went sailing on. The recession in the economy flattened out by the autumn, in time for plenty of forecasters to talk of a recovery starting by the year-end; in the event, it failed to arrive. A secretary of state for Northern Ireland, Peter Brooke, showed the patience of Job in bringing the province's politicians to the negotiating table; they left it within weeks, accomplishing nothing. Above all, perhaps, it was a year haunted by the prospect of a general election that was never called—though it came close in June, and probably in the late autumn too.

For the only man who knows how close, the year was something of a personal triumph. John Major faced daunting odds at the start. He was a prime minister recently foisted on the electorate by the sudden downfall of Margaret Thatcher. He inherited a parliamentary party deeply unsettled by her abrupt departure, and still riven with uncertainty over the issues that triggered it.

Major misses little

He faced the country as a politician with a short and colourless career at Westminster, whose success owed much to a supremely emollient temperament. This ensured plenty of jokes about the grey man in Downing Street—jokes that could easily have turned into popular scorn. Good luck and a devotion to detail saved him from this political death by derision. He ended the year firmly in control of his party, with the opinion polls reflecting a widespread public respect for his abilities—as well as a measure of continued amusement over his fabled greyness. Not a bad mixture for success in British public life.

His luck came by way of foreign affairs. These cast Mr Major first as the foremost ally of President Bush in defeating Saddam Hussein; then as the chairman of the G7 group of nations, which enabled him to play a walk-on part as one of Boris Yeltsin's lifelines to the West during the August upheavals in Moscow; finally, he was the anti-federalists' champion in the battle against the continent over the drafting of the Maastricht EC treaty. In terms of his own immediate political standing, Mr Major scarcely put a foot wrong through all this.

Home, sour home

The task facing him at home was trickier. Outside Westminster, the new prime minister had to defuse the explosive resentment built up over Mrs Thatcher's poll tax; within Parliament, the challenge was to finesse the Tories' divisions over Europe and win a fresh consensus over the future of the EC. Mr Major surprised his critics on both counts. A cautious approach left nothing to chance, though it prompted frequent charges of indecision and dithering. In the end he was vindicated. The poll tax was scrapped to (almost) universal relief. And in December, the prime minister returned from Maastricht with a deal over the EC's future which astonishingly left most shades of opinion confident that he had served their interests well. Even if he should prove to be one of Downing Street's briefest occupants this century, Mr Major has made his mark.

Will that be his fate? Keen to win a direct mandate for his own premiership but unwilling to risk all with a bold appeal to the electorate, Mr Major dillied and dallied over the timing of the election. He wanted first to see a consistent Tory lead in the opinion polls. This prospect flickered tantalisingly whenever foreign affairs dominated the news; when they faded, Labour inched ahead. The two main parties were both scrambling to recapture the middle ground between them, abandoned in the early 1980s. But the same strategy produced markedly different results on either side of the political divide.

As a torrent of policy papers restated Labour's post-socialist vigour, the party's shadow cabinet grew in stature. Despite obvious misgivings about Neil Kinnock as a future prime minister, the public seemed increasingly ready—in opinion polls, at least—to acknowledge Labour as a party ready to govern. The Conservative Party's move towards the centre was less successful. Ministers found it hard to stir the blood with talk of their post-Thatcher ambitions for the 1990s. She had turned "conviction politics" into a household slogan; the Major cabinet preferred to rely on a more traditional Tory ticket—trust us, as competent pragmatists, to fix what needs mending. The prime minister promoted the idea of a citizen's charter, which would help raise the standards of service offered by the public sector. It was meant to rebuff the notion that the Tories had a barren agenda for the 1990s; for many, it justified the charge. Meanwhile the list of things that needed mending grew longer—and the government looked less handy at fixing them as the year went on.

Kinnock scents it, at last

This impression was often unfair. Solid progress was made in changing the national health service, where a programme of difficult reforms began to win over support from the medical profession. But Labour found it easy to savage the government's intentions. The Tories had to work hard to rein back the public's alarm—though the reforms were seen by many overseas observers as a bold shot at something (ie, controlling the explosive cost of modern medicine) that now poses a challenge for politicians everywhere. In the same way, the Tories probably got less credit than they were due for working to improve standards in state schools. Kenneth Clarke, the education secretary, swept aside protests from the teachers' unions and insisted that too many classroom practices adopted since the 1960s were just plain wrong. But the Tories' ideas on education—on the contents of the national curriculum and on the best way to test pupils learning it—had been tuned and retuned a little too often since the 1988 Education Act. Labour decried the constant revisions as a back-breaking burden for teachers.

Damned thing won't start

Easily the bitterest blow for the Tories, though, was the poor performance of the economy. Having committed sterling to the exchange-rate mechanism (ERM) of the European monetary system late in 1990, the government had little choice but to stand aloof from the recession brought on by the excesses of the 1986-90 boom. As the economy deflated, interest rates would fall and a natural recovery would ensue without fresh inflationary pressures. Things went according to this plan for much of the year. The headlined rate of inflation fell from 9.0% in January to 3.7% by October. Interest rates dropped through a succession of half-a-percentage-point falls over the same period, from 14% to 10½%. A

price was paid in terms of steadily rising unemployment; but the level of pay awards in industry dropped much more quickly than many had dared hope. It looked by the autumn as though Britain might have adjusted to the disciplines of the ERM with far less domestic pain than had been experienced, say, in France in the early 1980s. Further cheer was provided in October by reports of a significant recovery in business confidence. The recession seemed to have ended with the second quarter's fall in GDP; a slow but timely recovery was on its way.

It never arrived. The third quarter's GDP figures showed an economy flat on its back. The hoped for boom in British exports had not happened. Retailers confirmed that the recession was still hitting household spending hard. November brought a stream of depressing statistics. The building and construction industry was enduring its worst slump, some said, for 40 years. The housing market in London and the south-east stayed virtually frozen. As disappointment over the non-recovery grew—and unemployment with it—the government's critics forgot about the battle against inflation and wondered why more had not been done earlier to reflate the economy.

The critics included many Tory backbenchers. With only months to go before the next election, they wanted the economy "kick-started"—a phrase much in vogue over the last weeks of 1991. But most fiscal remedies had to await the budget. So the reflaters turned to the chancellor, Norman Lamont, for a cut in interest rates. Unhappily for Mr Lamont, their pleas chimed with a move to higher rates by the other major currencies of the ERM. This scotched the chances of lower rates on the pound and threatened to push them higher still. Domestic policy and the dictates of ERM membership were tugging the chancellor in opposite directions—a risk inherent in

Castles for sale

membership from the start (and a prime reason for joining, given Britain's inflationary record). Those opposed to membership had been waiting 12 months for such a dilemma to materialise. But as it did so, Christmas arrived and the implications of the decision in 1990 to pin sterling to the ERM were left to be fully confronted in 1992. It was that kind of year.

January

Thursday 3rd
The Foreign Office ordered eight members of Iraq's London-embassy staff to leave the country within 24 hours and ordered the deportation of another 67 **Iraqi nationals**. The move reflected a growing pessimism in the country that war with Iraq could be avoided: the staff of the British embassy in Baghdad had been cut from 16 to six on new year's day.

Monday 7th
The first significant economic statistics of 1991 wiped out any lingering uncertainties about the **severity of the recession**. New car registrations for December 1990 revealed the sharpest year-on-year fall ever recorded for a single month; retail sales volumes for the three months to November 1990 reflected the worst underlying rate of decline since June 1981; and the Central Statistical Office reported that companies' gross trading profits for the third quarter of 1990 showed them falling at an annual rate of 3.1%—another worst since 1981.

An early morning **commuter train** from Kent ran into the buffers at London's Cannon Street station. Two people were killed and 250 were injured, some seriously. John Prescott, Labour's transport spokesman, demanded new laws against overcrowding on trains.

Sunday 13th
John Major, interviewed on television, dismissed speculation about an early election to establish a direct mandate for his own premiership. He had never been "a cut and run merchant", said Mr Major.

Wednesday 16th
The day after the expiry of the **deadline** for Saddam Hussein to withdraw from Kuwait, armed soldiers and tanks began to patrol Heathrow airport, while security was generally tightened at government and military installations in readiness for possible terrorist attacks.

Thursday 17th
The outbreak overnight of fighting in the Gulf prompted the first meeting of the cabinet's **war council** at 7am. John Major afterwards appeared on the pavement of Downing Street and said he hoped Saddam Hussein would swiftly decide to withdraw. In a seven-minute evening broadcast to the nation, Mr Major warned that the war would involve "danger and sacrifice". Most observers thought his downbeat, matter-of-fact tone chimed well with the national mood.

A group of cabinet ministers closely involved with the **poll tax** agreed on an interim financial package worth £1.1 billion ($2 billion) to ease its impact in 1991-92.

Saturday 19th
The annual five-nations championship **rugby match** between England and Wales, played at Cardiff's Arms Park, won a place in the records book when England scored its first victory there for 28 years. But it got plenty of a different kind of publicity, too: the English team afterwards refused to talk to the press, as a protest against the Rugby Football Union's hostility towards players earning money from the game.

Sunday 20th
Opinion polls showed strong public support for the government's **Gulf strategy**. A poll for the *Sunday Times* newspaper found that 80% supported British military involvement and 60% believed Kuwait's liberation was worth the loss of British soldiers' lives.

Monday 21st
Television pictures of two captured **British airmen** prompted widespread calls for Saddam Hussein's removal to be added to the list of the allies' war aims. Photographs of the airmen, one of whom had clearly been badly beaten, appeared on the front of every national newspaper the next day.

The government announced a new plan for the **homeless in London**, pumping £3m ($5.7m) into provincial projects to bail out desperate people before they even set off for the capital. Virginia Bottomley, a health minister, said many of the 3,000 people sleeping rough in the city might have stayed at home had they been given enough assistance earlier.

Tuesday 22nd
Nicholas Mosley, the son of the 1930s fascist leader, Sir Oswald Mosley, won the £22,000 Whitbread **Book of the Year** prize with a novel called "Hopeful Monsters".

A £950m ($1.8 billion) scheme to build an **east-coast motorway** linking the north-east with the Channel tunnel was proposed in a report sponsored by the European Commission, local councils and private companies. Supporters claimed the new road would give the north-east better access to European markets and would help create 60,000 jobs.

The Central Statistical Office celebrated its **50th birthday**—on a preliminary and seasonally unadjusted basis.

Monday 28th
Rolls-Royce, the country's leading manufacturer of aero-engines, unveiled plans to cut the workforce in its Derby factories by about 10% by the end of 1991. The statement came on the heels of a gloomy British Chambers of Commerce quarterly economic survey: 21% more manufacturers said they expected to shed jobs than increase them.

The Home Office ruled out any immediate moves to set up ITV "super regions" in the auction for independent **broadcasting franchises**, due later in 1991.

A letter to the *Independent* newspaper from 19 distinguished writers protested at the Home Office's imprisonment of a **Palestinian scholar** who had been living in Britain since 1975. The protest drew attention to a policy which had resulted in the jailing of 42 Iraqis and eight others, mostly Palestinians, pending their deportation.

Wednesday 30th
At its first meeting since the outbreak of hostilities in the Gulf, the national executive of the **Labour Party** gave overwhelming backing for the party leadership's support of the United Nations war aims. Labour opponents of the war, led by Tony Benn and a handful of other MPs, were swept aside by a large majority of the executive.

Saturday 2nd
The tabloids made a breakthrough in the **kiss-and-tell** school of journalism. The day before the *News of the World* could publish the girl's version of a sexual peccadillo by the brother of the Princess of Wales, a Saturday rival grabbed the headlines by publishing his own account of the story for free.

Tuesday 5th
Peace campaigners cheered, but local businesses groaned, when the American government announced that it had decided to close its **nuclear-submarine base** at Holy Loch on the Firth of Clyde.

Wednesday 6th
The **pound** rose on foreign exchange markets, reaching $2 for the first time since 1981.

Jaguar, the country's biggest maker of luxury cars, said it planned to shed 1,000 jobs in the face of steeply declining sales. Output would be cut by two-thirds within weeks.

Thursday 7th
The IRA launched a **mortar-bomb attack** on the war cabinet as it met in 10 Downing Street. One bomb exploded against a tree in the Downing Street garden, only yards from where John Major and his colleagues were sitting; the other two fell just beyond the garden. They were fired from mortar-tubes in a van parked a few hundred yards away in Whitehall. The terrorists blew up their van and escaped in the midst of a snowstorm, bringing the traffic in central London to a halt for the rest of the morning. Nobody in Downing Street was hurt.

Monday 11th
A severe bout of winter weather produced chaos for travellers all over Britain. The Automobile Association said conditions in the south-west were the worst ever recorded in its 95-year history. British Rail apologised for the fact that a third of its rolling stock had been temporarily put out of action, telling commuters in the south that the storms had brought "**the wrong kind of snow**".

Wednesday 13th
In a letter to *The Times*, six monetarist economists—including Margaret Thatcher's former personal adviser, **Sir Alan Walters**—warned that unless monetary policy was significantly loosened it might well push the economy into a 1930s-style slump. They added that Britain should also consider devaluing the pound.

Within a few hours of the letter's appearance, the Bank of England announced a half-a-point cut in interest rates, to 13½%. But Norman Lamont, the chancellor of the exchequer, said **fighting inflation** was still his first priority—and sterling held its ground in the foreign-exchange markets.

Thursday 14th
British troops in the Gulf sent hundreds of **Valentine greetings** to their sweethearts back home, courtesy of a BBC radio disc-jockey, who travelled to Saudi Arabia to conduct a satellite love-in.

Monday 18th
An IRA **bomb** exploded at London's Victoria station, during the morning rush-hour killing one man and injuring 38 other people. Another bomb had gone off at Paddington station a few hours earlier, with no casualties, and a row ensued over the reaction of the authorities. Police said other London stations had not been immediately evacuated because a warning call from the terrorists had been too vague. Security cameras at Victoria, which could have filmed the bombers, had been switched off.

Tuesday 19th
MPs got cross with the governor of the Bank of England, **Robin Leigh-Pemberton**. A select Commons committee wanted to follow up allegations of improper activities at a bank belonging to Harrods, the Knightsbridge store owned by the Egyptian Fayed brothers. Appearing before the committee, Mr Leigh-Pemberton insisted that banking law prevented him saying anything at all about the proprietorial role of the Fayeds.

The first reports appeared in the press that the cabinet was steeling itself to abolish the **poll tax**.

Thursday 21st
Interviewed on television, **Sir Bob Reid**, the new chairman of British Rail, urged the government to spend up to £2 billion ($3.9 billion) on improving the country's rail network. His supporters said he was determined to grasp the nettle; critics said he had gone native.

Sunday 24th
The **queen** made the first ever wartime broadcast of her reign: in a speech limited to just 90 words, she said the country's pride in its armed forces had already been justified by the successful start to the land battle in the Gulf.

Monday 25th
Lord Justice Woolf published his inquiry into the 1990 riot at **Strangeways prison**. It blamed the disturbance on poor conditions and harshly criticised the state of Britain's prisons in general. Kenneth Baker, the home secretary, reacted by announcing within hours a £36m ($70m) programme to put a toilet in every cell within four years, thus ending the present "slopping out" procedures.

Tuesday 26th
University finance got a dose of discipline. Institutions with good teaching and research records won extra government cash in the annual hand-out announced by the Universities Funding Council; low scorers were penalised with below-average increases.

Thursday 28th
John Major, responding to news of a ceasefire in the Gulf, described the **allied victory** as "one of the most remarkable military campaigns of all time". Margaret Thatcher broke her post-resignation silence in the Commons, with a speech from the backbenches cautioning that the "victories of peace will take longer than the battles of war."

Monday 4th

The government announced the **end of the duopoly** in telecommunications, set up prior to the privatisation of British Telecom in 1984 as a half-way house between the old monopoly regime and a fully liberalised market. A white paper declared the industry open to all-comers, on both local and long-distance lines. BT was required to cut its overall charges by 6¼% a year in real terms from August and international-call charges by 10% within a few months. Most industry observers, though, reckoned BT had been left better placed at the end of the duopoly than they had expected.

Ofgas, the gas industry regulator, asked **British Gas** to think again when the utility announced, with 24 hours' notice, a 35% jump in prices to new power stations. Ofgas said the increase would jeopardise six new power-station projects and should be suspended for a month. Advocates of a truly competitive gas market sharpened their pencils for a long campaign.

Wednesday 6th

In a confident **post-war mood**, prices surged to a record high on the stockmarket and holiday-makers flocked to the travel agents: bookings soared for a few days. Elsewhere, though, the recession continued to bite. Marks and Spencer told two-thirds of its graduate recruits for the autumn that they would have to wait 12 months before joining the payroll.

A report from the House of Lords select committee on science and technology stirred up the perennial debate about the state of the country's **manufacturing industry**. Unless the government moved to combat short-termism and the prohibitively high costs of investment, said the report, British-owned manufacturers could soon become an endangered species.

Monday 11th

Euro-sceptics in the Tory party got a nasty fright when John Major distanced himself from Thatcherite policies towards the European Community, with an enthusiastic speech in Bonn. On his first big overseas visit as prime minister, he told a German audience of his vision of Britain working "at **the very heart of Europe**".

Thursday 14th

The **Birmingham Six** finally won their freedom. Jailed in 1975 on 21 charges of murder, following the notorious IRA pub-bombings in Birmingham the previous year, the six Irishmen were acquitted after a second plea to the Court of Appeal. (The first was swept aside in January 1988.) Lord Justice Lloyd concluded a nine-day hearing by telling them: "Your appeals will be allowed. You are free to go." There were scenes of great emotion as the men emerged from the Old Bailey and held their arms aloft before crowds of cheering well-wishers.

A brainstorming session by a small committee of senior ministers endorsed the conclusion reached by John Major that the poll tax was **unsalvageable**. Their agreement to ditch it was approved by the full cabinet, and plans were announced for further discussions to be held about a replacement property tax on households. The government's dramatic about-turn over the greatest political failure of Margaret Thatcher's premiership drew only muffled protests from a few Tory MPs. Beyond Westminster, though, many local Tory associations bitterly opposed the decision.

Sunday 17th

Air Europe, a holiday airline grounded after the collapse of its parent company, ILG, sacked nearly 2,000 staff as hopes of a buyer faded. Other airlines, which examined Air Europe's accounts, said it was a miracle it survived so long.

Monday 18th

Doctors vied with each other in the press to agree with Norma Major that the strain of the job was getting too much for her husband. After President Bush had described him as "**wiped out**" during a weekend together in Bermuda, Downing Street said the prime minister was looking forward to a quiet Easter holiday in Spain. The *Sun* newspaper then published a photograph of the villa where he would be staying.

Tuesday 19th

There was only one bombshell in Norman Lamont's **first budget**: he raised value-added tax from 15% to 17.5% to pay for big cuts in the poll tax. The chancellor said it would allow the government to reduce community-charge bills by £140 ($250) each in 1991-92. Apart from a few sweeteners for business—notably a one-point cut in corporation tax and a flurry of measures for small companies—other tax changes bashed the rich. Company cars, higher-rate mortgage-interest relief and porta-ble telephones were all penalised; child benefit went up. The stockmarket sagged, but the pound held steady.

A telephone-operator who received a **bomb-hoaxer's call** asked him to hold on, then tipped off the police. They traced him to a pub and reached him 20 minutes later, still waiting for the operator with the receiver in his hand.

Wednesday 20th

Tibet's **Dalai Lama**, on a private visit to Britain that caused severe twitches in the more China-friendly parts of the Foreign Office, addressed a meeting of MPs and peers at Westminster.

Thursday 21st

Michael Heseltine, the environment secretary, pronounced the poll tax dead in the House of Commons and unveiled plans for an extensive future **restructuring of local government**. He said a new tax would be introduced by 1993-94, based on the assessed capital value of each household and taking some (modest) account also of the number of residents.

Tuesday 26th

Nigel Lawson, a former chancellor, attributed the government's protracted agonies over the poll tax to its own indecision about the replacement, and suggested this called into question its **ability to govern**. A furious John Major hit back by telling MPs that his government had done the things Mr Lawson had wanted but failed to do.

Thursday 28th

A Sheffield coroner recorded verdicts of accidental death on 95 football fans crushed to death at the **Hillsborough stadium** in Sheffield in 1989. Angry relatives said they would consider private prosecutions against some of the police officers involved.

April

Tuesday 2nd
Roger Cooper, a British businessman accused of spying by the Iranians, flew home after five years in a Tehran prison. "Anyone who has been to an English public school and served in the British army," he observed, "is quite at home in a third world prison."

Thursday 4th
A surge of support for the **Welsh Nationalists** pushed the Tories into a poor third place in a by-election in the safe Labour seat of Neath.

Monday 8th
After days of mounting concern throughout the West about the plight of **Iraqi Kurds** fleeing to the mountains to escape the soldiers of Saddam Hussein, John Major seized the initiative. He called for the creation of a Kurdish sanctuary in northern Iraq, protected by a multinational military force.

Eurotunnel announced that problems with its shuttle wagons would mean that the **Channel tunnel** could not offer a full service when it first opened in 1993. This did not deter a young German, who was arrested by police as he set out to walk home through the tunnel.

The Football Association announced, and the Football League denounced, a plan to create a **superleague** of 22 first division clubs in 1992-93 (falling to 18 within four seasons), equipped with civilised stadiums and better safety standards. The League, which will be left running only those clubs unable to qualify for the new premier division, accused the Association of trying to hijack the professional game.

Wednesday 10th
The three main political parties launched their campaigns for the May local-government elections, with Labour pledging to cut **local-tax bills** by £140. An opinion poll gave Labour a 4% lead over the Tories.

Thursday 11th
The Tories, already busily squabbling over the effectiveness of **John Major's leadership**, were shaken by an outspoken attack on him by the Bruges Group, a private lobby group widely associated with the more anti-European members of the parliamentary party. It accused Mr Major of "wobbling" over foreign policy and blamed him in part for an inconclusive end to the Gulf war. Margaret Thatcher, the group's president, had to leap hastily to Mr Major's defence.

London Zoo, the world's oldest, asked the Department of the Environment for £13m ($24m) to help it stave off financial disaster. It submitted a survival plan for its future, but denied press reports that it was having to consider killing off some of the 8,000 animals kept at Regent's Park. Government ministers suggested the zoo needed better management rather than more public money. But the thought of a massacre in the menagerie had many animal-lovers reaching for their wallets, and the private donations came pouring in.

Thursday 18th
One of Whitehall's most important jobs went to an outsider, with the announcement that **Sir Terence Burns** would succeed Sir Peter Middleton as permanent secretary to the Treasury.

Sunday 21st
The **London Marathon** attracted 23,559 starters, of whom 23,061 finished. The £31,000 ($53,000) prize for winning the men's race went to a teacher from Siberia who was earning £5 a month.

John Major dithered before remembering for an interviewer how many **O-levels** he has (six). Neil Kinnock, Labour's leader, claimed that everybody remembers that sort of thing and then got his own score wrong. (He claimed seven, but has eight.) The nation looked on, bemused.

Monday 22nd
The sharpest rise in **shop sales** for almost 12 years, unveiled for March, encouraged hopes that the worst of the recession might be over. But the CBI cautioned that a rush to beat the VAT increases announced in the March budget had encouraged the spending spree.

Tuesday 23rd
President **Lech Walesa** of Poland came to London to see the queen. At the start of a four-day visit, the ex-shipyard worker from Gdansk rode with her in a landau carriage through Windsor Great Park.

The government finally unveiled plans to replace the poll tax with a "**council tax**". Michael Heseltine, the environment secretary, told the Commons that the new, property-based tax would sort all 22.2m homes in the country into seven bands according to their market values. The top rate would be no more than 2½ times the bottom rate. The poor would be exempt. Alas, the poll tax would have to linger on, said Mr Heseltine, until April 1993.

The chancellor of the exchequer, **Norman Lamont**, told sceptical businessmen at the annual Institute of Directors' conference that the economy would recover in the second half of the year.

Gerald Ratner, the chairman and managing director of the country's biggest jeweller, jokingly described one of his lines, a decanter set, as "**total crap**". Mr Ratner was then hounded by the tabloids for days, and confessed that he would treat his own sense of humour with more caution in future.

Wednesday 24th
Manchester beat London in a run-off to decide which city would bid to become the host for the **Olympic Games** in 2000. The Mancunians' campaign was led by the Duke of Westminster.

Monday 29th
British Gas agreed to accept tough new rules from Ofgas, the industry's regulator, that would keep **gas-price rises** well below the rate of inflation for 17m households until 1997.

Tuesday 30th
After months of painstaking preparatory talks, Peter Brooke, the Northern Ireland secretary, at last sat down at Stormont Castle outside Belfast to begin an all-party conference on **Ulster's future**. Sinn Fein was excluded, because it would not agree to renounce support for the IRA's armed campaign.

May

Wednesday 1st
Some **car prices** charged in Britain were more than 50% higher, before tax, than those in some other European markets, a study by the Monopolies and Mergers Commission found. Curbs on Japanese car imports and tied distribution networks were found to be keeping prices up.

Monday 6th
Arsenal won the Football League championship. The North London team lost only one game all season.

Tuesday 7th
The **talks at Stormont** on Ulster's future ran into an unforeseen snag: where to hold them? The Irish government wanted them to be convened in Dublin, the Unionists preferred to talk in London. Neutral Strasbourg was dismissed as impractical: there were found to be no direct flights between there and Dublin. The wrangling continued.

Wednesday 8th
The Opposition leader, Neil Kinnock, presented the Labour Party's **economic manifesto** for the next general election. He said his party would put public services before tax cuts, would restore the full value of child-benefit, raise pensions and reverse the government's health-service reforms. He attacked Tory plans to cut the basic tax rate to 20%. A bitter squabble ensued over how Labour intended to pay for better public services.

Thursday 9th
Five weeks after the launch of the government's national health service reforms, the **British Medical Association** offered to defuse a continuing row over their impact by striking a compromise. The doctors told William Waldegrave, the health minister, that they would drop their opposition if the government agreed to put off the next stage of opting out by hospitals and agreed also to review the changes implemented so far. Mr Waldegrave turned down their offer.

Friday 10th
Addressing the annual conference of the Scottish Tories, John Major damped down **premature excitement** over the prospect of a general election and relieved some of the growing political pressure on his chancellor to cut interest rates.

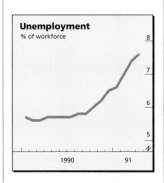

Unemployment
% of workforce

Monday 13th
Evidence of the **depth of the recession** continued to pile up, with seasonally-adjusted unemployment reaching 2.18m in April—that represented 7.6% of the workforce, up from 7.4% in March. The growth in average earnings, at 9% for the 12 months to March, continued to slow. And gloomy figures on consumer borrowing reflected again a general lack of confidence in the high street.

Wednesday 15th
As the deadline fell for bids in the auction to win 16 new **commercial television** franchises, 40 companies had put in submissions. There was no competition for three of the regions, but Granada Television found itself faced with an unexpected challenger at the last minute.

Ulster Unionists demanded and got **a private meeting** with John Major, after appealing to him to break the impasse reached over the future of the all-party talks on Northern Ireland. But then they assured him they wanted to persist with the struggling initiative; and they agreed to accept a yet-to-be-chosen independent chairman, for talks that would involve Irish government ministers sitting down at Stormont.

After 311 years, trading ceased at London's **Spitalfields** fruit and vegetable market.

Sunday 19th
A six-year-old girl was savaged by a **pit-bull terrier** in Bradford. Coming in the wake of a succession of similar incidents, the attack triggered a public outcry which at first wrong-footed the home secretary, Kenneth Baker, and then pushed the government into announcing emergency legislation to ban all fighting dogs. Breeds like the pit-bull terrier and the Japanese tosa had "no place in our homes", said Mr Baker.

Monday 20th
Two white papers on further and higher education included a proposal finally to abolish the distinction between **universities and polytechnics**.

Scrap the monarchy, abolish the House of Lords and get a written constitution—a few of the proposals in the Commonwealth of Britain bill put forward privately by **Tony Benn**, a Labour MP. Well, no harm trying.

Tuesday 21st
Neil Kinnock launched another Labour manifesto—one of a growing number setting out Labour's electoral platform—this time explaining the party's plans for London, centering on a new elected authority. The **Greater London Authority** would have strategic powers over transport, big building developments, and the police and fire services. Best of all, it would (allegedly) pay for itself.

Wednesday 22nd
The tendency for too many people to take **automatic pay rises** came under fire from the prime minister. He called for more restraint, in the wake of an article in the Bank of England's *Quarterly Bulletin* noting the continuing problem. Then the Bank revealed that its governor, Robin Leigh-Pemberton, had been given a 17% salary rise in 1990.

Tuesday 28th
Six months into his new job as transport secretary, **Malcolm Rifkind** appeared to turn the government's previous road-and-rail policies on their head by declaring himself "enthusiastically and unequivocally" in favour of a bigger role for the railways. Labour's John Prescott described the conversion as "greater than St Paul's on the road to Damascus."

Wednesday 29th
The Department of the Environment announced that the overall **rate of collection** for the 1990-91 poll tax in England by the end of March had reached approximately 85%. This compared with about 98% under the old rates and represented a shortfall of nearly £2 billion ($3.6 billion). The worst affected councils were two inner London boroughs, Lambeth and Islington, which respectively managed to collect only 66.6% and 68.6% of the total demanded.

Sunday 2nd
Norman Lamont, the chancellor of the exchequer, said he had ordered a Treasury investigation into reports that **the clearing banks** had not been passing on the benefit of lower base rates to small-business borrowers. Later in the week he summoned the chairmen of the banks to Downing Street to discuss the problem. The Treasury confirmed that any evidence of collusive behaviour by the banks could end up being sent to the Office of Fair Trading. (None was found.)

Monday 3rd
Control of Harrods Bank was taken away from the Egyptian Fayed brothers, owners of the swanky Knightsbridge department store. The Bank of England put it in the hands of independent trustees, a move almost unprecedented in British banking. The Bank's action came a mere three years after a damning report from the Department of Trade and Industry, criticising **Mohamed Fayed** (above, with friend, maintaining a low profile) and his brothers for the way in which they had acquired Harrods.

A meeting at the Commons between John Major and **Margaret Thatcher** sparked off speculation that the prime minister was asking his predecessor to stop stabbing him in the back. Mrs Thatcher had earlier been reported in a Sunday newspaper as saying that she had been wrong to trust Mr Major to carry the torch for Thatcherism—a rumour she strongly denied.

Tuesday 4th
A hoax caller whose bomb scare in February had shut down every main railway station in London was **jailed** for four years. The resulting delay to 500,000 commuters cost an estimated £25m ($48m). "I was bored," said the hoaxer.

Wednesday 5th
Five weeks after the apparent go-ahead for an all-party conference on Northern Ireland's future, Peter Brooke, the Northern Ireland secretary, at last persuaded Ulster's politicians to agree a date for the start of actual talks. Three IRA terrorists were **ambushed and killed** in the province by SAS soldiers.

A report from the Monopolies and Mergers Commission said the public was right to have a low opinion of the **London Underground**. It blamed a ramshackle service on chronic underinvestment and warned of higher fares.

Ownership of **fighting dogs** would be phased out by tough new laws against imports, said Kenneth Baker, the home secretary. Any current owner wanting to hang on to their little Tyson would have to neuter him, insure him for third party liability, get him a police permit and keep him leashed and muzzled in public places. But Mr Baker ruled out a mass slaughter.

Monday 10th
England's cricketers won their first **home Test victory** against the West Indies for 22 years, beating them at Headingley by 115 runs.

Tuesday 11th
Guards staged a sit-in at **Liverpool council**'s main security-control centre in protest against the council's plans for 1,000 redundancies. Strikes over the job losses had already paralysed many services in the city.

Wednesday 12th
John Major struggled at Westminster to defend his credibility over Europe against Tory right-wingers, after a leaked memo from the anti-federalist **Bruges Group** suggested he was frightened of vetoing plans for a single currency. Cabinet colleagues urged Mr Major to take a tough line.

Sharp remarks from John Drummond, controller of BBC Radio 3, about Nigel Kennedy, **a punk violinist**, struck a discordant note. Referring to Mr Kennedy's carefully cultivated cockney accent and extravagant clothes, Mr Drummond suggested he was in danger of turning himself into "the Liberace of the nineties".

Monday 17th
Tories hoping to avoid friction over European policy were let down by Margaret Thatcher. Speaking in America, she denounced federalists as "little Europeans" with "dangerous illusions". Then she warned her colleagues at Westminster that "we had better go back to full and open and free discussion . . . " Responding with unconcealed fury the next day, **Edward Heath** accused Mrs Thatcher of having a "tiny" mind: it was ignorant and deceitful of her, he suggested, to cast membership of the EC as the opposite of a noble sovereignty. Tory MPs were aghast.

Wednesday 19th
The South Yorkshire police agreed to pay more than £500,000 ($815,000) in damages and costs to 39 former **striking miners** who had sued them for their conduct during and after a battle between police and NUM pickets at Orgreave coking plant in June 1984—one of the most acrimonious encounters of the 1984-85 miners' strike.

Tuesday 25th
The prime minister waded into a row over **big pay rises** for the heads of the newly privatised industries. He condemned a 58% increase for the boss of National Power, but said it was not the government's place to interfere.

Wednesday 26th
In a passionate Commons debate on Europe, Margaret Thatcher attacked a draft treaty on political union, agreed at a summit of EC leaders the previous weekend. She told MPs it represented "the **greatest abdication** of national and parliamentary sovereignty in our history."

An opinion poll suggested that, whatever the politicians thought about the idea of a **federal Europe**, many ordinary people favoured it: 43% of those polled were for, 31% against.

Saturday 29th
Somebody up there likes **bookies**. By June 28th they stood to lose £50,000 ($90,000) to punters who had bet that it would rain in London every day in June. On the 29th the capital stayed dry. Next day—with the Wimbledon tennis championships scheduling a full day's play on the middle Sunday of its fortnight for the first time—the rain resumed.

Tuesday 2nd
The BBC announced that Michael Checkland, its director-general, would have to make way for his deputy, **John Birt**, in 1993. Mr Birt, who once worked for ITV, said he looked forward to making the corporation "as lean and efficient as any of its competitors."

The home secretary, Kenneth Baker, unveiled measures to stem a rising tide of **asylum-seekers**, now running at 1,000 a week. The handling of cases would be speeded up and economic refugees screened out. He said that the government had been forced to act because the numbers had surged from 5,000 in 1988 to over 30,000 in 1990.

Wednesday 3rd
Peter Brooke, the Northern Ireland secretary, told the Commons he had decided to break off the all-party talks on Ulster's future that began on April 30th, after 16 months of preparation. He assured the House that foundations had been laid for the future, but MPs heard him out in silence.

The prime minister signalled his support for radical **changes in education**. John Major said he would simplify testing, make teachers more accountable, and encourage the setting up of more city technology colleges and grant-maintained schools.

Thursday 4th
In a by-election in Liverpool Walton, caused by the death of Eric Heffer, the Labour Party inflicted a thumping defeat on the **Militant**-dominated Real Labour Party, whose candidate attracted only 2,613 votes.

Friday 5th
As the Bank of England moved to close down the Bank of Credit and Commerce International, more than 50 **local authorities** found themselves facing embarrassing losses, totalling about £100m ($165m). It emerged within days that the worst-hit was the Western Isles council in Scotland, with lost deposits of about £25m.

Saturday 6th/Sunday 7th
The Germans cleaned up at **Wimbledon**: Steffi Graf took the women's title and Michael Stich the men's, thrashing fellow German Boris Becker.

Two suspected IRA terrorists on remand in **Brixton prison** escaped with the aid of a handgun, hidden in a shoe, and an unsuspecting taxi-driver who picked them up after their break-out and took them to an underground station where they disappeared. The police mounted a huge manhunt; the home secretary, Kenneth Baker, called for a security inquiry; the opposition called for his resignation.

Tuesday 9th
Launching a much trailed white paper, the defence secretary, Tom King, proposed the biggest **defence shake-up** for 30 years. By the mid-1990s the army would be cut by 40,000 to 116,000, and the navy and air force would lose 15% of their manpower. Angry military men, supported by MPs of all parties, accused him of going a cut too far. (Weeks of lobbying ensued, as plans were drawn up to reorganise the army's regiments: in the end, some were merged but none was disbanded.)

The Confederation of British Industry added its support to calls for a central administrative body for **London**. It proposed a government-appointed London Development Agency.

Sunday 14th
The British driver, **Nigel Mansell**, won the British grand prix at Silverstone.

Monday 15th
London hosted a successful three-day **summit meeting** of G7 leaders. The discussions between the G7 leaders themselves were overshadowed from the start by speculation about their response to Mikhail Gorbachev, who appealed to them in person for help with his economic reform plans. The summit concluded in unprecedented fashion, with the Soviet president standing beside the western leaders on the steps of Lancaster House. With the final communiqué taking in a good many points pushed hard by Britain, the meeting was generally deemed a timely success for its chairman, John Major.

Tuesday 16th
British Airways said it was stopping its annual donation to the Tory party, worth £40,000 ($66,000) in 1989-90 and the same in 1990-91, because of the government's decision to give some of the airline's routes to a rival.

First blood in the battle for new **television licences** went to Scottish and to Central, two of the largest existing ITV companies, which emerged as sole bidders for their franchises with bids of less than £1m ($1.6m) each.

Thursday 18th
Unemployment was reported to have risen in June to 2.3m—the 15th consecutive monthly rise. A report from the European Commission said Britain's jobless total would top 3m before 1993.

The political consequences of BCCI's collapse continued to reverberate, with the revelation that a letter warning of **widespread corruption** inside the bank had been received in Whitehall in June 1990. Written by a member of the bank's own staff, the letter had been passed between various departments before being lost altogether.

Monday 22nd
John Major unveiled his long-awaited "programme for a decade"—a **Citizen's Charter**. The glossy brochure promised a better deal for consumers of public services: more published information on targets, more penalties for under-performance and more effective regulation of privatised utilities. Labour criticised the document for providing no extra cash for the public sector; but it won a generally favourable response from the press.

Wednesday 24th
Oftel, the telecommunications regulator, confirmed that competitors would not have to pay special fees to **British Telecom** to gain access to its lines until they had a market share of at least 10%. BT agreed—thereby escaping a referral to the Monopolies and Mergers Commission which had been threatened by Oftel's head, Sir Bryan Carsberg, during a protracted squabble between the two sides that preceded the deal.

August

Sunday 4th
The trade secretary, Peter Lilley, had to interrupt his summer holiday to defuse a row over Britain's exports to Iraq before the 1990 invasion of Kuwait. Customs statistics revealed sizeable **exports of uranium**. A nasty skeleton in the government's cupboard, said Labour. Nonsense, said Mr Lilley: only about 100kg of depleted uranium had been sent, in an 8.6 tonne consignment consisting mostly of industrial isotopes—plus dry ice and a lot of protective lead. But the furore rumbled on for a week.

Monday 5th
The government brushed aside critics of its health-service reforms by inviting applications for the third wave of self-governing **hospital trusts**. Announcing the names of 113 hospitals and units that had applied so far in 1991 for semi-independence, the government urged all NHS managers to join "a gathering momentum of change".

A report into the **escape** of two IRA suspects from Brixton prison revealed that police had given the prison authorities five months' warning that the pair were planning a break-out. Brixton's governor lost his job.

Thursday 8th
John McCarthy, a British television journalist held hostage in Beirut by the Islamic Jihad for five years, flew home. He arrived late in the evening at RAF Lyneham in Wiltshire, where he was welcomed by friends and supporters of the long campaign for his freedom, led by Jill Morrell—plus about 500 photographers.

Monday 12th
England defeated the West Indies in the **fifth Test match** at the Oval, to draw the summer series 2-2. Veteran Ian Botham hit the winning runs.

Tuesday 13th
Hopes that the recession might at last be **bottoming out** were encouraged by news of a 0.2% increase in manufacturing output for June, a surge in North Sea oil production, better than expected retail-sales figures for June and a new high on the stockmarket.

The police killing of a black man who was carrying what turned out to be an unloaded airgun sparked off a street **riot in Shropshire**. Community leaders demanded an inquiry.

The Prince of Wales caused more controversy in the architectural world. Moments before the patrons of the National Museums of Scotland announced the winner of a competition to design a **new museum** in Edinburgh, it was disclosed that the Prince had resigned as their president in protest at the way the winner had been chosen. Both sides blamed the other for the unhappy timing.

Wednesday 14th
The Inland Revenue unveiled a charter to make itself more user-friendly and to cut down on the mumbo-jumbo in its dealings with the self-employed. **Tax inspectors**, it said, should be fair, efficient and helpful (the same promises were made in 1986). Labour MPs said the charter was an "insult" to taxpayers.

The citizen's charter arrived on the football terraces. Cardiff City **football club** announced it would charge £1 ($1.70) less for entry to its ground if the team did badly in the league in the coming season—and £1 more if it should reach the top.

Saturday 17th
Two men took **sanctuary** in the cathedral of Newry, South Armagh, after the IRA threatened to kill them. The pair, who the IRA claimed were members of a criminal gang (sic), said they would stay in the cathedral for years if necessary to escape the gunmen. (They left 11 days later, claiming that the clergy had forced them to hide elsewhere.)

Sunday 18th
Plans were revealed in a Sunday newspaper for a new "**linear city**" east of London to meet the south-east's housing needs. The idea, the brainchild of Michael Heseltine, the environment minister, was said to envisage 30 miles of new developments along both sides of the Thames.

Tuesday 20th
John Major provided **Boris Yeltsin** with one of his few links to the outside world during the Soviet coup as the Russian leader found himself under siege in the parliament buildings in Moscow. Standing in front of hordes of pressmen in Downing Street, Mr Major passed on the gist of a telephone conversation he had just had with Mr Yeltsin: the pair had agreed on the need to have Mikhail Gorbachev freed and to keep his programme of reforms alive.

Wednesday 21st
Sir Edward du Cann, a former Tory MP and long-serving chairman of the Tory back-benchers' 1922 committee, resigned as chairman of Lonrho in the face of moves by the Department of Trade and Industry to have him disqualified as a company director. Sir Edward said he would contest the department's case.

Sunday 25th
Sunbathers scattered when a **powerboat** crashed on to a packed Devon beach, injuring two people, after getting lost in thick fog. Four other racers also crashed, two of them hitting moored boats.

An otherwise-peaceful Caribbean carnival in London's **Notting Hill** was marred by a tragic late-night murder. An argument between strangers led to a stabbing in the street; the victim was a prominent genetic physicist.

Tuesday 27th
John Major set off with his family for a three-day working holiday with George Bush at the president's Kennebunkport home in Maine. In a spate of interviews, he outlined his solution to the Soviet crisis—making aid conditional on economic reforms and defence cuts—and revealed that he would be visiting Moscow within days in his capacity as chairman of the G7 group of nations. At home, the Labour Party could only look on glumly as Mr Major's soaring **international profile** gave the Tories a sharp boost in the polls.

Thursday 29th
Sir Alastair Burnet presented his last television evening-news programme, after a long stint as anchorman for ITN's News at Ten.

Sunday 1st

After three nights of unrest, more trouble broke out in the inner cities. Youths confronted police in outbreaks of **rioting** on housing estates in Cardiff, Oxford and Birmingham. Senior police officers blamed drink, joyriding in stolen cars and a period of unusually hot and humid weather; their leaders called for the return of the Riot Act.

Monday 2nd

Press reports of a red-carpet reception for John Major in Moscow over the weekend triggered three weeks of growing speculation about the **prospects for a November election**. Mr Major's travels—he went on from Moscow to Beijing and Hong Kong—sent the Tories' rating in the polls racing up, the stockmarket reached a record high on the 2nd and base rates were cut on the 4th from 11% to 10½%.

Tuesday 3rd

The Trades Union Congress's annual conference pleased the Labour Party by rejecting a call from the National Union of Mineworkers' president, Arthur Scargill, for the repeal of all Tory **anti-union legislation**. Mr Scargill was described as "the last of the dinosaurs" and a "recruiting agent for the Tories".

Wednesday 4th

The government announced plans to spend £2.8 billion ($4.7 billion) on **widening and improving the M25** motorway round London. Dismayed public-transport lobbyists pointed out that this would exceed London Transport's entire budget for the next three years. Next day the transport department said it had turned down London Underground's request to be allowed to raise its ticket prices to raise cash for extra investment in the tube system. The department also ruled out extra capital grants.

The Advertising Standards Authority announced that it had "effectively banned" a poster promoting Benetton, a clothes company. The poster, showing a **new-born baby** covered in blood and screaming in the midwife's hands, had provoked 800 complaints in four days.

Saturday 7th

A new way to say "I love you"? A **streaker** was arrested for running naked down the pitch at Lord's cricket ground during a knockout-championship final. He explained to the magistrate that he was trying to persuade his wife not to divorce him. A bunch of red roses might have been simpler, said the magistrate—and fined him £50 ($90).

Sunday 8th

The dapper leader of the **Liberal Democrats**, Paddy Ashdown, beamed for the cameras as he kicked off his party's annual conference at Bournemouth. Carving out a distinctive niche for centre politics over the next few days, the party called for an end to slavery. It also promised better education for toddlers, teenagers and adults—paid for by an extra 1p on income tax, if necessary.

In a fierce attack on Church liberalism, the arch-traditionalist Archdeacon of York called for the **Church of England** to be split in two. It was intolerable to be identified with liberal clergy who marry gay couples in church, introduce feminist liturgies and refer to God as "she", he protested. His remarks set off a public debate that lasted several days: John Gummer, the agriculture minister and a member of the church's general synod, warned that unless the liberals eased off, "the Church of England will become a sect."

Monday 9th

Thousands of rugby nuts, golf freaks and opera buffs got the jitters when the country's biggest ticket agency, **Keith Prowse**, collapsed. Receivers were called in to sort out debts estimated at £7m ($12m).

More **rioting** broke out. On a housing estate in North Shields, Tyneside, anti-riot police clashed with youths who set buildings alight, looted shops and cut telephone and power lines. Other riots followed later in the week in Newcastle itself. John Major called it "unacceptable", and side-stepped attempts by opposition politicians to link the trouble to unemployment.

Tuesday 10th

A fresh set of statistics on the state of the economy pointed to a further easing of inflationary pressures and signs of a definite upturn. Even Labour seemed persuaded: rather than denying **economic recovery** it gave warning of another "boom-and-bust" cycle.

Monday 16th

Stung by polls showing that his popularity was sinking and newspaper gossip that some of his colleagues were sharpening their knives, **Neil Kinnock** insisted that he was a "very good captain of the team".

The elite **Magic Circle** of top magicians voted to admit women for the first time in 80 years

Tuesday 17th

A group of ten Tory candidates in safe seats endorsed **road-pricing**, and the London borough of Richmond announced a test scheme.

The case of **Judith Ward**, jailed in 1974 after confessing to an IRA bombing of an army coach that killed 12, was referred to the Appeal Court.

The prospect of an autumn **general election** dimmed after an opinion poll gave Labour a four-point lead—though the poll also suggested the opposition could have been ten points in front if it had been led by John Smith, the shadow chancellor. Two further polls in the next few days broadly confirmed the same message about the relative standing of the two parties.

Wednesday 25th

Looking haggard and frail, 77-year-old Jackie Mann flew into RAF Lyneham after 865 days as a **hostage** in Beirut. A Spitfire fly-past welcomed home the former wartime fighter pilot with a victory roll.

Two Labour MPs, Dave Nellist and Terry Fields, were suspended by party leaders over alleged links with **Militant**. A few days later, on **Sunday 29th**, the Labour Party conference at Brighton opened with a decisive vote in favour of the leadership's firm line.

Monday 30th

John Major finally ruled out a **November election**, on the eve of Neil Kinnock's speech to the Labour conference. The decision was less remarkable than its delivery: a private briefing from John Wakeham, one of Mr Major's closest cabinet allies, to the government's closest newspaper allies.

Tuesday 1st
Addressing the annual **Labour Party conference** in Brighton, Neil Kinnock chided John Major for postponing the general election and said he was running away from the electorate. In a well-received speech, the Labour leader played heavily on his party's role as protector of the national health service. A long ovation closed with a chorus of "We Shall Overcome".

Four former West Midlands detectives who investigated the 1974 **Birmingham pub bombings** were charged with perjury and conspiracy to pervert the course of justice.

Wednesday 2nd
The Department of Health banned a popular **sleeping pill**, sold under the brand name of Halcion, after a negative report on its side-effects from the Committee on the Safety of Medicine. The American manufacturer, Upjohn, had refused to withdraw the drug voluntarily and said it would fight to reinstate the pill, its second biggest product.

Thursday 3rd
The director of public prosecutions, Sir Allan Green, QC, resigned after being stopped by police near King's Cross. He is alleged to have been **kerb-crawling** in a neighbourhood notorious for its street prostitutes.

Billed as Britain's biggest sporting event since the 1966 football world cup, the **rugby union** world cup kicked off at Twickenham. Sixteen teams, including Zimbabwe and Japan (but not South Africa), got down to four weeks of hard scrumming and rucking for glory—or the opposite: two days later, Wales lost 16-13 to Western Samoa at Cardiff.

Wednesday 9th
After getting off to its tradi-tional, heavily pre-pro-grammed schedule the day before, the annual **Tory party conference** was almost de-railed in Blackpool's Winter Gardens by the appearance on the rostrum of Margaret Thatcher. Amid cries for a speech—only abandoned after her personal intervention—the party faithful gave her a five-minute ovation.

Malcolm Rifkind, the transport secretary, announced that the Channel tunnel's **fast-link railway** would go through east London. Sir Alastair Morton, chief executive of Eurotunnel, said the decision to scrap the British Rail alternative—a more direct route into the capital through its southern suburbs—was "a disaster". Others assigned it a historic significance, opening up east London to developers.

Forty overweight superstars limbered up for a five-day sell-out show at the Royal Albert Hall. None of them was called Pavarotti, but there was a Dumptruck and a Wolf: **sumo wrestling** was in town, with the first top-level tournament ever held outside Japan.

Monday 14th
With sectarian **tit-for-tat killings** increasing at an alarming rate in Northern Ireland, the Royal Ulster Constabulary announced that it had set up a special unit to track down loyalist terrorists. With remarkable disregard for allegations, still rife in the media, that security forces had colluded with Protestant gunmen in the recent past, the unit was christened the Loyalist Murder Co-ordinating Team.

Keen to enforce the value-for-money spirit of his Citizen's Charter, John Major intervened to hold down **rail-fare increases** on commuter lines offering sub-standard services—including one between London and his own constituency. Passenger lobby groups said the 7.9% price rise on most other routes was "unjustifiable".

Tuesday 15th
Rebellious Tory backbenchers failed to repulse plans for hefty **defence cuts**. In spite of army fears that 40,000 fewer soldiers would leave it fatally over-stretched, a majority of 258 MPs approved the proposals after a two-day debate. The losers vowed to go on fighting to save some famous regiments from inglorious mergers.

Wednesday 16th
The results were announced of the government's auction for **commercial television** licences. Thames Television, TV-am, TVS—three of the biggest companies contributing to the national network—and TSW were given the bad news by fax that they would have to stop broadcasting at the end of 1992. Only half the 16 new licences were awarded to the companies making the highest bids in their region. The boss of TV-am caused a sensation the next day by publicising a letter of commiseration from Margaret Thatcher, the original architect of the auction; she told him she was "heart-broken" at the outcome.

Monday 21st
The curtain came down on performances at the **Royal Opera House**, Covent Garden, because of a pay row between the management and the orchestra. The musicians, who had taken to playing in casual clothes instead of the traditional evening dress, had threatened to take extra intervals in a new production.

Tuesday 22nd
Two MPs demanded an inquiry into claims that Nicholas Davies, a *Daily Mirror* journalist, had links with the Israeli secret service. Mr Davies and Robert Maxwell, the newspaper's owner, said they would sue over the allegations—which had been published days before, in an American book on the arms trade—and the next day's *Daily Mirror* printed a fierce counter-attack. The MPs, it said, were "a pair of jackals scavenging in the rubbish heap, which is where they belong." This triggered days of intense coverage for what was predictably christened the **Mirrorgate affair**. The newspaper went on angrily protesting Mr Davies's innocence—then sacked him on the 28th for lying to the editor during an internal inquiry.

Tuesday 29th
Norman Lamont, by now a hard-press chancellor, seized on the first real signs of **rising business confidence**: in its regular quarterly survey of industrial trends, the Confederation of British Industry reported that businessmen expected demand to remain stable or improve over the next four months. Earlier surveys had shown expectations of lower demand ever since April 1990.

Saturday 2nd
The Poms lost to Australia by 12-6 in an exciting Twickenham final of the world cup rugby tournament.

Tuesday 5th
The news broke in London that **Robert Maxwell**, the owner of Mirror Group Newspapers and Maxwell Communications Corporation, had been found dead in the sea off the Canary Islands. The circumstances of his death prompted widespread speculation: he had disappeared from his private yacht during the night, as it was cruising on the open sea. Suspicions of suicide were fuelled by reports of a sharply worsening outlook for his business empire. But he was hailed as "the man who saved the *Daily Mirror*" on the front page of his own newspaper the next day, and most of the formal obituaries took a similarly generous view of his achievements.

Wednesday 6th
Norman Lamont, the chancellor, presented the customary autumn statement on **public-spending plans** for the coming fiscal year: he proposed extra dollops in 1992-93 for health, transport and social security. Mr Lamont claimed this reflected the Tories' commitment to "the most vulnerable members of society".

Thursday 7th
The government lifted its tally of **by-election defeats** since 1987 to eight, by losing one seat in the north-east to Labour and another, to the Liberal Democrats, in Scotland. This left the number of Scottish Tories trailing third at Westminster behind the two opposition parties.

Monday 11th
In a delicately worded speech at the annual Lord Mayor's Banquet at the Guildhall, John Major hinted that he was ready to compromise on **Eu-**

ropean integration and warned that he was against any hasty rejection of a single currency.

London Transport reacted furiously to an announcement that the government was stripping it of responsibility for the notoriously unreliable **Docklands light railway**. Ownership would be vested instead in the London Docklands Development Corporation.

Tuesday 12th
A flurry of economic statistics unsettled the City. Producer-price inflation dropped to 4.2% in the year to October, its lowest level for more than four years. The Treasury suggested this was an encouraging sign that core inflation was falling fast. But manufacturing output emerged for the third quarter at almost exactly the same level recorded in the second quarter, prompting fears of **stagnation**. Leading economists began to hedge their bets on any meaningful recovery before the end of the year.

Thursday 14th
Douglas Hurd, the foreign secretary, named two **Libyan agents** believed to be responsible for the bombing of the Pan Am jet that exploded over the Scottish village of Lockerbie in December 1988, killing 270 people. The government said it was demanding of Colonel Qaddafi that he hand them over to face murder charges in an English court.

Despite record losses, Ford offered 29,000 manual workers a two-year inflation-topping **pay deal**, worth at least 5% a year.

On the eve of re-organising itself as the Democratic Left, the **Communist Party** of Great Britain decided to come clean over its past financial links with the Soviet Union. Cash

payments, it said, had been received from the Soviet embassy in London from 1958 to 1979, often amounting to hefty sums—during the 1960s, as much as the equivalent of £1m ($1.8m) a year in 1991 pounds.

Tuesday 19th
Terry Waite, the Archbishop of Canterbury's former special envoy in Lebanon, came home after nearly five years as a Beirut hostage. He astonished onlookers with a powerful 13½-minute speech at RAF Lyneham. His reaction in captivity to receiving a postcard from Bedford, depicting the author of the Pilgrim's Progress in a relatively comfortable prison?: "My word Bunyan, you're a lucky fellow."

Thursday 21st
Support for a **referendum on Europe** began to strengthen, after a two-day debate in the Commons on the issues raised by monetary and political union. Margaret Thatcher demanded that the people's voice should be heard; John Major said he himself was against a referendum, but hinted that a future Parliament might take a different view. Next day, Mrs Thatcher left old allies blushing, and old enemies spitting, after she accused Mr Major of being "arrogant" and "wrong" in his response. Furious colleagues in vain urged Mr Major to censure her publicly.

Monday 25th
More recession gloom, this time courtesy of the **construction industry**. Backed by two new reports predicting steep falls in output, building bosses at an annual trade fair warned the government they were facing the worst crisis in nearly 50 years.

The pound dropped to its lowest level since entering the ERM in November 1990, triggering talk of a rise in **interest rates** and a pre-election sterling crisis—until it rallied.

Tuesday 26th
Michael Heseltine, the environment secretary, set the average **poll-tax bill** for 1992-93 at £247 ($455), a rise over 1991-92 of nearly twice the inflation rate. For the first time, it looked as though all councils might have to be rate-capped. Labour said the government's average bill was bound to be exceeded, as it was the result of "a fairy-tale exercise".

Several leading supermarket chains, including Sainsbury and Tesco, decided that breaking the law was cheaper than breaking the bank: they announced they would stay **open on Sundays** until Christmas. The attorney-general, Sir Patrick Mayhew, incensed many MPs on both sides when he told the Commons he could not intervene—enforcing the law was up to local councils. (This did nothing to spur the councillors on. As Christmas approached, the Sunday outlaws did a brisk trade while the government's critics grew more outraged each weekend.)

Monday 2nd
The suspension of trading in the shares of Mirror Group Newspapers and Maxwell Communication Corporation kicked off a traumatic week for the *Daily Mirror*. Its initial verdict on **Robert Maxwell** as "the man who saved the *Mirror*" gave way to increasingly bitter headlines as the paper tried to come to terms with what its dead proprietor had done—from "Millions missing from *Mirror*" (Wednesday), through "The increasingly desperate actions of a desperate man" (Thursday) to "The Lie" (Friday) and "Bugged!" (Saturday). Other papers watched in glee.

Tuesday 3rd
Kenneth Clarke, the education secretary, launched an inquiry into **primary school teaching**. Mr Clarke said he wanted to end the 25-year rule of "progressive" teaching, which emphasises developing skills over acquiring knowledge. The inquiry, leading to a report within two months, would be taken into account in devising teacher-training reforms early in 1992.

Thursday 5th
A red-faced junior minister had to inform the House of Commons that a missing consignment of **diplomatic mail** had turned up at the laundry of Wandsworth Prison. MPs rolled in the aisles, while the hapless minister parried a flurry of jokes about dirty washing and cats jumping out of bags. The Foreign Office, it emerged, had a contract with Wandsworth prison for the laundering of diplomatic pouches—and someone had sent along a full bag that should have gone to Ottawa.

The Court of Appeal broke with all precedents by apologising to three men whose convictions it had just overturned. The **Tottenham Three** had been given life sentences in 1987 for the murder of a policeman during a riot on a London housing estate in 1985. Three appeal judges said it was profoundly regrettable that the men had "suffered as a result of the shortcomings of the criminal process."

Monday 9th
Judge, jury and executioner: press attention became too much for a **High Court** judge called to a hearing involving Kevin Maxwell. Surrounded by cameramen, he lashed out. Unfortunately, his blow against media intrusion landed on the hapless cabbie who had arrived to take him to the court.

Wednesday 11th
Jubilant Tory backbenchers cheered as John Major arrived to tell the Commons of Britain's "leading role" at the **Maastricht summit**. The result, notably opt-outs from a single currency and a social charter, was "one in which we can clearly see the imprint of our views," he said. For Labour, Neil Kinnock called it "abdication, not negotiation". But the criticism that Tory MPs most feared never came: Margaret Thatcher told journalists the next day that she was "absolutely thrilled" with the outcome.

Monday 16th
The IRA varied a pre-Christmas fire-bombing campaign by putting a small but well-placed **bomb beside a railway line** in south London. It forced British Rail to close all mainline stations into the capital, disrupting the journeys of 500,000 commuters and costing an estimated £40m ($73m).

Ministers sat down with building-society bosses to devise ways of leaving as many **hard-pressed mortgagors** as possible still living in their homes—albeit as tenants. Further meetings followed on the 18th and the 19th, before the societies agreed to set aside as much as £1 billion against the cost of various refunding schemes. In return, the government cancelled stamp-duty payments on houses bought for up to £250,000 before August 1992 (a month later than the last possible date for the election, as it happened).

Monday 23rd
While much of the country got stuck into a week's holiday (or more) for the Christmas break, the City had a tense day as continental **interest rates** rose in the wake of the previous week's ½-point rise in Germany. But the pound, already trading perilously near the bottom of its range in the EC's exchange-rate mechanism, managed to hang on with no rise in base rates. (The cliffhanger continued in the last few days of the year. But to the government's relief, sterling managed a small recovery—and the stockmarket staged its biggest one-day jump of the year on the 31st, lifting the FT-SE index up 3%.)

Friday 27th
The England **cricket team** left for a tour of New Zealand and Australia—minus Ian Botham, who was to catch up with the tour after taking his pads off at the Bournemouth Pavilion where he was starring in "Jack and the Beanstalk".

Desert Orchid, one of the best loved horses in the history of **steeplechasing**, retired after falling in a race on Boxing Day. It was the end of an eight-year career reckoned to have cost the bookies £25m.

Sunday 29th
A rash of end-of-year surveys and reports suggested that a prosperous new year was the last thing most people were expecting. Company directors were markedly less optimistic than three months earlier; ordinary voters seemed to have grown gloomier; employment agencies warned of worsening job prospects. But the chancellor, Norman Lamont, was quick to stamp on **talk of devaluation**—from rattled Tory backbenchers, among others.

Monday 30th
One of the first direct shots in the 1992 election campaign was fired by Neil Kinnock. The Labour leader set his face **against tax cuts** as a way of boosting the economy. If the Tories were "daft or desperate" enough to cut 1p off the standard rate of income tax in a pre-election budget, said Mr Kinnock, a Labour government would put it back.

Tuesday 31st
The **new year's honours** included the CBE for the four returned Beirut hostages. Several sportsmen and artists on the list were less expected—except to those familiar with the new status of cricket and opera in Downing Street.

Folkestone waved farewell to its last **cross-channel ferry**, ending a service to Boulogne that began in 1843.

Among the **cabinet papers** for 1961 released under the 30-year rule was a string of letters recording one of Harold Macmillan's lesser known battles during his premiership: a campaign to press for bounty payments on grey squirrels. SuperMac pestered the agriculture ministry about it for 17 months. But grey men from the ministry sided against the idea and finally saw him off.

As we reported then

Back to the bulldog stuff

JANUARY 19TH *Britain's firm response to the prospect of war in the Gulf was a reminder of more than just its past involvement with the region: the crisis evoked a deep sense of identification with America and distanced Britain from its European neighbours*

NO OTHER western country, not even America, has been as ready to fight in the Gulf as Britain. Resolve to get on with the conflict has been far more apparent in Britain than elsewhere in Europe since long before January 15th—with not much jingoism on display, but little equivocation, either.

The lack of jingoism is logical. Britain's own interests are not as directly at stake as they were in the Falklands; nor is there the same need to keep deep doubts about the outcome of the conflict at bay. The odds on a victory in the Gulf, despite the possibility of a wider conflagration, look far better than they did when the British task force set sail for the South Atlantic in 1982.

The ready resolve is harder to fathom, but there is no mistaking it. A MORI poll on January 10th found that 75% of Britons thought force should be used against Iraq, if it did not remove its troops from Kuwait. Only 18% disagreed. By contrast, polls have shown that 70% of Germans, 53% of Frenchmen, 51% of Italians and 46% of Americans are opposed to war. When asked if the allied forces should try to remove Saddam from power, even if he pulled out of Kuwait, 53% of Britons said they should try and only 34% said they should not. Even the government's war policy—backed by a vote of 453 to 57 in the House of Commons—stops short of seeking to bring down Saddam.

A series of peace marches was held across the country at the weekend, and a rally in London attracted 40,000 people. But the peace campaigners were probably out of tune with most Britons. And pacifism is not what it was. The Oxford Union voted on the night of January 15th against fighting for Queen and Country in the Gulf, evoking shades of the famous vote in 1933 that is supposed to have spurred on Hitler's ambitions. But a wider poll of student opinion by the university's newspaper this week found 60% in favour of war.

The press has been unusually united. Every national newspaper now supports the use of force against Iraq, albeit some with reservations. The Guardian argued on Tuesday that sanctions should have been given more time; but it simultaneously published an article by its chief political columnist which demolished this argument.

BBC television showed a remarkably biased "Panorama", airing the case made by a (tediously small) selection of the war's opponents at some length while restricting any review of the arguments for war almost entirely to an interview with Dick Cheney, the American defence secretary. For the most part, though, broadcast news has been as balanced as the government could have wished.

The most striking sign of Britain's resolve has been its physical commitment to war preparations since last August. This may pale by comparison with that of the United States. The 35,000 British troops represent just 5% of the total allied forces in the Gulf. But Britain is contributing far more than any other of America's western allies: no other country apart from America has sent ships, aircraft and ground forces. And it has provided some crucial weaponry.

Why has Britain reacted so differently from its European allies? The simplest answer is that its political leaders have been the most committed. Mrs Thatcher took a tough stand from the first moments of the drama last August. This left her successor relatively little scope to amend the government's position. But Mr Major has complemented her approach by taking great pains to build the widest possible support for war. It is conspicuous that the outgoing Archbishop of Canterbury, Robert Runcie, whose love-thine-enemy sentiments over the Falklands so angered Mrs Thatcher, has publicly conceded approval of the case for fighting.

As the former leading colonial power in the Gulf, Britain could hardly escape a particular sense of involvement in Kuwait's fate. And Britain's relationship with America—which has blossomed again during this crisis—has strong roots in that region.

There are other factors at work, too. Military tradition has survived more robustly in Britain than in most countries. Although the proportion of British GDP spent on defence has declined from 5.2% in 1985 to just 3.9% in 1990, among NATO members only Greece and the United States spend more. So Britain is well equipped to fight—and has a tough professional army to do the job. The absence of conscription, in contrast to much of Europe, also makes it easier for British public opinion to accept casualties. There has been little opposition to the deployment of troops in Northern Ireland, though 618

soldiers have died there since 1969.

Unlike its neighbours, too, Britain has long been a stranger to military defeat. The victory in the Falklands war reinforced this feeling of invincibility. Nothing could have been better calculated to complement the aversion to appeasement that has run deep in British folk-memory since the days of Chamberlain and Munich in 1938. And the election victory for Mrs Thatcher that followed her Falklands triumph has left its mark on British politics.

Take two films. One is about the passing of cold-war comradeship, fading American interest in Europe and an uneasy British conversion to European union. The other is about an alliance restored, in an old colonial stamping-ground, for as good a cause as you get, with those continentals dodging and weaving. Guess which cinema the British will flock to.

Grocer profits

Source: Verdict Estimates

FEBRUARY 23RD *While most retailers had a miserable time in 1991, the big supermarket chains went on carving out fat profits*

TODAY'S subtly-lit supermarkets, where loganberries nestle up with the kiwi-fruit, are a world away from Jack Cohen's "pile it high and sell it cheap" Tesco's. After the price wars of the late 1970s, when many supermarkets were still conspicuous mostly for their general ugliness and grubbiness, the big chains decided to invest their way out of trouble. It has paid off.

They introduced rigid quality control, centralised distribution and electronic tills. With town centres increasingly congested and car-ownership rising fast, people were keen to shop outside town. So the supermarkets (with the exception of Kwik Save) also started closing their high-street shops and building big edge-of-town stores. A relaxation of planning rules under Margaret Thatcher made this expansion easier.

The supermarkets then found that they could charge bigger margins on goods that were peripheral to their core product-lines of processed foods. Shoppers liked the quality, the fresh fruit, the hot croissants and chilled meals. They still expected to get cheap baked beans, but would pay over the odds for high-quality fresh food.

The price gap between the supermarkets and other retailers has been shrinking ever since. Most surveys show that a basket of food still costs a bit less at a supermarket than it does at an independent grocer's; but *The Economist* did not find that this week. Of an arbitrary 13 goods, five were more expensive in the independents, seven more expensive in Sainsbury's, and one (tinned tomatoes) cost the same. White cabbage was selling for 12p a lb at the greengrocer's and 29p a lb in Sainsbury's. Hardly a scientific survey—but suggestive, nonetheless.

Fresh food is the most extreme example of the change that has come over the shops. Ten years ago, there were a few incidental boxes of onions in supermarkets; in the new-age groceries, the shopper is usually greeted at the door by a banquet of fresh fruit and vegetables glowing with health.

The supermarkets' muscle enables them to demand quality yet keep farmers' prices down, and the gap between what they pay and what they charge has widened. According to Verdict, a retail-industry analyst, the gross margin on fresh foods has increased from 21% in 1986 to 28% in 1990. For some items it is even greater. John Ricks, a farmer near Colchester, says his onions cost 9p a lb

wholesale; packing and transport costs 10p; in paper bags at the local independent, they cost 15p a lb. The supermarket price is 29p—a high premium for tough quality controls.

The speedy, low-inventory distribution systems that big retailers have invested in have made things even more comfortable. The supermarkets get paid cash by the customer a few days after the goods arrive in their shops, while they pay their suppliers between one and two months after delivery.

Suppliers admit they get more stability than in the past, but some complain of ruthless use of retail muscle. They say that supermarkets will overestimate next year's requirements and then force farmers to discount. Why does the farmer not switch to another retailer? "It isn't so easy," says one. "You've invested capital to tie in with their distribution system. And if you are recognised as a supplier of one, the others may not be interested. They insist on loyalty."

The retailers argue that their life is not all that cushy. Net margins on sales may be better than those of their foreign counterparts (see table over page), but they have to employ more capital to build the new prettily-lit, out-of-town shops that the British want. American retailers' building costs are lower, they say, because the price of land is lower. On the continent, planning controls are often so tough that retailers cannot build expensive new shops and are stuck with their ugly, cheap ones.

Yet British retailers still get a better return on their assets. Of the big foreign chains, only America's Albertson's makes a similar return; all the continentals do worse. Gerd Krampe, of Rewe Leibbrand, a German retailer, gave clear advice to a recent conference of British retailers on the question of expansion abroad: "You stay at home with your nice profits."

But if British food retailers are in clover, why does some foreign beast not intrude on their patch? For one thing, there are highish barriers to entry. Building an up-to-the-minute superstore costs around £25m ($49m). And until a company has the volumes, it will not be able to get the same good terms from suppliers.

A German retailer, Aldi, is trying to move in. It has opened a dozen shops with an intriguing new concept–pile it high and sell it cheap–and plans a chain of 200. It stocks a relatively small range of products and plans to hit the supermarkets in the processed-foods business. But Aldi says it has been running into some unexpected problems: the Office of Fair Trading is investigating Aldi's claim that suppliers, frightened of affronting their main customers, have been giving it the cold shoulder.

A judgment is expected any moment; but even if the OFT decides in Aldi's favour, the matter will still have to be investigated further by the Monopolies and Mergers Commission. It could be many years before the Department of Trade and Industry decides to take action–or not, as in the case of the brewers. Long before then, though, market laws look likely to prompt changes.

The biggest supermarket chains are still expanding furiously and expensively. On January 29th Tesco launched a rights issue to help finance an investment programme averaging £900m a year for the next three years. Sainsbury, which has concentrated on the south, has just opened its first store in the north-east and is moving into Wales

The great divide

Food retailers 1989-90

Britain	Net profits as % of: assets	sales
Kwik Save	14.6	3.8
Tesco	12.1	5.1
Marks and Spencer	11.7	7.2
Argyll	10.5	4.6
J.Sainsbury	10.5	4.8
Asda	5.8	3.9
average	**10.9**	**4.9**
Continental Europe		
Ahold (Holland)	5.7	1.4
Comptoirs Modernes (France)	4.9	1.7
Ava (Germany)	4.9	1.5
Delhaize-Le Lion (Belgium)	4.6	1.2
Carrefour (France)	4.2	1.7
Promodès (France)	3.9	1.3
Au Printemps (France)	3.8	2.3
Docks de France (France)	3.5	1.2
Asko (Germany)	2.4	1.5
Casino (France)	2.0	0.9
average	**4.0**	**1.5**

Source: Morgan Stanley Capital International

and Scotland.

There are plenty of distant, though real, risks. People's eating habits may change: as in America, take-aways may bite a chunk out of the market. An environment-minded government may increase petrol tax. This could discourage people from driving ten miles to buy their groceries.

And success will bring its own problems. So far, they have grown without competing too much against each other. But in three years' time Sainsbury will hit the North Sea. Tesco may not be able to get planning permission for any more stores. According to Ian Davis of McKinsey, a management consultancy, "they will inevitably end up competing with each other in their push for increased market shares."

It may be, too, that the small independents, squeezed for so long, are starting to fight back. In 1986-89, the average annual decline in their market share was around 1%; in 1989-90 it fell by 0.3%. Not surprising, when the corner-shop grocer is selling cabbage for 40% of the supermarket price.

A terrible truth unfolds

MARCH 2ND *The case of the Birmingham Six reached a dramatic conclusion, leaving deep misgivings in its wake about the whole British judicial system*

THEIR story began with a particularly heinous case of murder. It involved, three years ago, the longest criminal appeal to date in British legal history. Now its ending could prompt, within a few days, perhaps the starkest rebuff ever given to a Lord Chief Justice of England. Events surrounding the Birmingham Six go on breaking all precedents, as they have done since 1974.

That was the year IRA bombs exploded, early one Thursday evening in November, in two crowded pubs in Birmingham: 21 were killed and 162 injured. About 20 minutes before the explosions, five Irishmen left the city on a train connecting with a ferry to Ireland; a sixth companion stayed behind. A little over 24 hours later, all of them–the Birmingham Six–found themselves under arrest on suspicion of murder.

They appeared on murder charges in a magistrates' court the following Monday. The case appeared to have been sewn up with dramatic speed. The five bound for Ireland had been picked up queuing for their ferry. Apparently shocked at hearing about the scale of the carnage in Birmingham, four of them had volunteered long and elaborate confessions, which had led quickly to the arrest of the sixth man.

Meanwhile a forensic scientist said he had uncovered traces of nitroglycerine on two of their hands. And fast work by the police in Birmingham had started producing circumstantial evidence, too: friendships

with known IRA men, odd bits of behaviour before the bombings, suspicious remarks made at work and so on.

The six were remanded in custody in a Birmingham prison, where they were badly beaten by prison warders. They were convicted on 21 counts of murder the following summer. The judge, Mr Justice Bridge (as he then was), thought the prosecution had presented "the clearest and most overwhelming evidence I have ever heard". He also went out of his way to rebut a crucial part of the defence case–that the six men had had their confessions coerced out of them by the police. To believe this, he said, one would have to suppose the existence of a "conspiracy ... unprecedented in the annals of British criminal history" among the officers involved.

A flurry of smaller trials followed. Several prison warders were tried for assault. A doctor testified that the men had been badly beaten before reaching the prison; this was rejected, but the trial collapsed anyway. In 1976 the six were refused leave to appeal against their convictions. In 1977 they were allowed to bring a civil action against the police, for injuries allegedly received over that first weekend in custody; but the judge, Lord Denning, refused to countenance the notion of police brutality and contemptuously swept the suit aside.

Much had changed by the time that Douglas Hurd, as home secretary, decided

in 1987 that the case should return to the Appeal Court. The forensic evidence had begun to look flimsy, at best. The scientist employed in 1974 had been pushed into retirement on formal grounds of "limited efficiency"; his evidence had been widely challenged by the outcome of further tests. The circumstantial evidence was at least open to question: a Labour MP, Chris Mullin, even insisted that he had met IRA men in Ireland who claimed to be the real bombers.

Above all, the voluntary nature of the six men's confessions had been widely challenged. A book published by Mr Mullin in 1986 gave a different version of the men's first three days in custody, back in 1974. It claimed they had been deprived of sleep, physically intimidated and beaten until they were ready to sign written confessions which amalgamated their own gibberings with statements concocted by the police.

One thing, though, had not changed since Lord Denning's judgment of 1980: the intense reluctance of the judiciary to contemplate the possibility of dishonest police work. Lord Chief Justice Lane presided over the appeal with two other senior judges. Their 168-page dismissal of the appeal, in January 1988, relied heavily on the "wealth" of circumstantial evidence; it also clung to the last shreds of forensic evidence (presented by a second scientist, who later gave a press interview challenging the judges' interpretation of her testimony). But the crux of the judgment was a refusal to doubt the integrity of the policemen who had secured the confessions.

In sticking to this position, Lord Lane and his colleagues scarcely bothered with the views of some outsiders to the case, whose evidence might have upset the assumption of police innocence. The doctor who said the six had been beaten before reaching the prison in Birmingham, for example, was not given a hearing. Nor was any attention paid to the presence in the court's public gallery of the MP who claimed to have talked to the IRA. Two new witnesses who did get to the stand, claiming to have seen instances of physical intimidation by the police, were dismissed as liars.

Instead, their lordships produced a judgment oddly assertive of the absurdity of the defence's case. Lord Lane and his colleagues thought the idea that police officers might have assaulted one of the six "without even inquiring what it was [he] might wish to say is, to say the least, unrealistic". As for the allegation that the confessions might have been cooked, the judges thought them far too detailed and too inconsistent for that. In short, "the longer this hearing has gone on, the more convinced this court has become that the verdict of the [1975] jury was correct".

Last summer, new evidence prompted a second referral to the Appeal Court. Since then Sir Allan Green, the Director of Public Prosecutions (DPP), has been receiving reports from a fresh police inquiry into the case. And the longer this inquiry has gone

The Birmingham Six: arrested November 1974, set free March 1991

on, the more worried the DPP has become that the 1975 prosecution was unsound. On February 7th he said he was dropping the forensic case. Then, on February 25th, he announced that no evidence relying upon police testimony could be used. The convictions were therefore, in his view, no longer "safe and satisfactory".

The appeal is set to begin on March 4th. The acquittal of the six appears a formality; but the court seems keen, rightly, to have the

grounds for the DPP's change of heart fully aired in public. His disclosures, if they point to shocking dishonesty by the police, may yet provide some vestige of comfort for the individual judges who got the case so badly wrong. They are unlikely to offer much comfort for the judicial system as a whole: it stood by the police, in stubborn defiance of independent investigations, for far too long. Acknowledging that might be a first step towards a better system.

June's budget, in March

MARCH 23RD *A successful first budget by a new chancellor marked a historic break with the Thatcher years*

WHILE Norman Lamont was delivering his budget, he was dimly aware of a lurid figure bobbing gently at the end of the Commons chamber. Sir Nicholas Fairbairn MP, in tomato-flavour jacket, cream trousers and a garishly-striped tie, went to Loretto, the Scottish boarding school also attended by the chancellor, and was advertising the fact by wearing a medley of the old school uniform.

Loretto once specialised in cold baths, excessive quantities of fresh air and bare knees. Celebrating this Victorian masochism, its Latin motto still runs: Spartam nactus es, hanc exorna--roughly translatable as: you inherited Sparta, laddie, you adorn it. It is hard to think of a less appropriate battle-cry for Britain's sleek unSpartan new chancellor.

Margaret Thatcher, who was born a Spartan, albeit a Lincolnshire one, sat a few rows behind Mr Lamont's right shoulder, clad in puritan black and muttering a running commentary on his speech. It was not

complimentary. Hardly surprising, really: the budget, with its return to deficits and its U-turns on the poll tax, child benefit and higher-rate mortgage tax relief, was described by one senior Treasury person as "the end of Thatcherism".

After it, she hurried away, looking dismayed. Since her return from America, Mrs Thatcher has seemed to be swinging towards a decision to fight the next election and stay an MP. This would horrify John Major's cabinet, who fear her influence on the backbenches. Whether this week's bonfire of her sacred texts will encourage her to remain or quit is anybody's guess.

Labour MPs noted that the Tory party chairman, Chris Patten, who is widely seen as the most aggressively liberal influence in the government (he recently warned Thatcherite critics to "belt up"), nodded and smiled his way through Mr Lamont's speech in an almost proprietorial way. Mr Lamont, a chum of Mr Patten's from the days when they worked for the Conservative

research department, produced a budget that symbolised the new post-Thatcher thinking. He cracked down on some cherished perks of the wealthy. He introduced a mildly progressive switch from poll tax to value-added tax. He encouraged the notion of a growing national consensus by swiping pet ideas from the opposition--Tory rebel ones like fully uprating child benefit; Liberal ones like boosting profit-related pay; and Labour ones like a crackdown on offshore tax avoidance, and restricting mortgage-interest tax relief to the standard rate.

It was, in brief, a highly political package. Mr Lamont showed that even in a recession with no money to spare (there was a slight fiscal tightening) he could write and deliver a popular budget. One half-admiring Scottish left-wing MP described it as "clever--bloody clever" and a Labour frontbencher admitted: "This makes things a bit awkward". Though there were some cautious souls among the milling Tory members, most thought that the chancellor had prepared the way for an early election.

The pleasure on the Tory benches was heightened after the wretched few days of farce that had followed the apparent leaking by a junior member of the environment department of the cabinet's expected reforms of local government. Other ministers were livid–particularly since, despite denials and smokescreens, the leaks seemed pretty accurate. Michael Heseltine, the environment secretary, denied the leaks had come from one of his staff. But suddenly the mood of comradeship in cabinet was threatened. A flurry of backstabbing and counter-briefing started throughout Whitehall. It reminded some ministers of the worst days of Margaret Thatcher's administration.

It was no way to run a whelk emporium. But the budget and the drama of the poll-tax announcement turned the mood among Tory backbenchers within about ten minutes. So promptly did June election fever catch hold that Mr Patten had to step out smartly with suggestions that a later election might suit the government, just to keep Mr Major's options open. Mr Major, however, will shortly chair meetings of the inner manifesto-writing group and has given a strong impression to friends that he would prefer to go within a few months and win a fresh mandate for his different style of Conservativism.

He has a point. The significance of the shift in the philosophy of the Tory leadership, from populist right-wingery to–what to call it? One-nationism? Christian democracy?–cannot be exaggerated. It contains risks as well as rewards: those up-

Not so spartan Lamont

wardly-mobile voters, devoted to their newly acquired houses and the "great car economy", who were wooed by Mrs Thatcher, are unlikely to be much pleased by the budget. Many, particularly in the south, rather liked the principle–if not the size–of the poll tax.

But the new spirit reigneth, in small things as in great. Last weekend Mr Major had some guests to his official country retreat, Chequers. Among them was the for-

mer Labour prime minister, Lord Callaghan. Every prime minister is commemorated there with a painted window and plants a special tree. Lord Callaghan had never seen his window before, nor revisited his tree–for the simple reason that he had not once been invited back there during the Thatcher years.

Mr Lamont, who is seen by some on the right as a possible future champion, has delighted the Majorites and the Tory left, without overly offending anybody else. Those who viewed him as a rather lightweight, raffish figure catapulted into the job by the Major coup have been forced to admit that his first budget was clever, complex and stylish.

He has spent much of his career in the Treasury. Mr Lamont made a point of praising his old boss, Nigel Lawson, who became a non-person to true Thatcherites, airbrushed out of their family album after his resignation as chancellor in 1989. Mr Lamont neither expected nor got much applause for that. Mr Lawson himself liked the Lamont budget, except for the inevitable "distortions" caused by the need to include the poll-tax remedy in it. Indeed, Mr Lamont's delivery, mannerisms and style of budget-writing are all reminiscent of Mr Lawson.

As Mr Lamont luxuriates in the warm praise flowing around him this week, he ought to keep a picture of Mr Lawson nearby–a chilling momento mori for "brilliant" chancellors.

Low spirits in the Highlands

APRIL 13TH *The dour Scotsman ranks among the most familiar of British stereotypes. No laughing matter, according to one medical researcher*

IF CALM and freedom from stress are what you yearn for, living in the country could be just what the doctor ordered. Where better than the Scottish Highlands?

Plenty of places, if you are the gloomy type. Male suicide rates turn out to be far higher in the tranquillity of the Highlands than in any other part of Scotland. By contrast the central Lowlands, with their high population density, heavy industry and relative social deprivation, have the lowest male suicide rates in Scotland. Among the British, the Scots are the most prone to do themselves in. For each million of the male population, 150 Scots kill themselves a year, compared with 108 English and Welsh. Different jurisdictions define suicide differently, but the world average is 94.

Iain Crombie, senior lecturer

in the department of epidemiology and public health at Ninewells Hospital in Dundee, analysed the geographical spread of suicide in Scotland and reported his findings in the British Medical Journal. He counted suicides between 1974 and 1986 in

Poor conversationalists

each of Scotland's 56 local-government districts. Their pattern was constant. All eight Highland districts had at least 25% more male suicides than the Scottish average. The highest was well over twice the average. Out of the remaining 48, only two Lowland districts, Lothian and rural Dumfries and Galloway, had comparably deadly rates. Most of the Scottish Lowlands had rates at or well below the average.

Intriguingly, the geographical spread of suicide among women showed no such clear pattern. Women kill themselves much less than men anyway: there are 36 female suicides per million in England and Wales, and 60 in Scotland. The world average is just 28.

Dr Crombie is not sure what is driving Highland men to despair. Perhaps mental illness–the most important risk factor for suicide–is more common in the mountains. Maybe people just get lonely.

Can the regulators hold them?

JUNE 1ST **Privatisation was hailed in the 1980s chiefly for its managerial benefits. But the ultimate gains for the customers began to attract a lot more attention in 1991: were they coming through? With the privatised utilities regularly reporting bumper profits, many thought not**

BIG profits mean bad regulation. Or so you would think from the outcry that greeted British Telecom's announcement that its profits in 1990-91 were £3.1 billion ($5.7 billion). A quick calculation by the tabloids came up with £97 a second, which sounded a suitable shocker. The complaints have grown louder as British Gas and some of the water companies have also unveiled fatter profits this week, despite the recession. Tory backbenchers have joined Labour in demanding that something be done. So how well, after seven years, is Britain's new regulatory regime working?

Much of the current uproar is due to a simple confusion between big—which the monopolies' profits certainly are—and too big. BT is Britain's biggest, most valuable and most profitable firm. But its profits are a smaller proportion of sales (at 21.5%) and of capital (21.3%) than, say, Glaxo's (40% and 35.6% respectively), though Glaxo makes much smaller profits (£1.1 billion in its latest full year) because it is a far smaller company.

The profits of some privatised firms are made to look artificially big by historic-cost accounting. Firms in telecoms, water, elec-

tricity and gas tend to have more long-term assets, with lower historic-cost depreciation charges, than most businesses. Lower depreciation means higher bottom-line profits. The privatised firms have largely themselves to blame for this: most of them dumped current-cost accounting, which values assets at what they cost now, as soon as they went private. Their motives were no mystery: shareholders, unlike customers, like big profits.

Even so, some of the privatised monopolies' profits may well be too high. The regulators certainly think so. Their main method of control is the pricing formula known as "RPI-minus-x". This means that each firm must limit its product-price rises to "x" percentage points less than the rate of inflation. (So, for example, RPI-minus-3 at a time of 10% inflation allows prices to rise by 7%.) If the regulator reckons that the firm is earning too high a monopoly profit, it can raise "x". So far, the regulators have raised "x" each time they have reviewed it. BT's "x" started at 3% and is now 6.25%; British Gas's has gone up from 2% to 5%.

This is no surprise. To get public-sector managers to agree to be privatised, and to persuade investors to buy the shares, the

government had to offer the firms a good deal in the private sector. Water was the most brazen case; managers were encouraged to believe that they would be able to raise their prices to cover the costs of almost any quality-boosting investment. Once a firm is sold, though, the government has little reason to preserve such a friendly regime, and every reason—customer equals voter—to make life tougher.

All this looks cheery for the regulators, though it leaves them much to do. More worrying for them is the effect that changing the "x" has on investors and managers. Investors will have to take account of the risk of a change in "x"; this will almost certainly raise the firm's cost of capital. Managers could also get depressed; what, after all, is the point of striving to be efficient, as BT has been doing with its staff-cutting "Project Sovereign", if the resulting higher profits lead only to the regulator raising "x"?

The danger is that "RPI-minus-x" will turn into rate-of-return regulation—restricting companies' profits to a given rate of return on capital—which gives a firm few reasons to be efficient. But the system need not go this way. "RPI-minus-x" can work if the regulator has a good idea of how efficient the firm is, and how much better it could be.

This is most likely when technology is fairly mature, so the rate at which the regulator learns about the firm is faster than the rate at which the firm changes. In most of Britain's regulated monopolies, technology is nicely mature. Gas pipes, reservoirs and water pipes, runways, buildings and so on have little to boggle a regulator's mind. The big exception is telecoms, where technology is changing fast.

If the regulators are to stay on top, promoting competition is the key, even in technologically mature industries. Britain still lacks a clear policy on vertical integration. Electricity has been broken into competitive generation and monopolistic distribution, but Britain's gas and telecoms remain fairly integrated. "Yardstick" competition—comparing the performance of one local monopoly with other similar monopolies—has been a regulators' buzz-word for some time, but it has still to be seriously used.

"Unbundling" the costs and prices of all a firm's activities—as BT began to do when it charged for directory inquiries and cut ordinary call charges—reduces unnecessary regulation and should go much further. This is not easy, though, especially when working out the costs to competitors of using a monopoly system. The coming reform of the railways could underline the point: would-be private sector train-operators should look at the history of Mercury's troubles with BT before investing in rolling-stock to run on tracks controlled by British Rail.

It has been hard going for the regulators; but there is worse to come. In the run-up to privatisation, tough decisions were fudged. These will return in the 1990s, and regulators will be caught in the inevitable rows. Ofelect, the electricity regulator, will have to tackle the future of nuclear power and British Coal, and the risk of insecure supply. Ofwat will face growing public unease about higher water prices to finance an upgraded system. BAA's need for new airport capacity will run into environmental objections. And all the regulators will face the growing tension between price and quality.

Ofgas recently made it clear that if British Gas sacrificed quality to get higher profits, it would consider raising "x". The growing all-party interest in "Citizens' Charters" means that regulators will be spending much more time looking at quality--as well as how to bring choice into services that are still, all too clearly, not market-led.

A bad week for Asians

JULY 13TH **The collapse of the Bank of Credit and Commerce International exposed a rottenness that many top bankers said they had always suspected. But it came as a nasty shock to thousands of less worldly unfortunates—its customers**

STANDING around in bewildered crowds outside branches of the Bank of Credit and Commerce International, Asians have been swapping their small, painful stories: the family that had saved £40,000 ($55,000) for the daughter's dowry, the father who had sold his hotel and put the cash in the bank as capital for his sons' business. The £100m or so invested by 30 ill-advised local authorities may make up the largest chunk of the £250m of deposits endangered in Britain by the close-down of BCCI on July 5th; but the personal losses incurred by thousands of Asians account for the biggest share of suffering in the country.

Borrowers may be even worse off than depositors. Deposits are often spare cash. Borrowers whose loans are called in by the receivers may find they can no longer run their businesses. The bulk of those affected in Britain are borrowers: fairly recent immigrants tend to be building up businesses, not saving money. If most of the 120,000 accounts were held by the 1.5m-strong Asian population, then a broad cross-section of it will be directly affected. For many this will be the second blow: Asians are enthusiastic property-buyers, and plenty have seen their savings hit by the slide in property prices.

Asians banked with the BCCI partly because its Pakistani origins made them feel culturally at home. The bank had a policy of recruiting the best managers from overseas branches of Pakistani and Indian banks: they were cheap and, because they came from a society that works on contacts, would bring business with them. And, for those customers still unsteady in English, the bigger BCCI branches would have staff speaking Hindustani, Bengali, Gujerati and Punjabi.

There was also an economic reason for banking with BCCI. When the clearing banks turned up their noses at an Asian customer, BCCI would often come to the rescue. According to Dilbagh Chana, an insurance broker in Southall, "an Anglo-Saxon bank manager will use the yardstick he applies to an Anglo-Saxon client. But he may be ignoring, for instance, an immigrant's willingness to cut down on personal expenditure." Asians found the BCCI more willing than the clearing banks to lend larger sums on smaller security, and to be less nosey about the numbers.

The BCCI's attitude and network were also suited to some of the businesses Asians go in for. Hotels require a big up-front investment. Retailers often need a lot of short-term cash to finance their supplies. And, with branches all over the third world, the BCCI was more enthusiastic about financing trade with East and West Africa.

Some customers heard the rumours about the bank; a few even withdrew their custom. Those who stayed explain that they had heard about the alleged drug-laundering, but did not necessarily think it was going to do the bank's balance sheet any harm; anyway, they--like the councils who pay for expensive financial advice--trusted the Bank of England.

Many feel mistreated. Why did the Bank of England take so long to act? Why did it close the bank on a Friday, just before the time when Muslim businessmen, emerging from the mosque, usually withdraw the week's wages for their staff? Wouldn't the government, many ask, be offering more compensation if white people were involved? There are small political stirrings-- Pakistanis, Ugandan Asians, Sikhs, Hindus meeting separately--but Asian businessmen are not in the habit of political activity, so are mostly leaving it to their MPs to press for compensation.

For borrowers left in the lurch, there are few options. They can try three private Asian banks--the Equatorial Bank, Mount Banking Corporation and Meghraj Bank-- but these are small, conservative and no more likely than the clearers to be interested in the riskier business the BCCI took on. A nimble Asian accountant has sent letters to 41,000 businesses with his ideas on survival; but the prospects for many look bleak.

Directly or indirectly, few Asians in Britain will be unaffected. Asians mostly employ Asians and deal with Asians: those who import cloth sell to those who make up the clothes, those why buy spices from India sell to those who pack them and those who make food. Businesses will go under and finance for new ventures will be tighter. Asians, who have struggled hard to get where they have in Britain, may find that in future they have to fight harder still.

Last one out, switch off the lights

Responding to treatment

AUGUST 3RD *The Tories' health reforms triggered endless political rows in 1991. Behind the scenes, meanwhile, early signs emerged that they were working*

THE reforms of the national health service (NHS) may still be unpopular with the average voter, but there are encouraging signs that they are beginning to benefit patients. One survey suggests that the new self-governing hospital trusts formed in April have cut waiting lists by as much as a quarter. William Waldegrave, the health secretary, is so confident of success that he plans to push ahead with more radical reform.

On August 5th his department will announce that another 113 hospitals, and other units such as ambulance services, have applied to become self-governing trusts. Officials estimate that 300 general practitioners (GPs) want to run their own budgets. Self-governing hospitals and budget-holding GPs will be only the most eye-catching parts of the coming shake-up. Mr Waldegrave has no doubt that, however well the changes are managed, scares in the press and slanging matches in Parliament will continue.

Indeed, the political argument may get nastier, because the first year of the reforms has been little more than a dry run. The government tried to limit the impact of the changes by obliging health authorities to send their patients to the same hospitals as before. The new contracts simply described long-established customs. This limited disruption but produced few improvements.

The government has now decided to risk disruption. Duncan Nichol, the chief executive of the NHS, has instructed purchasers to shop around for the best care at the best prices when negotiating their contracts for next April, even if this means breaking with old habits. No matter that the local cottage hospital will go under: the important thing is to provide cost-effective services for patients. The new contracts will be negotiated in the autumn and start to operate next April. The full-blooded market will produce losers as well as winners.

Mr Nichol has also announced a timetable for introducing weighted capitation, an arrangement to give health authorities budgets according to the size and age of their populations, rather than the historical claims of their hospitals. This will lead to a dramatic shift in money to areas of population growth: notably from the inner cities to the suburbs.

Mr Waldegrave has been encouraged to push ahead with his reforms by John Major's "Citizen's Charter". The best way to get doctors to make precise appointments with their patients, or to guarantee that all patients receive treatment within two years--two top objectives in the charter--is to allow purchasers to place their contracts with the most efficient and patient-friendly hospitals, private as well as public.

Mr Waldegrave may also have been encouraged by the implosion of the British Medical Association. The BMA was always more of a worry for him than the Labour Party: voters trust doctors as much as they distrust politicians. Its successful publicity campaign against the health reforms scared the public and unnerved ministers.

Now the doctors have suddenly turned on each other, dispirited by their failure to force the government to back down and divided over tactics. Jeremy Lee-Potter, the BMA's new chairman, favours conciliation; his activists still want confrontation. The association's annual meeting in Inverness early in July was dominated by faction-fighting and name-calling.

More important, the reformed NHS is beginning to deliver the goods. A survey of the 57 existing hospital trusts by Newchurch, a consultancy, reveals striking improvements in organisation and efficiency since April. Trusts have increased their workload and speeded up patient treatment, cutting waiting lists by up to a quarter. They have started to get to grips with problems which have troubled them for decades. And they have made themselves more attractive employers by extending performance-related pay and non-monetary benefits like flexible working hours.

However, the NHS management executive sometimes gives the impression that such changes will not cause any pain. Thus Mr Nichol intends to vet all proposed changes in contracting patterns before December, to ensure that the overall impact is palatable. His main worry is that the combination of giving less cash to London together with freer contracting may put at least one London teaching hospital out of business. That could be fatal to the government in the run-up to the general election.

But over-generous treatment of London would distort the internal market and provoke protests elsewhere. The current allocation of money to London is hugely unfair: West Lambeth, for example, receives 34% more cash than it would under weighted capitation. The last thing health authorities in the home counties want to do is continue to carry the London teaching hospitals on their backs. Mr Nichol could have quite a fight on his hands.

Even if the Labour Party wins the next election, the NHS may not return to its old form. The creation of 100 more trusts and 300 more GP fund-holders next April will create a large vested interest in favour of the new system.

The trusts will employ 280,000 people; account for 35% of the NHS budget; and serve 25.2m people. At the same time, a third of eligible GPs will be running their own budgets. An incoming Labour government would find all this difficult to dismantle. It might even face a noisy BMA campaign to defend sensible ideas like the internal market from meddling politicians.

Flattened

The summer months brought another spate of the supposedly mysterious phenomena known as crop circles. But saturation coverage by the tabloid press eventually spoilt the fun

NOBODY likes to admit to having been fooled, especially when future book royalties are at stake. So it is no surprise that the "experts" on crop circles are fighting a rearguard action against the tide of confessional hoaxers now breaking over them. "Doesn't explain them all," they cry.

Crop circles, which are round areas of flattened corn that appear in the summer, have gained a dedicated following in the decade or so since they first appeared. Experts on them fall into two groups: flying-saucer, unknown-intelligence types, led by Patrick Delgado, and ball-lightning, we're-serious-physicists types, led by Terence Meaden. They agree on only one thing: that not all the circles could possibly have been made by mischievous men with ropes and planks.

This year, however, the chorus of self-confessed hoaxers can no longer be ignored. Among the confessed are:
• Dave Chorley and Doug Bower, who have been making circles together for 13 years, and who have more than once infiltrated crews of circle watchers to make circles while concealed by mist. They recently made a circle for *Today* newspaper, watched it pronounced by Mr Delgado as perfect and not man-made, then owned up.
• Fred Day, who has been making them all his life and has tried in vain to persuade newspapers to part with the prize money that they have periodically offered to anyone who solves the riddle.
• A group called the Wessex Sceptics, led by Robin Allen, who made one for Channel 4 Television's Equinox programme. It convinced Mr Meaden, who pronounced it 100% genuine; several dowsers, whose dowsing sticks went beserk; and a medium, who felt ill in the circle.
• A journalist on this newspaper.

The experts are hastily inventing new arguments: that circles cannot be made so easily in green corn as in ripe corn (untrue), that the recent appearance of circles in Canada proves that hoaxers cannot be the cause (illogical), that the sheer number of circles defies the hoax explanation (why?), that they can always tell hoaxes from genuine ones (see above), that circles pre-date 1978, when the first hoaxes were made (aerial photographs used by archaeologists show none before 1980), and that one or two man-

All in a night's work

made circles do not necessarily prove that all are man-made.

This last argument is logical, but applies to cars and polythene bags as well. The burden of proof still lies clearly with those who would prove that a car or a corn circle can be made by a mechanism other than man.

Island-hoppers

The start of a huge Japanese Festival focused attention on a growing ex-patriate community

TEN years ago there were 10,000 Japanese living in Britain. Today there are at least 44,000. The tide of Japanese investment is bringing a tide of Japanese expatriates–and with them everything from sushi bars to sumo wrestling.

The typical Japanese expatriate is still a company man spending three to five years abroad. Most commonly he (rarely she) will be a banker in his 20s or 30s; a small minority will be senior executives sent over to run a London headquarters or (less often) a plant in Wales or the north-east. Recently, more students are arriving too.

The biggest snag for a Japanese expatriate with a family is providing an education for his children. Stepping off the exams escalator at home risks sacrificing a job-for-life in a prestigious company. Parents with no option but to bring their children to Britain with them scramble for places in schools that teach the Japanese national curriculum.

The best known is the Japanese School in Acton, West London. It caters for 980 pupils–up from 657 in 1987–and is staffed by Japanese teachers on three-year secondments from the Ministry of Education in Tokyo. But three new schools have opened since the mid-1980s to ensure the maximum choice for Taro-chan. One, the Gyosei International School in Milton Keynes, takes 1,000 pupils and is the biggest Japanese school in Europe. Britain now has eight private Japanese schools, and six Saturday schools attached to Japanese-owned factories in Wales and the north-east.

Even with the schools problem resolved, there are other headaches. Top of the list for most is the language. English (or rather American) is Japan's second language. But eight years of parroting verbs and learning about sub-clauses is poor preparation for the patter of London cabbies and Geordie shop stewards. One woman who has lived in Britain for a decade summed up her frustration: what makes life so difficult is that the poor people do not speak English.

Another worry is social anarchy. Many Japanese find ethnic diversity a puzzle. The levels of violence and crime in contemporary Britain are profoundly shocking to them. Most dislike the lack of deference displayed by the poor to the rich and–even worse, in their eyes–the lack of consideration shown by the rich for the poor. One acute young banker mused that it was only after taking up residence in London that he could see where Karl Marx got his idea of the class struggle from.

A mini-industry has developed to make the Japanese feel at home. Those moving to Britain can choose among eight Japanese estate agents to find them a house, and seven Japanese removal companies to shift the mod cons which keep all Japanese houses ultra-clean and super-efficient. Once here, they look for a location that reflects their position in the social pecking-order. Around London it is St John's Wood and Hampstead for bosses; Finchley, Golders Green and Ealing for middle managers; Croydon for the lower ranks.

The unadventurous can live as though they have never left Tokyo: reading Japanese newspapers, buying their spectacles in Japanese opticians and suits in Japanese tailors, playing mahjong in Japanese clubs and singing "New York, New York" in karaoke bars. London has more than 60 Japanese restaurants and eight Japanese food shops to stave off the torments of English food. In the provinces there are regular food parcels from relatives in Japan and weekly lorry loads of supplies from London shops.

As they become more established, the Japanese are also growing more adventurous. There is plenty that they like about Britain: huge houses and (relatively) easy commuting, cheap and readily accessible golf courses. And the women enjoy their freedom and status. Japanese firms have recently started to worry that company wives do not want to go home. Perhaps Britain will change Japan as much as Japan is changing Britain.

The joints are jumping

OCTOBER 5TH *The recession spread as much gloom in the entertainment world as anywhere else in the economy. In London, though, young and seriously trendy nightclubs were, as their customers put it, the happening scene*

AT FOUR o'clock on a Sunday morning in Trafalgar Square, there are usually a couple of hundred people waiting at bus stops. Some wear scruffy bomber jackets, some shiny leggings, some are in black with their faces painted white. In Brixton, Notting Hill, Hackney and Camden, hundreds more wander along the pavements, some off to bed, some to another club.

London is Europe's main clubbing city. Rome and Madrid have big scenes, Berlin and Amsterdam have variety, but only London has the size and the mix. According to the British Tourist Authority, in 1989 4% of European tourists said they came to dance. The Japanese are joining in, too: Gaz's Rockin' Blues in the West End has a regular crowd of Japanese in impeccable designer scruff.

New York has the high-fashion film-star clubs, but London has a bigger grassroots scene. Part of London's advantage lies in its relative racial harmony. Blacks, who make most of the music, are essential to serious clubs. London imports black American music generated in places that American whites would not venture into--acid house came from black Chicago, for instance-- then produces a version for its mixed-race clubbers.

The recession has hurt some clubs. Members' clubs have had a bad time: people are unwilling to pay a big signing-on fee. Places that rely on tourism have suffered. The older, plusher end of the market has been hit: yuppies with mortgages have cut down on the champagne. Some clubs have closed, some changed hands. Adrian Flack, owner of the small and fashionable Brain Club in Wardour Street, says things are now picking up: "I can really relate to what the chancellor is saying." But the West End is still thick with rumours of closures.

To keep full, West End clubs

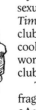

have been letting out their premises to promoters and disc jockeys who are in closer touch with the more resilient end of the market, known as the hardcore. The hardcore is under 22, does not own property and may well still live with its lucky parents. If it is in work, it has money to spend. It is serious about music, and will not be seen dead in a place that plays the charts. James Style, who writes on clubs for the *Independent* newspaper, reckons that there are 30,000 determined clubbers in London, compared with 20,000 in the mid-1980s.

Fashionable drugs encourage clubbing: they keep you awake all night. Ecstasy, at £15-20 a tab, is the most popular; for those with less money, speed is £12-15 a gramme (enough for ten people for an evening). Unlike alcohol, which makes young men aggressive, ecstasy convinces people that the world is their friend, so hardcore clubs tend to be rather amiable places.

Acid-house parties, the most visible symptom of the nightlife boom, were stamped on last year by new laws. Clubs, encouraged by the regular extension of dancing licences until 6am, have picked up the custom. According to Dave Swindells, clubs correspondent for *Time Out*, a listings magazine, new venues are opening more often: three years ago, a couple of new clubs opened in a year, whereas now there is a new one every month or two. About 50 heterosexual clubs are mentioned in *Time Out*. But by no means all clubs are listed. Advertising is not cool--serious clubbers rely on word-of-mouth--and unlicensed clubs do not seek publicity.

The hardcore market is highly fragmented. The biggest scenes are:
• Acid house. The music is fast and furious, the crowd is a bit maler, whiter and more working class than others. The clothes are baggy and deeply unsexy. No smooching.
• Hip-hop and rap. The people are younger, blacker and flasher--"Lycra-ed out", as other scenes put it. There is more sex in the air and an occasional whiff of violence.
• Funk/soul. Slower music: some clubs guarantee a maximum number of beats per minute. The customers smooch and chat.
• Reggae. Gentle Jamaican music, now having a revival.

Beyond these are the Latin, African and jazz scenes, grunge music (favoured by hippies), the Goths (black clothes, white-painted faces, found in the Intrepid Fox in Soho).

Since the customers are easily bored, venues offer different scenes on different nights, and promoters and DJs hop between venues. The DJ is the key to success. Top DJs have taken over much of the ground that pop stars used to occupy. As well as music, the customers want a bit of art: promoters employ artists to design light shows.

The business can be exceedingly profitable. A top DJ can make £700 an hour, appearing at three venues a night. Since inverted snobbery demands that the premises should not be too plush, rents are low. VOX, a popular new place in Brixton, happens in a former warehouse (customers are welcomed by a large "Loading and Unloading" sign, and descend into the club in an industrial lift). Other places are squatted: according to a promoter, if you find a good railway arch, spend £3,000 on hot DJs and incidental costs and get the word around, you could get in 1,000 people at £8 a head.

On the other hand, nobody may come. Fashion is a slippery business, and the fashionable are fickle by nature. This has discouraged the big entertainment chains, which leave the hardcore to young entrepreneurs with a feel for what their demanding peers want. The business is run by people in their early 20s, black and white, whose lack of interest in publicity probably has something to do with the tax authorities. Interviews with them are interspersed with calls from their parents asking if they will be home for dinner. Some make a lot, and many make a living.

There is some biggish investment going on, though. The most happening place at the moment, the Ministry of Sound, which opened two weeks ago, is huge, licensed for 1,200, with a sprung dancefloor and a sound system, said to be the best in Europe, that directs thunder at the dancers and quiet at the alcohol-free bar. Set in the grey concrete of south London's Elephant and Castle, the club has the atmosphere of a high-security jail. Searchlights scan the queue, fearsome bouncers frisk the customers down to the bottoms of their cigarette packets and police vans cruise suspiciously. It is supposed to give customers the frisson of an illegal acid-house party. They seem to like it.

In one way, recession has helped the club business: the property slump has increased the supply of venues. Sir Terence Conran's Docklands venture at Butler's Wharf collapsed last December; with the development in limbo, warehouse parties have started happening there. A DJ speculates that this Christmas, there will be a rash of illegal parties in unlet Docklands buildings. Why not, he suggests with a visionary gleam, in Canary Wharf?

The press after Maxwell

NOVEMBER 9TH *It took the world almost a month to see how badly stricken were the businesses that the late Robert Maxwell left behind. But the future of the Daily Mirror, flagship of his media interests, looked uncertain from the first day*

THE sudden death of Robert Maxwell on November 5th leaves a big gap in British public life. There will be less entertainment, fewer works of public charity, a smaller market for ailing football teams and fewer charges of commercial skulduggery. The City will be preoccupied for years with the indebted business empire he has left behind. But the biggest gap of all could yawn in British politics.

Under Mr Maxwell's ownership, the *Daily Mirror* was a staunch supporter of the Labour Party; indeed, the newspaper and its stablemates, the *Sunday Mirror*, the (Sunday) *People* and the (Scottish) *Daily Record*, were the only mass-circulation newspapers that backed Labour. The *Mirror*'s bias to the left provided a particularly important counterweight for the fifth or so of the electorate who read it every day. As Roy Greenslade, a former *Mirror* editor who fell out with Mr Maxwell, puts it: "Every upstanding Tory should be pleased that there is a paper like the *Mirror*, because if it did not exist a future Labour government would take harsher measures to control the press."

Legend has it that the *Mirror* has the power to decide elections. Maurice Edelman, in a history of the paper, argued that its support for Labour was decisive in the close elections of February 1951 and October 1964. After Mr Maxwell bought Mirror Group Newspapers in 1984, Labour politicians unsurprisingly tried to ingratiate themselves with the new owner. He had been a Labour MP between 1964 and 1970, so the paper's allegiance was never in doubt; yet at first Mr Maxwell's *Mirror* was sharply critical of some Labour policies.

After Neil Kinnock was elected leader, paper and party drew closer together. Mr Kinnock treated Mr Maxwell with deference; other members of the shadow cabinet followed suit. At Labour Party conferences, police and security men would suddenly descend to clear bystanders out of a hotel: a sure sign that Mr Kinnock was about to lunch with Mr Maxwell. *Mirror* reporters enjoyed privileged access to Mr Kinnock, especially at election time.

Statistical evidence of the paper's influence is thin. A survey by MORI this summer found that 65% of *Mirror* readers intended to vote Labour and only 21% Conservative. By contrast, readers of Rupert Murdoch's pro-Tory *Sun* newspaper actually preferred Labour by a margin of 46% to 39%. But this does not prove that the *Mirror* is more effective at converting its readers; it merely suggests that on balance Labour-voting working-class readers prefer the *Mirror*.

Indeed, the influence of the *Mirror* may actually be less than that of the *Sun*, because its bias is more evident. In a 1983 poll, 71% of *Mirror* readers were aware of the fact that their paper supported Labour whereas only 60% of *Sun* readers knew that their paper

backed the Tories.

Still, few practising politicians doubt that Labour would suffer if the *Mirror* went neutral, especially in the close election that looks likely for the spring. (Anyone who doubts it should look at the paper's relentless attacks on the health secretary in recent months, which have undoubtedly weakened the government.)

So is it likely that the paper will stop backing Labour? On the face of it, no. The two Maxwell sons who have taken charge, Ian and Kevin, say they will maintain their father's political credo; and the senior editorial staff, including Joe Haines, who used to be Harold Wilson's spokesman, remain sympathetic to Labour. Others point out that the *Mirror* has a commercial interest in backing Labour because there are so few papers available for Labour supporters.

This may not be enough. The Maxwell sons have had no involvement in politics; one close colleague guesses that both are Tory voters. They may try to stand behind their father's views, but they are most unlikely to wield the red pen as he did. In time, this could mean the return of a more detached editorial stance.

More important, the Maxwells may not retain control. If the banks lose confidence in the Maxwell empire, they could push for a sale; a strong surge in the newspaper group's share price on November 7th reflected the City's awareness of that possibility. And there is no guarantee that a new proprietor would conclude that a bias towards Labour sells more papers. A survey back in 1979 found that less than a third of *Mirror* readers thought it should have a pro-Labour bias. Mr Maxwell was not the kind of man to let details like that constrain his whims. His successors may be less robust.

Shares in Mirror Group Newspapers were suspended on December 2nd. Ian Maxwell resigned as MGN's chairman the next day. Journalists voted on the 4th to continue the paper's political traditions; but those in charge of breaking up the Maxwell empire said bidders for its 51% stake in the Mirror would be judged on commercial grounds.

Sozialpartnerschaft

NOVEMBER 16TH **The death of socialism challenged Labour politicians to come up with a fresh agenda, to reaffirm the party's evangelist spirit. The Bagehot column noted the vision of the moment: Britain as a country more like Germany**

IN PURSUIT of that chimera in a double-breasted suit, respectability, Labour politicians have spent much time and many words proving themselves dull. Like Lord Whitelaw, they have gone about the country stirring up apathy. They have been uncommonly successful. Miss Prim of Magnolia Lodge, Home Counties, used to fear that Neil Kinnock would tax her to death, or surrender her to the Red Menace. Now she merely fears that he would bore her to death.

It has all gone too far, as even Labour front-benchers admit. The party's Treasury spokesman, Chris Smith, said recently: "People have to feel not only safe about voting Labour, but a little excited too." Both big parties are searching for a magic extra ingredient. Tory-bashing—or Labour-bashing—will not be enough to shift bored, suspicious voters. That acidic American, H. L. Mencken, spoke for them when he said: "Under democracy, one party always devotes its chief energies to trying to prove that the other party is unfit to rule—and both commonly succeed, and are right."

The peculiar thing is this: Labour still has a radical programme. Dramatic changes to the constitution, including a bill of rights; a multi-billion-pound redistribution of income from higher-rate taxpayers to single mothers, the low-paid and pensioners; a keen (if sometimes incoherent) Europeanism. It would be possible to market all of this as being almost too exciting. One shadow minister says: "We will fight the 1992 election on a manifesto which will be more radical than in 1979, 1983 or 1987." Yet hardly anyone seems to have noticed. Perhaps British voters should all be more enthusiastic. Or more frightened.

A central problem has been language. The failure of socialist economics has led to a loss of socialist rhetoric. This snag, common to all left-leaning parties, will not go away. But there is the glimmer of an alternative vision in the speeches, interviews and conversations of Labour politicians.

It is, in essence, that Britain should be more German. Margaret Thatcher spent a decade trying to persuade her compatriots to be more American. Everything Mr Kinnock's team now stresses—a culture of long-termism in business; a more consensual society; devolution of power to the regions—seems hostile to the Anglo-American model of capitalist democracy, and sympathetic to the continental one.

This summer John Smith, the shadow chancellor, told the German chambers of commerce that he thought Labour's outlook was far nearer their social-market philosophy than anything offered by the Tories. Gordon Brown, the industry spokesman, enthuses about meeting Deutsche Bank executives to discuss the merits of a banking system that owns chunks of industry. For the conspiratorial, it is worth adding that the party's European-affairs spokesman, George Robertson, sports a decoration in his lapel. It is nothing to do with the British Empire—it is a Commander's Cross of the Order of Merit of the German republic.

None of this is so surprising. Much of

Chancellor-to-be Schmidt?

Germany's constitutional settlement derives from the work of British civil servants in the mid-1940s, during the heyday of Labour corporatism. And a phalanx of Labour politicians—including Mr Smith, Mr Brown and Mr Robertson—are Scots, brought up in the most consensual, corporatist part of Britain. Anyone who doubts that the Scottish culture is different should discuss it with the Scottish Council Development and Industry (sic), which brings together trade unionists and bosses. Or spend a couple of hours in the executive lounge of Edinburgh airport.

It may be that Mr Kinnock thinks this Germano-Scottish vision is too dangerous to push at touchy English or Welsh voters. And his team has been trained to wince at the word which underlies it, corporatist. The German alternative, social partnership, is a bit of a mouthful, especially in a Glasgow accent. But even Tory ministers concede that voters may find the German model more attractive than the American one. If there is a Labour vision, this is it.

There are two other aspects of Labour's potential radicalism that are rarely talked about, but worth pondering. The first is that Mrs Thatcher herself did not arrive in power with a revolutionary programme sewn into the lining of her handbag. She arrived, and pushed a bit, and found things and people giving way, so kept on pushing. Mr Kinnock's pared-down manifesto may provide few clues to what he would be doing as prime minister in five years' time.

The second is that there are the faintest hints that senior Labourites are reconsidering their attitude to a deal with the Liberal Democrats, should there be a hung parliament. The official position (which will be strenuously repeated in public, whatever the private thinking) is that Mr Kinnock should accept the premiership if he has the largest party, then announce a populist programme of legislation and dare Paddy Ashdown to join the Tories in voting it down. If he did, there would be a second election in which Mr Kinnock would finish the job and win an overall majority.

A bold and principled stand, but a dangerous one, too: no one could predict how that second election might go. Mr Kinnock might well go down as the prime minister who lasted only a few months. On the other hand, the momentum inside the Labour Party towards a more proportional voting system is already strong—and will not be stilled by Mr Kinnock's preference for the party's internal report on the matter to be shelved until after the general election. So if Mr Kinnock took a deep breath, agreed to a reformed voting system for the Commons, and did a deal with Mr Ashdown, he might be prime minister for—what? Ten years?

Granted, he would have made it far less likely that Labour would ever again form a Westminster administration on its own. But if Labour failed to consolidate itself in power, its future could be grim. And think, say some Labourites, of what the party could achieve if it held power throughout the 1990s, albeit in partnership with Mr Ashdown. There are plenty of ifs and buts in this argument. Could Mr Kinnock deliver his MPs' votes on this issue? Would his own cabinet stand for it? Would he? The important thing, though, is to note that this idea is about. And recall H.L. Mencken's other famous sneer: "A politician is an animal that can sit on a fence and keep both ears to the ground."

Contents

EUROPE

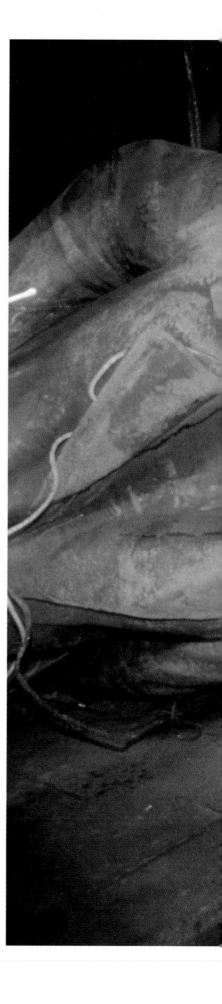

Three ways to change a continent

THE cartographers could hardly keep up. Europe ended the year with a dozen more countries than it had had at the start, and with a transformed political landscape. The Soviet Union disintegrated, and the unhappy experiment called Soviet communism came to an end. War returned to the Balkans. West Europeans (most of them, anyway) committed themselves to economic union and something like federalism. Anyone who thought that the excitement would die down after the collapse of the Berlin Wall was proved spectacularly wrong in 1991.

Why the Euro-frenzy, such a contrast from the old "Eurosclerosis"? Largely because the collapse of the Soviet empire requires a huge adjustment on both sides of the continent. In the East, a superpower comes apart; in the West, countries respond by coming together (eventually, some hope, to blend into a new superpower); in the middle, people struggle—

We agree it's over

some bloodily—to find their place. The result is a frenzy of change, which has been happening in three main ways across Europe.

One way is revolution, the dramatic but (so far) mainly peaceful overthrow of an old order. In January the Soviet Union was still Communist and in one piece, with a mini crackdown in the Baltic arranged to keep it that way. By the year's end the place had dissolved into 15 separate countries, some of them loosely connected in a new "Commonwealth". The turning-point was August's coup in which hardliners botched their attempt to save communism and the Soviet state. After that, the place simply crumbled, bringing down Mikhail Gorbachev with it.

Mr Gorbachev had manoeuvred desperately to keep his country together and himself in power. First he swung towards the reactionaries who had backed the Baltic repression (thus losing powerful allies in the reformist camp). In the spring he veered back towards reform, agreeing with the leaders of nine republics to work towards a big devolution of power in a new "union treaty". That lost him the loyalty of the reactionaries: their coup came just as a union treaty was about to be signed. The hero of the coup's defeat was not Mr Gorbachev but Russia's president, Boris Yeltsin. Power shifted definitively to the republics. Mr Gorbachev was left without a role, and pretty soon he lost his country too.

Did he have to lose everything? Maybe he was doomed to become the victim of the revolution he himself started. But he made several avoidable mistakes. He dithered over economic reform, allowing a degeneration into hyperinflation and slump. He failed to appreciate the force of nationalism and the depth of popular disenchantment with communism (instead, by remaining Communist Party boss, he ensured that he was fully associated with that disenchantment). And he lacked the courage to subject himself to a direct presidential election.

Mr Yeltsin made none of those mistakes. It was his election as Russia's president in June—coupled with the sort of courage he showed in resisting the hardline coup in August—that made him such a formidable force. After the coup, he proceeded to push aside the Communist Party and plan radical economic reform. Ukraine's wily leader, Leonid Kravchuk (a former Communist ideologue), learned the same survival lesson: espouse nationalism, ditch communism and get yourself elected. As a result he is now president of a new nation-state the size of France. Whether Messrs Yeltsin and Kravchuk can continue to survive so successfully is another matter; the relationship between Russia and Ukraine, full of early strains, will be the crucial one in the post-Soviet venture.

Meanwhile in Maastricht

In Western Europe, a far duller process of change—the smoked-filled room approach—was under way. It was a year-long negotiation by bureaucrats and politicians, behind closed doors, aimed at reforming the European Community through twin treaties, one on economic and monetary union (EMU), the other on political union. Cynics wondered whether the Community wasn't following an outmoded agenda and ignoring the new challenge of embracing the emerging democracies to the east; they pointed to the Soviet Union as a warning of how imposed federations can come to grief. At times during the year it seemed that the Community had indeed over-reached itself. But at the December summit in the Dutch city of Maastricht, a deal was duly done.

The "inter-governmental conference" on EMU had been solidly prepared, and so work proceeded fairly smoothly and largely according to German design (what really mattered to the Germans was ensuring the independence of the future

European central bank, and making would-be EMU members pass a demanding economic fitness test). An "opt out" clause had to be arranged for reticent Britain. But the EMU deal struck at Maastricht was if anything bolder than expected: for those countries fit for it, EMU will begin by 1999 at the latest.

The conference on political union, on the other hand, had been poorly prepared. Some countries, like Belgium and Italy, saw it as a chance to push the Community towards a federal United States of Europe. At the other extreme, Britain was determined to keep any further erosion of national sovereignty to a minimum. Arguments raged over the scope and mechanisms of any EC foreign and security policy, over visa policy and other matters of "internal security", over the powers of the European Parliament, and over the extension of EC decision-making into new areas and whether decisions should be taken unanimously or by qualified majority. The poorer members demanded money to make sure they did not get left behind in the future "European Union". There was also a struggle over structure: should everything be part of a single Community, as federalists wanted, or should foreign policy and internal security be left to separate, inter-governmental co-operation?

To reach a deal, federalist ambitions had to be scaled down drastically. Even then, because of the British government's visceral aversion to any expansion of the EC's role in social policy, the summiteers had to cobble together a special arrangement allowing 11 members to go ahead with new social laws without Britain. Yet the deal still gives the Community a powerful push in a federal direction. The European Parliament will have new veto powers; the Community will be able to make laws on a swathe of new topics, with more majority voting; and there is the embryo of a common foreign and security policy.

As usual, the driving force behing EC reform was the Franco-German alliance. France wanted to dissolve united Germany's power into the Community. Germany's leaders saw it as their mission to create a European Germany rather than a German Europe. Besides, the drama in the East made many feel that the Community had to prepare itself for new responsibilities, especially in foreign policy. Increasingly, the outside world expected the Community to act as a power in its own right. In 1991, the Community fluffed its first big foreign-policy test, the Gulf war. The Yugoslav crisis gave it a second chance to prove itself.

Back to the Balkans

Alas, Yugoslavia showed that a third means of change was still possible in Europe: war. No longer held together by East-West tension or Tito's superglue, Yugoslavia came unstuck. Slovenia and Croatia declared independence. Serbs decided to fight, if not for the continuation of Yugoslavia, at least for a "Greater Serbia" including large chunks of Croatia. By the end of the year several thousand people had died and many villages and historical buildings had been destroyed in a grisly war. To the dismay of believers in a new European enlightenment, reason had given way to historical hatreds and old-fashioned blood-letting.

But this Balkan crisis was different. It did not quickly spread. The European Community, by maintaining an (albeit strained) common front, helped to keep the conflict contained. What the Community failed to do was prevent the war from happening in the first place or stop it once it had started. It was asking a lot to expect the Community to sort out Yugoslavia's mess. But if the Community is to become the sort of power its boosters hope, that is the sort of job it will have to attempt.

For other Europeans, it was a year of painful adjustment. NATO agreed on a new post-cold-war strategy, based on fewer troops and more mobility. Germans grappled with the enormity of the task—and the cost—of unification. Albania opened up, and revealed its wretchedness. Other East Europeans struggled with a transition to market economics made all the harder by the abrupt collapse of their trade with the Soviet Union. Hungary, Czechoslovakia and Poland snuggled up to the European Community through association agreements reached after hard haggling.

The seven members of the European Free Trade Association also cosied up to the Community; they reached a deal on a "European Economic Area"

Dismantling Yugoslavia

(EEA), only to find it questioned by the European Court. But for several EFTA countries the EEA was anyway but a step to full EC membership. In 1991 Sweden applied to join (Austria had already done so), and Finland was close to following suit. It was a notable year for both countries: Swedes voted out their long-ruling Social Democrats, and Finns—their trade hit by the Soviet collapse—suffered a savage recession.

Not only were countries queueing to join the EC, a lot of foreigners were trying to get inside it. Coping with the soaring numbers of would-be immigrants and asylum-seekers, from Albanian boatpeople to Maghrebian migrants, emerged as one of Western Europe's great new policy challenges. Resentment against foreigners grew visibly: there were ugly attacks in Germany, France's far-right National Front flourished and anti-foreigner forces did well in elections in Belgium and Austria.

Ah, you can almost hear some faint-hearted people sigh, for the comfortable old days of cold war and Eurosclerosis.

Tuesday 1st
Years of soft-currency barter trade between the Soviet Union and Eastern Europe came to an end. Henceforth, trade would, in theory, be in **hard currency** only.

An economic mini-bang took place in **Czechoslovakia**, with the introduction of market-oriented reforms. Some prices were freed, the way was opened for the privatisation of small businesses, and limited internal currency convertibility was introduced.

As Europe's last Stalinist regime began to loosen up, nearly 3,000 **Albanian refugees** arrived in Greece. By the middle of the month the numbers would rise to some 8,000. Many were ethnic Greeks and would be allowed to stay. Many others would later be sent back across the border into Albania.

Thursday 3rd
The **Israeli consulate in Moscow** reopened. This was a step towards restoring ties between Israel and the Soviet Union, which broke diplomatic relations after the Six Day War in 1967. Soviet Jews danced for joy at the opening ceremony.

Friday 4th
Jan Krzysztof Bielicki, a keen free-marketeer, was voted in as **Poland's prime minister**.

Monday 7th
The Soviet defence ministry announced that it was to send paratroopers to enforce conscription in **seven rebel republics**: the Baltic three, Armenia, Georgia, Moldavia and parts of Ukraine. In Lithuania for example, over 80% of eligible recruits were avoiding the draft.

Poland refused entry to a train carrying **Soviet troops** and equipment home from eastern Germany. The Poles wanted money for allowing returning

Soviet troops to transit Poland. They also wanted agreement for an early withdrawal of the 50,000 Soviet troops still stationed in Poland.

Thursday 10th
"Vzglyad", a popular Soviet current affairs television programme, was taken off the air—further evidence of a tightening squeeze on **glasnost**.

Saturday 12th
Alfonso Guerra resigned as Spain's deputy prime minister after months of embarrassment over an influence-peddling scandal involving his brother, Juan. The left-wing Mr Guerra, since the 1960s the closest political ally of Spain's prime minister, Felipe Gonzalez, remained deputy general-secretary of the Socialist Party.

Sunday 13th
Soviet troops stormed the television building in Vilnius, **Lithuania**'s capital, killing 14 people and injuring at least 150. A "National Salvation Committee", made up of Communists loyal to Moscow, claimed to control the republic. Lithuania's elected leaders occupied the parliament building, determined to defend it from attack.

While questions were asked about the role (direct or indirect) of President Mikhail Gorbachev in ordering the use of such force, Russia's **Boris Yeltsin** rushed to Estonia on January 14th to meet Baltic leaders and declare his solidarity with them.

Mario Soares was comfortably elected to a second five-year term as president of Portugal. Mr Soares, formerly a Socialist prime minister, won 70% of the vote.

Lothar Späth, the influential Christian Democratic premier of Baden-Württemberg for 12 years, resigned amid allegations of corruption.

Monday 14th
Valentin Pavlov, a technocrat who had risen through the economic bureaucracy to become finance minister, was appointed Soviet prime minister. The next day **Alexander Bessmertnykh**, a diplomat who had spent much of his career in the United States, was appointed foreign minister. Mr Bessmertnykh's appointment was meant to reassure the West that the liberal policies introduced by his predecessor, Edward Shevardnadze, would continue.

Wednesday 16th
The European Community's muddled reaction to the build-up towards the Gulf war raised doubts about the aim of a single **European foreign policy**. Even Jacques Delors, president of the European Commission, was to call the EC's response "ineffectual". Germany came under particular criticism for its dreamy distance from use of force.

Albania's President Ramiz Alia agreed to postpone its **multiparty election** by seven weeks, to March 31st. The opposition wanted more time to prepare, and had demanded a three month delay.

Thursday 17th
King Olav V of Norway died, aged 87. His son was sworn in as King Harald V on January 21st.

Czechoslovakia started screening officials for links with the **secret police** in the Commu-

nist past. This led to the sacking, a week later, of the environment minister, Bedrich Moldan.

Friday 18th
In another ominous sign for Soviet reform, Mikhail Gorbachev's pro-market economic adviser, **Nikolai Petrakov**, resigned after protesting about the use of Soviet troops in Lithuania.

Sunday 20th
The Baltic crackdown spread. Four people died when pro-Soviet "Black Beret" troops stormed the interior ministry in Riga, the capital of **Latvia**.

In elections in the German state of **Hesse**, the centre-right coalition lost its majority and was replaced by a coalition of Social Democrats and Greens.

Tuesday 22nd
The Soviet Union declared strict limits on withdrawals from bank deposits plus the cancellation of 50- and 100-**rouble banknotes**. The idea was to stem inflation. The result was panic and fury.

Tuesday 29th
The first top official of **former East Germany** went on trial: Harry Tisch, ex trade union leader, was accused of corruption. Erich Honecker, the former East German leader, was also wanted for trial, but the Soviet Union refused to hand him over from his refuge at a Soviet military base in Germany, whence he was later spirited to Moscow.

Thursday 31st
France's defence minister, **Jean-Pierre Chevènement**, resigned. A founder-member of the Franco-Iraqi friendship society, he had become an embarrassment at a time when France was at war with Iraq. President Mitterrand replaced him with the dependable Pierre Joxe.

Friday 1st
A decision went into effect to deploy small groups of **Soviet soldiers** with policemen to patrol large Soviet cities. The idea, officially at least, was to curb rising crime.

As part of the move to market economics, food prices in **Bulgaria** rose by 500% or more. Fares on public transport rose by 1,000%. The next day interest rates went up from 15% to 45%.

Sunday 3rd
At a conference in Rimini, Italy's communists, the country's second-biggest party, formally reconstituted themselves as the **Democratic Party of the Left**. The change was influenced by the party's eroding support and the collapse of communism in Eastern Europe. A few communist nostalgics walked out, vowing to continue in the true faith.

Three by-elections were held in France, after three neo-Gaullist deputies had resigned in a challenge to their party leader, Jacques Chirac. The main challenger, **Michel Noir**, retained his seat in Lyons, but the rebels failed to get much real momentum behind them. One of them, Michèle Barzach, a former health minister, had withdrawn after a poor showing in the first round of voting in a Paris constituency.

Monday 4th
The foreign ministers of **France and Germany** launched a new plan for a common EC security policy. It called for closer links between the Community and the Western European Union, a defence alliance of nine EC members. Almost everyone could agree with that. But eventually, under the Franco-German plan, the EC and WEU would merge. Britain and Holland feared this would dangerously weaken NATO.

Wednesday 6th
The German government agreed on a further tightening of **arms-export controls**. Germany had been stung by allegations of German companies' involvement in supplying weapons and military technology to Iraq. Few people were optimistic that the tighter controls could stop the illicit arms dealing altogether.

Saturday 9th
Lithuanians voted overwhelmingly to become an independent, democratic state. In a poll arranged to pre-empt Mr Gorbachev's supposedly nationwide referendum on March 17th on the future of the union, turnout was 85%—and 90% of those who voted said Yes to independence. But a majority of ethnic Russians and Poles either stayed away or voted No.

Sunday 10th
Six regionalist parties in northern Italy, under the leadership of the **Lombard League**, formed a coalition called the Northern League. Umberto Bossi's Lombard League had been strikingly successful in regional elections in May 1990.

Tuesday 12th
The Soviet prime minister, Valentin Pavlov, claimed he had thwarted a **western plot** to flood the country with billions of roubles and thus overthrow the Soviet regime. Mr Pavlov, it seemed, wanted to repair his reputation at home after the unpopular currency confiscation in January. He succeeded only in ruining his reputation abroad.

Tuesday 19th
After weeks of arguing over air-time, **Boris Yeltsin** used a live interview on Soviet television to make a dramatic call for Mikhail Gorbachev's resignation.

Wednesday 20th
In Tirana's main square, Albanian students pulled down a giant statue of **Enver Hoxha**, the country's former dictator. President Ramiz Alia imposed presidential rule. But anti-communist demonstrations continued.

Thursday 21st
The Yugoslav republic of **Croatia** declared its laws to be above federal laws made in Belgrade. Croatia was following Slovenia's example. Both had already threatened to secede from Yugoslavia unless the other republics (especially Serbia) agreed to transform the country into a loose confederation.

Friday 22nd
The European Parliament unfroze a $1 billion **food-aid programme** to the Soviet Union. The aid had been blocked after the crackdown in Lithuania. The Soviet attitude towards the Baltic republics was deemed to have improved.

Turkey's President Turgut Ozal dismissed his defence minister (and nephew), Husnu Dogan. Mr Dogan had objected to a campaign by the president's wife, Semra Ozal, to become leader of the ruling Motherland Party in Istanbul.

Saturday 23rd
The anti-communist movement that led Czechoslovakia's "velvet revolution", **Civic Forum**, agreed to split. It would divide into the two main groups whose arguments had strained the movement's unity: a centre-right party under the finance minister, Vaclav Klaus, and a social democratic party calling itself the Liberals.

Monday 25th
The six **Warsaw Pact** countries agreed formally to wind up the pact's military structure by the end of March. The formal death of the pact's political organisation would take a little longer.

Bulgaria's former communist leader, **Todor Zhivkov**, went on trial in Sofia, charged with embezzlement. He was only the second of Eastern Europe's ousted communist bosses to face trial: the other, Nicolae Ceausescu of Romania, was shot after a show trial.

Tuesday 26th
Several of Germany's EC partners reacted with annoyance to a German draft treaty for **economic and monetary union**. It proposed delaying the establishment of a European central bank until 1997.

A Soviet diplomat was posted to **Albania**: the first since Moscow and Tirana broke diplomatic relations in 1961.

Thursday 28th
A Polish opinion survey showed **George Bush** ahead even of Poland's own Pope John Paul II as the most popular man in Poland.

March

Friday 1st

Soviet **coal miners** began a strike. Their demands: more money, and President Gorbachev's resignation.

Sunday 3rd

Latvia and Estonia held plebiscites on **independence** from the Soviet Union. In Latvia, 73% voted for independence; in Estonia 77% did.

Friday 8th

The number of **Albanian refugees** escaping by boat to Italy since the start of the month reached 17,000. The Italian port of Otranto was under a state of emergency. At Brindisi the authorities tried forlornly to stop the refugees landing, but faced riots among the Albanians.

Germany announced that it would raise taxes to spend an extra DM24 billion over two years to help increase investment and create jobs in eastern Germany, which was struggling with accelerating economic collapse.

Sunday 10th

Two people died and about 90 were injured in **clashes in Belgrade** between police and demonstrators. This was the first major violence among Serbs in recent years. Students and opposition leaders, several of whom were arrested, were protesting against the strong-arm policies of Serbia's Socialist (ex-Communist) leader, Slobodan Milosevic.

In Moscow, hundreds of thousands of people marched in support of **Boris Yeltsin**'s campaign against Mikhail Gorbachev. Mr Yeltsin's supporters rallied in other Russian cities too.

Some 8,000 people demonstrated in Bratislava, Slovakia's capital, to support **Slovak sovereignty**. The demonstrators wanted Slovak laws to be above federal laws made in Prague, and they wanted their own army.

Monday 11th

Spain's Socialist prime minister, Felipe Gonzalez, used a long-awaited **reshuffle** to bolster the pragmatists in his cabinet. He promoted Narcis Serra, his former defence minister, to be deputy prime minister (a job held until January by the leftist Alfonso Guerra). The influence of Carlos Solchaga, the finance minister and arch rival of Mr Guerra, was enhanced.

Friday 15th

The resignation of Borisav Jovic, a hardline Serb, as head of **Yugoslavia**'s eight-member collective presidency triggered fresh fears of a military intervention. Mr Jovic, who had tried and failed to get the presidency to agree to emergency measures, thus created a power vacuum which fellow hardliners hoped the army might fill. But the army did not oblige.

The Paris Club of creditor governments agreed to forgive **Poland** half of its debt. This was a big gesture of political support for Poland's effort to move to pluralist politics and economics.

Albania and the United States restored **diplomatic relations** after a break of 52 years.

Saturday 16th

Soviet-American talks in Moscow failed to resolve differences over **arms control**. The Americans were worried about Soviet compliance with the 1990 treaty on conventional forces in Europe.

Sunday 17th

Voters went to the polls in the **Soviet referendum** on the future of the union. Six independent-minded republics—the Baltic three, Armenia, Georgia and Moldavia—boycotted the vote. Elsewhere there were variations on the questions asked. This made the result confused. Turnout was 80%; 76% of these voters said Yes to Mr Gorbachev's question about a "renewed federation of equal sovereign states"; in Russia, 70% of voters approved Boris Yeltsin's idea of a directly elected president in their republic.

The right-wing Centre Party was the big gainer in **Finland**'s general election, at the expense of the Conservatives and Social Democrats in the outgoing coalition. The main reason: Finland's recession. Negotiations began for a new coalition led by the Centre Party.

Monday 18th

Monday protest marches, a feature of **East Germany**'s 1989 revolution, started up again in Leipzig, this time against economic conditions in former East Germany.

Tuesday 19th

Karl Otto Pöhl, president of the Bundesbank, called **German economic and monetary union** (GEMU) a "disaster", and suggested it was an illustration of the dangers of proceeding to European economic and monetary union (EMU) before there was sufficient convergence between the various economies. Chancellor Helmut Kohl swiftly replied that there had been no alternative to GEMU, and that the comparisons with EMU were misleading.

Thursday 28th

Tens of thousands of supporters of **Boris Yeltsin** rallied in Moscow despite Soviet attempts to ban the protest and the intimidating deployment of 50,000 Soviet troops in the heart of the capital.

Friday 29th

Italy lost its 49th government since the war. President Cossiga had surprised Italians by threatening to dissolve parliament and call elections. Italian presidents are usually mere figureheads. In the end, the Christian Democratic prime minister, Giulio Andreotti, merely had to resign and start putting together a new government. He had been under pressure for a renegotiation of the coalition pact from his main partner, the Socialists' Bettino Craxi.

Sunday 31st

The communists won **Albania's election**, the country's first multiparty vote in 60 years, although President Ramiz Alia was defeated in his Tirana constituency. They won 68% of the vote, mainly thanks to strong support in the countryside. The opposition Democratic Party won 25% of the vote, and triumphed in the towns. The vote left Albania divided, and violent.

About 90% of the electorate in the Soviet republic of **Georgia** voted for independence in a referendum held to rival the supposedly pan-Soviet vote on March 17th.

April

Monday 1st
Germany's RAF terrorists assassinated **Detlev Rohwedder**, the forceful head of the Treuhand agency responsible for privatising and liquidating state-owned firms in eastern Germany. He was a scapegoat for the trauma of eastern Germany's transition to capitalism.

Big price rises were imposed on already hard-pressed **Romanians**. The currency was devalued by 42%. The IMF had made tough reforms a condition for help.

Tuesday 2nd
The Soviet government introduced retail **price rises** averaging 60%. The next day, the three top Soviet financial officials said the budget deficit was running out of control and that the economy was on the brink of catastrophe.

Sunday 7th
Mass was celebrated in **St Basil's cathedral** on Red Square for the first time since 1917.

Monday 8th
The six "Schengen" countries (Benelux, Germany, France and Italy) introduced visa-free travel for **Poles**. The Poles were delighted; some far-right young Germans were not.

Wednesday 10th
About 140 people died when an Italian ferry collided with an oil tanker off Livorno. It was Italy's worst **maritime disaster** since the second world war.

Thursday 11th
Disaster struck Italy again when an explosion crippled an oil tanker, *Haven*, off the coast of Genoa. The tanker was carrying more than 700,000 tonnes of oil. The **oil spillage** threatened to be the Mediterranean's worst.

Saturday 13th
Italy's 50th post-war government was sworn in. Giulio Andreotti, a Christian Democrat, remained prime minister, but he lost one of his partners from the outgoing five-party coalition: because of an argument over portfolios, the small Republican Party refused to join the new government.

Monday 15th
The **European Bank for Reconstruction and Development** was formally inaugurated in London. Its mission: to help the countries of Eastern Europe to privatise and modernise.

Luxembourg, as president of the EC, presented a draft treaty on **political union**. It was a careful compromise which would serve as a working document but which left plenty of arguments to be settled on foreign policy, defence and the powers of the European Parliament.

Tuesday 16th
Brokers in white shirts and red braces began trading shares in Poland for the first time since the German invasion in 1939. The site of Po-

land's new stockmarket: the former communist-party headquarters.

Sunday 21st
A thumping **defeat for Chancellor Kohl**'s Christian Democrats in his home state of Rhineland-Palatinate brought his fortunes to a new low. His party lost power there for the first time in 45 years. The voters were venting their anger over the soaring costs of unification.

The conservative Independence Party emerged as the largest party in **Iceland's general election**. Its leader, David Oddsson, would become the new prime minister, in a coalition with the Social Democrats.

Tuesday 23rd
A **reconciliation** between Mikhail Gorbachev and Boris Yeltsin brightened the prospects for the Soviet Union. Together with leaders of eight other Soviet republics, they signed an agreement (which became known as the "nine-plus-one" agreement) to pull the country out of crisis through co-operation, not conflict.

Wednesday 24th
The agreement with the republics helped **Mikhail Gorbachev** survive a challenge from hardline Communists who threatened to oust him at a Central Committee meeting. Mr Gorbachev offered his resignation, but the comrades asked him to stay on.

A new centre-right **Finnish government** was formed. It was led by Esko Aho of the Centre Party, the main winner in March's election. For the first time in 15 years the Social Democrats were left out of government.

Vladimir Meciar was forced to quit as **premier of Slovakia**. A fierce nationalist, he had

broken away from the moderate Public Against Violence to oppose the federal government's free-market reforms which he thought would hurt Slovakia. His supporters rallied to his defence—a sign of Slovakia's increasing nationalist passions.

Thursday 25th
Spain eavesdropped on the infighting of its ruling Socialist Party. An intercepted carphone conversation of the party's number three, Txiki Benegas, was broadcast on radio. His criticisms of the prime minister, Felipe Gonzalez, reflected growing tensions between the pragmatic Socialists in government and left-wingers in the party.

Sunday 28th
Britain and France fell out at a meeting in Luxembourg over future plans for **European defence**. The French wanted the new EC treaty on political union to aim for a distinct European defence identity. Britain wanted to avoid anything that could undermine NATO.

Monday 29th
A big earthquake in the Soviet republic of **Georgia** killed more than 100 people and caused widespread damage. The quake was said to be even more powerful than the one which killed at least 25,000 people in neighbouring Armenia in 1988.

Tuesday 30th
The **Soviet coal strike** moved towards an end. As part of his new pact with President Gorbachev, Boris Yeltsin persuaded the miners to go back to work. The miners won a promise to sell some of their coal for hard currency. Mr Yeltsin won control of some of the pits for his Russian republic—plus the kudos of being the man who could solve the dispute where Mr Gorbachev had failed.

May

Thursday 2nd

Several people were killed as clashes began between Croatian police and Serb paramilitary groups. The clashes added to **Yugoslavia**'s rapidly worsening ethnic tensions. Croats accused the Serb-dominated army of failing to protect them, and held a big anti-army demonstration in Split on May 5th. A threat of martial law was averted when, on May 9th, the collective presidency managed to agree on measures which—temporarily—diffused the tension.

Monday 6th

Anger mounted in **Armenia** over the deaths caused as Azeri riot police, backed by Soviet troops, moved through Armenian-populated villages to disarm local militias. The Armenians suspected the Kremlin was siding with the Azeris to punish Armenia for its drive for independence.

Friday 10th

François Mitterrand celebrated his tenth anniversary as French president. He remained the most popular politician in France—and the most enigmatic.

Monday 13th

Two days of **riots in Brussels** ended with the arrest of nearly 200 North African immigrants. It was another sign of racial tensions affecting several big European cities.

Wednesday 15th

France got its first woman prime minister, **Edith Cresson**. Michel Rocard re-signed after three years in the job. President Mitterrand had decided it was time for a change, in advance of the general election due in 1993. But in the new cabinet the main ministerial jobs did not change hands.

Yugoslavia's crisis deepened. Its collective presidency should have rotated to a Croat. But **Serbia** and its allies blocked his election. This left Yugoslavia not only without a head of state—but also without a commander of its armed forces.

Thursday 16th

Karl Otto Pöhl announced he would resign as president of the **Bundesbank**, four years before his term was complete. Mr Pöhl had been critical of the way the government handled monetary union with the former East Germany.

Poland devalued the **zloty** against the dollar for the first time since its anti-inflation "Big Bang" introduced on January 1st 1990. Pressure to devalue came from the need to boost exports.

Sunday 19th

The general election in **Cyprus** was notable for the gains—unusual since the collapse of communism in Eastern Europe—by the Communists. They and other parties picked up seats at the expense of the centrist Democratic Party led by ex-president Spiros Kyprianou.

A referendum in **Croatia** showed that 94% of voters wanted Croatian sovereignty within a looser Yugoslavia. And 92% were against staying in Yugoslavia in its present form.

The **Pentagonale**—a club for regional co-operation between Italy, Austria, Hungary, Czechoslovakia and Yugoslavia—decided to admit Poland. Poland would officially join in July, turning the *Pentagonale* into the *Hexagonale*.

Monday 20th

The Soviet Union passed its long-awaited **foreign-travel law**. From January 1st 1993, Soviet citizens would no longer need exit visas, and would have the right to return. For years the West demanded that the Soviet Union grant its people the freedom to travel. In future the problem will be permission to enter the West.

Tuesday 21st

Grigory Yavlinsky led a team of **Soviet economists** to work on a plan for Soviet reform with economists at Harvard University. The idea was to come up with a plan that was radical, credible and could command western support.

Wednesday 20th

Britain and Albania at last agreed to restore **diplomatic relations**, broken since the second world war by disputes over British-held Albanian gold and compensation for two British destroyers sunk off the Albanian coast in 1946.

Thursday 23rd

Founded in 1705 by Peter the Great, but closed for the past seven decades, the **Leningrad stock exchange** reopened.

Sunday 26th

The first open direct election of a republican leader in the Soviet Union was held, in **Georgia**. The winner, with 86.5% of the vote, was Zviad Gamsakhurdia, a fierce nationalist who had already led a non-Communist coalition to victory in parliamentary elections in October 1990. No voting took place in South Ossetia and Abkhazia, two provinces of the republic in conflict with the Georgian majority.

The ruling Socialists in **Spain** did poorly in local elections, losing control of several big cities. The results made the conservative People's Party look, for the first time, like a potentially credible challenger to the Socialists in a general election. The poll was a disaster for the centrists of Mario Suarez, a former prime minister, who resigned from the leadership of his party.

Tuesday 28th

NATO defence ministers approved a sweeping reform of the **Atlantic alliance**'s forces, for the post-cold-war era. The central-front forces would be reduced from eight single-country corps to five multinational corps, all partly manned by reserves. A rapid-reaction corps would be created for use anywhere in Europe. France was upset; the plans undermined its hopes for the creation of a European defence identity.

Jacques Delors, president of the European Commission, wrote to complain to Luxembourg, the current EC president. Mr Delors reckoned Luxembourg's first draft of a new treaty on political union envisaged too small a role for the commission.

Wednesday 29th

Germany's opposition Social Democrats elected **Björn Engholm** as their new leader. The popular 51-year-old premier of Schleswig-Holstein thus became a likely candidate for chancellor at the next general election.

June

Saturday 1st
Pope John Paul II arrived in his native Poland for a ten-day visit, his fourth since he became pope but the first since the fall of communism. But that did not mean politics no longer mattered. Poland's parliament had just postponed decisions on whether to make abortion illegal. The pope used the visit to argue passionately against abortion.

Sunday 9th
In a referendum, **Italians** backed a change in voting rules aimed at cutting out electoral fraud. A fierce debate had begun over how to shake up Italy's politics. The referendum was at least a start. Its main sponsor, Mario Segni, a modernising Christian Democrat, claimed that the vote would "start an avalanche of desire for reform".

Tuesday 11th
A new, coalition government was named in **Albania**, ending the communists' 45-year monopoly of power. The communists kept 12 portfolios (including internal and foreign affairs) in the government of the new prime minister, Yilli Bufi. But the Democratic Party got seven posts, including that of deputy prime minister responsible for the economy.

Wednesday 12th
In the first ever direct election of a Russian leader, **Boris Yeltsin** was elected president of the Russian republic. He won 57% of the vote; his closest rival, Nikolai Ryzhkov, a former Soviet prime minister, won 17% (the turnout was 74%). Endorsement through the ballot box greatly strengthened Mr Yeltsin's hand in his power struggle with the un-elected President Gorbachev.

In other votes on the same day, the liberal mayors of Moscow and Leningrad—Gavriil Popov and Anatoly Sobchak—were both returned to office, their status enhanced. And Leningraders voted to change their city's name back to **St Petersburg**.

Sunday 16th
Luxembourg, as current EC president, unveiled a new draft **treaty on political union** with a far more federalist flavour than its previous version. Britain was dismayed at the references to the Community's "federal goal", and to its ambitions for a single currency and the "eventual framing of a defence policy".

Monday 17th
In Bonn, **Germany and Poland** signed a treaty designed to reassure both on future good-neighbourliness. The Poles wanted reassurances that there would be no German designs on their territory, the Germans wanted reassurances about the rights of Poland's German minority. Both sides seemed happy.

The Soviet prime minister, **Valentin Pavlov**, failed in an attempt to get special powers to rule by decree. It was seen as an attempt to reverse President Gorbachev's drift back towards liberal policies.

Tuesday 18th
Speaking in Berlin, the American secretary of state, **James Baker**, described his idea of a "Euro-Atlantic community", stretching "from Vancouver to Vladivostok".

Wednesday 19th
The **Soviet military pull-out** from Hungary and Czechoslovakia was completed. The celebrations that followed included a shaving party in Prague for Czechs who had grown beards when Soviet tanks invaded in 1968 and refused to shave until they left. But there was no celebration over the environmental mess the Soviet army left behind.

The membership of the Conference on Security and Co-operation in Europe (CSCE) had dropped from 35 to 34 with the disappearance of East Germany. It climbed back again to 35 with **Albania**'s admittance to the club.

Thursday 20th
The Bundestag, Germany's parliament, surprised itself and most of Germany by voting narrowly to move from **Bonn to Berlin**. The move of parliament and government would take several years, but the effects were immediate: gloom in Bonn, a scramble for property in Berlin.

Sunday 23rd
Mesut Yilmaz, a former foreign minister, replaced Yildirim Akbulut as **Turkey's prime minister**. At a party congress the previous week, Mr Yilmaz had won the leadership of the ruling Motherland Party. The party was worried about its chances of winning the general election due by November 1992.

Tuesday 25th
Slovenia and Croatia declared their independence. Two days later the Yugoslav army intervened, recapturing Slovenian border posts but getting cut off in the process. EC leaders, meeting at their (otherwise uneventful) Luxembourg summit, dispatched a *troika* of foreign ministers to mediate a ceasefire. They managed to unblock the election of a Croat, Stipe Mesic, to the head of Yugoslavia's presidency (and hence commander of the army). But the fighting continued.

Reactions to the Yugoslav crisis revealed a **split in the West** between those countries (such as France and Spain) determined to keep Yugoslavia together, out of fear of a plague of separatism, and those (notably Germany and Austria) stressing self-determination for the republics that want it.

Wednesday 26th
An opinion poll showed a drop of 16 points in the approval rating of **Edith Cresson** since her appointment as France's first woman prime minister in May. Her dismal performance—caused partly by her handling of the immigration issue—also affected the standing of President Mitterrand, whose approval rating was down to its lowest since 1985.

EC farm ministers rejected the European Commission's latest proposals to reform the disastrous **common agricultural policy**.

Thursday 27th
Deputies in **Ukraine** voted to delay further discussion of the proposed Soviet union treaty until September. Four days earlier thousands had demonstrated in Kiev against the treaty, which they saw as depriving Ukraine of its independence. The reluctance of the second-most-populous Soviet republic complicated President Gorbachev's efforts to rebuild a new Soviet Union.

Friday 28th
Inspectors from the International Atomic Energy Agency declared the Kozlodui **nuclear power plant** in Bulgaria unsafe, and said it should be closed. But the Bulgarians needed the electricity. Fear of a disaster was to prompt the European Community to send money and technical help to prevent accidents over the winter.

July

Monday 1st
Nine prominent Soviet politicians launched a new Movement for Democratic Reforms. Leading these liberals who had left (or were about to leave) the Communist Party was former foreign minister, **Edward Shevardnadze.**

Holland took over the European Community's six-month rotating presidency from Luxembourg.

The Soviet Union and five East European countries formally dissolved the **Warsaw Pact**. It will not be missed.

Thursday 4th
Chancellor Kohl went to Kiev to see **President Gorbachev**, and reportedly coached him on how to present his case for western help at the G7 summit later in the month. Mr Gorbachev was booed by crowds in the Ukrainian capital.

Friday 5th
Germany's second chamber, the **Bundesrat**, voted not to follow the Bundestag to Berlin. But there was little celebrating in Bonn. The Bundesrat said it would review the decision in a few years' time.

Sunday 7th
At the third attempt, the EC mediated a truce in **Yugoslavia**. This soon ended the fighting in Slovenia (where EC observers would be sent to monitor the ceasefire). But it did nothing to prevent the escalation of violence in Croatia between Serbs and Croats.

Friday 12th
A new **Bulgarian constitution**, supposedly designed for democratic politics, was signed into law. But many opposition deputies boycotted the event, claiming the new constitution favoured the (ex-communist) Socialist Party.

Wednesday 17th
Mikhail Gorbachev domi-

nated the G7 meeting in London, to which he was invited as a guest. He won seven encouraging pats on the shoulder, but no cash.

In an effort to reduce a national sport, **Italy**'s finance ministry published a list of more than 500,000 tax-dodgers. The list included some prominent businessmen and media personalities. The idea was to embarrass people into paying their taxes. Some hope.

Thursday 18th
Yugoslavia's collective presidency ordered the federal army to withdraw from **Slovenia**, in effect conceding that Slovenia was on its way to independence. Croatia objected that the retreating troops might be used to support the Serb militiamen who were moving to clear Croats out of mainly Serb-populated parts of Croatia.

Farmers in **Portugal** blocked roads in protest against their government's lack of support in the face of rising EC competition. The protests risked embarrassing the government just three months before an election.

Friday 19th
President Bush began a visit to Greece and Turkey, and tried to push them into progress in the **Cyprus dispute**. Mr Bush pleased the Turks more than the Greeks. Grateful to Turkey for its help during the Gulf war, he said it could count on his support in its bid to join the European Community.

Saturday 20th
Russia's newly elected president, **Boris Yeltsin**, issued a decree banning Communist Party cells from factories, farms and government offices—their main power base. The decree enraged Communists and embarrassed their leader, Mikhail Gorbachev, just before a meeting of the party's Central Committee.

Tuesday 23rd
The **Soviet Union** surprised the West by applying for full membership of the IMF, just a week after it had been offered "special associate status" at the London G7 summit. Clearly, the Kremlin was not satisfied with a status that would entitle it to advice, but no money.

Thursday 25th
At a meeting of the **Soviet Communist Party**'s Central Committee, Mikhail Gorbachev presented a new programme that would turn the party into a social democratic one in all but name. Conservatives decided not to fight the changes—yet.

Saturday 27th
Alexander Yakovlev, sometimes described as the **guru of glasnost**, resigned from Mikhail Gorbachev's team of advisers. Mr Yakovlev was involved in the new Movement for Democratic Renewal. His departure left Mr Gorbachev's team dangerously short of intellectual talent.

Monday 29th
Fuel was added to a fiery debate over **immigration** in France with the publication of a report arguing that the country's low birth rate meant that it could face a serious labour shortage early in the next century. One answer, the report argued, was renewed immigration. This shocked many people in France who thought that their country was already super-saturated with immigrants.

The presidents of **Russia and Lithuania** signed a state treaty in which Russia recognised Lithuania's independence—something the Soviet government had refused to do.

Tuesday 30th
A Berlin court ended some of Germany's agonising over how to handle the legacy of communism by halting the prosecution of former **East German spymasters**. The court argued that it was unfair to prosecute people for the sort of work that went on in any country.

Wednesday 31st
The European Commission at last delivered its opinion on **Austria's application** to join the European Community. The commission was generally in favour of Austrian membership, but with two reservations: it worried about Austria's neutrality and about the need for more EC institutional reform to ease decision-taking before Austria and other would-be newcomers swelled the numbers.

Six Lithuanian officials were killed in an attack on a border post with Belorussia. It was the bloodiest attack since the attempted **crackdown in Lithuania** in January. The incident came at an embarrassing time for President Gorbachev: he was hosting the superpower summit in Moscow with President Bush.

August

Thursday 1st
A particularly bloody day in **Yugoslavia**: at least 21 people died in fighting for villages in Croatia. As Serb forces continued to advance, western reactions continued to be divided: some politicians called for western military intervention, others scoffed at the idea.

After his Moscow summit with President Gorbachev, **President Bush** went to Kiev, where he warned Ukraine's independent-minded parliament against "suicidal nationalism based on ethnic hatred". This did not go down well with nationalists. It was later dubbed Mr Bush's "chicken Kiev" speech.

Friday 2nd
President Bush announced that the leaders of Greece and Turkey had agreed to talk about **Cyprus** in September at a UN-sponsored conference in America. A breakthrough in the long dispute over the divided island? Alas, no. Even the sensitive procedural details of the talks were still to be decided (and in the end Turkey used the excuse of its early election to put off the talks).

Sunday 4th
An EC peace-making mission to **Yugoslavia** ended in failure. Serbia blocked attempts to arrange a ceasefire. The head of the EC *troika* of foreign ministers said Yugoslavia was "facing catastrophe".

Tuesday 6th
Yugoslavia's collective presidency decreed a **ceasefire**. Despite some violations, the fighting abated. The Soviet government gave warning that a western military intervention could escalate the conflict into an all-European one.

Ivan Polozkov, the hardline boss of the **Communist Party of Russia**, resigned. He had been under attack for allowing the party to lose members and influence fast.

Wednesday 7th
Poland showed that it really had joined the ranks of the capitalists: it had a **financial scandal**. The scandal involved state guaranteed loans and the Art-B Corporation, hitherto a star of Polish finance.

Thursday 8th
Constantine Mitsotakis, **Greece**'s prime minister, sacked 12 ministers in a **cabinet reshuffle**. The most notable departure was that of his daughter, Dora Bokoyannis, whose presence in the cabinet had aroused jealousies and accusations of nepotism.

Thursday 8th
Yet another wave of **Albanian boat people**—some 17,000—forced their way to Bari in Italy, only to face dismal detention, police truncheons, then summary return to Albania. They were fleeing economic misery, not political repression. Many people in and outside Italy were critical of the Italian authorities' handling of the crisis.

Wednesday 14th
A bold **privatisation law** was passed in **Romania**. It envisaged 30% of Romanian capital being privatised through the distribution of deeds to Romanian citizens.

Friday 16th
Politicians in **Turkey** agreed to hold a general election in October, a year earlier than it was due. The ruling Motherland Party hoped for a boost at the polls from its new leader and prime minister, Mesut Yilmaz.

Monday 19th
The real Russian revolution took place: an attempted **coup against Mikhail Gorbachev** collapsed within three days. Mr Gorbachev was detained in the Crimea and prevented from returning to Moscow, where he was due to sign the new union treaty. An eight-man emergency committee took charge. But faced with the defiance of Boris Yeltsin at the Russian parliament, as well as popular protests and splits in the army, the junta had to choose between bloodshed or backing down. They backed down.

Around the Soviet Union, resistance to the coup was strong in places, but patchy. Many factories and mines responded to Mr Yeltsin's call to strike. In **Leningrad and Kishinev** there were mass demonstrations. **Estonia and Latvia** declared full independence, bringing themselves into line with Lithuania.

Thursday 22nd
Mr Gorbachev returned to Moscow, but showed in a press conference that he had failed to grasp the magnitude of the change that had taken place in his country. The coup leaders were arrested; one of them, the interior minister, Boris Pugo, committed suicide. The rest were charged with treason. Huge crowds celebrated in Moscow, cheering the hero of the resistance to the coup, **Boris Yeltsin**. They also toppled the statue of Felix Dzerzhinsky, the founder of the Soviet secret police.

Friday 23rd
The change in the balance of power in Moscow became clear during Mikhail Gorbachev's appearance before the **Russian parliament**. Mr Gorbachev got a stormy reception and had to accept decisions dictated by Boris Yeltsin. Among those decisions: the suspension of the Russian Communist Party. Mr Yeltsin also suspended *Pravda* and five other Communist papers. Mr Gorbachev had to read out a report showing how almost his entire (now sacked) government had betrayed him during the coup. The pre-1917 Russian flag was hoisted over the Kremlin.

Saturday 24th
Mr Gorbachev set about adjusting to the new, post-coup realities. He resigned as **Communist Party boss**, and gave party property over to the state. His military adviser and former chief of staff, Marshal Sergei Akhromeev, committed suicide. Hundreds of thousands of Muscovites turned out to bury those killed in the coup.

Ukraine declared its independence, subject to approval in a referendum; the next day Belorussia also declared independence. Among the Soviet republics rushing to assert their own sovereignty, Ukraine, with over 50m people, mattered more than any except Russia itself. In the wake of their independence declaration, Ukrainians were alarmed by a suggestion from Boris Yeltsin that borders might have to be reviewed. A delegation had to be dispatched from Moscow to Kiev to soothe worries.

Tuesday 27th
European Community foreign ministers agreed to recognise the three **Baltic states** (Latvia, Lithuania, Estonia). Denmark had broken EC ranks to recognise its Baltic neighbours the day before.

Thursday 29th
More than 70 years of Soviet communism came to an end when the Supreme Soviet formally suspended the **Communist Party**.

September

Monday 2nd
The United States at last joined the rush to recognise the **Baltic states** (though only after a long-awaited nod and wink from President Gorbachev). Two days later the ex-Soviet Union itself formally recognised the independence of Latvia, Lithuania and Estonia.

Thursday 5th
The Soviet parliament haggled its way to a new, provisional structure of government, dominated by the republics. The ex-Soviet Union became the **Union of Sovereign States**. There would be an interim, two-chamber parliament, made up of delegates from the republics; a State Council consisting of President Gorbachev and representatives from the republics; and an inter-republican economic committee. How would all this work in practice? Nobody knew.

Friday 6th
France upset its EC partners and **East Europeans** by blocking moves to liberalise meat imports from the East. Poland, Hungary and Czechoslovakia said it was not worth talking about association agreements with the Community unless the EC got serious about opening its markets.

Saturday 7th
An EC-sponsored **peace conference** on Yugoslavia opened in The Hague, chaired by Lord Carrington. It was not expected to produce quick results.

Sunday 8th
Macedonia became the third Yugoslav republic to vote for independence in a (cautiously worded) referendum. Some 95% of those who voted said Yes to independence. But the republic's Albanian minority and local Serbs abstained. Macedonia's neighbours—especially Serbia and Greece—immediately began thinking

of ways to make sure its independence did not happen.

Two parties opposing EC membership scored big gains in **Norway**'s local elections, complicating the debate on whether the country should apply to join the EC. With Sweden's application already in and Finland's expected in 1992, Norway risked being the odd-Nordic-out.

Ayaz Mutalibov was elected president of **Azerbaijan**, despite having supported the August coup in Moscow. The opposition tried to organise a boycott of the vote. Mr Mutalibov, the republic's incumbent president, was the only candidate.

Sunday 15th
The Social Democrats, in power for all but six of the previous 60 years, lost **Sweden's election**. The reasons: recession and a loss of faith in the "Swedish model" of socialism. The Conservatives were the main gainers. Their leader, Carl Bildt, set about forming a centre-right coalition government.

Monday 16th
Thousands of people rallied in **Georgia**'s capital, Tbilisi, to demand the resignation of the republic's president, Zviad Gamsakhurdia. Dissatisfaction had been growing about the dictatorial ways of Mr Gamsakhurdia, a veteran of the anti-communist opposition, since he was elected president in May.

Thursday 19th
EC foreign ministers decided against sending a **force to Yugoslavia** to keep (or make) the peace. France had been most tempted by the idea, Britain most strongly opposed.

Saturday 21st
A former (and would-be future) French president, **Valéry Giscard d'Estaing**, caused a

stir by warning of an "invasion" of immigrants and calling for nationality laws based on blood rather than place of birth or residence. He was accused of pandering to the far right.

Armenia held a referendum on whether to secede from the Soviet Union. As expected, 95% of the electorate voted for independence.

Sunday 22nd
The umpteenth **Yugotruce** between Serbs and Croats was declared, and—like all the others before it—was promptly broken. The Croats had been having some success in fighting back, besieging federal army barracks and capturing lots of weaponry.

The Soviet and Finnish foreign ministers agreed that the 1948 friendship treaty between their two countries would be renegotiated. The treaty had been the basis of **Soviet-Finnish relations**. Its replacement would mark the definitive end of what used to be called "Finlandisation".

Tuesday 24th
The former East German **spy chief**, Markus Wolf, was arrested when he returned to Germany after a year on the run.

Wednesday 25th
For the second time in 15 months, **Romanian miners** rampaged through Bucharest. In June 1990 they had attacked the government's opponents. This time, furious about low pay and rampant

inflation, their target was the government itself. The miners took a beating, and had to retreat—but not before President Ion Iliescu had announced the resignation of the free-market government headed by Petre Roman.

Sunday 29th
At a local election in the German state of **Bremen**, the far-right Deutsche Volksunion nearly doubled its share of the vote to 6.2%. Voters were expressing fears about immigration. (The Social Democrats who had been running the local government slumped from 51% of the vote to 39%). Across Germany, a wave of **attacks on foreigners** by neo-Nazis and skinheads was beginning to alarm the nation.

Some 200,000 **French farmers** demonstrated in Paris against cuts in subsidies and cheap imports from Eastern Europe. French smallholders have been getting relatively poorer, with many of them going out of business. The demonstration drew attention to their plight, but was unlikely to stop the trend.

Theodor Stolojan was named as **Romania's prime minister**. He had been finance minister and then privatisation chief in the previous government—which suggested that he would continue the policy of market reform.

Monday 30th
A severe embarrassment for **Holland**, which as EC president had tried to put its federalist stamp on the negotiations over constitutional reform. Near-universal opposition forced it to abandon its draft treaty on political union, which was unlikely to produce an agreement at the Maastricht summit in December. Foreign ministers agreed to return to the draft prepared by Luxembourg, the previous EC president.

Tuesday 1st
Leningrad formally reverted to its original name, **St Petersburg.**

Saturday 5th
The **Belgian government collapsed** for the usual reason: squabbling between French-speakers and Dutch-speakers.

Sunday 6th
Anibal Cavaco Silva was re-elected as **Portugal's** prime minister. His right-of-centre Social Democrats won a clear majority for the second time running, offering Portugal the prospect of another four years of stable government.

Tuesday 8th
Yet another truce was signed and broken in Yugoslavia. The historic ports of **Dubrovnic and Zadar** on the Croatian coast were under siege.

The Soviet Union agreed to move most of its **troops out of Poland** by the end of 1992. Soviet troops had already withdrawn from Czechoslovakia and Hungary, but negotiations with Poland had proved difficult. The failed coup in Moscow seemed to speed up agreement.

As part of a quickening disarmament race, NATO announced that it would unilaterally scrap up to half of its **nuclear bombs.**

Thursday 10th
Germany's main parties agreed on measures aimed at speeding the processing of **asylum-seekers.** They would

be put into big camps and their applications processed within six weeks; those rejected would be booted out promptly.

Saturday 12th
Askar Akaev was elected president of **Kirgizia**, one of the smallest remaining Soviet republics. Mr Akaev was considered such a fine democrat that nobody stood against him.

At a meeting of EC foreign ministers, **Britain and Italy** put forward a joint plan for European defence. The real novelty was that two big countries other than France and Germany should get together to try to shape the Community's future. France and Germany were not amused.

Sunday 13th
The communists, now called Socialists, lost power in **Bulgaria's general election.** The winner, with 35% of the vote to the Socialists' 33%, was the Union of Democratic Forces, an argumentative right-of-centre coalition led by 36-year-old Filip Dimitrov. But to govern Mr Dimitrov would need the support of the third party in parliament: the Movement for Rights and Freedoms, representing ethnic Turks, which won 7% of the vote.

Tuesday 15th
The **Franco-German riposte** to the joint British-Italian initiative on European defence came in the form of a joint letter by President Mitterrand and Chancellor Kohl. They set out plans for a European army (based on the existing Franco-German brigade) and called for common EC foreign policy on a long list of topics.

In the ethnically mixed Yugoslav republic of **Bosnia-Hercegovina**, Croat and Muslim deputies passed a resolution underlining their republic's sovereignty. Serb deputies objected and walked

out. While falling far short of a declaration of independence, the resolution was meant to show that Bosnia would resist being absorbed into a "Greater Serbia".

Having recently regained their independence, the three **Baltic states** (Latvia, Lithuania and Estonia) became members of the Conference on Security and Co-operation in Europe, which groups all European countries and North America.

Wednesday 16th
Armenia held a direct election for its presidency. The winner, with 80% of the vote, was the de facto incumbent, Levon Ter-Petrossyan.

Friday 18th
In the Kremlin, eight of the remaining 12 Soviet republics signed an outline Treaty on Economic Community. Notable for not signing was **Ukraine,** ever keener to emphasise its independence.

As part of the Middle East peace process, the **Soviet Union and Israel** re-established diplomatic relations, broken by the Kremlin after the Six Day War in 1967.

Sunday 20th
The **election in Turkey** marked a triumphant return for Suleyman Demirel, a former prime minister whom Turkey's generals had tried to ban from politics in the early 1980s. His conservative True Path party pushed well ahead of the ruling Motherland Party, but lacked an outright majority. Mr Demirel began to negotiate a coalition with the third-placed Social Democratic Populist Party.

Fringe parties (including some with an anti-foreigner message) did well in **Switzerland's general election.** But the four-party coalition—of Free Democrats, Socialists,

Christian Democrats and Centrists—that has run the country for four decades kept their comfortable majority.

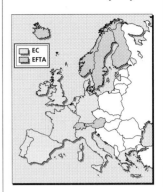

Tuesday 22nd
After 14 months of talks, the European Community and the seven-member European Free Trade Association (EFTA) agreed to create a **European Economic Area**, giving the EFTA countries access to the EC's post-1992 single market but without political rights to shape the rules. What started as an attempt to discourage the EFTA folk from applying to join the Community came to be seen by countries like Sweden and Austria as a mere stepping-stone to full EC membership.

Sunday 27th
Poland's first fully democratic general election in over half a century produced a mess: some 20 parties in parliament, none with more than 12% of the vote. The largest party was the centre-right Democratic Union, led by a former Solidarity prime minister, Tadeusz Mazowiecki. Only 42.5% of the electorate bothered to vote. The laborious task of coalition-building began.

Monday 28th
Russia's **Boris Yeltsin** seized the initiative on economic reform, without waiting for the other ex-Soviet republics. He announced plans for free prices, faster privatisation and land reform.

Sunday 3rd

Bartholomew I was enthroned as the Archbishop of Constantinople and the 270th **Ecumenical Patriarch**. He thus became the first among equals of the autocephalous church leaders of the 135m-plus adherents of Orthodox Christianity—mostly in the ex-Soviet Union and south-eastern Europe. One of his main tasks was expected to be to resist Catholic evangelism in the Orthodox heartland.

Monday 4th

Filip Dimitrov, leader of the Union of Democratic Forces, which defeated the Socialists (ex-Communists) in October's election, was appointed prime minister of **Bulgaria**. He formed a minority government that would rely on the support of the ethnic Turkish Movement for Rights and Freedoms.

Saturday 9th

The **NATO summit** in Rome approved a post-cold-war strategy for the alliance. It declared that NATO would continue to lead the defence of Europe (with the continued presence there of American troops), and it offered to treat the former Warsaw Pact countries as partners. The declaration was meant to secure NATO's future role amid the Franco-German talk of an emerging European "defence identity". NATO's new military strategy involved fewer soldiers and more reliance on mobile units.

On the anniversary of Hitler's *Kristallnacht*, a heartening demonstration against racism took place in **Norway**. Arne Myrdal, an anti-immigrant leader, had called a rally in Oslo. Some 10,000 people turned up, encouraged by the Lutheran church to protest peacefully. Almost all turned their backs on Mr Myrdal and heckled when he spoke. He had to abandon the rally.

Sunday 10th

France's **President Mitterrand** promised constitutional reforms before his term ran out in 1995. He did not spell out the details. He no doubt hoped the initiative would boost his flagging popularity.

Austria became the latest European country to see a sharp rise in the anti-immigrant vote. In Vienna's local election, Jörg Haider's Freedom Party—an odd mix of liberals and xenophobic populism—more than doubled its share of the vote to 23%.

Boris Yeltsin's Russia got a taste of the sort of separatism that was destroying Mikhail Gorbachev's Soviet Union. Mr Yeltsin declared a state of emergency in the rebellious region of **Checheno-Ingushetia** in the Caucasus. But, unable to enforce it, he had to back down the next day.

Thursday 14th

Several thousand people managed to flee the besieged Croatian port of **Dubrovnik** aboard a ferry sent to evacuate European Community peace monitors.

Sunday 17th

The horror of the war in Yugoslavia was brought home with the **fall of Vukovar**, a Croatian town on the Danube which had endured a grinding three-month siege by the Serbs and the Serb-dominated federal army. An exodus of survi-

vors of the siege began, amid allegations by both Serbs and Croats of atrocities.

Tuesday 19th

Turkey got a new government. Suleyman Demirel, whose True Path party came first in October's election, signed a coalition deal with Erdal Inonu of the third-placed Social Democratic Populist Party.

The Soviet Union got back its old foreign minister. Desperate to bolster his credibility, President Gorbachev announced the reappointment of **Edward Shevardnadze**, his friend and partner in foreign-policy perestroika, who had resigned 11 months earlier and given warning of an impending dictatorship.

Sunday 24th

The political mess in **Belgium** got messier. In its general election, extremists and cranks did well and most of the government parties got punished for the byzantine squabbling between its French- and Dutch-speakers which had forced an early vote. Wilfried Martens's four-party coalition lost 14 of its 134 seats in the 212-member parliament. The far-right Vlaams Blok won 10% of the vote in Flanders.

In a local election in the Italian town of Brescia, a regionalist party, the **Lombard League**, won a quarter of the vote, overtaking the Christian Democrats as the biggest party. The League, which attacks wasteful government in

Rome, had been worrying Italy's mainstream parties ever since its sudden surge in local elections in 1990.

Despite the failure of the August coup in Moscow, **Soviet hardliners** continued to make their mark. A former Communist, Rakhmon Nabiev, comfortably won a presidential election in the republic of Tajikistan. Two days later the ex-Communist leadership in Azerbaijan abolished the autonomous status of the Armenian-populated enclave of Nagorno-Karabakh, thus sharply increasing tensions with Armenia.

Monday 25th

The Democratic Party of the Left (ex-Communists) called for the impeachment of Italy's increasingly eccentric **President Cossiga**. They accused him of exceeding his constitutional powers in a row with the judiciary.

Mikhail Gorbachev's hopes of putting together a new union treaty suffered another blow when he chaired a meeting of the leaders of seven republics. They refused to initial his draft treaty, agreeing only to refer it to their parliaments.

Wednesday 27th

In response to the collapse of the Warsaw Pact and the changes in NATO strategy, **Italy** announced plans to cut its armed forces by a quarter, or some 90,000 men.

Thursday 28th

Hectic diplomacy continued in the run up to the European Community's summit at **Maastricht** in December. Spain threatened to veto political reforms if it did not get a promise of more EC money for poorer members, Chancellor Kohl said the reforms must be "irreversible", and John Major got a warning from Tory backbenchers not to give away too much.

December

Sunday 1st
Europe acquired a new state the size of France, and the Soviet Union lost a vital republic. In a referendum, **Ukrainians voted** nine-to-one in favour of independence. They also elected Leonid Kravchuk, a Communist ideologue turned nationalist champion, as president. Canada led the movement by foreign governments to recognise Ukraine as an independent state. President Mikhail Gorbachev warned of "catastrophe".

Tuesday 3rd
Pre-Maastricht ministerial meetings sorted out most of the European Community's treaty on monetary union, but big decisions on the treaty on political union were put off to the summit itself. In many cases, it was British reluctance that prevented agreement. Among the most contentious issues: the extent of EC powers in social policy, the EC's role in foreign and security policy, immigration, and the powers of the European Parliament.

The European Community crept further towards recognition of **Yugoslavia's** breakaway republics by restoring trade and aid links, where possible, to Croatia, Slovenia, Macedonia and Bosnia & Hercegovina. In effect, this meant EC sanctions were targeted on Serbia and its ally Montenegro. The next day, Germany cut transport links with Serbia and Montenegro.

Wednesday 4th
The Democrats pulled out of **Albania's** ex-communist-led coalition, complaining that the former communists were exploiting their presence in the government to shift the blame for the country's economic crisis. Bread riots were spreading, and crime was rampant.

Thursday 5th
After more than a month of post-election haggling in **Poland**, President Lech Walesa nominated Jan Olszewski as prime minister. Mr Olszewski, a defence lawyer for dissidents in communist days, was to take over once he had put together a centre-right coalition government. It took him a further 18 days—and plenty more arguments with Mr Walesa—to do so.

Sunday 8th
Leaders of Russia, Belorussia and Ukraine met in Minsk and declared the **death of the Soviet Union**. Instead, they said, they were setting up a "Commonwealth of Independent States", with headquarters in Minsk. Mikhail Gorbachev, fighting for his political life, denounced the decision as unconstitutional.

In a **referendum in Romania** voters approved a new constitution. Opposition leaders complained that the referendum fixed Romania as a republic without giving Romanians the chance to vote specifically on whether they would like to restore the monarchy.

Tuesday 10th
At the end of their two-day summit, EC leaders agreed on the **treaty of Maastricht**, setting the so-called European Union on course for a single currency and far closer political co-operation. Britain kept open the option of not joining the economic and monetary union (EMU), but other EC members that met the economic "convergence criteria" would move to EMU by 1999 at the latest. Britain also rejected any increased EC role in social policy, so the other 11 decided to press ahead with that on their own.

The Maastricht deal gave more power to the **European Parliament**, which will have the right to veto laws in several areas. **More policy areas**—including consumer protection, health and education—came under the EC's competence. Rules to encourage a tighter EC **foreign policy** were agreed upon, and closer links with the Western European Union would make it, in effect, the European Union's **defence** wing. Poorer members won a promise of **more money** from the EC budget.

Thursday 12th
Ukraine declared it was taking control of all non-nuclear forces on its territory. The Soviet state's collapse spread to **Aeroflot**, the state airline. Many airports had to close because of lack of fuel.

Sunday 15th
The European Court of Justice threw into confusion the painfully negotiated EC-EFTA pact to create a 19-nation **European Economic Area** (EEA). It said the plan to set up a joint court to settle disputes in the EEA would undermine the Community's founding Rome treaty. The negotiators would have to try again.

Tuesday 17th
The European Community barely managed to avoid an open split over **Yugoslavia**. Pressed hard by Germany to recognise Slovenia and Croatia, the other members agreed to recognise all would-be independent Yugoslav republics by January 15th, provided they passed certain tests of good behaviour. But Germany threatened to go ahead with recognition anyway, leaving merely the "implementation" to January 15th.

Thursday 19th
The formal end of the Soviet Union drew closer. **Boris Yeltsin** decreed that Russia was taking over the Kremlin and most ex-Soviet ministries. Mikhail Gorbachev was left nominally in charge of only the defence and nuclear-power ministries.

Sunday 22nd
In Alma Ata, Kazakhstan's capital, 11 of the 12 Soviet republics agreed on the creation of a **Commonwealth of Independent States** to replace the Soviet Union. Independent-minded **Georgia** was the only republic not to sign up. It was preoccupied with its own power struggle: heavy fighting was taking place in Tbilisi, the capital, in the attempt to oust President Gamsakhurdia.

Wednesday 25th
Mikhail Gorbachev announced his resignation as Soviet president. The next day the Soviet Union's parliament formally voted the country out of existence.

Monday 30th
At a meeting in Minsk, leaders of the new ex-Soviet Commonwealth confirmed that the **strategic nuclear arsenal** would continue to be under a unified command. But they failed to agree to keep a single conventional army. Ukraine, Azerbaijan and Moldavia planned to set up their own forces.

As we reported then

Supertsar without superpolicy

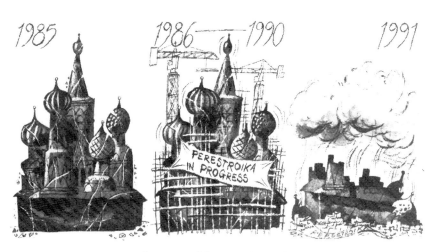

JANUARY 5TH, MOSCOW **At the start of the year it was becoming ever clearer that Mikhail Gorbachev was more interested in modernising his own, and the Communist Party's, grip on power than in radically changing the Soviet system**

IF GORBACHEV the Great is looking more and more like Mixed-up Mikhail, it is not just because he has an impossible job. He has made several big mistakes. One was his failure to hold a direct election for the presidency last year. Mr Gorbachev might well have won such a vote, and added to his formal powers the authority he now lacks. Then there was his failure to embrace the Shatalin plan for market reforms, which, for all its faults, would have meant a clear break with the centrally planned past. And he was far too late in proposing a new deal to the various republics. His current offer would have seemed attractive to them a couple of years back, but not now.

With luck, Mr Gorbachev may also have left it too late to make a fourth big mistake: returning his country to dictatorship. Optimists reckon that reform has already gone too far to allow that. But the pessimists include Edward Shevardnadze, whose sudden resignation as foreign minister set the tone at the meeting from December 17th to 27th of the Congress of People's Deputies, the Soviet super-parliament.

Mr Shevardnadze, worn out by the struggle for reform, used his resignation speech to the Congress to give warning that a new dictatorship was in preparation. A hardline tirade by General Vladimir Kryuchkov, the head of the KGB, strengthened the impression that conservative forces were on the rise. So did Mr Gorbachev's nomination of Gennady Yanaev, a Communist apparatchik, for the new post of vice-president (a fine choice, said that figurehead of Soviet conservatism, Yegor Ligachev). The Congress approved most of the new powers Mr Gorbachev had requested, including direct control over the government and over a new security council. These are powers which, if abused, could quickly turn him into a dictator.

What has brought about the change in Mr Gorbachev? Perhaps, in a sense, there has been no change. Nearly six years since Mr Gorbachev came to power, it is still unclear what sort of future he has in mind for the Soviet Union. Suppose for a moment that Mr Gorbachev himself does not know what he has in mind; assume that he is just a moderniser with no clear idea where modernising leads. The one certainty is that he has consistently sought to secure his own position, mostly by presenting himself as a sensible centrist between the extremes to his right and left.

He has continued to cling to the middle ground, but that ground has been shifting. So long as radicals were on the rampage, staying in the centre meant leaning ever farther towards liberal reform. Now that a reaction is setting in, Mr Gorbachev is leaning back towards the conservatives to keep his balance.

And he is still on his feet. At last month's meeting of the Congress he showed again how he can play on the mutual fears of reformers and conservatives to get his own way. He won few friends, but he won the votes that mattered to him. The Congress approved in principal his draft union treaty (though the vote was taken in the absence of deputies from some of the most independent-minded republics, who boycotted the Congress). It accepted Mr Yanaev as vice-president (but only after an embarrassing failure in the first vote and some heavyweight intervention by Mr Gorbachev). And it granted Mr Gorbachev most of the new powers he had requested (though it rejected his clumsy proposal for local inspectors to help enforce presidential decrees).

Now that he has these powers, what will he do with them? People are unlikely to pay much more attention to his decisions just because there has been some fiddling with the constitution. And enforcing his policies is only part of the problem. The other part is having coherent policies in the first place. Mr Gorbachev still lacks them in the two areas that matter most.

One is the economy. Mr Gorbachev has again postponed a decision on what sort of economic system he is aiming for by referring the question of private land ownership to a referendum; when this will take place and exactly what it will ask are not yet decided. Meanwhile, he enters 1991 without an economic plan or budget (so everyone is having to improvise with last year's targets), and without a prime minister to blame for mismanagement (Nikolai Ryzhkov, who for months had been under pressure to resign and was about to be sidelined anyway, had a heart attack on December 25th). Most ominously, Mr Gorbachev faces a drastic loss of revenue to the central budget from the rebellious republics.

The three Baltic states are refusing to pay anything. But the biggest loss will come if the giant Russian republic carries out its decision, taken last week, to cut its contribution to the central budget by more than four-fifths. Unless Mr Gorbachev can persuade—or force—Russia and others to back down, he will either have to print roubles even more furiously than before (result: hyperinflation), or else he will be unable to pay for the huge central bureaucracy and, more seriously, for the army. Of all the challenges thrown at Mr Gorbachev by Boris Yeltsin, the president of the Russian republic, this is easily the greatest.

Thus the muddle over the economy is inseparable from Mr Gorbachev's other main policy muddle: the relationship between the centre and the 15 Soviet republics. "Preserving the union" has become his first priority: a "sacred cause", he called it in his new year's message. His strategy for achieving this by persuasion is not convincing.

The Federation Council, upgraded as part of his constitutional changes approved by the Congress, is meant to give the republics a share of central power and responsibility. But it promises to be an unwieldy body, including the heads of 20 "autonomous republics" as well as those presidents of the 15 fully fledged republics who agree to turn up to its meetings. Mr Gorbachev's pro-

posed Union Treaty is, like the matter of land ownership, to go to a referendum. But that will not settle the trickiest question: whether those republics which are determined not to be part of the Soviet Union will be allowed their independence, or whether they will be kept in by force.

Fears of a crackdown have been strongest in the Baltic republics and Moldavia. The Moldavians, given an ultimatum by Mr Gorbachev to settle their ethnic conflicts by the year's end, decided to compromise rather than test the president's readiness to resort to force. Several bombs have gone off

in Latvia; the locals think these were planted to give the army a possible excuse to move in. On December 29th, in response to "provocations and threats made by the Soviet military leadership", the foreign ministers of Estonia, Latvia and Lithuania issued a statement calling on the Soviet Union to renounce the use of "further military force" against the Baltic countries.

For now, Mr Gorbachev is just managing to continue what he does best: keeping his show on the road. The trouble is that nobody knows where the road leads. And the show threatens at any moment to turn ugly.

Look on the bright side

JANUARY 26TH, WARSAW *Bad news about Eastern Europe was drowning out the good news. Wrongly. We aimed to redress the balance, starting in Poland*

GLOOM and doom are all the rage in Eastern Europe. Poland, one year after starting a strict anti-inflation programme, is said to be a particularly terrible place. Statistics are cited to prove the depth of popular misery: falling real wages, rising unemployment, a catastrophic drop in production, a general collapse of living standards. But look more closely at the statistics, look at what is really happening on the streets and in the shops, look at how people's lives are changing, and it becomes clear that things are not nearly as bad as they are painted.

True, the Polish reform has had its faults. Privatisation has been too slow. The dominant state industry still awaits a proper shake-out. Inflation remains 5% a month, a big improvement on a year ago but still worrying. Yet all these faults suggest that the reform, far from being too bold, has not been bold enough. The government reckoned that Poles were having to cope with about as much economic pain as they would tolerate. Life has certainly been tough in Poland over the past year. But has it really been tougher than before?

Official figures greatly exaggerate the drop in industrial production (which is said to have fallen by almost a third last year). One reason is that previous years' figures were bloated by communist managers with an interest in padding their production numbers to get bonuses or promotion. Performance was measured against the plan, not the market. Now, in contrast, managers are tempted to under-report their performance, to avoid taxes.

If some factories are now producing fewer feet-breaking shoes and unusable machines than they were a year ago, so much the better. And if others are producing smaller amounts of goods that people actu-

ally want to buy, fine. One steel factory in Silesia found that it could no longer afford to make the heavily subsidised, high-quality steel it used to produce before the new budgetary regime, so it began to make smaller quantities of low-quality steel, which it found could be exported to Germany at a profit. Factories reducing production in or-

The enterprise culture

der to change their technology or improve quality—even factories going bankrupt—are excellent signs of industrial restructuring. Many economists say bankruptcy figures in Poland are still too low.

But what really distorts the official statistics is that they are based almost entirely on the state economy. They fail to account for the boom in private enterprise. Any visitor to Poland immediately sees what the figures fail to reflect. Every Polish town now has its

street market, where everything from imported toothpaste to once-unavailable Polish ham can be bought. Queues have virtually disappeared.

Some estimates of the size of the private sector do exist. The Polish government's statistical office believes that the output of private industry (excluding farming) grew by 50% over the past year, and that it now accounts for 18% of national income, up from 11% in 1989. The number of people employed in private enterprise, the government's statisticians guess, grew by more than 500,000 in 1989, bringing the total to between 1.8m and 2m people.

Keeping it private

But much of Poland's private industry goes unrecorded. Private traders, plumbers, carpenters and truckers under-report their income, fearing Poland's high taxes. Average income in the private sector is probably about three times that in the state sector, but no one knows for sure.

What about the "30% drop in the standard of living" so often referred to? This number comes from comparing the figures of 1990 with those of 1989—a year of hyperinflation, when wages grew astronomically. A comparison of 1990 with 1987 yields a drop in real wages of only 2-3%. Even this fails to account for some unmeasurable changes. Polish housewives no longer have to spend two hours a day in queues, and they can choose between 15 brands of mineral water, when once only one diesel-flavoured Polish brand was on offer.

Another seldom-mentioned change in the Polish standard of living is the increase in dollar purchasing-power brought about by the newly stable zloty. At the black-market rate for the dollar, the average Polish monthly wage in October 1987 was $40. In October 1990 it was $131. This means that, though many foreign goods are still way out of reach for most Poles, others are suddenly at fingertip-end. Psychologists speculate that much of the current dissatisfaction with the economy is caused by the presence of previously unattainable consumer products like video recorders, which are now available but still too expensive for most Poles.

The most misleading figures are those on unemployment. Commentators, both in Poland and abroad, are fond of repeating that unemployment went "from zero to 1.2m" in the past year: up to about 7% of the labour force. But "zero" refers to the communist era, when unemployment officially did not exist. When the government first began to register the jobless and offer unemployment money, thousands of people, including housewives, who had never held jobs signed up. Traders and other private entrepreneurs also signed up in order to supplement their unregistered incomes.

The ministry of labour suspects that about half of the unemployed have indeed been laid off, but other evidence suggests that at least in some parts of the country the proportion is much lower. In most big cities advertisements for workers, from plumbers to car mechanics, go unanswered for weeks.

If the news is really not so bad, why hasn't the government said so? Partly because for the past year the finance minister, Leszek Balcerowicz, and the former prime minister, Tadeusz Mazowiecki, stuck to a policy of preparing the nation for the worst. The current government wants to change this approach, which helped Mr Mazowiecki lose last month's presidential election. Yet it still finds that the official statistics-gathering system is designed to measure the state economy, but not the rapidly growing private one. It is also true that public complaining, impossible under the old regime, has grown enormously with the advent of a free press. Things may well have been a lot worse five years ago. But back then there was no open way to blame the government, and no way at all to vote it out.

Welcome to the seething south

MARCH 2ND *Once, a bit of bother in the Balkans could lead all the way to world war. Times have changed, but old trouble was bubbling up all across south-eastern Europe. We sounded the alarm*

THE trouble starts with the disintegration of empires. Last time it was the Ottoman and Habsburg empires, now it is the Soviet one. Then as now, tensions soon rise over disputed borders, national minorities, drives for independence. Happily, though, Europe is not about to return to 1914 and war among the great powers. The Balkans are no longer the powder keg of Europe. Which means that the region's troubles are as much an opportunity as a worry: a chance at last to sort out some of the inherited mess.

The big difference this time is that the region is no longer linked by a network of alliances to the struggles of outside powers. Before the Soviet retreat from Eastern Europe, it was possible to imagine an east-west fight over who controlled, say, a collapsing Yugoslavia. Not any more. Nor are there today strategic resources in south-eastern Europe that might tempt foreigners to intervene. The days when Romanian oil or Yugoslav grain could matter militarily (as they did for Hitler) have long passed.

So local arguments should on the whole remain local. That does not mean that outsiders can just ignore them. Consider some of the tensions that are now resurfacing.

Greece is again worried about Turkey. Yugoslavia is indeed breaking apart. With luck, it could be an amicable divorce; at worst, there could be another violent bust-up between Serbs and Croats. Kosovo, a Serbian province 90% populated by Albanian-speakers, is on the brink of rebellion. One thing that could help push it over the brink is more upheaval next door in Albania proper, which after 45 years of Stalinism is about to have a multi-party election—if it does not first have either a neo-Stalinist crackdown or a Romanian-style revolution.

Romania itself is, with Bulgaria, relegated in western eyes to a second-class club of ex-communist countries, behind the first-class trio of Czechoslovakia, Hungary and Poland. Reform communists still have a share of power, the economies of both countries are in a desperate state, and both have trouble with ethnic minorities (Hungarians in Romania, Turks in Bulgaria). Hence the prevailing western view—maddening for the Romanians and Bulgarians—that they are likelier than the Central European trio to revert to some sort of dictatorship.

Across the Romanian border lies one of the restive Soviet republics, Moldavia, whose mainly Romanian-speaking population are almost as independence-minded as the Balts. Earlier this month Moldavia's president, Mircea Snegur, visited Bucharest and said he favoured confederation with Romania. A week later, faced with a Communist backlash, he offered his resignation. Farther east, in Georgia, most of the locals are even more determined to "return to Europe", which to them means leaving the Soviet Union. It will not happen smoothly. Already clashes with the pro-Soviet Ossetian minority have left more people dead than January's crackdown in Lithuania.

None of these difficulties is merely a private, parochial affair. All are liable to affect the outside world, for a variety of reasons.

Some spillover into neighbouring countries is inevitable, not least in the form of refugees. Italy and Austria are particularly worried about instability on their doorstep. Already, Austria's army is policing its frontier with Hungary to keep out unwanted Romanian migrants. Greece is doing its best to keep out—or send back—refugees from Albania, unless they are fortunate enough to be ethnic Greeks.

As the European Community prepares to remove its internal frontiers after 1992, trouble in the Balkans will add to pressure to tighten the EC's external border controls. Failing agreement on that, the Community's frontier-free plans are likely to face delays. Yet at the same time the southerners will be pressing the Community to include them as closely as possible in the process of European economic integration.

Western governments may well have to decide how to respond to the creation of new countries. At what point, for example, should an independent Slovenia get official recognition? And how much help should it be offered to make itself viable as a separate state? An attempted Georgian or Moldavian breakaway would raise the problem, as Lithuania has, of how far to support local wishes at the expense of relations with the Soviet Union.

Countries that feel nervous about their neighbours will seek outside help. Now that the Warsaw Pact is as good as gone, Romania and Bulgaria are beginning to search for security links with the West, arguing that they are on Christendom's front line with Islam. To avoid trouble in the family, NATO allies will have to keep a watchful eye on relations between Greece and Turkey.

The West will also be asked for money, lots of it. South-eastern Europe is poor. GDP per head is on average only about a quarter of that in the European Community.

The region's problems should not be exaggerated. Romania and Bulgaria, for example, are reforming faster than is commonly believed in the West. All the more reason to beware of neglecting them and hampering their efforts by failing to give enough support. Most Yugoslavs see the sense of negotiating rather than fighting their way out of their current conflicts. The need for western economic help, and the desire to be accepted in western democratic clubs, can be used as bargaining levers to discourage repression of minorities and to promote tolerant politics. Properly handled, there is plenty of hope in the Balkan upheaval.

The gap left by Rohwedder

APRIL 6TH, BONN *The assassination of the boss of the Treuhandanstalt, the agency in charge of privatising former East German firms, brought home the trauma involved in German unity*

GERMANY'S Red Army Faction, once the so-called Baader-Meinhof gang, is now into its third decade of violence, with a new generation of terrorists if anything more cold-bloodedly sophisticated than the last. By shooting Detlev Rohwedder in his Düsseldorf villa on April 1st, the group stuck chillingly true to its policy of selecting the best for slaughter.

Like Alfred Herrhausen, the boss of the Deutsche Bank blown to bits in his car in late 1989, Mr Rohwedder stood out even among the country's business elite. He successfully made the change from politics (the federal economics ministry) to industry (the Hoesch steel group), which Germans rarely manage. He had the managerial toughness to haul Hoesch back to profit in the 1980s combined with a social conscience which made him a card-carrying Social Democrat. And he had an ironic wit that charmed foreigners but baffled a lot of his countrymen.

All that made him the ideal man for Germany's least popular job: boss of the Treuhand agency, responsible for privatising or liquidating some 8,000 mostly doddery firms in what was East Germany. The Treuhand was originally set up in early 1990 by East Germany's last communist-led government, not to privatise but to preserve "people's property" and jobs for party hacks. When Mr Rohwedder took over last summer he reversed the strategy, decentralised the outfit to 15 regional offices, sacked senior managers tainted by the old regime and built up more than 2,000 staff.

Easterners used to job security howled over his decisions to close loss-making firms (including even the Interflug airline) for which no serious buyers seemed in the offing. Capitalists on the prowl for property at rock-bottom prices smarted under Mr Rohwedder's public condemnation of their "Wild West approach". Politicians complained that the Treuhand was either too slow or too heartless. Probably, Mr Rohwedder reflected, it was part of the Treuhand's role to act as scapegoat in the early trauma of economic union.

He would not have stuck to his post, braving so many attacks, without a hefty dash of patriotism too. Born in Thuringia in eastern Germany in 1932, he often showed in private conversation a passion he rarely revealed in public for the cause of a united Germany. When Helmut Kohl offered him the Treuhand post, Mr Rohwedder accepted, well knowing what he was letting himself in for.

Much the same goes for Herrhausen, signed up by Mr Kohl to help co-ordinate the west German economic drive in the east shortly before he was murdered. Did the commitment to unity by both these men make them a special target of the terrorists? Not necessarily, though in the past few weeks more has become known of the links between the Red

A patriot becomes a scapegoat

Army Faction and the Stasi, the former East German secret police, many of whose top agents remain at large. German state prosecutors say the Stasi not only gave succour to the group's terrorists fleeing from West to East Germany over the past decade, which was known, but trained them in long-range shooting and in the use of explosives. It is not yet clear what return commitment the Stasi got, for instance in selecting victims, for the help they gave.

The latest murder will not of itself alter the Treuhand's work. It may cause the agency's most outspoken critics ("Rohwedder-hangman", read a placard in one recent demonstration by jobless in the east) to pipe down. A good replacement may even be at hand in Mr Rohwedder's deputy, Birgit Breuel, a strong-willed former finance minister of Lower Saxony. It will take courage to take on so tough a job.

Edith the First

MAY 19TH, PARIS *French presidents like to change their prime ministers from time to time. President Mitterrand's choice of Edith Cresson had novelty value—and proved disastrous*

THE appointment of Edith Cresson, France's first woman prime minister, will mark a change in style. Where Michel Rocard was prudent and low-key to the point of being a trifle grey, Mrs Cresson, on past form, is likely to be blunt and colourful.

Although more a social democrat in the Mitterrand mould than a doctrinaire socialist (she is not automatically opposed to privatisation, for example), she is a woman of strong views, especially when it comes to the protection of France's national interests. As minister for trade and industry (1983-86) and again as minister for European affairs (1988-90), she was outspoken in her protectionist distrust of the Japanese.

"Japan is an adversary who does not respect the rules of the game and whose overwhelming desire is to conquer the world," she thundered in a newspaper interview carefully timed to coincide with the official visit of the Japanese prime minister to Paris in January last year. "Those who can't see that must be blind. Japanese investments are not like others. They destroy jobs." She returned to the attack in another interview six months later, this one timed to coincide with a supposedly conciliatory return visit by Mr Rocard to Tokyo: "We hear all too often that we must open up our markets, which really means first to the Japanese. In the name of what must we abandon France?" Mrs Cresson has never been known for her tact.

Although she had a lot of support from like-minded industrialists, such as Jacques Calvet, the head of Peugeot, she often clashed with Roger Fauroux, the industry minister in Mr Rocard's government, who favoured the opposite approach. "Japan de-

Japan's basher

serves respect," he cried in response to one of Mrs Cresson's more colourful outbursts. "If we don't sell cars to the Japanese, it could be because theirs are better." Mr Fauroux was not expecting a place in her government. Her difficulty in working with those she disagrees with is a weakness.

She felt on a limb at the ministry for Europe and quit the government in October 1990 with characteristic brio: "I was fed up talking in a vacuum," she said. "The political power of France is in danger of being weakened because of insufficient industrial mobilisation. There's a world economic war going on, and France is not leading it." Since last October she has been working for Schneider, a big French industrial group.

Born on January 27th 1934, into a well-to-do but left-wing family (her father was a senior civil servant), she became an active Socialist in 1966 after meeting François Mitterrand. Appreciated by him for her drive and intelligence, as well as for her obvious feminine charms, she has stayed in his inner circle of friends and political colleagues.

After working as the Socialist Party's national secretary for youth, she won a seat in the European Parliament in 1979 and then became minister of agriculture in the first Socialist government two years later. She got along poorly with male-chauvinist French farmers. As a reward for winning the only big town (Châtellerault) from the right in the 1983 municipal elections, she became minister of trade and tourism, adding industry in 1984. Mrs Cresson relishes tough jobs.

Married with two children, she has a degree in business studies, a doctorate in demography, and speaks good English. Like Margaret Thatcher, to whom Mrs Cresson is sometimes compared, she is no feminist. But she has never doubted that women were as able as men. To her "men are irreplaceable in only one area—one's private life."

The road to war

JULY 6TH *War in Europe was meant to be a thing of the past. Alas, Yugoslavia proved otherwise. A mini-battle in Slovenia spread to a deadly fight for Croatia*

TOO often, wars happen as a result of miscalculations made in a fog of misunderstanding. Protagonist and antagonist make mistaken decisions on the basis of misread signals. By the time they realise their mistakes, it is too late, and getting out of the resulting mess becomes even more complicated than the trouble that led to it in the first place. All of that applies to the nasty little war, the first of its kind in Europe since 1945, which Yugoslavia drifted into on June 27th, and which has already claimed dozens of dead and scores of wounded.

For months Slovenia and Croatia, the two westernmost republics, had been clamouring for an agreement to transform Yugoslavia into a loose grouping of sovereign states. Otherwise, they said, they would be obliged to secede by the end of June, a policy supported by referendums in both republics. They got a predictably dismissive answer from Serbia, the largest republic, and from the Serb-dominated Yugoslav army.

Western governments also tried to discourage them. For the West, the Croats and the Slovenes were repeatedly told, Yugoslavia's unity was the highest priority. President Bush said in March that the United States "would not reward" those who seceded unilaterally. His secretary of state, James Baker, said during a short visit to Belgrade last month that the United States would not recognise the two republics' independence "under any circumstances". The main effect of these warnings was not to deter Slovenia and Croatia, but to encourage some of Yugoslavia's generals in the belief that the West would not object—and might even reward them—if they moved to keep Yugoslavia in one piece.

The Croats and Slovenes duly declared their independence, wrong-footing their opponents by doing it a day early, on June 25th. As expected, the federal government in Belgrade pronounced the move illegal, but made no attempt to negotiate. Clearly following a prearranged plan, the army went into action against Slovenia on June 27th, claiming the federal government's authority. (The army's commander-in-chief, Yugoslavia's collective eight-member presidency, had been inoperative since May 15th, when Serbia blocked the election as its chairman for one year of a Croat, Stipe Mesic.)

But the army's Blitzkrieg against Slovenia did not go according to plan. Slovenia's resistance proved fiercer than expected. The Slovene territorial forces were defending their own land, with the full support of the population. Slovenia's territorials also benefited from having fended off attempts by the Yugoslav army to disband them in 1990, when the Communists stepped down from power in the republic. They kept about 40% of their equipment. (In Croatia, in contrast, the disarming of the territorials was almost totally successful.) The West, far from welcoming the army's attempt to crush Slovenia, suddenly changed its tune. It condemned the army's intervention, mounted several mediating missions, and even started talking about immediate recognition of Croatia and Slovenia.

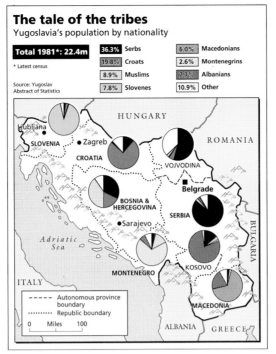

The tale of the tribes
Yugoslavia's population by nationality

Total 1981*: 22.4m		
* Latest census	36.3% Serbs	6.0% Macedonians
	19.8% Croats	2.6% Montenegrins
Source: Yugoslav Abstract of Statistics	8.9% Muslims	7.7% Albanians
	7.8% Slovenes	10.9% Other

HUNGARY
Ljubljana
SLOVENIA · Zagreb
ROMANIA
CROATIA
VOJVODINA
Belgrade
BOSNIA & HERCEGOVINA
SERBIA
· Sarajevo
Adriatic Sea
BULGARIA
MONTENEGRO
KOSOVO
ITALY
MACEDONIA
ALBANIA   GREECE

----- Autonomous province boundary
.... Republic boundary
0   Miles   100

All this unnerved the army's top brass, causing it to pause. The army's morale began to crack, notably among young conscripts. In Belgrade, a group of mothers fought their way into the Serbian parliament and demanded the return of their sons from Slovenia and Croatia. The Slovenes even managed to capture some tanks, proudly displaying them, and their captured crews, on television. Instead of cowing the Slovenes into quick submission—and freeing themselves for the harder task of subduing bigger Croatia, Yugoslav army units found themselves cut off and surrounded in humiliating circumstances in various parts of the Slovene countryside.

The army was particularly upset by a Slovene demand that as part of any ceasefire its units should go back to barracks leaving all their equipment behind. This demand led to the failure of two successive ceasefires mediated by EC foreign ministers sent to Belgrade and Zagreb. The terms of both

ceasefires were: first, the return of all soldiers to barracks; second, suspension for three months of the implementation of the Slovenian and Croatian independence declarations; and, third, the unblocking of Mr Mesic's election as head of the collective presidency.

On July 2nd on Belgrade television, General Blagoje Adzic, chief of staff, a Serb and a leading hawk, angrily repudiated a third ceasefire, arranged on the same day by the collective presidency under Mr Mesic, who had by then been installed under EC pressure. General Adzic said the army accepted the challenge of total war that had been imposed on it, and would end it soon with a complete victory. Next day a large armoured column left Belgrade for Croatia. By the afternoon it had reached the Croatian border, but stopped there. In Slovenia a return to barracks proceeded. The fighting died down, and by July 4th a nervous calm prevailed.

The army is in a dilemma. If it allows the civilian leadership, under EC pressure, to push it back to barracks, it risks shrinking drastically or even disintegrating as part of any deal over the dissolution of Yugoslavia. If, however, it acts to take power, it risks getting embroiled in conflicts that could lead to further humiliations, desertions and eventual break-up. Growing anti-war feelings in Serbia could even be forcing the army to abandon the war in Slovenia and concentrate instead on trying to secure, in alliance with Serbia's populist president, Slobodan Milosevic, a Greater Serbia, including large chunks of Croatia and Bosnia & Hercegovina.

There is still a danger that the core of some 70 hardline officers who make up the army's political leadership, led by General Stevan Mirkovic, a former chief of staff and also a Serb, may decide in favour of "decisive action": in other words, an outright coup. But nothing could now come as a surprise in Yugoslavia—not even a sudden outbreak of reasonableness.

The missing children

AUGUST 3RD *Southern Europeans are having fewer babies? Some northern Europeans are having more babies? Why? And what does it all mean for the future?*

IF PEOPLE mean power, Europe's is dwindling. In 1900 about a third of the world's population lived in Europe. Now, about a tenth does. And with Europeans having fewer babies than ever, their share of the world will shrink further.

In 1979 only 3% of the French thought

the ideal family should have one child. By 1989 that had risen to 19%. More and more parents have matched ideal to reality: the average number of babies that a French-woman bears during her lifetime has dropped from 1.95 in 1980 (and 2.48 only ten years before that) to 1.81 in 1989. Across

Europe the two-child family has become the norm. As a report by Britain's Family Policy Studies Centre points out, the fertility rate in the European Community has dropped in the past 30 years from an average of 2.6 children per woman to 1.6.

Europe's lowest birth rates are now in its deep south: 1.5 children per mother in Greece and Portugal, 1.3 in Spain and Italy. These extraordinary figures reflect a shift in timing, as young women postpone starting a family. But they also reflect a new taste for small families. Asked their ideal family size, 13% of Greeks, 21% of Portuguese and 22% of Spaniards plump for an only child. The proportion of Spaniards who like the idea of three or more children is, at 21%, smaller even than in Germany.

Why this distaste for procreation? Asked directly, in a survey by the European Commission, EC citizens think that uncertain economic prospects are the main explanation, followed by the lack of suitable housing, the growth of job opportunities for women and the shortage of good child care. Jobs for women may be a particularly powerful influence. The British Social Attitudes survey finds Italians more enthusiastic about working mothers than more northerly countries. To the statement, "A woman and her family will all be happier if she goes out to work," 48% of Italians assent—compared with 25% of the Dutch, 21% of the Irish and only 18% of Britons.

The rise in women's earnings, relative to those of men, may have made them more reluctant to cut their working hours to raise a family. Children impose costs in cash, and time. Employed women spend less time on household chores than their housewife sisters; but when work in the home is added to work outside, employed mothers put in the longest hours of all women.

The consequences of the vanishing babies will increasingly be felt in the labour market. Some time in the first quarter of the next century the number of people of working age will start to decline. At the same time the number of old people will be increasing.

A report by France's Institute for the Study of Statistics and Economics, INSEE, spells out the effect on France. On current trends, by 2025 the number of people of working age in France will have returned to its 1985 level. The proportion of elderly people in the population is likely to increase by more than a 1985 projection had expected. Almost half the rise in female life expectancy between 1985 and 1990 was accounted for by women aged 75 and over. The life expectancy of elderly men also rose faster than

So long, farewell, auf Wiedersehen, adieu

at any time over the previous 15 years.

The shortage of young workers may eventually drive up their pay. In Britain, where the number of 16-year-old school-leavers will hit its lowest point for over 30 years in 1993, teenage pay has perversely tended to decline, not rise, relative to adult wages. One reason may be that more youngsters are staying on at school; the dim ones still leave early, but earn less than their brighter friends would have done.

A more serious consequence will be the growing burden of paying for the care of the old. Fewer workers will have to pay the pensions and health-care costs of more elderly people. Moreover, the high divorce rate means that the old may be less likely to look after each other. In Britain one woman in 39 aged 65 and over, and one man in 44, are divorced. By 2025 these numbers are expected to rise to one in eight and one in 12.

What is to be done? "Horizon 2000", the INSEE report, sets out several possibilities for France. One—controversial, given

the large numbers of French people who think their country is already super-saturated with foreigners—is to allow more immigration. At present fertility rates, the workforce would need an annual influx of 142,000 immigrants between 2000 and 2009, 148,000 the following decade and 180,000 between 2020 and 2029 to prevent a fall in the working-age population.

INSEE's other options are to raise the age of retirement, to attract more women into the workforce and to raise productivity. Of these, the most politically difficult but economically attractive is the first. Keeping the old at work helps in two ways: it increases the number of taxpayers and diminishes the number of people living on financial support. Raising the retirement age by three years would be enough to keep the working-age population at its 2010 level right through to 2040, though the median age of the labour force would go up.

Some European politicians think that government policy can raise the birth rate. Malcolm Wicks of the Family Policy Studies Centre characterises this as "elderly male politicians trying to encourage young women to have more children than they want." In Western Europe, France has been trying hardest for longest to bribe the birth rate, with no family allowance for a first child but rising payments for the second and third. The upshot, notes Kathleen Kiernan, a British demographer, is that France's fertility rate of 1.8 children per woman precisely matches that of Britain, where benefits for a three-child family are almost half the French level, and where child tax allowances do not exist.

In fact, the decline in child-bearing may now be ending. In several European countries—Germany, Norway, Denmark, Bel-

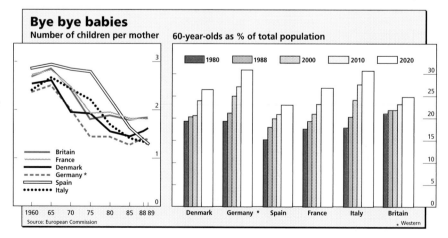

Bye bye babies
Number of children per mother

- Britain
- France
- Denmark
- Germany *
- Spain
- Italy

1960 65 70 75 80 85 88 89
Source: European Commission

60-year-olds as % of total population

1980 1988 2000 2010 2020

Denmark Germany * Spain France Italy Britain

* Western

gium and Britain—fertility rates in 1989 were higher than in the mid-1980s. Most remarkable of all is Sweden, where fertility fell to 1.6 in 1983 but recovered in 1990 to 2.1, the rate at which the population stabilises. Sweden's rising fertility rate has now drawn abreast of Ireland's declining one.

Sweden may be an example of govern-ment intervention that works. Jan Hoem of Stockholm University thinks the rise may be connected with changes in the rules on maternity benefit, making it possible for a mother to take two periods of equally well-paid leave if a second child is born within 30 months of the first. If so, the timing of births may be more affected than the num-ber of babies. All over northern Europe, women are hearing the ticking of the biological clock. As a result, fertility rates will rise before levelling off—though women may still have fewer children than needed to stop the population shrinking. Europe's new parents will continue to have smaller families than the ones in which they grew up.

Cheer up, it's working

AUGUST 10TH, BONN *Nearly a year after unification Germans were gloomy about the prospects for their country. We were more optimistic*

THE economic shake-up stands to turn much of the eastern part of Germany into the most modern region of the country before the decade is out. It will also help to rid the western part of rigidities that have plagued it for too long. You would not think so, to hear Germans moan.

At least once a decade Germans fret that their economy is going down the plughole, and their country's precious stability with it. In the late 1960s the cause was a mini-recession, in the mid-1970s it was the oil crisis, in the early 1980s a seemingly growing lead by foreign rivals in technology and fresh ideas.

Now unity is the culprit. According to an EMNID opinion poll published in July, most *Wessis* (westerners) believe their economy and living standards are in danger because of the large sums being shunted over to the shambolic east. Most *Ossis* (easterners) judge *Wessis* to be arrogant know-alls, unwilling to share their wealth. Only 3% of *Ossis* reckon the eastern economy is doing well. Not surprisingly: in July the jobless total topped 1m for the first time. By year's end nearly half the labour force there may be unemployed or idle.

No wonder that trade unionists give warning of a "hot autumn", and that the ruling Christian Democratic Union under Helmut Kohl, the chancellor, is getting a drubbing in both parts of Germany, especially the east. Since January support there for the Christian Democrats has plunged from 39% to 29%; it has soared from 26% to 41% for the opposition Social Democrats, who said before last winter's general election that unity would prove trickier and more costly than the government claimed.

The Social Democrats were right. East German industry turned out to be largely a junkyard (albeit one with better-supervised junk than elsewhere in Eastern Europe). At the exchange rate fixed for German economic and monetary union in July last year, its products were uncompetitive in the West, unaffordable by East Europeans and largely shunned (at least at first) by east Germans. Legal tangles and incompetent or non-existent administration blocked investment; eastern wage rises that far out-stripped productivity, designed to help stop labour drifting to bigger money in the west, pushed people out of work.

To pay the bills the government borrowed heavily and raised taxes (after promising not to), nudging inflation last month up to an un-Germanic 4.5%. Worried by rising prices and a D-mark made groggier by Germany's mainly unity-induced current-account deficit, the Bundesbank looks set to raise its key interest rates again soon. Pessimists see this as a prelude to recession, bigger deficits and still worse friction between embittered *Ossis* and *Wessis*.

I spy a Wirtschaftswunder

There are two reasons for taking a rosier view. Despite much rotten news from the east, the upswing is under way there.

Witness the newly stocked and painted shops, the building sites and the lorry-queues on the autobahns. Over the past 18 months 2m people have found new jobs (admittedly small comfort for the lots who have not). Some 370,000 more small businesses have started than have failed.

After a slow start the Treuhandanstalt, the trust agency charged with privatising former state-owned industry in the east, has now sold 2,600 firms and is selling on average 20 more each day. Public and private west German investment in the east will this year top DM60 billion ($35 billion, more than 2% of all-German GDP). Next year the figure will be higher. The result should be a modernisation benefiting the east not unlike the reconstruction of the west after 1949.

Eastern German GDP is likely to rise in 1992 by around 10% in real terms, after plunging by more than a fifth this year. Cold comfort to *Wessis* who are probably heading for slower growth. On the other hand western Germany's export performance may improve, because many products that went to feed the first spending spree in the east after monetary union will be redirected abroad, where demand is expected to pick up. The result could be an improved German current account, which would help to steady the D-mark.

The other reason for optimism is that unity is dealing a new blow at western Germany's all-too-cosy system of state subsidies, over-regulation and closed shops. For instance, the government can hardly go on paying DM10 billion a year to protect west German hard-coal miners when tens of thousands of brown-coal miners in the east

The future looks brighter

are losing their jobs. It can hardly block more private enterprise in the telecoms and road-building businesses when state companies are clearly unable to meet the unity challenge.

Nor is it just the German state that needs to become more flexible. There is plenty of scope for more competition in the electric-power industry and in trades like painting and decorating. Much more variation between the different regions is needed in the national wage agreements negotiated by the trade unions, in order to curb excessive wage rises in the east.

So far the government's response looks feeble. Its claim in July to have cut DM10 billion-worth of subsidies (from an annual total of more than DM100 billion) is largely bogus. But the pressure is mounting. Without drastic savings the government knows it will have to court still more unpopularity by raising federal tax rates and social-security deductions again. Without a radical shake-up the federal railways and post—both fac-

ing huge new burdens in the east—will plunge still deeper into the red and even the federal telecoms may no longer show a profit. So the bosses of all three are asking for an end to the protected civil-servant status of many of their staff, which brings with it over-manning and blocks initiative.

There are going to be plenty more struggles connected with Germany's unification, in west as well as east. But, for all the *Angst*, the outlook is brighter than the gloom-mongers currently believe.

Is Europe's boat full?

AUGUST 17TH **Albanian boat people focused attention on one of Western Europe's trickiest problems: how to handle the huddled masses pressing to get in**

POOR, miserable Albanians flooding the Italian port of Bari are merely the latest and most vivid reminder that a lot of people are desperate to enter Western Europe. The muddled reaction of the Italian authorities caused dismay inside Italy as well as out: first policemen's truncheons and tear gas, then summary return to Albania for thousands of hungry and frightened people. As if to meet the criticisms, 500 or so of them were to be sent to refugee camps in Italy and the government, with German help, took steps to deliver food to ports in Albania.

Shocking as the scenes on the Bari docks were to Europeans who thought that boat-people were an Asian or American phenomenon, few governments in Europe think that the Italians, at root, were wrong. Albanians were fleeing poverty more than repression, they think, and letting them in would have been an irresponsible invitation to other economic refugees or asylum-seekers searching for a place on a crowded continent. But were they right?

Each year hundreds of thousands of people come to Europe claiming to be political refugees. They seek a haven under the 1951 United Nations Convention on the Status of Refugees, which all EC members accept. This obliges them to take in anyone with a "well-founded fear of being persecuted for reasons of race, religion, nationality, membership of a particular group or political opinion."

Numbers to do with asylum-seekers need treating with care. But it is clear they are rising. In the early 1970s, Europe's asylum-seekers were a few thousand at most. In 1983, the number of those seeking haven in the 21 countries of the Council of Europe had jumped to 70,000. In 1989 (the most recent year for which figures are available) it was 350,000. This year, the number of applications will probably exceed 500,000. Where asylum-seekers come from has also changed. In the 1950s and 1960s most were from Eastern Europe. Since the 1970s they have tended to come more from the third world. A majority of asylum-seekers in Britain come from sub-Saharan Africa, most of those in France from North Africa.

As the number of applicants has grown, the proportion granted asylum has fallen. Only 4.4% of applications were approved in Germany last year. In Britain the acceptance rate fell from 64% in 1980 to just half that in 1989. In France less than a fifth are successful. Not only are more people claiming asylum as the easiest route into Europe, the Europeans have also become tougher-minded about treating as political refugees people fleeing economic hardship.

This does not mean that all those turned down have to leave. In Britain, where 50,000 cases await decision, it takes an average of 14 months for an initial finding. In Germany the wait is longer. As many EC states let asylum-seekers work in the meantime, applicants are often well integrated by the time a decision comes. One-third of those whose applications are rejected are allowed to remain. Others stay on illegally.

Refugee organisations argue, with force, that the asylum problem is overdone. Many third-world countries have far higher numbers of refugees relative to their populations than does the rich EC. Yet immigration of any sort is a political flashpoint in Europe.

Politics here clashes with principle. Recalling their countries' behaviour during the second world war, French and Germans have been especially loth to change a post-war tradition of almost unquestioning asylum. Yet both are tightening their rules. France's Socialist government has threatened deportation of rejected asylum-seekers (and other aliens) who have remained illegally. Germany's ruling conservatives are pushing, against the wishes of their liberal coalition partners, for a revision of the constitution, which grants asylum by right to victims of political persecution.

EC governments are being tougher about visas in general. This does not help them with the refugee who arrives with no papers and stutters "asylum" at passport control. But it may reduce the growing number of people who arrive on a short-term visa and then ask for asylum. Some EC countries are sending out passport officials to check papers before would-be refugees leave their own countries. They are getting tough with airlines that carry passengers with no papers.

The handling of asylum requests is also changing. France now gives applicants a

Not ants, Albanians

small monthly allowance instead of a work permit. The time of review is being cut there to a few months. Refugee organisations favour speedier reviews so long as these do not become rubber-stamp refusals. Amnesty International welcomes the British decision to more than quadruple the number of hearing officers. But it frowns at the government's plan to limit asylum-seekers' access to independent legal advice.

As barriers come down inside the Community, governments see a need to align policies on refugees and immigration. EC governments have already reached two agreements on this. A convention on asylum is meant to prevent asylum-seekers from shopping for the best havens, and to prevent officials shunting them to more receptive neighbours. The idea is that the country they first arrive in deals with them.

Under an accord on the crossing of external borders, EC countries have agreed that, for a given foreign country, they should aim to demand the same type of visa.

Refugee advisory groups fear that almost all such steps endanger the rights and protection of true political refugees. "Our fear", an Amnesty official says, "is that there'll be a levelling down, not a levelling up; that there'll be a Fortress Europe."

Anatomy of a botched putsch

AUGUST 24TH, MOSCOW *More than 70 years of Soviet communism came to an end with the failure of the August coup in Moscow. The Soviet inner empire started to unravel—and with it the power of President Mikhail Gorbachev. The power of Russia's Boris Yeltsin, the hero of the resistance, increased dramatically*

HELICOPTERS beat the air over Moscow for days before. But the eve of the coup was Soviet Air Force Day, so no one thought twice about them. The announcement on the morning of Monday August 19th that Mikhail Gorbachev, holidaying in the Crimea, was "ill" and that his duties had been taken over by his vice-president came out of a blue sky.

Yet the coup not only could have been predicted, it was—by Mr Gorbachev's former adviser, Alexander Yakovlev, who resigned from the Communist Party on August 16th, giving warning that the party was preparing a "Stalinist coup".

He was wrong about the party. The state of emergency was imposed by a junta consisting of the prime minister, the heads of the three security services (defence ministry, KGB, interior ministry) and representatives of the "military-industrial complex", the vast chunk of the economy controlled by the armed forces. The usurping vice-president, Gennady Yanaev, tried to portray it as ordinary constitutional procedure following the illness of the president. But the semblance of constitutionality was a fiction.

The timing made clear the purpose of the coup. That Monday, Mr Gorbachev was due back in Moscow, intending to sign a new union treaty the next day. The treaty would have delegated nearly all significant central-government powers to the republics, which were to be recognised as "sovereign states". The junta's first decree was that the constitution of the Soviet Union took precedence over republican ones, and that decisions of the emergency committee had to be obeyed by republican governments.

Yet, though the day of the coup must have been decided some time in advance, it was poorly prepared and conspicuously lacking in military precision. Tanks did not appear in the streets of Moscow until nearly midday, six hours after the announcement of Mr Gorbachev's "illness". And when units of the Taman motorised rifle division

and the Katemirov airborne division did roll into the city, it was in an uncoordinated jam, with tanks queuing up for miles along Moscow's outer ring road.

The lack of ruthlessness and planning became more and more apparent as the hours passed. The only person of significance arrested was Mr Gorbachev himself. Boris Yeltsin, Russia's president, was left free to lead the opposition. He went to his parliament building, known as the White House, where he denounced the coup and called for a general strike. The failure to arrest Mr Yeltsin reveals the committee's blurriness of purpose: until he uttered his defiance, Mr Yeltsin had broken none of the committee's decrees; when he did, it was too late to arrest him.

Contrast what happened next with the imposition of martial law in Poland in 1981. There, within hours, nearly all of Solidarity's leaders were in prison, blanket censorship had been imposed and all telephone communications cut so that nobody in one part of the country knew what was going on anywhere else. In the Soviet Union, telephone lines remained open and miners' leaders inside the Russian parliament began to organise strikes by telephone.

Western press and television operated freely. The junta even lost control of its own media. No soldiers arrived to censor the opposition press, even though the junta had said that all but eight newspapers were being closed down. The next day several liberal newspapers banded together to bring out a special joint edition. On the day of the coup itself Soviet television viewers were regaled with the sight of Mr Yanaev being asked what he thought of Mr Yeltsin's call for a national strike—which broadcast the strike call over the country.

Those first few hours of dithering were decisive, because they gave Mr Yeltsin's supporters a chance to rally. In the early hours of the coup it seemed that even the tanks had failed to rouse the Russians out of their

famous passivity. Inside the Russian parliament people were playing computer games. The massed demonstrations that filled the centre of Moscow earlier in the year to support Mr Yeltsin failed to materialise. No rattle of gunfire sounded in the streets. How different, it seemed, from the night of January 13th in Vilnius, when troops stormed Lithuania's television centre.

Yet, from Monday afternoon onwards, every hour that went by saw the committee losing control of one part of the country after another. First the strike began to take hold as miners in half the pits in Russia's main mining areas—the Kuzbass and Vorkuta—walked out. Within a day of the coup the garrison commanders of 11 Russian cities opted to support Mr Yeltsin. Then the republics, too, began to line up behind him. Even part of the Communist Party entered the fray against the coup when its deputy leader, Vladimir Ivashko, demanded to see Mr Gorbachev.

By midday on Tuesday, the second day of the coup, it still seemed possible that its leaders, given enough ruthlessness, could assert their authority. At this point, with events hanging in the balance, two things tipped the advantage to Mr Yeltsin.

How the tide turned

The first was the appearance of serious dissatisfaction in the upper levels of the armed forces. General Vladimir Polyakov, a candidate for head of a new Russian branch of the KGB, said that members of that branch regarded President Yeltsin, not General Vladimir Kryuchkov (the KGB's chairman and a junta member), as their head. For the army, General Konstantin Kobets joined Mr Yeltsin at the White House to say that soldiers were not obliged to obey their superiors. General Kobets had been a rising star in the Soviet general staff, with close ties to the chief of staff himself.

That only ten tanks defected to Mr Yeltsin (under the barrels of forces loyal to the coup leaders) was widely misunderstood. Their small number was taken to show that the bulk of the army would carry out its orders. But military reluctance expressed itself in a different way: through passive resistance.

Imposing a coup in a country as large as the Soviet Union means relying on local commanders. Their willingness to obey orders varied. In the Baltic states General Fedor Kuzmin, accustomed to violence after the events in Lithuania in January, sent his troops to all three capitals. But in Georgia the independence-seeking president persuaded the local commander not to deploy his troops by disbanding Georgia's own national guard. Leningrad's mayor, Anatoly Sobchak, persuaded the military commander there, General Alexander Samsonov, to allow mass demonstrations in the centre of the city by promising not to call for a strike (which went ahead anyway at several plants). The junta's inability to secure the country's second city was extraordinary evidence of its failure of will.

Significantly, during the whole 60-hour fiasco nothing was heard from the chief of staff, General Mikhail Moiseev (who was appointed acting defence minister after the coup failed). The likely explanation is that he was unwilling to throw the full weight of the armed forces behind the putsch.

But this alone was not enough to explain its collapse. The second thing that decided the issue was the surge in active resistance in Moscow and Leningrad. This meant that the coup could succeed only through the most ruthless oppression. And that was something the coup leaders were unwilling, or unable, to order.

On Monday afternoon the first barricades went up in the centre of Moscow as people began to respond to Mr Yeltsin's appeal to defend their parliament. By Tuesday night the building had become a defensive encampment bristling with steel bars, concrete blocks, buses slewed across the roads—anything that could be pressed into service as a makeshift barricade. Behind the barricades were the handful of dissident tanks, and a huge crowd gathered in torrential rain and mud to defy coup and curfew.

General Kryuchkov himself, according to a Russian KGB officer, decided not to storm the parliament. When fighting did erupt in the streets of Moscow that night, it was 200 yards away near the American embassy. Four people died.

Back to Gorbachev

The failure to storm the parliament was a test that the junta failed. Unwilling to fill the streets with blood, yet unable to control the country in any other way, the conspirators turned against each other. A baffling series of rumours began, with one member after another reported to have left the group. First the prime minister was said to be ill and to have been replaced by his deputy (this was true). The defence minister and the KGB chief were said to have stepped down (this was not true). But even the rumours were revealing, because they pointed—correctly—to the junta's loss of nerve.

Narrowly escaping arrest at one of Moscow's airports, four of the committee's members fled the capital at midday on Wednesday to make some sort of appeal to Mr Gorbachev in his dacha in the Crimea. But it was too late. As the defence ministry ordered all troops to leave Moscow, the praesidium of the Soviet parliament formally reinstated Mr Gorbachev in power. In the small hours of August 22nd he returned triumphantly to Moscow.

This was not a carefully prepared counter-revolution. It was a botched continuation of an abortive constitutional coup d'état that had taken place a month earlier. On June 17th the prime minister asked parliament to reduce Mr Gorbachev's powers, and was supported by the men who made up this week's junta. Parliament rejected the demand and President Gorbachev, flanked by the defence, KGB and police chiefs, laughingly observed that "the coup is over".

The deal is done

*DECEMBER 14TH, MAASTRICHT **The year-long negotiations to reform the European Community climaxed in the Dutch town of Maastricht. History was duly made***

THE treaty of Maastricht marks a step forward for the European Community on a par with the Treaty of Rome which created it 34 years ago. The treaty—one part covering economic and monetary union (EMU) and the other, political union—creates a so-called European Union and sets its course for years ahead. Determined not to let their deadline slip, and aware of the urgency of sorting themselves out to face the upheavals in the East, the EC's leaders bulldozed their way to a super-deal that may eventually make the European Union a superpower.

Believers in a federal Europe insist that the treaty lays down the main elements, if only in embryo, of a future European government: a single currency, common foreign and defence policy, a common citizenship and a parliament with teeth. Those of a more pragmatic bent say that it marks a sensible step forward, helping the EC to meet the challenges of Eastern Europe (through tighter foreign policies) and creating a more efficient market (through a single currency).

These views do not clash, and so after the Maastricht summit on December 9th and 10th, all 12 leaders liked the results. France's President Mitterrand had got the Germans to commit themselves to a single currency and to a foreign and defence policy. Germany's Helmut Kohl won agreement that EMU should follow a German design and that the European Parliament should have more power. Felipe Gonzalez, the Spanish prime minister, won promises of "cohesion" (more money) for the poorer members.

The problem for John Major, Britain's prime minister, was that the main thing he wanted from the deal was that it should not do too much. But his success in blocking more EC powers over employment law allowed him, too, to claim a triumph.

The Dutch presidency's draft treaty had proposed letting the EC make laws by majority vote in new areas such as working conditions and worker consultation. Mr Major argued that this would make the EC uncompetitive. So on the summit's second day, its chairman, Ruud Lubbers, the Dutch prime minister, presented a greatly watered-down "social chapter". This was acceptable neither to France, Italy nor Belgium (which wanted more), nor to Britain (which wanted still less).

By early Tuesday evening most of the treaty was agreed upon, but there was deadlock on the social chapter. At 7pm the meeting was stopped so that Mr Lubbers could talk to Mr Major. They called in Mr Kohl. Mr Major showed them a new and even more watery draft, but they told him it would not do. When asked if he could accept Mr Mitterrand's suggestion that Britain should opt out of employment law, Mr Major said no—perhaps reckoning that a social opt-out, on top of the one he had already negotiated on EMU, would be embarrassing at home. But, he said, he would buy the other 11 "opting in" for an arrangement to make social laws without Britain.

So at the 11th hour Mr Major's friendship with Mr Kohl proved useful. Mr Kohl said he would support this ploy and, when the summit reconvened, proposed it. There was little resistance to such an unprecedented institutional fix. It was late, everyone wanted to go home—and so much that had already been agreed upon might be sacrificed if the talks broke down. The result was a concoction that may have far bigger consequences—if the idea catches on in other areas or with future EC members—than the bleary-eyed summiteers realised.

A protocol attached to the treaty says that 11 EC members will make social laws on the basis of the initial Dutch draft. The European Commission, Parliament and Court will play the roles they would in EC legislation. But Britain will be absent from the Council of Ministers. The Treaty of Rome's existing social chapter remains unchanged. If the commission planned a social law, it would ask the British if they wanted to be involved. If they said yes, the commission would propose a normal EC law. If no, it would propose a law to the 11.

This strange beast may never be uncaged. A Labour Party victory in next year's election would allow Britain to opt in. And as Mr Lubbers said, at his 2am press conference: "History teaches us that if one or two members lag behind, they always follow."

Mr Major, in any case, was delighted. He also won a protocol giving Britain alone the right not to join the single currency. But on the summit's first day he had to accept the setting of a date for EMU. Mr Mitterrand and Italy's Giulio Andreotti wanted a date to make the passage to EMU "irreversible". Mr Kohl agreed, so 1999 it was.

Conveyor belt to the ecu

The procedure for moving to the single currency will begin in 1996. Finance ministers will decide, by qualified majority, which members meet certain "convergence" criteria. A summit will then decide, again by majority, whether at least seven countries are ready for EMU, and if so, whether and when it should start. If no date is set, another summit will meet before July 1998 to decide, again by qualified majority, which members are ready. Those countries will automatically adopt the ecu as their single cur-

rency in January 1999.

Mr Major defeated the federalists on the overall shape of the treaty. The European Union's "federal goal" was deleted, in favour of "an ever closer union among the peoples of Europe, where decisions are taken as closely as possible to the citizens." He also struck out a clause declaring that in the long run the European Union's two inter-governmental "pillars"—for foreign policy and internal security—would merge with the Community, where the European Parliament and Commission play a larger role. The article calling for a treaty revision in 1996 to "strengthen the federal character of the union" has lost its federal trappings.

Mr Major also liked the wording on subsidiarity. The EC should act "only if . . . the objectives of the proposed action cannot be sufficiently achieved by the member-states and can therefore, by reason of the scale or effects of the proposed action, be better achieved by the Community."

Yet despite Mr Major's successes, much of the treaty reflects French and German interests. Hence the idea of common foreign policies: the Council of Ministers, having agreed unanimously on a common policy, may also decide, again unanimously, that certain measures needed to implement the policy should be taken by qualified majority vote. On Britain's insistence, even once they have agreed on a common policy, countries will be allowed to act on their own "in cases of imperative need".

The deal on defence, said Britain, involved France accepting the thrust of October's British-Italian paper. France said Brit-

ain had bowed to the Franco-German counter-proposals. The French are a little closer to the truth. The treaty talks of "the eventual framing of a common defence policy, which might in time lead to a common defence." The nine-member Western European Union is an "integral part of the development of the European Union", which may "request . . . the WEU to elaborate and implement decisions and actions of the Union which have defence implications."

The French said that means the WEU (which, the summit decided, all EC members could join) is subordinate to the European Union; the British said the wording means it is not. France got its review of defence arrangements in 1996, but Britain got the treaty to say that these arrangements should be compatible with NATO.

Mr Gonzalez was happy with his deal on cohesion. The principle that poorer countries should pay less into the EC's budget appears in a binding protocol. And by 1994 a "cohesion fund" will be set up to help pay for environmental and transport projects.

Federalists were pleased to see EC powers extended to consumer protection, health, education, and "trans-European networks" (telecoms, transport and energy projects). Ministers will vote in these areas by majority. But environmental rules on planning, tax and choices between energy sources will require unanimity, as will chapters on industrial policy and culture.

Mr Kohl used his weight to give more power to the European Parliament. It gains the right to veto laws on consumer protection, health, education, trans-European networks, culture, environment strategy, research and the single market. But Mr Mitterrand overturned the agreement reached last month to add another 18 German Euro-MPS (and to cut the number of commissioners to one per country). From January 1995 commissioners will serve five-year, rather than four-year, terms so that their terms coincide with the parliament's.

Mr Kohl made little progress with his demand for an EC role in asylum and immigration policy. But Mr Major had to accept that the EC will decide on the list of countries whose citizens will need visas to enter the EC. Decisions will for now require unanimity, but in an "emergency" the council may vote by qualifed majority, which after 1996 will be the rule. In 1993 a summit will consider moving asylum policy to the EC.

The Community's leaders can congratulate themselves on having pulled off a job that at times over the past year seemed beyond them. But they cannot afford to rest on their laurels. They have to get the treaty through their parliaments. Then there are the small matters of the budget, new members, war in Yugoslavia and the collapse of the Soviet Union.

Contents

ASIA

Cutting the apron strings

IS ASIA beginning to stand on its own feet? To apply such a mundane metaphor to 3 billion people—who range from Afghans to Koreans, from Australians to Japanese—may strain belief. Yet in 1991 the cold war ended, and for the first time in over four decades America and the Soviet Union were happy to relax their geopolitical grip on Asia. From now on, Asians will be increasingly responsible, and their governments accountable, for their own actions and their destinies.

Consider the most dramatic and welcome results of the loosening grip of outside power: in September, the United States and the disintegrating Soviet Union agreed to stop by year's end all military support for their proxies in Afghanistan's civil war; in October, prodded by their foreign sponsors to a peace conference in Paris, the warring factions of Cambodia agreed to end more than a dozen years of fractricidal war; and in December, after 38 years of unrelenting animosity on both sides of their demilitarised zone, North and South Korea formally agreed to end their state of war.

The cooling (extinction is too premature a description) of those flash-points could not have happened without the changes initiated by Mikhail Gorbachev. Without Soviet support, the Kabul regime in Afghanistan must surely sue for peace—just as the Phnom Penh regime in Cambodia did once its backer, Vietnam, had lost its own Soviet economic support. Nor was it coincidence that the ending of Soviet aid preceded North Korea's belated amiability. The collapse of Russian and European communism and the demonstration of America's might in the Gulf war confirmed the obvious: in 1991 Asian countries could no longer play on the politics of superpower rivalry.

Unhappily, it does not follow that Asia will now be at peace with itself. One reason is that the flash-points that have cooled could still ignite. The Khmers Rouges, for example, are a necessary partner in Cambodia's peace, but remain unacceptable in its democratic future. In Afghanistan, if the mujaheddin find it hard to co-operate in wartime, they may find it even harder in peacetime. And in the Korean peninsula there can be no guarantee of stability while the North seeks the ability to wage nuclear war.

A second reason is that there are points of potential or actual conflict that will not be erased simply because the cold war has become a memory. In disputed Kashmir the armies of India and Pakistan are on constant alert. In the high Himalayas, China holds land claimed by India, and India holds land, east of Nepal, claimed by China. In the South China Sea, because of competing nationalisms and the prospect of finding fields of oil

Glorious farewell

and gas, the innocuous-looking Spratly Islands are squabbled over by China, Taiwan, the Philippines, Malaysia, Vietnam and Brunei.

But the most important reason is that without the presence of the superpowers to keep the peace, their erstwhile proxies are more likely to turn squabbles into conflict, arguments into war. The easy temptation, now that communism is no longer an attractive option anywhere in Asia, is to assume an era of growing trade between former enemies. The countries of Indochina, for example, are beginning to trade with ASEAN, and ASEAN's more entrepreneurial members, Singapore and Thailand, were in 1991 already investing in Vietnam and Cambodia. Yet it is equally easy to see an era where economic competition revives ancient jealousies and ethnic tensions. The Thai government may dream of a *suwannaphume*, or "golden land", linking Thailand to Vietnam and the rest of Indochina, but that dream will first have to overcome the traditional antipathy between the Thais and Vietnamese. Regional tensions, from the Himalayas to the Korean peninsula, are just as likely as regional friendships—especially when so many of Asia's countries are so well equipped for war.

While large armies do not, of course, necessarily make war more likely, there is an uncomfortable correlation in Asia between the biggest armies and the points of actual or potential conflict. India has more than 1.25m under arms; Pakistan over half-a-million; China 3m; North Korea 1.1m; South Korea 750,000; and Vietnam half-a-million on active service. As a 1990 report by America's Department of Defence had already noted: "The 1990s will be a decade of transition in the Asia-Pacific region. Political volatility and turbulence will characterise key countries—China, the Soviet Union, North Korea, Cambodia and the Philippines, to name a few. Political uncertainties are exacerbated by the major changes in generational leadership that will occur, such as in China, North Korea, Singapore, Vietnam and Indonesia . . . "

A promising report card

But despite that sombre prognosis, 1991 evoked more optimism than alarm, and not just because of the hopeful signs towards the end of the year in Afghanistan, Cambodia and the Korean peninsula. China, for example, chose not to use its UN Security Council veto to obstruct the American-led effort to humble Saddam Hussein; and India, the world's most populous democracy, triumphantly completed a general election despite an undercurrent of sectarian violence and despite the traumatic assassination of its former prime minister, Rajiv Gandhi, in May. Just as impressively, the new minority Congress Party government of Narasimha Rao proceeded to introduce the economic liberalism that had always been anathema to India's policy-makers—even while it was producing the economic miracles of South-East Asia.

Arguably, the governments of China and India had little choice. The regime of Deng Xiaoping and Li Peng may have feared America's "hegemonism" after the collapse of the Soviet Union, but it also needed to escape the ostracism that had followed the bloodshed of Tiananmen Square in June 1989. Similarly, the Rao government's economic bravery was dictated as much as anything by the desperate need for help from the International Monetary Fund. But whatever the motives, the behaviour of the two giants, who will dominate their continent by sheer weight of numbers, was at least sensible.

India marked up

But what of the country which, by its economic clout and overseas investment, will help define Asia's future just as much as China and India? In 1991 Toshiki Kaifu was the most popular prime minister that Japan had ever had. Yet he failed in his attempt to send troops, even as non-combatants, to help the American alliance in the Gulf war; he failed to reform an electoral system that breeds corruption and money-politics; and, in October, he had ignominiously to withdraw from the contest for the presidency of the Liberal Democratic Party—and for the prime ministership that goes with it.

Mr Kaifu's successor, the English-speaking Kiichi Miyazawa, was as sophisticated and intelligent a prime minister as any of Japan's trading partners could wish. But the truth was that Japan's politics was characterised throughout the year by its familiar introspection and corruption (in contrast to the "clean" Mr Kaifu, Mr Miyazawa, who had been involved in the Recruit scandal of 1988, was by December again being accused of unsavoury links to big business). The little amount of foreign policy initiative that was shown was either to rebuff Mikhail Gorbachev's plea for aid on his visit to Tokyo in April or to warn North Korea to dismantle its nuclear programme (a demand that followed the visit to Tokyo in November by America's secretary of state, James Baker).

Does Japan's introspection matter? When the 50th anniversary of Japan's attack on Pearl Harbour was commemorated on December 7th, a common reaction was that Japan had achieved in peace the Greater East Asia Co-Prosperity Sphere it had failed to win by war. Perhaps so, but only because the American victor of that war had subsequently held back the advance of commu-

nism and kept the region's peace.

In which case, Japan and the rest of Asia should note America's abandonment in 1991 of its Clark Field air base in the Philippines and its promise to leave the Subic Bay naval base within three years. Those decisions had been under consideration ever since America began to take seriously Mr Gorbachev's peaceful intentions, and ever since the decline of Soviet power became unmistakable. What brought them into being was the volcano that in June covered Clark with a layer of ash, the anti-bases nationalism of the Philippine senate and the determination of the American Congress not to waste the "peace dividend" of the new Soviet-American friendship on defending Asia from itself.

The question is how well Asia will react. Singapore, as pragmatic as ever, in 1991 arranged a level of co-operation with America's troops in Asia that gives them more-or-less permanent access to Singapore's port and repair facilities; and Japan and South Korea will doubtless both heed at the financial level Mr Baker's plea in November to "share the burden" of keeping Asia at peace.

But those will be only half-remedies until Asia sorts out its new balances of power. That will mean defining a new relationship between Pakistan, which is cut off from American aid because of its nuclear capability or near-capability, and India. Pakistan's fear of India and its loss of American support (indeed, in 1991, America was wooing India) are turning the country's attention towards its Muslim neighbours to the west and north; India, meanwhile, is improving its relations with China, whose prime minister, Li Peng, visited Delhi in December.

Such political shifts, wherever they occur, will be more smoothly managed if Asia can escape the economic troubles that in 1991 so dramatically slowed the English-speaking countries of the West. With luck it will: an increase in trade within Asia is reducing the region's vulnerable reliance on the American market, and in most countries economic growth is handsomely outstripping population growth. But all that, in turns, depends on trade with Japan and investment from Japan. As Asia stands on its own feet, Japan will have to keep it upright.

January

Tuesday 1st

Hong Kong's gamblers bet over HK$833m ($113m) on an afternoon's horse-racing at the Happy Valley course. Meanwhile, press reports said over 70,000—out of a population of under 6m—had applied in 1990 for certificates of no criminal conviction to help them emigrate before 1997, when the British colony reverts to China.

The Liberation Tigers of Tamil Eelam began a "goodwill" **ceasefire in Sri Lanka.** Some other Tamil groups opposed to the LTTE said the ceasefire was to allow the Tigers to acquire more weapons.

Thursday 3rd

President Corazon Aquino asked the **Philippine Congress** for powers to suspend labour laws and enforce price controls because of the anticipated Gulf war. The Philippines imports its oil and had relied on remittances from some 500,000 Filipino workers in the Gulf region.

Singapore's parliament voted 75-1 to amend the constitution: the nation's presidency, hitherto ceremonial, would now carry executive powers, including a veto over the spending of the country's financial reserves. The president would also have powers over the Internal Security Act, which allows indefinite detention without trial.

Saturday 5th

A Beijing court jailed seven dissidents for their part in the 1989 **pro-democracy** demonstrations. Two were spared because of their "willingness of repentance".

Tuesday 8th

Japan's prime minister **Toshiki Kaifu** was greeted in Seoul by demands that Japan apologise for its past colonisation of Korea. Japan's finance minister was greeted in Beijing by smiling hosts hoping for Japanese loans.

Thursday 10th

The governor of the Bank of Thailand said the era of fast growth for **Thailand** was over: GDP would grow by an average of 7-8% compared with the average of 11.5% over the past four years. The OECD average for 1987-90 was 3.4%.

Singapore's prime minister Goh Chok Tong predicted that the countries of **Indochina** would abandon communism within five years.

Friday 11th

Sri Lankan troops resumed military operations against **Tamil rebels,** saying they had used a ceasefire merely to acquire more arms.

Saturday 12th

"China alone has the right to speak on behalf of the Hong Kong people," said a Chinese official. The remark came during talks in Beijing over plans for a new **Hong Kong airport.** China worried that the cost of this and associated projects—originally put at $16.3 billion—would empty the coffers by 1997, when China takes over the British colony.

Thursday 17th

The **Philippines**, with a foreign debt of over $27 billion, reached a "substantive agreement" with the IMF, promising new taxes to reduce the government's budget deficit. The agreement was expected to trigger pledges of $3 billion from foreign aid donors.

Tuesday 22nd

Japanese officials announced a 13% fall in the December trade surplus compared with that a year earlier, ending 50 months of rises. Higher oil prices and tight monetary policy were blamed.

Wednesday 23rd

Rebels on the island of **Bougainville** signed a treaty ending a two-year fight to secede from Papua New Guinea.

Friday 25th

Japanese men should do more housework, according to a government report, in order to make marriage more attractive to women and so boost the declining birth rate. Of women aged 25-29, 37.3% were still single in 1989 compared with 20.9% in 1975.

Saturday 26th

Student leader **Wang Dan**, top of China's most-wanted list after the 1989 protests in Tiananmen Square, was jailed for four years.

Singapore, where land is scarce, said the cost of burial, if required for religious reasons, would rise by 8% to **encourage cremation**. Without such reasons, the cost would rise by 33%.

Sunday 27th

Four boats with 29 Vietnamese on board sailed into Hong Kong, bringing to 390 the number of **boat people** to arrive so far in January--more than double the total for January 1990. There were 43,992 boat people in Hong Kong awaiting determination of their fate. Another 7,900 had been classified as refugees, allowed to settle in the West.

North Korea warned South Korea to cancel its **joint military exercise** with America, Team Spirit, or risk a break in recent high-level contacts. Team Spirit in 1990 involved 200,000 troops. The 1991 exercise, scheduled for March, was to be scaled down by 30% in deference to North Korea.

Wednesday 30th

India's prime minister **Chandra Shekhar** imposed direct federal rule on Tamil Nadu because of activity by militant Tamils from Sri Lanka. In Punjab, Sikh militants killed at least 23; in Kashmir, two Indian soldiers and four Muslim militants were killed in an attack on an army convoy.

South Korea, officials said, would contribute an extra $280m and 150 non-combat personnel to the allied effort against Iraq. Earlier, South Korea pledged $220m and sent a 154-member medical team to Saudi Arabia. This contrasted with its agreement to lend the Soviet Union $3 billion over the next three years, following 1990's normalisation of relations.

Thursday 31st

The Executive Yuan, or cabinet, of **Taiwan** approved a six-year economic plan that would involve spending of $308 billion, mainly on renewing and enhancing the island's inadequate infrastructure. The plan assumed annual economic growth of 7% from 1991 to 1996. Even if the plan missed its goal, America, constantly in a trade deficit with Taiwan, was expected to appreciate the effort.

February

Friday 1st
China agreed to take from Japan more than 1,000 **ethnic Chinese** who arrived in Japan in 1989 posing as Vietnamese refugees but were not recognised as such by Japan. China had said it would not take them back because they had come from Indochina. The change paved the way for expected visits by Japan's prime minister and foreign minister.

The American State Department, in its annual report on **human rights**, said China had sentenced more than 1,000 people to jail for their part in the 1989 democracy movement; at least another 335 were held without trial. By contrast, the report praised Mongolia and Nepal for moving towards democracy.

Thursday 7th
Radio Pyongyang reported that North Korea's ruling Workers' Party had **crushed a plot** against the planned transfer of power from President Kim Il Sung to his son, Kim Jong Il. President Kim, the "Great Leader", had ruled since 1948; his son, the "Dear Leader", was said to be unpopular with the army.

Friday 8th
China's senior leader, **Deng Xiaoping**, in remarks reported by a Hong Kong magazine, said people in the British colony "should not have too many unrealistic illusions" about their transfer to Chinese sovereignty in 1997. "The opposition party", which organised support in Hong Kong for democracy in China, "has to be kicked out of the political establishment."

Sunday 10th
On the eve of the sixth round of talks in Manila to renew the lease on **American bases** in the Philippines, the chief American negotiator said America could "survive, prosper and prevail" without

them. The present agreement, covering America's biggest overseas bases, was scheduled to expire in September. The talks were on the price and duration of an extension.

Monday 11th
Corazon Aquino became the first Philippine president to testify in a trial. In a libel suit against two Filipino journalists she denied she had hidden under her bed during an attempted coup in 1987.

Tuesday 12th
A Beijing court sentenced two long-time **dissidents**, Wang Juntao and Chen Ziming, to 13 years in prison for their role in the 1989 democracy movement. Their money-raising and organisational abilities probably contributed to the length of their sentences, by far the worst since the Tiananmen crackdown.

North and **South Korea** agreed to form united sports teams for two international championships. South Korea said it hoped for a joint team at the 1992 Olympics.

Wednesday 13th
Japanese investigators found a leak in a tube in a **nuclear reactor**, four days after Japan's worst ever nuclear-plant accident. Some 39 nuclear-power stations provide 27% of Japan's energy.

Japan reported that its trade surplus for January was $987m, more than triple the low level of a year earlier. Workers launched their annual *shunto*, or **spring offensive**, with a claim for an 8-9% pay rise for fewer hours.

Monday 18th
South Korea's President Roh Tae Woo replaced two cabinet ministers and the mayor of Seoul after a **bribery** scandal. Meanwhile, North Korea cancelled a fourth round of talks, due to begin with the south,

in protest at American-South Korean military exercises.

Tamil separatists killed 44 government soldiers in an ambush in Sri Lanka.

Thursday 21st
A nuclear reactor north-west of Tokyo shut down automatically because of abnormal pressure. It was the second **nuclear incident** in Japan in less than two weeks.

Friday 22nd
Opposition leader Kim Dae Jung accused South Korea's President Roh Tae Woo of personal involvement in a **property scandal** which involved at least $1.3m in bribes.

Of China's state-run enterprises, 31% lost money (in record amounts) in 1990, officials announced. Meanwhile, **Xu Jiatun**, who fled to California shortly after retiring in February 1990 as China's chief representative in Hong Kong, was expelled from China's national legislature and denounced as a traitor. Mr Xu once described capitalism as a "great creation" of mankind.

Saturday 23rd
Thailand's military leaders imposed martial law in a bloodless **coup**, citing intolerable corruption during the 30-month administration of prime minister Chatichai Choonhavan, Thailand's first elected prime minister in 12 years. The coup was the latest of 17, successful and other-

wise, since the end of the absolute monarchy in 1932.

Tuesday 26th
A delegation from Taiwan's opposition Democratic Progressive Party (DPP) began a two-week visit to mainland China, with which Taiwan was still technically at war. Many DPP leaders had favoured **independence** for Taiwan. This was treason since both the communist government in Beijing and the Kuomintang one in Taipei believe in a united China.

Australia lifted all **sanctions** against China except for a ban on arms sales and security contacts. The sanctions were imposed in protest at the suppression in June 1989 of China's democracy movement.

Wednesday 27th
Bangladesh held its first free parliamentary **elections** in 20 years of independence. The centrist party of Begum Khaleda Zia, widow of an assassinated president, won most seats–but not enough for a majority in parliament.

A Singaporean MP said his countrymen were too busy **making money** to make babies. Singapore's government is concerned at the declining birth rate.

Thursday 28th
The Philippine government said the number of **communist insurgents** had fallen from a peak of 25,000 in 1987 to about 14,000.

Only 65,674 applications were received for the full **British citizenship** offered to 50,000 Hong Kong heads-of-households to persuade the commercially and professionally valuable to stay in Hong Kong up to and beyond China's takeover in 1997. Hong Kong officials had predicted there would be over 300,000 applications.

Saturday 2nd

Thailand's new military junta named Anand Panyarachun, a career diplomat, as caretaker prime minister pending a general election. Bankers and businessmen applauded.

Ranjan Wijeratne, Sri Lanka's deputy defence minister and the leader of the offensive against Tamil separatists, was **killed by a car bomb** in the capital, Colombo.

Sunday 3rd

A third of Hong Kong's registered voters turned out for local **elections**. Those registered are only half of the 3.6m eligible, but officials described the turnout as an "encouraging" prelude to the first-ever direct elections, in September, to the colony's Legislative Council.

Monday 4th

China jailed three Hong Kong men for terms of up to five years for helping Chinese **dissidents** from the 1989 democracy movement escape.

Wednesday 6th

India's prime minister **Chandra Shekhar resigned,** accusing his coalition partner, former prime minister Rajiv Gandhi, of undermining his four months in office.

Hong Kong's financial secretary raised the **tobacco tax** by 200% in his budget. He cited health concerns; cynics cited the need to pay for Hong Kong's planned airport, part of an infrastructure package costed at $16.3 billion.

Monday 11th

American fighter aircraft took part for the first time in exercises in Singapore as part of an agreement allowing **American forces** increased access to Singapore's military bases. Singapore was anxious that America maintain its military presence in the area, despite opposition in the Philippines to American bases there.

Tuesday 12th

Bob Hawke, Australia's prime minister since 1983, announced a package of tariff cuts and tax incentives to pull the country out of recession. Business leaders said the measures were correct, politically brave—but not enough to inspire investment.

Wednesday 13th

A United Nations consultant pronounced that **Vietnam's 1990 "Year of Tourism"**, designed to earn foreign exchange and encourage investment, had been a dismal failure. Only 187,000 tourists visited Vietnam in 1990. The UN gave Vietnamese officials a 1,500-page report telling them how to correct mistakes such as too few hotels and too much red tape.

Thursday 14th

Papua New Guinea's prime minister Rabbie Namaliu announced that criminals would be **tattooed on the forehead** to help deter rising crime in his nation of almost 4m people. Other measures would include a night-time curfew and the reinstatement of the death penalty.

Malaysia's foreign minister said the Association of South-East Asian Nations (ASEAN) was moving towards **dialogue with the Soviet Union**. The ASEAN members—Malaysia, Brunei, Thailand, Singapore, the Philippines and Indonesia—are traditionally allied to America and hostile to communism, but Malaysia wanted a role for the Soviet Union as a counter to the emergence of America as the only superpower.

Friday 15th

China agreed to make a **soft loan** to the Soviet Union, supplying food, textiles, cigarettes and consumer goods worth $733m. Soviet officials failed in efforts to call the loan a "barter trade", even though China was said to be seeking Russian fighter aircraft at bargain prices.

Saturday 16th

Threatened with arrest, American officials removed a 10lb bag of **American rice** from a Tokyo food exhibition. Japan bans virtually all rice imports, citing the need to maintain national self-sufficiency in rice. Cynics say the reason is the political power of Japan's farmers. The result is that Japanese consumers pay several times the world price.

Tuesday 19th

Begum Khaleda Zia, widow of President Ziaur Rahman, who was assassinated in May 1981, was appointed Bangladesh's first **woman prime minister**. In the February 27th elections, her Bangladesh Nationalist Party won 139 of the 300 seats in parliament. Meanwhile, deposed President Ershad pleaded not guilty to possessing illegal weapons.

Wednesday 20th

Chinese judicial officials told visiting American lawyers that there would be no more trials connected with the **1989 democracy movement** (an assertion contradicted three days later in the official *People's Daily*). At the same time, Beijing's highest court rejected the appeals of three intellectuals jailed for their part in the 1989 protests.

Eduardo Cojuangco, an estranged cousin of President Aquino and a **crony** of deposed Philippine president Ferdinand Marcos, announced he would run for the presidency in 1992.

Thursday 21st

Japanese newspapers claimed that Japan would give up to $28 billion in aid to the Soviet Union if it returned islands occupied since 1945. The dispute over the **Kurile islands** seemed certain to figure in the April visit by President Gorbachev to Tokyo.

Monday 22nd

The annual session of China's National People's Congress opened in Beijing. Prime Minister Li Peng frankly acknowledged the severity of the country's **economic problems**—but offered no convincing remedy. The finance minister, whose 1990 budget was overspent by 69%, allowed a 12% increase in defence spending.

Wednesday 27th

Singapore commandos stormed a **hijacked** Singapore Airlines airliner, freeing all passengers and killing four Pakistani hijackers. The hijackers had demanded the release from jail of the husband of ousted Pakistan prime minister, Benazir Bhutto.

Friday 29th

"Red" Prince Souphanouvong, 81, who fought alongside Lao and Vietnamese guerrillas against America's presence in Indochina, resigned from the leadership of the communist party of **Laos**. Meanwhile, neighbouring Cambodia said the scheduled congress of its communist party had been cancelled.

Tuesday 2nd
Afghanistan's President Najibollah called a day of mourning after the loss the previous day of the garrison town of Khost. Victorious **mujaheddin** guerrillas set up a new administrative council for the town—a snub for the official capital, Kabul.

Wednesday 3rd
Britain's foreign secretary, Douglas Hurd, became the most senior British official to visit Beijing since the Tiananmen crackdown of 1989. He went to seek **China's backing** for an expensive new airport in Hong Kong.

Saturday 6th
Japanese officials, wary of **trade blocks**, expressed doubts at Malaysian plans for an East Asian Economic Group. Malaysia's minister of trade and industry said in Tokyo that the group would complement, not compete with, existing organisations.

Monday 8th
Members of Taiwan's National Assembly threw documents, water and punches at each other at the opening of a session designed to reform a political structure dominated by elderly, often **senile, politicians** elected on the Chinese mainland over 40 years ago. The opposition said the reforms, pensioning off the mainland representatives, did not go far enough.

Arswendo Atmowiloto was sent to prison for five years for a **blasphemous gimmick**. In an Indonesian magazine he had published a popularity poll in which the Prophet Muhammad came 11th, behind men such as Saddam Hussein. Mr Arswendo, a Christian, came 10th.

Ichiro Ozawa, secretary-general of Japan's ruling Liberal Democratic Party, resigned after the LDP's official candidate was beaten in the previous day's Tokyo's gubernatorial election by the 80-year-old incumbent. Most pundits believed Mr Ozawa's demise would be only temporary.

Wednesday 10th
Imelda Marcos filed a $3.6m criminal and civil suit against the Philippines' foreign secretary. The widow of President Marcos complained that the government's refusal to give her a passport to return to the Philippines from America violated her constitutional rights.

Friday 12th
South Korea's defence minister suggested a pre-emptive attack against a suspected **nuclear-bomb plant** in North Korea. He later retracted, saying journalists had misinterpreted private remarks.

Monday 15th
Thailand's National Legislative Assembly, acting in a single sitting, changed the country's **unions** into associations with no right to strike. The assembly was appointed by the ruling military junta soon after the February 23rd coup.

Tuesday 16th
President Mikhail Gorbachev arrived in Tokyo for a three-day **summit** with Prime Minister Kaifu. The Soviet president was hoping for Japanese aid and investment. Mr Kaifu was hoping for the return of islands, at the southern end of the Kurile chain, seized by Soviet troops at the end of the second world war. Both men were disappointed.

Prime Minister Rabbie Namaliu said that during his absence on a visit to China the Papua New Guinea army had raided the rebel-held island of **Bougainville**. This came despite an agreed end to hostilities. The PNG provincial affairs minister called for those responsible for the raid to resign.

Wednesday 17th
The **Philippine Supreme Court ruled** that the government could not have voting rights for shares in the San Miguel Corporation, the Philippines' biggest company, seized from cronies of the late President Marcos. The ruling restored three seats on the board to Eduardo "Danding" Cojuangco, the estranged cousin of President Aquino.

Friday 19th
China protested that the meeting, two days earlier, between President Bush and the exiled Tibetan spiritual leader, the **Dalai Lama**, had "hurt the feelings of the Chinese people and harm our bilateral relations".

Saturday 20th
America announced it would establish an office in Hanoi to help search for Americans **missing in action** during the Vietnam war. Since the war ended in 1975 America has embargoed trade with Vietnam and mounted a diplomatic boycott to press for the recovery of the MIAs and a settlement to the Cambodian conflict.

Monday 22nd
Burma's armed forces' government officially ruled out any transfer of power to the parliament elected in May 1990. General Than Shwe said political parties in **Myanmar** (as Burma now calls itself) were "subversive" and "unfit to rule". Most leaders of the National League for Democracy, which won 80% of the parliament's 485 seats had been arrested since the election.

Friday 26th
Yasuhiro Nakasone, Japan's former prime minister, was welcomed back into the Liberal Democratic Party. He had resigned in 1989 after being implicated in the Recruit shares-for-favours scandal.

Saturday 27th
South Korea's interior minister resigned following the beating to death the previous day of a student demonstrator by Korean riot police. The killing sparked off widespread street **demonstrations** against the government of President Roh Tae Woo.

Sunday 28th
Taiwan sent a delegation from the "Strait Exchange Foundation" to Beijing "to establish channels for dialogue". Taiwan's President Lee Teng-hui was due formally to end the state of war with the communist mainland on May 1st.

Wednesday 1st
Capitalist Taiwan officially **ended its state of war** with communist mainland China. The decision meant that emergency measures could be lifted and Taiwan could become fully democratic, so ending the political stranglehold of old guard members of the Kuomintang elected on the mainland before the communist victory in 1949.

Thursday 2nd
A South Korean student died after setting himself on fire a day earlier. President **Roh Tae Woo apologised** for the police brutality that had sparked a week of violent student demonstrations.

Friday 3rd
Several members of the dissident **Petition of 50** group were refused permission to leave Indonesia. Apparently, they might have criticised Indonesia and so jeopardised the country's access to foreign aid. In banning their travel an official disclosed that 17,000 Indonesians were on a government blacklist.

Thailand lifted martial law. It had been imposed by the junta of General Sunthorn Kongsompong after the bloodless coup of February 23rd.

Thursday 9th
A spokesman said China was prepared to lose its **most-favoured nation** trading status with the United States rather than submit to pressure on human rights. The loss of MFN status would make China's exports to America liable to high tariffs. In 1990, China had a trade surplus with America of over $10 billion.

Saturday 11th
President Ranasinghe Premadasa's United National Party won a sweeping victory in **Sri Lanka's local elections**. The party claimed its victory was a vote of confidence in the war against the Tamil Tiger secessionists.

Sunday 12th
The **Kingdom of Nepal** held its first free, multiparty elections in 32 years. The prime minister, Krishna Prasad Bhattarai, unexpectedly lost to a communist. Although the pro-India Nepali Congress Party just won a majority, the strong showing of the communists, who resent India's influence, promised a difficult parliamentary session.

Monday 13th
Jeffrey Kitingan, a politician in the Malaysian state of Sabah, was arrested under the **Internal Security Act**. Malaysia's ruling United Malays National Organisation, which two days earlier had won its first ever by-election in Sabah, suspected a plot to take resource-rich Sabah out of the Malaysian federation.

In **Myanmar**, as the military regime calls Burma, 34 members of the National League for Democracy, including 24 elected MPs, were jailed for up to 25 years for treason. The party won a landslide victory in the election of May 1990, but the military then refused to let the parliament convene.

Wednesday 15th
Jiang Zemin became the first boss of the Chinese Communist Party to visit Moscow since Mao Zedong in 1957. His trip helped show that relations between **communism's two biggest powers** were normal after the tensions that followed the break in relations in 1961. Even so, there was little substance in the agreements signed with Mr Jiang.

The identity of Japan's next prime minister, after Toshiki Kaifu, became in doubt with the **death of Shintaro Abe**. The former foreign minister had been in line to succeed Mr Kaifu in October 1991. Many predicted the job would now go to Noboru Takeshita, who resigned as prime minister in 1989 amid a financial scandal.

Monday 20th
In talks with Japan conducted in Beijing, **North Korea** refused to open its nuclear facilities to international inspection. Japan said this was a condition for the normalisation of diplomatic ties.

Tuesday 21st
Former prime minister, **Rajiv Gandhi, was assassinated** near Madras, just one day after the first day of voting in the Indian general election. The two final days of voting were postponed until June. Whereas Rajiv's mother, Indira Gandhi, had been assassinated in 1984 by Sikhs, the suspects this time were Tamil extremists.

Wednesday 22nd
South Korea's prime minister, Ro Jai Bong, resigned. President Roh Tae Woo hoped that this, and later a cabinet reshuffle, might calm the annual spurt of student protest.

Thursday 23rd
British and Chinese officials admitted they had failed (for the time being) to agree on plans for **Hong Kong's new airport**. In return for its support, China wanted a say in all large Hong Kong decisions before 1997, when the British colony reverts to China.

Monday 27th
"Trying to chart a moral course through a world of lesser evils", President **George Bush** said he would renew most-favoured nation trade status for China for another year. It was certain that many in Congress would oppose the president, objecting to China's arms sales and poor record on human rights.

Tuesday 28th
North Korea announced it would follow South Korea and apply for separate **membership of the United Nations**. This reversal of policy followed a Soviet promise not to veto the South's application and by hints that China would not cast its veto either.

Wednesday 29th
India's Congress (I) Party named veteran politician **Narasimha Rao** as its president in place of the assassinated Rajiv Gandhi. Mr Rao, in poor health and not a contestant in the general election, was a compromise. The party had first offered the post to Mr Gandhi's Italian-born widow, Sonia. She refused.

Thursday 30th
Australia's treasurer (chief finance minister), Paul Keating, challenged the prime minister, Bob Hawke, to contest the **Labor Party's leadership**. Mr Hawke said a 1988 promise to step aside for Mr Keating after the 1990 election no longer held because Mr Keating, at Christmas 1990, had criticised his leadership.

June

Saturday 1st
Three officials dismissed after the 1989 crackdown on **China's democracy movement** were given deputy ministerial posts. They included Hu Qili, a former member of the Politburo Standing Committee. The next day, around 50,000 Hong Kong Chinese gathered to mourn those who died around Beijing's Tiananmen Square on June 3rd-4th 1989.

Sunday 2nd
Cambodia's prime minister, Hun Sen, agreed that Prince **Norodom Sihanouk**, leader of the Cambodian resistance movement, should head a Supreme National Council to guide the country pending elections.

Monday 3rd
Bob Hawke, Australia's prime minister since 1983, survived a challenge for the leadership of the Labor Party from the treasurer, Paul Keating. Many observers, however, believed Mr Hawke's victory would be Pyrrhic—and that Labor would, in any case, lose at the next general election, due by 1993.

Tuesday 4th
China officially admitted the death, by suicide at the age of 77, of **Jiang Qing**, the widow of Mao Zedong and a member of the disgraced "Gang of Four". Jiang had been imprisoned since 1976.

Thursday 6th
Pakistan's prime minister, Nawaz Sharif, called on America, the Soviet Union and China to sponsor talks on **nuclear non-proliferation** in South Asia. India set off a nuclear explosion in 1974. Fears of Pakistan's determination to match India led to a ban in 1990 on American military aid to Pakistan.

China strained Hong Kong's self-confidence by saying it reserved the right to scrap all of the British colony's laws after sovereignty is transferred to China in 1997. The Chinese government was angry at the passing of a **Bill of Rights** for the colony.

Friday 7th
North Korea said it was ready to discuss international inspection of its nuclear facilities. It was unclear whether the North would still insist on the removal of American nuclear weapons from South Korea.

Sunday 9th
Mount Pinatubo, a volcano extinct for six centuries, erupted in the Philippines, causing the evacuation of 14,500 Americans from the nearby Clark Field air base. The possibility of three more years of eruptions added new doubts to protracted negotiations to renew the lease on the American bases at Clark and Subic Bay.

Tuesday 11th
America's Central Intelligence Agency said a report it had commissioned on Japan did not reflect the views of the experts who had contributed to it. The CIA report, **Japan 2000**, said Japan was bent on "unequivocal economic dominance" of the world.

Indian paramilitary **troops rampaged** through the Kashmir capital, Srinagar, after one of them had been killed by a sniper. The result of this and other incidents on the same day was a death toll of 46 and the imposition of a curfew.

American officials said the United States would not resume **arms sales to Pakistan** until Pakistan proved it did not have a nuclear bomb and was not building one.

Thursday 13th
America's House of Representatives voted to halt all aid and **military sales to India,** unless it stopped making nuclear weapons.

A **Bangladesh tribunal** sentenced deposed President Ershad to ten years' jail for the illegal possession of guns.

Saturday 15th
The **Indian general election** ended. Congress emerged as the single biggest party but failed to win a majority because of the popularity of the pro-Hindu Bharatiya Janata Party. Voting, spread over three days, began on May 20th but after the murder of the Congress leader, Rajiv Gandhi, was then delayed until June 12th and 15th.

Monday 17th
China accused the Vatican of interfering in its affairs by appointing a dissident Chinese priest, Gong Pinmei, as cardinal. Cardinal Gong, 90, lives in exile in America. Formerly bishop of Shanghai, he was arrested in 1955 and spent 30 years in prison. The Vatican does not recognise China's communist government.

Wednesday 19th
Reginald Bartholomew, an American under-secretary of state, ended a visit to Beijing without getting a guarantee that **China** would not sell its missiles to Syria and Pakistan. He said, however, that China was considering signing the Nuclear Non-Proliferation Treaty.

Thursday 20th
India's Congress Party chose Narasimha Rao to be the **next prime minister.** Aged 70 and in ill-health, Rao did not stand in the parliamentary elections. Under the Indian constitution he was given six months to find a seat through a by-election.

Sunday 23rd
At a meeting in Pattaya, a Thai seaside resort, the Vietnam-backed Cambodian government and three guerrilla groups agreed to an indefinite **ceasefire** in their 12-year-old war. Two days later, the resistance groups' leader, Prince Norodom Sihanouk, said he would return to Cambodia to head a "super government" in Phnom Penh.

Tuesday 25th
Prime Minister Li Peng said China would stop buying Boeing airliners if America revoked China's **most-favoured-nation** trade status. President Bush had pledged to renew it, but was facing opposition because of China's poor human rights' record.

Wednesday 26th
The commander of **American forces in the Philippines** said the Subic Bay naval base and Clark Field air base would be repaired after damage from the Pinatubo volcano. The volcano had erupted as negotiations were close to conclusion on renewing the bases' lease, scheduled to expire in September.

Thursday 27th
Vietnam's Communist Party ended its seventh congress with a new leader and revamped Politburo. Do Muoi, 74, became party leader in place of Nguyen Van Linh, 76. Half the 12-man Politburo retired, including the anti-Chinese foreign minister, Nguyen Co Thach. The new, younger Politburo pledged to continue economic reform.

Monday 1st
The National People's Congress, China's parliament, decreed that in one year's time **smoking would be banned** in public places and on public transport. China is the world's biggest cigarette market, with over 200m smokers (the most famous being 86-year-old senior leader Deng Xiaoping).

Tuesday 2nd
Kim Jong Il, the son of North Korean dictator Kim Il Sung, was officially referred to not just as the "dear leader" but also as the "great leader"—a term hitherto reserved for his father. South Korea saw the description as evidence that Kim Il Sung was **preparing to step aside** for his son, for whom support in the armed forces is relatively weak.

The ruling **Bangladesh** Nationalist Party proposed a return to Westminster-style parliamentary democracy. One constitutional amendment would change the presidential system into a parliamentary one; a second amendment would allow the acting president, Shahabuddin Ahmed, to resume his job as chief justice.

North Korea formally applied for **United Nations' membership**. Previously, the North had refused to apply separately from South Korea, arguing that this would preserve the unacceptable division of the Korean peninsula.

Thursday 4th
Britain and China announced

agreement on a new **Hong Kong airport**. China's backing was needed to finance the airport, part of a scheme originally costed at $16.3 billion. Britain's prime minister, John Major, agreed to visit China. Hong Kong's fiscal reserves were not to be exhausted in 1997, when the colony reverts to China.

Friday 5th
Mumtaz Rathore, the former prime minister of the Pakistan-controlled **Azad Jammu and Kashmir**, was arrested in Islamabad a week after Kashmir's voters had swept him from power. Mr Rathore, a supporter of the former Pakistan prime minister, Benazir Bhutto, claimed the elections had been rigged against him by Pakistan.

The executive secretary of the **Philippines'** cabinet, Oscar Orbos, resigned, apparently to free himself for the presidential elections scheduled for May 1992. Six days later, the defence secretary, Fidel Ramos, resigned for the same reason.

Monday 8th
Former army commander Chaovalit Yongchaiyudh, head of the New Aspiration Party, warned **Thailand's** ruling military junta that it risked a popular revolt if it reneged on its promise to hold elections. The junta had ousted the corrupt civilian government of Chatichai Choonhavan in February.

Wednesday 10th
South Korea offered to open its military facilities simultaneously with **North Korea** if the North proved it was not developing nuclear weapons. The North had signed the Nuclear Non-Proliferation Treaty, but—pending the removal of American nuclear weapons from the South—not an accord allowing inspection of its facilities.

America's House of Representatives overwhelmingly voted to attach conditions, especially concerning human rights, to the renewal of **China**'s Most Favoured Nation trading status. A subsequent Senate vote, however, allowed President Bush to veto the conditions.

China opened its grain reserves to feed millions left homeless in the worst **flooding** in a decade. Officials said more than 200m people were in some way affected.

Friday 12th
A security van containing $21.5m-worth of banknotes was hijacked in Hong Kong's **biggest-ever armed robbery**. An innocent Taiwanese woman was questioned at the airport when $4m in cash was found in her carry-on bag.

Tuesday 16th
Thai officials decided to buy a $4m airship to monitor Bangkok's **traffic jams**, which are worsened by the addition of 400 new cars a day. Japan's solution was to impose a fine of $1,400 for overnight parking in a no-parking zone.

Wednesday 17th
America offered to pay aid and grants worth $203m a year to renew the lease on the Subic Bay naval base in the **Philippines** for another ten years. Other payments would add $350m in the first year. The Clark Field air base, covered in ash from the Mount Pinatubo volcano, was to be abandoned. The Philippines had earlier insisted—unrealistically—on $825m a year for a lease of only seven years.

Cambodia's warring factions agreed in Beijing to allow the United Nations to monitor their ceasefire. A Supreme National Council of the three guerrilla groups and the Vietnam-backed government in Phnom Penh would represent

Cambodia at the UN.

Monday 22nd
Taro Nakayama, Japan's foreign minister, told the six ASEAN foreign ministers meeting in Kuala Lumpur that ASEAN should hold annual **security talks** with Japan, Australia, New Zealand, South Korea, America, Canada and the EC. The ministers were unsure how to react. So was America.

The ASEAN ministers at their Kuala Lumpur meeting rejected western pleas for **economic sanctions against Myanmar**. Money earned by trade with, in particular, Thailand, has allowed the Burmese military junta to survive.

Tuesday 23rd
The **Social Democratic Party of Japan**, the leading opposition party (and formerly known as the Japan Socialist Party), chose the moderate **Makoto Tanabe** as its leader. His predecessor, Miss Takako Doi, resigned after poor election results. Mr Tanabe's willingness to allow a role for Japan's army was later blunted by party traditionalists.

America's secretary of state, James Baker, flew into **Mongolia** promising aid worth up to $25m. Earlier, he had appealed to rich Asian nations to help the economy of Mongolia, whose changes, he said, were "truly democratic".

Sunday 4th

Pakistan's former prime minister, Benazir Bhutto, led a **12-hour fast** protesting against legislation by her successor, Nawaz Sharif, to give the government sweeping powers against suspected criminals.

General Suchinda Krapayoon, leader of **Thailand**'s bloodless coup of February 23rd, assumed the post of supreme military commander. He replaced his fellow coup leader, General Sunthorn Kongsompong.

Monday 5th

Romulo Kintanar, commander of the communist New People's Army in the Philippines, was **captured** with his wife in a Manila hospital. They had been captured before, in March 1988, but had escaped during the senior warden's birthday party.

American officials said that photographs from Soviet magazines had been doctored to appear as Americans **missing in action** in Vietnam. Almost 2,300 Americans are listed as MIAs in Indochina.

Tuesday 6th

The mayor of Hiroshima apologised for Japan's aggression in the **second world war**. A few days later a Japanese government spokesman said America, as well as Japan, should apologise for the war in the Pacific.

Wednesday 7th

The ruling party of **Vanuatu** voted to replace Walter Lini as its president and so as the

prime minister of the Pacific nation. Mr Lini, party leader since independence in 1980, said the vote was illegal and refused to step down.

Sunday 11th

Japan's prime minister, Toshiki Kaifu, laid a wreath at the Hero's Monument in Beijing's Tiananmen Square. A day earlier, China announced it would sign the Nuclear Non-Proliferation Treaty. Mr Kaifu's visit symbolised **China's rehabilitation** after the bloodshed of June 1989.

Friday 16th

Thailand, source of much of the world's opium, passed a law to permit the freezing and confiscation of the assets of suspected **drug traffickers**.

Indonesia released 226 detainees suspected of being guerrillas fighting for the secession of Aceh, a province of Sumatra noted for its Muslim fundamentalism.

Monday 19th

A court in Seoul **imprisoned five police officers** who had beaten a student to death in a campus protest in April. The killing sparked weeks of riots across South Korea.

Tuesday 20th

Two Chinese Red Cross officials arrived in **Taiwan** to see 18 fishermen from China detained in Taiwan. The visit was the first by officials from the mainland since 1949, when China's Kuomintang government under Chiang Kai-shek arrived in Taiwan in flight from Mao's communists.

A Tamil suspected of planning the assassination of Rajiv Gandhi was found dead, with six companions. Their suicide, in a house in Bangalore surrounded by police, ended a **three-month manhunt** among Tamils in India.

Wednesday 21st

As nominations closed, **Singapore's opposition** conceded the ruling People's Action Party a majority in the general election set for August 31st. The opposition, with only one elected member of parliament, decided to concentrate its efforts by nominating candidates to only 40 of the 81 seats at stake.

Sunday 25th

South Korea said it had asked Japan to be discreet in its **normalisation talks** with North Korea. The South believed that such normalisation should await progress in the dialogue between the two Koreas and a decision by the North to open its nuclear facilities to international inspection.

Tuesday 27th

The Philippines' government agreed that America could use the **naval base at Subic Bay** for another ten years in return for $203m a year in American aid to its former colony. But the deal was subject to approval by two-thirds of the Philippine senate. With elections due in May 1992, it seemed unlikely that the senate would change a nationalistic stance against the base.

Meeting at the Thai resort of Pattaya, the Vietnam-backed government of **Cambodia** and the three Cambodian resistance groups agreed to reduce their armies by 70% and to put the remaining troops under UN control. The decision was another sign of progress by the rival Cambodian leaders towards peace after 12 years of war.

Wednesday 28th

The **Asia-Pacific Economic Co-operation** forum announced that China, Taiwan and Hong Kong would all be eligible to attend the third session of APEC in Seoul in November. Taiwan would attend as "Chinese Taipei". APEC

was founded under an Australian initiative to link the countries around the Pacific, but China's political sensitivities had prevented comprehensive membership.

A **motion to impeach** President Ranasinghe Premadasa was presented to the speaker of Sri Lanka's parliament accusing the president of a gross abuse of power. Many MPs believed that executive presidency should be abolished. Mr Premadasa decided to suspend parliament until September 24th to give would-be impeachers a chance to change their minds.

Friday 30th

Soviet President Mikhail Gorbachev sent a letter to South Korea's President Roh Tae Woo. In answer to **South Korean congratulations** on surviving the abortive coup of August 19th, Mr Gorbachev asked for "practical support" for the Soviet economy.

Saturday 31st

In **Singapore's general election** the People's Action Party saw its share of the vote fall to 61% from 63% in 1988. Moreover, four opposition members were elected, compared with one before. Prime minister **Goh Chok Tong** said the result was a setback for his liberal style. He had threatened during the election campaign to reduce public services to constituencies that voted against the PAP.

September

Monday 2nd
Britain's prime minister, John Major, shook hands in Beijing with Li Peng, so becoming the first western leader to visit **China** since the Tiananmen bloodshed of June 1989. Critics called the visit, made to sign an agreement for a new airport in Hong Kong, a kowtow. He responded by attacking China over human rights.

Tuesday 3rd
Singapore said it would allow the *Asian Wall Street Journal* to raise its circulation from 400 copies a day to 2,500. Complaining about unfair reporting by the foreign press, Singapore had four years earlier cut the newspaper's sales from 5,000 a day.

Thursday 5th
Australia's defence minister said that, because of the end of the cold war and a smaller American presence in the region, the country's **military budget** could not be cut. As "middle powers" filled the vacuum, he said, "that could threaten the stability of our region."

Sunday 8th
South Korean television said that China's senior leader, Deng Xiaoping, had sent a message to the South Korean government calling for full **diplomatic relations**. China, a close ally of communist North Korea, had nonetheless developed greater trade over the years with the capitalist South.

Monday 9th
Vietnam's foreign minister, Nguyen Manh Cam, began a five-day visit to China, paving the way for normal **Sino-Viet-namese relations** 11 years after the two countries fought a brief border war after Vietnam's invasion of Cambodia.

The Philippine senate, sitting in committee, voted 12-11 against a new 10-year lease agreed by the government for America's **military base** at **Subic Bay**. The senators maintained their opposition in a formal vote a week later, despite the jobs and financial aid that the lease would bring.

Wednesday 11th
Japan said it was considering a plan to give "**tacit**" **recognition** to North Korea when the two Koreas separately joined the United Nations on September 17th. A spokesman said this would encourage the North to be a responsible member of the world community.

Jiang Zeming, boss of the Chinese Communist Party, warned the party to "exercise **absolute leadership**" over the army". Mr Jiang's speech, carried by the state-run newspapers, was apparently prompted by the failure of the Soviet army to back the August coup against President Gorbachev.

Thursday 12th
Communist insurgents in the Philippines declared a **unilateral ceasefire** in support of senators opposed to America's continued military presence at the Subic Bay naval base.

Friday 13th
America and the Soviet Union agreed to cut off their military aid to Afghanistan by January 1st. The **arms embargo** seemed more likely to hurt the government in Kabul, hitherto a Soviet protégé. America's clients, the mujaheddin, had alternative suppliers in Pakistan and Saudi Arabia. On the other hand, the government had massive military stockpiles.

Four researchers from China's Academy of Social Sciences, a leading think-tank, began a month-long visit, paid by the Ford Foundation, to study **human rights** in America and Canada. China had traditionally pooh-poohed the western concept.

Sunday 15th
The liberal-minded United Democrats won a landslide victory in the **first ever direct elections** to Hong Kong's Legislative Council. Candidates backed by China were all defeated. But the elections covered only 18 of the council's 60 seats. Of the 3.6m eligible to vote, just half registered—and of these only 39% voted.

Monday 16th
The Philippine Senate formally rejected a new lease for America's naval base at **Subic Bay**. Constitutionally, the lease needed to be ratified by a two-thirds Senate majority. President Aquino talked of a national referendum to change the Senate's mind. The confusion worsened when she revoked an earlier eviction notice on the Americans.

Tuesday 17th
Robert Gates, President Bush's nominee to be the new boss of the CIA, told a Senate committee that there should be **more American spies** in China. This, he said, was the lesson to be drawn from events in the Soviet Union.

Hong Kong and Vietnam agreed to resume direct **air links**, which were broken in 1975 after the Vietnam war. The decision was thought to be connected to a tentative agreement for the repatriation of Hong Kong's Vietnamese boat people, currently numbering over 64,000.

Wednesday 18th
Japan's ruling Liberal Democratic Party said it would support legislation to allow Japan to provide troops for UN **peacekeeping** operations. This would reverse a post-war ban on the dispatch of soldiers overseas.

Monday 23rd
President Aquino abandoned her call for a national referendum to extend America's stay at the Subic Bay naval base. Senators opposed to the base had threatened to impeach her. Nonetheless, an immediate **American withdrawal** seemed unlikely, which meant the base would become an issue in the 1992 elections.

Tuesday 24th
Taiwan's legislature opened a new session in such **uproar** that the prime minister, Hau Pei-tsun, had to deliver his address from behind a cordon of security men.

Thursday 26th
India's Congress government said it accepted recommendations, made ten years earlier, reserving 27% of government jobs to "backward" castes, in addition to the 22.5% already reserved for untouchables and tribal people. **Positive discrimination** had been a demand of the opposition Janata Dal, and in 1990 had caused widespread bloodshed.

Monday 30th
A Japanese parliamentary committee decided to scrap an electoral reform package on which **Toshiki Kaifu** had staked his future as prime minister. Mr Kaifu threatened to call a general election—a fit of anger which then forced him to abandon his plan to stand again for his party's presidency and the accompanying prime ministerial term.

Wednesday 2nd

In a cabinet reshuffle New Zealand's prime minister, Jim Bolger, **sacked** his minister of Maori Affairs, Winston Peters, who had been a critic of the government's free-market economic policy.

President Aquino reached an agreement with the Philippine Senate that American troops should have three years in which to leave the **Subic Bay** naval base. There was no obligation for the Americans to pay compensation, although earlier they had offered at least $2.18 billion in aid in return for a new ten-year lease.

Diplomats said Vietnam had tentatively agreed to accept the forcible return from Hong Kong of **boat people** found not to be genuine refugees. Of the 64,000 boat people in Hong Kong, only a minority were likely to qualify as refugees, with a right to settlement in the West.

Thursday 3rd

Japan's finance minister, Ryutaro Hashimoto, said he would **resign** after the annual meeting of the IMF later in the month. He accepted that his ministry should have prevented a recent series of Japanese financial scandals.

Sunday 6th

Police said Indian troops, seeking to combat Muslim separatism, killed ten people in house-to-house searches in **Kashmir**. Witnesses said the troops fired on unarmed civilians.

A team from Western Samoa, a nation of just 170,000, beat the Welsh team in Cardiff in the **rugby** world cup.

Monday 7th

The speaker of Sri Lanka's parliament dismissed an **impeachment** resolution against President Ranasinghe Premadasa, saying there were not enough valid signatures. The resolution had accused the president of abusing his power.

Francis Seow, a former solicitor-general, was found **guilty in absentia** by a Singapore court of tax evasion. Mr Seow has been a constant critic of the government.

Thursday 10th

America opened an investigation into **China's trade barriers**. China had dismissed American complaints over the rise of its trade surplus with America, expected to rise from $10 billion in 1990 to over $15 billion in 1991.

China rejected an offer by the **Dalai Lama** to return to Tibet to help prevent violence by Tibetan nationalists. The Chinese said the Dalai Lama, who went into exile in 1959, must first renounce the call for Tibet's independence.

Friday 11th

Shin Kanemaru and Noboru Takeshita, the two most powerful men in Japan's ruling Liberal Democratic Party, agreed that **Kiichi Miyazawa** should become the LDP's next president, and so Japan's next prime minister.

Saturday 12th

Sonia Gandhi, the widow of the assassinated former prime minister, Rajiv Gandhi, formally declined to contest a by-election in the Amethi constituency. Her decision meant that for the first time in India's 44 years of independence there would be no presence in parliament for the Nehru-Gandhi family.

Monday 14th

The **Nobel peace prize** was awarded to Aung San Suu Kyi, the leader of Myanmar's opposition. Because she had been placed under house arrest by the military junta in July 1989, it was not known whether she knew of her prize.

The Soviet Union announced an immediate reduction in its military presence on four islands, occupied in 1945, at the southern end of the **Kurile** chain. The islands are claimed by Japan, which the week before had promised the Soviet Union $2.5 billion in aid.

Vietnam's prime minister, Vo Van Kiet, told *Le Monde* that **non-communists** would be allowed to join the Vietnamese government.

Tuesday 15th

China said it had begun work rebuilding the **railway** to Vietnam. The link, across Friendship Pass, was destroyed during a brief border war in 1979, when China attacked Vietnam because of its occupation of Cambodia.

Wednesday 16th

The UN asked Thailand to deploy troops to stop **Khmer Rouge** guerrillas from forcing refugees to return to Cambodia from camps in Thailand. Influencing the 350,000 refugees would be important in any future Cambodian election.

Hong Kong officials admitted that an agreement for the repatriation of Vietnamese **boat people** had been delayed. Some boat people still threatened to commit suicide rather than be forced back to Vietnam.

Two bombs in Rampur, in northern India, killed 55 people. The **terrorism** was attributed to Sikh separatists.

Monday 21st

Singapore refused to accept ten **Vietnamese boat people** who had been picked up at sea by a Panamanian-registered ship. Officials said this was because two western countries (thought to be Norway and Holland) had not fulfilled promises to resettle 148 boat people already there.

Tuesday 22nd

A government spokesman said China's legislature would approve China's accession to the **Nuclear Non-Proliferation Treaty** at a session beginning on October 25th. As it turned out, he was lying.

Wednesday 23rd

The government in Phnom Penh, the three Cambodian resistance factions and 18 governments signed a **peace accord** in Paris to end 13 years of civil war in Cambodia. Few signatories, however, expected a smooth process towards free and fair elections.

Sunday 27th

Kiichi Miyazawa was elected leader of the Liberal Democratic Party, and so **Japan's prime minister-designate**. A fluent speaker of English, he resigned as finance minister in December 1988 over a corruption scandal.

Tuesday 29th

Britain and Vietnam finally signed an agreement that would allow for the **forced repatriation** of Vietnamese boat people from Hong Kong.

Friday 1st
Anwar Ibrahim announced a **Malaysian budget** promising economic growth of 8.5% in 1992. Critics, accusing Mr Ibrahim of trying to win popularity in his party's conference in 1992, said the economy would overheat.

Sunday 3rd
Myanmar denied reports that the winner of the Nobel peace prize, **Aung San Suu Kyi**, under house arrest since July 1989, was critically ill. Two days earlier, the Nobel awards committee in Oslo had said she was on hunger strike.

Monday 4th
After almost six years' exile in America, **Imelda Marcos** returned to the Philippines. The government of Corazon Aquino had allowed her return in order to file criminal charges against her. These would be part of an effort to recover $350m illegally banked in Switzerland by Mrs Marcos and the late President Ferdinand Marcos.

Zahir Shah, the 77-year-old exiled **king of Afghanistan**, was stabbed at his villa in Rome, but not seriously injured. Some Afghans believed that the king, who had been deposed in 1973 after ruling for 40 years, should assume a role in the emerging peace settlement for Afghanistan.

Taiwan's prime minister held **private talks** with the Democratic Progressive Party. There have been frequent brawls in parliament between the DPP, many of whose members re-

nounce Taiwan's claim to China, and the ruling Kuomintang over the pace of democracy.

Tuesday 5th
Do Muoi, leader of Vietnam's Communist party, and Vietnam's prime minister, Vo Van Kiet, arrived in Beijing for five days of talks. The visit marks a **normalisation** of Sino-Vietnamese relations, soured in 1979 by a brief border war.

Storm-driven **floods** swept through the central Philippines, killing at least 2,000 people (later estimates said 7,000) on the island of Leyte. Illegal logging, precipitating landslides, was blamed.

Wednesday 6th
After the king of Bhutan said he could not attend for reasons of domestic security, Sri Lanka **cancelled** the summit scheduled for the next day of the seven-nation South Asian Association for Regional Cooperation. It was thought that India had decided to undermine the meeting and was behind Bhutan's action.

Japan and other Asian countries expressed surprise at President Bush's decision to cancel **a trip to Asia** planned for the end of the month. The president was worried about his poor rating in recent American opinion polls.

Saturday 9th
Hong Kong bundled 59 Vietnamese **boat people** on to a Hercules aircraft for the first forced repatriation of boat people since December 1989.

Sunday 10th
A group of 37 Australian soldiers arrived in Phnom Penh, the first UN **peacekeepers** provided for in the Cambodian settlement signed in Paris in October. They were armed with pistols and the promise of 1.5 tonnes of lager to come.

Monday 11th
America's secretary of state, **James Baker**, began an Asian tour in Tokyo by telling Japan to be more active in promoting democracy and free trade. But the greater thrust of his trip was to arrange international pressure to halt North Korea's nuclear programme.

Tuesday 12th
Indonesian troops opened fire at a funeral in **East Timor**, killing around 50 mourners. Indonesia occupied the island after Portugal withdrew in 1975. The occupation was not recognised by the UN and was resisted by Fretilin guerrillas.

Thursday 14th
To greetings from jubilant crowds in Phnom Penh, Prince Norodom **Sihanouk** returned to Cambodia after 13 years' exile. However, the newly-arrived American envoy said the Khmers Rouges could still come to power if the impoverished countryside were kept in neglect.

Friday 15th
In a communiqué signed in Moscow, representatives of the Soviet Union and the Afghan mujaheddin agreed that Afghanistan's Soviet-backed **President Najibullah** should hand over to an "Islamic" interim government. The same communiqué also denounced the 1979 occupation of Afghanistan by Soviet troops.

Sunday 17th
India's prime minister, **Narasimha Rao**, won a parliamentary by-election by 580,000 votes—the biggest margin ever in any democracy. Mr Rao became the leader of the Congress Party after the assassination in May of Rajiv Gandhi. By law he had to become a member of parliament within six months of becoming a minister.

James Baker ended a trip to China having made little

progress on **human rights**. China made only small concessions to the American secretary of state on weapons sales and trade.

Wednesday 20th
Amid hints of pre-emptive military action, American and South Korean defence officials said North Korea's **nuclear arms** programme must be stopped "in advance, without fail." The following day, America halted its long-planned troop reductions in South Korea.

Thursday 21st
Holland **suspended aid** to Indonesia pending an explanation of the massacre earlier in the month in East Timor.

Monday 25th
Japan agreed to reduce its **drift-net fishing** by 50% from June 30th and to stop it by the end of 1992. Ecologists accused Japan, Taiwan and South Korea of destroying fish stocks by using nets up to 65 km (40 miles) long.

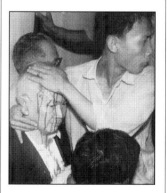

Wednesday 27th
His head streaming with blood, **Khieu Samphan**, the nominal leader of the Khmers Rouges, was forced to return to Bangkok only hours after arriving in Phnom Penh. Angry Cambodians had almost lynched him, holding him partly responsible for perhaps as many as a million deaths. The Khmers Rouges said they would still stay with the peace process.

Monday 2nd

Hong Kong officials announced that in November only 7 Vietnamese **boat people** had arrived in the British colony—compared with more than 300 in November 1990. The drop followed the introduction of forced repatriation for Hong Kong's boat people, who now numbered some 56,000.

Australia declared a large part of its longest river system a natural disaster. Over 1,000 km (620 miles) of the Darling River in New South Wales, the country's most populous state, was clogged with **toxic algae**, causing havoc for farmers.

The francophone Union of Moderate Parties was the biggest winner in a general election in **Vanuatu**, with 19 out of 46 parliamentary seats. By mid-week it agreed on a coalition with the Anglophone National United Party. Maxime Carlot became the country's first French-speaking prime minister.

Tuesday 3rd

Japan's foreign minister, Michio Watanabe, expressed "deep **remorse** over the unbearable suffering and sorrow Japan inflicted" by starting a war with America 50 years earlier. He added that Japan was not seeking an apology for the American atom bombs dropped on Hiroshima and Nagasaki.

The lower house of Japan's Diet (parliament) broke new constitutional ground by passing a bill allowing troops to join UN **peacekeeping forces** overseas. However, political ineptness by the prime minister seemed to presage the bill's defeat in the upper house.

Wednesday 4th

For the first time in Hong Kong's colonial history the Legislative Council **rejected** a British decree. It voted against an agreement by Britain and China limiting to one the number of foreign judges on the five-man Court of Final Appeal, which will be set up when British rule ends in 1997. It argued more foreigners would help judicial independence.

Thursday 5th

Prince Sihanouk said the political alliance between the Cambodian faction led by his son, Prince Ranariddh, and the regime in Phnom Penh of Hun Sen had been dropped. This followed opposition from other Cambodian factions and from China.

Friday 6th

Australia's prime minister, **Bob Hawke**, replaced his treasurer (finance minister) John Kerin with Ralph Willis. After 8 years in office Mr Hawke's Labor Party government had become very unpopular because of the country's worst recession in 60 years.

Saturday 7th

Thailand's National Legislative Assembly, appointed by the military junta, passed the kingdom's 15th **constitution**. The senate, also military appointees, would now be able, with the help of only 46 MPs, to topple a government. Elections were planned for March, but critics said the new constitution would in fact prolong military power.

Monday 9th

The chief of Indonesia's armed forces, General Try Sutrisno, vowed to "wipe out all separatist elements" once a government inquiry had been completed into the November 12th **massacre** in East Timor, a former Portuguese colony which was occupied by Indonesia in 1975.

Tuesday 10th

Troops in Myanmar (Burma) broke up student demonstrations in support of **Aung San Suu Kyi**. The demonstrations, the first since the democracy movement was crushed in 1988, were on the day that the detained politician should have been collecting her Nobel peace prize.

Wednesday 11th

Murli Manohar Joshi, president of the Bharatiya Janata Party, began a "unity pilgrimage", to go from India's southern tip to Kashmir. Critics said it was an appeal to **Hindu chauvinism** which would lead to communal violence. The BJP said the aim was to unite against secessionism.

Li Peng became China's first prime minister for 31 years to visit India. His five-day trip made little progress over the two countries' border disputes, but India, which gives sanctuary to Tibetan refugees, did affirm that it considered **Tibet** to be part of China.

Thursday 12th

The Philippine Senate **ousted** Jovito Salonga as its president, replacing him with Neptali Gonzalez. Mr Salonga, the leader of the Liberal Party and a probable candidate in the 1992 presidential election, had been criticised for obstructing urgent government bills.

Friday 13th

South Korea and the economically desperate North signed a **non-aggression pact**, 38 years after the end of the Korean war. The South, which later said there were no longer any nuclear weapons on its soil, said ratification of the pact would depend on the North opening its nuclear industry to inspection.

Wednesday 18th

Japan's ruling Liberal Democratic Party dropped plans for a new tax to finance more foreign aid. This was seen as a new **setback** for the prime minister, Kiichi Miyazawa.

Thursday 19th

After 8 years in office and four election victories for the Australian Labor Party, Bob Hawke was **deposed** as Australia's prime minister by his parliamentary colleagues and replaced by Paul Keating. Australia was suffering its worst recession for 60 years.

Saturday 21st

Taiwan's ruling Kuomintang (Nationalist Party) won 71% of the vote in an **election** for a new National Assembly. The pro-independence Democratic Progressive Party won a disappointing 24% of the vote.

Sunday 29th

China's National People's Congress authorised the government to sign the **Nuclear Nonprofileration Treaty**. America had accused China of exporting nuclear technology.

Monday 30th

A month after being nearly lynched by protesters **Khieu Samphan**, official leader of the Khmers Rouges, returned to the Cambodian capital, Phnom Penh, for a meeting of the Supreme National Council. Son Sen, the other Khmer Rouge representative on the council, did not return.

Tuesday 31st

North and South Korea agreed to ban **nuclear weapons** from their divided peninsula and to submit their nuclear facilities to mutual inspection.

As we reported then

Two voices

JANUARY 5TH *The memory of Tiananmen Square still haunts China's ageing leadership. For arch-conservatives, the year's paramount need was for a return to orthodoxy. But this would nullify more than a decade of economic reform by China's senior leader, Deng Xiaoping*

GREETINGS for the new year to the Chinese readers of the *People's Daily*:

It is imperative to persist in the four cardinal principles [adherence to socialism, the dictatorship of the proletariat, the leadership of the Communist Party, and Marxism-Leninism and Mao Zedong thought], oppose bourgeois liberalisation, smash the 'peaceful evolution' schemes of antagonistic international forces and inspire patriotism and socialist consciousness.

Greetings, too, from President Yang Shangkun to the foreign listeners of Radio Beijing:

China continues to open its door wide to the entire world, and friends from around the world are welcome to visit China.

Over the next ten years, China will become economically more liberal, internationally more friendly:

The leadership is guiding the Chinese people to implement firmly the reform and open policy put forward by Deng Xiaoping.

Since "bourgeois liberalisation" is code for western, capitalist influences, and since "peaceful evolution" is code for the capitalist subversion of communism, perhaps Mr Yang forgot to read his newspaper. More likely, China is still trying to reconcile the irreconcilable: Marxism with a market economy, central control with the reality of powerful politicians in the provinces. The *People's Daily* tells the Chinese what they are supposed to believe; Mr Yang tells foreigners what he would like them to believe.

How long this muddle can last is anyone's guess. It was supposed to be resolved at the long-awaited, and delayed, meeting in Beijing of the party's Central Committee on December 25th-30th. Some 171 full members and 107 alternate members (with 300 other sundry officials looking on)

met to agree on the new "proposals for the ten-year programme (1991-2000) and eighth five-year plan (1991-95)". In practice, they agreed only to more muddle.

The communiqué offered plenty of jargon. "The responsibility system with the household contract linking output to payment as the main form is in keeping with the present level of the productive forces in China's rural areas and must be maintained as a basic system for a long time to come ... Further efforts should be made to enhance the vitality of the enterprises, especially the large and medium-sized state-run enterprises ... It is necessary to handle properly the relations between the central and the local authorities."

The simple translation is, first, that the 750m people in the countryside, including 90m who work in what amount to private

factories, cannot be sent back to the commune, however much China's old-guard ideologues might wish. They must be allowed to make profits in a free market that co-exists with the planned economy. Second, the state will continue to prop up inefficient state enterprises. This may mean forcing the worst of them to merge with the best; it will certainly mean a widening of China's budget deficit. Third, the state will attempt to squeeze more tax revenue from provinces intent on keeping as much money as possible for themselves.

The less simple translation is that the battle continues between economic reformists and those hardliners, led politically by the prime minister, Li Peng, and ideologically by the 86-year-old Chen Yun, who believe that quick reform leads only too quickly to bourgeois liberalisation and peaceful evolution—witness the student democrats in 1989 in Beijing's Tiananmen Square and the collapse of communism in the countries of Eastern Europe.

In which case, who is winning? It is tempting to pick the reformers. The seventh five-year plan just ended may have had its ups and downs, producing high growth in the first half of the plan's period, followed by inflation and then austerity in the second half, but overall it was a success: the economy grew by 7.5% a year, incomes for city-dwellers almost doubled and last year's grain harvest was the biggest ever. The province of Guangdong, the five special economic zones and the 14 "open cities" are proof of the plan's promise to bring prosperity through economic liberalism. Last month Shanghai even launched a computerised stock exchange.

But if the reformers are in the ascendant, why did their fragile 86-year-old leader, Deng Xiaoping, find it necessary to make an appearance on December 26th at a local election? Given that Chinese elections have no element of uncertainty and that Mr Deng had not appeared in public for almost six months, perhaps he felt the reformers on the Central Committee were in urgent need of help. Mr Li has made it plain that there will be no more special economic zones in the next ten years, and the praise in the communiqué for the Dengist reforms smacks of ritual.

The most likely surmise is that the hardliners are now more powerful than the reformers, but are unable to press home their advantage. The reason they are more powerful is that economic liberalism did, indeed, help cause the tumult of 1989, by inspiring a dangerous mix—an overheated

economy, rampant corruption and rejection of the party. Equally to the hardliners' point, Mr Gorbachev's Soviet Union is a discouraging example of what happens when the party loosens its control of the economy and the people.

But the reason they cannot press on to victory is transparent: the central planning dear to people like Mr Li and Mr Chen stands no chance of coping with 20m or more urban unemployed, a labour force that will grow by 95m in the next five years

and rising expectations of wealth. The Central Committee reaffirmed an old pledge by Mr Deng: China's GNP will quadruple between 1980 and the end of the century. So far, China is more or less on course. But to remain so, it will have to give the market its freedom: no more fixed prices, no more production quotas, no more refusal to let bad enterprises go bust. Until then the eighth plan, due to be rubber-stamped in March by the National People's Congress, will be planning only muddle.

Indonesia's Muslim dilemma

FEBRUARY 23RD, JAKARTA *As the leader for 25 years of the world's largest Muslim country, President Suharto's political skills are not in doubt. Nonetheless, those skills faced a new test in the aftermath of the American-led war against Iraq*

THE Javanese have a legendary fruit called the *simalakama*. It kills your mother if you eat it and your father if you don't. Indonesia's President Suharto, a good Javanese, may ruefully be recalling the legend these days as he ponders over what attitude to take about the Gulf war. America, Japan and the other allies fighting Iraq provide the investment and aid money that supports Mr Suharto's ambitious development programmes. On the other hand he does not want to jeopardise his shadowy courtship of Indonesia's 160m Muslims.

Well, maybe not 160m. All Indonesians must have their chosen god stamped on their identity card. (This precludes them from being irreligious communists.) Some 90% choose Islam, but many chain-smoking, beer-drinking "ID-card Muslims" are less than fanatical about their faith.

They are, however, almost universally cross about the bombing of their brethren in

Iraq, the schooling ground for many of Indonesia's brightest Muslims. (There is little love lost, on the other hand, for Kuwait, whose price-busting oil policy hit Indonesia and other producers.) Whether or not they support Saddam Hussein's call for a holy war, there is a feeling that Islam should be solid for Iraq. Add in the poor world's anti-Americanism and the mixture is potent: no one was very surprised that a bomb was planted in the American ambassador's residence in Jakarta soon after the war began. The demonstrators against the war in the streets of the capital are using the weapon of Islamic solidarity to have a go at the western powers, and some are indirectly critical of Mr Suharto, who is assumed to be the West's friend.

The 69-year-old president is well aware of the potential of Islam as a political tool, and during his 25 years in power has done his best to regulate the influence of Muslim

politicians. Muslim political parties were involved in regional rebellions during the rule of President Sukarno in the 1950s. By 1973 Mr Suharto had forced the Islamic parties into a single body—the United Development Party, whose leaders were carefully screened. This screening proved so uncomfortable for the group's largest component, the Nahdatul Ulama (NU) that, in 1984, it pulled out of competitive politics altogether.

The NU, a conservative, village-based organisation, turned to school-building and social work instead. Mr Suharto has been tempting it back into his orbit by, for example, encouraging a Chinese business group to help it set up a bank, thus giving the NU's members a useful stake in the economic largesse that the government can dispense.

Golkar, Mr Suharto's own political grouping, has also done its bit to co-opt Islam. Its coalition of bureaucrats, soldiers and other groups includes Muslim youth organisations and Islamic advisory councils. The Muslim organisations that remain outside the fold, such as Muhammadiyah, an NU group with modernist ideas, dare not dabble in politics. (Nevertheless, Mr Suharto's step-brother, Probosutedjo, recently gave a lecture to a Muhammadiyah conference in which he argued the need to re-elect the president in 1992.)

Not content even with this level of political castration, Mr Suharto has instructed the security forces to keep a close watch on what is said in mosques. Preachers are paid to speak about the wisdom of Pancasila, the state philosophy. The army stamps with efficiency on any uppity religious leaders. Soldiers wiped out a village in south Sumatra's Lampung province in 1989 because a zealot was thought to be preaching fundamentalism (it has emerged he was just griping about land ownership).

With the lucrative business contracts that used to keep the generals happy being diverted to Mr Suharto's children, his military power-base is developing cracks, although so far they are barely perceptible. If the army is going to be troublesome, Mr Suharto needs the Muslim masses clearly on his side to ensure he will have his way in next year's election. Even if he stands aside, which is unlikely, he will want to retain the privilege of picking his successor.

To this end Mr Suharto has a number of gifts to distribute. One was handed out last week. Pupils in state schools were given permission to wear the *jilbab* headscarves that are the badge of good Muslim women. For years the headscarf was frowned upon on the ground that it encouraged dissent among children of different religions.

State banks, much to their chagrin, have been ordered to provide cheap insurance for pilgrims to Mecca: some 800 Indonesians died in the *haj* last year. The government has announced with great fanfare the

formation of Islamic courts for Muslim marital and social disputes. In fact, according to lawyers, the new courts are little different to the ones they replace, but they appear to be generally welcomed.

Such concessions are designed for the Muslims who make up Indonesia's poor rural majority. More educated Indonesians, though, expect more sophisticated prizes. With this in mind, Mr Suharto has encouraged the formation of the Indonesian Association of Muslim Intellectuals, a group of thinkers, many of them educated in the West and several of them cabinet ministers. Mr Suharto has been criticised for having too many Christians in his circle, among them the defence minister, some of his economic advisers and Chinese tycoons who control four-fifths of the country's private

industry. The new association is a way of drawing attention to the Muslim technocrats around the president.

Thinking about the dilemma captured in *simalakama* legend, Mr Suharto has clearly decided that, if he has to make a choice between wooing the Muslims and placating the West over the Gulf, the Muslims will have his full attention. The Americans do not like receiving frequent reports of pro-Iraqi demonstrations throughout the Islamic world. But, like the anti-war protests even in America's ally Japan, they do not have any effect on the course of the war. That being so, the West can shrug its shoulders and live with them. For his part, Mr Suharto can tell himself that the war will not be a lasting problem. Keeping his Muslims loyal will be.

Japan's pampered children

FEBRUARY 9TH, TOKYO *Not surprisingly, the world's most successful economy has begun to suffer the problems of affluence—especially among its young. The generation gap splits the Japanese family*

THE Japanese child is not as its parents were: disciplined, spartan in habit, perfect in every way. According to a report about children between the ages of four and nine now being studied by the Japanese cabinet, little Kazu is more than a bit spoilt. At least half of the 695,600 children in the study have their own televisions, radios and tape recorders. A third have their own telephones.

The good news in the report is that children are taller than they used to be because they are getting more to eat. Desks and chairs in Japan's 47,000 state schools have had to be made bigger to accommodate the new intake of pupils. But many of the children are overweight. This may be due to a change in diet—less rice, more junk food—and because the children lack exercise. For the many who live in high-rise apartments, a park may be only a picture in a book. Some children told researchers that they had never picked flowers. They also seem to lead solitary lives. Their favourite "game" is watching television.

All this is worrying to a government concerned that the new generation is going to be disturbingly unpredictable in its attitude to work. But it hardly needs a psychiatrist to explain why the changes have happened. Little Kazu is being indulged with all his expensive

toys simply because his parents are trying to make up to him for the restrictions of urban living.

The signs are that indulged children tend to become unmanageable when they reach their teens. "They have no interest in anything," says Dr Kiyoshi Ogura, a child expert. "They live from day to day with no goal in life." Dr Ogura blames women who are more interested in advancing their careers than mothering their young children.

Spare the yen and slim the child

These are left (like many of their western counterparts) for most of the day and part of the evening in pre-school nurseries.

The strains on Japanese children have been a talking point for years. Until recently, though, criticism has mainly been confined to the rigid educational system. The education ministry acknowledged the problem and proposed to ease the curriculum in state schools. But parents were against such reforms. Some were alarmed enough to move their children to strictly run private schools. They took the view that, however materially indulgent home life might be, school life should remain rigidly tied to exams.

February remains the one month that many a Japanese schoolchild dreads. He faces the examinations that are the climax of 14 years of gruelling education. The results will decide if he will win a place at a good university and the job in government or industry that automatically follows. Japanese companies are more concerned with the university an applicant went to than the degree he got.

Pity the modern Japanese child for the confusion in his life. Pity Japan Inc for the possible drying up of the supply of what an American anthropologist, Thomas Rohlen, has called "generations of disciplined workers for a techno-meritocratic system". Saturnine Dr Ogura sounds despairing: "I am very worried about the future when these kids take over. They could turn the world against us."

Lifeguard Bob

MARCH 16TH, SYDNEY *Australia is "the lucky country", but by the start of the 1990s its population was having to take some strong economic medicine. The odds of a quick cure, however, did not look good*

WHEN the sun shines and the surf is strong, when your sportsmen triumph around the world and your average incomes are 15th highest in the world, it is hard to believe that your economy is a mess. The clue—that, in this century, those incomes used to be the highest of all—is buried too deep, and anyway the beach looks good today.

That is the trouble with Australia. The country's real problems are economic, but get too little attention. Its contrived problems are political, and are in the headlines every day. They stem from the fact that federal Australia has too many layers of government, all of them elected too frequently. So when the central government tries to tackle economic issues, its effectiveness is quickly dissipated, and its nerve usually fails in the face of a new opinion poll and with the prospect of an imminent election.

Bob Hawke's Labor government has tried hard to overcome these handicaps. This week, eight years after it was first elected, it showed that it is still trying. It produced a package of measures designed to acknowledge, in Mr Hawke's words, "that this tough, increasingly competitive world of 5.5 billion people does not owe, and will not give, 17m Australians an easy prosperity." The package is potentially far more serious than anything contained in the annual budget. But its potential will be realised only if enough of those 17m Australians recognise that their prosperity will indeed not be easy any more.

The surest way to achieve that recognition is to let the world into Australia. For decades it was kept out by trade barriers, so Australians were allowed to slide into uncompetitive ways. Formal tariffs were high, 30% or more. But the truer measure of "effective protection" that economists like to calculate showed that some industries could charge prices double those abroad before facing competition from imports.

The Hawke government started reducing tariffs in 1988, and now plans to go further. Between 1993 and 1996 tariffs will be reduced from their 10-15% range down to a single rate of 5%. It sounds sensible, but it has two flaws. One is that several industries are exempt: cars, lorries, clothing, textiles and footwear are to be handled much more delicately, even though they are the ones that need the biggest jolt.

The other weakness is the emphasis on reducing tariffs, as if that were the sole test of trade virtue. In fact tariffs are the least-bad form of protectionism. Throughout the 1980s governments everywhere have been slipping in anti-dumping laws, "voluntary" export restraints and a host of protectionist measures masquerading as health and safety standards. Australia has not been above such tricks, and this week's package promises that "the government will not allow unfair competition from dumped imports which damage local industry." Protection is dead, long live protection.

That is too cynical. Mr Hawke's government has done much to liberalise parts of the economy, and this week's measures continue the trend. But one area of economic life remains untouched: the labour market. Australia has more than 300 trade unions, many of them tiny and therefore desperate to make some kind of mark. Large firms in Australia typically have to negotiate with five different unions. All companies are legally bound to match the wages and conditions laid down in federal (and sometimes state) awards for their industry. The result of pervasive union power is Luddite—automation in Australia's motor industry is only a third as advanced as in Western Europe—and deeply damaging to productivity.

The damage is greatest in the public sector. When the OECD ran its ruler over the performance of public utilities, it found that their output per worker in Australia was less than half the average of its 24 members. Since nationalised industries account for more than a quarter of the country's non-housing investment (compared with less than 10% in America and Japan), the inefficiency of the public sector washes right through the rest of the economy.

This week's package of measures contained nothing on trade-union reform, and nothing but a few pieties on shaking up the public sector. The lacuna is easily explained: a Labor government finds it hard to be tough with its labour supporters, particularly when it is unpopular with the rest of the voters.

Just how unpopular is shown by some recent opinion polls. Labor is trailing the Liberal-National opposition by 12 percentage points, despite the boost it has had from sending warships to the Gulf. Mr Hawke gained personally from his stance on the

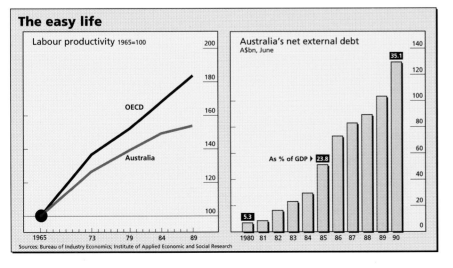

The easy life

Labour productivity 1965=100

OECD

Australia

Sources: Bureau of Industry Economics; Institute of Applied Economic and Social Research

Australia's net external debt A$bn, June

35.1

As % of GDP ▶ 23.8

5.3

war: 48% of those questioned approve of his performance as prime minister, his highest score for almost a year. But on virtually every specific issue the opposition is now seen as more likely than Labor to achieve results.

Much of Labor's malaise can be put down to the economy. Australia led the world into recession last year, and a few people whose sense of humour is stronger than their sense of economics talk optimistically of its being the locomotive that will lead the world out of it too. Meanwhile, the pain is palpable: unemployment is rising steeply, many small businesses (particularly in construction) are going bust, and yet inflation remains a stubborn 7%.

The blame is pinned on the sleek suit of the treasurer (finance minister), Paul Keating. Mr Keating has long been regarded, particularly by himself, as the obvious successor to Mr Hawke. He is clever, determined and (a vital quality in Australian politics) capable of phrases that would bring blushes to a bar-room brawl. Recently, though, he has lost his touch. His approval rating has fallen to 22%. He used to be an asset to Mr Hawke, as well as a threat. Suddenly, he seems to be neither.

The main beneficiary of Mr Keating's difficulties may not be Mr Hawke himself, but the leader of the opposition, John Hewson, a former professor of economics at the University of New South Wales. Like Mr Keating, he is young, and makes the economy his forte. He was critical of this week's industry package, saying it was not radical enough. But even industrialists whose natural home is the Liberal Party wonder privately whether Mr Hewson would have the steel to take on the unions.

If his chance comes at all, it will come too quickly. The curse of political economy in Australia is the short period—a maximum of three years—between federal elections, with state elections providing ample distraction in between times. It is not a coincidence that the new programme of tariff cuts does not really start until July 1993, four months after the latest date for an election. Mañana is not just a habit. It is a constitutional imperative.

....

Mr Keating ousted Mr Hawke as party leader and prime minister on December 19th.

Then there were six

APRIL 13TH, BANGKOK *Corruption is endemic in Thailand. But one reason given for the military coup earlier in the year was that the civilians had let it get out of hand. The junta promised some corrective measures*

KLAEW THANIKUL died as any self-respecting gangster should—in a hail of bullets. At dusk on April 5th, his car was overtaken by a pick-up truck as it was passing through Nakhon Pathom, a small town west of Bangkok. Gunmen in the truck opened fire on the car, killing Klaew and his bodyguard and injuring a dozen people in a nearby restaurant. The intriguing question is, did the army order the hit?

The leaders of the military coup which toppled Thailand's elected government in February said they intended to fight evil in Thai society. This was bad news for the seven *jao poh* (big brothers) who control most organised crime in Thailand. The seven have grown fat on the proceeds of gambling, prostitution, heroin and logging (which is banned). "They will be asked to stop their illegal activities. If they refuse to comply, they may face drastic legal action, or probably special methods," said the junta's interior minister in March.

A pamphlet circulated in Bangkok shortly before Klaew's death gave a foretaste of what these special methods might entail. It alleged that Chalerm Yoobamrung, the army's least favourite minister in the old government, had been seized by soldiers and handed over to the Khmers Rouges, who had executed him inside Cambodia. (Mr Chalerm has not been seen in public since the coup.) The army denies this allegation, as it does any suggestion of involvement in Klaew's murder.

The previous government's attempts at cracking down on organised crime were half-hearted. Last year, Thai television viewers saw a squad of commandos knocking politely on the door of a *jao poh*. The commandos were allowed in to perform a gentle search only after they had taken off their boots. This *jao poh* supported one of the government parties. Another *jao poh* was an adviser to a government minister.

After the coup, most of the godfathers appeared to have got the message that the army was serious. Klaew claimed that he had been misunderstood and was not all that rich. The other six *jao pohs* are said to be trying to turn legitimate in case they, too, are misunderstood. Some are now dealing in property, and are said to be doing well. There is talk in the junta of using the weapon that got Al Capone—the taxman.

Death among the blossoms

MAY 25TH, DELHI *Political violence is endemic in the world's largest democracy. But the pre-election murder of Rajiv Gandhi seemed to threaten Indian unity*

FLOWERS always decorate Indian election campaigns. The heat sweetens their smell. Rajiv Gandhi, his car bouncing towards a rally in Sriperumbudur in southern India, was covered in garlands by hands that reached through the open window. He was determined to be accessible during the campaign: in the past he had been accused of being too aloof. As they arrived, he asked the local candidate, with whom he was travelling, what he should speak about. The candidate thought village development the most suitable subject. Mr Gandhi walked towards a platform to begin his speech and was blown to pieces by a bomb, along with 14 other people. The bomb may have been concealed in a bouquet of flowers.

Mr Gandhi was killed on May 21st, the day after the first of three days of voting in the general election. The electoral process stopped abruptly with the death of the man most likely to be prime minister. As the army was deployed to keep order, the remaining two polling days were postponed until June 12th and 15th.

The expected violence broke out at the news of his death. Supporters from his Congress Party burned buses, cars and shops and attacked police stations. Police fired on protesters. At least eight people were killed and many more injured; but things could have been much worse. After his mother's assassination, in 1984, some 3,000 Sikhs were killed in Delhi.

Part of the reason there has been so little bloodshed is that nobody yet is certain who killed Mr Gandhi or why. The Tamil Tigers, a separatist group in Sri Lanka, are suspects, since Mr Gandhi had complained that they were becoming a parallel government in Tamil Nadu. He used this as an excuse to force the prime minister, Chandra Shekhar, to sack the pro-Tiger state government earlier this year. One theory is that the bomb was detonated by remote control, a method used to kill Ranjan Wijeratne, Sri Lanka's defence minister, earlier this year. Another possibility is that a woman had a bomb wired to her, and that it went off as she gave flowers to Mr Gandhi. The Tigers have denied responsibility; but they usually do.

Sikh terrorists killed Mr Gandhi's mother, and had vowed to get him too. During this election campaign, they have killed an average of 15 people each day in Punjab, including eight candidates, and have tried to kill two prominent candidates in Delhi. But Mr Gandhi had plenty of enemies who would like to boast of his murder: a group like the United Liberation Front of Assam, separatist terrorists in the north-west of the country, could equally well be the culprit. A caller to a newspaper claimed responsibility on behalf of the "Commander of the Combined Forces"; but this is reckoned to be a hoax.

It is clear, though, what killed him: the current of political violence that runs from separatist terrorism to the small-time brutality of local hatreds. Around 200 people were killed in the six weeks of election campaigning, and nearly 200 on the first day of voting. Over the past year, some 2,000 people have been killed in Hindu-Muslim riots, and about 150 in protests against job reservations for particular castes. Illegal arms and bomb factories have been set up in many parts of northern India to fuel the conflicts.

The violence fills the void of modern India: the institutions on which independent India was proudly built no longer work. The state is seen as corrupt and callous, incapable of delivering justice or prosperity to the people. India's old-style intellectuals, who preach democracy, secularism and Fabian socialism, are falling silent, belatedly aware of their impotence. Violence is both cause and effect of this failure.

Hoodlums hired by virtually all parties use arms and muscle at election time, partly to capture polling booths, partly to repel attempted captures by rival parties. Booth-capturing is no longer seen as an outrage and has become a normal part of electoral strategy, particularly in lawless Bihar. In booths where the presiding officer reports a capture, a second poll is made. But in many booths the presiding officer is in cahoots with the captors, or may be too terrified of local toughs to protest. Hoodlums have longer arms than the law.

The current Indian election was spread over three days to enable security forces to move from one area to another; but even so the chief ministers of Uttar Pradesh and Bihar are reported to have used musclemen to capture booths in the first round of the election. The election commission has therefore countermanded voting in several seats and

ordered a repoll in more than 1,000 booths. Never before has there been such open abuse of power by those who are supposed to set standards for the people.

The police and civil service are seen as oppressors and terrorists. The law courts are venal and can take decades to decide a case. The rule of law does not seem to work in settling people's grievances. What seems to work is violence and money, and all political parties are engaged in a mad race to maximise the use of both. Indians believe that nothing much happens to bandits any more since so many of them have links with politicians, and some have even become ministers.

The army, long seen as standing above the fray, dirtied its reputation in Kashmir earlier this year. Sent in to suppress separatism, its behaviour has only fostered the movement. Stories of torture, murder and mass rape are widespread.

Indians' disillusion with the state is compounded by the failure of successive governments to deliver economic growth. Politicians cling to the rhetoric of socialism while supporting a system which delivers great riches to few businessmen, and profitable cuts to the civil servants and politicians who hand out licences. Indira Gandhi swept the 1971 election crying *"Garibi hatao"*—end poverty—and Indians, still poor, feel cheated.

Most Indians have no chance of bettering themselves. They live in little rooms and spend their days on overcrowded streets. Nerves fray easily. On the pavements, pedestrians bump into each other rather than step aside, and small offences turn quickly into shouting matches. Among frustrated people, violence sparks easily.

Amid this moral decay, religious, ethnic and caste crusades have a growing appeal. People find a purity in them which they do not find in secular, national parties. And an increasing number of people are willing to

kill in the name of causes which they find holier than the discredited law of the land. Hence the burgeoning popularity of the Bharatiya Janata Party: a fringe party of Hindu extremists only a few years ago, it looks as though it could be part of a government after the election.

As institutions weaken, individuals take over. So Congress, clinging to the Nehru-Gandhi dynasty as the country's only stable political landmark, elected Sonia Gandhi, Rajiv's Italian-born widow, as party president. That decision exposed the party's bankruptcy: with no leader of stature to replace Mr Gandhi, they turned to a woman whose only political asset was her name, which, the party hoped, would bring in the sympathy vote that swung Rajiv into power after his mother's death in 1984.

Sonia Gandhi, however, has shown an extreme distaste for politics. When Rajiv was persuaded to go into the family business by his mother in 1980, Sonia was against it. She was happier being the wife of an airline pilot.

Sonia refused the party presidency, not surprisingly; and the stockmarkets, which had plunged at the news of Rajiv's death and risen at the news of her election, plunged again. Her decision has left Congress headless and embarrassed at having exposed its weakness.

The party is unlikely to give up on Sonia. It is worth remembering that, when Indira asked Rajiv to go into politics after his brother's death in 1980, he put out a statement saying that he had no such intention. Sonia might be persuaded to keep a seat warm for her daughter: Priyanka is only 20 (the minimum age for a seat in the lower house is 25) but is said to be sharp and keen on politics.

After all these years, a non-family member will have little authority. One possibility, P.V. Narasimha Rao, is a former foreign minister whose ill-health means he cannot hope to become a permanent head of the party. For that reason, he might be acceptable as a temporary chief. Sharad Pawar, chief minister of Maharashtra, is by far the strongest Congress state leader. Narain Dutt Tewari of Uttar Pradesh could be a contender if he wins the state election being held alongside the parliamentary one; but he may be beaten by the BJP. There is some talk of a collective leadership, but that would not last.

Congress might still garner sympathy votes. Before the assassination, opinion polls gave the party 225 to 310 seats out of 537. Votes have been cast in 40% of the seats. Congress might just be able to form the next government alone; if not, it would try to split bits off other parties. If that did not work, a coalition would have to be built.

One possibility, given the strong showing of the BJP and the equally strong antipathy to its views amongst other parties, is a secularist line-up. Indians of many parties have been terrified by the prospect of escalating Hindu-Muslim violence, highlighted in Meerut in Uttar Pradesh during the first round of voting, when 19 people were killed. Such an alliance would bring together Congress, the breakaway Socialist Janata Dal run by Chandra Shekhar, and the Janata Dal of V.P. Singh. The Communists, implacable enemies of the BJP, would give their support.

That prospect may be less depressing than a future dominated by the BJP, but it leaves little room for optimism. Coalitions have never worked in India, which is why the country has always returned to the comforting but damaging embrace of Congress and the Nehru-Gandhi family.

In August a Tamil suspected of organising the assassination committed suicide to evade capture.

In pursuit of sympathy

JUNE 1ST, DELHI **The assassination of its leader posed a problem of succession for India's Congress Party—and the chance to be more than a political vehicle for the Gandhi family**

RAJIV GANDHI'S ashes were divided into 35 lots. His widow and children took two urns to Allahabad, where the Ganges and the Yamuna rivers join. His son Rahul scattered them on the water, then turned to his mother, weeping. One urn was emptied from an aircraft over the Himalayas. The other 32 were squabbled over by Congress Party politicians, then carried off to India's states to be used in a desperate attempt to collect the "sympathy vote".

India's politics, shabby at the best of times, has rarely looked shabbier than in the week after Rajiv Gandhi's death on May 21st. The Congress Party lapsed into acrimonious argument: how should it exploit its leader's murder, and who should succeed him as party president? After Sonia Gandhi's refusal, the party divided: some thought they should persist in pressing Mrs Gandhi; some thought the prime minister, Chandra Shekhar, a former Congress man, should be co-opted; and some thought there should be a leadership ballot.

Given the need to get some sort of leader in place before the closing rounds of voting in the election, due on June 12th and 15th, the party settled on a compromise. It elected a leader who would be an unlikely prime minister–P.V. Narasimha Rao, a former for-

eign minister. Mr Rao is in ill health and is not contesting the election.

Mr Rao's principal qualification for the job is his loyalty to the Gandhis. During the controversial "emergency" that Indira Gandhi imposed in 1975-77, he was a loyal general secretary of the party. After Mrs Gandhi lost the election in 1977 he was a standard-bearer for the party in parliament. When Mrs Gandhi returned to power in 1980 he was rewarded with the foreign ministry.

Constitutionally, he could become prime minister if Congress won the election, though he would then have to win a parliamentary seat within six months. But no one believes his political future will extend very far. That is why heavyweights such as Sharad Pawar, chief minister of Maharashtra, and N.D. Tiwari, former chief minister of Uttar Pradesh, can accept him.

The voters may be less accommodating. By failing to provide a political heir to Mr Gandhi, Congress risks dissipating the sympathy it is hoping to create: grief for Rajiv may give way to worries about the cohesion of Congress. A worried Congress attempted to persuade the election commission to bring forward the dates for the next rounds of voting. The commission refused.

But Congress's real challenge is to con-

vince the electorate that it will return to being the sort of party it was half a century ago: a decentralised affair, with strong grassroots leaders. Jawaharlal Nehru and his daughter Indira Gandhi (latterly in partnership with her younger son Sanjay) drew power to themselves and abandoned that tradition; Rajiv likewise. How can Congress, having tried to recruit the last available Gandhi, now carry conviction as a party of principles, not personalities?

Despite promising pre-election opinion polls, the signs from the voting on May 20th, before the assassination, are against Congress. Voting took place in 40% of the constituencies. Exit polls in Chandigarh and Delhi suggest a swing of 7% to 9% away from Congress in these cities, with the Bharatiya Janata Party gaining most from its message of Hindu chauvinism.

Yet the non-Congress parties' gain in seats may be less than the swing suggests. In the previous election, Congress's opponents had an electoral pact. Now they do not. And voting still has to take place in Congress strongholds in the south and west. In Tamil Nadu the regional party opposing Congress is linked to the Tamil Tigers of Sri Lanka, who are thought to have been behind the assassination.

The BJP, however, thinks it has found a strong card. Before Mr Gandhi's death, Congress was campaigning as a force for stability. That stability was embodied in the Gandhi family. Without Rajiv, the party looks like a group of fratricidal factions. Many Indians, stunned by the assassination, are looking for comfort and security. L.K. Advani, the BJP leader, believes that he and Hinduism provide a better focus for such yearnings than the factions swearing temporary loyalty to Mr Rao. Unlike Congress, the BJP has always been a disciplined party. Mr Advani has urged his supporters to go out and campaign with a "killer instinct"–an unfortunate phrase.

What of V.P. Singh, head of the Janata Dal and prime minister for a year until November 1990? Since he never seemed in control of his party's factions when he was in power, and his party ultimately split, he cannot convincingly offer the country stability. Indeed, he now seems in danger of losing yet more factions to Congress.

A new political alignment therefore suggests itself. Whereas, since 1947, the key question before voters has always been whether they were for or against the Gandhi family, now the question could be whether voters are for or against the BJP.

This, oddly, could help Congress if it could unite around a leader. Chandra Shekhar (who leads the tiny Socialist Janata Dal Party) thinks it should be him. He and Mr Singh were in Congress until they fell foul of the Gandhi family. Mr Shekhar is a leader without a party, whereas Congress is a party without a leader. Even the Marxists, once implacable foes of the Gandhis, are talking of the need for all secular forces to unite in the country's hour of need. But is Congress yet ready for Mr Shekhar?

Later in the month Narasimha Rao formed a minority government which undertook radical economic reforms.

Genghis-grit

JULY 13TH, MONGOLIA **The collapse of communism is not confined to Europe and the Soviet Union. One of the world's poorest countries, sandwiched between Siberia and China, is trying democracy too**

NOBODY could accuse the heirs of Genghis Khan of being wimps. Seventy years after their first "revolution", and almost a year after their first democratic election, Mongolians still have little to celebrate--and not much to celebrate with. Theirs is a vast country of steppes, mountains and desert, about the size of Western Europe, trapped between China and the Soviet Union. Although animals outnumber the 2.1m humans by ten to one, meat is rationed. So is vodka, the local tipple. But still Mongolia's government is pressing ahead with a brave (and desperate) attempt to make the transition from central planning to a market economy in little more than two years. If it works, the "Mongolian model" will be to North Korea, Vietnam and China what Hong Kong and the other little dragons have been to the rest of Asia.

And if it doesn't? The chances of failure are high. In the first five months of this year both food production and industrial production dropped by 10% compared with the same period last year; foreign trade (hit

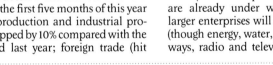

hard this year by the change to convertible-currency trade with the Soviet Union) plummeted by 54%. There are acute shortages of everything from petrol and electricity to consumer goods. Unemployment, like the budget deficit, has been rising fast.

Which is where the Genghis-grit comes in. Unlike Mikhail Gorbachev next door, who wants large dollops of western help as a bribe to get a market economy going, Mongolia is simply doing it. Earlier this month the government slashed its 1991 budget by 30%. Last month the local currency, the tugrik, was devalued by almost 600% (there are now 40 to the dollar). The economic transformation, which began in earnest last year, is picking up speed.

A new banking system is in the making; so is a stock exchange; more and more prices are being set free. The first privatisations (of state shops and small enterprises) are already under way. Privatisation of larger enterprises will take up to two years (though energy, water, the railways, the airways, radio and television, and post and telecommunications will remain under central control). Eventually, the government estimates, 57% of state-owned assets will have been put into private hands. Since Mongolians have little cash to invest, all citizens born before May 31st this year are being issued with vouchers to buy shares.

Yet even Mongolia's fierce determination cannot easily overcome the barriers created by its long isolation as more or less the 16th Soviet republic, its inhibiting lack of hard currency and its huge debt (Mongolia and the Soviet Union agree that the debt amounts to something like 10 billion transferable roubles, but have not yet agreed what that comes to in real money). "Fraternal" socialist countries used to account for over 90% of Mongolia's foreign trade--but are now too hard up to help.

Earlier this year Mongolia joined both the IMF and the Asian Development Bank in the hope of getting the technical assistance and cash that it needs. Food aid has already come from America and others. But it is Japan that seems most determined to take Mongolia under its wing. Japan's prime minister, Toshiki Kaifu, is due to visit Mongolia in August, doubtless bringing aid. If the Mongolian model can prod Asia's other communist laggards into reform, then Japan reckons it will be money well spent.

As close as teeth and lips

AUGUST 10TH, HONG KONG **The south of China has always tried to prosper beyond the gaze of the central government. We wondered whether this tradition could be Hong Kong's salvation when the British leave in 1997**

AT LO WU, on the border between Hong Kong and China, travellers get from one side to the other by walking across a footbridge that spans a little stream. Fifteen years ago the bridge was usually empty. These days it has regular rush hours, when the crush of people waiting to pass through immigration control is so heavy the bridge cannot be seen under the commuters.

The traffic in goods is just as thick: on an average day, 14,000 trucks cross the border. They take out of Hong Kong the raw materials and half-finished goods that the 16,000 Hong Kong-owned factories in next-door Guangdong province turn into toys, shoes, clothes and stereos. They bring back most of Hong Kong's food and a large share of the manufactured goods it exports to the rest of the world. Hong Kong the trader has been reunited with its Chinese hinterland.

Yet the return to this natural economic state--after the artificial separation of 1950-78 brought about by the mainland's isolationist policies--has come at an awkward time. In the middle of 1997 the British colony reverts to the sovereignty of a China that, for now at least, is run by a communist dictatorship determined to stamp out any western notions of democracy and liberty that it finds sprouting on Chinese soil. A central point in the 1984 agreement between Britain and

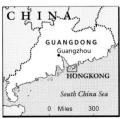

China on Hong Kong's future is that the territory should maintain its own identity after 1997 and so continue its way of life. Might this aim be undermined by Hong Kong's growing Guangdong connection?

Not in a social or economic sense. The 65m people of Guangdong are being bent (extremely willingly) to the ways of Hong Kong's 6m fellow Cantonese, not vice versa. Just across the border in Guangdong lies Shenzhen, one of the five "special economic zones" (three of them in Guangdong) that China has set up to attract foreign investment and technology. Although Shenzhen is on Chinese soil, the currency almost universally used is the Hong Kong dollar: indeed, some 20% of Hong Kong's banknotes and coins are thought to be circulating in Guangdong.

Up the Pearl river in Guangdong's capital, Guangzhou (more familiar to westerners as Canton), most of the money changing hands is Chinese yuan. But televisions are tuned to Hong Kong channels and watches set to Hong Kong's standard time rather than the summer time decreed by China's government.

People in Guangdong have good reason to admire Hong Kong. Their little neighbour accounts for three-quarters of Guangdong's foreign trade (and Guangdong itself accounts for more than 40% of all of China's exports). Hong Kong is also responsible for the lion's share of direct foreign investment in the province: 80% of the $17 billion-worth approved by the Chinese authorities.

It has been a fruitful partnership. Labour in Hong Kong costs at least five times as much as labour in Shenzhen (which has the highest wages in Guangdong). A 50-year lease on undeveloped land in Hong Kong costs at least 30-50 times as much. Hong Kong companies employ more than 2m factory workers in Guangdong; manufacturing employment in Hong Kong itself is down to around 700,000. Hong Kong is fast becoming a high-wage service economy, the marketing and management headquarters for manufacturing in southern China.

The export-driven restructuring of Guangdong's own economy has been even more startling. A sleepy agricultural province has been turned into China's most formidable industrial power. Shenzhen, which was mostly farmland in 1979, has a population of 1m that is growing by 20-30% a year and an industrial output that in the first half of 1991 was 40% bigger in real terms than it had been a year earlier. In Guangdong as a whole, industrial output in the first half of 1991 was up by more than 25%.

If there is a threat to Hong Kong in all this, it is (predictably) political. One worry is that the American Congress, angered by China's poor record on human rights (and America's trade deficit) might withdraw China's most-favoured-nation trading status (MFN). If this happened, Hong Kong could move its factories out of Guangdong at a fast clip; but it would hurt. The threat seems gone for this year—President Bush has more than enough votes in the Senate to sustain his grant of MFN to China—but it will reappear when the question of renewing MFN comes up again in June 1992.

A more insidious, though also more ambiguous, matter is Chinese government interference. The authorities in Beijing are known to be furious with Andrew Chow, the head of a Hong Kong-based company called Tian An China that has a large and successful property-development business in Guangdong and other parts of southern China. They are convinced that Mr Chow helped Xu Jiatun, a former head of China's Xinhua press agency in Hong Kong (which serves as its informal embassy in the colony), escape to America last year.

To widespread disbelief, Mr Chow firmly denies this charge; but he also says that three Chinese government outfits (including the Hong Kong branch of Xinhua) want to sell their 10% stake in the unlisted parent company of Tian An China. Everyone believes their motivation is political: on its business merits, Tian An is a star.

Does it matter? After the *Asian Wall Street Journal* ran a front-page story on the subject this week, Tian An's share price

barely flickered and there was no unusual trading volume. But, says Mr Chow, the rumour about China's displeasure has been current in Hong Kong for three months; over that period Tian An's shares "should have performed better."

The real danger signal would be trouble on Tian An's part in getting the government approvals that are vital for its developments in China. Of that, says Mr Chow, there has been no hint. Nor, say most observers, will there be any: the approvals are handed out by provincial and local officials, most of whom (in Guangdong anyway) do their utmost to differ from the line taken in Beijing.

This happens with purely political matters as well. Guangdong, comfortably distant from the dour autocrats in Beijing, has long been the most relaxed part of China. It is by no means free, but a study by John Kamm, a Hong Kong-based American businessman, shows that the clampdown in Guangdong after the Tiananmen Square killings of June 1989 was far less severe than that imposed elsewhere in China: fewer dissidents arrested, none executed. Christian churches are tolerated in Guangdong, foreign radio broadcasts unjammed.

Guangdong's ability to protect its people from Beijing is usually credited to Ye Xuanping, who was governor of the province until he was kicked upstairs to a job in Beijing this spring. The well-connected Mr Ye (his father was a famous army marshal and a close comrade of Deng Xiaoping) has refused to stay upstairs. He had his choice of successors in Guangdong and still spends most of his time there, making public appearances often enough to reassure everyone that he is looking after their interests.

In private, Guangdong officials profess eagerness for more political contacts with Hong Kong. Delegations of civil servants (50 or so from the Hong Kong side so far this year, 30 from Guangdong) ferry between these Cantonese cousins. Beijing restricts political contacts to the extent it can. Hong Kong should encourage them: given that it has to go back to China, it should nestle as far as possible under Guangdong's wing.

Pontius Pilate and the US base

SEPTEMBER 21ST, MANILA *America's bases in the Philippines, its former colony, had been taken for granted in keeping Asia's peace—until the Philippines' politicians rediscovered a sense of nationalism*

THE vote went as predicted. On September 16th the Philippine Senate decided that it no longer wanted American soldiers, sailors and airmen to be based in the country. It voted 12-11 to reject a treaty that would have given new life to the expiring lease on the huge American base in Subic Bay. This should have been a solemn moment: the

American army has been in the Philippines for around 100 years. But solemnity was impossible in the hubbub caused by a plan to override the senators. The government of Corazon Aquino wants to hold a referendum in the belief that most Filipinos would like the Americans to stay. "People power", which President Aquino used to depose Ferdinand Marcos in 1986, is on the move again.

If the opinion polls are correct, people power could win again. Most Filipinos believe that American money—up to $800m a year according to the most inventive Philippine calculators (the agreement actually says $203m a year)—is needed to keep the Philippines afloat. Some of the senators who voted against a new lease claimed they were not anti-American: they just thought the Americans were not offering enough.

Filipinos at large might be less grasping.

Yet a vote in the legislature is a vote. Is it constitutionally proper to overturn it by appealing directly to the people? Teodoro Benigno, a former government minister and an ally of Mrs Aquino when she was battling against the Marcos gang, says that people power as a spontaneous uprising may have been fine once, but questions whether it should be used as a method of government. If the voice of the people is all that matters, he says, "then lower taxes, lower gasoline prices must be granted, because that is what the people want."

The president of the Senate, Jovito Salonga, turned to the Bible for confirmation that a referendum would be bad. Consider, he said, the first well-documented referendum in history. Pontius Pilate, the governor of a Roman colony, asked the crowd to decide who should be punished, Barabbas, a bandit, or Jesus, a man of peace. "There is no indication that Jesus Christ got even one vote in that electoral exercise," said Mr Salonga. "We have buried the treaty and it now lies cold in its grave. Do not disturb the peace of the dead." In the Philippines, where over 90% of the people are Christian, Mr Salonga's biblical words could carry a lot of weight.

It is not certain that a referendum will be held. The Supreme Court will be asked to rule on its legality. Opponents say that, although referendums are allowed under the constitution, they should be kept to local issues, not foreign treaties. Mrs Aquino says she wants to hold the vote by December–assuming, that is, that she is able by then to collect the 3m signatures, 10% of registered voters, needed to bring the issue to the ballot. But even if she is, the Supreme Court

The street referendum...

could deliberate on the matter until next May, when, if the referendum is allowed, it would become entangled with elections for local councils, Congress and the presidency.

The Americans have become mere spectators in this pantomime. Should they pack their bags, as they said they would if the Senate vote went against them? They have long maintained that the lease was not up on September 16th, as the Philippine government maintained, but in a year's time. Mrs Aquino has now found it convenient to agree with the Americans, and has revoked an eviction notice the Philippines gave in May last year. She says that the Americans will have to be given a formal year's notice to quit, and she has no plans to issue such a notice now. Business-minded people go further: they point out that under Philippine company law even small companies

are allowed three years in which to wrap up their affairs. In any event, Mrs Aquino told the Americans in a note sent to their embassy in Manila less than an hour after the Senate vote, there is no need even to think about saying goodbye until after the referendum is held.

For years, though, the Americans have been exploring possible alternatives to Subic Bay. Guam, Saipan and Hawaii, among other places, ensure they will not be homeless in the Pacific. Singapore has said it will help. The Vietnamese have even offered the Americans use of Cam Ranh Bay, now that what remains of the Soviet Union no longer needs it. But this may have been a piece of mischief to make the point that the region is no longer under communist threat, a view shared in America by those who believe Subic should have been abandoned long ago. Neighbouring Clark air base, once also deemed essential, has been made unusable by a carpet of volcanic ash, and no one seems to be much troubled by the loss.

The Senate, apparently exhausted, has gone into recess for two weeks. When it reconvenes it will discuss when exactly the Americans should go. At least one senator, though, is not on holiday. Juan Ponce Enrile, an old ally of Mrs Aquino turned implacable foe, said on September 18th that she should be impeached. Allowing the Americans to stay without a new treaty was treasonous, he said. Proceedings to impeach the president could be started with the consent of one-quarter of the members of the House of Representatives. Mrs Aquino's supporters dominate the house and can easily stop any move to impeach her. But they will have a noisy time arguing about it.

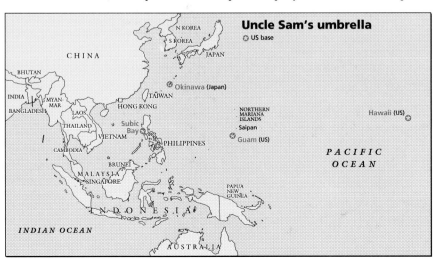

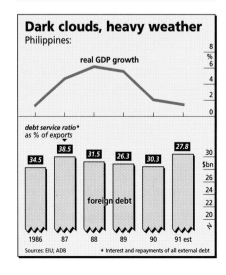

Dark clouds, heavy weather
Philippines:

Getting to know Mr Miyazawa

NOVEMBER 2ND, TOKYO *Both the outgoing and the incoming prime ministers of Japan were to find that the real power lies with others*

AFTER the amiable but weak Toshiki Kaifu, the tough and astute Kiichi Miyazawa. Japan's next prime minister is clearly a more formidable personality than the man he is replacing. Yet, as Mr Kaifu has done, Mr Miyazawa will have to do as he is told by the men who matter most in Japanese politics. These are Shin Kanemaru, the chairman of the Takeshita faction in the ruling Liberal Democratic Party, and Noboru Takeshita, a former boss of the faction that bears his name. Mr Miyazawa's own cabal and the much smaller one that Mr Kaifu belongs to do not have the strength to make prime ministers. The large Takeshita faction does. What this means for Miyazawa is that if he displeases his masters he can expect to be as summarily dumped as Mr Kaifu has been.

The elevation of Mr Miyazawa, who is 72, came on October 27th when he was elected president of the Liberal Democrats. Because the party has a majority in the lower house of the Diet (parliament), its president becomes prime minister.

The president is elected by the party's 395 members of parliament and, indirectly, by its 1.75m rank-and-file members, who were allocated 101 votes. With the Takeshita and some other factions behind him, it was predicted that Mr Miyazawa would win overwhelmingly. He got 285 votes out of a possible 496, but it was no landslide. It seems that among the 230 Diet members who had promised to vote for Mr Miyazawa, a fair number switched to two rival candidates, Michio Watanabe or Hiroshi Mitsuzuka.

It seems likely that most came from the Takeshita camp. Both Mr Kanemaru and Mr Takeshita are old-fashioned power-brokers with a strong distrust, if not actual loathing, of such an elitist and ideas-man as Mr Miyazawa. They agreed to support him only after failing to persuade one of their own kind, Ichiro Ozawa, to stand: he recently had a heart attack and anyway considers himself, at 49, too young for the job.

To the Takeshita faction, Mr Miyazawa's sole virtue is that he is one of the "Recruit generation". He was forced to resign as finance minister in December 1988 after lying about his involvement in the Recruit bribery case. Having him back in office means that other Liberal Democratic figures who were implicated in the shares-for-favours scandal can come out of hiding too.

By depriving him of a landslide win, the Takeshita men are giving him notice that his independence as prime minister will be limited. They allocated at least some of their support to Mr Watanabe. Although his own faction has only 67 members, the popular "Mitchie" received 120 votes. His was the real success of the election. He is likely to be foreign minister and deputy prime minister in the new cabinet. He could be the prime minister to follow Mr Miyazawa.

Mr Miyazawa has had to agree to let the

Miyazawa starts, Kaifu departs

Takeshita faction remain in charge of the finance ministry: Tsutomu Hata will take the job that has been held by Ryutaro Hashimoto. Another Takeshita man, Tamisuki Watanuki, will be the party's new secretary-general--the job that Mr Ozawa did so effectively during the Kaifu government.

For the sake of unity, two other influential party posts will go to lesser groups. The Watanabe faction's Koko Sato is to become chairman of the party's decision-making executive council. Mr Sato received a two-year suspended prison sentence for taking bribes during the Lockheed scandal of 1976. If Mr Miyazawa's appointment is seen as the burial of the Recruit affair, Mr Sato's marks the end of the party's other misdemeanours. Yoshiro Mori, from the Mitsuzuka faction, will be the new chairman of the party's policy research council. Mr Mori was another Recruit recruit.

Mr Kanemaru, known as the party's godfather, has taken it into his head to destroy the 81-member Mitsuzuka faction. Mr Mitsuzuka did not seek Mr Kanemaru's advice when taking over the faction after the death of Shintaro Abe last May. He then sacked his rival within the faction, Mutsuki

Kato. Only after pleas by party colleagues did Mr Kanemaru allow the Mitsuzuka faction a place in the new cabinet.

With his cabinet picked for him, Mr Miyazawa is not going to have much scope for his own policy ideas. The popular view is that his first move will be to stimulate the weakened economy. This he attempted to do when he became finance minister in 1986. Mr Miyazawa knew what was needed: he had been a bureaucrat within the finance ministry before turning to politics; he also had the backing of a powerful prime minister, Yasuhiro Nakasone.

Yet, for all the things going for him, it still took Mr Miyazawa a year to persuade his officials of the need to stimulate the economy–and that was when Japan was in the throes of a high-yen recession. When he eventually announced a supplementary budget in 1987, it was too much and too late. This time, Mr Miyazawa is likely to find even less freedom to act.

Mr Miyazawa's fate will be decided, though, more by how well he handles political problems at home and diplomatic issues abroad during the next 12 months. His first test will come soon. George Bush will be in Japan on November 29th and 30th, a week before the 50th anniversary, on December 7th, of the Japanese attack on Pearl Harbour, which brought America into the second world war. This sensitive matter apart, foreign-ministry officials are worried about the consequences of the visit. They expect that Mr Bush will make many demands, the first being that Japan should comply with GATT proposals to convert all non-tariff import barriers to tariffs. This would scupper the Liberal Democrats' promise to farmers that "not a single grain" of foreign rice will be allowed into the country.

With an upper-house election due in July, the ruling party is going to have to work hard to prevent the traditionally loyal farming households from showing their displeasure, as they did after Japan's beef and citrus markets were liberalised three years ago. Their abstention from the polls contributed to the Liberal Democrats' loss of its upper-house majority in the 1989 election. The party is desperate to control the upper house again. It will be Mr Miyazawa's task to ensure that it does–or comes close to doing so. If he fails to deliver the goods, the Takeshita faction could well be looking for a new prime minister by next summer.

The lost world of Laos

DECEMBER 7TH, LUANG PRABANG **Of the countries swept by communism and the ripples from the Vietnam war, the poorest was—and still is—Laos**

IN 1961 King Savang Vatthana of Laos believed that his tiny country faced extinction. He wrote:

> Our country is the most peaceful in the world. At no time has there arisen in the minds of the Lao people the idea of coveting another's wealth, of quarrelling with their neighbours, much less of fighting them. And yet, during the past 20 years, our country has known neither peace nor security.

For a time it seemed that Laos was indeed being obliterated. As the war in Vietnam intensified, American aircraft increased their bombing of the Ho Chi Minh trails, which ran through Laos. Laos received the equivalent of a planeload of bombs every eight minutes around the clock for nine years. After the seizure of power by the communist Pathet Lao (Land of the Lao) in 1975, Laos cut itself off from the non-communist world. It was not until 1989 that its government admitted that the old king and his queen had died in a "re-education camp" in northern Laos several years previously.

Today in Luang Prabang, the former royal capital, there is at least peace. Too much peace, say the town's more ambitious inhabitants, who fret at being trapped in a twilight zone only tenuously connected to the 20th century. Few can afford the airfare to Vientiane, the capital. The road is terrible and said to be unsafe because of bandits. The journey by river can take more than a week to cover 225 kilometres (140 miles) because of rapids on the Mekong.

Luang Prabang's only sign of industry is the remains of a Soviet-built factory on the road to the airport. No one is sure what it was supposed to produce: there was never enough electricity for its machines.

With nothing else to do, many young men have chosen a life of contemplation in one of Luang Prabang's 36 monasteries. A town that can support such a large idle population is well-off by modern Lao standards. The majority of the country's 4.1m people live in poverty that would be considered bad even in Africa.

A report on the Lao economy by the World Bank begins with the caution that all figures it uses "constitute educated estimates rather than confirmed facts". The Bank estimates that Laos's GDP per person is $180, making it one of the poorest countries in the world; health spending is less than $1.60 a person, and falling; 90% of the country's primary schools need extensive improvements or reconstruction. Teachers earn around $7 a month, if they are lucky--in some provinces the government cannot afford this much and pay is months in arrears. Life expectancy in Laos is 42 years, 20 years less than it is in Thailand.

Unlike Vietnam and Cambodia, where American pressure has restricted access to large-scale foreign aid, Laos has been successful in getting a good share of aid in recent years. "This country's capacity to absorb aid is total," says a representative of one of the largest donors to Laos. "You pour it in and it just disappears."

Laos's difficulties in turning aid into productive investment are a result partly of war damage and partly of Soviet advice. They are mainly, however, a result of the Pathet Lao's decision to "re-educate" its former enemies. After 1975 some 40,000 skilled Laotians were banished to the north to build dirt roads and work in the fields.

Most detainees have now been allowed to go home. Amnesty International knows of only eight men who were picked up in 1975 or 1976 and are still being "re-educated". The government has never said what offences these eight committed, but it evidently has no plans to release them soon.

By denying itself access to almost all the country's skilled manpower, the government guaranteed that its communist experiment would fail. To his credit, Kaysone Pomvihan, the dominant figure behind the Pathet Lao since the party's formation in 1955, recognised this failure early. In 1985 he introduced the New Economic Mechanism, which began the difficult process of ending central planning.

At 71, Mr Kaysone still takes the big decisions in Laos. He is close to Vietnam; he is half-Vietnamese, his wife is Vietnamese, and the Pathet Lao depended on North Vietnamese support during the war.

Mr Kaysone and his aged Vietnamese friends seem to agree on two matters. First, that economic reform is possible without political liberalisation: three government officials who criticised the party were arrested in October 1990, and are now in solitary confinement in a Vientiane jail. Second, they both regard Thailand with a mixture of contempt, fear and envy.

Relations between Laos and Thailand have improved enormously since 1988, when the Laotian army humiliated the better-equipped Thais in a skirmish over a hill. At the end of November the foundation stone was laid for the first bridge across the Mekong connecting the two countries. Trade is booming. Laos depends on Thailand, which controls its access to the western world and is the sole market for Laos's biggest export–hydroelectric power.

Laos fears it could end up as a commercial colony of Thailand. At the party congress in March, Sisavat Keodounphan, the army's chief of staff and the mayor of Vientiane, was sacked from the Politburo. Mr Sisavat was involved in some of the more lucrative deals with Thai companies to chop down Laos's remaining forests. His dismissal was supposed to send a signal that, though capitalism is now officially encouraged, dodgy deals with Thais are not.

Alas, Mr Sisavat's disgrace was short-lived. He has since been made minister for agriculture, "which is like putting Dracula in charge of the bloodbank," says a diplomat in Vientiane. When Mr Sisavat's Thai friends leave with the last tree, Laos will be poorer still and environmental degradation will take up where the bombers left off. King Savang's fear that Laos faced extinction could yet be realised.

Contents

INTERNATIONAL

A poison that gave strength

EVERYBODY knew it existed. But not until it disappeared was it clear how widely the cold war had spread its poison. The collapse of the Soviet empire in eastern Europe and the unification of Germany were the post-cold-war wonders of 1990. By 1991 the benefits had started to spread to farther-flung parts of the world. Freed from the complications of an East-West struggle that was never their own, the Middle East, Africa and Central America spent a giddy year striving to reinvent themselves.

Some of the most startling changes came in the Middle East. Stuffed with weapons and oil, abutting the frontiers of the Soviet Union—for decades this region had justified its reputation as an explosive cockpit of superpower confrontation. At least twice, in 1956 and 1973, it had been possible to imagine a third world war starting there. And yet, in 1991, something previously unthinkable happened: Mikhail Gorbachev's Soviet Union looked calmly the other way while an American expeditionary force pounded and humiliated Saddam Hussein's Iraq. For a while, Iraq had been one of the Kremlin's closest Arab friends. The western world's war against Russian influence in the Middle East—a war coiling back via the contest the British knew as the "Eastern Question" to the early parts of the 19th century—was over; and the West had clearly won it.

From the Soviet defeat, much followed. Arab states such as Syria, which had enlisted the Soviet Union in their struggle against Israel, saw that they had to detach themselves and move towards the United States instead. The United States, in turn, allowed itself to think freshly about its proper relationship with Israel. The Jewish state—dependable, democratic, militarily proficient—was accepted as a natural American ally when a Soviet shadow still darkened the region and its oil. After the Gulf war the case for this special relationship looked feebler. Not only had the Soviet threat disappeared, but several Arab states, notably Saudi Arabia and Egypt, had proved that they too could be dependable friends of America. Indeed, the one thing that put Arab loyalty in jeopardy during the Gulf war was the strength of the Israeli-American alliance. It would have been odd if the special relationship had survived the Gulf war unscathed.

It didn't. The war ended in February. By October the American secretary of state, James Baker, had bullied the Israelis, Syrians and Palestinians into dropping their reluctance to negotiate with each other. In agreeing to attend a much-ballyhooed peace conference in Madrid at the end of that month, all three parties had to make sacrifices. Syria had never before made it so clear that it was accepting the permanence of the Jewish state. The Palestinians had to drop their claim that Yasser Arafat's Palestine Liberation Organisation was their sole legitimate representa-

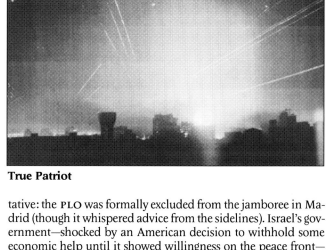

True Patriot

tative: the PLO was formally excluded from the jamboree in Madrid (though it whispered advice from the sidelines). Israel's government—shocked by an American decision to withhold some economic help until it showed willingness on the peace front—had to brace itself against Arab demands for the return of all the territory that Israel had captured in the 1967 war and had spent the subsequent quarter-century colonising.

By the end of the year, despite the sterility of a brief follow-up meeting in Washington in December, it was still possible to hope that the Arab-Israeli conflict, deprived of the oxygen with which the cold war had fuelled it, might begin to burn itself out. After all, something similar was already happening in other parts of the world. In Africa, from Horn to toe, old struggles, and some old ways of thinking, were coming to an end as the superpowers withdrew their aid and weapons.

In Ethiopia in May, the tottering Stalinesque regime of Haile Mariam Mengistu finally collapsed. The dictator fled to exile in Zimbabwe; rebels from the secessionist province of Tigre marched into Addis Ababa, and the Eritreans set about consolidating their independent coastal state. Although the Ethiopian empire died mainly by its own hand, the timing owed much to the fading of the cold war. Until the end of the 1980s a flow of Soviet money and weapons had propped Mengistu up. When the supply was turned off, the tide of battle turned decisively against him. In Somalia, likewise, the regime of Siad Barre found itself unable to play its old trick of playing off one superpower against the other, and then blackmailing both. Left to its own devices the regime swiftly discovered that it had none. It fell apart, leaving grim clan warfare.

As in the Horn, so in southern Africa. Since 1975 there had been no peace in Angola, despite

Shamir squeezed

the withdrawal of Portugal, the former colonial power. After the Portuguese left, the cold war had stepped into the vacuum. For more than a decade the Americans had backed Jonas Savimbi's UNITA movement in a bush war in the south, using neighbouring Zaire as an entrepot for supplies. South Africa intervened on the side of UNITA. Soviet arms and Cuban soldiers propped up the governing party, the MPLA, which held Luanda, the capital.

By 1989, however, superpower disengagement was pushing Angolans back to the peace table. May 1991 brought a negotiated settlement, under which the UNITA and MPLA armies would merge and the country would prepare for multi-party elections under international supervision.

Peace in Angola made that Zairean entrepot matter a good deal less. By mid-1991, not coincidentally, Zaire's dictator, Mobutu Sese Seko, was looking less comfortable on his gilded perch. This was the year, after all, when the word "democracy" was on every European's lips. When François Mitterrand hinted that France would no longer prop up non-democracies in its former African dominions, half a continent of autocrats began to lose their footing. The slips and falls were not confined to French-speaking Africa. Kenneth Kaunda of Zambia let opposition parties challenge him in a free election, and was promptly swept out of office. By year's end a similar fate was stalking Daniel arap Moi. That principled defender of single-party rule changed his mind within days of the rich countries taking a decision to suspend new aid for Kenya.

The end of the cold war had meanwhile played some part in coaxing South Africa's white rulers away from apartheid—and in persuading the African National Congress that there was no future in a Soviet-supported "armed struggle". Even the Americas were affected. Throughout the 1980s the United States had treated conflict in Central America as the southern front of a global war against communism. By 1991, once the Nicaraguans had voted their revolutionaries out of power, this no longer made sense. The United States ceased to support unsavoury right-wingers in El Salvador just because the Soviet Union was supporting unsavoury left-wingers in Nicaragua. As for Cuba, that loyal foot-soldier against capitalism, it ended 1991 in unglorious isolation: cut off without a rouble by its former paymaster, bereft of new ideas, more pitied than feared by the neighbours it had once been able to terrify.

By putting all these changes together, it is tempting to conclude that the world's regional conflicts were nothing more than

Siad Barre goes

a product of the cold war, and will therefore vanish with its passing. Even during 1991, alas, plenty of evidence suggested otherwise. The cold war, it is true, was a polariser of politics. When the world was divided into armed camps, the superpowers tended to put only one big question to third countries. Are you with us or against us? The blemishes of friends were then systematically overlooked, the virtues of foes systematically ignored. The cold war was also a hijacker of regional conflicts: it made some of them—such as Israel versus the Arabs—a lot more explosive because of the danger that the superpowers might be sucked into their clients' local wars. But it did not invent all local conflicts, and its disappearance will not necessarily solve all of them.

For proof of this Europeans need look no further than their own backyard: at the ethnic struggles ravaging Yugoslavia and bubbling up inside the former Soviet Union. But in the third world, too, where the early consequences of the end of the cold war seem so benign, it is a similar story. Without a big brother to protect them, rascals like Somalia's Siad Barre and Ethiopia's Mengistu fell from power. All very welcome—except that the states they ruled have fallen apart too. One thing the cold war helped to do was to keep the lines on the world's map in a fixed place. With its passing, some tribes in Africa, Europe—and maybe soon the Middle East—feel freer to redraw borders; often in blood, with brute force as the cartographer of first resort.

Through much of 1991, the world consoled itself with the hope that the gap left by the cold war could be filled by something else, the "new world order" of countless editorial articles. At the minimum this would comprise a robust United Nations, stronger international law, tougher arms-control, wise advice from the rich democracies for the poor and primitive who wanted to join their club. The regional squabbles that had not disappeared with the cold war would be tidied away by the newly dominant

Mengistu goes too

Americans. So, towards the end of the year, it began to turn out. December 31st brought a peace agreement in El Salvador. And did not October's Arab-Israeli peace conference in Madrid show that even the most stubborn of conflicts must eventually end, given the sustained attention of the United States?

Perhaps. But a big question as 1991 ended was whether the attention of an increasingly introspective United States was any longer a given. If the cold war was poisonous it was also an organising principle around which great powers mobilised their energies. Victory left a desire for rest, plus a whole world of troubles from which the victors turn away at their peril.

Tuesday 1st

Rebels of the United Somali Congress claimed to have cornered the unloved president, **Siad Barre**, in a bunker at Mogadishu's military airport. He fled into the bush with a small group of bodyguards 25 days later. He had ruled Somalia since 1969.

A controversial **goods and services tax** came into effect, courtesy of Canada's Conservative government. The Senate opposed the tax, so the prime minister, Brian Mulroney, packed it with supporters, almost starting yet another constitutional row.

Wednesday 2nd

A helicopter carrying three American military advisers was shot down in **El Salvador** by guerrillas of the Farabundo Marti National Liberation Front. The American government said two of the three had survived the crash but were shot dead by their captors.

Nicaragua's army admitted that some of its officers had stolen a stockpile of surface-to-air missiles and given them to left-wing guerrillas in neighbouring El Salvador. The president, Violeta de Chamorro, declined requests to sack the (formerly Sandinist) army commander.

Thursday 3rd

President Bush offered to "go the **extra mile for peace**" in the Gulf, by sending his secretary of state, James Baker, to meet Iraq's foreign minister, Tariq Aziz, in Geneva on January 9th. He also said there would be "no negotiations, no compromises, no attempts at face-saving, and no rewards for aggression."

Sunday 6th

Jorge Serrano, an engineer, was elected president of **Guatemala**, though more than half of the country's 3.2m registered voters did not bother to turn out. The new president described his Solidarity Action Movement as a part of "the modern centre right".

Monday 7th

A former Haitian minister of the interior, Roger Lafontant, tried to organise a coup, to prevent the newly elected president from taking office. It failed, and the **new president**, Father Jean-Bertrand Aristide, emerged from hiding, to a joyous reception from the people.

Tuesday 8th

Canadian police tried to stop a lorry which was violating traffic rules in an Indian reservation in Quebec. This caused a fight between policemen and **Mohawk Indians** armed with guns and clubs. A dozen policemen and 11 Mohawks were injured.

Wednesday 9th

James Baker and **Tariq Aziz** talked for nearly seven hours in Geneva. Afterwards, Mr Baker said Iraq had been inflexible. There had, he announced ominously, already been "too many Iraqi miscalculations."

Saturday 12th

Both houses of the American Congress agreed a joint resolution authorising the president to **use force** in the Gulf.

Sunday 13th

UN Secretary-General Javier Perez de Cuellar met Saddam Hussein briefly in Baghdad. "God only knows," he said afterwards, whether there would be **war**.

Monday 14th

France suggested that the Security Council might issue a statement linking Kuwait with the **Palestine** issue. America's UN ambassador retorted that his government was not in favour of "artificial linkage". Predictably, Iraq's National Assembly voted unanimously to back Saddam Hussein.

Tuesday 15th

A leader of the **Medellin drugs cartel**, Jorge Luis Ochoa, gave himself up on the understanding that the Colombian government would not extradite him to the United States.

According to UN Resolution 678, this was the **last day** by which Iraqi forces should have withdrawn from Kuwait. The Iraqis did not withdraw.

Wednesday 16th

The **war started**. The nighttime bangs and whizzes around Baghdad were shown live on America's Cable News Network. Mr Bush promised to knock out Iraq's nuclear-bomb and chemical-weapons facilities. "Our objectives are clear," he said. "Saddam Hussein's forces will leave Kuwait. The legitimate government of Kuwait will be restored to its rightful place and Kuwait will once again be free."

Thursday 17th

Iraq fired eight **Scud missiles** at Israel. They were to be the first of many. Israelis donned gas masks, although all the Scuds turned out to be armed with conventional warheads.

Friday 18th

Israel's defence minister, Moshe Arens, said that Israel would certainly react to the Scud attacks, but would not say when. Jordan's King Hussein called the American-led assault on Iraq "brutal". Mr Bush urged Israel to **show restraint**.

Sunday 20th

Saddam Hussein said he had only used a fraction of his military power. Iraq fired Scud missiles at Riyadh and Dharhan, in Saudi Arabia. Several were intercepted by American **Patriot missiles**. General Norman Schwarzkopf claimed that Iraq's nuclear installations had been put out of action.

Tuesday 22nd

Erskine Sandiford's Democratic Labour Party was returned for a second term of government in a general election in **Barbados**.

Wednesday 23rd

General **Colin Powell**, America's top soldier, said his strategy for dealing with the Iraqi army in Kuwait was simple: "First we are going to cut it off. Then we are going to kill it." The German chancellor, Helmut Kohl, said his country would have to help foot the bill for the war. Japan made similar noises, vaguely.

Monday 28th

Saddam Hussein told America's Cable News Network that Iraq would win the war. The next night President Bush gave his annual "state of the union" message to Congress, and promised that America would win. As Mr Bush was speaking, Iraqi troops launched a **raid across the border**, briefly capturing the Saudi town of Khafji. Several American marines were killed.

Tuesday 29th

Nelson Mandela and Chief Mangosuthu Buthelezi met each other for the first time in 30 years, in the hope of stopping members of Mr Mandela's African National Congress and Mr Buthelezi's mainly Zulu Inkatha movement from killing each other. Clashes between the two organisations killed more than 3,000 people in **South Africa** in 1990.

February

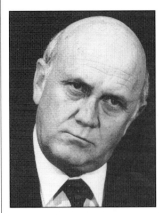

Friday 1st
At the opening of Parliament in Cape Town President F.W. de Klerk promised to knock down three pillars of **apartheid**: the Group Areas Act and Land Acts (telling people of different colours where they can live and own land) and the Population Registration Act (giving people their official colour). Far-right members of Parliament stalked out during the speech. The European Community said it would lift sanctions once the laws had been repealed.

In another attempt to curb inflation, Brazil introduced a freeze on **prices and wages**, and stopped the index-linking of savings and certificates of deposits. Union leaders complained that wages were set at too low a level and that the price freeze would not be policed effectively.

Saturday 2nd
The head of a Brazilian farmworkers' union, Expedito Ribeiro de Souza, was murdered. The murder recalled the killing of the leader of the rubber-tappers' union, Francisco "Chico" Mendes. Both men had campaigned to preserve the **Amazon rainforest** and antagonised cattle ranchers who want more land for pasture.

Sunday 3rd
The Israeli cabinet acquired a **controversial new member,**

Rehavam Zeevi of the Moledet party. With the addition of Moledet, Yitzhak Shamir's Likud-dominated coalition government controlled 66 seats in the 120-seat parliament. But the appointment of Mr Zeevi, a retired general, was opposed by several cabinet ministers. Mr Zeevi's party, more hawkish than Likud, favours "transferring" Arabs from Israel and the occupied West Bank and Gaza.

Tuesday 5th
Colombia's constituent assembly, elected in December, met to discuss **constitutional reforms** to end political violence. In its opening session the assembly called on Colombia's various guerrilla factions to give up armed struggle. Two guerrilla factions, the Revolutionary Armed Forces of Colombia and the National Liberation Army, launched a new offensive.

Wednesday 6th
King Hussein of Jordan upset the Americans by making a bitter attack on their policy towards Iraq in a speech on television. He saluted Iraq's "heroic army" and did not mention its invasion of Kuwait. Three days later, America said it was reviewing its economic aid to Jordan.

Thursday 7th
Haiti's new priest-president, Jean-Bertrand Aristide, was sworn into office in Port-au-Prince. Threats to his life had driven him into hiding after the December election, which he won with a large majority. Mr Aristide promised to uproot corruption and persuaded the army to purge its high command.

Tuesday 12th
American aircraft hit a bunker in Baghdad with two bombs, **killing hundreds**. The White House said it had been "a command and control centre that fed instructions directly

to the Iraqi war machine". Western journalists visiting the bunker afterwards said all the casualties they saw were civilians.

Thursday 14th
Peru's council of ministers resigned for a second time in as many months because of arguments over economic policy. The country's woes were augmented by the first cholera epidemic to hit Latin America in more than a century. The United States, Japan, and several European and Latin American countries banned food imports from Peru.

Friday 15th
Iraq's Revolutionary Command Council said it was willing to **withdraw from Kuwait** and accept Resolution 660 if a number of other conditions, including an Israeli pull-out from occupied Arab lands and the cancellation of Iraq's debt, were met. Mr Bush called the peace offer "a cruel hoax".

Saturday 16th
Enrique Bermudez Varela, a founder and former military chief of Nicaragua's anti-Sandinist "contra" rebel movement, was **shot dead** in Managua. The Sandinists said they had nothing to do with the assassination.

The on-again, off-again war between Colombia's government and its **drug-smuggling** cartels turned violent when a bomb killed more than 20 people, including ten policemen, in Medellin.

Sunday 17th
Aristides Maria Pereira, president of **Cape Verde** since independence from Portugal in 1975, was voted out of office in the first free election he had dared to call.

Tuesday 19th
Reforming the army was said to be on the agenda in **peace**

talks between the government of El Salvador and the guerrillas of the Farabundo Marti National Liberation Front. The guerrillas said the United Nations, which had arranged the talks in Costa Rica, proposed giving them a zone they could control while becoming a political movement. Government negotiators said the only idea was for a zone where the guerrillas could disarm and disband.

Thursday 21st
Saddam Hussein said in a defiant speech on the radio that Iraq had no honourable choice except the one it had taken in the Gulf. A few hours later his foreign minister, Tariq Aziz, said Iraq had accepted a Soviet **peace plan**.

Friday 22nd
Mr Bush told Iraq to begin an immediate and unconditional withdrawal from Kuwait by 5pm GMT on Saturday if it wanted to avoid a **land war**.

Sunday 24th
Coalition armies entered Iraq and Kuwait. In the afternoon General Norman Schwarzkopf announced that the troops were proceeding with "**dramatic success**" and that casualties had so far been remarkably light.

Wednesday 27th
The Iraqi armed forces no longer posed "an offensive regional threat", said General Schwarzkopf in Riyadh. He announced that 29 Iraqi divisions had been destroyed or "rendered inoperable", with 3,000 tanks already destroyed and another 700, belonging to the Republican Guard, about to be knocked out by American armour. Mr Bush said in a television broadcast from Washington that the **offensive** would end at midnight, New York time: "Kuwait is liberated. Iraq's army is defeated. Our military objectives are met."

Sunday 3rd

General Norman Schwarzkopf met Iraq's generals in a tent to negotiate an **interim ceasefire** agreement. The Iraqis, worried about an armed insurgency already under way in Basra and other Iraqi cities, agreed immediately to release prisoners of war and hostages, and give General Schwarzkopf details of the minefields they had laid. The American general agreed that Iraq would be allowed to continue using its helicopters, though flights by fixed-wing aircraft would be banned. Later, when the helicopters were used to kill Iraqi Kurds, General Schwarzkopf said he had been "suckered" during the talks in the tent.

Wednesday 6th

Eight Arab countries which fought against Iraq in the Gulf war issued a joint statement after a meeting in Syria. The **"Damascus Declaration"** called for the creation of a "new Arab order", an Arab peace force for the Gulf and an end to the Arab-Israeli conflict. It excluded the customary reference to the Palestine Liberation Organisation being the sole representative of the Palestinians. The eight participants—all six members of the Gulf Co-operation Council plus Egypt and Syria—resented the PLO's support for Saddam Hussein during the Gulf war.

Sunday 10th

A Palestinian from the Gaza Strip stabbed four Israeli women to death as they waited for a bus in a suburb of Jerusalem. He told police the murders were "a message" for James Baker, the American secretary of state, on the eve of his first ever visit to Israel. On the day of the stabbings Mr Baker was in Riyadh, outlining a four-point American **peace plan for the Middle East**. Its elements included a new "regional security structure", arms control, help for poorer countries and a solution for the Arab-Israeli conflict.

Tuesday 12th

South Africa's government tabled a **white paper** setting out plans to reform the various laws that had restricted the places where black people could live or own land. Once the laws were changed, a government minister said, "anybody will be able to buy land anywhere in South Africa". The ANC complained that the government was offering no compensation to blacks who had been moved forcibly as a result of apartheid.

Thursday 14th

Kuwait's emir, Sheikh Jaber al-Ahmad al-Sabah, **returned home**, a fortnight after his country had been liberated from Iraq. Fighting between government forces and rebels was reported from both the north and south of Iraq. James Baker, visiting Damascus, said he discerned a "window for peace" between Israel and the Arabs.

Friday 15th

President Fernando Collor unveiled a National Reconstruction Plan for **Brazil**. The plan called for the scrapping of state monopolies and subsidies, cutting the number of state employees and introducing profit-sharing schemes for workers.

Wednesday 20th

Kuwait's cabinet resigned, amid mounting criticism of the government's performance since the end of the Iraqi occupation.

In Washington Ms April Glaspie, the former American ambassador to Iraq, told a Senate committee that in July 1990 she had given Saddam Hussein **a tough warning** against invading Kuwait. She claimed that an Iraqi transcript of the meeting had been doctored to make it sound as though she had been too polite to Mr Hussein.

Saturday 23rd

Ernesto Diaz, Cuba's most famous **political prisoner**, was set free after 22 years in jail. He said he did not regret his attempt to overthrow Fidel Castro's communist government.

Sunday 24th

Benin's President Mathieu Kerekou lost a **general election** after 18 years in power.

South African police **shot dead** 11 supporters of the African National Congress during a rally in Deveyton, a black township outside Johannesburg. One policeman was also killed. The police said they had come under attack. ANC officials said the shooting was unprovoked.

Tuesday 26th

The presidents of Brazil, Argentina, Paraguay and Uruguay met in Asuncion and signed an agreement to establish a **common market**, to be known as Mercosul, by the end of 1994. The aim was to end all trade barriers and co-ordinate economic policy.

Mali's President Moussa Traoré, who took power in a coup in 1968, was overthrown after three days of pro-democracy rioting in which more than 100 people died. His place was taken by a military ruling council, led by Lieut-Colonel Amadou Toumani Toure.

Wednesday 27th

A 36-person commission led by two Quebec businessmen, Michel Belanger and Jean Campeau, called for a referendum to decide whether **Quebec** should become independent or remain part of English-speaking Canada. The referendum, it said, should be held by October 1992—which might give the province's premier, Robert Bourassa, time to negotiate a better deal with the rest of Canada.

In **South Africa**, a group of unidentified men carrying automatic weapons burst into a house in Alexandra, a township near Johannesburg, and killed 15 people who were attending a funeral vigil. All the murderers and their victims were black. Archbishop Desmond Tutu said "the culture of violence" seemed to be taking root in the black community.

April

Monday 1st

Assassins in **Chile** killed Jaime Guzman, a right-wing senator, prompting demands from the army for a bigger role in fighting terrorism.

Wednesday 3rd

The UN Security Council passed **Resolution 687**, bringing the Gulf hostilities to a formal end. The resolution said Iraq's chemical and biological weapons, plus its ballistic missiles, would be destroyed under international supervision. Material that could be used in nuclear weapons would have to be surrendered. Only then would Iraq be allowed to start exporting oil, though a proportion of its revenues would be set aside for compensation.

The Iraqi government recaptured Sulaymaniyah, the last main Kurdish stronghold in northern Iraq. Hundreds of thousands of **Kurdish refugees** streamed towards the Turkish border. Turkey said they could not cross.

In Canada, William Vander Zalm, the premier of British Columbia, resigned after being accused of mixing **private business interests** with public responsibilities. It all arose from the sale of an amusement park, Fantasy Gardens, to Taiwanese businessmen whom the premier had buttered up at public expense.

The African National Congress asked South Africa's law and order minister, Adriaan Vlok, to outlaw the carrying of "traditional weapons" by Zulus, who make up most of the membership of the Inkatha movement, the ANC's main rival. The weapons include spears, wide-bladed swords called pangas, and heavy clubs.

Friday 5th

In Resolution 688 the Security Council condemned the repression of the civilian population in Iraq and demanded an immediate end to it. Britain and America said their aircraft would begin **dropping supplies** by air to Kurdish refugees in northern Iraq.

The ANC said it would stop talking to **South Africa**'s white rulers unless the government agreed to several demands including the sacking of two cabinet ministers (Adriaan Vlok and Magnus Malan), disbanding an anti-insurgency unit, banning the carrying of traditional weapons at mass rallies and stopping the police using live ammunition at such events.

Sunday 7th

Kuwait's emir, Sheikh Jaber al-Ahmad al-Sabah, promised a new election for the parliament he abolished in 1986, but not until August or September 1992.

Monday 8th

At a summit in Luxembourg the European Community adopted a British proposal to provide Iraq's Kurds with **international observers** or protectors so they could return home. On some estimates about half of Iraq's 4m-5m Kurds had become refugees. Iran said it had taken in about 800,000. Turkey closed its border, but 400,000 refugees crossed it anyway.

Mexico's president, Carlos Salinas de Gortari, addressed Canada's parliament about the merits of a **free-trade area** for Canada, the United States and Mexico.

Tuesday 9th

Israel's foreign minister, David Levy, told James Baker in Jerusalem that Israel would agree to attend a regional **peace conference**. The American secretary of state said "many details" had still to be worked out.

Wednesday 10th

America said that Iraq must not fly helicopters or aircraft, or engage in military action on the ground, north of the 36th parallel, lest this endangered the international effort to bring **humanitarian relief** to Iraq's Kurds.

Sunday 14th

American forces in southern Iraq began withdrawing into a buffer zone straddling the Iraqi-Kuwaiti border, in readiness for handing over to a UN **peacekeeping force**.

Monday 15th

The European Community's foreign ministers agreed to relax **sanctions on South Africa** by lifting a ban, imposed in 1986, on the import of iron, steel and gold coins.

Tuesday 16th

America, Britain and France said they would move troops into northern Iraq to set up **protective zones** for Kurdish refugees. President Bush said the aim was to get the refugees off the mountains and into areas where food, clothing and shelter could be provided. He said America did not intend to occupy Iraqi territory permanently.

Yitzhak Shamir, Israel's prime minister, met Valentin Pavlov, the Soviet prime minister, in London. They discussed the possibility that the Soviet Union would **renew relations** in return for a seat at the Arab-Israeli peace conference proposed by America.

Brazil's acting health minister announced that the **cholera epidemic** sweeping through Peru had crossed the border. One case was confirmed and several more suspected in the Amazon region.

Thursday 18th

Iraq and the United Nations signed an agreement on the care and safety of **Kurds** and other Iraqi refugees. The agreement had nothing to do with the American, British and French operation in northern Iraq, which the Iraqis condemned.

Saturday 20th

Health ministers from eight Latin American countries held a meeting in Bolivia to co-ordinate their fight against the region's **cholera epidemic**. They were told that the disease had affected nearly 160,000 people in Peru alone.

Sunday 21st

Canada's Conservative prime minister, Brian Mulroney, **reshuffled** his cabinet. His main change was giving Joe Clark, the external-affairs minister and a former prime minister, the job of preventing Quebec from leaving the federation.

Saturday 27th

Negotiators trying to end the civil war in **El Salvador** said they had made a breakthrough during talks in Mexico City. The government and the rebels signed an agreement committing the government to bring the army under tighter civilian control and increase the independence of the judiciary. A commission appointed by the United Nations would investigate human-rights abuses.

Wednesday 1st

The official Lebanese army began entering areas previously controlled by various private militias. At Syria's urging, the militias had begun to disarm in accordance with a **peace plan** agreed by the Arab League in the Saudi town of Taif in 1989. The Taif agreement called for an end to Lebanon's civil war, a new constitution and privileges for Syria, which has a large army in Lebanon.

Wednesday 8th

Egypt announced that it was withdrawing its troops from **Kuwait**. President Hosni Mubarak said the troops were coming home because they had completed their mission. Rumour had it that Egypt wanted more aid from the Gulf states for the part it played during the Gulf war.

Thursday 9th

Richard Cheney, the American defence secretary, said that the six member-states of the Gulf Co-operation Council had accepted American plans for a new **security structure** in the Gulf. He declined to give details of the plans.

Sunday 12th

Zulus in **South Africa** rampaged through a squatter camp near Johannesburg, killing at least 27 people with knives and spears.

America's secretary of state, pursuing his **peace mission** in the Middle East, spent six hours talking to Syria's President Hafez Assad in Damascus. Officials said that Mr Baker made "no particular progress".

Monday 13th

A court in South Africa found **Winnie Mandela**, the wife of Nelson Mandela, guilty on charges of kidnapping and being an accessory to assault. The judge called Mrs Mandela an "unblushing liar" and sentenced her to six years in jail. Mrs Mandela said she would appeal. Her husband said he was sure she would be cleared, but that the case would not affect negotiations between the ANC and the government.

Thursday 16th

James Baker, America's secretary of state, wound up the fourth of his Middle East **peace shuttles** after two days of talks in Israel. His plan to hold a peace conference was still being held up by a difference between Syria and Israel on the role of the United Nations. Syria wanted the UN involved; Israel said its participation would obstruct direct talks between the parties in conflict.

Monday 20th

Poland's president, Lech Walesa, addressed the Israeli parliament in Jerusalem. He asked **forgiveness** for the fate of Poland's Jews in the second world war. Israel's Polish-born prime minister, Yitzhak Shamir, lost his family in the Holocaust. He once said that Poles took in anti-Semitism with their mothers' milk.

Tuesday 21st

Ethiopia's Marxist dictator, President **Mengistu Haile Mariam**, fled the country after ruling it for 14 years. He took refuge in Zimbabwe while anti-government rebels, led by fighters from the province of Tigre, closed in on Addis Ababa. The government he left behind appealed for a ceasefire. The rebels, of the Ethiopian People's Revolutionary Democratic Front, said they would press on regardless.

Wednesday 22nd

Tunisia's government claimed to have uncovered a **coup plot** by Islamic extremists and had arrested 300 of the plotters. The interior minister said the coup was being organised by Islamic militants of the Ennadha party, with accomplices in the army. Sceptics said the coup allegation was trumped up, to discredit the Islamic opposition and divert attention from the killing of several students in a clash with the police.

James Baker, the American secretary of state, told a congressional hearing that Israel's creation of **Jewish settlements** in the occupied territories was an obstacle to peace in the Middle East. President Bush added his voice the next day. He said he had asked Israel not to move ahead with more settlements.

In Brazil, three of the biggest trade unions started a two-day **general strike** in protest against the government's policy of wage- and price-freezes.

Friday 24th

Israel airlifted more than 14,000 **black Jews**, known as Falashas, out of Addis Ababa in a secret operation, co-ordinated with the United States. The Americans had asked rebel troops not to enter the capital until the evacuation was over.

Monday 27th

Rebel troops of the Ethiopian People's Revolutionary Democratic Front entered **Addis Ababa**, after getting the go-ahead from the United States. An American official had been mediating between the rebels and what remained of the Ethiopian government at talks in London. The Americans said the EPRDF, formerly Marxist, was now promising to set up a democratic government.

Tuesday 28th

Having secured control of Addis Ababa, the EPRDF said that it had agreed during American-sponsored talks in London to form a **transitional government**, in co-operation with two other rebel movements—those which had been fighting for the independence of Eritrea and of the Oromo people. The rebels agreed to hold an election within a year.

Wednesday 29th

President Bush unveiled an **arms reduction** plan for the Middle East. It would entail freezing the purchase and production of surface-to-surface missiles and, eventually, removing nuclear and chemical weapons from the region. He said the five permanent members of the UN Security Council should limit their sales of conventional weapons to those needed for their customers' legitimate defence needs.

Thursday 30th

Visiting Israel, Richard Cheney, America's defence secretary, said America's commitment to **Israel's security** was "unshakeable". He agreed to deliver more F-15 fighters, and to continue paying for development of Israel's anti-missile missile, the Arrow.

June

Saturday 1st
Meless Zenawi, leader of the Ethiopian People's Revolutionary Democratic Front, arrived in Addis Ababa promising that his **interim administration** would pursue no vendettas against remnants of the former Ethiopian government. But scattered violence continued in the capital.

Sunday 2nd
Kuwait's government confirmed its plan to hold full parliamentary **elections**— though not until October 1992. Fed up with the government's autocratic instincts, the opposition howled.

Wednesday 5th
Amid **rioting** on the streets, the government of Algeria imposed a four-month state of siege and called off the general election that had been due at the end of the month. One theory held that the government aborted the election because the opposition Islamic Salvation Front (FIS) was going to win; another that the FIS started the riots because it expected to lose.

South Africa's white parliament repealed the Land Acts and Group Areas Act. Later in the month it repealed the Population Registration Act and reformed the Internal Security Act. For years these laws had been considered the **pillars of apartheid**. The new legislation—and, said the government, the formal end of apartheid—came into effect on June 30th.

Mr F.W. de Klerk made a **state visit** to Kenya, the first by a South African president. After meeting President Daniel arap Moi, he foresaw an Africa consisting of four trading regions, based on Kenya, South Africa, Egypt and Nigeria. South Africa's GDP, he pointed out, was almost as big as the combined GDP of 40 black African countries.

Israel dropped its previous objection to **European participation** at a Middle East peace conference. An EC spokesman said the conference seat would be taken by whichever government held the Community's rotating presidency at the time.

Sunday 9th
At King Hussein's instigation, Jordan adopted a **national charter** relaxing press controls and legalising political parties. However, groups linked to or financed by other Arab governments would remain banned.

Monday 17th
South Africa's President F.W. de Klerk said that 1991 would go down in history as the year apartheid ended. He was speaking after parliament repealed the **Population Registration Act**, under which every South African had been given an official colour. The repeal of the act was praised later in the week by General Ibrahim Babangida, president of Nigeria and chairman of the Organisation of African Unity.

Tuesday 18th
Nicaragua's opposition Sandinist party started a **boycott** of the National Assembly. It claimed that legislation by Violeta Chamorro's government, allowing former owners to recover confiscated property, was reversing the land redistribution the Sandinists had introduced when they ran the government.

A fortnight after imposing a state of siege, **Algeria** acquired a new government. The new prime minister, Sid Ahmed Ghozali, promised to lead the country towards fresh elections, following the postponement of those scheduled for June 27th.

Wednesday 19th
Pablo Escobar, boss of Colombia's Medellin **drugs cartel**, gave himself up and went to a prison he had helped to design. Half a dozen cronies followed suit a few days later. Earlier, the government had changed the law so that drug traffickers could no longer be extradited to the United States.

King Hussein of Jordan appointed a **new government** after the resignation of the prime minister, Mudar Badran. His replacement, Taher Masri, was considered less friendly to the country's Islamic fundamentalists and keener on making peace with Israel. The Muslim Brotherhood, which had been represented in Mr Badran's cabinet, was left out of Mr Masri's.

Saturday 22nd
A South Africa **peace summit**, sponsored by churchmen and businessmen, brought together South Africa's warring groups. Representatives of the government, the African National Congress and the Inkatha movement set up a committee to work out ways to end political violence. At

least 20 people were killed in township clashes the following weekend.

Sunday 23rd
The Israeli army admitted, after a television programme, that it was using **undercover units** in its battle against the Palestinian uprising in the occupied West Bank and Gaza Strip.

Wednesday 26th
Kuwait's government announced that 29 people sentenced to death for **collaborating** with the Iraqi occupiers would not be executed after all. The original verdicts had caused dismay among Kuwait's wartime allies. They prompted James Baker, the American secretary of state to concede in Congress that, even after liberation, Kuwait did not enjoy the "optimum" type of government.

Thursday 27th
A committee set up under Keith Spicer by Canada's federal government published a report calling for reforms of the Senate and constitutional changes recognising Quebec as a **unique province** within Canada.

Friday 28th
UN inspectors scouring Iraq for **nuclear-weapons sites** were fired on by Iraqi soldiers. It was the Iraqis' second attempt in three days to interfere with the inspectors' work. President Bush hinted that he would take military action if Saddam Hussein failed to let the inspectors see what they wanted, as laid down under the ceasefire agreement at the end of the Gulf war.

Sunday 30th
The Algerian authorities arrested Abassi Madani and Ali Belhadj, two prominent leaders of the opposition Islamic Salvation Front. It accused them of planning an **armed conspiracy**.

INTERNATIONAL

July

Monday 1st
Troops in **Algeria** closed several mosques and arrested 700 people, following continuing disturbances by supporters of the main opposition party, the Islamic Salvation Front, which wanted to set up an Islamic state in Algeria.

Fighting erupted in **southern Lebanon** between the Palestine Liberation Organisation and the Lebanese army. The army captured the port of Sidon, as part of its continuing drive to restore the whole country to the control of the central government.

Tuesday 2nd
The African National Congress met in Durban for its first national conference inside South Africa for more than 30 years. At the five-day meeting the Congress elected **Nelson Mandela** its president and called for the creation of a constituent assembly and interim government to oversee the end of apartheid.

In Addis Ababa, the new rulers of Ethiopia agreed to let the province of Eritrea hold a **referendum on independence**. In return the Eritrean People's Liberation Front promised to let the rest of Ethiopia use the Eritrean port of Asab for access to the sea.

Thursday 4th
After four days of fighting against the Lebanese army the PLO accepted a **peace accord** under which it would withdraw its heavy weapons from Lebanon and cease raids across the border into Israel.

Colombia promulgated a **new constitution**, reforming the electoral and judicial systems and giving congress more power to keep tabs on the executive. President Cesar Gaviria described it as a peace treaty, because it would enable former guerrillas of the M-19 organisation to compete for office.

Monday 8th
Iraq gave the United Nations a new list of its nuclear activities, admitting for the first time that it had been trying to **enrich uranium**, in breach of the Nuclear Non-Proliferation Treaty, which it had signed.

The five permanent members of the UN Security Council met in Paris for two days to discuss ways of **cutting arms sales** to the third world, especially the Middle East. They said the region should be made free of weapons of mass destruction, and of surface-to-surface missiles.

Wednesday 10th
Ignoring the pleas of Nelson Mandela, and of some opponents in Congress, President Bush announced that America would **lift sanctions** against South Africa. But a ban on the sale of arms and nuclear materials remained in place.

Sunday 14th
Syria said that it had accepted American proposals for an Arab-Israeli **peace conference**. All eyes turned to Israel.

Monday 15th
Western troops withdrew from Iraqi Kurdistan, following the establishment of a **safe haven** for Kurdish refugees. Allied commanders said some of the forces would stay on in Turkey, to keep watch on the haven. Kurds complained that they were once again at Saddam Hussein's mercy.

Tuesday 16th
The **Group of Seven**, meeting in London, called for the strengthening of the UN, peace in the Middle East and a slow-down in the arms race. The seven leaders asked Israel to stop building Jewish settlements in the occupied territories, and the Arabs to drop their economic boycott of Israel. The summit added its voice to calls for the UN to help arms control by keeping a register of arms sales.

Wednesday 17th
The **Group of Seven** ended its meeting with an offer of technical help but no money for its controversial visitor, the Soviet Union's Mikhail Gorbachev. At the same time Presidents Bush and Gorbachev reached final agreement on the Strategic Arms Reduction Treaty, which could cut their respective nuclear arsenals by about one-third.

Monday 22nd
South Africa's cabinet started an emergency meeting at a **secret location** to discuss revelations that the government had donated nearly £370,000 ($630,000) over six years to the Inkatha movement and other rivals of the African National Congress.

Tuesday 23rd
Madagascar declared a **state of emergency** after a day of protests organised by the six-party opposition. The opposition called for an end to the socialist constitution, free elections and the departure of President Didier Ratsiraka, who had been in power for 16 years.

Sunday 28th
Kuwait made its first **oil shipment** to the outside world since the Gulf war. The oil minister said the emirate was producing 115,000 barrels a day (b/d) compared with 2m b/d before the Iraqi invasion.

Monday 29th
South Africa's President F. W. de Klerk **demoted** two ministers. Adriaan Vlok, the minister for law and order, and Magnus Malan, the defence minister, had been implicated in the covert transfer of government funds to black organisations opposed to the African National Congress. The following day, Mr de Klerk announced the immediate cessation of all such payments.

Wednesday 31st
Presidents Bush and Gorbachev signed the Strategic Arms Reduction Treaty (START), under which the United States and the Soviet Union are to cut the number of long-range **nuclear weapons** they possess by about 30%. They also announced plans to co-sponsor an Arab-Israeli peace conference in October. James Baker, the American secretary of state, flew to Jerusalem to see if Israel would accept an invitation.

Rolf Ekeus, head of the United Nations commission supervising Iraqi disarmament, said that Iraq had lied about its stockpile of **chemical weapons**. Inspectors had discovered 46,000 chemical shells and warheads in Iraq instead of the 10,000-11,000 Saddam Hussein had owned up to. Some warheads were armed with a nerve gas called Sarin and were fitted to Scud missiles. Mr Ekeus complained that the Iraqi authorities were still failing to co-operate properly with members of his commission.

Thursday 1st
Yitzhak Shamir, the prime minister, said Israel would indeed attend a peace conference sponsored by the United States and the Soviet Union, provided that there was a "satisfactory" solution to the problem of **Palestinian representation**. Israel's position was that no Palestinians from the Palestine Liberation Organisation, East Jerusalem or beyond the occupied territories could attend the peace talks.

The African National Congress called on South Africa's government to **resign**, following revelations that it had secretly funded the Inkatha organisation. Unimpressed by President F.W. de Klerk's cabinet reshuffle and a promise to halt all such payments, the ANC said an interim government was needed to oversee the negotiation of a new non-racial constitution.

Sunday 4th
A Greek **cruiseliner**, the *Oceanos*, sank in high seas off the coast of South Africa. Most of the 580 passengers aboard were rescued. They accused the crew of fleeing first.

In **Zimbabwe** 83 children and four teachers were killed when a bus overturned.

Monday 5th
The Turkish army launched an **invasion** of the Kurdish "safe haven" inside northern Iraq. The Turks said that guerrillas of the Kurdish Workers' Party (PKK) had begun using the haven as a base for attacks on Turkey. During the operation, which lasted a week, a number of Kurdish civilians, as well as some PKK guerrillas, were killed. The Turks apparently mistook their refugee camps for PKK bases.

Thursday 8th
John McCarthy, a British journalist who had been a **hostage** in Lebanon for more than five years, was set free. His captors gave him a letter addressed to Javier Perez de Cuellar, the secretary-general of the UN, proposing to exchange Arab prisoners held in Israel and Europe for the remaining westerners held in Lebanon. Edward Tracy, an American hostage held for five years, was released three days later.

Friday 9th
In **South Africa**, white police and white demonstrators clashed violently in Ventersdorp, a farming town west of Johannesburg. Three of the civilians died. It was the first fatal battle between police and members of the Afrikaner Resistance Movement, a far-right group that opposes the ruling National Party's efforts to end apartheid.

Saturday 10th
A campaign to unseat **Madagascar**'s president, Didier Ratsiraka, turned violent. The government said 11 people were killed and many more wounded when they launched an attack on the presidential palace. Opposition spokesmen said scores of people had been killed in a variety of incidents. Strikes and demonstrations against the president had been going on for ten weeks.

Sunday 11th
Iraq let UN inspectors visit its **supergun**, a vast cannon with a barrel more than 50 metres long. The gun, installed in rugged mountains north of Baghdad, was assembled but not yet capable of firing. Before the Gulf war Iraq had denied possessing such a weapon.

Thursday 15th
The UN Security Council adopted **Resolution 706**, under which Iraq would be permitted to sell $1.6 billion-worth of oil over six months. The catch was that the sale would have to be supervised by the UN and the proceeds put into an escrow account. After deductions for war reparations and UN expenses, the money could then be used to buy food and humanitarian supplies. Iraq said no. Another Resolution, 707, said UN inspectors could use their own helicopters to scour Iraq for hidden nuclear- and missile-sites.

The government reached agreement with the African National Congress and the Inkatha Freedom Party on a plan to end **political violence** in South Africa. The plan, to be signed officially in September, laid down a code of conduct for political parties and the security forces. It would also establish a "peace secretariat" to investigate violent incidents.

Sunday 18th
Mexico held elections for six state governorships, half the seats in the Senate and for the 500-seat Chamber of Deputies. The ruling Institutional Revolutionary Party won all the governorships and all but one Senate seat. The opposition complained of fraud. On August 29th, under pressure from President Carlos Salinas, the PRI victor in the state of Guanajuato stood down in favour of an opposition candidate.

South Africa's **United Democratic Front**, which campaigned against apartheid during the 1980s while the African National Congress was banned, dissolved itself. At its peak, it had a membership of some 3m people. Meanwhile 30 people who had been held prisoner as spies by the ANC in exile returned to South Africa. Some of them said they had been tortured.

Tuesday 27th
Delegates to a national conference in **Togo** defied the president, Gnassinbé Eyadéma, and voted in an opposition leader, Kokou Koffigoh, as prime minister. The president, who had run Togo for 24 years, ordered troops to surround the building where the conference was held.

Wednesday 28th
Javier Perez de Cuellar, the UN secretary-general, issued a report saying that **Africa** was facing a tragedy. He said rich countries should cancel Africa's debts and increase aid for the continent.

Thursday 29th
General **Michel Aoun**, the Lebanese army officer who aspired to evict Syrian troops from Lebanon, left the country himself on board a French submarine.

Kuwait claimed to have repelled an Iraqi attempt to land troops on Bubiyan island, the strategic mudflat Iraq claimed for itself before the Gulf war.

Wednesday 4th

The ruling National Party unveiled its plans for a **post-apartheid** constitution for South Africa. It called for universal suffrage, together with checks and balances. These included a veto-wielding upper house, a collective presidency with three to five members, and cabinet seats for all major parties. The African National Congress denounced the plan as a subterfuge to protect the white population's "accumulated privileges".

Friday 6th

President Bush asked Congress to delay for 120 days a decision on granting **loan guarantees** of $10 billion for Israel, which said it needed the money to absorb Soviet immigrants. The president said that granting the loans could disrupt efforts to convene an Arab-Israeli peace conference.

Sunday 8th

President Carlos Menem's Peronist Party did well in **Argentina's mid-term elections**. It gained four seats in the 254-member Chamber of Deputies, for a total of 123 compared with the Radicals' 87 and the Centre Democrats' ten.

Unidentified gunmen using AK-47 rifles massacred more than 20 members of South Africa's Inkatha Freedom Party, the main rival of the African National Congress in South Africa. The ambush prompted a spate of violence and counter-violence which raised the death toll to above 90 within three days. The ANC said the killings may have been the work of a "**third force**" intent on aggravating relations between the two black groups, which had hoped to sign a peace accord one week later.

Wednesday 11th

President Gorbachev announced that the (former) Soviet Union was opening talks with Cuba about **withdrawing** its 11,000 soldiers from the island. America's secretary of state, James Baker, called it "a very substantial gesture".

Israel released 51 Lebanese prisoners, and returned the remains of nine dead guerrillas, as part of a **prisoner exchange** organised by the UN.

Saturday 14th

The government, the African National Congress and the Inkatha Freedom Party signed a **peace accord**, aimed at curbing political violence in South Africa. It laid down codes of conduct for the police and for political parties, set up a peace committee to monitor incidents, and established procedures to investigate complaints and expose the causes of violence. Archbishop Desmond Tutu called it "a historic day".

Sunday 15th

Iraq reported that its prime minister, Saadoun Hammadi, had been **dismissed** from his job. President Saddam Hussein, a Sunni Muslim, had given the job to Mr Hammadi, a Shia, after the Gulf war, ostensibly to introduce political reforms. Some observers said the dismissal showed that Mr Hussein was growing in confidence. Others thought that Mr Hammadi had been executed after trying to mount a coup.

Monday 23rd

President Bush asked the UN General Assembly to repeal the 1975 resolution describing **Zionism** as a form of racism. The Palestine National Council, the "parliament" of Yasser Arafat's Palestine Liberation Organisation, began a week-long meeting in Algiers, agreeing to co-operate with American plans for an Arab-Israeli peace conference, but rejecting Israel's conditions for taking part.

Tuesday 24th

Iraqi soldiers blockaded 44 UN **inspectors** in Baghdad who were trying to remove boxes of files containing information about Iraq's nuclear-weapons programme. After a siege of several days, during which the United States hinted at renewed military strikes against Iraq, the inspectors were allowed to carry off their booty. David Kay, the team leader, said later that the documents showed that Iraq had come close to producing a nuclear weapon before the Gulf war.

France and Belgium sent paratroops into Zaire, to rescue foreign nationals endangered by an **army mutiny**. Zairean soldiers had run amok in the capital, Kinshasa, because the regime of Mobutu Sese Seko had failed to pay them. Trouble spread to the southern towns of Kamina and Kolwezi as well. Opposition groups blamed "frustration", caused by Mr Mobutu's blocking of a national conference which had been convened in August to discuss political reforms.

Brian Mulroney, Canada's prime minister, unveiled a new **constitutional blueprint** designed to heal the rift between French-speaking Quebec and the rest of the Canadian federation. The new proposals were designed to please Quebec by recognising its "distinctiveness and linguistic duality", and please the western provinces by creating an elected Senate with "more equitable" regional representation. Equally controversially, the blueprint also called for the free movement of goods, services and capital within Canada.

Jackie Mann, an Englishman who flew Spitfires in the second world war, was released after being a **hostage** in Lebanon for 28 months. He had been held, often in chains, by a gang calling itself the Revolutionary Justice Organisation. Israel had released 51 Lebanese prisoners 13 days earlier, as part of an exchange organised by the secretary-general of the United Nations.

Wednesday 25th

Britain and Argentina signed an accord normalising military arrangements around the **Falkland Islands**, for which the two countries went to war in 1982. The accord reduced the amount of notice each side must give about air and naval movements. But Argentina said it still refused to recognise British sovereignty in the Falklands.

Sunday 29th

President Jean-Bertrand Aristide of Haiti, fled after an **army coup**, led by the new provisional commander, Brigadier-General Raoul Cedras. The United States, the Organisation of American States and the UN refused to recognise the new regime.

October

Friday 4th

Four Israeli F-15 fighters made a **reconnaissance flight** over Iraq. Iraq complained to the UN secretary-general. The United States complained to Israel.

Sunday 6th

An Israeli court sentenced Abie Nathan, an Israeli **peace activist**, to 18 months in jail for having a meeting with Yasser Arafat, chairman of the Palestine Liberation Organisation. "Without speaking to the enemy there won't be any chance of peace in our area," Mr Nathan said.

Monday 7th

Kurdish guerrillas **shot dead** 60 unarmed prisoners from the Iraqi army, on the third day of fighting on the fringes of the Kurdish "safe haven" in northern Iraq. Massoud Barzani, leader of one of the main Kurdish groups in Iraq, condemned the killings.

Despite a heavy police presence, unidentified attackers **shot dead** 18 black South Africans returning from the funeral of a prominent member of the African National Congress. The ANC accused the police of assisting the killers.

Tuesday 8th

The Organisation of American States voted unanimously to **embargo** trade with Haiti, and freeze its assets abroad, until the military coup there was reversed.

Wednesday 9th

Hundreds of Israeli Jews, some of them armed, occu-

pied several houses in an **Arab neighbourhood** of East Jerusalem. They claimed to have purchased the properties, but agreed to leave all but one pending a court decision. One of the squatters, an Israeli cabinet minister, said she hoped the action would destroy America's efforts to convene an Arab-Israeli peace conference.

Thursday 10th

Cuba's Communist Party held its first congress since 1986. Fidel Castro, the 65-year-old president, told delegates during the four-day meeting that the western notion of democracy was "garbage". He and his brother Raul, the armed-forces minister, kept their jobs in a newly elected Politburo and Central Committee.

Friday 11th

Turkish aircraft attacked targets in the Kurdish **safe haven** in northen Iraq. The Turks said they hit bases of the Kurdish Workers' Party, a guerrilla group fighting for an independent Kurdish state in southern Turkey. The Kurds said the victims were civilians.

Sunday 13th

Algeria's parliament adopted a **new electoral law**. The country's next attempt to run a free and fair election was set for December 26th, although the main opposition party, the Islamic Salvation Front, was still threatening to boycott the vote.

Monday 14th

After a fortnight of haggling, **Zaire's** President Monutu Sese Seko agreed to let one of his opponents, Etienne Tshisekedi, become the country's prime minister.

Saturday 19th

Nigeria held **election primaries** in all 30 states, as part of a plan by President Ibrahim Babangida to restore the coun-

try to democratic rule. Only two parties, the National Republican Convention and the Social Democratic Party were allowed to compete. Both had been formed under the guidance of the military rulers.

Sunday 20th

Israel's cabinet voted to accept a Soviet-American invitation t o a **Middle East peace conference**, to be held in Madrid at the end of the month. On the previous day the Soviet Union restored diplomatic relations with Israel, which it had severed in 1967.

Monday 21st

Jesse Turner, another **American hostage in Lebanon**, was set free by his captors after Israel's release of 15 Lebanese prisoners earlier in the day. Mr Turner had been held for just under five years.

The **Commonwealth** ended its two-yearly meeting in Harare, with a call for all of its 50 member countries to respect human rights. Britain had the usual tiff over South African sanctions, but not the flaming row that had been customary when Margaret Thatcher was prime minister.

Sunday 27th

Colombia held elections for a new Senate, Chamber of Deputies and—for the first time in in the country's history—27 state governors. President Cesar Gaviria's Liberal Party did best, although only about a third of the electorate bothered to vote. One novelty was the participation of the M-19 Democratic Alliance, which won nine seats in the Senate, 15 in the lower house and two governorships. M-19 used to be a guerrilla outfit.

At a meeting in Durban, South Africa's African National Congress and Pan-Africanist Congress joined together to form a single **Patriotic Front**, to negotiate

with the government. Two organisations left out of the Front were the Zulu-dominated Inkatha Freedom Party and the Azanian People's Organisation.

Wednesday 30th

Israel and its Arab neighbours sat across a table in Madrid's Royal Palace for their first **comprehensive peace conference** since the founding of the Jewish state in 1948. The United States and the Soviet Union were the main sponsors. After three days of televised speeches Israel held separate, direct talks with teams from Syria, Lebanon and a joint group of Jordanians and Palestinians. The Palestine Liberation Organisation was not allowed to attend.

Thursday 31st

President Kenneth Kaunda stepped down as president of **Zambia** after his United National Independence Party was routed by Frederick Chiluba's Movement for Multiparty Democracy in the country's first free election for two decades. The MMD won 125 of the 150 seats in parliament.

Argentina's President Carlos Menem issued a decree introducing **sweeping deregulation**. He banned all restrictions on the sale of goods and services, closed down the national grain and meat boards and did away with most regulations and taxes on imports and exports.

Sunday 3rd

As part of the peace conference in Madrid, Israel held **bilateral negotiations** with delegations from Syria, Lebanon and a mixed team of Jordanians and Palestinians. They adjourned after failing to agree where to meet next.

Gunmen shot dead 16 people at a barbecue in the centre of Lima. Peru's government said the massacre was another outrage by **terrorists of the Shining Path movement**, but some Peruvians said a right-wing murder squad was responsible.

Monday 4th

Millions of South Africans began a two-day **general strike** in protest against the introduction of a 10% value-added tax. In the course of the week 76 miners were killed in fights at the President Steyn gold mine in the Orange Free State. Mine owners said strikers had attacked non-strikers. The union said it was the other way round.

Israeli settlers set up a new **Jewish settlement** in the Golan Heights, which Israel captured from Syria in 1967. The inauguration ceremony, attended by several cabinet ministers, came one day after Syrian diplomats had met Israeli diplomats in Madrid and demanded Israel's withdrawal from the Heights.

Wednesday 6th

Hussein Kamal, who had been considered the second-most powerful man in **Iraq**, was removed from his job as defence minister by President Saddam Hussein. His job was taken by Ali Hassan al-Majid.

Thursday 7th

President Carlos Salinas of Mexico announced sweeping **land reforms**, which would at last allow individual owners to buy and sell land belonging to the *ejidos*, Mexico's venerable farming collectives.

Sunday 10th

President F.W. de Klerk of South Africa started a three-day **state visit to Israel**. He said he wanted to improve trading relations with Israel, but had no intention of discussing military co-operation.

Robert Maxwell, the British publishing tycoon, was buried in Jerusalem. Israel's president, one of the mourners, praised Mr Maxwell's contributions to Israel's security and economy. Conspiracy theorists took note. Mr Maxwell had died at sea, in mysterious circumstances, shortly after a book had accused him of helping Mossad, the Israeli intelligence service.

Thursday 14th

Britain and America accused two Libyans of having planted the bomb on a Pan Am jet that killed 270 people in and above the Scottish town of **Lockerbie** in December 1988. Both men were said to be agents of the Libyan intelligence services, who had acted with other conspirators still to be named. Britain's foreign secretary, Douglas Hurd, said that Colonel Moammar Qaddafi should hand them over to be tried.

Left-wing guerrillas of the Farabundo Mundi Liberation Front called a **unilateral ceasefire in El Salvador**. The announcement raised hopes that a UN-mediated peace plan, drawn up in September, might produce a formal peace treaty by the end of the year.

Monday 18th

Two more western hostages, **Terry Waite and Thomas Sutherland**, were released from Lebanon. Mr Waite, a special envoy of the Archbishop of Canterbury, was kidnapped in January 1987 while trying to negotiate the release of other hostages, including Mr Sutherland, a Scottish-born American kidnapped in 1985.

Tuesday 19th

Kenya's energy minister, Nicholas Biwott, was sacked by President Daniel arap Moi. The sacking came after a Scotland Yard detective told a judicial commission that the minister was his **prime suspect** in the murder of the country's foreign minister, Robert Ouko, in 1989.

Thursday 21st

The Security Council chose an Egyptian diplomat, Boutros Boutros Ghali, as the next **United Nations secretary-general**. Mr Boutros Ghali had the advantage of being able to portray himself as an Arab and an African, as well as a fluent French speaker. Against him was only his age, at 69, and a suspicion that he might prove to be a trifle dull.

Friday 22nd

Yitzhak Shamir had an unfriendly meeting with George Bush in Washington. The Israeli prime minister had hoped to discuss the time and place of the next round of **Arab-Israeli peace talks**, but the Americans issued the invitations—for Washington on December 4th—just before the two men met. Mr Shamir's colleagues said that he had been humiliated.

Saturday 23rd

Ian Richter, a British businessman accused of bribery, was set free after **six years in jail in Iraq**. Another jailed Briton, Douglas Brand, had been released in June. Though the British said there had been no deal, the freeing of Mr Richter resulted in Britain letting Iraq use £70m ($125m) of frozen assets to import food and medicines.

Tuesday 26th

Kenya's President Daniel arap Moi ordered the arrest of Nicholas Biwott, the energy secretary he had sacked a week earlier. Police also arrested a former head of internal security who, along with Mr Biwott, had been implicated in corruption, and in the murder of the foreign minister, Robert Ouko. The arrests coincided with a meeting in Paris of rich-country donors. They said they would **suspend further aid to Kenya** for six months, pending "economic and social reforms".

Wednesday 27th

The United States said it would press ahead with the next round of **Arab-Israeli peace talks** in Washington on December 4th, even though Israel said it would not attend until the 9th.

Thursday 28th

Troops loyal to President Gnassingbe Eyadama, one-party ruler for 24 years, organised a **coup in Togo** against the pro-reform prime minister, Joseph Kokou Koffigoh.

South Africa's pro-apartheid Conservative Party won a **landslide victory** in a parliamentary by-election in the Orange Free State.

Monday 2nd

Joseph Cicippio, **an American hostage**, was set free from Lebanon after more than five years. Alann Steen came out the following day.

Kenya's ruling party decided to move to a **multi-party democracy** after nearly ten years as a single-party state. The decision was formally confirmed by a party conference the following day. Daniel arap Moi, the president, suggested the change one week after rich countries decided to suspend new aid to Kenya.

Troops loyal to the ever-ruling president of Togo stormed a government building and **captured the new prime minister**, who had been planning political reforms. Later, France sent troops to neighbouring Benin, and called for the reforms to continue.

The United States gave Iran $278m in **compensation** for weapons paid for by the former shah but never delivered. American spokesmen said the deal had nothing to do with the release of western hostages from Lebanon.

Wednesday 4th

Terry Anderson, the last of the **American hostages** in Lebanon, was released after six and a half years. His freedom set back hopes for a comprehensive deal that would also set free two remaining German hostages, a captured Israeli pilot, and several hundred Lebanese prisoners held by Israel.

Syrian, Lebanese, Jordanian and Palestinian negotiators turned up at the State Department in Washington for a second round of **Arab-Israeli** peace talks. Israel's negotiators were not there, having named December 9th as the day they wanted to resume negotiations.

The chief of Libyan intelligence said in a newspaper interview that he was investigating American and British charges against two Libyans suspected of destroying **Pan Am 103** over Lockerbie in 1988. He said the men had been arrested but would not be extradited as the British and Americans had requested.

Sunday 8th

Overruling the government's own legal adviser, Israel's cabinet gave permission for Jewish settlers to move into a number of houses in Silwan, an **Arab suburb of Jerusalem**. The settlers claimed to have acquired the properties legally, but Teddy Kollek, the city's mayor, said the move was provocative.

Tuesday 10th

Arab and Israeli negotiators met for **peace talks** at the State Department in Washington. Israel's meetings with Syria and Lebanon went smoothly. Its talks with the Palestinians and Jordanians were held up by a procedural argument. The Palestinians and Jordanians came as separate delegations. Israel said they had to act as a joint delegation. This issue was then discussed for three days in a corridor outside the negotiating room.

Nicholas Biwott, a former Kenyan cabinet minister who had been accused of **arranging the murder of a colleague**, was released from jail because the police said they could not find enough evidence against him.

Javier Perez de Cuellar, the UN secretary-general, said Iraq had been responsible for causing the 1980-88 **Iran-Iraq war**. The ceasefire agreement between the two countries, signed in 1988, had called for an independent investigation of the origins of the war.

Wednesday 11th

A stormy meeting of the **Organisation of the Islamic Conference** broke up in disarray in Dakar, a day earlier than planned. Yasser Arafat, chairman of the Palestine Liberation Organisation, departed in tears after the 45-nation organisation voted to delete its customary call for a *jihad* (holy war) against Israel.

Saturday 14th

Nigeria held **gubernatorial elections** in each of its 30 states. The military government allowed only two parties to compete: the National Republican Convention on the right and the Social Democrats on the left. The elections were part of an army plan to restore the country to civilian government.

Sunday 15th

Nearly **500 people drowned** when an Egyptian ferry sank in the Red Sea, after hitting a reef. Nearly 200 other passengers were rescued.

Monday 16th

The UN General Assembly repealed a resolution it had passed in 1975 equating **Zionism and racism**. The vote was 111 to 25, with 13 abstentions. Despite their peace talks with Israel, most Arab states voted to maintain the original resolution.

Wednesday 18th

The Arabs and Israelis **adjourned their peace talks** in Washington, having made little or no progress. All they could agree on was that they would meet again—in Washington—in January.

Friday 20th

In a helicopter raid, Israeli soldiers abducted three suspected guerrillas from **South Lebanon**. Israel released them the following day, after admitting that they had grabbed the wrong men.

A multi-party body, the **Convention for a Democratic South Africa**, held its inaugural meeting in Johannesburg, to begin drafting a post-apartheid constitution. President F.W. de Klerk accused the African National Congress of retaining its private army, despite promising to disband it. The ANC's president, Nelson Mandela, accused the government of condoning violence by the security services. The militant Pan-Africanist Congress accused Mr de Klerk and Mr Mandela of having made a secret deal on power-sharing.

Thursday 26th

In the first round of parliamentary **elections in Algeria**, the Islamic Salvation Front performed better than the ruling National Liberation Front, which had ruled Algeria since independence. The Islamists won 188 seats, against 15 for the FLN and 25 for the Socialist Forces Front. A second round was set for mid-January. In it, the FIS would need only 28 more seats for a majority.

Tuesday 31st

Javier Perez de Cuellar spent his last day as UN secretary-general negotiating a **ceasefire agreement in El Salvador**. Though it was the latest of many, it looked more promising than most.

Countdown

JANUARY 5TH *After Christmas, the deadline which the United Nations had set for Iraq to evacuate Kuwait suddenly seemed alarmingly close. Many observers were sure that Saddam Hussein would back down at the last moment; we looked for evidence in vain*

NOT since last August's invasion of Kuwait has an American-led war against Saddam Hussein looked so likely, or its human costs so high. After January 15th Resolution 678 of the United Nations Security Council allows any country, at the request of Kuwait, to remove the Iraqis forcibly. The American forces in and around the Arabian peninsula are now close to full fighting strength, with about 1,500 tanks and 1,300 aircraft already in place. British and American troops are being vaccinated against anthrax, after reports that Iraq has added biological weapons to its arsenal of missiles and chemicals.

If George Bush or Saddam Hussein is secretly preparing to climb down, neither gives any sign of it. The Iraqi president spent new year's eve stirring stew for his soldiers in Kuwait. He told them that Iraq had 60 divisions ready for war, compared with his enemies' 18, and would therefore win any battle for Kuwait, which was part of Iraq's "body and soul". Mr Bush continues to say that Iraq must fulfil to the letter the UN's demand for an immediate, complete and unconditional withdrawal. In December word was leaked to American newspapers that the president had resolved to fight, if war was necessary, even if it meant destroying his chances of re-election.

This unflinching march to the brink does not make it inevitable that war will begin the moment the deadline expires. The Americans and their allies have always made it plain that January 15th was merely the point after which war would become authorised, not necessarily the date for attack. Not all the American forces destined for the Gulf will have arrived there in time. Even so, striking on or soon after January 15th would help Mr Bush underline, for the benefit of critics at home and abroad, the clear legal authority the UN has given him for military action. Barring some abrupt turn in the diplomacy, the chances of fighting having begun in the next few weeks are high.

What has made the approach of the deadline even more worrying is the apparent still-birth of Mr Bush's proposal at the end of November to meet Iraq's foreign minister, Tariq Aziz, in Washington, and to send his own secretary of state, James Baker, to Baghdad. Iraq accepted the proposal, but it seemed to evaporate, ostensibly because of an argument about dates. On January 3rd, under pressure from Congress, Mr Bush offered a new idea: a meeting between Mr Baker and Mr Aziz, in Switzerland, between January 7th and 9th.

The diplomatic impasse between Iraq and America has concentrated minds elsewhere. In December, when a meeting between Mr Baker and Mr Hussein still looked possible, the European Community decided against starting talks of its own with the Iraqi leadership. Separate talks, it was felt, would encourage Mr Hussein to detect a rift between the Europeans and Americans, and so draw the sting of the approaching deadline. This week the Community had second thoughts. Jacques Poos, the foreign minister of Luxembourg (which has just taken over the Community's presidency), hoped that he would be allowed to visit Baghdad on its behalf.

It is hard to imagine the countdown to war continuing without an intensification of diplomacy. Yet getting talks started—whether between the Europeans and Iraq or, better still, the Americans and Iraq—is not the same thing as avoiding war. What makes war likely is not that America and Iraq are not talking. It is that they are not talking because they see no way to settle their differences. Indeed, even before the argument over the date of Mr Baker's trip to Baghdad, the Americans said that he would not be negotiating, only warning Mr Hussein to submit.

In any game of brinkmanship, it is possible that one side will collapse suddenly. If Mr Hussein has decided to do so—by ordering a full or partial withdrawal from Kuwait before January 15th—he will find it less humiliating to say so to the European Community, or to Arab mediators, than to Mr Baker. He can also be expected to make the most of whatever face-savers the mediators can offer him.

Mr Poos hints that one such face-saver could be a promise of talks on Palestine. Since August 12th Mr Hussein has repeated like a gramophone the refrain that he will not budge from Kuwait until Israel gives up the West Bank and Gaza. But, in its Venice Declaration of 1980, the Community has already accepted the right of the Palestinians to self-determination. With American acquiescence, the UN has recently endorsed the principle that an international peace conference on Palestine might be useful at an appropriate time. Little more can be offered without handing Mr Hussein the propaganda victory the Americans and Europeans insist on denying him.

Besides, there is no solid reason to assume that Mr Hussein's will is going to be the first to break. Over the past five months, despite everything that has gone wrong with his adventure in Kuwait, he has calmly refused to bow to pressure, whether political, economic or military. On January 2nd NATO agreed to send 42 fighter aircraft to defend Turkey. On the same day Mr Hussein raised the pay of his soldiers and promised a glorious future. Perhaps he really believes that he can win a war in the Gulf. Perhaps he will strike first.

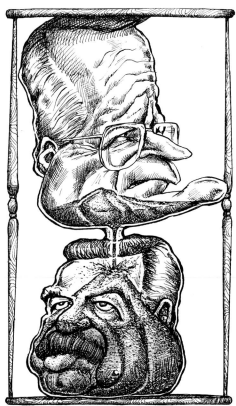

Before you feed on me

FEBRUARY 2ND **Two weeks into the Gulf war, doubts about the effectiveness of the allied bombing campaign set in. Was the military strategy going wrong?**

LONG before the war to free Kuwait began, George Bush's administration promised that, when it did, it would be "sudden, massive and decisive". It was indeed sudden. Measured by the number of aircraft sorties (more than 30,000 in the first two weeks), it has been massive too. But most people expected the decision to come faster than it has. Is Saddam Hussein winning simply by having survived this long?

At briefings in Riyadh, Washington and London, officials merely scoff. Mr Hussein, it is pointed out, promised rivers of blood. Instead, allied losses after a fortnight were still under 40 killed. The best of his air force, having failed to intervene in the land war, has fled to Iran. While Iraqi troops and armour inside Kuwait are pounded around the clock, allied forces prepare confidently for their own ground offensive. Everything, in short, is going to plan in the best of all possible plans.

And yet, and yet. Two weeks into the war, on January 28th, the man whom many Americans imagined to be cowering in some bunker gave a cool interview, in a dark blue suit, on America's Cable News Network. Kuwait, he said as he had said so many times before the war, would forever remain part of Iraq. He had not one doubt in a million that he would win the war; his missiles, after all, could carry nuclear, biological or chemical weapons. The following night, while Mr Bush was promising victory in his annual "state of the union" message to Congress, Iraqi tanks drove across the border and shot up the Saudi town of Khafji. The Americans announced the death of 11 of their marines.

Those tanks were repulsed. But the interview, and the cross-border raid, showed that Mr Hussein has lost none of his ability to frighten his enemies, or to take them by surprise. The interview underlined the failure of allied bombing to shock a supposedly brittle and unpopular regime into immediate collapse. The border raid proved that at least part of Iraq's army had some fire, if not much food, in its belly. The spectre of an Iraqi secret weapon—a crude atomic bomb, deadly toxins?—hovers at the back of everybody's mind. All this adds up, in the circumstances, to a psychological success for Mr Hussein.

Yet psychology, in the end, does not win wars. In his now famous nerve-steadying briefing after the first week, America's General Colin Powell said he intended to cut off and destroy the Iraqi army in Kuwait. After the second week, on January 30th, General

Norman Schwarzkopf, the American commander in Saudi Arabia, gave an equally bullish progress report.

The Iraqis, he said, had given up trying to co-ordinate their air defences, leaving allied aircraft free to roam the skies. At least 70 of the hardened shelters in which Iraq's aircraft had sat out the start of the war had been destroyed, along with all of the 30 fixed sites, and many of the mobile launchers, from which Iraq could fire Scud missiles at Saudi Arabia and Israel. As for isolating the Iraqi army in Kuwait, tens of bridges had been smashed and military convoys attacked. The quantity of supplies reaching Kuwait from Iraq had fallen from 20,000 tons a day to 2,000 since the beginning of the war. On some days, he said, 400 tons of bombs were falling on Iraq's Republican Guard divisions.

To some old-timers, slick briefings that emphasise the good news and "prove" it with numbers and videofilms are uncomfortable reminders of Vietnam. In Vietnam the number of lorries hit, sorties flown and

bridges smashed sounded impressive. They turned out to be a better measure of allied effort than of any real weakening in the fighting ability of the enemy. The difference this time is that all the attrition has so far been on one side.

Mr Hussein has already lost a lot of his power without killing a lot of his enemies. This means that he has not yet achieved a key strategic aim: to inflict so many casualties on the Americans and their allies that public opinion turns against the war. A second aim, to lure Israel into the battle and so widen the war, has also been a flop. Israel, uncharacteristically, continues to sit tight and count the political rewards of restraint.

All this could of course change. Israeli restraint may not survive a poison-gas attack on Tel Aviv (although Iraq's ability to deliver one has probably declined since its best low-level bombers departed for Iran). And to raise the number of American casualties, Mr Hussein may try to liven up the front line in Kuwait, which has been eerily calm for much of the war.

Until now, the bulk of the allied ground forces have been deployed beyond the range of Iraqi artillery, biding their time until the order is given to start their own offensive. Most of the heavy armour is many miles to the west of Khafji, apparently preparing for a scythe-like sweep around the western border of Kuwait. If the Khafji attack was an effort to lure allied forces into messy and costly border skirmishes, it seems unlikely to succeed.

Mr Hussein's best hope must still be that his well-entrenched defenders will put up a bloody fight when the allies eventually move in. But that fight, too, might be more one-sided than he hopes. Conscious of the danger of being drawn into trench warfare, the allies will almost certainly aim to outflank the strongest Iraqi defences, forcing Iraq's armoured divisions out of their shelters and into an unfamiliar war of manoeuvre. In that sort of fight the American forces, with close air support and hundreds of tank-busting helicopters, would still have a huge advantage.

Europe stirs, Islam boils

So much for the military balance of power. How has the political balance shifted since the start of the war? Mr Bush's pleasantest surprise since fighting began must have been the rallying around of most of the hitherto squeamish Europeans. Anti-war protesters have held big demonstrations in several capitals. But Iraqi tactics—the humiliation of captured pilots, the unprovoked missile attacks on Israel—appear to have persuaded many other Europeans that the war is necessary.

Britain was always reliable. In France opinion has flip-flopped. A poll in *Le Figaro* on January 25th showed 65% in favour of French participation in the war, as against 57% a week before fighting started. Approval for Mr Bush's "action" had soared from 53% to 71%.

The war is now also popular in Germany: a poll in *Der Spiegel* this week revealed that 66% of Germans considered it "necessary". Germany has promised to add another DM8.3 billion ($5.6 billion) to the DM5.3 billion it had already promised for the war effort. "There can be no safe little corner in world politics for us Germans," said Chancellor Helmut Kohl; "We have to face up to our responsibility whether we like it or not." With Scud missiles landing on Israel, Germany is rediscovering some old guilts: after the German foreign minister's tour of Scud wreckage in Israel, an Israeli delegation has arrived in Bonn with a list of

defence equipment it wants to acquire.

The stiffening of Mr Bush's European allies, together with solid support at home (he was interrupted by applause umpteen times during his "state of the union" message to Congress), is excellent news for the alliance. Not so the reaction from the Muslim world. There Mr Hussein's defiance of America has won him millions of admirers. In Jordan, it is reported, hundreds of newborn babies are being named after him. Moroccans, whose soldiers are formally part of the anti-Saddam coalition, held a general strike to show support for the Iraqi leader. Pakistan's army chief, accusing America of provoking the war, says the Pakistani soldiers helping to defend Saudi Arabia at Saudi Arabia's request are strictly neutral.

Most of these reactions appear to be driven by general anti-Americanism, plus sympathy for a fellow Muslim. But they are helped along by a suspicion that the war aims of the anti-Saddam coalition have grown beyond those set by the United Nations. What, third-world onlookers want to know, has bombing Iraqi power stations, government buildings and refineries got to do with the freeing of Kuwait? Even Egypt, a stalwart member of the coalition, has found it necessary under the pressure of public protests to shed some crocodile tears for Saddam. If he would only leave Kuwait, the

Egyptian foreign minister said this week, he could once again enjoy Egypt's close friendship.

It was perhaps to answer these fears that Mr Bush emphasised in his message to Congress that, though intent on destroying Iraq's ability to sustain the war, America did not seek to destroy Iraq itself. On the same day James Baker, the secretary of state, and Alexander Bessmertnykh, the new Soviet foreign minister, said jointly that Mr Hussein could have a ceasefire in return for "an unequivocal commitment" to leave Kuwait. The commitment, though, would have to be coupled with "immediate, concrete steps leading to full compliance with the Security Council resolutions". A hint of "linkage" with Palestine drew protests from Israel, and was half-disowned by the White House.

As far as the Americans are concerned, the ceasefire was offered in the expectation, and perhaps the earnest hope, that Mr Hussein would ignore it. A fortnight after the war began, Mr Bush sounds just as confident of victory as Mr Hussein does, and with better reason. But his claim that the whole world supports America in the Gulf is wrong. Rightly or wrongly, public opinion in much of the Muslim world is appalled. Even in defeat, the harm Mr Hussein has done is liable to spread way beyond the Middle East.

Guess who's still running Iraq

APRIL 6TH, BAGHDAD **Saddam Hussein's attack on the Kurds was the first sign that the Gulf victory was less complete than advertised. The victors, however, were in no mood to resume the struggle**

IT WAS, to be sure, a famous victory. But, less than two months after the liberation of Kuwait, the world is having to come to terms with the fact that Saddam Hussein has somehow managed to survive his misadventure in the Gulf. The separate rebellions that flared against him in the far south and far north of his country are sputtering to a close. In the south the Iraqi army has snuffed out the Shia revolt in Basra and the nearby towns and cities. In the north the Kurdish insurrection, which opened with such high hopes a mere three weeks ago, has collapsed as abruptly as it started. Hundreds of thousands of Kurds are now flocking in terror through snowbound mountains towards the Turkish border.

Western reporters fleeing alongside the Kurds in Iraq report that whole towns and villages are emptying, the prosperous middle class joining the poor in a headlong dash northwards. Iraqi helicopter gunships are said to have strafed the road from Arbil to Salahuddin, one of the main escape routes. Kurdish spokesmen in Damascus allege that the Iraqi Republican Guard has

also massacred many civilians in the recaptured towns, but evidence of this is scarce. A lot of Kurds are clearly fleeing not because of fresh massacres but because they remember previous ones—notably the Iraqi air

KURDISTAN

TURKEY

SYRIA

Zakho
Dohuk
Mosul
Salahuddin
Arbil

IRAN

Kirkuk
Sulaymaniyah
Tuz Khurmatu
Tikrit

IRAQ

Euphrates

Baghdad

Tigris

0   Miles   100

force's killing of hundreds of Kurds with cyanide gas at Halabja and other villages at the end of the Iran-Iraq war nearly three years ago.

Kirkuk, the biggest prize seized by the Kurdish guerrillas, fell to a government counter-attack on March 28th. The other Kurdish strongholds tumbled in swift succession. On April 2nd the government was confident enough to take a group of foreign journalists to the city of Arbil, which normally has a population of several hundred thousand. Apart from young soldiers from the Republican Guard, it was all but empty, with corpses and burnt-out tanks abandoned in the streets. Two days later the government announced the capture of Sulaymaniyah. The Americans say that Iraqi forces have started levelling "substantial portions" of Tuz Khurmatu.

Why they failed

A week ago the Kurds were full of victory. Now they are on the run. Why did their revolt collapse so fast? One reason appears to have been a lack of military co-ordination between Masoud Barzani's Kurdish Democratic Party, which is strong in the northern part of Iraqi Kurdistan, and Jalal Talabani's Patriotic union of Kurdistan, which gets its support mainly in the south. Since 1987 these and smaller guerrilla bands have been working together in a united Iraqi Kurdistan Front. But each of the various groups appears to have followed the instructions of its own leader, with little effort to draw up a realistic military plan for defending Kurdistan against superior firepower.

The Kurds' military strength has anyway always been slighter than it appeared. The Iraqi Kurds can probably field no more than 30,000 peshmerga, the veteran guerrilla fighters who fled into Iran, Turkey and Syria in 1988 after the failure of their previous uprising against Saddam Hussein. Having crossed back last month, when much of the Iraqi army had been sent south to suppress the Shia rebellion, the peshmerga made short work of the demoralised garrison troops who had been left behind. The guerrillas' numbers were boosted by tens of thousands of army deserters, plus defectors from the pro-government Kurdish militia known as the *jash*.

At their peak last week these forces probably amounted to about 200,000 men with light weapons and some captured armour. Even so, they were no match for the organised Republican Guard units sent with tanks and guns to recapture the towns and villages. In classic guerrilla fashion the Kurds plan to melt away and continue their struggle from the hills. But doing so will be harder than it was in the past.

After crushing the 1988 rebellion Saddam Hussein ordered the razing of thousands of mountain villages and moved their inhabitants to prefabricated settlements near the main towns. This was a deliberate policy to deprive the peshmerga of the cover and sustenance that the villages once provided. Much of Kurdistan is now an empty, free-fire zone at the mercy of Iraqi aircraft and helicopter gunships.

The American air force has shot down two Iraqi fighter-bombers since the war ended. It has no orders to shoot down the helicopters that are being used against the Kurds. Television film of the horrors in Kurdistan has made Americans feel sorry for the Kurds, but it has not persuaded them that America can or should do much to help.

Two prominent Democrats—George Mitchell, the majority leader of the Senate, and Lee Hamilton, the chairman of the House of Representatives sub-committee on Europe and the Middle East—say they would like the Iraqi gunships shot down. But neither man is prepared to go further than that. Mr Mitchell says the policy of non-intervention is "generally a correct

one"; Mr Hamilton that America does not have the will to restart the war.

Behind their comments lie two calculations. The first is that the American public, basking in the aftermath of a war fought for clearly defined ends, would not want to engage in one whose objectives were murky. The second is that America would squander the goodwill it has built up with its Arab and other regional partners if it connived in the break-up of Iraq—even if that were seen to be in America's interest, which the administration doubts. President Bush has made it plain, by word and lack of deed, that he will stick as close as a limpet to Turkey's President Turgut Ozal, who recently had a successful visit to Washington. If Mr Ozal does not believe that military assistance to the Kurds is sensible—and for reasons of his own, he does not—President

The Republican Guard was here

Bush is unlikely to gainsay him.

Mr Bush's chief preoccupation is to extricate the American army from Iraq. The passage on April 3rd of Security Council Resolution 687 brings him a step closer to that aim. under its terms, which Iraq and Cuba bitterly resisted, Iraq must let a UN commission inspect its military installations, remove its nuclear fuel, destroy or render harmless all chemical and biological weapons and all ballistic missiles with a range exceeding 95 miles (150 kilometres). Thereafter Iraq would have to submit to an arms embargo banning the delivery of spare parts as well as purchases of new weapons. Only then would it be allowed to resume exports, although a proportion of oil revenues would be set aside to compensate countries damaged by its invasion of Kuwait.

At one point this week France expressed interest in adding another condition to this list of punishments, by stipulating that the economic sanctions still in force against Iraq would not be lifted until Iraq stopped repressing the Kurds. This found no favour with the other permanent members of the council. They offered to compromise by drafting a separate resolution, or perhaps only a presidential declaration, concentrat-

ing on the Kurds' humanitarian needs. And not even the French advocate the dismemberment of Iraq and the creation of an independent Kurdish state.

So Iraq's dictator defies the world and lives to tell the tale? For the moment. But the sort of repression he is using to restore control at the extremities of his defeated country may not protect him from the disenchantment in Baghdad and his own Sunni heartland around Tikrit. Saddam Hussein used to be careful to balance the terror he used against opponents with rewards for Iraqis who stayed loyal. Now, with no largesse to distribute, the regime is trying to prop up public support in two ways.

First, it is tacitly confessing to mistakes at home and promising to correct them. Official speeches in recent days have been larded with promises of democracy, administrative reform and an end to nepotism—along with more customary hymns of praise for the "honest struggler", Saddam Hussein.

The government now explains that it has wanted since the early 1980s to bring in democracy, but was blown off course by the war against Iran and, lately, by the "aggression" inflicted by the Americans and the Zionists.

At the same time the propaganda effort to persuade Iraqis that it was a good idea to invade Kuwait and go to war against America and its allies is unceasing. "Sooner or later", Saadoun Hammadi, the newly appointed prime minister, said on television on March 30th, the scope of Iraq's achievements would become clear:

> The citizen in Iraq and the Arab homeland and the free Muslims and free people in the world will see that Iraq has paid a price for a just and a noble aim: namely, resisting imperialism, Zionism and the old system. A just struggle for this cause or any other serious cause is not expected to be without a price.

A few Iraqis may still believe this sort of thing. But their numbers are liable to fall once Resolution 687 takes effect. The Iraqi regime has submitted to a variety of richly deserved humiliations since the end of the war. It has admitted in public that its annexation of Kuwait was illegal. It has handed over lists of all the plunder it took, and promised to return it.

Now the government that saw itself as the first Arab superpower is being told to let UN inspectors enter Iraq and blow up the Scud missiles which, when fired at Israel, became symbols of its power. Maybe they will blow up Saddam Hussein's reputation at the same time.

The time of cholera

APRIL 27TH **In an otherwise upbeat year for Latin America, something old-fashioned began to kill people again**

THE sickness will not go away. Cholera, brewed in the foulness where sewage runs into the drinking water, is an ever-present menace to the poor of Africa and South Asia. In refugee camps, and where sanitation has been smashed by war (as in Baghdad and Basra) it is the aid-workers' nightmare. The disease has now reinvaded the American tropics, whence it had been absent since migration from Asia was cut off by the world upheavals of 1914-18.

Peru is the first victim. Nobody yet knows who took the disease there. How it spreads is all too obvious, in the filthy shanty-towns to which poor and ignorant countryfolk are driven by misgovernment and terrorism. One of the few luxuries within their reach is ceviche, a delicious mess of chopped raw fish with onions and lemon; since fish feed near sewers, and are caught by people who wash (if at all) in sewer-water, they are perfect for spreading infection.

As the cholera panic spread, Peru's normally sensible president, Alberto Fujimori, sought to calm it by eating (with his cabinet ministers) a dish of ceviche, on television. The panic died down, the fish-vendors' business picked up, the cabinet survived–but thousands whose fish was less fresh began to suffer the cholera pangs; explosive diarrhoea and rapid dehydration, which can lead to rapid death.

The result was disastrous for Peru's economy too. Neighbouring countries closed their borders, both to travellers and to goods that might carry the infection–particularly fish, Peru's speciality. But the cholera has spread into Ecuador, where tens of thousands of people live in shanty-towns without clean water. Worse, it was carried across the Andes into Peru's provinces on the upper Amazon, whence it is inexorably moving downstream into Brazil–much richer than Peru, but with even worse social

services.

Peru's hospitals and clinics, short of medicines and everything else, managed to defend the people against the worst ravages of the disease. In past epidemics, the doctors reckoned that one in ten of those infected would die. In Peru, some 140,000 people have been treated, and more than 1,000 have died. It is very bad. It could have been much worse.

Last December a similar outbreak of cholera struck Zambia–another nation crippled by misgovernment and low copper prices. The number of cases is not recorded; the number of deaths is officially put at 855, and may have been much higher, since diarrhoea is so common there that it often goes unreported. The authorities closed most schools and institutions, and ran a hygiene campaign on radio and television. Overseas aid came in from many quarters (including South Africa); the landlocked Zambians brought in health officials from all their neighbours to try to limit the spread of the disease, which nevertheless struck Malawi. The worst is over: of 130 nursing centres opened in Zambia at the height of the epidemic, the authorities have now closed 80. Only about 100 patients remain in care.

Given reasonable precautions and a small amount of money, cholera can be effectively fought. New and simple techniques of rehydration make most deaths– except of the very young and old– preventable. The onset of infection should be preventable too. All you need is a clean water-supply and an efficient way of getting rid of human excrement. Investment is better than cure. In Bangladesh, where cholera broke out a month ago and may already have infected 30,000 people, they know that perfectly well. They just can't afford it.

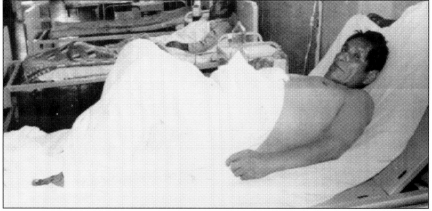

It was preventable

An Iraqi prison diary

MAY 4TH **Our correspondent crossed into Iraq with Kurdish guerrillas in March. His report was delayed by nearly three weeks he spent in an Iraqi prison**

BAKHTIAR, a Kurdish rebel, took a pen to my hand. "This is the city," he said drawing a circle. He added two solid dots on the left and bottom of my palm: "This is the Iraqi army." Our Kurdish guide was wrong. As we attempted to flee Kirkuk, he, I and two other reporters drove directly into an ambush.

Having taken cover behind a house, we watched a column of tanks descend from a mountain pass. With a French-Vietnamese photographer I spent 18 hours hiding in a

ditch. The Iraqi soldiers were camped directly on top of us. We last saw Bakhtiar, who was armed, and Gad Gross, a German photographer on assignment for *Newsweek*, running behind a house. Soon after sunrise, they were discovered; they surrendered but within minutes both had been executed.

We were found in our ditch an hour later; the presence of an Iraqi officer during our capture may have been the only reason

why we too were not killed. It was March 29th. My blindfold was made of thin cloth so I could still see a bit.

It was then that I knew that the Kurdish rebellion would soon be finished. I could hear and see the outlines of dozens of tanks, artillery, armoured personnel carriers and other heavy vehicles. Whole divisions were massing for a counter-offensive. The Kurds had no pre-knowledge of this build-up. And, their enthusiasm apart, they had no strategy capable of prevailing against the vastly superior firepower of the Iraqi army. Saddam Hussein was clearly planning to retake all of Kurdistan. He recaptured most of it in less than four days.

The Kurds were simply over-confident: the initial liberation of Kurdistan had gone too well, with local villagers and armed guerrillas overrunning local military posts and even bases. But these posts had been defended by regular army conscripts whose performance gave little indication of what to expect from the special forces and Republican Guard divisions. Their tanks and helicopters made all the difference.

Blindfolded, we underwent interrogations. During the most severe ones, I was accused of being a CIA agent and told that if I confessed I would go free, but if I "continued to lie" I would spend "many years" in jail. In the event, without any confessions, I was released "on the personal order of President Saddam" after 18 days.

One evening a prisoner was dragged out of his cell. We heard him making strange sounds, interspersed with the sound of heavy wood meeting flesh. The soldiers made him crow like a rooster, laughing when a real rooster crowed as if to answer his call. During his ordeal, the sound of guards playing ping-pong competed for our attention. A prisoner with a rare beautiful voice began to sing, almost wail, in prayer. The sounds of pain, mirth and prayer blended strangely.

The guards' instrument of choice was a heavy rubber hose. We listened, and occa-

They forgot about the tanks

sionally watched, as men were beaten. Some were hit on the soles of the feet. If a prisoner raised his hands to defend himself, he would be savagely beaten around the head and body. The guards also had a collection of heavy sticks, some as thick and twice as long as a baseball bat. I watched as

one blindfolded man cried out in the cell-block yard: about five guards surrounded him, their hoses and sticks flailing. One playfully held his broom handle like a pool cue as he repeatedly poked the weeping man in the head.

"Stun guns" which give electric shocks were another favourite. A black man, perhaps from Sudan, was hosed down and then made to stand outside on an overcast day. He was interrogated while he stood there shivering. When the answer failed to satisfy, a guard zapped him with the stun gun, watching him fall helplessly. We sometimes heard faint but terrible cries coming from elsewhere in the prison. We tried to ignore them but they persisted. They were the screams not of fear or sharp pain but of a man in long agony.

The prisoners we were with seemed to be neither hardened criminals nor important enough to be political prisoners. But they were all under suspicion and, in Iraq, to be under suspicion is as good as being charged with a crime. If a person is suspected of being against the regime, the suspicion can result in his being abused and held incommunicado in jail.

There was a larger-than-lifesize portrait of Saddam next to one of my cells. A Kurd I was with spoke no English except to reiterate that "Saddam is a donkey!" Perhaps, I thought, but this donkey is still up on its legs and kicking.

The man who killed millions

MAY 25TH *For more than a year Ethiopia's empire had teetered on the brink of collapse. The end came in a rush*

AT THE bitter end the dictator ran for it. President Mengistu Haile Mariam, who misruled his country for 14 years, fled on May 21st to Zimbabwe, where his retreat was prepared. The rebels, whose advance had brought them within 50 miles (80 km) of the capital, Addis Ababa, were undecided whether to fight on.

Mr Mengistu handed over the reins, *ad interim*, to Lieutenant-General Tesfaye Gebre Kidan. He commanded the government troops in Eritrea, and chaired the court martial in 1989 which disposed of 12 of his fellow-generals for plotting an anti-Mengistu coup. Yet he passes for a moderate within the fierce revolutionary council, the Dergue. His appointment as vice-president in April was intended to buy time.

If the rebels were prudent they would hold the line where it is, and take advantage of the peace talks that the American State Department has by steady diplomacy arranged for them in London. But they are divided. The junta is dominated (as Ethiopia has always been) by men who speak Am-

haric. The main rebel movements represent other regions. The Eritrean People's Liberation Front stands for secession (following a referendum) of its own relatively developed region. The Ethiopian People's Revolutionary Democratic Front, whose leaders are Tigreans, wants autonomy and elections, but no votes for feudalists and capitalists. The smaller Oromo Liberation Front, which also favours devolution rather than secession, speaks for the people outsiders call the Galla, the second-largest of Ethiopia's many peoples. (A smaller complication is the presence near Addis Ababa of nearly 20,000 Falashas, black Jews whom the Israelis may now be tempted to rescue in an Entebbe-style commando raid.)

The failure of the Mengistu regime is shown by the success of this uneasy coalition. Ethiopia's army is immense, with some 430,000 men; but they are mostly unwilling conscripts, and the Soviet Union has cut off their supplies. By some accounts front-line soldiers on both sides have lately taken to doing local deals with each other,

so fewer people die than the officers report.

The chief victims are, as usual, civilians. The harvest has been bad. With fighting on the highways, it is harder than ever to shift food to where it is needed. Earlier this year the World Food Programme was reckoning that some 5m people were at risk of famine in the north of the country; if so, some 1.2m tonnes of grain would be needed to feed them, of which a bit over half has been pledged by donors.

As the rebels advanced, the roads were blocked to civilian traffic. Food, whether as aid or as normal trade, could not be moved from the ports to the people who needed it. The aid agencies were starting to sound panicky, as well they might. The horrors of the Ethiopian famine of 1984-85 are too vivid to be easily forgotten. As long as President Mengistu held on, there was a real chance that it might all happen again. If the Americans with their peace talks do get the parties together, their first business will be to arrange a truce so that food can move.

It is hard to see how such a regime could have survived for so long, after bringing such unexampled disaster on its people. Ethiopia, fortunately, is a special case. The

The proletariat did not say thanks

jump a multi-ethnic feudal state, with no transition, into communism. They slaughtered kulaks, and transformed vast, unproductive private estates into vast, unproductive state farms. Farmers who stored food from a good harvest were shot for hoarding. Merchants who bought food in surplus areas for sale in drought districts were shot for profiteering. Provincial discontent, however justified, was met with repression.

Soviet aid for the army was not matched by aid for civilian development. By the end the regime was spending more than 70% of its revenue on weapons, and practically nothing on roads, water supplies, schools and the rest. Pressure from western governments, unwilling to contemplate another famine on their domestic television screens, forced the junta last year to loosen up control of farms and trade; but too late.

junta that overthrew the old Emperor Haile Selassie in 1974 brutally eliminated the tiny, rich and greedy elite around him. That left nobody who could run anything. Soviet ministries were ordered to fill the gaps, and sent their discards. Ethiopia became a punishment station for rejects from one the world's most incompetent bureaucracies.

Under that influence the Ethiopian soldiers tried, literally, to imitate Stalin; to

Other African countries find natural sponsors in the West, in the form of their former colonial masters. Ethiopia's period under colonial rule, by the Italians in the late 1930s, was too short to earn much salutary guilt from the ex-colonists. If Ethiopia falls apart, nobody outside will weep for it; nor, if it holds together, will any outsider pay the vast bill for putting it to rights.

Syria's shadow over Israel

JULY 20TH *During the Gulf war President Bush promised America's Arab allies that, after victory, he would make a fresh attempt to sort out the Arab-Israeli conflict. Israel's most implacable enemy appeared to believe him*

WITH impeccable timing, President Hafez Assad of Syria has done himself some good, put Israel on the spot and perhaps even advanced the chances of an Arab-Israeli peace. After brooding on the matter for six weeks, Mr Assad chose the eve of the London economic summit, with the high and mighty gathered together, to say Yes to the letter that George Bush sent to him and to Israel's Yitzhak Shamir on June 1st. Mr Shamir had replied by return, but only with an uncompromising No.

With a bit of good news to speed him on his way, James Baker, America's secretary of state, is off on his fifth peace-seeking trudge round the area since the end of the Gulf war. But this time the full blast of his persuasive powers will be directed at Israel, where he arrives on July 21st. One of Mr Baker's predecessors, Henry Kissinger, used to give Mr Assad (whom he nevertheless outwitted) the accolade of smartest statesman in the region. Syria's astute dictator has shown that he still deserves the praise.

Mr Bush's letter had suggested a procedural compromise for starting the stuck negotiations on an Arab-Israeli peace. Egypt is at peace with Israel already. Jordan, dithering, will go along with whatever the others decide. The Palestinians have almost reached the point of acknowledging that they have no other options. Syria—and Israel itself—were the standouts.

The Syrians had wanted any talks with Israel to be held in the framework of an international conference at which the United Nations, as well as the United States and the Soviet Union, would take part. The Israelis wanted no UN participation and the conference to be no more than a one-day ceremonial send-off for the talks. The American compromise suggested that the UN, like the European Community, should be given a single non-speaking walk-on part at the opening conference, and that the confer-

ence itself should then be dissolved but periodically reconvened for progress reports, as the negotiators wish.

Never mind, the Americans told the Syrians in a series of private "clarifications" during the six-week brooding period, that this procedural compromise is heavily weighted Israel's way; what really matters is the substance of the talks, if talks there are to be. In agreeing to face-to-face talks with Israel, Syria claims to have been reassured by America's continuing commitment to the UN Security Council resolutions that call on Israel to trade lands they occupied in 1967 in return for secure and recognised boundaries—a commitment formally endorsed by the G7 summiteers in London.

But at the same time as they were tempting the Syrians with talk of substance, the Americans were laying a trail of procedural titbits to lure the Israeli government—which flatly rejects land-for-peace trade—into reconsidering its rejection of the American compromise. Israeli foreign-office officials now mutter, unattributably, that a silent UN observer might not be an insuperable obstacle. Fine, but one of America's enticements allows the Israelis to veto the choice of Palestinians in a joint Jordanian-Palestinian delegation; this could give the Israelis the opportunity of almost indefinite delay.

Delay might not distress Mr Assad too much. To be sure, he dearly wants to get back the Golan Heights for Syria, and better still to win the hero's mantle by procuring for the Palestinians a home of their own. Meanwhile he is not doing badly. He has seen his main Arab rival, Saddam Hussein, done down; he has peacefully swallowed war-torn Lebanon, to general congratulation; he has the Palestinians cowed; and he has wrongfooted Israel.

Mr Assad has earned America's gratitude, first by helping it in war and now by helping it in peace. This gratitude, if expressed in something more than words, would be particularly useful since the Soviet Union, which once stood by Syria, now wants to get back what it can of its Syrian debts. The Americans say they will not repeat the mistake they made with Mr Hussein—forgetting that the man they are tilting towards is a dictatorial, often brutal, ruler with links to terrorism and at least one horrendous massacre on his copybook. But Syria now has obvious uses. Its army, it is still hoped, may provide an Arab stiffening for Gulf security. And Mr Assad's apparent flexibility gives Mr Bush a chance to prove the good faith of his post-war pledges on the pursuit of an Arab-Israeli peace.

Grousing that it has been tricked, Israel is on the defensive, and not only about the peace conference. The routing of the Palestinians in southern Lebanon weakens Israel's own case for holding land in Lebanon. When their own men are killed there—as some were this week—they take revenge by bombing raids that kill civilians. Worse, recent revelations of nuclear goings-on in Iraq have prompted fresh calls for inspection and control of bomb-making in the Middle East; Israel cherishes its nuclear secrets.

Israel's distress at the turn of events with Syria is acute. Mr Shamir may yet deploy his ultimate defence. If pressed into a corner by Mr Baker, he could call for an early general election. This would concentrate voters' minds on the great questions of peace and territory, baffle the divided and demoralised opposition Labour Party—and hold up the peace process yet again.

The Titicaca tonic

AUGUST 31ST, THE ANDES *Fancy a good rub-down with a live guinea pig? Nor did we, despite the enthusiasm of our correspondent in the Valley of the Moon*

FOR the overweight who have tried everything, a really new offer: lose weight at altitude on coca-based products. The last word in exotic slimming clinics is about to open on the Bolivian side of Lake Titicaca, at 3,810 metres (12,500 feet) above sea level. The first guests have already booked.

The venture is being launched by the Darius Morgans, father and son. Father has an international travel business—that is, a hydrofoil service across the lake between Bolivia and Peru. He also has a showman's eye, running tours to the "Valley of the Moon", a moderately strange set of rock formations close to La Paz, and to "Witch Doctor Street" in La Paz, where tourists can shudder as the local Aymara Indians buy folk remedies and ingredients for magic. (A llama fetus is regularly buried in the foundations of a new house, for good luck. A pig fetus makes a curse against an enemy.)

Darius Morgan, Jr, has added folk medicine to the slimming business. Coca is well-known for reducing hunger, thirst and fatigue—the Spaniards made sure their Indian slaves got their coca rations regularly. But the clinic's guests will not have to

chew the leaves, which have the consistency of holly, less the prickles. They can take it in a syrupy extract, or chew coca-based gum.

Mr Morgan, Jr, has set up a small museum of folk medicine at the company's hotel-and-clinic complex by the lake, to display the lore of the Kollawaya people, a tribe well known as travelling healers and diagnosticians. Western doctors might study one Kollawaya technique, which is to listen carefully to what the patient and his family and friends say about his illness. Another technique involves rubbing down the patient with a live guinea pig. A genuine Kollawaya practitioner will be available to guests, along with a programme of sensible diet and exercise.

The Morgans are plugging into the international spa and health-centre circuit, a newish tourist-industry niche. It is an original way of selling Bolivia, which has hitherto been a mere appendage of Peru's cultural-tourist circuit. Until this year Peru was receiving 200,000 foreign visitors a year, Bolivia 15,000.

This season the numbers are down by more than half, what with recession in the United States, the Gulf war, the murderous activities of Peru's Shining Path terrorists, and an epidemic of cholera. Peru's own tourist industry has fragmented, with hundreds of freelance "travel agents" and guides squabbling to sell tickets and hotels to a trickle of travellers. The prospects for revival look uncertain. Coca drinks and guinea-pig massages could be the key to survival.

All capitalists now

SEPTEMBER 28TH, ANGOLA *The end of the cold war has made many regional conflicts look unsustainable. One corner of Africa is ripe for a happy ending*

LOADED with journalists and marshalled by public-relations men, Jonas Savimbi's aircraft set off this week from Johannesburg for Luanda, the Angolan capital where for years he has been presented as the arch-fiend. On the way he stopped to recruit friends in the smaller towns where his UNITA party gets its main support. Meanwhile, President Jose Eduardo dos Santos was being marshalled by his rival public-relations team from Washington to London and Brussels, on the tour that Mr Savimbi has made so often.

Angolan politics, and Angola's quest for foreign friends and investors, have moved into a new era. If the transition to free elections can be peacefully completed within the year set aside for the job, it will be an African triumph all the more astounding for its lack of drama.

Angola, with only 10m people, is twice the size of France. Its soil is rich, its minerals precious. Portugal, its former proprietor, never had the resources to develop it, and was too inward-looking to let anybody else do so. When the Portuguese dictatorship collapsed in the mid-1970s, Angola fell apart too. The settlers went home.

The capital was taken over by the few Angolans whom the Portuguese had educated, who were very left-wing because their former bosses had been so right-wing. They formed a government and called themselves the Angolan Popular Movement (MPLA), with Soviet patronage and Cuban military backing. Among the factions that dominated the countryside, the most effective by far was Mr Savimbi's UNITA. It smartly dropped its far-left stance, thus securing the patronage of the Americans and—more significant—the South Africans, who provided bases and soldiers.

The Americans, having fostered the civil war, arranged an end to it. South Africa pulled out. So did the Russians, drawing the Cubans after them. The MPLA government now says it wants a free-enterprise economy as badly as Mr Savimbi does; Mr dos Santos's latest trip was designed to persuade the United States and the Europeans that he means it. Hampered by some senators' loyalty to Mr Savimbi, President Bush is not yet sending an ambassador to Luanda, but American oil companies have never stopped working profitably in Angola. Many European companies are eager to get back old assets and exploit new ones, once there is peace and an elected government.

The shooting war has given way to a better, electoral one. Under an agreement made in Lisbon last May, the government's soldiers, and UNITA's, will be withdrawn into camps. Maybe half of each will be merged in a new national army. The rest will be pensioned off (which could mean trouble ahead from officers who see the end of their careers). In a joint commission, the political parties are to agree on an electoral law and a voting system. Ample advice is available from western countries, both on military and on political reform.

The elegant Mr dos Santos, who graduated from the Soviet Oil and Gas Institute in Baku, Azerbaijan, thinks it possible that all parties will be offering free-enterprise policies, so that the choice will be mainly one of personalities, between him and his rival, the polyglot Mr Savimbi, who studied in Switzerland. Others suppose that tribal affinity may sway the voters. The MPLA's main strength is in the cities and along the coast, where people are of many tribes, or none. Mr Savimbi's people, the Ovimbundu, are the country's largest, with more than a quarter of the population. The Bakongo of the north may rebuild their own party. If, as seems probable, the electoral system turns out to resemble Portugal's, a coalition government could emerge.

Few cold-war stories have such a chance of a happy ending. If Southern Africa, with all its problems, is to prosper, it needs regional, not merely national, economic solutions. For Zambia and Zaire, Angola offers the best outlet to the sea. Its southern peoples are indistinguishable from those of northern Namibia. Its mines and farms are like South Africa's. If they can only get through this election year that opened with the main contenders' travels this week, Angolans should be playing a bigger role on a wider scene sooner than anybody expected.

Something rotten in Kenya

OCTOBER 5TH, NAIROBI *Kenya was once a model for East Africa. In 1991 it began to look dangerously wobbly*

THE energy minister is urging a consumer boycott of Ford cars. "The name", he explains, "stinks". His advice, issued because an opposition group uses FORD as an acronym, is among the more benign pronouncements from Kenya's politicians. They are working themselves into a frenzy as they refuse to join the pluralist tide sweeping black Africa.

The last such agitation culminated in July 1990 with violent riots in most large towns. Once again, cabinet ministers and their backers are, through bellicose statements propagated by the official press, providing the challengers' best publicity. At one rally a minister called on citizens to visit beer halls and "crush any government critic". A week later 14 ministers gathered to hear the vice-president call opponents traitors. One of his colleagues said clubs would be wielded, if necessary, to end talk of multiple parties.

Once again figures in the ruling Kenya African National Union (KANU), eager to show loyalty, have declared their leader, Daniel arap Moi, president for life. Once again Mr Moi has vowed to crush opponents "like rats". As before, the spectre of the unsolved murder of the foreign minister—a man reputed to be bright and honest, in an official culture riddled with mediocrity and corruption—hangs over the scene.

The present row revolves around six businessmen and out-of-favour politicians who have formed the Forum for the Restoration of Democracy—the FORD of official distaste. They call it a forum rather than a party, and keep its numbers low, hoping to avoid problems with the official registrar. That official earlier this year refused to register, and hence legalise, a political party proposed by Oginga Odinga, a former vice-president, now a member of FORD.

The group sought permission to hold a public meeting on October 5th at Nairobi's Kamukunji grounds. The unhappy precedent is that, last year, opposition figures requested leave to hold a meeting at Kamukunji, and were turned down; riots nonetheless began there on the date of the forbidden meeting. This time the government kept FORD's request tied up in the courts, until on October 3rd the Forum withdrew its application. Its members, carefully legalistic, do not urge attendance without a permit. There could still be trouble.

Disgust over widespread rigging during

the last parliamentary elections, in 1988, remains. The economy is faltering. Some private economists reckon there was no growth over the past year, while the government says growth is just outpacing the rate of increase in the population, which is at least 3% a year. Price increases and decontrols, recommended by the World Bank and the IMF, affect the commodities like flour and sugar that poor Kenyans rely on. Some essential goods are running short. The universities have been closed indefinitely since July, when students were asked to pay more, and rioted.

Corruption, long mentioned only sotto voce, is beginning to rise to public view. Some Kenyan athletes at the recent All-Africa Games in Cairo appeared in mis-matched uniforms after their proper kit "disappeared". Denmark recently suspended its aid because, it said, a $40m rural-aid fund had been robbed. The United States has been quick to complain when government critics are arrested, with the State Department's senior Africanist making the point explicit and public. Even the British, long shy of criticising Kenyan excesses, sound less friendly. The foreign secretary, Douglas Hurd, said on a recent visit that his government would prefer multiparty democracy for Kenya.

Kenyan lawyers stubbornly, and publicly, argue the case for a choice of parties.

Moi oh Moi

An official inquiry into the death of the foreign minister, Robert Ouko, has ground on for more than 200 days. In the wings is what is presumed to be a damaging affidavit from the dead man's brother. He fled to asylum in the United States after, he says, he was tortured by police. Ugly incidents occur: somebody fired shots at a car driven by Mr Odinga's son, and the head of the Law Society says thugs have stoned his car.

Everybody is uncomfortably aware that

Odinga and Ouko are Luo names. The Luo are Kenya's second-largest group of tribes, the largest being the Kikuyu, with more than a third of the population; President Moi is Kalenjin, a smallish and hitherto obscure rural group.

Kenya is being pushed closer to tribal fractures, and to violence. Last weekend a mob, complaining of abuse by the ruling party's youth wing, sacked a KANU office in a Nairobi slum. The same day a crowd emerging from a football match stoned cars and shouted slogans in favour of FORD. The crowd, and both teams, were Luo. Many of the most vitriolic members of parliament are Kalenjin, seemingly ill-disposed to lose the prizes their group has grasped under Mr Moi's patronage. Kikuyu leaders had been less prominent in this year's argument until Charles Rubia, a main leader of last year's ferment, re-issued in late September the calls for pluralism for which he was detained 15 months earlier.

More violence is feared. Embassies are jumpy; the Americans advise their citizens to stay away from the city centre next weekend. The British have special reason to worry. On October 7th the Queen, on her way to Zimbabwe for the biennial Commonwealth conference, is due in Nairobi for an overnight stay, and a photo-opportunity with President Moi.

Words, and glares, in Madrid

NOVEMBER 2ND, MADRID *For the first time since 1948, Arabs and Israelis met face-to-face to discuss the possibility of living in peace. But the conference in Madrid showed the need for American mediation*

AS HOSTS, George Bush and Mikhail Gorbachev strove to fill Madrid with the clang of swords being beaten into ploughshares. As guests, the Israelis and Arabs pretended, in their set-piece opening speeches from the Royal Palace, to go along with this. "Let us declare, here and now, an end to war, to belligerency and to hostility," said Yitzhak Shamir, Israel's prime minister. Huddled back in their respective hotels, the delegations produced a different sound: the scrape of bayonets being sharpened for battle. The battle is for the mind of America.

In the far-off days before the Gulf war, Israel and America were united in opposing an international peace conference. They produced learned arguments to prove that such a conference would certainly fail. But what really worried the Americans was giving the Soviet Union a seat at the top table; and what bothered Israel's Likud government was that a conference would show too

clearly—to Israeli voters as well as to the wider world—that the price of peace was Israel's withdrawal from more of the territory captured in the 1967 war.

How the world has changed. At the opening of the Middle East peace conference in Madrid on October 30th, President Gorbachev's feeble presence at the top table was more of an embarrassment than a threat to an America fresh from victories in both the cold and the Gulf wars. Israel's fears were becoming true, but with an unexpected twist. The superpower that stood loyally behind it during the cold war had ceased to be an intimate ally and transformed itself into a mere "honest broker".

For a while, on the eve of the conference, it looked to Israel's delegation as though the breach with America could grow even wider. The Israelis had invested arduous diplomacy in shaping the conference their way. They had managed to exclude the Pal-

estine Liberation Organisation, confine the United Nations to observer status and establish that peace should emerge from direct talks between the enemies, not by superpower edict. On arrival in Madrid, however, the Americans abruptly announced that the Palestinian half of the joint Jordanian-Palestinian delegation would have as much speaking time as a full delegation. More surprises of this sort, grumbled Binyamin Netanyahu, Israel's deputy foreign minister, might jeopardise America's standing as an honest broker.

Mr Bush made amends, and more, on the conference's first day. His short opening speech was everything Mr Shamir could have wished for. Mr Bush spoke of the need for territorial compromise, but said the United States had no map of final borders. He spoke of the need for "fairness" for the Palestinians, but said nothing about Palestinian self-determination, let alone statehood. Instead, he held out the promise of the Palestinians gaining "meaningful control over their own lives and fate". In a clear warning to President Hafez Assad of Syria, he said the United States expected "real peace", anchored in treaties and trade, not just non-belligerency. And he made no reference to Israel's planting of settlements in the occupied West Bank and Gaza.

If this was music enough in Israeli ears, Mr Bush's description of how he saw the conference procedure unfolding was a veritable symphony. The real work, he said, would take place in the bilateral talks between Israel and its various Arab interlocutors. The plenary conference would not impose or veto agreements, or reconvene without the consent of all the participants. The United States was happy to be a "catalyst", but making progress would depend on give-and-take between the parties to the dispute, who would have to live with the consequences of their decisions. As if to underline America's determination to leave the delegations to their own devices, Mr Bush thereupon swept off to the airport.

Like guests invited to a party whose host locks the doors and then vanishes, the Arab and Israeli delegations were left to wonder what they had let themselves in for. Mr Bush said almost casually that he did not expect peace to be negotiated "in a week, or a month, or even a year". The next step in this tortuous process is to be a series of bilateral meetings between Israel and the three Arab teams: the Syrians, Lebanese and, jointly, the Palestinians and Jordanians. A little later, multilateral talks on topics such as water and arms control are to convene as well. These talks may add Egypt, the Gulf states and the Maghreb to the circle of negotiation, though Syria will probably stay away.

To judge by the haggling over where these meetings will take place, movement will be glacial. On the Israeli-Palestinian front there is at least a road map, inherited from the Israeli-Egyptian peace treaty of 1979. The parties are to reach agreement, within a year, on a five-year period of self-government for the occupied territories, with negotiation about the territories' final status put off until the third year. The Israelis will expect an end to the Palestinian uprising, the intifada, in return for which the Palestinians will expect a chance to build the institutions of statehood.

On the wider Arab-Israeli front no such map exists, and the chief cartographers—Mr Shamir and Mr Assad—continue to regard each other as mortal enemies. The bilateral talks between Syria and Israel are to be conducted by officials, not politicians, and are expected to reach a dead-end early on. At that point both parties will look to the Americans to propose a compromise, possibly by separating the notion of sovereignty over the Golan Heights, which Syria demands, from physical possession, which Israel says is essential for its security.

Nobody in Madrid took too seriously Mr Bush's claim that he will stand loftily aside while the region sorts out its own troubles. It is accepted glumly that with no America to administer reward and punishment, the negotiations would quickly break down. The Palestinians, showing new maturity in the world of international diplomacy, made the best they could of the "meaningful control" offered in Mr Bush's opening performance. The Israelis, though gratified by the president's words, are uncomfortably aware that within a few months Mr Bush must decide what to do about Israel's request for $10 billion of loan guarantees. That could be the moment when the administration revives the call for a freeze on West Bank settlements.

Mr Shamir, a taciturn man, seems at last to have grasped the extent of the calamity threatening to befall his country's relations with America. He chose, unusually, to make his speech in English, and began by thanking the United States for "a strong friendship with Israel in an alliance that has overcome occasional differences". He challenged the Arabs to show, by holding the bilateral talks in Israel and in Arab countries, that they were serious about accepting the Jewish state into the region. But he gave no hint of new flexibility on the territorial issue, and warned his listeners that to concentrate exclusively on territory would be "the quickest way to an impasse". With predictable symmetry, the Arab foreign ministers reiterated their demand for Israel to withdraw from all of the territory it gained in the 1967 war.

For all the inspiring talk, the gap between the two sides remains dispiritingly large. But Madrid was not just a party piece, put on by reluctant guests to satisfy a demanding host. Simply by showing up, the leaders of the Middle East have broken with the patterns of the past and aroused expectations back home. For the first time Israel will be negotiating with Palestinians whose transparent links with the PLO give them real standing in the occupied territories. And, for the first time, all Israel's neighbours have agreed to drop the pretence that they can evict Israel from the occupied territories without first making peace with it. Peace is still far off, but the Middle East will not be the same again.

Terry and Ollie

NOVEMBER 23RD *The release of Britain's most famous hostage, Terry Waite, stirred new debate about what he had been doing in Lebanon in the first place*

HE WAS the ideal intelligence asset: committed, brave, gregarious, trustworthy, able to take people into his confidence, and with an appearance of utter integrity. There can be little doubt that agencies of Ronald Reagan's administration, notably the CIA and the National Security Council (NSC), made use of Terry Waite in their efforts to free the western hostages held in Beirut. They would have been fools not to. The questions that remain, now that Mr Waite is free, are how far he knew that he was being used, how far he was happy to go along with it, and how much he knew about the other fish the Americans were frying.

Clearly Mr Waite was kidnapped, and held captive for five years, because the men in Islamic Jihad thought he was an American agent. Little was needed to give them that impression; Mr Waite's well-publicised use of an American military helicopter to get from Beirut to Cyprus in 1986 would have been enough. As it happened, there was considerably more "evidence" than that.

Mr Waite was implicated in the Reagan administration's arms-for-hostages deals simply by appearing in the picture when Benjamin Weir, Lawrence Jenco and David Jacobsen were released. All turned out to have been traded for arms. In December 1986 small items appeared in the British press linking Mr Waite to Oliver North, the marine lieutenant-colonel at the centre of the arms deals. In January 1987 Mr Waite was kidnapped. The press seemed to decide not to compromise him further.

But evidence continued to trickle out of Washington. Memoranda came to light in which Mr North had plainly debriefed Mr Waite and passed his information on to his superiors. In December 1985 he called him "our only access to events in Lebanon". Mr North's notebooks, made public in 1989, show at least a dozen meetings between the two men and frequent telephone calls. To some, all this is evidence that Mr North—and, through him, the CIA—were "running" Mr Waite. He is even said to have been given a transmitter hidden in a belt buckle, by which Mr North could track him in Beirut and possibly find the hostages. Mr North calls this "hogwash".

Only two men, Mr Waite and Mr North, can say for certain what their relationship was. Mr North cannot bring himself to say that he feels responsible for Mr Waite's kidnapping, although he says he is sorry that he did not dissuade him from his last mistaken trip to Beirut in January 1987; but he is adamant that the Americans did not use him. ("He was an agent, if anything, of humanity.") Both men insist that nothing was ever said about arms deals. They cannot deny that each was essential to the other.

In the small circle of people engaged in trying to rescue the hostages, Mr Waite had a name as a miracle-worker. As the special envoy of the Archbishop of Canterbury, Robert Runcie, he had rescued British missionaries from Iran in 1981; in 1984 he had rescued four Britons from Libya. Some time that year he was approached by the American Presbyterian church to try to rescue Mr Weir, a Presbyterian minister.

In that work he went to the United States and met Mr North, who was responsible for hostage matters within the NSC. The context was always ecclesiastical and humanitarian: the two men usually met in the house of the presiding Episcopal bishop of New York. They seem to have become close. Both were deeply committed and intensely religious; both had a liking for the bold stroke, and a streak of recklessness. Mr Waite enjoyed the limelight, while Mr North worked in the shadows. It might have seemed to be a

perfect combination.

At the beginning, the two seem merely to have traded information. Mr Waite's technique of patient and kindly negotiation was one of many avenues the Americans were exploring to free the hostages. Mr Reagan's men were also considering a military raid, ransom and arms sales. Other, crazier plans were floated every month.

Mr Waite, for his part, had no reason to distrust the Americans' motives: Mr North was welcomed at Lambeth Palace. At the same time Mr Waite must have known that he was dealing with entities beyond the Presbyterian church. Mr North always presented himself as the voice of the administration; he could rustle up Pentagon helicopters and security, for which Mr Waite was grateful on his missions.

Robert McFarlane, Mr Reagan's national security adviser from 1983 to 1985, has said that Mr Waite at first approached the American officials with caution. Enthusiasm seemed eventually to get the better of him. In time, it seems, Mr North began to tip him off about "good moments" to go to Beirut. The moments coincided with the release of hostages who had been ransomed for arms.

Mr Waite can hardly have failed to no-

tice that hostages seemed to come out without his intervention. When Father Jenco was released, in July 1986, Mr Waite was in Jordan; he was told to go to Damascus to meet him. Already useful to the Americans, he allowed himself, perhaps out of hubris, to become a lot more useful than he should have been.

By the autumn of 1986, when the Iranian arms deals were exposed, Mr Waite was both deeply involved with the Americans and apparently off Lord Runcie's leash. His last mission to Beirut showed him at his best and worst. He went as the agent of churches in the United States and Canada, and announced at a press conference that he had "two hostages in my sights: [Terry] Anderson and [Thomas] Sutherland."

Walid Jumblatt, the Druze leader in Lebanon, says that he saw Mr Waite climb off the aircraft with two suitcases full of dollar bills, church ransom for the hostages. A reporter at Associated Press in Beirut, assigned to keep Mr Waite safe and out of view, described how he would stroll out on his balcony, huge, bearded and obvious. Determined to show he was his own man, he was taking more risks than ever. His bravery and his motives cannot be impugned. His wisdom can.

Coming soon: Coca-Cola

DECEMBER 7TH *Half a year after Eritrea won its war to break free from Ethiopia, our East Africa correspondent reported from Asmara on a nation-in-waiting*

WHEN Ethiopia's army held Asmara, the capital of the country's Red Sea province, soldiers sometimes shot civilians who strayed too close to government-occupied buildings. People walked in the middle of the street. Such are the hangovers from Eritrea's 30 years of secessionist war, against first an emperor then a violent cabal of communist *apparatchiks*.

The province, at the northern edge of what the maps still call Ethiopia, is now virtually ruined, its fields drought-scorched and their tillers fled, its industry moribund, its treasury emptied, its main port wrecked by Ethiopian bombing. Eritrea is home to perhaps 3.5m people. Unlike the rest of Ethiopia, it was colonised—by the Italians, who ran the place for 50 years until they were ejected by the British during the second world war. Haile Selassie was overthrown in Addis Ababa in 1974 by a group of officers who, under Mengistu Haile Mariam, ran their dominions with rigid and repressive Stalinism.

By the time the Eritrean People's Liberation Front vanquished Ethiopia's northern army last May, some 50,000 rebel soldiers had died. The EPLF said all along it was fighting for independence. On taking con-

trol it said it would postpone that goal for two years, and ratify its separation by an internationally supervised referendum. This restraint was applauded by foreign powers and by Ethiopia's new government—the product of a separate guerrilla army, from the neighbouring province of Tigre, which took Addis Ababa as the EPLF won its war in the north.

Eritreans will certainly vote for independence. Visitors who raise the possibility of a "no" vote are greeted with incredulous laughter. Meanwhile, Eritrea's rulers brook no interference from their *de jure* superiors in Addis Ababa. Unwilling to accept the accreditation of diplomats posted to Addis Ababa, the Eritreans exist in a diplomatic limbo. But Eritrea needs help desperately, and humanitarian agencies normally work through country-to-country deals. Eritrea's leaders may move the referendum date forward.

The guerrilla army has been enlisted for civilian construction. Some 100,000 men will work for two years without pay, receiving only food and clothing, as when they were bush fighters. They are already rebuilding roads and terracing hillsides. The provisional government, acknowledging the

need to compete in world markets, welcomes investors. Foreign businessmen are trickling in, attracted by a liberal investment code with tax holidays, duty-free imports and repatriation of profits. Far from whining about colonial exploitation, officials talk confidently of economic take-off.

Optimism is widespread. Ask a waiter if Coca-Cola is available, and he will say "not yet". The harbourmaster at Massawa, where nearly every building has been hit by bombs, says everybody he knows is hopeful. The expectation of happier times rests on widespread confidence in the EPLF, which seems to fit in easily among the civilian population. There are no guns on Asmara's streets, prominent men wander the city without escort, and the old regime's roadblocks are off the rural roads.

Contents

BUSINESS

No rest for the weary

"**W**HEN the going gets tough, the tough get going" is the kind of macho posturing, so beloved of American managers in the booming 1980s, that went out of fashion in 1991. As recession in America, Britain, Canada and Australia dragged on and on, many companies that had prided themselves on their aggressiveness and acquisitiveness found themselves struggling just to stay upright. Even in Japan and continental Europe, where economies continued to grow, 1991 was a year of disruption and gloom. Instead of pursuing grand expansion plans, many managers had to concentrate on cutting costs, sacking employees and dickering with their banks. Weary work indeed.

Bright-eyed

Beleaguered businessmen are all too inclined to believe that the current recession is unique—unexpected, worse than earlier downturns and destined to go on indefinitely. In fact, all recessions have a lot in common: they expose companies' weaknesses, they are predictable and they do, eventually, come to an end. This downturn, though it has continued for longer than expected, will prove to be no exception.

Nevertheless, in many respects the recession of 1991 was different from those in the 1970s and the preceding one in 1981-82. The most important difference was that the 1991 recession was relatively mild and confined to Anglo-American economies, failing to cause more than slower growth in Japan, Germany and France. Despite this, the recession caused real upheaval, bankrupting many more firms than earlier recessions and playing havoc with the prosperity and plans of the world's biggest companies. One reason for this was that the Gulf war in the first two months of 1991 added to the feeling of uncertainty which recessions invariably generate. Another is that the globalisation of business, though sometimes exaggerated, has undoubtedly led to the globalisation of hard times. Even companies based in Japan and Germany were hurt by recession in America and elsewhere.

As a result, the recession accelerated fundamental changes already under way in some industries. The most graphic examples are the computer and airline industries. The Gulf war dealt a dev-astating blow to the airlines. For the first time, air travel almost stopped on some busy international routes. This not only helped send the weakest carriers—Pan Am, Eastern, and Britain's Air Europe—to the wall in 1991, it also forced desperate airlines to compete more fiercely with each other outside the already deregulated American market. Government-enforced cartels in Europe and Asia looked more vulnerable. Airlines pushed their regulators into granting more routes and fare-cuts. Deregulation looks sure to move quickly in the next few years, especially in Europe.

The collapse in air travel early in 1991 was nevertheless only a giant hiccough in the long and steady rise in air traffic, from which volumes in Europe and America have not yet fully recovered. The big dip will have one lasting effect, though: a new cost consciousness among business travellers. Scores of big firms grounded their employees during the war for fear of terrorism. In doing so, they made the not-so-startling discoveries that many business trips were unnecessary and most of the rest unnecessarily expensive. Companies have sent employees back into the skies, but in smaller numbers and in cheaper seats. Business class may be doomed as a lucrative money spinner for airlines. By the end of 1991 the competition for business travellers was becoming as price sensitive as the scramble for tourists.

For the computer industry, 1991 was an even more fateful year. After decades of growth through thick and thin, the industry finally looked as prone to the vicissitudes of the business cycle as any metal-bender. Whenever economies slow, capital-spending budgets are usually slashed first and deepest. With computer equipment now accounting for a big proportion of many firms' capital spending, computer makers can no longer count on technological advances to keep them invulnerable to any big cuts in capital budgets.

But hard times in 1991 also made it painfully clear that rapid technological change was transforming the economics of the computer industry itself in ways which the industry's leaders had yet to fathom. Many of the biggest companies seemed paralysed, frantically shedding jobs and sometimes chief executives. Most of

Bush-whacked

Europe's big computer makers—Bull, Olivetti, and Siemens-Nixdorf—lost money. Many of America's did so too. Once-stellar managers such as Olivetti's Vittorio Cassoni, IBM's George Conrades and Compaq's Rod Canion, found themselves shoved aside, demoted or out on the street.

The depth of the changes shaking the computer industry were best shown in the crisis at IBM, which in 1991 suffered its first drop in sales since the 1940s. For the past four decades "Big Blue" had so dominated its industry that, until recently, it seemed unassailable. Still the biggest computer maker by far, IBM is now under attack from all sides. The success of personal computers has lowered the barriers to entry for a horde of new competitors and eaten into the sales and profit margins of large mainframe computers, the biggest source of IBM's profits.

Throughout 1991 IBM struggled to come up with a strategy to cope with these changes. Early in the year it quarrelled with Microsoft, its long-time partner in computer software. Within months it had struck up alliances with Apple, once an arch-rival in the personal-computer market, and a host of other firms making both software and hardware. As profits continued to slide, the chairman John Akers announced on November 26th the loss of 20,000 (out of 350,000) jobs and a drastic decentralisation of the mammoth firm. But the details of the overhaul remained vague. Racked by low morale, IBM ended the year sad and puzzled.

For a number of other industries, 1991's recession was just as unpleasant, but its effects probably will be less enduring. Retailers everywhere suffered from lower consumer spending. Some American and British retailers went bust. But when economies recover, retailing will emerge largely unchanged, even if different companies own the shops. The year's downturn has pushed America's car makers deeply into the red and sown panic among Europe's car industry about the prospect of Japanese competition. But, with a few notable exceptions, most firms will survive until good times return.

In contrast, the contraction of the defence business, which really began to bite in 1991, will continue well beyond the recession. With the collapse of communism, many defence suppliers were forced to look elsewhere for business. Some ventured into the small, but burgeoning market for environmental-control equipment. McDonnell Douglas, one of those hurt most by defence cuts, announced in November that it planned to sell 40% of its commercial-aircraft business to a government-backed Taiwanese company and was looking for additional Asian investors. If successful, McDonnell Douglas could once again become a strong rival to America's Boeing and Europe's Airbus.

In 1991 the supposed excesses of the 1980s also continued to exact a toll. Gigantic debt burdens, and an unexpected decline in advertising spending, hurt many of the media and advertising conglomerates assembled so quickly in the 1980s. Robert Maxwell's empire tottered and then, after his mysterious death at sea, collapsed, revealing that he had been a crook. Rupert Murdoch narrowly escaped bankruptcy and then, under the watchful eyes of his bankers, began the long climb back from the brink. Time-Warner, shackled by $8.5 billion of debt, sold part of its film and television business to two Japanese firms for $1 billion and scoured the globe for other partners. Saatchi & Saatchi and WPP, competing global networks of advertising and marketing firms clumsily cobbled together a few years before, were saved by refinancings, but neither may survive in their present form.

During the year the number of takeovers, which had already plummeted in 1990, remained low. But takeovers did not disappear altogether. Despite the computer industry's woes, AT&T fought and won an acrimonious battle to acquire NCR, America's sixth-largest computer maker. One acquisitive British conglomerate, BTR, launched a hostile bid for Hawker Siddeley, an engineering company. Another conglomerate, Hanson, took a 2.8% stake in ICI, Britain's biggest manufacturer and the world's fourth-largest chemical company but then, for reasons still not clear, did not bid for the whole firm as expected. In continental Europe, where hostile takeovers are rare, three ill-natured bids dominated the news for months: Pirelli's for Continental, a German rival in the ailing tyre industry, Krupp for fellow German steel maker Hoesch, and Accor, a French hotel company, for Wagons-Lits, a Franco-Belgian tourism group. Pirelli's bid failed, Krupp's succeeded and, at the end of the year, Accor's was suspended while the EC Commission studied its effect on the travel market.

In any recession there are winners as well as losers. But until good times return the winners remain difficult to spot. The same has been true in 1991. Sadly, one group of obvious losers has been the countries of Eastern Europe. Western firms, initially so keen to do business in the region, were chary of committing large sums to countries where the rules of business were yet to be established and economies were in a tailspin. Investment in Eastern Europe did not dry up entirely, but it was a trickle, not the hoped-for flood. If western economies grow this year, Eastern Europe's plight may be eased somewhat. But that is a big "if", which also casts a pall of uncertainty over companies in Western Europe, America and Japan.

Businessmen will remember 1991 as a year of anxiety, in which a war that threaten the world's oil supplies gave way to political change of baffling speed and outlook, all overshadowed by the prospect of deepening and spreading recession.

Thursday 3rd

Another big **Japanese property company collapsed**. After chalking up debts of ¥500 billion ($3.5 billion), Tokyo-based EIE International was rescued by five large Japanese banks. The rescue was set to be Japan's second-largest ever.

For the first time since 1979, **western semiconductor companies** gained market share from Japanese rivals last year, according to Dataquest, a market researcher.

Monday 7th

While **De Beers**, South Africa's big diamond miner, increased sales overall by 2% in 1990 to $4.2 billion, diamond sales in the second half fell by 5% over the same period of 1989. Sales dropped in Japan and the eastern American states, but held up well in Texas and in Germany and Italy.

Dick Cheney, America's defence secretary, cancelled the **A-12 fighter** project, delivering a blow to General Dynamics and McDonnell Douglas.

With 67 Boeing 747s, the largest fleet in the world, and 64 747-400s on order, **Japan Airlines** announced the purchase of 14% of a subsidiary of Lockheed, an American aerospace group, which maintains 747s.

Standard & Poor's, an American credit-rating agency, downgraded long-term corporate **credit ratings** in a record 768 cases in 1990. Industries most at risk in 1991, said S&P, were retailing, airlines, cars and casinos; defaults on corporate debt could run to $15 billion-20 billion.

Tuesday 8th

Joining the ranks of Continental and Eastern, cash-starved **Pan Am** filed for bankruptcy under America's chapter 11. The move was designed to ease a merger with TWA, which promised a bridging loan only if Pan Am sought protection from creditors.

Wednesday 9th

Eastman Kodak's drugs subsidiary, Sterling Drug, and Sanofi, a French drug company owned by oil giant Elf Aquitaine, moved to combine operations to save on R&D and marketing.

Friday 11th

Ford and Chrysler, two of the three biggest American car makers, and the United Auto Workers union asked for new limits on the number of **Japanese cars** sold in America, covering local production as well as imports. General Motors, America's biggest car maker, opted out of the campaign.

Saturday 12th

Robert Maxwell, a large British publisher, decided to float off part of Mirror Group Newspapers. Assets included the *Daily Mirror* and *Sunday Mirror*, but the *People*, a Sunday tabloid, was not to be part of the flotation.

Monday 14th

A month after the death of Armand Hammer, his successor at **Occidental**, Ray Irani, announced a badly needed restructuring programme. The firm said it planned to cut $3 billion of its $8 billion debt through asset sales, improve cash flow and sharply reduce dividends.

Tuesday 15th

A 50% drop in the value of British purchases in 1990 made **Japan**, for the first time, the biggest buyer of American companies. This was mainly thanks to Matsushita paying $6.1 billion for MCA, which accounted for 53% of Japan's spending.

American companies accused Japanese manufacturers of **withholding technology and parts** to hinder competition. The General Accounting Office started to examine allegations that critical parts were either delayed or not available, except to Japanese affiliates.

In an unprecedented move, the biggest accounting firm in the world, **KPMG Peat Marwick McLintock**, said it would lay off around 300 of its 1,875 partners in America.

Wednesday 16th

A British luxury-car maker, **Rolls-Royce**, said it was cutting its workforce by 340 because of recession in Britain and America, the markets which in 1990 had accounted for 2,000 of its total sales of 3,300.

Friday 18th

In chapter 11 for nearly two years after labour problems, and crippled further by the Gulf war, America's **Eastern Air Lines** at last closed down after 62 years in the air.

Monday 21st

Continental, the Germany tyre manufacturer, issued a tough and final rejection of the merger approach from Pirelli, the Italian tyre company. Pirelli insisted its bid was "friendly", but pressed on with it despite the decision of the Continental board to break off talks.

France's state-controlled car maker, **Renault**, got a capital boost of FFr10 billion ($2 billion) from the government and from Volvo, a Swedish car maker with a 20% stake. The European Commission, which in 1990 made Renault start repaying FFr6 billion of state aid, did not object.

Tuesday 22nd

A range of ozone-friendly coolants for air conditioners and refrigerators, designed to replace CFCs, was unveiled by the Delaware-based **Du Pont** Chemical company. The range would compete with one already produced by ICI, but General Motors said it wanted Du Pont to supply a coolant for its 1994 cars.

Wednesday 23rd

Faced with an airline industry desperate for cash, America's transport department said it would relax restrictions on **foreign investment** in American airlines. The ceiling of 25% ownership was to be raised to 49%. This would allow Holland's KLM to keep a big investment in Northwest Airlines.

Thursday 24th

General Cinema agreed to acquire Harcourt Brace Jovanovich, a debt-laden American publishing house, for about $1.4 billion. Disgruntled bondholders threatened to block the deal.

Tuesday 29th

McDonnell Douglas, the American aircraft maker, and Fujitsu, Japan's largest computer maker, announced a partnership in factory automation that may include joint R&D and marketing.

February

Monday 4th

Taking advantage of the recession to cut some of its flab, **General Motors** said it was to cut 15,000 white-collar jobs, out of nearly 100,000, by 1993. America's largest car maker also announced cuts in capital spending of $500m a year, to about $7 billion, and a 47% drop in its dividend.

The French state-owned electronics conglomerate, Thomson, entered the **European telephone-equipment market,** aiming for a 10% market share in five years. Though well established in the American market, Thomson had been curbed in Europe by a 1983 market-share agreement wih Alcatel Alsthom, a French competitor.

Tuesday 5th

New Zealand's Sir Ron Brierley sold his 20% stake in Britain's **Vickers**, maker of tanks and Rolls-Royce cars, ending a two-year dispute with the company's management. Against Vickers's wishes, Sir Ron had long wanted to sell Rolls-Royce Motors off.

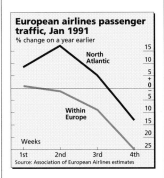

European airlines passenger traffic, Jan 1991
% change on a year earlier

North Atlantic

Within Europe

Weeks

1st 2nd 3rd 4th

Source: Association of European Airlines estimates

Thursday 7th

It became clear that the **airline industry was in crisis.** Transatlantic traffic had collapsed. Within Europe, traffic plummeted 25% in the last week of January over the same period last year, hit by fears of terrorism because of the Gulf war. Air France saw a 23% drop in passenger numbers. British Airways halved its

number of Concorde flights to New York and cancelled Concorde's Washington flights. Pan Am announced 4,000 job cuts and a reduction of more than 35% in its transatlantic flights. TWA defaulted on a $75m debt payment.

Friday 8th

Germany's national airline, **Lufthansa,** decided it could no longer afford to take over Interflug, so dooming the flag carrier of the former East Germany to oblivion. Nearly 3,000 jobs were lost. The news was a blow to east Germany's stumbling privatisation programme.

Only 18 months after it was opened, **Saab Automobile** said it would close its Malmo plant. The Swedish car maker also said it was likely at least to double its losses to SKr4.64 billion ($780m) in 1990, the first year in which it had been jointly owned by Saab-Scania and General Motors.

British music, lighting and defence conglomerate, **Thorn EMI**, made an offer for Thames Television which valued the largest commercial television company at £124m to £149m ($298m). Thorn already held 56% of the shares.

Thursday 14th

Carlo De Benedetti, through his beleaguered French holding company, Cerus, pulled out of Société Générale de Belgique, a huge Belgian com-

pany he tried to take over in 1988. He announced the sale of his 10% stake to Compagnie de Suez, a French investment group, for FFr2.1 billion ($424m).

Friday 15th

Four western companies agreed to participate in Japan's government-supported R&D project to develop a "**hypersonic" jet engine.** United Technologies' Pratt & Whitney unit, America's General Electric, Britain's Rolls-Royce and France's Snecma were to join Japan's three leading aircraft makers in a consortia organised by Japan's Ministry of International Trade and Industry.

Wednesday 20th

After yet another European airline made cuts—**Air France** said it would reduce its wage bill by FFr600m ($118m)—the EC decided to allow temporary subsidies and to relax rules on route-sharing.

Fanuc, a Japanese machine-tool maker, dropped plans to buy a 40% stake in Moore Special Tool, an American precision-tool manufacturer, after some **congressmen objected** to a foreign company owning a large stake in a firm capable of making parts of nuclear weapons.

Thursday 21st

One of the fastest-growing companies of the 1980s, the now-ailing **Saatchi & Saatchi**, announced a second financial rescue package. The first in mid-January ran into criticism from some of its bond-holders.

Monday 25th

Sweden's Wallenberg family, through its Investor and Providentia investment companies, paid SKr12.8 billion ($2.3 billion) for **complete control of Saab-Scania**. With foreign ownership rules soon to be changed in Sweden, the

car and aerospace group needed protection from foreign takeover attempts, said Peter Wallenberg.

Hit by the recession, a snobby clothing store in London's Piccadilly, Daks Simpson, accepted a £65m ($125m) **takeover bid** from Sankyo Seiko, one of the largest textiles and clothing companies in Japan.

Wednesday 27th

Westinghouse Electric took a $975m write-off on its credit business and announced that it would reduce its scope. Other big finance subsidiaries of American manufacturers had also run into difficulty—a blow to those arguing that industrial companies should be allowed to own banks.

Thursday 28th

Procter & Gamble and L'Oreal were revealed as possible bidders for **Revlon**. The two companies were negotiating with Ronald Perelman, the financier who won control of the company in a bitter 1985 takeover battle. Mr Perelman, with more than $3 billion in debts, was in need of the cash.

Holland's ailing electronics giant, **Philips**, announced losses of a net 4.2 billion guilders ($2.3 billion) in 1990 after running up nearly 4.7 billion guilders of restructuring costs. Observers began to wonder whether Mr Jan Timmer, a Philips veteran, recently appointed president, was tough enough for the job.

Monday 4th

One of the world's largest makers of shaving products, **Gillette**, signed a $60m joint-venture agreement to start manufacturing for the first time in the Soviet Union.

Germany's **Deutsche Aerospace**, a subsidiary of Daimler-Benz, decided to take a 50% stake in a new consortium to develop a family of 80-130-seat regional jets. France's Aerospatiale and Italy's Alenia said they would each take 25%. This annoyed Europe's Airbus Industrie consortium. The German and French aircraft companies are its two biggest partners, and Alenia is a subcontractor for arch-rival Boeing.

Tuesday March 5th

Marvin Roffman, a securities analyst sacked after he refused to withdraw **derogatory remarks** made about Donald Trump's Taj Mahal casino, was awarded $750,000 against his former firm, Janney Montgomery Scott.

A panel of federal judges declared that a growing backlog of personal-injury **asbestos cases** clogging the courts was an impending disaster, and urged Congress to come up with a national solution. For every case settled or tried, two new ones arose. The panel said that money now available from private industry for asbestos injuries would not be enough.

A British publishing and banking conglomerate, **Pear-** son, sold its 22% stake in a Dutch publisher, **Elsevier**, for £313m ($595m) to Goldman Sachs, an American investment house. The sale ended hopes that the two companies, which took stakes in each other in 1988 to fend off hostile approaches from Rupert Murdoch and Robert Maxwell, would merge.

Sunday 10th

In the continuing wrangle over its $6.1 billion hostile takeover bid, America's **teleglomerate**, AT&T, said it would raise its offer for NCR, a computer company, from $90 a share to $100, if NCR was prepared to discuss merger terms. NCR stuck to its demand for $125 a share.

Monday 11th

After three months of negotiation, **Heathrow airport** opened its gates to new airlines. The pact allowed United Airlines and American Airlines to proceed with buying the transatlantic routes of ailing Pan Am and TWA. In return, British airlines were to be allowed to fly direct from some American cities to the Caribbean, South America and other destinations.

It was revealed that **Microsoft**, the world's largest software company, had been under investigation by America's Federal Trade Commission for alleged anti-competitive practices since June 1990.

Tuesday 12th

Olivetti's chairman, **Carlo De Benedetti**, was indicted by a Milan court for fraudulent bankruptcy in connection with Banco Ambrosiano. He was its deputy chairman just before its $1.2 billion collapse in 1982, Italy's biggest banking scandal.

In a futile effort to bolster the **price of oil**, OPEC agreed to a voluntary but modest cut in production of 1m barrels a day from the current 23.3m b/d. But Saudi Arabia, faced with hefty war bills, refused to help bolster prices by cutting back production after increasing it during the Gulf crisis from 5.4m b/d to 8.5m b/d.

An expansive **Robert Maxwell**, wearing a blue baseball cap and a red bow-tie, announced he had struck a deal to buy the crippled *New York Daily News*, after winning the unions' agreement to cut 800 jobs. The paper's Chicago-based parent, the Tribune Company, agreed to pay Mr Maxwell $60m—the loss expected for the first quarter—to take the troubled tabloid newspaper off its hands.

Wednesday 13th

Shareholders of **Continental**, a German tyre maker, voted to lift restrictions on the voting rights of the firm's shares. Italy's Pirelli claimed a partial victory in its efforts to take over Continental, even though the firm's shareholders also rejected a proposal for a merger between the two firms.

Monday 18th

After spending more than two years trying to get on the board of **Lockheed**, America's sixth-biggest defence business, Harold Simmons, a Dallas billionaire, gave up and sold nearly all his 19.8% stake at a loss of $42m.

A famous east German optics company, **Jenoptik Carl Zeiss**, announced that it was going to have to shed more than 20,000 jobs, roughly 80% of its workforce, before its contemplated merger with Carl Zeiss in west Germany. This was dismal news for thousands of other firms in the former East Germany. Zeiss had been one of the country's industrial flagships. The western firm of the same name was formed by employees of the original company who moved to West Germany after 1945.

Friday 22nd

Despite an official ban, from 1982-89 **West German companies** supplied Iraq with around DM1 billion ($595m) worth of arms, and the technology to help make nuclear weapons, poison gas and missiles. Embarrassed, Germany promised to tighten trading laws.

Monday 25th

Private detectives employed by the Kuwaiti government revealed that they had discovered that Saddam Hussein had **hidden assets** in more than 40 banks around the world, $2.4 billion of which were not frozen by UN sanctions. Kroll Associates of New York said that around $10 billion of Iraq's $200 billion oil revenues had been skimmed off in 1979-89. A network of Iraqi front companies were said to own around $1 billion of shares in European countries, including an 8.4% stake in France's Hachette, the world's sixth-largest publisher.

Tuesday 26th

Europe's biggest **joint semiconductor research programme**, JESSI, booted ICL, Britain's biggest computer maker, out of three of the five projects in which it was taking part. Fujitsu of Japan bought 80% of ICL in 1990.

Wednesday 27th

Britain's debt-crippled **Saatchi & Saatchi** won shareholder approval for a £225m ($395m) rescue package. Earlier, the advertising group had announced a pre-tax loss of £5.2m ($10.1m) for the final quarter of 1990.

April

Monday April 1st

Elsevier, a Dutch publisher of newspapers and scientific books, agreed to buy Robert Maxwell's **Pergamon Press** for £440m ($780m), and announced plans to sell its 9% stake, worth around £180m, in Pearson, a British conglomerate, to help pay for the deal. In March Pearson sold its 22% stake in Elsevier for more than £300m.

In a terrorist attack by the Red Army Faction on his home in Düsseldorf, **Detlev Rohwedder**, head of the Treuhandanstalt, was shot dead. In charge of privatising east German industry, he and the agency had been criticised over their efforts to close hundreds of loss-making companies. Less than 18 months before, Alfred Herrhausen, head of Deutsche Bank, was killed by a bomb.

Thursday 4th

After months of negotiations, **WPP**, a British advertising and marketing group, tied up its $1 billion debt-restructuring package.

Friday 5th

America's **IBM** said it would cut 10,000 more jobs as part of the computer company's long-term restructuring and cost-saving effort. Together with the 4,200 jobs just departed through the sale of its typewriter division, the cut would reduce its payroll by 3.7% to 359,000. Some 10,000 voluntary job-cuts were made in 1989.

Monday 8th

Suspected of running an **illegal cartel**, several large steel companies, including British Steel, France's Usinor-Sacilor, Germany's Peine-Salzgitter and Arbed of Luxembourg, had their offices raided by officials from the European Commission, it was revealed.

Tuesday 9th

Bottled water may not be as pure as drinkers think—even after Perrier's problems in 1990. A study by the Food and Drug Administration of the $2-billion industry in America found bacteria tainting some brands, and one, popular at the White House, that gets its supply from the same underground source that feeds San Antonio's ordinary taps.

Wednesday 10th

Part of Revlon's $3-billion cosmetics business was bought by **Procter & Gamble**. The $1-billion purchase of the mass-market beauty products, including Max Factor, popular in Japan, and the German-based Betrix, would add an international angle to P&G's top-seller in America, Cover Girl.

Monday 15th

Birgit Breuel was appointed head of the **Treuhandanstalt**, the agency privatising east German businesses, following the murder of Detlev Rohwedder.

Tuesday 16th

After months of wrangling, it was announced that Giancarlo Parretti, the Italian financier who took over in 1990 as head of **MGM-Pathe Communications**, was leaving, to be replaced as chairman by Cesare De Michelis, brother of Italy's foreign minister. Lenders were reluctant to provide new loans as long as Mr Parretti stayed in charge of the company.

For the sixth month running, **Japanese company failures** increased. Bankruptcies in March rose 57.3% from a year earlier, to 773. In the same period the bankrupt companies' debts leapt more than ten times to ¥791.3 billion ($5.8 billion), the second-highest on record.

Wednesday 17th

Britain's **Robert Maxwell** launched the flotation of 45-49% of his Mirror Group Newspapers, in the hope of raising around £250m ($448m) to reduce his corporate debt.

Monday 22nd

AT&T's four-month old hostile bid for NCR turned a lot friendlier when **Ma Bell** met the computer company's asking price of $110 a share, though none of the $7.5 billion total purchase price was to be in cash.

With an eye to cutting costs, AT&T Microelectronics and **Japan's NEC** said they would jointly develop basic technologies to make new generations of chips.

American **oil companies** did well in the first quarter, helped by fat profits on refining. Mobil's net earnings rose to $710m, up by 78% on the same period of 1990. Amoco, not far behind, rose 72% to $803m. Strong gains came from other oil producers too, including Texaco, Chevron and Occidental.

Tuesday 23rd

A consortium led by Lockheed and also involving Boeing and General Dynamics beat a rival consortium of Northrup and McDonnell Douglas to win a $65 billion-95 billion order to build the next generation of America's **stealth fighter**. Over 20 years the Lockheed-led group will develop and produce 648 aircraft. It was announced that

Pratt & Whitney would build the engines.

With more and more restaurants dropping the expensive charge card, **American Express** promised to lower its fees, but only to those outlets that filed charge records electronically. In Japan Amex was to join Sumitomo Bank in issuing personal charge cards and make loans.

Wednesday 24th

Suzuki announced plans to take a 40% stake in a joint venture to make **cars in Hungary**. It would be the first Japanese car maker to go into business in Eastern Europe.

Tuesday 30th

The shareholders of **BSkyB**, Britain's money-losing satellite TV broadcaster, agreed to put up £200m ($360m) of new cash to keep the business going. Formed by a merger in November 1990 between Rupert Murdoch's Sky Television and its rival BSB (which had been backed by a consortium of large media companies), BSkyB was still losing £6m a week despite drastic cost cutting.

America's recession continued to extract a punishing toll on the country's biggest car makers. Ford and General Motors reported heavy first-quarter losses. Ford lost $884m on sales of $21.3 billion, compared with earnings in 1990's first quarter of $506m on sales of $23.6 billion. GM lost $461m on sales of $29.2 billion compared with earnings of $619m on sales of $30.1 billion the year before.

May

Wednesday 1st

Shell and British Petroleum announced **major oil finds** in the Gulf of Mexico. To exploit them, the companies said they would have to push deep-water technology to its limits. But the fields could be huge.

Thursday 2nd

The **video shop** may be doomed. Three American communications firms—AT&T, Tele-Communications Inc and US West—said they were test-marketing a system that allows cable-TV users to watch any one of more than 1,000 movies and filmed events, without leaving home.

Monday 6th

The computer industry's price cutting gathered pace. Japan's **Toshiba**, market-leader in portable computers, cut prices in America by 19-33%, claiming economies of scale. And competitive pressure finally forced IBM to cut its workstation prices by as much as 60%.

AT&T's tussle for NCR finally ended when America's fifth-largest computer maker accepted the telecom firm's $7.5 billion bid. AT&T hoped that NCR would revive its loss-making computer business.

An American government report claimed that some Japanese companies were **withholding production technology** from American semiconductor makers, among other unfair trade practices. Hitachi, one of the firms accused, replied that no American firms had ordered from it.

Tuesday 7th

For $1.1 billion, **Comcast** bought Metromedia's Philadelphia-based cellular-telephone operations. The sale underlined a growing interest by cable-television companies in mobile phones—but the price was considered low.

Wednesday 8th

Jon Peters, co-chairman of **Columbia Pictures**, said he would leave to set up his own production company, tied to Columbia. The move came only 18 months after Sony of Japan paid a high premium for Mr Peters's services.

Thursday 9th

The sudden resignation of **Horst Urban**, the chairman of Continental, a big German tyre maker, meant a resumption in merger talks with Pirelli. Mr Urban had long resisted the Italian tyre maker's attentions.

Friday 10th

Saturn, the independent subsidiary which General Motors set up to pioneer new manufacturing and management techniques for the rest of the giant American car maker, issued its second recall for **faulty cars**. Saturn said it would replace all 1,836 vehicles shipped with a bad batch of engine anti-freeze. Problems had plagued Saturn since it began producing and selling cars in the autumn of 1990.

Sunday 12th

Three months of hostile takeover talks ended when **Square D**, a leading American electrical-equipment company, admitted defeat to France's debt-laden **Schneider** and accepted its generous $2.23 billion offer.

Monday 13th

Just a week after being acquired by AT&T, computer maker NCR unveiled a range of large, computers using **parallel processing** to boost computing speeds, the first major computer company to use this technology for commercial computers aimed at a wide market of business customers.

Tuesday 14th

Britain's leading takeover expert, **Hanson**, paid £240m ($417m) for a 2.8% stake in **ICI**, Britain's chemicals giant and its largest manufacturing company. Rumours abounded of a possible bid, a step which could cost Hanson about £11 billion. The British group, led by 69-year-old Lord Hanson, could easily afford it.

Wednesday 15th

Sony became the first company to unveil a commercial version of a compact-disc machine that can record as well as play. The announcement means that a **battle of formats** is likely to develop between Sony's recordable disc, incompatible with existing CDs, and Philip's digital compact cassette, a tape format which also permits home recording of digital music.

The European Commission agreed on a directive to ban all **tobacco advertising** in the Community from 1993. To become law the directive needed to be approved by a majority of member governments, many of whom, such as Britain and Germany, opposed it.

Rupert Murdoch's media empire, **News Corp**, went deep into loss in the third quarter. Its post-tax operating loss of A$204.7m ($160m) included A$190m to pay for repackaging its $7.6 billion of debts.

Thursday 16th

Japan's **Bridgestone** said it would invest $1.4 billion more in Firestone, the American tyre company which it had been struggling to turn around since 1988.

Tuesday 28th

In a deal worth around $4.3 billion, Saudi Aramco, Saudi Arabia's national oil company, and a Japanese group of companies agreed to build and operate **oil refineries** in the two countries.

Wednesday 29th

In a deal worth £230m ($400m), a British computer maker, **ICL**, 80%-controlled by Japan's Fujitsu, said it would merge its information-systems division with those of Nokia Data, Finland's largest public company and Scandinavia's largest information-technology group.

Japan's foreign ministry summoned the French ambassador to protest at Japan-bashing by France's new prime minister, Edith Cresson, who had remarked that Japan was an unfair trader and had destroyed the American car industry. Relations would be damaged if she did not tone down her remarks, Japan's foreign ministry said. The action came after the Cresson government had said it might block **Japan's NEC** from taking a 5% stake in Bull, France's ailing and state-owned computer maker.

Thursday 30th

Boxer-turned-tycoon **George Walker** lost his job as boss of Brent Walker, the British leisure group he helped build. The company was struggling to service a crushing $2.1 billion of debt.

June

Monday 3rd

A Swiss pharmaceutical group, Roche, jumped into the European market for over-the-counter drugs by buying Nicholas Laboratories, maker of British favourites **Aspro and Rennie**, for $821m from the Chicago-based Sara Lee Corporation.

Having recently bought NCR, a big American computer maker, **AT&T** sold its 19% shareholding in Sun Microsystems, a Californian computer maker which bought back some of its own shares, for $580m.

Tuesday 4th

The world's largest steel producer, **Nippon Steel**, signed a $200m deal with Oracle Systems, a big American software company, to take a 49% stake in Oracle's Japanese subsidiary. Nippon said it wanted access to software for its computer-making division.

In a first step towards full ownership, **BP** paid Ptas20.7 billion ($192m) for a 24.9% stake in Petromed, a Spanish oil and gas company. Corporacion Banesto, Petromed's owner, also promised to sell BP its remaining 46% stake in Petromed at the same price per share.

Thursday 6th

It emerged that Apple and IBM, once **bitter rivals** in the personal-computer market, were holding talks. Apple was considering whether to licence a powerful new microprocessor from IBM, and IBM was attracted by Apple's software technology, which it could use to boost its troubled OS/2 operating system software.

America's **Whirlpool** paid $610m to buy the 47% stake held by Philips, its partner in its European appliance business. Whirlpool used the joint venture to learn about the European market, but wanted to exploit opportunities in the European Community's single market on its own.

Monday 10th

The boss of Toyota's European operations said that European car makers, in trying to limit sales of **Japanese cars in Europe**, were thinking small. Europe would become the biggest market in the world, said Junji Numata who added that Toyota planned to expand sales there by a third over the next six years.

Tuesday 11th

A French ad group, **BDDP**, took over Wells Rich, a New York agency, by raising its 40% stake to 70%. BDDP said it wanted to create a "multicultural" advertising network.

Wednesday 12th

Raul Gardini was ousted as boss of the family holding company, Serafino Ferruzzi, to be replaced by Arturo Ferruzzi, sole heir to Italy's second-largest private business. A rift between Gardini and the Ferruzzis grew after he lost his battle with the government to control Italy's chemicals industry.

France's Nipponophobe prime minister Edith Cresson allowed state-owned computer maker **Bull** to re-open talks with Japan's NEC on technological co-operation and NEC's plan to acquire a 5% stake in the French firm.

This was a reversal of one of the first actions taken by Madame Cresson upon taking office in May.

Friday 14th

A new 105-seater **twin-engined jet** based on McDonnell Douglas's MD-90 is to be developed, it was announced, in conjunction with a Chinese aircraft maker (where the aircraft would be built), Pratt & Whitney (who would supply the engines) and Northwest Airlines (who might use it).

Sunday 16th

In a race to make **artificial blood**, a small biotechnology company based in New Jersey, DNX, said it had managed to breed three genetically altered pigs which produce human haemoglobin.

Monday 17th

A German industrial company, **Viag**, received permission from the European Commission to go ahead with its purchase of America's Continental Can. The deal, for an undisclosed price, created Europe's second-largest packaging company.

America's computer giant, **IBM**, claimed to be the first foreign firm to have set up a wholly-owned subsidiary in the Soviet Union.

Unilever, an Anglo-Dutch detergent and food group, said it would buy 80% of a **Polish detergent maker** for $20m. Pollena Bydgoszcz, to be renamed Lever Polska, was auctioned by the Polish government, which retained 20% of the privatised firm. In another deal, America's **Procter & Gamble** agreed to pay $44m for Rakona, a big Czechoslovakian detergent maker.

Monday 17th

Pepsi Cola announced plans to invest $60m over five years—to update its Polish bottling plants.

Tuesday 18th

Massachusetts-based **Wang Laboratories**, beset by losses, said it planned to sell IBM computers under its own label, virtually abandoning its long struggle to be a top computer designer and manufacturer on its own. Big job losses would follow.

Friday 21st

America's Food and Drug Administration proposed new rules on listing **additives in food**. This meant relabelling most packaged goods sold in supermarkets.

Monday 24th

In a move that would almost double its size, Carrefour, France's biggest operator of **hypermarkets**, agreed to buy one of its rivals, Euromarché, for FFr5.2 billion ($825m). France's no-frills hypermarkets make almost one-fifth of the nation's retail sales.

The pride of Europe's car companies was dented when Mazda recorded **Japan's first victory** in the Le Mans 24-hour race. Germany's Porsche said it was withdrawing temporarily from grand-prix racing.

Tuesday 25th

After Germany decided to shift its seat of government from Bonn to **Berlin**, Sony became the first foreign multinational to decide to locate its European headquarters in Berlin. The Japanese consumer-electronics giant would be moving from Cologne.

Friday 28th

Following probes into Microsoft and Nintendo, America's Federal Trade Commission said it was directing its latest antitrust investigation at **Intel**, which has a near monopoly as a maker of microprocessor chips for IBM-compatible personal computers.

Tuesday 2nd

America's biggest car maker, **General Motors**, reached agreement with its union to run three assembly shifts of 120 hours a week, a tactic GM had used to great effect in Europe.

Thursday 4th

IBM and Siemens said they were to join forces to produce next-generation memory chips at IBM's chipmaking facility in France. Production of chips four times more capacious than today's biggest memory chips was to begin in 1992.

Germany's Volkswagen agreed to produce an **electric-powered car** jointly with Switzerland's SMH, the maker of the cheap, but trendy Swatch, which saved the Swiss watch industry from extinction. The car, priced at about $6,300, was to go into production in three or four years and would be sold under the Swatch name.

Monday 8th

Continental, the German tyre company in everlasting talks with Italy's Pirelli, appointed a new chief executive: Hubertus von Grünberg, head of the automotive division of ITT in America.

Tuesday 9th

The Commerce Department decided that Japanese makers of portable-computer screens were **dumping** their products in America.

Six states filed suits against TRW, one of the leaders in America's **credit-reporting** industry, charging it with persistent errors in consumers' details, failing to correct errors, and illegally selling information to junk-mail firms.

Wednesday 10th

President Bush ended America's trade embargo against **South Africa**, saying the five conditions that Congress had imposed because of South Africa's apartheid policies had been met.

Friday 12th

A French supplier of telecommunications equipment, **Alcatel**, paid $625m for a subsidiary of Rockwell International that makes products for telephone communications networks. As a result of the deal, Alcatel's 4% of the American transmission market jumped to 15%.

Monday 15th

After 15 years of legal tussles, it was agreed that **Kodak** would pay $925m to **Polaroid** for infringing its instant-photography patents.

Tuesday 16th

More scene changes for **Maxwell Communication** when Kevin Maxwell, chief executive and son of Robert, decided to demerge and refloat MCC's American companies to bolster its shaky finances. Those interests, which included Macmillan, a large publisher, formed more than 70% of the assets of the British conglomerate.

West European new-car registrations Largest markets
Jan-Jun 1991, % change on a year earlier

Germany*	+50.7
Italy	−2.7
Spain	−16.4
France	−16.6
Britain	−24.8

* Includes eastern Germany in 1991
Source: Industry estimates

The boom in **used-car sales in east Germany** continued fueling demand for new cars in the western half of the country, while elsewhere in Western Europe sales dived by 11.9% in the first six months of 1991. French car makers suffered, with Peugeot dropping 10%. But the biggest losers were Saab (down 16.3%), Volvo (18.4%) and Jaguar (35.4%).

Accused so often of dumping, Japan fought back. An independent Japanese report criticised American and European **anti-dumping** measures. The report said that the GATT rules were being departed from with increasing frequency.

Friday 19th

Warning that computer markets remain bleak, **IBM** said that its profits in the second quarter dived 92% compared with 1990, to $114m. **Compaq**, once a rising star, announced an 81% fall in the same period. **Digital Equipment**, the world's third-biggest computer firm, lost $617m in the year to July 1991.

Saturday 20th

Since 1983, foreign direct-investments of **multinational companies** have grown three times faster than world trade, it was reported. Four-fifths of the total was accounted for by America, Japan and the EC.

Monday 22nd

Two American gene-splicing experts, **Cetus** and **Chiron**, got themselves spliced in a $660m share swap. The merger followed the sale to Switzerland's Roche, for about $300m, of the rights to Cetus's revolutionary genetic fingerprinting technology, a sale which helped staunch Cetus's losses.

Tuesday 23rd

One of Germany's industrial giants, **Daimler-Benz**, bought a 34% stake worth FFr2.4 billion ($403m) in Sogeti, the holding company that controls Europe's largest computer-services group, Cap Gemini Sogeti. By 1996 Daimler could have a majority stake.

Despite announcing a hefty loss only days before, Digital Equipment bought the loss-making computer division of **Philips**, Holland's struggling electronics giant. The purchase, for an undisclosed sum, did not include Philips' PC business.

Debt-crippled **Unisys**, another American computer maker, lost $1.3 billion in the second quarter, including a $1.2 billion restructuring charge. It was to cut 10,000 more jobs, consolidate plants and trim its product-range.

Thursday 25th

A court decision to allow America's **Baby Bells** to compete in information services could lead to explosive growth in the market or a stifling monopoly, depending on whom you listened to. Lobbyists for much smaller competitors besieged Congress hoping for legislation to prevent the intrusion.

Monday 29th

An Australian transport group, TNT, and the post offices of five countries decided to set up a joint venture called GD Net to provide an **express parcel-service worldwide** which would take about 20% of the market. Other countries would later be able to join the venture.

Wednesday 31st

The EC and Japan agreed to a plan to limit Japan's share of the **EC car market** until the end of the century. Japan's share would be allowed to rise steadily until 1999, when the EC would lift all barriers. A dispute about whether the output of Japanese factories in Europe should be included was fudged, with both sides claiming victory.

Monday 5th

Soichiro Honda died, aged 84. He founded Honda Motor, the motorcycle and car company that became a symbol of Japan's post-1945 industrial success. The son of a blacksmith, Mr Honda began by fitting second-hand military engines to bicycles.

Andrew Lloyd Webber, creator of such musicals as "Evita" and "Cats", sold a 30% stake in his **Really Useful Holdings** to Polygram, a record company, for £78m ($134m). That was a really useful deal. Just eight months earlier, in December 1990, he had bought the entire company back from shareholders for £77.5m.

Tuesday 6th

After scrapping one controversial rights issue, **Time Warner**, an American publishing and entertainment group, succeeded in raising $2.76 billion on its second attempt. The money was used to reduce the group's $11 billion of debt.

Sony announced a plan to raise $2 billion to $3 billion in equity in America and Japan, partly by selling stakes in Sony Music (formerly CBS Records) and other entertainment firms. The Japanese firm wanted to repay some of the debt incurred when buying **Columbia Pictures** in 1989.

New York's **Corning** put its low-margin pots and pans business into a new $800m-a-year joint venture for consumer housewares formed with Vitro, Mexico's largest glass manufacturer. This freed Corning to focus on its high-margin business: laboratory services, optical fibres and special materials.

Friday 9th

Two car makers with small sales in the **American car market** decided to pull out. France's Peugeot and Britain's Sterling, a part of the Rover Group which sold luxury cars there, decided not to stick out the recession.

Monday 12th

Britain's second-largest accountancy firm, KPMG Peat Marwick, agreed to pay £40m ($68m) in damages to **Ferranti**, a beleaguered electronics company whose purchase in 1987 of International Signal & Control, a firm audited by Peat Marwick, proved a disaster when a £215m fraud was uncovered. Ferranti had initially hoped to claim £400m.

After **Delta** raised its price, Pan Am received approval from the bankruptcy courts to sell its European and transatlantic routes, its north-east shuttle and 45 planes to America's third biggest airline. Delta paid $416m for the assets, and promised to invest $305m in Pan Am and to assume $668m of its debts.

Tuesday 13th

Pentland, a British consumer products group, took a 20% stake in **Adidas** worth DM134.5m ($78m) to help bail out France's Bernard Tapie, once a pop singer and now a socialist politician and financier heavily in debt. Later in the year, Pentland sold its stake in America's Reebok, a rival of Adidas's.

Japanese corporate failures rose by 81% in July from the year-earlier period. It was the tenth month in a row of year-to-year rises.

Friday 16th

Four big oil companies agreed to pay a total of $180m to settle an antitrust dispute in California. **Chevron, Texaco, Mobil and Royal Dutch/Shell** claimed they did not rig the price of oil pumped from the Wilmington oilfield. Local and state authorities said they did. Other oil companies had already settled.

Tuesday 20th

America's media and entertainment conglomerate, **Time Warner**, dropped its anti-takeover defence. Shareholders had threatened to use the poison-pill vote at the firm's September annual meeting to show disapproval of a controversial $3.5 billion rights issue.

Japan's fourth-largest car maker, **Mazda**, said it planned to launch a new range of luxury cars, called Amati, in North America. The move upset European luxury-car makers who in July, for the first time, saw Mercedes and BMW outsold in America by Toyota's Lexus and Nissan's Infiniti.

Monday 26th

Scientists announced the birth of the **world's first transgenic calf**, which carries a gene for the production of an important human-milk protein in cow milk. The bull calf was the result of a collaboration between GenPharm International, a California-based biotechnology company, and the Dutch agriculture ministry. It means cow milk will have anti-bacterial and other essential properties, making it suitable for human babies.

Tuesday 27th

The profits of Japan's largest electronics company, **Matsushita**, dropped 25% in the three months to the end of June, to ¥95.7 billion ($692m), due mainly to its $6.1 billion acquisition of MCA, a big American entertainments group. In Europe the EC Commission said it would relax competition rules to allow a joint venture between Matsushita and Philips, the Dutch electronics giant, to go ahead.

Wednesday 28th

Brent Walker, a troubled British pubs and betting-shops group, asked the Serious Fraud Office to nose through its files. The founder of the company, former boxer George Walker, was booted out in May.

AT&T signed an agreement with Japan's Nippondenso, a car-components maker allied with Toyota, to exploit AT&T's **smart-card technology** in Japan. The card looks like a credit card but contains a tiny computer that can store information. The partnership will explore various uses for the card, including personal identification, security, automatic toll collection.

Fujitsu, Japan's largest computer maker, invested $40m in Hal Computer Systems, a California start-up by Andy Heller, once one of IBM's star researchers. Named after the computer in the movie "2001: A Space Odyssey", the company planned to use widely available components to create a full range of computers which would help turn it into one of the biggest firms in the industry. Despite such lofty ambitions, the company had still not said when its first product would appear.

September

Monday 2nd
A consortium led by **Westland** and America's **IBM** won a £1.5 billion ($2.53 billion) defence order to supply an initial 44 Merlin EH101 helicopters to Britain's Royal Navy. The decision came as a blow to two big British firms, General Electric Company and British Aerospace, which had put in a rival bid.

Thursday 5th
Searle, a big American pharmaceutical subsidiary of Monsanto, bought a 12% stake at a cost of $106m in Hokuriku Seiyaku, a **Japanese drugs maker**, as part of its plan to increase its share of the Japanese drugs market.

A missile alliance was announced by Europe's aerospace industries. Thomson and Aerospatiale, both French state-owned companies, and Germany's MBB, a division of Daimler-Benz, said they would co-operate to make a new generation of short-range anti-aircraft missiles.

IBM's Japanese subsidiary said it planned to sell a supercomputer made by rival NEC to a customer, construction-machinery maker Komatsu. This was the first time IBM had resold a supercomputer made by another company, which marked another step in the computer giant's strategy of seeking more alliances and partnerships.

Monday 9th
An engineering, defence and car giant, **British Aerospace**, launched a £432m ($747m) rights issue after warning that its profits for the year to December were likely to be half expectations. It announced half-year pre-tax profits of £86m, down from £146m in the first half of 1990. The half-year profits of **Rolls-Royce**, a British aero-engine maker, also tumbled, from £115m to £11m.

Tuesday 10th
Japan's leading electrical-machinery manufacturer, **Hitachi**, reduced its profit forecast by nearly 30% and said it would cut capital spending by 20% for the year to next March. Prices for 4 megabit DRAM memory chips had more than halved in the past year.

Wednesday 11th
Japan and the European Community are heading for a row over details of last month's deal on **EC car trade** after 1992. Yutaka Kume, chief executive of Nissan Motor, denied that Japan agreed to limit Japanese car production in Europe, as the EC seemed to believe.

Friday 13th
America's Northwest Airlines pulled out of plans to operate the **Trump Shuttle** after it failed to reach agreement with 100 baggage handlers. The deal would have relieved Donald Trump of $135m of personal debt.

Monday 16th
Hanson made an agreed takeover bid of £351m ($612m) for **Beazer**, Britain's fourth-largest housebuilder which had got into debt by expanding into America. The acquisition stopped the proposed flotation of CHB Group, Beazer's British half.

America's **General Electric** took a charge of $1.8 billion against first-quarter results, turning its $999m profit into an $801m loss. The reason: a new accounting rule for pensioners' health benefits.

The American machine-tool industry called for an extension to a **voluntary restraint agreement** that has protected it from Japanese and Taiwanese competition since 1987. The industry cited national security and poor profits as reasons.

Germany's beleaguered sports-car maker, **Porsche**, turned down an offer from Mercedes-Benz, a German luxury-car maker owned by the Daimler-Benz group, to take a minority stake in the family-controlled company. Porsche said it wanted to stay independent. It expected to produce only 27,000 cars this year, half its 1985-86 total, and planned to cut 550 jobs.

Tuesday 17th
Williams Holdings, a British conglomerate, made a hostile takeover bid of £750m ($1.3 billion) for the remainder of **Racal Electronics** a day after the defence, security and data-communications company spun off its profitable cellular-telephone operations.

Wednesday 18th
WH Smith, a British retailer, and **Virgin Group**, the trading company founded by Richard Branson, announced a joint venture that would control 30% of Britain's music-retailing business.

Friday 20th
Hawker Siddeley Group, a British aerospace and defence contractor, rejected a a £1.5 billion ($2.5 billion) **takeover bid** from BTR, an acquisitive British conglomerate, beginning a prolonged battle.

Monday 23rd
America and the EC agreed to work together on enforcing their **antitrust and competition laws**, sharing information and evidence in investigations of multinational companies. The regulators' main target appeared to be alleged anti-competitive behaviour by the Japanese.

Tuesday 24th
One of the Baby Bells, **Bell Atlantic**, launched a $1.7 billion agreed takeover of Metro Mobile CTS, the second-biggest independent operator of cellular-telephone networks.

One of the world's biggest record companies, **Polygram**, said it would build up its movie business by investing $200m over the next three years. The company, 80%-owned by electronics giant Philips, would increase its stake in two small film-production companies.

Wednesday 25th
Blamed for a botched rights issue on September 9th and gloomy profit forecasts, the chairman of British Aerospace, **Sir Roland Smith**, resigned. Though his post was a non-executive one, he took an active part in running the firm. Sir Graham Day, boss of Rover car group, became chairman.

Monday 30th
The American government, Alaska and Exxon agreed on $1.25 billion to settle claims arising out of the 1989 **Exxon Valdez oil spill**. The deal was criticised for being little different from a previous failed agreement.

October

Tuesday 1st
Following the resignation of its chairman, **British Aerospace**, Britain's biggest manufacturer and exporter, was the target of rumours that British financial institutions, continental defence firms and perhaps Britain's GEC were dreaming up ways to break it up. It all came to nothing.

Wednesday 2nd
The European Commission blocked the proposed purchase of Boeing's Canadian subsidiary, **de Havilland**, by France's Aerospatiale and Italy's Alenia, causing outrage in both France and Italy. Commission officials argued the deal would have reduced competition in the commuter-aircraft market.

Two of **France's biggest advertising agencies** merged. Eurocom and Roux Seguela Cayzac & Goudard created continental Europe's largest agency, and the world's sixth biggest.

In a significant and surprising deal **IBM** and **Apple**, previously rivals, said they were to collaborate. Apple said it would use an IBM processor for future generations of Macintosh computers, and Motorola would supply the chips. Apple and IBM would also work on a new operating system to be compatible with computers from both companies.

Monday 7th
A big American conglomerate, **Westinghouse Electric**, announced a restructuring programme including 4,000 job cuts and a provision of $1.68 billion. The company made a net loss of $1.5 billion in the third quarter.

Robert Maxwell's Maxwell Communication sold its Macmillan directories business in the United States to **Reed International**. Reed paid $145m for the American Who's Who, and for 17 business directories under National Register Publishing.

Tuesday 8th
The world's largest glass company, Britain's **Pilkington**, announced it would move its flat-glass headquarters from St Helens to Brussels and would cut 750 jobs over the next two years.

Wednesday 9th
A day after American courts confirmed the right of regional "baby bell" telecoms companies to provide **electronic information services** in America, US West teamed up with France Telecom to do just that. France Telecom's Minitel terminals in France make it the world's biggest videotext supplier.

Four **European airlines**, Scandinavian Airlines System, Swissair, Austrian Airlines and British Midland, confirmed plans to create a partnership, called the European Quality Alliance (EQA), which would make them Europe's second biggest airline after Aeroflot.

Thursday 10th
As a prelude to a full merger, **Fried Krupp**, a German steel group, bought 24.9% of Hoesch, a troubled German rival. The merger, which would create a firm with sales of DM28 billion ($17 billion), would need approval from regulators. Hoesch later said it opposed the merger.

Friday 11th
Italy's largest car maker, **Fiat**, said it would buy 51% of the Polish state-owned FSM car factory. Fiat's total investment in the factory would be $1.36 billion, most of which would be spent over the next six years.

Tuesday 15th
The third-quarter net earnings of **IBM**, the world's largest computer manufacturer, plunged 85%, down from $1.11 billion in the same period last year to $172m, accompanied by warnings of worse to come. It also announced a three-month delay in introducing a version of its OS/2 personal-computer operating system.

Monday 21st
Picture-Tel, of Massachusetts, unveiled its new personal computer-cum-video telephone, useful for the growing **video-conference** business. IBM plan to sell the devices, which would cost some $5,000, towards the end of 1992.

Tuesday 22nd
General Motors and **Ford**, America's two biggest car makers, reported third-quarter losses of $1.1 billion and $574m respectively.

Wednesday 23rd
Rupert Murdoch's **News Corporation** said it would float its Australian commercial printing and magazine interests as a separate company. The assets in question generate about A$600m ($475m) a year in revenues. Mr Murdoch's company will hold a 45% stake in the new enterprise.

Thursday 24th
Rod Canion, president of **Compaq Computer**, the manufacturer of IBM-compatible PCs, lost his job. He was replaced by Eckhard Pfeiffer, head of Compaq's European operations. The dismissal followed news of Compaq's first-ever quarterly loss.

Monday 28th
The European Commission rejected plans to introduce competition quickly to **Europe's gas and electricity markets**, and to impose an anti-global-warming energy tax. Before Europe sets a tax, Japan and America must do the same, said energy ministers.

Tuesday 29th
Steve Ross, chairman of **Time Warner**, agreed to sell two 6¼% stakes in his company's film and cable businesses to Toshiba and C. Itoh for a total of $1 billion. The deal gave the Japanese firms some well-known films; it helped Time Warner reduce its debt.

Fujitsu announced a 41% fall in pre-tax profits for the six months to September 30th. Most of the fall was due to weak demand for 4-megabit computer chips—an industry-wide problem.

British Aerospace's £432m ($732m) rights issue failed spectacularly. Existing shareholders bought just 4.9% of the new shares, leaving underwriters with the rest. No surprise, after a forecast loss and the resignation of its chairman, Sir Roland Smith.

Whyte & Mackay, a subsidiary of American Brands, saw its £350m ($602m) bid for Invergordon, a Scottish whisky distillery, lapse. Whyte as left with a stake of 42.4%, too small to take control.

Friday 1st
Japan's Fujitsu dropped plans to **donate a $15m super-computer** to an American project studying the greenhouse effect after pressure from the American government and Cray Research. They regarded the gift as a disguised form of dumping.

Tuesday 5th
The dramatic death at sea of **Robert Maxwell** triggered the suspension of share-dealing in Maxwell Communication Corp and Mirror Group. His sons, Kevin and Ian, took control of their father's complex and troubled empire, now laden with debt of more than £2 billion ($3.9 billion).

Responding to a hostile takeover bid of £1.5 billion ($2.7 billion) from BTR, a British conglomerate, **Hawker Siddeley**, a British engineering group, announced it would sell a large part of its businesses and said it would increase its final dividend by 30% on end-year profits, forecast to be down by 7.4% to £130m.

Wednesday 6th
Philips, a Dutch consumer-electronics manufacturer, agreed to help **Gilbert Hyatt**, an American inventor, obtain licence fees from other manufacturers on patents he owns covering basic microprocessor technologies. Philips will take a portion of any fees earned.

Thursday 7th
IBM, an American computer maker, and **Intel,** a microprocessor chip maker, agreed to develop an entire computer based around a single silicon chip. This should cut the cost of personal computers.

Monday 11th
The world's **oldest cotton mill**, opened in 1784 by Sir Richard Arkwright in Derbyshire, closed with the loss of 97 jobs.

Finance ministers agreed that sales of **duty-free goods** on journeys within the EC would be phased out by July 1999. Britain had hoped for a 15-year reprieve.

As Italy's Olivetti slid further into difficulties, its chairman and chief executive, **Carlo De Benedetti**, took full control of the computers and office-equipment group. The move was an embarrassment to Vittorio Cassoni, managing director since 1988.

Moving ever further from the **Swedish model**, Sweden announced that it would sell 35 state-owned companies for as much as $50 billion.

America's biggest car maker, **General Motors**, announced it would have to take a non-cash charge of up to $24 billion because of new accounting rules for pensioners' health benefits.

Tuesday 12th
The testing and approval of **new drugs** should be speeded up, and the cost of their development cut sharply, following an agreement by drug regulators from America, the EC and Japan to harmonise procedures. The United States also announced a radical plan to restructure its **Food and Drug Administration.**

Monday 18th
Shares in **Maxwell Communication** took another batter-ing after the Serious Fraud Office started to investigate a £55m ($98m) loan made by Swiss Bank Corporation to a private company controlled by the Maxwell family. The shares had lost two-thirds of their value since Robert Maxwell's death. As bankers worked on a plan to freeze loan repayments pending a debt restructuring, IBCA, a credit-rating agency, put the group on its watch list.

Wednesday 20th
America's **McDonnell Douglas** agreed to sell 40% of its commercial-aircraft business—worth $2 billion—to Taiwan Aerospace. The Taiwanese company said it was also holding talks with Aerospatiale, a French group, over a possible helicopter deal.

Friday 22nd
Tainted by a share-support scandal ever since its takeover of Distillers in 1986, **Guinness** agreed to pay £92m ($165m) in compensation to Argyll, a grocery chain which had been a rival bidder. Two of Guinness's advisers in the Distillers takeover, Morgan Grenfell and Cazenove, said they would contribute another £8m.

Two Berlin property developers paid DM4.8 billion ($3 billion) for most of **Interhotel**, a big east German hotel chain, after a rival bidder, Sixt, pulled out.

There were no buyers at all for 18m shares being floated in **Sony Music Entertainment**, until the Japanese firm's consumer-electronics parent cut the price by 20%. The issue's flop persuaded six other firms to postpone flotations, adding to the Tokyo stockmarket's gloom.

Monday 25th
Harcourt Brace Jovanovich, a debt-ridden publisher and insurer, said its shareholders approved its $1.3 billion acquisition by General Cinema, after it had warned them that a failed bid might result in chapter 11 proceedings.

Helped by better trading results, Rupert Murdoch's **News Corporation** wrested a three-year extension and improved terms for $3.2 billion it owes to its main banks.

In the largest of a series of takeovers in France's retail industry, a 40.6% stake in **Au Printemps**, a Paris department-store and mail-order group, passed from the hands of Maus Nordmann, a deeply indebted Swiss holding group, to Pinault, a French timber and furniture conglomerate. The deal was worth FFr3.3 billion ($610m).

Deutsche Aerospace, part of the Daimler-Benz group, is to set up a $2 billion venture with France's Aerospatiale and Italy's Alenia to develop and make a new 90-120-seater jet aircraft. Separately, Aerospatiale and Alenia dropped their bid for Canada's de Havilland.

Tuesday 26th
The world's largest computer company announced a huge reorganisation. **IBM** made big senior-management changes, including pushing aside George Conrades, once considered a future chairman, then announced that it would make its businesses more independent. It said it would cut at least 20,000 jobs in 1992 and take a $3 billion restructuring charge against 1991 fourth-quarter earnings.

A German electrical group, **Siemens**, took a large stake in East European energy. It will have a 67% share in a $170m venture being formed with Skoda-Pilsen, Czechoslovakia's biggest maker of power stations.

December

Sunday 1st

After struggling for 14 months, Italy's **Pirelli**, a tyre and cable maker, gave up its bid for Continental, a German rival. The failed bid, which cost $287m, left Pirelli expecting a loss of 670 billion lire ($530m) in 1991.

Tuesday 3rd

PepsiCo said it was forming a joint venture with **Thomas J. Lipton**, a subsidiary of Unilever, to sell new types of drink based on tea. Coca-Cola and Nestlé reached a similar agreement in 1990.

Wednesday 4th

After failing to emerge from chapter 11 bankruptcy protection, **Pan Am** grounded its aircraft after 64 years in the business. Delta, an American rival, withdrew an earlier rescue offer, and no other saviour stepped forward.

Thursday 5th

After a week of scandalous revelations, **Robert Maxwell's sons**, Ian and Kevin, asked administrators to run their debt-ridden private companies. Their father was discovered to have borrowed secretly around £350m ($620m) for these companies from the two Maxwell-controlled public companies, **Mirror Group Newspapers** and **Maxwell Communication Corporation** and another £425m from their pension funds. Including bank loans, the private companies' debts were revealed to be at least £1.6 billion.

Monday 9th

After a five-hour session with

IBM's top managers, who tried to explain the company's restructuring plans, Wall Street analysts returned to their offices and promptly cut their earnings estimates for the company. Its share price fell to a new low.

Tuesday 10th

Raul Gardini, an Italian tycoon and ousted chairman of Ferruzzi, made a FFr1.65 billion ($306m) business comeback by taking over the food-processing activities of Sucden, an indebted commodity trader, in partnership with Jean-Marc Vernes, a French banker. With the purchase of Cocoa Barry, a leading cocoa processor, and Vital and Sogeviandes, both meat traders and processors, Mr Gardini, who made his name building an agribusiness empire, was back on familiar ground.

Nippon Steel, the world's biggest steel producer, renegotiated a deal it made in June with Oracle Systems, a big American software company. It would now take a 25% stake worth around $100m in Oracle's Japanese subsidiary, down from 49%. The revised deal reflects the software company's healthier finances, but still puts the steel maker in the computer business.

The French government postponed its partial-privatisation programme because of the depressed state of the stockmarket. The FFr2 billion ($371m) sell-off of shares in **Elf Aquitaine**, the country's largest state-owned firm, was to have been the first in line.

United Airlines acquired the largest chunk of **collapsed Pan Am** when it paid $135m for most of the airline's Latin American and Caribbean routes. Pan Am's unsecured creditors filed a $2.5 billion lawsuit against Delta. They accused the airline of reneging

on a deal to invest in a reborn Pan Am.

Wednesday 11th

Orion Pictures, the biggest independent Hollywood studios and distributor of "Dances with Wolves", filed for bankruptcy.

Thursday 12th

Richard Branson, the boss of Britain's **Virgin Atlantic Airways**, asked the non-executive directors of British Airways to investigate allegations that BA set up a dirty-tricks department to discredit his airline.

Europe's greenery bandwagon gained momentum when **EC environment ministers** agreed to a Community-wide label to identify products which do least damage to the environment.

Monday 16th

A consortium led by Conrad Black, the Canadian publisher of Britain's *Daily Telegraph* newspaper and owner of 88 publications in America and Canada, won the bidding battle for Australia's bankrupt Fairfax group, publisher of the *Sydney Morning Herald*, the *Age* and *Australian Financial Review*. Mr Black's consortium paid A$1.4 billion ($1.1 billion) for Fairfax, whose future had been uncertain ever since its banks put it into receivership in December, 1990

Tuesday 17th

In a rare move which could herald tougher anti-trust enforcement in Europe, a controversial bid by **Accor**, a French hotel group, for **Wagons-Lits**, a Franco-Belgian travel company was suspended by the European Commission, which decided to investigate whether a merger between the two companies would give it too big a share of the market for motorway services and hotels in France.

Wednesday 18th

In a move of ominous political consequence, **General Motors**, the world's largest car maker, announced that it planned to close 21 factories and eliminate some 70,000 jobs (out of more than 400,000) by 1995. The move follows expected losses on GM's North American car operations of $8 billion in 1991.

France announced a plan to form a **state-owned, high-tech conglomerate** embracing consumer electronics, nuclear energy and semiconductor chips. According to Edith Cresson, the prime minister, parts of the Thomson electronics group and the Commissariat à l'Energie Atomique would be merged into a new firm. The move followed French disappointment at the watering down of provisions for a European industrial policy in the European Community's Maastricht treaty earlier in the month.

Friday 20th

Fried. Krupp said that it had finally acquired a controlling 51% of the shares in rival German steelmaker Hoesch. Krupp's interest in merging with Hoesch, to cope with slumping demand in the European steel market, had first been revealed in October, sparking a row between the two firms.

Fujitsu, Japan's leading computer maker, said that it would cut investment in **chip manufacturing** by 40% to ¥90 billion ($700m) and that construction of new chip capacity would be postponed to 1993 or later. The decision reflects the overcapacity in the entire Japanese chip industry.

Sunday 22nd

Williams Holdings, a British industrial conglomerate, conceded defeat over its £700m ($370m) bid for electronics group Racal.

As we reported then

A chastened man

JANUARY 19TH *After dazzling growth through scores of acquisitions, Rupert Murdoch's News Corporation tottered on the edge of bankruptcy*

ASSUMING he survives, Rupert Murdoch plans big changes in the way his News Corporation is managed. He even claims he will begin to delegate. Yet managing has always been his speciality. He built a globe-spanning company virtually from scratch on a mountain of debt. He turned sleepy, money-losing newspapers into (sometimes sleazy) money-spinners. He transformed a gaggle of local television stations in America into a network rivalling the three big national ones and invaded British broadcasting with satellite television.

His touch disappeared in November, when a cash shortage forced News Corp to seek a Brazilian-style rescue from its banks. Since then, the value of the company's Australian shares has dropped by nearly three-quarters. Yields on some of its bonds have soared to almost 50%, the sky-high return investors usually expect on the debt of basketcases like Peru. Many investors must be betting that Mr Murdoch will be dethroned, his empire dismembered.

It could happen, but probably won't. Mr Murdoch's bankers are in the last, most difficult stages of a restructuring of News Corp's debt that should keep the company going. The deal includes $600m of new money, which will be used to pay outstanding bills for the company's capital-investment programme. All 27 banks in the lending group have agreed to advance this sum.

The trickier element of the package is to stretch over three years payments on $6.8 billion of existing debt. Without this, the company will not be able to repay bank loans due by the middle of this year. To wrap up this rescheduling, News Corp needs the agreement of 150 banks, some of which are reluctant to extend their exposure. All but a few have now said they will approve the plan. Citibank is worried enough to have assigned Bill Rhodes, the bank's chief negotiator with Latin American debtors, to the job of corralling the stragglers.

Why is Mr Murdoch now at the mercy of his bankers? Because, he admits, "I had taken my eye off the financial side" of the business. News Corp financed hugely ambitious acquisitions and investments with short-term bank borrowings, and paid scant attention to cash flow. In the year to June 30th 1990, News Corp spent A$1.7 billion ($1.3 billion) on capital investment, primarily for its British newspaper and television operations. Although the company made an operating profit, such heavy spending meant more cash was leaving the company than coming in. As a result, News Corp continued to pile up debt. The company borrowed A$2.8 billion in 1990, mainly short term, to finance capital spending and acquisitions. That brought debt to nine-tenths of shareholders' equity.

Banks tolerate such shenanigans when times are good. But by the autumn of 1990 Australia, Britain and America–the three economies in which News Corp does most of its business–were slipping into recession and banks were no longer lending money so freely. With $3 billion of debt coming due for repayment between September 1990 and June 1991, Mr Murdoch had to seek aid from his banks.

The banks are demanding a stiff price for extending their loans. Mr Murdoch will add one percentage point to the spread he already pays on News Corp's debt. He will also pay a 1% fee up front and another 1% success fee on the debt remaining after three years. The higher spread will cost News Corp an extra $100m or so each year. To meet repayment targets, Mr Murdoch will have to sell assets, possibly at distress prices. And he can no longer ignore the financial disciplines that lesser magnates live by. Unlike his existing loan agreements, the new covenants set tough standards for cash flow and interest cover.

Meeting the new financial standards will not be easy. Terry Povey, an analyst at ANZ McCaughan, says cash flow will barely cover interest payments this year. That leaves News Corp little margin should the recession deepen. The company must also raise enough new money to knock $800m off its debt by the end of the year.

News Corp executives point out that they have already eliminated a £100m-a-year loss by merging Sky, its British satellite television company, with its rival BSB and taking the merged company off the balance sheet. They reckon that a massive investment in colour-printing facilities in Britain and Australia will pay off in lower costs and higher advertising revenues. Mr Murdoch's American movie studio, 20th Century Fox, is at last making hit movies. Lower interest rates in America will also help.

Mr Murdoch says the bruising experience of near-bankruptcy has left him "chastened". He is considering things he would have thought unthinkable just a few months ago. His long-standing opposition to reduc-

How do you do it Mr Murdoch?

ing the Murdoch family's half-share in News Corp is a relic of his bumptious past. He now says he is willing to issue new voting equity in the company (once the share price recovers), even if that means diluting his control. News Corp has grown too big, he says, to be run as a one-man show.

He also concedes the need to improve the management of his far-flung company. He will soon appoint a chief operating officer, probably from within the company's ranks. He talks of travelling less, and delegating more authority to his deputies in Britain and Australia. He is learning, he claims, "to let other people do the work."

If this really happens, Mr Murdoch will head a different sort of business. News Corp can no longer afford to stalk the world for promising new acquisitions. Instead, it will concentrate on improving the profitability of its existing assets. Committee meetings may replace Mr Murdoch's roving, impul-

sive style. The reconstruction of the company's balance sheet will inevitably clip Mr Murdoch's wings. In short, News Corp may soon resemble a traditional company. Perhaps this is unavoidable. But it will make less compulsive viewing.

....

Mr Murdoch got his deal from the bankers and then demonstrated his survival skills yet again by remorselessly selling businesses and slashing costs throughout his empire. By the end of the year, News Corp was back in favour with both bankers and investors.

Young love, great riches, first tiff

FEBRUARY 23RD   *Microsoft's partnership with IBM made Bill Gates, Microsoft's founder, a billionaire and helped IBM become the biggest personal-computer maker in the world. We explained why the relationship was fraying.*

THEY were the glamour couple of the 1980s. The unlikely marriage between tousled Microsoft and buttoned-down IBM created the hottest products in the decade's hottest industry, personal computers. Celebrated everywhere, the duo had no reason to question their good fortune, and no need to wonder which their friends really liked best: IBM's earnest reliability or Microsoft's youthful creativity. Now a setback has brought long-buried differences to the surface. Computer-industry gossips wonder if the marriage can survive.

Premature though speculation of divorce may be–both Microsoft and IBM are quick to pledge their commitment to each other–even minor flaws in their domestic harmony will be closely watched. Together, IBM and Microsoft set the technical standards that helped fuel the explosive growth of personal computers in the 1980s: "IBM-compatible" hardware and Microsoft's DOS operating-system software, the basic program needed to run any computer. Together, both companies are trying to set a new standard for the more complex computing world of the 1990s: a jointly developed operating system called OS/2. But customers have been slow to embrace OS/2. The frustration is driving Microsoft and IBM apart. The eventual result may be new leadership for the personal-computer industry, or no clear leadership at all.

Since they first began holding hands, Microsoft and IBM have shared barely a care. The men from Big Blue originally came to Microsoft's founder, Bill Gates, to license the programming languages that he had written for the early personal-computer enthusiasts, most of whom had built their own machines. IBM also needed an operating system. Gary Kildall, whose Digital Research created the CP/M operating system for the first generation of personal computers, did not jump at IBM's offer. So in 1980 IBM came back to Mr Gates, then 25, who quickly bought a rudimentary operating

system from another young company, renamed it DOS, and fixed it up for IBM.

DOS now sells about 17m copies a year, and Mr Gates's 40% stake in Microsoft is worth about $4 billion. Today's success was created largely by yesterday's success. Because it was IBM that jumped into the computer market with Microsoft in 1981–as opposed to yet another bunch of blue-jeaned entrepreneurs–would-be competitors reckoned the couple's technology might be worth copying. Microsoft's willingness to license DOS helped rivals to copy it and then use that technology as the basis for their own innovation.

Almost everybody in the computer industry expected something similar to happen with OS/2. It hasn't. Since its launch in 1988, sales of OS/2 have grown to only about 300,000 a year. Nobody knows why. Perhaps the relatively high price of the more powerful personal computers needed to run OS/2 has put off budget-minded companies. Perhaps buyers are put off by the complexity of learning a new technology. Or perhaps OS/2 simply solved problems that do not trouble most customers. Whatever the reason, OS/2's adversity is pushing Microsoft and IBM apart.

Microsoft responds to slow OS/2 sales with a youthful eagerness to do better. "We were wrong," admits Steve Ballmer, a top Microsoft executive. He says both he and Mr Gates thought OS/2 would outsell DOS by 1992 at the latest. It will not. So Microsoft is now concentrating its efforts on a product customers do want to buy: Windows.

Windows does the most visible part of the job OS/2 was designed to do. It helps users to juggle a variety of programs at once, each in its own window on the screen. It is nowhere near as good as OS/2 at managing complex tasks, like getting computers to cooperate across a network. But customers do

not seem to care. In nine months on the market, the latest version of Windows has sold 3m copies. Microsoft is now trying to market Windows as a stepping stone to OS/2, by making it easy for users of Windows and writers of programs for Windows to migrate to OS/2 eventually.

Microsoft's enthusiasm for Windows annoys IBM. For Big Blue, OS/2 is just one piece of a grand vision about how all of a company's computers can work together. Any gains it might make by fiddling with its strategy for OS/2 would be offset–perhaps more than offset–by the confusion such fid-

Am I blue?

dling would engender about IBM's overall strategy. So IBM is publicly sticking to OS/2, though it is also quietly hedging its bets by incorporating into its grand scheme other products with many of the same capabilities.

Piece by small technical piece, these strategies are eating away at the consensus that originally made OS/2 seem a certainty as the computing world's next-generation technical standard. Microsoft has set up Windows as a rival to a component of OS/2 called Presentation Manager, which is still backed by IBM. Perhaps in retaliation, IBM has signed an agreement with Novell, a maker of personal-computer networks. This could make Novell's products an alternative to Microsoft's networking software, called LAN Manager. And IBM is financing an ambitious project by a young Californian company, Patriot Partners; it would let software companies write programs compatible with OS/2 and Unix, an operating system with similar capabilities originally created by AT&T's Bell Labs.

With more and more options to choose from, customers and software developers are increasingly reluctant to plump for just one. What makes this a particular problem

for Microsoft and IBM is that, while the consensus on OS/2 is unravelling, its chief rival, Unix, is at last making headway. When OS/2 was announced, Unix was dismissed as a flop. Now various versions of Unix have been boiled down to two.

About 1m copies of Unix were sold in 1990. A recent poll by DMR, a Canadian information-technology consultancy, shows that nearly as many American companies are planning to adopt Unix as OS/2. This raises the possibility that OS/2–and, with it,

IBM's partnership with Microsoft–will get caught in a vicious circle, much like DOS got caught in a virtuous one. Slow sales will encourage Microsoft to innovate and IBM to hedge, which will make customers cautious, which will slow sales, which will encourage further tiffs between the two companies.

....

A few months later, IBM established an alliance with Apple in both hardware and software. Meanwhile, Microsoft became the target of a government investigation because of alleged abuses of the company's dominant position in the software market.

Falling off the learning curve

FEBRUARY 23RD, TOKYO *With the price of Japanese memory chips plunging, America seemed slightly more inclined to enjoy the sensation than to fight it*

JAPANESE manufacturers of memory chips are poised on the brink of a bloody price war. The price of a 1-megabit dynamic random-access memory (DRAM) chip–the current workhorse of the Japanese semiconductor industry–has tumbled 40% since September, to around $4.50. Falling prices for 1-megabit chips erode prices for the coming generation of 4-megabit DRAMS. At $17 a chip, the price of 4-megabit DRAMS is already probably too low for semiconductor manufacturers to recoup the cost of the new production lines needed to make them. The last time Japanese chip makers faced a ruinous price war over a new generation of chips, they were saved by American stupidity. This time they may not be so lucky.

In 1985, when Japanese chip makers last started slashing prices, America's government insisted that they raise them in order to protect the (virtually non-existent) American DRAM industry. That agreement is about to expire. Although America's electronics industries are keen for the government to renew the parts of this agreement that call for the Japanese to buy more American chips, their ardour for price-fixing has cooled. Instead of government-rigged prices, they want little more than a reaffirmation of existing anti-dumping rules. That may not be enough to save the Japanese from cutting each other's throats.

The main market for Japan's semiconductor makers–the American computer industry–has been sinking deeper into slump since August 1990. Now chip sales in Japan are beginning to collapse as well. As a result, big DRAM producers like Toshiba, Hitachi, Mitsubishi Electric and NEC have 4-megabit chips piling up in their warehouses, just as they start opening additional factories. Over the past year Japanese semiconductor firms have spent a colossal ¥850 billion ($6.7 billion) building more production lines for 4-megabit chips.

Each has been trying to outbid the rest in an attempt to gain market share and so ex-

ploit economies of scale. Between them, Japanese semiconductor firms will produce 120m of the new 4-megabit chips for the year ending in March. According to World Semiconductor Trade Statistics, customers are expected to buy 100m of these chips at most. All told, demand for memory chips fell more than 16% in 1990.

Behind the brave faces of Japanese DRAM makers, anxieties are beginning to

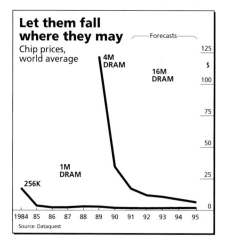

Let them fall where they may
Chip prices, world average
Forecasts
256K
1M DRAM
4M DRAM
16M DRAM
$
125
100
75
50
25
0
1984 85 86 87 88 89 90 91 92 93 94 95
Source: Dataquest

show. Most are now talking about launching the next-generation DRAM, the 16-megabit chip, as soon as next month. Previously it was not expected to reach the market until 1992. Over the past couple of months all the leading Japanese DRAM suppliers–including Hitachi, Toshiba, NEC, Mitsubishi Electric and Fujitsu–have started shipping "engineering samples" of 16-megabit chips. So have Texas Instruments in America and Siemens in Europe.

For the first time in its brief history, the semiconductor industry is going to be making, and trying to sell, three generations of memory chips in large volumes at the same time. Prices should tumble as each cannibalises sales of the others.

A 4-megabit chip ought to sell for five

times as much as a 1-megabit device, the price premium justified by the smaller space and lower power needed to provide four times the amount of memory. Dataquest, a market-research company, is now forecasting that a 4-megabit chip will cost barely three times more than a 1-megabit chip by next year. More painful still, 16-megabit chips will hit the market at only nine times the price of existing 4-megabit DRAMS. New generations of memory chips are usually 30-40 times the price of the industry's mainstream product.

Pundits are now beginning to wonder whether Japanese chip makers may be preparing to "leap a generation". Hitachi, Fujitsu, Toshiba, Mitsubishi Electric and Matsushita hurried out experimental 64-megabit models last week. For semiconductor makers not already committed to building 16-megabit production lines, the case for going straight for the 64-megabit device looks increasingly attractive. Fujitsu recently showed that 64-megabit DRAMS could be made using fairly conventional lithographic equipment, based on ultra-violet light rather than exotic lasers or x-rays. In January Fujitsu announced that it will spend ¥100 billion ($770m) next year getting its plant in Miyazaki prefecture ready for making 64-megabit chips.

Meanwhile, Japanese and American officials have begun negotiating a renewal of their pact on semiconductor trade. The Americans are asking for 20% of Japan's chip market, up from 13% today. Japanese officials plead that they do not have the power to carve up the market in this way. They also calculate that the Americans already have 18% of the Japanese market. There has not yet been much debate about prices. But the Americans do not seem likely to force the Japanese to overcharge them for chips again.

....

Half way through the year America and Japan signed a new chip-trade agreement. It did not set minimum prices but made it impossible for either government to complain if Japan's chip makers formed a price-rigging cartel.

....

The flight of Icarus

MARCH 16TH **Saatchi & Saatchi and WPP soared on the promise of global marketing. But both nearly crashed under the weight of debt**

KNOWN in the 1950s as the "hidden persuaders", advertising agencies shed their relative obscurity to become some of the most visible and envied businesses of the 1980s. Britain's Saatchi brothers, Maurice and Charles, became media stars on both sides of the Atlantic as they built the world's largest advertising group through a dizzying series of acquisitions and then diversified into consulting, market research and a variety of other corporate services. A wave of mergers swept the advertising industry as imitators tried to copy the Saatchis. The most notable was Martin Sorrell, the Saatchis' former finance director, who put together an empire even bigger than theirs in only three years.

Mr Sorrell and the Saatchi brothers seemed to represent a new breed of entrepreneur. The new men, it was said, had the vision to exploit global markets and the will to marshal the emerging class of highly educated, independent professionals needed to compete in dozens of countries at once.

Reality turned out to be harsher. Both Mr Sorrell's WPP and Saatchi & Saatchi are now fighting for survival. At an extraordinary general meeting on March 27th Saatchi & Saatchi's shell-shocked ordinary shareholders will be asked to approve a plan that will dilute their ownership of the company from 100% to 16%. The plan is the second recapitalisation proposal made by the company since January. If it is rejected, Saatchi & Saatchi will still be no nearer to finding a way of making a scheduled £211m ($390m) payment to bondholders in July 1993. And WPP has spent the past couple of months asking its 30 banks to reschedule its £297m of debt. A deal has yet to be agreed upon. On March 7th the company announced it was paying no dividend to ordinary shareholders for 1990 and that shareholders' funds were minus £244m.

Both companies will probably scrape through more or less intact, though who will control them in the future is unclear. Saatchi & Saatchi's shareholders, as well as its equally unhappy bondholders–who are about to be offered shares instead of cash–have little choice but to accept its plan. A break-up of the group might pay off Saatchi & Saatchi's bankers, but could leave shareholders and bondholders virtually empty-handed. Similarly, the banks will probably give their nod to WPP's refinancing only because dismantling the ad agencies, public-relations firms, design groups and market-research consultancies so hastily assembled by Mr Sorrell could lose them much of the money they have already lent the company. In the middle of a recession in America and Britain, the bits of both empires could be sold only at fire-sale prices.

The problems of both companies are the direct result of hubris. After building their ad agency into London's biggest and most successful–a business they were good at–the Saatchi brothers went on to pay too much not only for American ad agencies but for management and computer consulting businesses they knew little about. In 1987 they even took a quixotic tilt at two big British banks, Midland and Hill Samuel. By 1989 their own company was in so much trouble that they had to recruit Robert Louis-Dreyfus, a wealthy Frenchman who had successfully managed and then sold a market-research company in America, to run the group for them.

Mr Sorrell was a more skilful dealmaker until he made a hostile bid for Ogilvy & Mather in 1989, eventually winning the company for $864m. Almost everyone in the advertising industry considered that too high a price for the New York-based ad-agency network. Fresh from successfully turning around another old Madison Avenue agency, J. Walter Thompson, Mr Sorrell did not listen, borrowing heavily to buy a relatively well-managed business. Many observers thought he insisted on buying Ogilvy only to make WPP the world's biggest marketing conglomerate and so surpass his mentors. Mr Sorrell denies this. Anyway, when he issued a profits warning last November, WPP's share price collapsed, losing 70% of its value in two days.

Even apart from such blunders, the plight of the two groups also raises serious doubts about the grandiose rationales offered by both Mr Sorrell and the Saatchis for building global advertising and marketing conglomerates. Saatchi & Saatchi and WPP contain two separate, global ad-agency networks each. Such internal duplication seems extravagant just as many of their bigger clients are unbundling their own operations or discovering the competitive advantages of localised marketing.

Nevertheless, both Mr Sorrell and Maurice Saatchi, who remains Saatchi & Saatchi's chairman, are unrepentant. The combative Mr Sorrell claims many big companies, not just his own, were surprised by the rapid economic slowdown in Britain and America at the end of last year. Although he admits that WPP is "aggressively" financed, he says that consolidating its borrowings into a single medium-term loan should avoid a breach of loan covenants later this year and see it safely through the recession.

Improved margins at Ogilvy & Mather, says Mr Sorrell, prove that buying it made sense. Aside from a few small disposals already announced, WPP will sell none of its businesses. He insists that his pet theory of "cross-selling" advertising, public-relations, promotional and other marketing services to the same client is working. On the other hand, he now says WPP is "complete" and he does not plan any big acquisitions, even when good times return.

Just as well. Mr Sorrell's reputation, his biggest personal asset, has taken a beating. "He's not an advertising man. He's a bean-counter who counted the beans wrong," snipes the boss of one rival ad agency. "The banks can find someone else to do that for them." One London analyst agrees: "His credibility is zilch." Mr Sorrell shrugs off such comments. But it is true that, if WPP really is no longer interested in takeover deals, Mr Sorrell no longer looks so essential to the group, which is more a collection of autonomous fiefs than a single company. If its financial problems become worse, someone else could run it–or break it up.

The same argument applies to Saatchi & Saatchi. But who is in charge there is less clear. Mr Louis-Dreyfus has the title of chief executive. He has spent months negotiating the company's rescue package with its bankers, shareholders and bondholders. He has also sold the company's consulting businesses, at a huge loss, and introduced tighter financial controls. And yet the Saatchi brothers remain on the board and Maurice states categorically that they still consider Saatchi & Saatchi their company. They vetoed a proposal to change the name of the group, which is also the name of one of its two global ad-agency networks.

Both Mr Louis-Dreyfus and Mr Saatchi say that control is not an issue, because all three get on together perfectly. Mr Louis-Dreyfus is at pains to stress Maurice's skills with big clients like Mars and Procter & Gamble, and Charles's skills at concocting winning ideas. He calls them geniuses. Maurice Saatchi returns the compliment.

In fact it looks as if Mr Louis-Dreyfus and the brothers have been sending different messages to different audiences. To investors and bankers, they have been saying that Mr Louis-Dreyfus is firmly in charge,

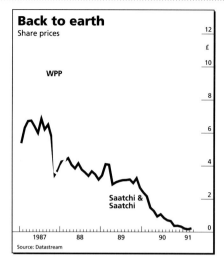

Back to earth
Share prices

WPP

Saatchi & Saatchi

1987   88   89   90   91

Source: Datastream

because any hint to the contrary would kill the rescue attempt. To some senior employees and certain clients, they seem to have indicated that ultimate control rests with the men whose name is above the door.

If or when Saatchi & Saatchi recovers from its financial travails, there could be a bust-up. With two new directors from large investor groups joining the board, it looks evenly balanced between Saatchi loyalists and those who might back Mr Louis-Dreyfus. And after Mr Louis-Dreyfus purchases £1m of the £55m in new shares the company is issuing, he will own 0.64% of the company's equity, more than either of the brothers, who together will own 1.07%. If Mr Louis-Dreyfus has to take up any of the $4m share-offer to management which he is underwriting, then his stake could be much larger than that of the brothers' combined.

Who controls the company matters, because of Maurice Saatchi's adherence to his original ideas. The case for selling a broad range of services to multinationals, from ad-

vertising to computer expertise to management advice, could still make sense, he insists. And global brands, sold in scores of countries with the same basic message, is still the way of the future. Plenty of sceptics disagree, including Mr Sorrell, who calls such reasoning "specious".

Mr Saatchi gives the strong impression that he is biding his time until he can take the reins at the company once again. That would horrify bankers and investors, who have watched Saatchi & Saatchi's market capitalisation plummet from more than £1 billion in July 1987 to less than £40m in early March. (WPP's market capitalisation dropped from £345m to £67m over roughly the same period.)

In fact, the idea of global services conglomerates is flawed, whether global brands dominate markets in the future or not. The problem is not so much that such businesses have no assets and depend on their ability to hold on to highly skilled people. After all, high-tech factories without the right people to run them are not worth much either. The problem is that it costs so little to set up an advertising agency that any talented employee can establish a rival firm, and probably will. There are also huge diseconomies of scale in managing thousands of creative people spread across the world.

Even if some clients want to deal with an ad agency with offices in scores of countries, no agency needs two such networks, as both Saatchi & Saatchi and WPP have. When their balance sheets are restored and the American and British economies recover, it will be time to dismember both empires. Is Mr Louis-Dreyfus the man to do it? Or, for that matter, Mr Sorrell?

Saatchi & Saatchi was hauled back from the brink when its refinancing package was approved at the end of March. WPP got its banks to agree a refinancing a few months later.

The wrong choice?

APRIL 27TH *Why we thought AT&T's acquisition of NCR, a big American computer maker, was a mistake*

IT WAS in December last year that American Telephone & Telegraph (AT&T) put in its first takeover bid for NCR, an American computer-maker. Five months later, the two firms are within a whisker of agreeing on a deal. While NCR's shareholders are celebrating, Ma Bell's are likely to suffer the inevitable hangover. Not only is AT&T probably paying too much, it should not have been trying to buy the firm in the first place. That is because AT&T's best bet for maintaining growth is to divide its manufacturing businesses from its telephone arm, not to buy more of them.

AT&T's original offer valued NCR at $6.1

billion, or $90 a share. At 15 times NCR's falling earnings, the offer was already generous. Now the deal looks likely to go through at a whopping $7.5 billion, about $110 a share.

Ma Bell is prepared to pay so much because the firm's chairman, Robert Allen, is convinced that the computer and telecommunications industries are converging. In the technical sense he is correct. Telephone switches are just big computers in disguise. Companies that use computers have been connecting them to each other for a decade, often using AT&T's telephone lines. Taking note, AT&T assumed that success in one

business meant success in the other. It set up its computer division in 1984, as soon as it was allowed to.

The assumption was wrong. Computer-making essentially remains a manufacturing industry, telecoms a service business. To succeed, telephone companies need marketing flair. Once-stuffy AT&T has surprised everyone by displaying plenty of this. The company has concocted new gimmicks such as cut-price Mothers' Day calls or new services such as call-blocking facilities for single women. It has also been deftly successful with its new Universal credit card.

But making and marketing computers require a different set of skills: manufacturing efficiently, shipping products rapidly and then providing complicated technical support to finicky business customers. Though the technology that telecoms and computer firms use is similar, success in telecoms services does not necessarily bring success in the computer, or telecoms-hardware, business. Painfully, AT&T has already been forced to recognise that. Analysts reckon AT&T has invested $2 billion in its computer division since its birth, and that it is still losing $200m a year.

Even when the purchase of NCR is complete, computers will still make up less than a fifth of AT&T's business. More than 60% of AT&T's $36 billion of sales comes from telephone calls, the remainder from sales of telephone equipment–the big computer-like switches that work telephone exchanges, and the smaller ones, called PABXs, that offices use to route calls internally. And here lies a contradiction at the heart of AT&T's original business, even before it tried to get into computers.

Since trustbusters broke up America's Bell system in 1983, AT&T's biggest switch-customers have been the seven regional "Baby Bells" born of the break-up. But they are also some of AT&T's toughest rivals in telecoms services. AT&T and the Babies do not compete on the provision of basic telephone services, since under the terms of the break-up AT&T may carry only long-distance calls, the Baby Bells only local ones. But they do compete in advanced services like electronic mail and computer-data networks. These can run off either the public-telephone network, or off the smaller PABXs that control businesses' own in-house telephone systems. While the Baby Bells try to sell corporate customers advanced services using their own networks, AT&T offers the same lot of customers PABXs which allow them to do exactly the same things. Mean-

while, it sells big switches to the Baby Bells themselves.

It is hardly surprising, then, that AT&T's switch-sales to the Babies have suffered as a result. Ten years ago AT&T supplied all of America's exchange-switches. Now that share has fallen to 42%. Most of the rest has gone to foreign-based switch suppliers such as Canada's Northern Telecom, Japan's NEC and Germany's Siemens.

Hamstrung at home, AT&T needs to do more business abroad. Only 13% of the firm's sales come from outside America. Mr Allen has said he wants to see that percentage double by the mid-1990s. But that will make AT&T's service and equipment-manufacturing businesses step on each other's toes again.

Over the past few years foreign telephone companies, and the Baby Bells, have been snapping up stakes in newly privatised telephone companies in New Zealand, Mexico and Argentina, and mobile-telephone franchises even in rich countries such as Britain and Germany. Curiously, AT&T has stood aside from this scramble, apart from filing a joint offer to build Poland's mobile-telephone system.

Ma Bell's coyness is hard to fathom. It may be afraid to annoy foreign network-operators with new local services and so jeopardise the chances of selling them equipment, which has accounted for much of AT&T's recent growth.

Staying friendly with foreign telephone firms also helps in other ways. The customers AT&T is keenest to serve are global firms wanting global services. Last September AT&T launched a "virtual private network" covering Japan, Britain, France, Canada and Belgium, which gives firms luxuries like coded dialling over public networks. Another service allows firms with offices in different countries to have centralised telephone bills. Setting up such products needs the co-operation of foreign telephone-network operators. AT&T could find such co-operation elusive if it was also competing with them.

The obvious way for AT&T to escape the conflicts of interest between its equipment and service businesses is to split them, perhaps doling out new shares in the two new firms to existing shareholders on a pro-rata basis. At least that would give each half of the business a free run to compete with a growing horde of competitors.

Though that might benefit AT&T's shareholders, the idea is heresy to most employees of the firm. AT&T fought hard to hang on to its equipment businesses through telephone deregulation–the Justice Department took the firm to court on the issue in 1949 and again in 1974. And having just fought for NCR, Mr Allen is unlikely to propose such a break-up.

Hanson liked the look of ICI

MAY 18TH **Hanson's startling acquisition of a 2.8% stake in ICI, one of Britain's biggest manufacturing companies, made everyone think that Lord Hanson, the firm's boss, was about to bid for the whole company**

THE purchase by Hanson on May 14th of a stake in ICI, Britain's biggest manufacturer and the world's fourth-largest chemical company, has at least one classic hallmark of the way the acquisitive British conglomerate works–it was as unpredictable as the outcome will be. Admitting the following day that it was the mystery purchaser who had electrified London's stockmarket, Hanson would say only that its £240m ($420m) purchase of a 2.8% stake was "required for investment purposes". No one was content

with that.

London is abuzz with speculation about the intentions of Lord Hanson, a consummate dealmaker who, with his partner Lord White, has built the firm named after him into Britain's fifth-largest firm by acquiring, and often selling, dozens of companies. In fact, Lord Hanson's intentions seem clear. By buying the stake in such a headline-grabbing fashion, he has sent ICI, coping poorly with the recession despite successive bouts of restructuring, into the arena. Either Han-

son itself will soon make a bid for the company or it will provoke someone else into doing so, perhaps in concert with its own bid. Alternatively, an intimidated ICI may be forced to break itself up and dispose of some of its disparate businesses, much as BAT, a sprawling British conglomerate, was forced to do to fend off Sir James Goldsmith's £13 billion bid in 1989. Whatever happens, ICI's shareholders will benefit.

Many British politicians, union leaders, workers and managers will not see it this way. Howls of outrage began as soon as Hanson's interest became public. And Britain's Conservative government, facing a general election, will not be happy to have to referee a contentious battle for one of Britain's top companies. ICI is a pillar of Britain's industrial establishment, its legal name–Imperial Chemical Industries–reflecting its origins in empire and its role as one of the country's corporate leaders. The company has long considered itself virtually bid-proof. One of Britain's biggest export-earners, it is also one of its biggest employers, with 53,700 employees in Britain, out of a total worldwide workforce of 132,100. Perhaps just as important, some 70% of its £679m R&D budget is spent at home.

Aware of ICI's status, the 69-year-old Lord Hanson may nevertheless feel that a bid for the company would give him a spectacular finish to a spectacular career. It would also represent the final triumph of Britain's thrusting Thatcherite businessmen over the country's often still-stodgy corporate establishment.

Hanson can afford to bid for ICI, whose value at the £11.94 Hanson is thought to have paid for its shares is £8.4 billion. Hanson would probably have to pay about £11 billion to buy the company, but estimates of its break-up value exceed £14 billion. Hanson's own market value is about £10.7 billion. But it has £7 billion in the bank (though net cash after accounting for existing debt is only £232m) and total borrowing powers of £17 billion. That would be plenty to buy ICI, though the purchase would leave Hanson heavily in debt. It would have to get rid of bits of ICI pretty quickly.

That may not be too difficult, even in a recession. Despite years of efforts by ICI to refashion itself–which did make it more international and produced a gush of profits when times were good–the company is still spread thinly across an array of separate products and markets. The company's businesses range from research-intensive products such as pharmaceuticals to bulk-commodity products such as PVC, which goes to make plastic buckets. In such a span there are few, if any, synergies. Other firms already heavily committed to bulk chemicals would probably be interested in the commodity operations. On the other hand, if Hanson decided to keep the bulk-chemical business, there are also plenty of potential buyers for the drugs division, in an industry that has seen a wave of mergers in the past few years as pharmaceutical companies have tried to achieve economies of scale in marketing and R&D.

A decade ago profits plummeted for the world's chemical industry. Frightened by the prospect of a repeat performance in the next economic downturn, ICI and other chemical companies decided to diversify into less cyclical businesses in which more value is added. The product portfolios of other big chemical companies also span the range from low-margin bulk chemicals to high-margin special chemicals and drugs.

But most others are more focused on a smaller number of products within this range. ICI has many products, in many different markets.

In 1985 ICI bought the chemicals operations of Beatrice, an American firm, for $750m; in particular it sought the firm's advanced materials, tough plastics that are used by the aerospace industry. In 1986 it bought Glidden, another American company, for $580m, making ICI the world's biggest paint manufacturer. In 1987 came the $1.7 billion acquisition of America's Stauffer Chemical, whose agrochemical business ICI retained, selling the rest for $1.15 billion. At the same time, ICI began ploughing much more money into R&D, directing a third of its spending towards the high-risk but potentially lucrative business of developing new drugs.

But despite all this change, in 1990 ICI saw its pre-tax profits drop by 36% to £977m, on sales of £12.9 billion. Demand for bulk chemicals again plummeted as the recession spread through America and Britain, ICI's main markets.

Meanwhile, its special-chemical businesses have not done as well as ICI hoped. In 1990 ICI's paints and other speciality products (not including drugs) enjoyed a

mere 2.8% trading margin, compared with a 5.7% margin for its bulk-chemical businesses, even after bulk chemicals reported a 60% fall in profits. As other companies have also piled into special chemicals, such products became less profitable. Special chemicals have also been hit by the recent recession in America and the rest of Europe. And according to Jeremy Chantry, a chemicals analyst at Kleinwort Benson, ICI's acquisition of Beatrice has also run into problems. Its advanced-composite business has sucked up huge amounts of ICI's research budget, but is still losing money.

A fierce debate has raged within the company about how to respond to these problems. Some board members have even considered large disposals–ie, a carve-up of the company perhaps not dissimilar to what Lord Hanson might have in mind. The company's embattled chairman, Sir Denys Henderson, has had to eat his words about the company being recession-proof. "When I suggested that I saw no return to the dark days of recession, I was clearly wrong," he acknowledges in ICI's latest annual report.

At its annual results meeting in February, ICI announced the reorganisation of the company into seven international centres, which will cost £300m to do: materials, industrial chemicals, drugs, farm chemicals, specialities, paints and explosives. Every business would be scrutinised and unpromising ones would go, the company pledged. "There will be no sacred cows," said one board member.

Since February, ICI has announced the closure of its loss-making fertiliser business (critics argue that this could more easily have been sold several years ago). It has also closed a plant making Melinex (a plastic) in Brazil, a bold move since it was only three years old and cost £40m to build in one of ICI's more promising markets.

Hanson, however, would be bolder. One obvious candidate for spin-off is the business making bulk industrial chemicals, including all the company's petrochemicals and plastics, which accounts for nearly a third of ICI's sales. Again, some analysts believe that ICI might have done better to dispose of this when the commodity-chemical business was far more profitable.

Lord Hanson would almost certainly be more ruthless than Sir Denys. And he may well relish, rather than fear, the huge row that will take place if he bids for the company. But aside from understandable squeals of pain from managers and workers worried about their jobs, it is difficult to see what arguments could be marshalled to stop a Hanson bid if shareholders wished to sell. Job cuts look inevitable at the company whether Hanson buys it or not.

Both ICI and Hanson are among the world's top producers of titanium dioxide, the white pigment in most paints and plastics. But Hanson could easily allay competition fears by promising to dispose of ICI's titanium-dioxide business. And given ICI's mediocre performance, there is little justification for the argument that it has to remain so big to compete in world markets. In the past 25 years ICI's shares have underperformed London's stockmarket by half. Hanson's shares have outperformed the same market by 3,000%. Those are the figures the big institutional shareholders who hold stakes in both ICI and Hanson will be looking at–as indeed they should.

Speculation about a Hanson bid continued for months, fuelled by Lord Hanson's own public statements. But a bid never came.

Pile 'em high, sell 'em cheap

NOVEMBER 2ND *Once an icon of technological wizardry, personal computers have become a commodity. Other types of computers are headed in the same direction. This change is shaking the computer industry to its foundations*

HANG on tight. The computer industry is teetering on the edge of trauma. Just how fast things are changing was demonstrated on October 25th in the boardroom of Compaq, one of the world's most successful personal-computer firms. Rod Canion, Compaq's co-founder and president, entered a board meeting to discuss a restructuring plan and left without a job, replaced by his second-in-command, Eckhard Pfeiffer. Compaq's directors sacked the popular Mr Canion because they were convinced that he could not cut the firm's costs fast enough to halt a precipitous slide in its fortunes. The lesson from Mr Canion's fate is an uncomfortable one: personal computers have become a commodity item. Making good computers is no longer enough to succeed. Everybody can do that.

If making good computers is not enough to bring success, what is? The struggle to answer that question is causing havoc in the computer industry. Compaq's recent history illustrates how deep the problems run. The firm has consistently led the industry with some of the best personal computers on the market. And it has sold them through a network of dealers who pride themselves on their ability to tailor the basic machines to their customers' needs. This strategy is based on the common belief in the computer industry that corporate customers want "solutions"–complete systems of software and hardware which solve business problems at the flick of a switch. The snag is that, even if many customers want "solutions", most are not willing to pay a premium for them. The price of a complete computer system is being dragged down to the sum of its parts.

So Compaq, like many other firms, has seen its margins squeezed from two directions. The first is the increasing innovation and sophistication in the components business. Much of the past decade's improvement in computer performance has come from packing more and more circuits on to each silicon chip. The closer together the circuits, the faster a signal moves from one to another. But to take advantage of this extra speed, computer-makers have to give up much of their own scope for innovation. The more circuits are packed on each chip by semiconductor companies, the fewer chips need to be arranged on each circuit board by computer-makers–and the less time they have to come up with unique arrangements if they are to take advantage of the newest, quickest chips.

Meanwhile, at the other end of the value chain, the increasing sophistication of computer users is also dragging value out of the business of assembling computers. Users are insisting on machines that adhere to technical standards which will enable new machines to work with the huge, and ever growing, number of old machines they already own. This leaves still less room for companies to innovate and make their computers different from anybody else's. And customers are less willing to pay for service and hand-holding, especially if they already own lots of machines.

Compaq's results show the squeeze. Pretax profits fell from $454m in the first nine months of 1990 to $65m in the same period of 1991, on sales down by 8% to $2.4 billion. But Compaq is not alone. Across the industry, small firms which have concentrated on doing a few things excellently have flourished at the expense of larger ones which have taken the conventional wisdom about "solutions" seriously and tried to do a lot of things well. As a result, the share of computer-industry revenues accounted for by the 50 biggest firms has fallen sharply.

Specialists have thrived by letting others do the work that they cannot do best. Thus Microsoft, by concentrating on software, benefits from any advances made in the hardware industry. Dell, Northgate and other pioneers of mail-order personal-computer sales have concentrated on cutting costs and increasing service in distribution. Japanese firms have prospered thanks to their strength in chips. Arthur Andersen and EDS have grown huge by building systems from others' hardware and software rather than trying to create their own.

Specialising is easier to describe with hindsight than to pull off. There have been many more flops among specialists than successes. In a recent article in the *Harvard Business Review* entitled "The Computer-less Computer Company", Andrew Rappaport and Shmuel Halevi of The Technology Research Group, a management-consulting firm, tried to generalise about the sorts of things which western computer firms should and should not do.

Their article has sparked heated debate.

In essence, Messrs Rappaport and Halevi argue that there is little advantage in manufacturing computers, so western firms should concentrate on design, software and "integration" of complete "solutions". Though thought-provoking, the distinction seems over-simplified. As a recent study by McKinsey points out, five of the ten fastest-growing computer companies between 1985 and 1990 were hardware firms: Sun, Dell, Compaq, AST and Apple. Nor, contrary to popular belief, are profits in software consistently higher than those in hardware.

Besides, many industry executives point out that it takes a lot of knowledge about manufacturing processes to succeed in software and design. Microsoft works closely with a chip maker, Intel, to tune its software

for Intel chips. Though Sun will not manufacture the microprocessors that will power its next generation of workstations, the design is based on in-depth knowledge of a specific manufacturing technique developed by Texas Instruments at the same time.

Building the relationships needed to support such complex links is difficult. Many firms have not even seriously tackled the prerequisite: picking apart their products to decide where they excel and where they should tap the excellence of others. Even the most dedicated generalists are beginning to try. IBM is buying growing quantities of components and technology from outside suppliers. In September it smashed a long-standing taboo by selling its own

disk drives and other components to rival firms to incorporate into their computers.

The most interesting experiment is taking place at Sun. Six months ago the company split itself into three bits, each with its own mission. One subsidiary promotes Sun's version of the Unix operating system. Another builds Sun workstations. The third sells Sun-brand printers and other peripherals.

Sun is still trying to find out how to get these subsidiaries to work independently yet co-operatively. But the early signs are encouraging. Oddly, the best way to improve the whole job of computer-making may be the opposite of the best way to design the machines: put more distance and flexibility between different parts of the company.

The shadow Maxwell leaves

NOVEMBER 9TH, LONDON AND NEW YORK   *Robert Maxwell's media empire was an autocracy. He built it. He ran it. He saddled it with crushing debts. With him dead, we predicted it would crumble*

I SHALL not answer your scurrilous and ignorant questions about the indebtedness of my private interests. If you print such things, I shall sue. My private affairs are no one's business but my own." So said Robert Maxwell in an interview with *The Economist* earlier this year. The bluster was typical; so was the obfuscation. The late Mr Maxwell's private interests are bound up inextricably with his two public companies, Mirror Group Newspapers (MGN) and Maxwell Communication Corporation (MCC). It is a tangled, mysterious relationship that may be about to fall apart.

Mr Maxwell's empire is chin-deep in debt—at least £2.4 billion ($4.2 billion) worth. In this it is emblematic of an era in which media kingdoms were rushed into being—and let costs be damned. Mr Maxwell was a caricature of a late-1980s tycoon: charismatic, egocentric, worried more about the size of his companies than about the strategies to guide them. In the words of one of his press officers, he was "an attractive monster with a touch of genius." He was also the only one who fully understood the byzantine structure of his holdings.

Now he has been replaced by his sons, Kevin, who takes over MCC, and Ian, who now heads MGN. Both—Kevin especially—are likely to find the coming weeks a sobering experience. To pay off MCC's debts, big asset sales in America will be needed. Before trading was suspended on news of Mr Maxwell's death, shares in the company, as well as in MGN, had been trading at woefully low levels. Much of the stock has been mortgaged to secure other, private loans from a far-flung syndicate of banks. There are rumours that some of these loan covenants are

close to being breached. True or not, some bankers are getting restless.

Through a complex web of private trusts, foundations and holding companies–the centre of which is in Liechtenstein–the Maxwell family controls 68% of MCC and 51% of MGN. MCC has debts of about £1.4 billion; MGN's total is around £300m. In

addition, Maxwell's private vehicles are at least another £750m in debt. To borrow much of that, Mr Maxwell pledged millions of his shares in MCC and MGN to the banks as collateral. Bankers call this "pig on pork"; it is not a term of endearment.

Nor an uncommon practice. But it means that the firms' share prices are critical. If their value drops below a certain percentage of the loans they secure–in this case, 145%–the Maxwells must pay back the loans or provide more collateral. On the morning of November 5th, mere hours before Mr Maxwell was reported missing, MGN shares were trading at their lowest since they were floated in April. MCC's share price, after months of decline, was at an eight-year low.

This followed a week in which the City of London was full of speculation that some of Mr Maxwell's bankers were considering calling in their loans. Rumours were especially rife about Midland, a big British bank heavily exposed to the Maxwell family. Other banks with large exposures are said to be Crédit Lyonnais, Crédit Suisse, National Westminster, Lloyds and Barclays.

Meanwhile, Goldman Sachs, an American investment bank with close ties to Mr Maxwell, sold 2.2m MCC shares. During this year Goldman has held as much as 5% of MCC and 10% of MGN as security for two personal loans to Mr Maxwell, totalling less than $100m. But it decided to call in part of that collateral (ie, by selling the shares) after Mr Maxwell repeatedly failed to repay the loans when this was requested.

The threat of other banks doing the same increased when shares in both MCC and MGN resumed trading on November 7th. Bankers were anxiously watching to see whether the "Max Factor" would survive the end of the Max. MGN's share price opened at 93p, 20% up on its suspension price; apparently investors believe MGN is better off without him. MCC's shares, however, opened at 75p, a 38% fall. Should that slump continue, some banks may panic.

Not all of Mr Maxwell's bankers are nervous—at least not on the record. The American ones, led by Bankers Trust, say they are not concerned because their exposure is slight. The British ones, led by the clearing banks, say their loans are secured with assets: property, helicopters, perhaps even Mr Maxwell's yacht. They add that, private debts aside, both public companies are on course to make their next scheduled repayments. MCC, whose debt is the more worrying, must come up with £441m in October 1992, and £624m two years later.

This would be more comforting if MCC were not so troubled. Its interim results are due at the end of the month; they will probably be dismal. Analysts reckon pre-tax profits will fall to around £75m, compared with £90m for the same period last year. As much as £50m of that will come from the

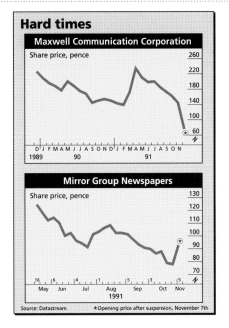

Hard times

Maxwell Communication Corporation
Share price, pence

260 / 220 / 180 / 140 / 100 / 60

D J F M A M J J A S O N D J F M A M J J A S O N
1989   90   91

Mirror Group Newspapers
Share price, pence

130 / 120 / 110 / 100 / 90 / 80 / 70

16   6   4   1   5   3   5
May Jun Jul Aug Sep Oct Nov
1991

Source: Datastream   *Opening price after suspension, November 7th

sale last March of Pergamon Press, a scientific publisher that was the Maxwell empire's crown jewel. Those profits will barely cover interest payments on MCC's debts; the company will probably need to dip into reserves if it wants to pay a half-year dividend.

That is not all. In July Mr Maxwell said he was thinking of demerging MCC's American interests, which provide 90% of the company's operating profits, and floating them on the New York stockmarket. These include Macmillan, a big publishing house, and Official Airlines Guide (OAG), a flights timetable—two businesses that together cost

$3.35 billion, lumbering the company with much of the debt it is struggling to shed.

Now the demerger seems to be off. Instead, MCC has been selling assets; on November 7th the firm said it would sell its stake in Berlitz for about $260m. So far the disposals have commanded good prices. The next wave may not. OAG, which is up for sale, may fetch only two-thirds the $750m price Mr Maxwell paid. Some analysts estimate that MCC's total assets may be worth as little as £900m: £500m less than its debts.

MGN is in better shape. It is profitable; its share price might double if it were owned by another publisher. The banks, which hold nearly 20% of MGN's stock as collateral, might make sure that this happens.

Already, they have met with Kevin and Ian Maxwell; these talks will continue. The banks will ask hard questions about the private debt; about the *European* and the *New York Daily News*, two privately held, loss-making newspapers. Such questions would not arise were the private debts separate from the public ones, or if the banks were sure what the total private debts were. But neither is the case. Indeed, no bank seems to have a full view of Mr Maxwell's holdings.

They are not alone. Recently a former lawyer for MCC said she had tried for seven months to get hold of a full list of all Mr Maxwell's public and private companies and their links to one another. She failed. A similar fate may await the younger Maxwells and their nervous bankers.

....

Only weeks later all of Maxwell's private and public companies were in the hands of administrators.

Asia bids for a stake in aerospace

NOVEMBER 23RD, HONG KONG   *News that a government-backed Taiwanese company was planning to take a 40% stake in McDonnell Douglas's commercial-aircraft business heralded the emergence of immense Asian influence in the world's aircraft industry*

MCDONNELL DOUGLAS has the good sense to prefer losing an argument to losing its shirt. The debt-ridden American defence and aerospace company has long been a vocal critic of the subsidies that helped Europe's Airbus Industrie displace it as the world's number-two maker of commercial aircraft. On November 20th McDonnell Douglas announced a deal in principle to sell 40% of its commercial-aircraft business to a brand-new Taiwanese company called Taiwan Aerospace. Talks are continuing with other Asian companies, from Singapore to South Korea, to bring them in on what may become a trans-Pacific version of the Airbus consortium. McDonnell Douglas itself is likely to enjoy a government sub-

las itself is likely to enjoy a government subsidy or two from all this, with the nice twist that the taxpayers paying for them will be Asian rather than American.

A lot of details have yet to be settled, and both the American and Taiwanese governments will have to agree to the deal before the end-January deadline the companies have set for themselves. But if the deal goes through, McDonnell will transfer all of its commercial-aircraft business to a new company headquartered in the United States. Taiwan Aerospace, perhaps together with other Taiwanese investors, will pay $2 billion to acquire 40% of the new company. McDonnell Douglas will retain a majority share and management control of this new

company, but small slices of equity may yet be sold to other Asian partners.

Something of this sort was essential if McDonnell Douglas was to stay in the commercial-aircraft business—which could be a matter of life or death for the company. McDonnell Douglas is America's biggest defence contractor. But last year it relied on commercial-aircraft sales for 34% of its $16.2 billion in revenues, and, with defence spending shrinking, success in the commercial market will become increasingly vital. Unfortunately, McDonnell Douglas is an also-ran in that market.

At the moment the company makes only two types of commercial jetliners: the two-engined MD-80 and MD-90, and the three-engined MD-11, an updated version of the company's venerable DC-10. The order book does not look bad. At the end of October McDonnell Douglas had 265 firm orders and 373 options for the two-engined

aircraft, and 154 orders and 179 options for the MD-11. Nevertheless, the company has steadily been losing market share to Boeing and Airbus. Unlike its two rivals, it does not have a full family of aircraft to offer its customers. The proposed MD-12, a long-range jumbo jet that would directly compete with Boeing's 747-400, would remedy that.

The trouble is that McDonnell Douglas cannot afford the estimated $4 billion needed to develop the MD-12, which it hopes to start rolling off the production line in 1997. In the first nine months of this year, the company's after-tax profits slipped 31%, to $212m (on sales up 15%, to $13.7 billion). More important, its balance sheet is still laden with $2.7 billion in debt.

This explains why McDonnell Douglas's managers have been scouting for a deep-pocketed partner. Asian candidates have several attractions. First, Asia is still a lower-cost producer than America or Europe in many types of manufacturing. Second, in the highly politicised world of aircraft sales, producing parts in a country offers a natural advantage in trying to sell jets to that country's airline. And selling aircraft in Asia is going to matter over the next 20 years, as the region's passenger traffic booms.

But is Taiwan Aerospace the right partner? On the face of it, the choice is peculiar. Only seven weeks old, the Taiwanese company is the proud owner of an empty factory in central Taiwan—but has never made so much as a rivet, let alone used it to put together something as complicated as a fuselage or wing.

Yet the company has a big advantage: the full support of a government determined to build a strong aerospace industry and with a cash pile to back up its determination. According to Taiwan Aerospace, 29% of its initial $250m capital is coming from the Taiwanese government, and the rest from private Taiwanese companies.

The firm has other big ideas, too. As well as negotiating the deal with McDonnell Douglas, Taiwan Aerospace is also talking to Aerospatiale, a French state-owned aircraft-maker, about a joint project to make helicopters.

The government's main motive is national security. At China's insistence, the United States (and every other country with the know-how) refuses to sell Taiwan advanced military aircraft. General Dynamics has been trying, without violating the American ban on the transfer of advanced technology, to help the Taiwanese develop their own jet fighter, but progress has been slow. What Taiwan's industry learns from the MD-12 deal cannot hurt the military effort; and it would certainly help in building up a large, capital-intensive industry with a network of suppliers boasting a highly skilled workforce, something that the otherwise admirable Taiwanese economy has lacked.

However modest Taiwan Aerospace's capital now seems, the money needed for the MD-12 deal can easily be found. Central Investment Holding, for example, an arm of the Kuomintang (Taiwan's ruling party), is said to have $40 billion to invest. McDonnell Douglas is planning to use the $2 billion it gets from Taiwan to reduce its debt sharply; it will then finance development of the MD-12 with revenues from sales of its other aircraft.

The idea behind the MD-12 deal is that pieces of the aircraft would be made by various aerospace companies in Asia, brought together for sub-assembly in Taiwan and then shipped to America for final assembly in a factory specially built for the purpose. There are several other potential partners in Asia. Singapore Aerospace, an aircraft-maintenance specialist two-thirds owned by the Singapore government, is eager to participate in full manufacturing.

South Korea's government is pushing aerospace as hard as Taiwan's. At least two

Korean companies—Samsung Aerospace and Daewoo Heavy Industries—might be interested, though McDonnell Douglas is irritated at both, and at the Korean government, over its last-minute loss of a military-aircraft sale earlier this year.

At first glance the participation of Japan's three aircraft companies—Mitsubishi Heavy Industries, Fuji Heavy Industries and Kawasaki Heavy Industries—in any McDonnell Douglas-led consortium looks unlikely. All three share a 21% risk-bearing stake in the development of Boeing's 777. Nevertheless, the Japanese companies might still join a McDonnell Douglas consortium too. They have been careful to keep their options open. For example, Mitsubishi remains a contractor on the MD-11. And on the same day that McDonnell Douglas confirmed its deal with Taiwan Aerospace, Europe's Airbus acknowledged that it had been talking to the three Japanese firms about joining its project to build a "superjumbo" jet capable of carrying more than 600 passengers on long-haul routes sometime early in the next century. Development costs alone for such an aircraft could be as much as $9 billion. With their financial clout, Mitsubishi, Fuji and Kawasaki could yet buy their way into almost any airline project, whether it be led by Boeing, Airbus or McDonnell Douglas.

Plenty of things can go wrong. Engineering talent exists in Taiwan and other fast-growing Asian countries, but it is already in short supply. As the price of such skills rises, the cost advantage of manufacturing parts of aircraft in Asia will diminish. Many Asian carriers, particularly Singapore Airlines, which has just cancelled a preliminary order for 20 MD-12s in favour of Airbus models, may not be as willing as expected to purchase aircraft made by a McDonnell Douglas-led Asian consortium. Politics should prove less of an obstacle than some people fear. With McDonnell Douglas ailing, American fears of Asian investment are likely to be muted. And China, where McDonnell Douglas already has a joint venture producing MD-80s, is far likelier to want a piece of the action than to be miffed by Taiwan's involvement.

If the deal works, it will herald a rather different commercial-aircraft industry at the end of the century. Three strong competitors could be fighting it out instead of two and an also-ran. Even if this deal flops, it looks more and more likely that Asia will play a much bigger role in the business of building aircraft. Boeing, aware that its 747 monopoly of the market for long-haul jumbos will be threatened by the end of the decade, is also considering building an even bigger jumbo. Like McDonnell Douglas and Airbus, it will probably have to look East for the billions of dollars it will cost to get the new jet off the ground.

Recycling in Germany

NOVEMBER 23RD *Companies selling in Germany will soon have to take back and recycle their packaging. And eventually their products, too. This could be the beginning of a worldwide trend*

LAST April Germany's federal government ratified a new packaging law that is tougher than anything introduced in any other country. Its aim is to reduce the amount of waste going to landfill and incineration. As from December 1st companies must take back and recycle packaging used during transport, or arrange for somebody else to do so. From April 1st 1992 that law will extend to "secondary" packaging–intermediate layers such as gift wrapping or the cardboard box around a whisky bottle. From January 1st 1993 it will cover all packaging, from yoghurt pots to butter wrappers.

The ferocity of the new obligations is extraordinary. By July 1st 1995 80% of packaging waste must be collected–a figure that other recycling schemes have not managed even in middle-class suburbs. Germany's provision applies to everyone. Of the collected materials, 90% of glass and metals must be recycled, and 80% of paper, board, plastics and laminates. Incineration, even if used to generate power, is ruled out. The legislation shows no interest in what the recycled materials will be used for or who will buy them. That is a problem for companies.

To cope, companies have set up the Duales System Deutschland (DSD), which will run its own waste-collection system. Depending on the size of their containers, participating companies will pay up to 20 pfennigs (12 cents) an item. In exchange, their product will carry a green dot showing that their packaging can be recycled and thus qualifies for collection under the DSD scheme. Firms that do not join will have to make their own arrangements. Payments for the dot will pay for the DSD.

For transport packaging, the DSD offers no help. Instead, a number of companies have been set up to offer recycling services. Some specialise in particular materials–

Resy, backed by waste-paper merchants and paper-packaging firms, specialises in handling cardboard; others concentrate on aluminium, clothes hangers and plastic materials. All insist that the packaging be handed to them free of nails and sticky tape; charges are hefty.

To companies in Germany, the arrangements are exasperating. To those outside, they are often a nightmare. David Perchard, a British consultant specialising in packaging issues, says simply finding out what is required has been almost impossible. The different deadlines for collecting different types of packaging have meant nit-picking definitions. The cardboard box in which a cooker is sold to a customer is transport packaging, and must be collected from this December; a cardboard box in which a toaster is sold is sales packaging, and will not have to be taken back until 1993. Dotty.

Hewlett-Packard, an American computer company, has redesigned its packaging worldwide to make it easier to recycle in Germany. Where possible it has switched from plastic to cardboard, altered some products to make them less vulnerable to knocks, and surveyed its German customers to see whether they would accept products in re-used boxes (they would).

For America's Bristol-Myers Squibb, which sells hair colourants and other personal-care products in Germany, the immediate problem has been to incorporate the green dot on to labels whose colour printing is already expensive and delicate in order to reflect precise hair colours. Steph Carter, who has managed the company's packaging development, sees a different problem. In Britain, companies still put products in the biggest possible package. In Germany, customers who see a big package round a small container say "I'm not buying that–look at

all the waste."

For smaller firms, the difficulties are harrowing. The obligation to take back packaging around foreign products rests not with the manufacturer but with the importer. Many small companies have been given impossible requirements by their distributors. Britain's Industry Council for Packaging and the Environment is collecting horror stories to support a protest to the European Commission. One company was told by its distributor to use "biodegradable" nails in its crates. Fruit and vegetable shippers are especially unhappy. Their European trade body, Eucofel, says there is no provision for recycling the wooden crates in which 65% of Germany's fruit and vegetables arrive, and that the law forbids them to be burnt.

Other EC countries are now mimicking Germany. Holland and France have both made tough deals with industry to encourage more recycling of packaging; Austria is even proposing a legal obligation on the consumer to return packaging to the retailer. As for Germany, it plans to extend the obligation to take back and recycle to manufacturers of cars and of electronic goods such as computers and televisions. German companies are already practising hard: Volkswagen has learnt how to strip down a car in 20 minutes and has promised to take back and recycle for free its latest Golf.

All this has serious implications for the EC's internal market: such unilaterally imposed rules are precisely the barriers to trade that are henceforth supposed to be harmonised away. German manufacturers face the same strictness as foreigners, but foreign companies, especially small ones, may find retailers more reluctant to risk taking their goods. The German packaging industry will undoubtedly gain. German companies will prefer to buy a standard container, made from materials that they know to be readily recyclable; and packagers will acquire a cheap source of raw material, as companies hunt for something to make out of their collected waste.

The Brussels commission hesitates to take Germany to court. It has been struggling for months to produce its own directive on packaging waste. A draft produced in October suggested freezing the Community's output of waste at its current (estimated, for all figures of this sort are highly suspect) level of 150 kg a head, recovering 90% of packaging waste and recycling 60%– all within ten years. That was attacked from many directions. The trouble is, as the chart shows, that Europe's members vary widely in their enthusiasm for recycling.

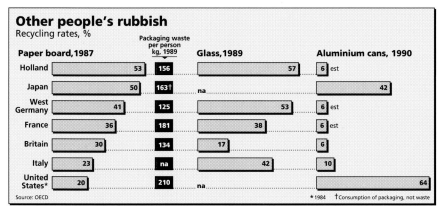

Other people's rubbish
Recycling rates, %

	Paper board, 1987	Packaging waste per person kg, 1989	Glass, 1989	Aluminium cans, 1990
Holland	53	156	57	6 est
Japan	50	163†	na	42
West Germany	41	125	53	6 est
France	36	181	38	6 est
Britain	30	134	17	6
Italy	23	na	42	10
United States*	20	210	na	64

Source: OECD   *1984   †Consumption of packaging, not waste

Contents

FINANCE

Debt's revenge

IT WAS not a year for the financially faint-hearted. In the 12 months that began with the threat of nuclear war in the Persian Gulf and ended with the decomposition of the Soviet Union, financial fraud and fragility managed more than their usual share of headlines. The background to both was stalled or slowing economic growth in America and Britain, Japan and Germany. High real interest rates curbed the boom of the 1980s but put the financial system under greater strain than their advocates had anticipated. The value of real assets (property, art) plunged in most places; shares fell in Japan and limped along elsewhere for most of the year from mid-summer; debt deteriorated along with the finances of recession-bound debtors. If greed was the hallmark of the 1980s, insolvency looked like that of the 1990s.

All this meant that a year which opened with gloomy financial forecasts ended with even gloomier ones (the stockmarket rally in late December notwithstanding). The Gulf war was won, communism was dead, Japan and America cut interest rates to their lowest level in decades—yet economic recovery still looked elusive. Behind the gloom lay another fear, that two trends of the 1980s—deregulation, and the accumulation of debt—had produced a financial system that was different in kind from what had preceded it: less secure, more volatile, more open to abuse by insiders, less responsive to changes in monetary policy. Some of the fear was misplaced: the preoccupation with fraud, for example. Some was not: notably, concern over the health of banks.

Take fraud first. For many, 1991 will linger in financial folklore as the year when scandal broke loose worldwide. Not that fiddling was anything new. Throughout the year, America's courts were dealing with the fallout from earlier insider trading, Britain's with its Blue Arrow and Guinness share scams, France's with shady deals during an American acquisition by Pechiney in 1988. Japanese who had recently learned that top politicians took corporate kickbacks in the Recruit scandal cannot have been very surprised to learn that big securities houses were bribing investors. Yet the large-scale fraud that surfaced last year in one market after another was nonetheless impressive.

Executives at several Japanese banks resigned or took pay cuts when fraudulent loans were re-

Maxwell's world caves in

Gutfreund unbowed

vealed. Big brokers from Nomura down admitted that they had been compensating favoured clients for losses. Nomura's chairman, as powerful a man as almost any in Japan, took responsibility and resigned; the firm expressed its shame in letters of apology to its (other) customers. Salomon's John Gutfreund, chairman of America's oldest primary dealer in Treasury bonds, admitted publicly neither responsibility nor shame for his firm's repeated fiddling and forging in bond auctions there, but he went too. In Germany hundreds of equity traders were investigated for tax evasion.

The two most disruptive scandals, however, were those involving the Bank of Credit and Commerce (BCCI) and Robert Maxwell's complex media empire. For years, it turned out, the bank, headquartered in Luxembourg, had been cooking its books, hiding bad loans, faking new ones, and being generally helpful to drug-runners and other crooks. When its London offices were closed in July by the Bank of England, BCCI left 800,000 depositors in 70-odd countries to whistle for about $9 billion in uncovered liabilities. But most of BCCI's customers were Asian businessmen and other third-world depositors; the West's financial sophisticates had had little to do with it. Quite a different story was revealed on the death in November of the Czech-born, British-based Robert Maxwell. His siphoning off of pension assets, apparent share-support schemes and other malarkey were made possible by the eagerness to do business of many of the most established names in European and American finance.

For all the half-enjoyable *frissons* which revelations of really big wrongdoing produce, more scandals were sadly to be expected last year. When asset prices and investment returns are rising, fraudsters have more incentive to transgress and people more willingness to trust the untrustworthy. Ebbing financial booms leave unattractive detritus on the beach. A second reason has to do with deregulation. It would be nice to think that what seemed evidence of more fraud was in fact proof of more zealous crook-catching. Last year's cases suggest rather the reverse: that as markets deregulate, the opportunity and encouragement to sin increase faster than financial policemen's ability to catch on to it. But both are temporary phenomena.

Of greater interest is whether the events of 1991 fostered long-

Nomura bowed

erm changes in the economics of financial services, and in how they operate. The year brought disaster to many banks and insurers, but record profits to many securities firms.

As bad debts mounted, 124 American banks went bust, with $64 billion in assets—almost twice as much as in the next-worst year, 1988. The country's biggest bank, Citicorp, suspended its dividend. Pre-tax profits in the first half fell at Britain's four big clearing banks, and one, Midland, made a loss. Japan's 12 biggest commercial banks reported their second year of falling profits in the 12 months to March 1991, and the outlook for 1992 was worse. Banks in healthier western Germany, by contrast, expected good profits in 1991, but feared they would slip the year after.) With capital impaired and tougher ratios to meet in 1993, most banks lent less, and at greater spreads over their cost of funding.

Insurers, too, watched aghast as risks became reality in unprecedented, hence underpriced, quantities. Competitive underwriting in the 1980s had left many property/casualty insurers with a barrowful of dicey business. Economic downturn made it dicier—raising claims, lowering asset quality and reducing investment returns for many. In America, at least 70 insurance companies went bust. All Britain's big composite insurers made pre-tax operating losses in the first half of 1991. Germany's Allianz was set to report, at group level, an underwriting loss for the year—the first ever for Europe's largest insurer. Outside investors ("names") departed in droves from Lloyd's of London.

So what? Let's buy

Securities firms and markets bucked the depressing trend. Share prices mostly rose once shooting started in the Gulf, then hung about or drooped from mid-year until a last round of interest-rate cuts in America and Japan sparked a rally in December. These were jittery times, however. World stockmarkets flirted with 1987-style disaster in August (when Russia's hardliners got fed up with Mikhail Gorbachev) and again in November (when investors tired of bad economic news in America). Nonetheless, America's Dow Jones Industrial Average gained 20% over the year, ending it at an all-time high. In Britain, France and Germany share prices were higher at the end of the year than at the beginning; in Japan they were 4.5% lower.

Companies were stirred by higher share prices and lower interest rates to restructure their balance sheets, replacing expensive old debt with cheaper new bonds or equity. New issues of securities soared in America and Britain. In Japan, where an informal ban had prevented new equity issues since April 1990, there was a tentative revival of warrant bonds and, towards the end of the year, a hint that straight corporate bonds might become a serious source of finance for companies. New issues of international bonds totalled $228 billion, well up on 1990. New ecu bonds were nearly twice the previous year's, as Europe's politicians negotiated the details of the Community's coming monetary union.

All this translated into fat earnings for securities firms, even though mergers and acquisitions dropped off, by more than a

third worldwide. Wall Street had its best year since 1986, and so did British securities firms. Japan's firms, trapped by falling markets and scandal, were the exception.

Even among banks and insurers, beneath the horrible headlines healthier things were happening. Through mergers, no less than failures, America's too-numerous banks thinned out and Japan's began to do so. The insurance market started to shed capacity, not only at Lloyd's; this implied higher rates and somewhat better profits in 1992. Private-sector borrowers seemed to be sobering up and reducing debts after their credit binge of the 1980s. Private investment was flowing again to Latin America and other developing markets, as the spectre of third-world default paled beside the problems of first-world property developers and small businessmen. As 1993 neared, European financial firms continued to hunt for allies in other countries, and banks and insurers made often rational decisions to join hands. Despite these moves, spurred in some measure by the frauds and failures of 1991, the legacy of the year is likely to prove pernicious.

For evidence, look for progress, or lack of it, on two fronts: the unchaining of financial institutions in America and Japan, and the creation of a single market in Europe. Proponents of broad banking reform in America, including the curiously ineffectual President Bush, failed to convince Congress to free banks from restrictions on what sorts of business they can do and where—rules which have kept them fragmented, weak and prone to unprofitability for more than half a century. In Japan, official proposals to let banks do more things emerged timid and half-baked. The drive in Brussels to allow financial firms to operate across borders, subject mainly to home-country regulation, seems to have run into the sand; draft directives to free investment services and most insurance remain drafts.

In all cases, the inability to reconcile the competing claims of different interest groups was a powerful reason to retain the status quo; but fear of freedom, of failure and of further deregulation, was another. For this, the financial fraud and fragility that made 1991 a year full more of spills than thrills were directly responsible. Such fear of change—leading, perhaps, to some measure of re-regulation—may well overshadow financial markets long after this economic recession has lifted.

Wednesday 2nd

Stockmarkets reopened for the new year in sombre mood, after a mainly gloomy 1990. In New York, the Dow had closed the old year at 2,634, down 4½% in 12 months; London's FT-SE at 2,143, was down 11½%. Toronto had fallen 18%, Frankfurt 22%, Paris 24%, Zurich, Milan and Madrid 25%, and Stockholm 31%. Tokyo was glad not to be reopening till a day after the rest: at 23,849, the Nikkei was nursing a 1990 loss of 39%. Few traders foresaw better times round the corner. The few were proved right.

Thursday 3rd

With dud-loan trouble mounting among **America's banks**, the Federal Deposit Insurance Corporation (FDIC) was reported seeking $25 billion over three years from the industry to keep itself afloat.

Sunday 6th

Bank of New England was taken over by the FDIC. Laden with bad property loans, the bank, with $22 billion in assets, had revealed it was heading for insolvency, leading to a run. Likely cost to the FDIC: $2½ billion.

Tuesday 8th

Would Germany help its EC partners by lowering **interest rates** or upvaluing the D-mark in the European Monetary System? No, said Bundesbank chief Karl Otto Pöhl. Facing a large budget deficit, Germany would go on doing what he thought best for it.

Wednesday 9th

Amid fears of a **credit crunch**, with frightened banks unwilling to lend even if loan demand rose as interest rates fell, American bankers had a new wheeze: a bank-financed fund to buy new preference shares in shaky banks.

With hopes rising of a **Gulf compromise** in American-Iraqi talks, world stockmarkets soared, then slumped as hopes were dashed.

Friday 11th

Its three biggest banks facing $1¼ billion write-offs for 1990, **Norway's** government announced plans for a state deposit-insurance fund.

Monday 14th

With **Gulf war** ticking nearer, gold soared above $400, the sickly dollar strengthened and equities fell worldwide.

Wednesday 16th

In 1985-90, **Japanese** companies issued $160 billion of bonds with **warrants** entitling holders to buy the equity at a should-be cheap price. Should be, but wasn't, after the 1990 Tokyo stockmarket slump. For the first time, one such warrant expired worthless.

World stockmarket index
January 1st 1970=100

Source: Morgan Stanley Capital International

Thursday 17th

With the **Gulf war** going well, share prices rocketed: Frankfurt's DAX index and Paris's CAC-40 by 7½%, the Dow and Nikkei averages by 4½%, London's FT-SE by a modest 2½%. Gold lost $30.

Four **South African** financial companies linked to tobacco group Rembrandt agreed to merge. The result, if it happened, would be the country's largest bank.

Friday 18th

A new board and chairman at Sweden's second-largest bank, **Nordbanken**, found an extra $350m of doubtful loans in the woodwork, bringing its 1990 provisions to $900m.

The board decided to pay no dividend for 1990. The government, holding 71% of the bank, wanted it privatised, and soon. Few could see how.

The **French** government said that new capital issued by **state-owned enterprises** would no longer carry a government guarantee.

After three years of public-debt repayment, the British authorities announced a new issue of **gilts**—government bonds—the first in 2½ years.

Monday 21st

The **Treuhand**, privatiser extraordinary in former East Germany, announced plans to borrow DM20 billion ($13.3 billion) in 1991.

Tuesday 22nd

New York's beleaguered **Citicorp**, America's biggest bank, said it hoped to cut costs by $1½ billion a year and to raise between $4 billion and $5 billion in fresh capital. Some foresaw an eventual merger.

Thursday 24th

Britain's law lords declared all interest-rate **swap deals** made by local councils unlawful: the councils had exceeded their powers. British and foreign bankers, standing to lose £600m (nearly $1.2 billion), judged the decision otherworldly and warned of lawsuits. The government said it was "considering" the issue—already 18 months old.

Friday 25th

London's stock exchange, handicapped internationally by an old-fashioned settlement system, put off till 1992 plans to replace share certificates with electronic records.

Monday 28th

Five seats on **Thailand's stock exchange** were auctioned to foreigners. They fetched an average of $9½m apiece. Few but the buyers could see why.

Japan and America talked on opening **Japan's financial markets** to outsiders, but made no progress. Would Congress get tough?

Wednesday 30th

A big World Bank bond issue led to tensions between **Switzerland's big three banks**. The three used to handle the underwriting of bond issues in a cartel, dissolved in December on government instructions. This time the lead manager, Swiss Bank Corporation, had trouble cajoling its rivals into taking part.

Britain's **Securities and Investments Board** put out 40 core rules for stockmarket and other financial trading. The aim was less regulation, not more; in an earlier version, the SIB rulebook had been famous for its fiddling detail.

Thursday 31st

The Bundesbank raised **interest rates** half a point. Austria and Holland followed suit. Many feared the rest of Europe would feel it must do the same. It did not.

Mega-financier **Jimmy Goldsmith**, who had already announced his retirement from business, sold £300m ($580m) of shares in British baker and food firm RHM.

Bond Corporation, leaking exflagship of mega-financier **Alan Bond**, defaulted on a $350m payment due in Australia, but managed to stay afloat nevertheless.

Friday 1st

After Germany's January 31st interest-rate hike, the Fed cut **American rates** half a point. The sliding dollar slid further.

The many bankers to Rupert Murdoch's **News Corporation** agreed an $8 billion refinancing—not before time.

South Korea allowed foreign securities houses to set up branches there. Most yawned: they were being asked to put up too much capital, and still did not know when they would be allowed seats on the Seoul stock exchange.

Tuesday 5th

America's Treasury sent Congress plans for **reforming the banking system**. The 1930s Glass-Steagall act, barring banks from securities business, would go. Non-financial companies would be allowed to own banks. Banks would be allowed branches nationwide. Regulation would be based on the strength of a bank's capital, with nationally chartered banks and thrifts overseen by a new Federal Banking Agency. Deposit insurance would be narrowed. Industry lobbyists rushed in, mostly hostile. Sceptics predicted a rough ride in Congress.

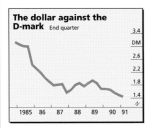

The dollar against the D-mark End quarter

1985 86 87 88 89 90 91

Wednesday 6th

Despite central-bank intervention, the **dollar** fell below DM1.45, its lowest ever. The fall lifted sterling over $2, last seen in 1981. In purchasing-power terms, the dollar was wildly undervalued, but experts foresaw no early upturn. Almost at once, they were to be proved wrong.

Dutch insurer **Aegon** revealed that it held a 10% stake in rival Nationale Nederlanden, challenging Nat Ned's agreed merger with a big bank, NMB-Postbank. Like other holders of Nat Ned, Aegon sought better terms in the merger. But it also feared this spread of Europe's *bancassurance* trend.

Monday 11th

After four weeks of Gulf euphoria, **Wall Street**'s Dow Jones average closed at 2,902, higher than before the Kuwait invasion. But the New York Stock Exchange faced staff cuts, to bring its dealing costs down towards those of off-exchange markets.

Soon-to-be **European Bank for Reconstruction and Development** (of post-communist east Europe) was reported planning to hire Boris Fedorov, former finance minister of the Russian republic.

The trial opened in London of **County NatWest** executives accused of handling a rights issue by **Blue Arrow**, an employment agency, in a misleading way that produced a false market in the shares. It was expected to be Britain's biggest-ever securities case.

Wednesday 13th

Chairman and chief executive George Ball quit Wall Street securities house **Prudential-Bache**, after another year of losses. The losses were due, not least, to the way he had pushed Pru-Bache in the 1980s into investment banking.

Someone (but who?) was keen on **Generali**, Italy's giant insurance company. Amid bid talk, Milan pushed its shares up 4½%. No bid turned up.

Britain launched a 2.5 billion ($3.4 billion) **ecu government-bond offer**, Britain's first and the market's biggest ecu issue ever.
Cerus, French arm of Italian

financier **Carlo De Benedetti**, announced the sale of its remaining shares in Société Générale de Belgique to French holding company Suez. Mr De Benedetti's French ambitions lay in ashes.

Thursday 14th

Under pressure to lower **Japanese interest rates**, hiked during 1990, central-bank governor Yasushi Mieno said no. Debt-laden property companies (and their lenders) shivered: two had gone bust in January, owing $3.4 billion.

Friday 15th

The **Reichmann** brothers, developers of London's vast Canary Wharf project in the revived London docklands, raised £403m ($790m) by selling shares in a brewing company. London offices had not been letting like hot bagels.

Tuesday 19th

Italy issued the first-ever 20-year **ecu Eurobonds**, 2.5 billion ecus worth.

The **Mexican government** named the first three state-owned banks to be sold off in an 18-bank privatisation, due to be completed during 1991.

Wednesday 20th

The European Commission published a draft directive aimed at freeing sales of **life insurance** EC-wide. Supposedly, it would come into force in 1993; in practice, national disagreements made the mid-1990s a likelier date.

Thursday 21st

A Saudi prince, holding 4.9% of troubled **Citicorp**, said he would put in $590m for new convertible stock, equivalent to a further 10%. To meet regulations, he later said he would sell his 4.9%.

Union Bank of Switzerland said it would buy **Chase Manhattan**'s institutional asset-management business, managing $30 billion.

Friday 22nd

Sears Roebuck could issue **Visa** cards, said an American court, despite a Visa association by-law denying membership to those, such as Sears, already issuing rival cards.

Monday 25th

A military **coup in Thailand** sent stockmarket prices there down by almost 7½%. Foreign investors were already wary of Thai stocks.

Tuesday 26th

Loan losses at **Swedish banks** in 1990 had been the worst ever, said regulators: in all, SKr17.7 billion ($3 billion).

Wednesday 27th

After a half-point cut in mid-month, **British banks lowered base rates** a further half point to 14%. Yet again, markets wondered whether the exchange rate would take fright. Yet again, it didn't.

Foreigners rushed into an auction of **Spanish government bonds**. After abolition of a 25% withholding tax in January, these high-yielders had become a world favourite, not least in Japan.

Thursday 28th

Ceasefire in the Gulf left stockmarkets unimpressed, but still well up since the end of 1990. The Dow Jones index had risen 9.4%, the Nikkei 10.7%, London's FT-SE 11.1%, Frankfurt's DAX 10.3%. Paris was up 12.7%, Toronto 6.3%.

Friday 1st

Insurer Aegon stopped trying to block Holland's **Nat-Ned/NMB Postbank** merger. The merger went ahead.

Saturday 2nd

Nigeria and its commercial-bank creditors agreed a $5.8 billion debt rescheduling: eg, an optional debt buy-back at maybe 40 cents on the dollar.

Monday 4th

The Federal Reserve told **Bank of Credit and Commerce International** to shut down its remaining operations in America.

Tuesday 5th

Britain's **Midland Bank** announced poor 1990 results, a dividend cut halving the year's total—and (nudged by the Bank of England) the midsummer replacement of (ex Bank of England) executive chairman Sir Kit McMahon.

Wednesday 6th

The **World Bank** said its president of five years, **Barber Conable**, would give way in the summer to Lewis Preston, ex-chairman of J.P. Morgan.

Swiss financier **Werner Rey**'s Omni Holding applied for protection from its creditors. Mr Rey lost his posts.

Citicorp sold a further $500m of convertible stock.

London's FT-SE index briefly surpassed its record level of January 1990, while the **Dow** flirted with 3,000.

London futures market LIFFE launched an ecu bond contract, five months behind MATIF in Paris.

Friday 8th

America's thrifts lifeboat, **Resolution Trust**, agreed to sell Lincoln Federal, centre of the Keating affair. Cost to taxpayers: $2.6 billion.

Monday 11th

Central banks, which had intervened a month earlier to hold up the **dollar**, intervened to hold it down. They failed.

Tuesday 12th

Tokai Bank said it would take over small Sanwa *shinkin* bank, the first such **bank rescue** since Japan's stockmarket slumped and property began to follow it down. But probably not the last.

Financier **Carlo De Benedetti**, cleared earlier in the 1982 Banco Ambrosiano affair, was reindicted by a higher court. All nonsense, he said.

Wednesday 13th

Three days of heavy foreign-exchange trading in Tokyo by **Hanwa Kogyo**—official business, steel stockholding—set the yen yoyoing. Hanwa made $20m. The banks that lost it raged: forex markets are for banks to make money in, they implied, not their customers.

Thursday 14th

London's FT-SE index closed above 2,500, for the first time.

Japanese securities house Nomura revealed it held 7% of **Britain's electricity-generating companies**, privatised earlier in the month. Hence the shares' embarrassing 40% premium over their launch price. Whitehall was furious.

Friday 15th

Poland's official creditors, owed $33 billion, agreed to forgive half of it. **Brazil**, nego-

tiating with banks to which it owed $9 billion in unpaid interest alone, paid off $480m.

Spain's central bank ended a requirement that companies borrowing abroad deposit 30% of borrowings with it. It also cut intervention rates by one point to 13.5%, easing upward pressure on the peseta, near the top of its ERM range.

Saturday 16th

South Korea named the first four foreign securities firms that would be allowed to open branches in Seoul. Japan's big four, which had applied, were not among them.

Tuesday 19th

Britain's budget forecast public borrowing of £8 billion ($15 billion) in 1991-92. **Gilts traders**, short of new issues, were relieved, not dismayed.

Spain's **Banco de Santander** said it would buy a $220m stake in First Fidelity Bancorp, big in New Jersey banking.

Wednesday 20th

America would forgive not half but 70% of $2.9 billion that **Poland** owed it, George Bush told visiting President Walesa. Other creditors were uneasy. What about us? said Latin American debtors.

Tobacco and consumer-products group **RJR Nabisco**, best known child of the junk-bond era—through a $25 billion leveraged buy-out in 1989—said it would raise $1.5 billion in equity and debt to pay off some of the junk.

Hong Kong company **Jardine Matheson** said regulators had agreed to allow it a form of stockmarket listing that would let it move its primary listing to London. In 1984 it moved legal domicile to Bermuda.

Thursday 21st

Italy's parliament voted for a

long-overdue **capital gains tax**: 25% on realised gains (after inflation-indexing) or 15% on a share's rise in the nine months before the sale.

Tuesday 26th

Bank of England governor Robin Leigh-Pemberton said direct controls on mortgage lending might be needed. Ineffective and impractical, said a miffed Treasury. The governor also suggested his bank should be independent of government control.

British insurer **Prudential Corporation** revealed the cost of its venture into estate agency: 1990 trading losses in that business of £34m ($62m). Worse, it had spent £330m getting into the business—and had recouped less than £30m selling four-fifths of it.

Tuesday 26th

In private, Fed chairman **Alan Greenspan** was accused by presidents of its regional outposts of exceeding his authority in cutting interest rates.

Wednesday 27th

Deutsche Bank announced net profits down 20% at DM1.07 billion ($635m). Blame dubious loans, not least to Eastern Europe.

Thursday 28th

The soaring **dollar**, below DM1.45 in early February, went over DM1.70.

British **property developer** Sheraton Securities International went into receivership, with debts of £350m ($640m).

April

Monday 1st
In a reviving junk-bond market, America's **Resolution Trust Corporation** had in the first three months of the year sold $1.75 billion of such bonds inherited from the bust thrifts in its care.

Tuesday 2nd
The **Soviet Union** ended its tourist rate for the rouble—about 16 cents—and said it would open a currency market on April 9th. Till then the tourist rouble would be fixed at less than 4 cents.

Thursday 4th
The council of Germany's **Bundesbank** rejected nomination of the Social Democrat mayor of Saarbrücken as president of the bank's Saarland outpost. A row followed. Parliament on April 26th overruled the rejection.

Friday 5th
The **French government** decreed that state-owned companies could issue shares to private-sector ones, as part of collaborative deals.

Swedish insurer **Skandia** reported profits two-thirds down in 1990. No tears from merger-minded Skandinaviska Enskilda Banken, holding an option to buy 28% of Skandia's equity.

Monday 8th
Brazil and the banks to which it owed $60 billion agreed on the $8½ billion of interest in arrears: Brazil would pay $2 billion during 1991, the rest being converted into ten-year bonds. And the principal?

And the $60 billion or so owed to official creditors? Much haggling lay ahead.

Wednesday 10th
Is **insider trading in junk bonds** illegal, as it is in equities? American law is not clear. And how much goes on? The SEC had launched an investigation to find out, reported the *Wall Street Journal*.

Thursday 11th
California insurance regulators took over First Executive Corporation, which had reported fourth-quarter losses of almost $470m. Holders of Executive Life insurance policies were told they were safe.

Friday 12th
Dresdner Bank, Germany's number two, revealed it planned a 7% share swap with BNP, France's (state-owned) number one, as part of a worldwide collaboration.

Monday 15th
The **European Bank for Reconstruction and Development** opened officially. Headquarters: London. Chairman: Frenchman Jacques Attali. Disgruntled shareholder: the United States, with a 10% stake but no man in the number two slot it thought it had been promised.

Few did better out of the early-1991 boom on **Wall Street** than shareholders in Wall Street itself: two big securities houses, Paine Webber and Smith Barney, reported first-quarter profits doubled from those of a year earlier. Brokerage shares were up 60%, on average, since end-1990.

Wednesday 17th
For the first time ever, the **Dow Jones** average closed above 3000, at 3004.

Monday 22nd
Fleet/Norstar, of Rhode Island, emerged as the FDIC's favoured bidder for bust Bank of New England. Price: only $125m, plus a $500m injection—and the FDIC would keep the bust bank's dud loans and take back any others that went sour within three years. Backing Fleet/Norstar with $283m: Kohlberg Kravis Roberts, former leveraged-buyout kings. A breach in America's wall between banking and other business? Not technically—not quite.

Tuesday 23rd
The **Treuhand** said it would raise DM2 billion ($1.2 billion) in commercial paper to help reshape east German industry.

Dutch central bank governor Wim Duisenberg called for budgetary discipline, saying the government's finances were in a "quicksand".

Wednesday 24th
Bad news for the already hard-hit **fine-art market**: Japanese police raided the homes of a former managing director and of a former president of trading firm Itoman, looking into prices paid for western paintings. Were all those record prices fakes?

Friday 26th
Germany's upper house of parliament rejected proposals by Bundesbank governor **Karl Otto Pöhl** to cut the number of *Land* representatives on the bank's central council. One per *Land* already meant 11; five newcomers from east Germany would make 16. Unwieldy, said Mr Pöhl, mean-

ing harder to whip into his line of stern monetary virtue.

Gold fell briefly below $355, its worst since mid-1990.

America's comptroller-general said the deposit-insuring FDIC **could be insolvent** by the end of the year, and called for a hefty special levy on banks to prop it up.

Sunday 28th
American corporate raider **T. Boone Pickens** said he would give up his two-year-old attempt to get nominees on the board of Japanese manufacturer Koito, and would sell his 26% stake.

Monday 29th
Christiania Bank, Norway's number two, reported a first-quarter pre-tax loss of $38m, after $90m of bad-loan provisions, mainly for property lending. Already awaiting an injection from Norway's bank guarantee fund, it suggested the central bank should help.

Tuesday 30th
After Sunday's Group of Seven meeting, where the Americans had argued for lower interest rates and most others said no, America acted on its own. **The Fed cut its discount rate** to 5½%. The ex-soaring dollar fell by 5 pfennigs—which still meant only to just under DM1.72.

The deadline for bids to privatise Britain's state-owned **Export Credits Guarantee Department** saw only two bidders still in the ring—one Italian, one Dutch.

May

Wednesday 1st
American banks lowered prime rates another half point to 8½%, the lowest level since early 1988.

Thursday 2nd
Banamex, Mexico's largest bank, already 30% privatised, was one of four named for the next round of privatisation.

Announcing 1990 earnings down by 78%, CS Holding, owner of **Crédit Suisse**, said it would put 20% of the bank's shares on the market. It had lost $587m at CS First Boston, its investment-banking arm.

Monday 6th
January-April **Euromarket issues** had run at $22 billion a month, 50% up on 1990 levels.

Wednesday 8th
Hung Yuan, a semi-legal **Taiwan** finance operation, went bust, as thousands of small depositors tried to draw out their money. Chairman Shen Chang-sheng had already drawn seven years in jail.

Thursday 9th
London's **Futures and Options Exchange** launched four property-based futures contracts. Nice idea—if it flew, as few expected. (It didn't.)

Monday 13th
Deutsche Bank and friends were planning a **Europe-wide credit-rating agency**, said the *Financial Times*. Speculative grade, sniffed Moody's and Standard and Poor's.

Tuesday 14th
Two **Spanish banks**, Central and Hispano Americano, announced a merger. It would create the country's biggest bank, with assets of $85 billion, overtaking the recently announced state mergers that would produce Corporacion Bancario de Espana.

Italian insurer **Generali** announced a huge (and oddly structured) rights issue: $1.4 billion. For expansion, it said. Takeover defence, said some.

Wednesday 15th
Owing over $4 billion, **Japanese condominium developer** Asahi Juken admitted it had had to seek its creditors' help. Trading house C. Itoh would lead the bail-out.

Thursday 16th
Bundesbank president Karl Otto Pöhl said he would quit in October. For personal reasons, he said; policy clashes with the government and in the bank's council, said others.

Japan's big four securities firms reported 1990 profits down 50-70%.

Troubled American insurer **Equitable Life** looked at a rescue plan that would bring in $1 billion from ambitious French one **Axa-Midi**.

Friday 17th
Federconsorzi, an Italian semi-state agricultural-services co-op, was put under the control of three government commissioners, owing more than $3 billion. Foreign banks claimed their loans should be repaid in full: they had regarded Federconsorzi as an arm of the state. More fool you, said the state.

Monday 20th
The SEC accepted a **New York Stock Exchange** plan for after-hours trading. The Big Board faced pressure from off-exchange dealing and screen-based rivals.

London securities houses revealed 1990 revenues down by a third, staff down by only an eighth—and losses of £350m ($600m).

Wednesday 22nd
The president of **Kyowa Saitama Bank**, Japan's number eight, resigned over loans to a speculative group.

Sunday 26th
British banks were not passing on interest-rate cuts to small firms, lamented a Sunday newspaper. Politicians rushed to join a pre-electoral bank-bashing orgy.

Monday 27th
Japan's top 11 commercial banks reported another year (to March 31st) of shrunken profits: down 23%. Assets fell too, by a combined $100 billion.

Trouble for **Crédit Lyonnais**. How much, through a Dutch subsidiary, had it lent Italian financier **Giancarlo Parretti** to help him take over film-maker MGM? Over $700m said some. The Dutch stock-market authorities, like French parliamentarians, wanted to know more.

Turkey launched its 1991 privatisation campaign, hoping to raise $750m.

Tuesday 28th
After looking sick in Tokyo's 1990 slump, **Japanese warrants**—the right to buy equity at a future date and price—were back in favour: warrant-linked Eurobonds totalling $850m were issued this day on dollar yields of 4%, and promptly traded upwards.

Wednesday 29th
Germany named **Helmut Schlesinger** to succeed Karl Otto Pöhl as **Bundesbank** president; new vice-president and likely successor, Hans Tietmeyer. Mr Pöhl would now go early, on July 31st.

Two top men quit as **Finland's biggest bank**, Kansallis Osake Pankki, revealed unexpected losses. The central bank was flexing its muscles.

Shareholders of British insurer **Prudential Corporation** denounced the 43% pay rise received by its chief executive in 1990, when profits fell 37%.

Thursday 30th
Britain's government named the share price for its £2.9 billion ($5 billion) privatisation of **Scottish electricity companies**. Projected yield: 5.1%, far below earlier electricity sell-offs—proving they had been give-aways, said Labour critics.

Friday 31st
The FDIC took control of **Goldome**, an upstate New York savings bank with $11 billion of assets. New York competitors got the better pieces, the FDIC would end with a $1 billion bill.

After good economic news, the **Dow soared to a record close** of 3027.

A **Swedish** parliamentary committee approved legislation that would let **banks and insurance companies** merge.

Brazil's national monetary council approved rules for direct stockmarket **investment by foreigners**. Two days earlier, the government had named a steel company, Usiminas, for privatisation; foreigners could buy 40%.

June

Tuesday 4th

Banking advisers to **Japan's** finance ministry endorsed moves to breach the wall between **banking and securities dealings**. But full freedom was still far off. Securities houses feared competition from banks' branch networks.

Italy's government tried again to sort out **Federconsorzi**, a bust farm-supplies co-op: bank creditors would be paid off with equity in a successor company. Meanwhile Banca Nazionale del Lavoro, half-owner of a Federconsorzi associate, Agrifactoring, was refusing to stand by Agri-factoring's debts. Some foreign banks began to cut down deals with BNL.

Wednesday 5th

Media group **Time Warner**, owing $11 billion, revealed plans for a bizarre $3.5 billion rights issue. The price would depend on how many shares were subscribed for. So accepting shareholders could not know their commitment. Wall Street frowned, Time Warner's share price slumped.

Thursday 6th

The **European Bank for Reconstruction and Development** (EBRD) named an American deputy to its president Jacques Attali: Ron Freeman, the head of Salomon Brothers' investment banking in Europe. At last, a real banker, said Mr Attali's critics.

Sunday 9th

Britain's Office of Fair Trading rejected calls for an investigation of British banks, accused of **gouging small business**: no evidence of any cartel, it said. But the media fantasy of the big, bad banker seemed set to run and run.

Thursday 13th

The **New York Stock Exchange** began after-hours electronic trading. The 75-minute session brought little business.

Friday 14th

American property tycoon **Donald Trump** reached agreement with bank creditors. He would lose slabs of his empire, but escape personal guarantees for $650m of its debts.

SWIFT, a **bank-owned global payments system**, refused to let fund-management companies join it.

Saturday 15th

South Korea said it would open its stockmarket to foreign investment in January 1992. Open? Foreign stakes would be limited to 10% in any company, less in most.

Tuesday 18th

British insurers disclosed their combined 1990 losses: £1.5 billion ($2.7 billion).

Frankfurt's stock exchange launched an **insider-dealing** investigation of some Deutsche Bank employees. One top man was later dismissed—for other reasons, Deutsche said.

Crédit Lyonnais brought suit to stop Giancarlo Parretti meddling with the management of MGM-Pathe, heavily in debt to the French bank.

Wednesday 19th

Europartners—a link between Commerzbank, Crédit Lyonnais, Banco di Roma and Banco Hispano Americano—faced break-up. At its 1970 launch, it had been hailed as a sign of banking's Eurofuture.

Insurance company Norwich Union forced out the board of Tace, an environmental-control company. A rare case of **British shareholders using their muscle**.

Monday 24th

The presidents of **Nomura Securities and Nikko Securities resigned**. Japan's number one and number three securities houses had admitted they had compensated favoured clients for stockmarket losses—and had had dealings (unknowingly, they said) with a well-known gangster. World stockmarkets slid.

Wall Street's turnaround confirmed: its securities houses made $957m after tax in January-March 1991, after losing $128m in the previous quarter.

OECD experts recommended that regulators impose **capital-adequacy requirements on securities firms**.

Tuesday 25th

First EBRD loan: $50m for Bank of Poznan, **Poland**.

India's new finance minister hinted that the long-standing 40% limit on **foreign stakes in Indian companies** might be eased.

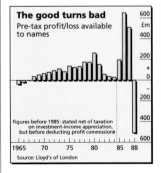

The good turns bad
Pre-tax profit/loss available to names
£m
Figures before 1985: stated net of taxation on investment-income appreciation, but before deducting profit commission
1965 70 75 80 85 88
Source: Lloyd's of London

Wednesday 26th

Lloyd's of London disclosed a loss for 1988 of £510m ($900m). With more horrors awaited for 1989 and 1990, the ancient insurance market was talking of reform. Limited liability, corporate capital?

NCNB and C&S/Sovran, two big banks in America's southeast, admitted to merger talks. The result could be **America's third-biggest bank**.

Thursday 27th

Germany's constitutional court ruled the government must collect tax, now widely dodged, on **interest income**. How? Fears of a withholding tax (tried and dropped in 1989) sent next day's bond and share prices tumbling.

Britain's TSB Group reported six-month losses of £150m ($270m), due mainly to loan disasters at its Hill Samuel merchant-banking arm, bought in 1987. Another British **institution that rushed into a new business** and fell on its face.

A new twist to **Japan's securities scandal**. Nomura's former president said the finance ministry had known all about Nomura making good clients' losses. Not us, said the ministry. Share prices crumbled.

Friday 28th

The House of Representatives banking committee voted through its version of the administration's plan for **American banking reform**. Much of the original plan survived.

Sunday 30th

The first half of 1991 saw $121 billion of **Eurobond issues**, up from $79 billion in the same period of 1990. Ecu-denominated bonds easily displaced sterling as the second-favourite currency, after the dollar. Lead manager: as in 1990, Nomura, with 10% of the market. But **syndicated loans** were down to $100 billion from $184 billion a year earlier; with several economies sluggish, banks and borrowers alike were cautious.

July

Monday 1st

Japan's central bank cut a half-point off **interest rates**. Nothing to do with the Nomura-Nikko scandal and crumbling share prices, the bank insisted. Oh no? said the stockmarket, soaring 3½%.

Tuesday 2nd

British banks were neither colluding on interest rates to small-business borrowers nor overcharging them, a Treasury investigation concluded.

Thursday 4th

After two days sliding, **Tokyo shares** fell lower than they had stood before Monday's interest-rate cut.

Friday 5th

The **Bank of Credit and Commerce International** was closed by regulators in seven countries, co-ordinated by the Bank of England. BCCI, incorporated in Luxembourg and the Cayman Islands, and 77%-owned by the sheikh of Abu Dhabi, had been found to be riddled with fraud, said the British central bank. The sheikh, who had put in $1 billion in 1990 to meet BCCI losses, and was preparing a restructuring, was not consulted. Nor was he pleased.

A fresh blow for Australian financier **Alan Bond**. With his public empire already crippled, Dallhold Investments, his personal vehicle, was put into liquidation, owing $750m.

Monday 8th

Japanese shares hit a 1991 low, as the finance ministry ordered the four big securities houses not to sell to corporate investors for four days; a slap on the wrist for the way they had compensated favoured clients for losses.

A flotation price was fixed for **Australia's** government-owned **Commonwealth Bank**. Nearly 30% of its equity would be sold, for $1 billion—Australia's biggest-ever issue.

Tuesday 9th

Japanese companies were back at their old game of issuing **bonds with equity warrants** attached: $925m of them on this one day.

Wednesday 10th

Boosted by South Africa's return to international respectability in sport—and by America's dropping of sanctions—**Johannesburg share prices** soared to a peak, 39% above their January low.

Friday 12th

Time Warner bowed to criticism of its bizarre proposed rights issue (see June 5th). Instead it would make an orthodox three-for-five issue, fully underwritten.

Monday 15th

New York's **Chemical Bank** and **Manufacturers Hanover** agreed to merge. The new Chemical Banking would be America's number two, with a combined (mid-1991) total of $135 billion in assets.

Tuesday 16th

Citicorp reported second-quarter net earnings over 80% down, to just $43m—3 cents a share (even cut, its dividend was 25 cents). At America's number five, Security Pacific, earnings fell 76% to $47m.

A survey showed **Japanese banks' loans to property companies** trebled to ¥50 trillion ($365 billion) in five years to March 1991. To build roosts for homing chickens?

Wednesday 17th

The Chicago Board of Trade unveiled plans for trading in **pollution permits** issued under American environmental legislation.

Thursday 18th

Confirmed: **French insurer Axa-Midi** would inject $1 billion into American one Equitable Life, eventually getting 40%-plus of its equity.

Monday 22nd

Another American bank merger: south-eastern NCNB and C&S/ Sovran (see June 26th) agreed to unite, as **NationsBank**. It would be America's number three, with $118 billion of assets.

More resignations at **Nomura Securities**: chairman Setsuya Tabuchi and vice-chairman Yoshihisa Tabuchi (who had only just quit as president).

In full-page newspaper advertisements, **Abu Dhabi denounced** the Bank of England's "abrupt" closure of BCCI. Seeking an immediate winding-up, the British central bank was rebuffed: the high court gave BCCI's owners eight days to mount a rescue.

Tuesday 23rd

Robin Leigh-Pemberton, governor of the **Bank of England**, admitted it had been warned of possible fraud at BCCI as early as April 1990.

Wednesday 24th

More freedom for **foreign investors in India**: in 32 industries, the government said, they would be allowed up to 51% of joint ventures, instead of 40%. More freedom also for big Indian groups to expand.

Thursday 25th

Fuji Bank, Japan's number four, admitted three Tokyo branches had taken part in issuing forged certificates of deposit for ¥260m, nearly $2 billion, enabling holders to borrow that amount from non-banks. Fuji was not alone. The device had enabled clients to borrow while bank lending was restricted.

Monday 29th

BCCI, its founder, Agha Hasan Abedi, and its former chief executive, Swaleh Naqvi, were **indicted on fraud charges** in New York. The bank had raised $20 billion in deposits, of which $5 billion might have been lost—"the largest bank fraud in history"—said the New York prosecutor.

Leading industrial companies were among 231 **Japanese** investors named as having had nearly $1 billion of stockmarket **losses made up by the big four brokers**. So were three (unnamed) "company officials", but not one politician. How convenient, said a sceptical world.

Tuesday 30th

German mega-insurer **Allianz** revealed pre-tax profits down 9%—and its stake in Dresdner Bank up to 23%: below the level that provokes investigation, but the cartel office decided to take a look anyway.

Another **rebuff for the Bank of England**: the high court gave BCCI's owners a further four months to rescue it, after the Abu Dhabi authorities said they would put in £50m ($85m) to tide over shareholders and employees.

August

Thursday 1st
Britain's largest bank, **Barclays**, blamed most of a 37% drop in first-half profits before tax, to £378m ($684m) on bad loans to small businesses. It warned of a tougher line in future.

Germany's **Deutsche Bank** reported a 23% increase in first-half operating profits, to DM3.16 billion ($1.8 billion), despite its costly expansion into eastern Germany.

Friday 2nd
The American Senate's banking committee narrowly approved a **banking-reform bill** expanding banks' activities and shoring up the FDIC's bust bank-insurance fund. Trouble for the controversial bill loomed in the House.

Monday 5th
Toshiki Kaifu, Japan's prime minister, promised **tough securities laws** to deter stock-market scandals. The Nikkei share average lost 195 points.

Tuesday 6th
Pre-tax profits at **National Westminster**, Britain's second-largest bank, fell by 77% in the first half. The bank said it was still lending actively to small businesses—but charging them more.

Wednesday 7th
Bank regulators in Luxembourg, where the crooked and bust Bank of Credit and Commerce International (**BCCI**) is registered, threatened to liquidate its operations in Europe unless depositors outside Britain received some compensation from its owners.

Commercial Union, a large British composite insurer, reported a pre-tax loss of £26.3m ($47.6m) for the half-year. A year earlier, CU had been the only one of Britain's big composite insurers in profit.

A French consortium, includ-

ing Mutuelle Assurance Artisanale de France and an offshoot of Crédit Lyonnais, offered $3 billion for the business and junk-bond portfolio of California's **Executive Life**, the second-largest insurer ever to go bust in America.

Thursday 8th
Second-quarter after-tax profits fell by 83% at **Sotheby's**, the art auction firm. Buyers had stopped bidding absurd prices for Impressionist and contemporary pictures.

Friday 9th
Salomon Brothers said that it had **broken Treasury-bond auction rules** that limit bidders to 35% of the securities on offer, faking customer orders to do so. The firm suspended four employees—not enough to halt federal investigation.

Monday 12th
BankAmerica agreed to buy **Security Pacific** for $4.4 billion. The merger of the two Californian banks would create the country's largest by assets after Citicorp.

Tuesday 13th
Japan unveiled its fourth and largest **bank-loan fraud**. A manager at a small credit union, Osaka-based Toyo Shinkin, helped a restaurant-owner, Nui Onoue, forge ¥342 billion-worth ($2.5 billion) in certificates of deposit on which she borrowed from other financial institutions. Toyo Shinkin's entire deposit base was only ¥360 billion.

Cross-border lending between banks fell by $54 billion in the first three months of the year, said the Bank for International Settlements. It was the biggest decline the BIS had ever recorded, and increased fears that a severe credit crunch was looming.

Wednesday 14th
Goldman Sachs declared that it owned stakes worth £143m

($241m) in two companies controlled by **Robert Maxwell**. Most was collateral for broking loans to the beleaguered media tycoon himself. The late disclosure was a technical breach of Britain's company law—and a bigger breach of common sense.

Salomon's chairman, **John Gutfreund**, and other top brass admitted they had known of the firm's bid-rigging in bond auctions in April but failed to report it to the authorities until August 9th.

Sunday 18th
Salomon's board of directors accepted the resignations of chairman John Gutfreund and two others. Warren Buffett, a large shareholder, was named interim chairman; Deryck Maughan, a British employee, became chief operating officer. The Treasury barred the firm for a time from bidding for government bonds on behalf of customers.

Monday 19th
Shares plummeted worldwide on news of an attempted **coup in the Soviet Union**. Stocks fell most heavily in Frankfurt, where they closed 9.4% down. Dollars and oil prices rose.

Scandinavia's banking woes deepened. **Christiania Bank**, Norway's second largest, revealed a first-half net loss of NKr1.64 billion ($230m). A

government-backed emergency bank fund pumped in NKr2.1 billion.

Wednesday 21st
A **rally in share prices** around the world strengthened on news that the Soviet coup had collapsed. The D-mark cheered up too.

Eagle Star, a British insurer, announced a pre-tax first-half loss, of £189.3m ($317m), linked to problems in its mortgage-indemnity business. Other insurers were to follow.

Friday 23rd
Norway's third-largest bank, **Fokus**, reported big first-half losses and got its second capital injection from the government in three months.

Monday 26th
Swedish financier **Erik Penser** lost command of Nobel Industrier. Nordbanken, Sweden's second-largest bank and Nobel's biggest creditor, took control, in a complex rescue of the defence conglomerate and its financial unit.

The Mexican government announced it had sold 71% of Banco Nacional de Mexico (**Banamex**), the country's biggest bank, to private investors for $3.2 billion. It was the seventh of 18 banks the government planned to sell.

Saturday 31st
A government official told Japan's parliament that the finance ministry suspected **Nomura** of having manipulated stock in Tokyu Corporation to profit Inagawakai, Japan's second-largest gangster group.

September

Monday 2nd
London share prices soared on takeover rumours, expectations of a cut in interest rates and an opinion poll favouring the Conservatives. The FT-SE 100 rose to a record 2679.6.

Tuesday 3rd
Commerzbank and **Crédit Lyonnais** dropped plans for cross-shareholdings and further co-operation. Another blow for cross-border banking alliances? **Dresdner Bank** and France's **BNP** looked set to consummate their partnership.

Wednesday 4th
The British Treasury dropped scandal-tainted **Salomon Brothers** as lead manager of the American portion of the £5 billion ($9 billion) sale of its remaining stake in British Telecom.

Thursday 5th
As Wall Street purged itself post-Salomon, **Shearson Lehman** suspended one of the heads of its worldwide equities division and another employee for alleged improprieties in an equity offering.

Delinquency rates on **American insurers' commercial real-estate loans** rose by 13% in the second quarter of the year, it was announced. This heightened fears about many insurers' solvency.

Not reassuring
Operating pre-tax profit/loss, £m

Source: Company reports

Sun Alliance, Britain's largest composite insurer, increased mortgage-indemnity premiums by 50%. Sun and other insurers had been hard hit by the increase in mortgage defaults.

Friday 6th
Union Bank of Switzerland fired one executive in America and suspended another for phoney trades in a security the bank was underwriting.

Monday 9th
National Westminster chose Salomon Brothers, rather than its own merchant bank, County NatWest, to manage a £140m ($240m) issue of preference shares.

Argentina returned to the capital markets with a $300m two-year bond issue led by J.P. Morgan. The Latin debtor had not yet agreed a full rescheduling with its commercial-bank creditors; the high-yielding bonds sold well nonetheless.

Wednesday 11th
British Aerospace stunned stockmarkets with the news that its 1991 profit would be half the figure expected. It chose the moment to launch a £432m ($745m) rights issue.

Gold prices fell to a five-year low on worries that Soviet problems would release tonnes into the market.

The Treasury and the Federal Reserve took the first step towards changing America's **government-bond auction rules** by requiring customers to confirm their bid in writing before they receive securities.

Prudential, Britain's largest life insurer, announced a 41% increase in first-half pre-tax profits, to £170m ($275m). Though higher taxes eroded earnings, the Pru's results were the first good news for many moons from British insurers.

The **City of London**'s net overseas earnings rose by 10%, to £14.1 billion ($25.2 billion), in 1990. Fans said it showed that London was holding its own against rival financial centres.

Thursday 12th
The World Bank barred two scandal-tainted Japanese securities houses, **Nomura and Nikko**, from participating in its bond issues. The Bank had banned Salomon Brothers more broadly in August.

Friday 13th
In a $40 billion deal that would create **Austria's largest financial institution**, Osterreichische Länderbank and Zentralsparkasse, two savings banks, agreed to merge.

Monday 16th
Five employees of Dresdner Bank resigned after an audit showed that they had violated the bank's **insider-dealing** controls. The Frankfurt prosecutor's office said that 150 securities traders were now under investigation for tax fraud.

Hit, like its rival Sotheby's, by buyers' reluctance to pay exorbitant prices for Impressionist and contemporary paintings, **Christies International** saw first-half pre-tax profits fall from £40.1m to £3m ($5m).

Thursday 19th
As Scandinavia's banks got deeper into trouble, **Finland's Skopbank**, an investment bank owned by the country's savings banks, had to be rescued by its central bank.

Friday 20th
The latest to leap on America's bank-merger bandwagon, **Bank of Boston** and **Shawmut** agreed to a merger that would create New England's largest and America's ninth largest bank, with assets of $56 billion.

The British government chose **Goldman Sachs** to replace disgraced Salomon Brothers as lead managers for America in its sale of British Telecom shares.

Saturday 21st
A two-day meeting of EC finance ministers at Apeldoorn in Holland seemed to resolve many of the disputes blocking progress towards a treaty on **economic and monetary union** in December.

Tuesday 24th
Japan's finance ministry suspended the four biggest **Japanese securities houses** from participating in new issues of government bonds for one month. The slap on the wrist was announced just as the houses revealed that they had paid an additional ¥43.5 billion ($330m) to selected customers in compensation for stockmarket losses.

Wednesday 25th
The latest in British *bancassurance*, **Abbey National**, a building society-turned-bank, announced plans to buy Scottish Mutual, a life insurer, for £285m ($497m).

Friday 27th
Gold prices rose on news from Grigory Yavlinsky, a top Soviet economic adviser, that Moscow's gold reserves had dropped by two-thirds to 240 tonnes. They would have risen far more if traders had believed him.

Monday 30th
The **dollar** slid to DM1.67, its lowest level in five months, on fears that the American economy was weak and further interest-rate cuts inevitable.

October

Tuesday 1st
Sal Oppenheim, a German private bank, said **Karl Otto Pöhl** would become a partner. This ended speculation about the plans of the former head of the Bundesbank.

Wednesday 2nd
Europe's biggest insurer said it would make its first underwriting loss this year. German **Allianz** blamed higher claims, and purchases in Eastern Europe.

The **London Futures and Options Exchange (FOX)** closed its property-futures market after regulators found that exchange officials had encouraged traders to fake volume.

Thursday 3rd
RJR Nabisco, the archetype of the highly-leveraged 1980s, announced new plans to shed its junk-bond image. It proposed swapping some $3 billion-worth of preferred shares for common stock and issuing $1.9 billion in new securities.

Monday 7th
Bear Stearns, an American securities firm, gave top executives a **25% average pay increase** for the year to June. With earnings again buoyant, Wall Street looked set to repeat its errors of the 1980s.

Richard Outhwaite, an insurance underwriter at **Lloyd's of London**, was sued for negligence by 987 members of a syndicate that lost more than £200m ($350m) under his management. It was the largest legal action ever to involve the insurance market.

Westinghouse Electric, an American conglomerate, announced a net loss and a $1.68 billion provision in the third quarter, mainly to cover bad property loans and investments at its financial subsidiary. It confirmed suspicions that America's property crisis was not nearly over.

Tuesday 8th
Nicholas Brady, America's Treasury secretary, announced that **bank-capital rules** would be eased to spur bank lending, thus reviving the economy. Even some bankers doubted the proposals would serve either purpose.

Thursday 10th
The beginning of American banks' third-quarter results saw after-tax profits at **J.P. Morgan** soar by 79%, to $341m, helped by trading gains in developing-country debt and other markets. Barnett Bank and First Wachovia, two regional banks, saw increased profits, while Bank of New York's fell.

Friday 11th
South African companies prepared to return to world capital markets after nearly a decade as Liberty Life, the country's third-largest life insurer, announced a $141m international share issue.

Monday 14th
The Norwegian government intervened to save **Christiania Bank**. The country's second-biggest bank was declared technically insolvent.

Tuesday 15th
Citicorp revealed a third-quarter loss of $885m and suspended its dividend for the first time this century.

American **securities firms** did well in the third quarter. At Merrill Lynch, the largest, earnings more than trebled, to $160.2m, while PaineWebber's increased fourfold.

Thursday 17th
London's stock exchange announced a new delay in implementing its **paperless settlement system**. It was rescheduled for April 1993—18 months later than planned.

Monday 21st
More than 60 Americans filed suit in New York, charging that **Lloyd's of London** broke American securities laws.

Tuesday 22nd
Net income at **Morgan Stanley**, a securities firm, jumped by 69%, to $121.8m, in the third quarter, proving that Wall Street's profits rally was not confined to retail houses.

The latest in a string of financial figures to resign, the chairman of **Industrial Bank of Japan (IBJ)**, Kaneo Nakamura, stepped down over its dealings with Nui Onoue, a bust restaurant-owner and financial speculator.

Wednesday 23rd
Three of the four biggest **Japanese securities houses**—Nomura, Daiwa and Nikko—reported first-half profits down by 64-70%. The fourth, Yamaichi, lost money. So did nine smaller firms.

Thursday 24th
After-tax profits at **American**

Express, the travel and card group, fell to $31m in the third quarter, down from $344m a year earlier. A $265m provision against credit-card losses was the main culprit.

Friday 25th
In the wake of the Salomon scandal, American Treasury officials published new rules to relax the grip of the 39 primary dealers on the **government-bond auctions**.

Monday 28th
A £432m ($745m) rights issue by **British Aerospace** failed spectacularly. Shareholders bought only 4.9% of the new securities. The flop, following another earlier in the month, raised fears that other companies would find it harder to raise capital.

Holland issued a draft treaty on EC **economic and monetary union**. It would have let Britain opt out of monetary union and made possible a single European currency as early as 1997.

Mexico's government sold 51% of **Bancomer**, the country's second-biggest bank, to a group of private investors for $2.55 billion. It was the eighth bank to be privatised in a programme that had already raised some $8 billion.

Tuesday 29th
Salomon Brothers made a provision of $200m against better than expected third-quarter earnings to cover possible costs arising from its government-bond fiddling. The pool from which employee bonuses were to be paid was reduced by $110m.

Thursday 31st
Den norske Bank, Norway's largest bank and the only big one to have stayed out of state hands, asked the government for its second dose of capital this year, after large third-quarter losses.

November

Monday 4th

Moody's, a credit-rating agency, downgraded $7 billion-worth of debt of **American Express**, the travel and card giant. The move was prompted by trouble in Amex's core business, Travel Related Services.

The banking committee of America's House of Representatives overwhelmingly rejected controversial broadbased **banking reform**.

Wednesday 6th

Salomon Brothers' new bosses announced a management shake-up that strengthened bond-trading and shrank equities. Among the casualties was Stanley Shopkorn, one of Wall Street's best-known equity traders.

Friday 8th

General Motors, the beleaguered American car maker, said it would take a charge of $16 billion-24 billion to conform with a new accounting standard on **pensioners' health benefits**. Ford and Chrysler also faced big noncash charges.

More problems for America's biggest bank: Citicorp confirmed that it fired the top officials of its profitable **credit-card** processing division for overstating revenues.

Germany's Munich Re, the largest **reinsurance** company in the world, blamed storm damage for a 41% decline in its net group profits, to DM104.9m ($66m), in the year to June. It was the worst year for the firm since an earthquake levelled San Francisco in 1906.

Tuesday 12th

The German government unveiled plans to **tax interest on investments**. In 1989 the government had to repeal a 10% withholding tax that prompted a flight from the German capital markets even before it had taken effect. This time foreigners and small domestic investors were to be exempted.

Barings, parent of Baring Brothers, a long-established British merchant bank, helped managers of **Dillon, Read**, a similarly blue-blooded American investment bank, buy its freedom from its insurance-company owner, Travelers. Barings secured 40% of the firm, its managers 60%, and Travelers $117m.

Wednesday 13th

The American Senate voted to **cap credit-card interest rates**, limiting them to four percentage points above the taxmen's late-payment charge. Banks reeled, as the cap would have forced them to reduce interest from an average of 18.9% to 14%, sharply reducing gains on one of their few profitable businesses. The move was later killed.

Thursday 14th

Finland uncoupled the **Finnish markka** from the ecu to which it had been hitched since early in the year, after speculative pressure had pushed up short-term interest rates to 30%. The markka plunged.

California's insurance commissioner chose a French group headed by Crédit Lyonnais's Altus Finance to buy **Executive Life**, the second-largest insurer to fail in American history. The French promised to pay a total of $3.45 billion for the insurer, and to take away most of the junk in its portfolio. Rival bidders said they would appeal the choice.

Friday 15th

America's ever-dimmer economic prospects pushed down New York **share prices**, in the fifth largest fall in Wall Street's history. The Dow Jones Industrial Average dropped by 120 points to 2,943. Most foreign stockmarkets, made jittery by their own exchange- and interest-rate worries, followed New York down as soon as they could, before rallying, patchily.

Monday 18th

Pre-tax profits rose by 34% at **S.G. Warburg**, Britain's largest merchant bank, in the six months ending September 30th. Booming corporate finance and fund-management business accounted for much of the increase over a depressed 1990.

Tuesday 19th

Salomon Brothers said that it had fired more than 130 investment bankers, stock traders and analysts during October. It was one of the biggest cuts of senior staff that the securities markets had seen in recent years.

Thursday 21st

The G7 agreed to defer principal repayments of $3.6 billion on **Soviet foreign debt** and to provide $1 billion as part of a gold swap deal.

Crédit Foncier de France launched FFr1 billion-worth ($183m) of **French-franc mortgage-backed securities**, the first ever in that currency. They proved popular.

Monday 25th

Thirty banks, headed by National Westminster, agreed in London to freeze repayments until December 20th on £850m ($1.5 billion) of loans to the family of **Robert Maxwell**, the media tycoon found mysteriously dead and less mysteriously broke on November 5th. At least two banks, Swiss Bank Corporation and Citicorp, were reluctant.

Japan's seven trust banks reported sharp falls in pre-tax profits for the half-year. Disastrous stock and property markets were the cause.

Wednesday 27th

The American Congress finally passed a **banking bill** which would replenish the Federal Deposit Insurance Corporation and tighten regulation, but left untouched restrictions on banks' activities. Thus ended the attempt to secure broad banking reform, which President Bush's administration once billed the most important piece of legislation that session.

Thursday 28th

Dresdner Bank, Germany's second largest, said partial operating profit had risen by 13% in the first ten months of the year—despite a doubling of the bank's reserves for loan losses, including Soviet debt.

The number of **individual shareholders in Britain** jumped in 1991 from one in four to one in three adults, to 12.75m people, as a result of privatising the country's electricity companies, the Treasury said.

Formal **complaints about British banks** by their customers increased by 62% in the 12 months to September, according to the Banking Ombudsman's Office.

Friday 29th

The **World Bank** decided to resume its dealings with Salomon Brothers, three and a half months after the securities firm's bond-auction fiddling came to light. Many reckoned that meant scandal-tainted Salomon had turned the corner.

Monday 2nd

Tokyo share prices fell by 3%, to below 22,000 for the first time since August, on fears of a weakening economy. New York rose, London resisted, continental share prices fell. Tokyo later rallied, but uncertainly.

A British High Court postponed winding up the **Bank of Credit and Commerce International** (BCCI) to let provisional liquidators negotiate compensation for depositors with the bust bank's Abu Dhabi shareholders. Not without cost: the liquidators had run up $200m in overheads since July, a report disclosed. The bank's assets stood at only $1.16 billion at the beginning of December, its liabilities at $10.64 billion.

In the most costly state bail-out of any Norwegian bank to date, **Den norske Bank** was promised NKr5.9 billion ($923m) to cover its losses and take over troubled Realkreditt, a mortgage lender.

Thursday 5th

Despite protests from share-holders, the Paris bourse cleared two controversial **takeover bids**, François Pinault's for 66% of Au Printemps, a retailer, and one by a holding company controlled by Italy's Agnelli family for Exor, which owned about 34% of the makers of Perrier water. The latter was to encounter more regulatory hurdles before final approval.

When many banks elsewhere were reporting ever direr results, Germany's **Deutsche Bank** said that operating prof-

its had risen 26% in the first ten months of the year. The gains came mainly from a surge in lending and canny foreign-exchange trading. **Commerzbank** followed suit four days later, despite higher provisions against Soviet debt.

Monday 9th

Nippon Telegraph & Telephone announced that it had chosen an American securities house, Morgan Stanley, to co-manage Japan's first domestic fixed-price corporate bond. The move seemed to signal the awakening of that long-dormant market at a time when depressed share prices and tight bank credit had closed off companies' traditional sources of funding.

Wednesday 11th

As one company after another went bust, to the apparent surprise of its auditors, Britain's Accounting Standards Board announced sweeping new proposals to provide clearer **financial reporting**. A few days later its American counterpart came up with a controversial rule requiring companies to report updated values for financial assets and liabilities. Banks were especially unenthusiastic.

Monday 16th

Maxwell Communication Corporation (**MCC**) filed for protection from its creditors for its American assets under chapter 11 of America's bankruptcy laws. Four-fifths of MCC's assets were in America, but most of its big creditors in Britain. These, understandably, protested: they wanted to deal with MCC under British insolvency procedures, which are tougher on bust companies' bosses.

Tuesday 17th

Commercial banks could not but agree to give the crumbling **Soviet Union** until the second quarter of 1992 to re-

sume repayments of principal on its debt. The smart ones promptly boosted their loan-loss reserves.

Norwich Union, a British insurer, said it was cutting bonuses to policyholders because the return on equities had dropped since the 1980s and was unlikely to improve in the 1990s. Other insurers looked set to do the same.

Thursday 19th

Alarmed by the rising tide of repossessions, Britain's government persuaded its **mortgage lenders** to make available up to £1 billion ($1.9 billion) to help homeowners who had fallen behind in their loan payments remain in their houses.

Liquidators of **BCCI** agreed to surrender the bank's American assets, valued at some $550m, as part of a guilty plea to federal and state charges against it. About half the assets were to be returned to the liquidators for distribution to creditors worldwide.

Friday 20th

A British High Court judge appointed three Price Waterhouse partners as administrators of the bust **Maxwell Communication Corporation** (MCC), pleasing the firm's bank creditors and irking its directors.

Monday 23rd

In a belated response to the Federal Reserve's one-percentage-point cut in the discount rate on December 20th, **American share prices** soared. With investors seemingly confident that the economy was now set for recovery, the Dow Jones Industrial Average rose 88 points to almost 3023. The dollar fell.

Thursday 26th

A California state judge formally approved the sale of **Executive Life**, a failed insurer,

to a French investor group led by a subsidiary of Crédit Lyonnais, for $3.55 billion.

Monday 30th

A Delaware court confirmed the removal of **Giancarlo Parretti**, an Italian financier and failed movie mogul, from the board of MGM-Pathe Communications, a struggling Hollywood studio. This greatly relieved its main creditor, Crédit Lyonnais, which had striven for months to have him removed. The luckless Mr Parretti had meanwhile been detained for questioning by the Italian authorities on (unrelated) alleged tax evasion.

The Bank of Japan's discount-rate cut, to 4.5%, spurred **Tokyo share prices**. The Nikkei share average closed the year at almost 22,984—down, nonetheless, by more than 1,000 points over the previous 12 months.

Tuesday 31st

A British High Court approved an agreement between the British administrators of **MCC** and the "examiner" appointed by a New York bankruptcy court to smooth insolvency proceedings. The agreement, which was subject to approval by the American court on January 3rd, would have given British administrators control over MCC's assets, with a duty of consulting the American court and examiner on major decisions.

Share prices in Europe and America closed the year sharply higher. The Dow Jones Industrial Average reached a record 3,168.8, up 21% on the year. Britain's FT-SE 100 index scored its biggest one-day rise of the year to end at 2,493, up 16% over the 12 months. Shares were 16% higher in France and 13% up on Germany's DAX index over the year, but slightly down in Milan.

As we reported then

Run-resistant money

JANUARY 12TH ***The need for bank regulation and deposit insurance is often taken for granted, especially when banks look wobbly, as America's did in early 1991. We suggested that a deregulated, uninsured banking system might work better—partly because the very idea of a "bank" would change***

WHEREVER financial institutions take deposits, it seems, governments provide some form of deposit insurance. In many countries this backing is formal and explicit. America's system, for instance, is run by the Federal Deposit Insurance Corporation (FDIC)—a government agency. British deposit insurance is a mixture of public and private: after the authorities intervened to deal with the secondary-banking collapse of the 1970s, they obliged banks to set up their own deposit-insurance scheme. Elsewhere, insurance is simply an understanding that the government will not allow depositors to lose their savings.

The need for the government to guarantee, in one way or another, the integrity of the banking system goes virtually unchallenged. Understandably so. The depression of the 1930s demonstrated that the banks have a unique place in the economy. A loss of confidence in the banking system can lead to a flight from deposits to cash. The result can be a vicious circle of curtailed spending, deepening financial weakness and economic slump. Deposit insurance prevents this by protecting the banking system from runs.

Until America's savings-and-loan fiasco, the argument looked watertight. But now the drawbacks of deposit insurance have become clear. Insurance relieves depositors of any need to monitor their banks' performance. Insured banks (or thrifts) can continue to attract deposits even though they may be engaging in reckless lending. The institutions can pile up bad debts for years. When the time comes to clean up the mess, the eventual cost to the government insurer can run to hundreds of billions of dollars. Insurance may prevent system-wide runs, but this protection comes at the price of imprudent banking and a potentially enormous cost to the public purse.

One answer is to combine limited insurance with vigorous regulation. The FDIC promises to insure deposits only up to a ceiling of $100,000. This gives bigger, and hence more sophisticated, depositors an incentive to keep a watchful eye on their bank-

ers. Regulation manages risk more directly—by forbidding, or making more costly, certain sorts of lending. But there are difficulties.

In dealing with the troubles at Bank of New England, the FDIC's nerve failed: it felt obliged to guarantee all deposits, not just those of less than $100,000. This will surely weaken supervision-by-depositors throughout the system. Nor is regulation a panacea. The drive to deregulate economies during the 1980s reflected disenchantment with the costs of intrusive government. Often regulators have proved at least as prone to mis-

takes as the people and firms they are meant to regulate.

A radical alternative to the insure-and-regulate approach is to ask how a largely unregulated, uninsured banking system might work. A key point is that deposit insurance is a subsidy. True, in many insurance systems banks pay premiums. But in America, at any rate, these premiums have been grossly inadequate—witness the cost of clearing up the thrifts, and the near-insolvency of the FDIC. Insurance lets banks operate with much less capital than they would otherwise need; without insurance (explicit or implicit), they would have to impress depositors with their financial strength.

This implicit subsidy is harmful because bank deposits are, by their nature, potentially destabilising. Savers usually regard a deposit as "safe", in the sense that it is a claim to a fixed amount of money. But this is what makes deposit-takers so vulnerable to a loss of confidence. If depositors suspect that the value of a bank's assets (mainly loans) is less than the value of its deposit-liabilities, they have a one-way bet: they have a lot to lose by leaving their deposit in the bank and nothing to lose by taking it out. This is why, when asset values fall, banks are prone to runs. Insurance deals with the problem, but only at a cost.

Suppose instead that a bank account were a claim not on a fixed amount of money, but on a share of an underlying investment—a basket of certificates of deposit, treasury bills and other safe, fixed-income instruments. The value of the account would fluctuate with the value of the assets in the basket. But the great advantage of such an instrument is that it would be naturally resistant to runs. Any fall in the value of the assets would be immediately reflected in the value of the deposit, so there would never be a one-way bet. A run on the institution would therefore be much less likely. Moreover, any fall in the value of such assets would automatically mean an increase in their yield; the income paid to new depositors would rise. If a run did start, it would be partially self-correcting.

If cheques could be written on such accounts, the result would be a lot like "money"—but much less threatening to the stability of the financial system. Actually,

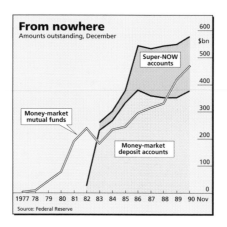

From nowhere
Amounts outstanding, December

Super-NOW accounts

Money-market mutual funds

Money-market deposit accounts

600
$bn
500
400
300
200
100
0

1977 78 79 80 81 82 83 84 85 86 87 88 89 90 Nov

Source: Federal Reserve

this sort of money has existed in America since the 1970s, under the name of money-market mutual funds. MMMFs are not insured, yet they grew from $10 billion in 1978 to nearly $250 billion in 1982. That growth was one reason why Congress then passed legislation allowing banks to offer new sorts of interest-paying accounts: money-market deposit accounts and, later, super-NOW accounts (requiring notice of withdrawals above a given sum). Both are vulnerable to

runs because they are fixed claims. Also, they are insured—ie, subsidised. Even so, MMMFs have continued to grow alongside the subsidised competition.

So financial innovation, itself a product of deregulation, makes it possible to imagine a safer, though uninsured, banking system. In this imaginary world, uninsured interest-bearing deposits would be at a competitive disadvantage against MMMFs, which would grow apace. Fixed-claim de-

posits would doubtless still be offered, but the banks would have to back them with more capital and conservative portfolios of safe assets; these accounts would pay little interest. Companies would be able to borrow much less from banks, and would therefore have to raise more finance by issuing debt and equity. This would be a very different financial system, to be sure—but one in which risk and return might be better aligned than at present.

Levitation

FEBRUARY 16TH *World stockmarkets leapt after the start of fighting in the Gulf. High hopes and easy money were the main reasons. But they had more solid support than that*

ASSUME that: (1) the Gulf war will continue to go as smoothly as a Tomahawk missile; without (2) Israel being dragged in or Saudi oil supplies disrupted; while (3) the Fed's belated pushing on a piece of interest-rate string turns out to work; and (4) the rest of the world's central banks, not least the Bundesbank, follow its lead; with (5)—especially in Britain, France and Japan—similar effectiveness. Make all these assumptions and you can reckon cheerily that, unlike most other people, you know why the world's stockmarkets, after their bounce as the war began, have been near-euphoric ever since.

Alternatively, you can believe that where Wall Street goes most other markets will follow. And you may be as near the truth.

Whatever the reasons, the markets have been defying gravity. New York was bumbling along with the Dow standing around 2,500 before the first bombs fell. Last Monday, February 11th, it went over 2,900, up 2½% in a day. Frankfurt had already risen as fast that day, Tokyo did so on Tuesday. Zurich and Madrid rose around 2%, London, Brussels and Amsterdam 1½%. Some technical corrections were bound to follow, and mostly did. But the mood was still lighter-than-air.

Why? New York has had technical help from short covering, but the market owes its fundamental thanks to the Fed, whose soft heart shoved bank shares up by 20%-plus in the first week of February. In London the early lead was taken by the slump-proof water stocks. Given the state of the British economy, that was sensible enough; but next came the newly privatised electricity distributors, utilities too but not slump-proof at all. Then came just about every equity that could drag itself out of bed, or even sick-bed.

In Tokyo the foreigners, fresh from the bath they took there last year, were crowding back for more. True, Tokyo's rise has been less enthusiastic than others, and has

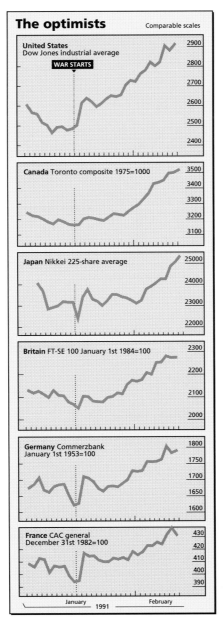

The optimists — Comparable scales

United States — Dow Jones industrial average — WAR STARTS — 2900 / 2800 / 2700 / 2600 / 2500 / 2400

Canada — Toronto composite 1975=1000 — 3500 / 3400 / 3300 / 3200 / 3100

Japan — Nikkei 225-share average — 25000 / 24000 / 23000 / 22000

Britain — FT-SE 100 January 1st 1984=100 — 2300 / 2200 / 2100 / 2000

Germany — Commerzbank January 1st 1953=100 — 1800 / 1750 / 1700 / 1650 / 1600

France — CAC general December 31st 1982=100 — 430 / 420 / 410 / 400 / 390

January — 1991 — February

taken the Nikkei index only back up toward last October's levels. Yet stocks there, by any other market's standards, even after last year's collapse, are still at go-go heights: what are grey-suited men doing grabbing for them as if the Japanese stockmarket were the Folies Bergères?

The answer, there as on Wall Street and almost everywhere else, Paris included, was a night-club-like mixture of overheated hopes and easy money: with interest rates falling, investors were determined to believe that better times must be round the corner.

Only a minority worried that, on the way to—and even after—the corner, the business news will be littered with slumbering demand, fallen profits and the occasional corporate corpse. Even the Bundesbank's raising of interest rates on January 31st got a paradoxical welcome: inflation fears were lessened, and the rise could be happily construed as offering still greater scope for rates to come down later. So buy. Up went the Frankfurt market, by 1½% that day, and it has seldom looked back since.

London and New York are the bravest exponents of this readiness to look forward to the rosy dawn and forget the night that remains. The logic of it is that the gloom and the risks are already discounted in the market. Maybe, but at what levels? Both markets were saying this when they stood 10% and more lower than they do now. Both are still saying it.

Yet there is more than an Indian rope trick keeping the markets up. Especially in Britain and the United States, the big investing institutions are heavy with cash, which some day will look for a home. That is hardly an economic fundamental, but it is a potent adjunct to stockmarket hope. When the day comes—some supposed, mistakenly, that it had dawned last Monday—market-makers will rush prices smartly up. And, bizarrely, the faster prices rise, the greater, for a time, demand will probably be, as cash-holders hasten to buy while stocks last.

Sorry, Auntie, I goofed

FEBRUARY 23RD *Britain's unit trusts, touted as the right place for the small investor, strikingly underperformed the market in 1990-91*

AT NOON on Friday, February 15th, Britain's rising equity prices, at 2303.8 on the FT-SE 100 index, stood within millimetres of their level—2303.2—at exactly the same moment 12 months earlier. Great news, you might think, for Aunt Agatha, who had begun to fear that, instead of taking young Billy Whizzquid's advice and putting her savings under the professional management of a unit trust, she would have done better to put them under her mattress.

Alas, not so. If she had cashed in her units at that day's prices, just two of 102 "UK general" trusts recorded by Finstat (a *Financial Times* subsidiary) would have given her back 100% or more of the money she put in a year earlier. The average would have been 88.4%, and 12 trusts achieved less than 80%. Among 127 "UK equity income" trusts, just two again were winners; the average was 87.2%, and 19 scored less than 80%.

Still, Auntie could have done far worse than that. Capital growth, above all, is what the industry sells to distinguish itself from boring old building societies. Had Auntie been fool enough last February to believe it, she had a choice of 190 "UK growth" funds—and in 187 of them the growth was negative. The highest flier soared to just

102.1%; the average was 79.3%; and the worst performer of all—stand up, MGM Special Situations Growth—managed 44.2%.

True, this is not quite fair to the industry. Young Whizzquid and his City friends cannot be expected to toil on Aunt Agatha's behalf for nothing, and the spread between offer prices and bid—between what she puts in and what she could take out five minutes later—is around 6%. Finstat's figures are dragged down by that spread, as a market index is not. On the other hand, Finstat—unlike an index—adds back 12 months' income, assuming it to be reinvested in the trust. That bridges much of the spread, albeit not all: it is worth maybe 5%, less 1% or so for the annual management fee that keeps Whizzquid on his toes.

True too, the FT-SE 100 is not the only index around. The 667-share FTA All-Share index on February 15th was still 4% below its level of 12 months before. Why pick the FT-SE to compare unit trusts with? The short answer is, why not? Any fool can buy a blue-chip index; Aunt Agatha could do it for herself, if she had the money and a stockbroker. Unit-trust managers are paid for the share-picking and dealing skills that enable them to do better than elderly aunts (how much

better is a question: supposedly index-tracking funds scored only from 88.4% to 93.2% over the period).

In sum, Auntie—and about 1.75m other Britons—was unwise to put her trust in units last year. Good news, at least, you might think, for that industry's rivals, the investment trusts. Wrong again. The FTA investment-trust index over the same period achieved 88.2%. True, that includes holdings abroad in earthquaked markets like Japan, so the comparison is a mite unfair. But the moral is the same. Aunt Agatha would indeed have been wiser to stuff her money under a mattress; or, better, in—yes—a building society, a bank or even, like great-grandpapa, 2½% Consols.

A job for Atlas and Hercules

MARCH 30TH, WASHINGTON *The naming of a new president for the World Bank prompted some suggestions for overdue reform*

"THE World Bank that Mr [Lewis] Preston takes over", crooned the *Washington Post* a week ago, "is in sound condition." Financially maybe, otherwise not. Insiders admit that by both external and internal measures, it has failed badly during the 1980s to live up to its promise. Notably it did not respond coherently to the third world's debt burden, and to ten years of stalled poor-country growth, probably because it did not overhaul its own ponderous bureaucracy.

A retired chairman of J.P. Morgan, Mr Preston, the bank's new president, will need all his organisational skills if (rightly) he decides in September to make that bureaucracy his first target. What it needs is some Herculean stable-cleaning. His predecessor, Barber Conable, who retires after five years in the seat, understood the size of that task when he arrived. But he used the wrong tools. In theory, he sacked thousands of staff. But he then told each layer of manage-

ment to appoint the layer below it. They duly reappointed old friends, and the Bank's already notable tendency to fiefs and feudalism was reinforced.

Mr Conable therefore hands over a 6,000-strong Bank with annual staff costs of over $900m, $150,000 a head, bloated by perks such as first-class air travel. On top of this, add 1,000 consultants, hired to do the work which the bank is—let us pretend—too understaffed or overworked to do for itself. The figures are absurd. So is the concentration in Washington. Only one-tenth of the staff work in poor countries. When World Bankers do visit those countries, unco-ordinated teams fall over each other. Czechoslovakia's finance ministry, for instance, is in despair these days as ten separate teams, each with a score of staff, crawl around its country.

Lack of direction led to meandering aims at the World Bank during the 1980s.

True, during his tenure Mr Conable quickly identified a number of themes—notably the environment and the role of women—that are now becoming central to development policy. Yet only recently has he been affirming what he sees as the Bank's main job: to attack outright poverty—measured, for instance, in crude terms of calorific intake. That ought to have been the World Bank's priority all along.

That it was not is largely due to the Bank's over-chummy relationship with client-country governments. Economic orthodoxy over the past decade has rightly stressed the role of the private sector in development. The Bank readily accepts this. Yet in practice it has strengthened some countries' public sectors at the expense of their private ones. Its lending has reinforced India's inept socialist policies. In Colombia industries have been kept in the public sector just to get World Bank finance.

Some insiders argue that the Bank is ill-adapted to encourage private enterprise, because its articles of agreement forbid it to lend to the private sector. These people, as well as America's Treasury, argue for changes to the articles. Others say the best way to get private sectors working is to reform the public sector: the World Bank can use its clout with poor countries to insist on structural reforms when it lends them money. A bit late: the bank's growth in lending, and therefore its leverage, except in a few countries like China, Vietnam and Argentina, is likely to slow in the coming years.

The conflict between public and private sectors is affecting relations between different bits of the World Bank group. The International Finance Corporation (IFC), the Bank's private-sector arm, can make loans to the private sector as well as equity investments. There are celebrated examples of bad communication between the Bank and the IFC; and the two have confused clients by offering different prices for the same services. A wide-ranging review (dread words) is now going on

to resolve the conflicts.

It is more than just goodwill that rests on the outcome. The IFC badly wants to double its capital with an injection of $1.3 billion from its government shareholders. America's Treasury is blocking the move. It thinks that even the IFC, particularly in the area of privatisation, is not adventurous enough. It also wants the IFC to be less transaction-hungry and to talk more to governments

about policy. That would mean that the World Bank would talk less to governments. One of the Treasury's main reasons for bullying the IFC is in order to get at the Bank.

This is the world into which Mr Preston steps. He is a man used to having his orders carried out, and there is no doubt that he has the toughness needed for cleaning out the bank. An east-coast patrician in the style with which George Bush feels comfortable, he will also not flinch at meeting the rich heads of poor states. In taking the job, Mr Preston, who two years ago insisted that J.P. Morgan shake the dust of third-world debt from its feet, now shows commendable sympathy for the world's ill-fed poor. There's the rub. The World Bank presidency has a habit of surrounding its occupants with a warm, well-meaning aura. More than at any time in his 64 years, Mr Preston now needs his cool, commercial banker's brain. And no sympathy at all for the well-fed hordes who stand in what should be his way.

Grey peril

MAY 11TH, WASHINGTON, DC *Many of America's private-sector pensions are publicly guaranteed. Another huge bill for the hard-hit taxpayer?*

WHAT next after the thrifts bail-out? Washington's favourite answer is down-the-tube banks. A less well-known candidate is private pensions, which could over the next decade cost American taxpayers $30 billion.

The Pension Benefits Guaranty Corporation (PBGC) is a curious off-budget animal created by Congress in 1974 to "insure" defined-benefit pensions when companies go bust or close down their pension plans. Total pension liabilities guaranteed by the corporation are put at some $800 billion. Since they are covered by private pension-fund assets exceeding $1 trillion, that should not be a worry. But assets have a way of disappearing when needed. And, within the total, hundreds of plans are underfunded, meaning the PBGC will have to pick up the bill if the company shuts its plan down.

Hence the PBGC's loss last year of some $900m, taking its cumulative deficit to nearly $2 billion. Recently it listed the 50 biggest underfunded pension plans that it guarantees. Big names include LTV, Uniroyal, Pan Am and Continental Airlines (both in chapter 11 bankruptcy), Bethlehem Steel, Chrysler and General Motors. The PBGC reckons unfunded, government-guaranteed liabilities amount to $20 billion-30 billion. Of that, some $8 billion is in "trou-

bled" firms in vulnerable industries like airlines, steel and cars.

James Lockhart, the PBGC's executive director, hopes his list will shame companies into putting more cash into their pension plans. Since few have any cash to spare, his hope looks vain. He has three other ideas to avoid a bail-out. One is to raise insurance premiums. But they were increased by 20% last year, and though higher premiums are charged on underfunded plans, the differential is not nearly big enough. Mr Lockhart admits that about half the present premium represents a subsidy from the well-funded to the underfunded plans, creating a direct incentive to underfunding.

Hence the second idea: persuade Congress to change the rules, either to make underfunding harder or to penalise it through still-higher premiums. The minimum level of funding that is acceptable for PBGC insurance is too low. Raising it or charging higher, risk-related premiums seems sensible–which may be why it will not happen. No congressman with jobs to fret over wants the blame for imposing new burdens that a rickety company might claim were pushing it into bankruptcy. That, after all, is why Congress allowed pension underfunding in the first place.

The third idea is to raise the PBGC's status in bankruptcy proceedings, so that it can get more money out of a bust company. Now it has to wait in line behind preferred creditors, and there are limits on what it can recover. And though the PBGC is often the biggest single creditor, it is not usually represented on creditors' committees. So the agency has a good case for higher status. But again it may not get much sympathy on Capitol Hill. Promoting its claims would mean downgrading banks, which have stronger lobbying power and can react by stopping loans to troubled companies with underfunded pension liabilities.

Mr Lockhart might instead look at another solution: to ask whether a public-sector PBGC is needed at all. Defined-benefit pension plans usually cover better-off workers, who hardly deserve taxpayer guarantees and support. The PBGC's existence has made it easier (and more tempting) for companies to underfund pension plans without upsetting their staff–the sort of moral hazard familiar from the thrifts debacle. And having Congress set rules and premiums inevitably invites the sort of trouble that the PBGC has got into. If companies and their staff need some kind of guarantee for their pensions beyond normal funding, they could devise a private PBGC that would charge commercial rates.

Trapped in the rubble

*JUNE 29TH, TOKYO **In mid-summer, Tokyo markets were rocked by a scandal involving top securities houses. It was yet another blow to a shaky financial system—and there were more to come***

LAST year was the one when even the Japanese discovered that what goes up eventually comes down. 1991 is proving another truism: the bigger they come, the harder they fall. And exceedingly painful the collapse of the great Japanese financial reach-for-the-skyscraper is proving.

The stockmarket led the way down. With the Nikkei still 40% off its all-time high, while the central bank stubbornly holds interest rates up, there was little chance that the effects could be laughed aside as a temporary blip. As ever, the collapse of a towering speculative market is exposing some ugly sights amid the rubble.

Lots of share speculators have been charged with multi-billion-yen tax scams. The presidents of three big banks have resigned in recent months in embarrassing circumstances. Most sensational of all, on June 24th Yoshihisa Tabuchi (above, right), president of mighty Nomura Securities, had to resign, as did Takuya Iwasaki (above, left), president of Nikko, Japan's third-largest broker. Although both men were moved upstairs to vice-chairmanships, the public humiliation was real. Mr Tabuchi, a proud samurai figure to the army of Nomura salesmen, was as powerful a man as any in Japanese finance.

The hope is that this sacrifice of big shots will appease public anger and stop a nasty scandal spreading further. That may prove optimistic: it depends how many awkward questions the Japanese press now asks. No one doubts there is more dirt to dig up.

The scandal that brought down the Nomura and Nikko bosses has two aspects. First, both firms admitted to lending money in the late 1980s to Susumu Ishii, the former boss of one of Japan's gangster groups. Some believe this money was used to manipulate the share price of Tokyu Corporation, a ramp in which Nomura's role is now being investigated. Second, both firms admitted that they had made good investment losses suffered by favoured clients, including one government pension fund.

Neither type of action would of itself have shocked observers of Japan's financial markets; their surprise has been that the scandals surfaced at all. Rumours about gangster contacts have long swirled around almost every big financial group in Japan. The reason is the constant need of organised crime to launder money. And the guaranteeing of investment returns has become popular in Japan's domestic fund-management industry in the past 15 years. Indeed it is seen as a necessary way of winning business (even, when gangsters are involved, of staying alive). Of course, the guarantor risks a huge liability. But this used to be viewed by Japanese brokers as of only academic concern, because until 1990 the Tokyo market kept going up.

Financially if not legally, the public outcry over big companies being let off losses while the small investor suffers will have longer-term implications than the brokers' alleged links with gangsters. This is because of the sheer size of the losses piled up in the

system. Japan's four big securities firms (Daiwa and Yamaichi owned up to the practice last year) have now admitted to paying a total of ¥65 billion ($475m) between 1988 and 1990 to compensate mostly corporate clients for losses. This is just the amount discovered so far by the tax authorities. It was they who blew the whistle on the affair and who are presumed to have revealed the details to the press. If the securities firms had not tried to claim their compensation payments against tax, many believe the scandals would probably never have come to light.

A sum of ¥65 billion is tiny in a market that has seen ¥200 trillion wiped off share values since early last year. So far, what the brokers have admitted to paying out in compensation relates mainly to *eigyo tokkin* accounts. These are the dodgiest sort of *tokkin*, a form of tax-exempt trust fund which expanded, to a peak of ¥43 trillion, in the late 1980s as Japanese companies went on a speculative binge. Some ¥3 trillion of *eigyo tokkin* money is still around. These are corporate accounts managed on a discretionary basis by stockbrokers offering informally guaranteed rates of return. Here the brokers probably face obligations of at least ¥1 trillion—more than all their 1990 profits put together.

Yet this is only part of the story. Guaranteeing returns is so much part of the investment business that it spans virtually every activity, from trust banks managing pension funds to stockbrokers with shady individual clients. The funds thus informally guaranteed are vast. Peter Tasker, a Tokyo-based strategist at Kleinwort Benson, says: "The money to fill in that little hole simply does not exist."

So dire is the situation that it has led some to suggest a machiavellian interpretation. This is that Mr Tabuchi and Mr Iwasaki were ordered to resign by the finance ministry because it became clear that the securities firms could not honour their obligations. So sacrifice some heads in the interest of letting the firms off the hook financially.

This seems too clever by half. First, the way the scandal oozed out does not look orchestrated. For example, Nomura's first reaction was to try to deny the allegations. Second, the overrated mandarins at the finance ministry are almost as big losers from this affair as the brokers, who had less reputation to lose.

The Japanese press is now calling for an independent securities regulator. For it has not gone unnoticed that the finance ministry's securities bureau has known about the compensation payments since last year. It is also true that, by its periodic commands to the big securities firms to support the stock-market, as happened both after the October 1987 crash and in October last year, the finance ministry itself encourages a manipulative view of financial markets. It also creates a problem of moral hazard: the brokers act on the assumption that they are themselves underwritten against risk. Thus, when it paid compensation to investors, Nomura probably thought its action justified, because it was supporting the market. As indeed it was: but for this, the investors would have been that much more likely to liquidate their *eigyo tokkin* accounts, causing still more selling pressure. That may also be why the finance ministry chose to keep quiet.

All this is what happens when you mess with markets.

Losses unlimited

JUNE 29TH   Lloyd's, London's 300-year-old insurance market, ran into trouble in 1990-91. Its tradition of unlimited liability buckled under the strain

THE chairman of Lloyd's, David Coleridge, must have expected the furore that swept over him at the annual general meeting on June 25th. The members—or "names"—of Lloyd's who provide the capital needed to underwrite its insurance were understandably unhappy with an overall loss of £509m ($825m) for 1988 (Lloyd's closes its accounts three years in arrears). Never, said one member, had he seen so many gloomy faces. The main culprit was a huge increase of £577m in reserves to meet claims from earlier years: 1988 on its own returned a small profit. To cap it all, Mr Coleridge warned that 1989 and 1990 were likely to produce further big losses.

Lloyd's last recorded an overall loss in 1967. The 1980s were mostly good years: the few years that made underwriting losses saw more than enough investment profits to compensate. Mr Coleridge talked optimistically at the meeting of an overdue rise in premiums for marine and non-marine business coming through, and of a good year in 1992. Even so the 1988 losses, early cash calls for losses in 1989 and 1990, and the spate of recent bad publicity for Lloyd's will probably trigger a new round of resignations among names before August 31st, the deadline for giving up underwriting in 1992. And with the American courts continuously extending insurers' liability for pollution claims against companies, who is to say the names will be wrong to go?

The prospect worries Lloyd's. Some 6,000 names have resigned in the past three years, reducing their number to 26,500. Many more would have liked to go but are locked in to "open years"—accounts that have so many claims outstanding they cannot be closed. Lloyd's points out that because names leaving have been poorer than those staying, its underwriting capacity is at a record of $11 billion, only half of it currently used. But if an upturn in the market coincides with a flood of resignations, its market share could quickly shrivel.

At the heart of the members' concerns is unlimited liability. This tradition is a historical accident. When Edward Lloyd was running his coffee-house in the 1680s, limited liability did not exist. Lloyd's was given a fillip in 1720, when Parliament gave two corporate insurers a monopoly and banned other companies and partnerships—but, thanks to an oversight, not individuals—from underwriting. When company law was revised to introduce the concept of limited liability in 1837, Lloyd's had become too steeped in its habits to switch. So its members remain liable without limit.

The popular phrase has it that names at Lloyd's are liable to their last collar-stud if things go wrong. That is not quite true, even for members unwise enough not to have taken out stop-loss insurance. Lloyd's will not bankrupt any member or even make him homeless; instead it will take a charge on his house and limit him to a small income. A hardship committee chaired by Mary Archer helps out in the worst cases. In such instances—or where members refuse to cough up—Lloyd's has a central fund of around £400m to draw on to ensure that claims are met. Where there has been a clear case of fraud by underwriters, brokers or policyholders, the corporation of Lloyd's will often pick up some of the bill—as it did in the 1920s for the Harrison syndicate and in the 1970s for the Sasse syndicates.

Yet even this version of unlimited liability is proving inadequate for the 1990s. In an era without exchange controls, there is no easy way of stopping names siphoning assets overseas. Many already transfer ownership to other family members. And often the response to cash calls in recent years has been to reach for a lawyer, not a wallet: a fifth of names are in dispute with their syndicates or each other. For all these reasons the Lloyd's task-force currently studying its future is looking hard at unlimited liability.

To scrap it would let corporate capital into the market. The trouble is that Lloyd's could then become little different from any

Those were the days

other commercial insurer. And though its brand-name has value, and the underwriters and brokers have plenty of expertise, its cost and client structure hardly equip Lloyd's to compete head-on with the big American or European companies. In one sense, unlimited liability is what has enabled Lloyd's to be an insurance innovator, boldly going where no limited company would go. In doing so it has creamed off lots of good reinsurance and catastrophe business, though it may now be paying the price.

The trick will be to find a way to limit liability that does not involve a total switch to a limited-company structure. There is talk in the market of requiring members to join a stop-loss or umbrella syndicate; of enlarging the central fund; or of making names spread their risks around the market more. One way or another, old-style unlimited liability is unlikely to survive.

The many façades of BCCI

JULY 13TH   LONDON, LUXEMBOURG, NEW YORK AND HONG KONG   BCCI was a stuccoed sham, concealing fraud by switching fictitious assets from one front to the next. The reputation of the world's bank regulators was among its victims

BANK of Credit and Commerce International is not the biggest bank to fail in recent times, but it is certainly the oddest. Indeed, strictly speaking, it has not even failed. Most of BCCI ceased to function on July 5th, a week after regulators discovered that some top executives had been committing extensive fraud for years. In one FBI-style raid, regulators in seven countries seized its assets. In the following days, authorities in most of the remaining 62 countries where BCCI had operations shut those down too. Its vast international network, controlled by a Luxembourg holding company, is now in the hands of liquidators.

The saga will not end here. Almost 1m depositors want to know why regulators did not discover the fraud earlier and why they could not rescue the bank with help from its owners in Abu Dhabi. Sheikh Zayed bin Sultan al-Nahyan, ruler of Abu Dhabi and the bank's biggest individual shareholder, wonders why regulators closed the bank when he was prepared to bail it out. Regulators themselves will have to devise better ways of handling dubious banks.

Luckily, BCCI is uniquely baffling and unusually corrupt. The brainchild of a Pakistani banker, Agha Hasan Abedi, it became one of the biggest privately owned financial institutions, with apparent assets of $20 billion when it was closed. Its two main arms were incorporated in the havens of Luxembourg and the Cayman Islands, its senior managers operated from London, its businesses ranged from seemingly respectable European banks to mysterious off-shore investment companies. Unusually, BCCI had no lender of last resort; since 1988 its operations have been supervised, with mixed success, by a "college" of regulators from seven countries, led by the Bank of England and Luxembourg's Monetary Institute, BCCI's home-country supervisor.

Hidden by this corporate jungle, BCCI indulged in a great deal of mischief. It first gained notoriety in 1988 as banker to Panama's now-deposed dictator-cum-drug-dealer, Manuel Noriega; last year, one of its main units pleaded guilty to charges of laundering drug money. Now the bank is under investigation for secretly taking control of a large bank in Washington, DC.

It was outright fraud, however, that felled BCCI on July 5th. Rumours of false accounting and fictitious loans had surrounded the bank for years, but regulators repeatedly failed to substantiate them. According to the bank's auditor, Price Waterhouse, that is because the bank hid each fraud behind another one. "We satisfied ourselves with a whole pile of evidence that the items we queried were all right," says Ian Brindle, chief of Price Waterhouse's British accounting practice. Investigators were fooled, he says, "because you can't go on the basis that everything you see and touch is a lie". Commissioned by the Bank of England to investigate in March, Price Waterhouse finally unearthed the fraud with the help of a former BCCI executive.

It discovered a "bank within a bank", created to hide losses on bad trades and loans, and controlled by top officials. When holes appeared in the balance sheet, the secret bank plugged them by raising deposits without recording these in the books. While naive depositors put their money in, managers and others close to the bank were pulling it out. Deposits rose by $3.3 billion in 1989, to $22.1 billion; deposits from "related parties" dropped by $481m to $336m.

To keep regulators guessing, BCCI shuttled assets and liabilities among its many subsidiaries. Bad loans on the bank's books would disappear into offshore accounts when regulators came calling; good assets would conveniently emerge. In 1988 alone, subsidiaries and affiliates paid $152m of fee income to one another. All this was incidental to other seamy sidelines: laundering money for drug dealers, and helping clients evade taxes and exchange controls.

The cost of BCCI's malarkey is bound to be huge. Investigators say the losses may be about $4 billion; others suggest $15 billion, three-quarters of the bank's stated assets. Even $4 billion would put BCCI's frauds among the largest in history.

Its victims are chiefly small businesses and individuals, many of them in Asia, Africa and Latin America, where the bank has three-quarters of its branches. In Pakistan, where branches remained open after regulators seized the bank's assets, depositors rushed to empty their accounts. Nigerian branches, backed by the central bank, traded normally after the seizure. But most depositors were out of luck—especially the 40,000 customers of BCCI's Hong Kong subsidiary. On July 6th the banking com-

Not just a pretty face

missioner there assured depositors that the local bank was "sound and viable" and urged them not to pull their funds out of the bank. They did not. By the morning of the next business day the government had shut down the bank, locking HK$11 billion ($1.4 billion) of customers' funds inside. Depositors in Britain, BCCI's biggest market, never had a chance to retrieve their money.

Sophisticates mostly knew enough to steer clear of BCCI. The bank held only $2 billion from other banks, not much in relation to its size. Not all big institutions were smart, however. Britain's local authorities may have placed £100m ($160m) with BCCI, mainly through London money-brokers. In America, banks and other financial institutions have an estimated exposure of $500m.

Many depositors are as angry at the regulators as at BCCI. Some assail them for acting too slowly, standing by for years while BCCI looted its tills. Regulators respond that they could not act without proof of wrong-

doing. That arrived only on June 27th, when Price Waterhouse delivered its report to the Bank of England. Many believe that Britain's central bank knew of fraud at BCCI long before that. One banker familiar with BCCI asserts that by 1988 the Bank of England had realised that BCCI was crediting fictitious income to bad loans.

The more bitter complaint is that regulators shut the bank down needlessly. Sheikh Zayed had injected $1 billion into BCCI in 1990, and a further $660m days before regulators seized it. His associates say he was willing to pour in billions more.

BCCI was also poised to announce a reorganisation that seemed to have the blessing of the Bank of England. It would have split into three regional banks, and its European base would have moved from secretive Luxembourg to London. It had hired senior British bankers to run the European bank, which would have got fresh capital. Its corrupt managers, says one banker, had al-

ready been purged. Why, depositors wonder, could the bank not start afresh with new money and new managers? The regulators reply that it was so soaked in fraud as to be beyond redemption.

Whatever their complaint, British depositors, notably, are angry. They are covered by a (private-sector) protection scheme only up to 75% of, at most, £20,000; already the government is under strong political pressure to bail them out, and the Bank of England faces at least one lawsuit.

The full truth about BCCI crimes will emerge slowly, probably in courtrooms packed with angry creditors and unrepentant felons. Meanwhile, the prosaic business of settling its debts will occupy liquidators and regulators. The Bank of England hopes to persuade Sheikh Zayed to bail out depositors, on top of the large sums he has already put in. If he refuses, lawyers will set to work sorting out the competing claims of creditors in more than 60 countries.

Rotten at the core

AUGUST 17TH NEW YORK *Salomon's bond-auction fiddling meant big trouble for the firm but bigger changes in the way the world's largest government-bond market works*

IN A mea culpa that left Wall Street gasping, Salomon Brothers admitted publicly on August 14th that its chairman, John Gutfreund, its president, Thomas Strauss, and a vice-chairman, John Meriwether, had known since late April of irregularities in its Treasury-securities department yet had undertaken no coherent action to stop them until July. Rumours of wrongdoing at Salomon were spreading even before the firm confirmed some of them on August 9th, but nobody knew how high knowledge of them went. This week's answer: right to the top.

Salomon broke rules designed to stop a single bidder from dominating the market in government securities and faked records to cover it up. It is a damning admission for America's oldest primary dealer, a firm that has raised more money for Uncle Sam since 1917 than any other. The repercussions will be all the greater because the market in question is not in any sense marginal, like the junk-bond market, nor can the investors affected be seen as a clutch of get-rich-quick speculators. Treasury bonds are at the heart of America's capital markets, and those who buy and sell them include its most powerful institutions.

Civil suits are being brought against Salomon and individual executives. The firm warns that its

actions may also attract criminal fines and other sanctions including censure, suspension and even exclusion from the government-bond market. It has been "reviewing" matters with the regulators since August 9th and intends to appoint a committee of outside directors to review them further. Appalled investors knocked $1.1 billion—or 26%—off the value of its shares in the week to August 15th.

The main offences that Salomon has admitted to involve breaking a rule imposed a year ago that prohibits a single entity from bidding for or purchasing more than 35% of a Treasury issue. In the December auction

of four-year Treasury bonds (notes, to Americans), Salomon bid in its own name for 35% of the $8.6 billion issue. It also placed an order for another $1 billion as purported agent for a customer who had not, in fact, authorised it to do so. The firm walked away with 48% of the issue. In February's five-year bond auction, Salomon submitted three bids for 35% of the $9-billion issue: one in its own name and two, unauthorised, for clients. It ended up with 57% of the bonds.

A bizarre fiddle, also in February, is interesting not because Salomon broke the 35% limit but because it shows how far out of control its securities operation was spinning. A managing director (now suspended) seems to have persuaded a client to carry out a "practical joke" which went awry, leaving Salomon with an unintended $1 billion-worth of that month's 30-year bond issue.

April and May were more complicated. Salomon not only bid for 35% of the April five-year bond issue on its own account but also asked for $2.5 billion on behalf of a customer, buying back $600m of it at the auction price. The manoeuvre may have been a way of guaranteeing clients a specific quantity despite auction uncertainties.

In May the firm bid as usual for 35% of the $12.3 billion two-year note issue in its own name, repurchased $500m from a customer in circumstances that remain mysterious, and failed to disclose another commitment to buy $497m of the securities when they were issued. At the end of the day it owned 44% of the notes.

Salomon also bid at that auction as authorised agent for two well-heeled clients, including George Soros's Quantum Fund, for a further packet worth up to $6 billion. That brought the firm's total position, as principal and agent, to some 85%. This substantial holding by Salomon and others squeezed dealers who had sold the notes short before the auction and had to scramble to buy them back, other dealers say. The shortage of stock in the market raised the price of the securities sharply, increasing the overall value of the issue by $254m.

Liar's poker redux

Salomon Brothers has blown the whistle on itself, astutely, before the government did it. The firm has suspended Paul Mozer and Tom Murphy, the managing directors in charge of Treasury trading, and two others. Yet the scandal cannot be other than a jarring set-back for the firm's chairman, John Gutfreund. He had been striving to restore Salomon to the prominence it enjoyed in the mid-1980s as Wall Street's leading trading firm, before internal feuding, uncoordinated international expansion and commercial reverses lowered its profile.

His efforts seemed to be succeeding. Salomon had record profits of $451m in the first half of this year. Recently, the firm managed a $3 billion rights offering for Time Warner. But Salomon's worldwide franchise rests on its reputation in Treasury securities. The revelation that he concealed wrongdoing in Salomon's core business may mean that Mr Gutfreund will never now realise his desire to become, once again, the "King of Wall Street".

Whatever happens to Salomon Brothers, America's loose-flying secondary market in government securities (the world's largest, with average daily trading of $118 billion in 1990) is likely to be more tightly regulated. So, too, is the primary market, a privileged group of some 40 firms which have not seen such a squeeze since Japanese banks tried to corner the market in 1986.

Huge leverage and declining interest rates make the Treasury market one of Wall Street's most profitable—and competitive—arenas. Last year it generated $800m in pre-tax profit for firms, half of which went to just five houses. A particularly steep yield curve in recent months has made the market even more lucrative than usual.

Salomon (like other dealers) was able to buy Treasury securities by putting down only 1% of their face value ($10m to buy $1 billion-worth, for example). Then the firm borrowed $990m with the notes as collateral. As the interest rate on Federal funds (the rate at which banks borrow short-term from the Federal Reserve) fell faster than rates on longer Treasury securities, preferred non-bank customers like Salomon were able to borrow on terms only slightly worse than the banks' own. They paid interest at rates up to 150 basis points less than the interest earned by holding the notes.

This "positive carry"—borrowing at a rate of 5.75% and earning between 6.9% and 7.25%—gave government securities an annualised return on investment of nearly 50%. Further profits could be gleaned by curtailing the supply of securities to the market so that their prices would rise.

Yet the biggest everyday problem with the government-securities market is neither leverage nor fiddling but simple murkiness. The Salomon affair will renew calls in Congress to let in more sunshine. The Treasury says that it is sufficiently concerned by evidence of unusual "concentration of ownership" in recent auctions to consider changing its rules. Some lawmakers would prefer to switch regulatory authority to the Securities and Exchange Commission (SEC) from the understaffed Treasury. Neither prices nor positions are now made public; dealers have also been allowed to keep information about their positions in bond-based options and futures offshore.

The SEC would probably tolerate none of that, and would also require firms to hold more capital to back their holdings of government securities. For all their glee that Salomon is being brought low, its rivals will not thank it for that.

....

Mr Gutfreund et al resigned; Warren Buffett, a large shareholder, became interim chairman and Deryck Maughan, a Salomon executive, chief operating officer. They sold a new squeaky-clean Salomon to officials and clients. By year-end, Salomon looked past the worst—and the government had begun to open up its bond auctions.

Deep in bad debt

NOVEMBER 2ND, TOKYO *Japan finally began to face the fact that its banks are stuck in a quagmire of bad debts, as bankruptcies rose and property and share prices fell. Short-term interest rates looked bound to fall—and did*

THE financial establishment in Japan is gingerly facing up to the credit problems of its banks, the world's largest. The *Nihon Keizai Shimbun*, the country's main financial daily, ran a lead story on October 24th about the growth of non-performing loans. It is the first time the newspaper has given the issue such prominence and shows that the topic is no longer taboo. In similar vein the finance ministry has decided to hold hearings on problem loans. Yet the steep decline in the quality of Japanese banks' loan portfolios has been evident for months.

Just how many bad loans are out there is anybody's guess. Japanese banks are not required to disclose non-performing loans. They can even report income from a loan for a year after they have stopped receiving interest on it. The *Nihon Keizai Shimbun* estimated that interest is not being paid on some ¥1.5 trillion ($11.5 billion) of city (commercial) bank loans and on another ¥1.5 trillion of loans held by long-term credit banks and trust banks. Though an understatement, the estimate is interesting. It suggests that the problem lies disproportionately with the much smaller trust banks and long-term credit banks: city banks account for 75% of the loans extended by the three types of bank together, but for only half the estimated bad debts.

Other estimates published in October appear to support that conclusion. *Kinyu Business*, a monthly business magazine, looked at banks' exposure to companies that have gone bust or had to reschedule their debts. The three long-term credit banks are owed ¥2.4 trillion by these debt-

ors alone. That represents 11 times their operating profits last year and 38% of their "hidden assets" (the unrealised gains on the shares they own). Given the lack of adequate provisions against dodgy loans, it is these unrealised share gains that are Japanese banks' effective loan-loss reserves. Worst hit of the three long-term credit banks is the smallest, Nippon Credit Bank. If the magazine's figures are right, it has ¥937 billion of these problem loans, which equals nearly 90% of its hidden assets. Long-Term Credit Bank has ¥857 billion and Industrial Bank of Japan (IBJ) ¥625 billion.

Kinyu Business finds the trust banks in equally grim shape. That is hardly surprising, since they have concentrated on property lending. Their problem loans total ¥2 trillion, eight times last year's operating profits and 31% of their hidden assets. Mitsui Trust is in the worst condition, with ¥570 billion of the total. One of the trust banks' biggest headaches is Juso, a company which they set up, together, with capital of ¥800 billion to provide housing loans to individuals. In the late 1980s Juso lent heavily to property companies instead. It now has debts of ¥2 trillion, and wants the trust banks both to reduce its interest payments and to forgive some of its debts. It may succeed. The trust banks' joint investment in the firm equals 23% of their total capital, so their own survival may depend on Juso's.

By contrast, *Kinyu Business* put city banks' problem loans at ¥2.8 trillion, which is only twice their reported profits last year and 13% of hidden assets. Some banks seem to have avoided trouble better than others. Sanwa, Mitsubishi and Dai-Ichi Kangyo have so far been mostly absent from the list of creditors in publicised bankruptcies and reschedulings; Fuji, Mitsui Taiyo Kobe and Sumitomo have not. Sumitomo's problems

Japanese banks' loan fragility

	Operating profits*	Loans	% of all loans on which non-payment of interest would
	¥bn	¥bn	wipe out profit
Long-term credit banks			
Industrial Bank of Japan	90.9	24,396	6.21
Long-Term Credit Bank	55.9	19,304	4.82
Nippon Credit Bank	19.2	11,453	2.79
City banks			
Dai-Ichi Kangyo	150.1	34,107	7.33
Mitsui Taiyo Kobe	98.7	37,835	4.35
Sumitomo	263.2	31,791	13.80
Fuji	175.4	30,968	9.44
Mitsubishi	161.3	30,748	8.74
Sanwa	210.3	31,263	11.21
Trust banks			
Mitsui	47.7	6,706	11.86
Mitsubishi	55.7	7,513	12.36
Sumitomo	60.1	6,920	14.47
Yasuda	41.4	5,797	11.90

Source: Salomon Brothers   *excludes securities sales

stem mainly from the scandal-infested Itoman, an Osaka-based trading company. If the bank's loans to related companies are included, Sumitomo is owed some ¥650 billion by the Itoman group.

These figures merely tally up known disasters; many more have yet to be made public. David Atkinson, a financial analyst at Salomon Brothers in Tokyo, forecasts that the non-performing loans of city banks, trust banks and long-term credit banks will reach ¥20 trillion, or about 7% of total loans, by the end of March 1992. He thinks that banks will not actually write bad debts off their balance sheets but will allow non-performing loans to accumulate, perhaps planting some on compliant affiliates (as Sumitomo has done with Itoman) until the property market recovers in three to five years. Bank earnings will be hit but their capital, he reckons, will not be wiped out.

This is the least damaging outcome that can be expected. But Salomon also admits a bleaker, less likely, possibility. If soaring bankruptcies became too much for banks to bear, they would have to write off some of these debts. In this case Mr Atkinson says that non-performing loans could total ¥59 trillion and debt write-offs ¥20 trillion. This would eliminate a big chunk of the banks' unrealised share gains, which amounted to ¥28.6 trillion at the end of March, when the Nikkei index was around 26,000. (On October 31st the index closed at 25,222.) Capital ratios would also suffer. Japan's banks are allowed to count 45% of their unrealised gains towards required capital.

If the banks do start writing off bad debts, it will push the stockmarket much lower. Bank shares account for 24% of the Topix index, Japan's version of America's Standard & Poor's 500 and the measure by which most fund managers are judged. If share prices fall generally, banks will have even slimmer unrealised gains with which to absorb loan losses—and hence an even greater capital shortfall.

All this raises the scary prospect of an imploding banking system, with falling asset prices and dwindling bank credit. Monetary policy is likely to be guided increasingly by the need to stave off a crisis in domestic banking. That is just what has been happening in America.

So short-term interest rates will most probably keep falling. They are now about 30 basis points (three-tenths of one percent) above yields on government bonds and may fall below bond yields for the first time in more than two years. Expect Japan's banks to respond to this fall in short-term rates relative to long ones just as their American counterparts have done—by buying safe bonds rather than making risky loans.

The dawning lure of distant shares

NOVEMBER 16TH *As markets in industrialised countries staggered from crisis to crisis, there was good news on another front. Stockmarkets in developing countries are growing up, just as rich investors are feeling ready to invest in them*

"EMERGING MARKETS" once seemed an optimistic term. Now it is really happening. The stockmarkets of Asia and Latin America, plus a handful of others classified as "emerging" by the International Finance Corporation (IFC, the private-sector arm of the World Bank), have collectively grown fourfold since 1985. Last year they provided $22 billion of fresh money for companies. Scarcely a month goes by without a British

or American investment manager launching a fund to take a slice of these markets; on November 14th Peregrine Brokerage, a Hong Kong firm, unveiled a new index of Asian stocks to help British fund managers measure their performance. The IFC reckons that foreigners' stake in the young markets has grown from next to nothing a decade ago to around $17 billion.

By the end of the decade, this sum may

seem paltry. For reasons unconnected with the individual charms of these markets, the world's big savings institutions—pension and mutual funds, insurance companies—are keener to spread their assets internationally; Salomon Brothers, an American investment bank, reckons that the value of cross-border equity flows increased 20 times during the 1980s. As they diversify, fund managers usually establish benchmarks to guide their asset allocation. A popular solution is to allocate money in proportion to the capitalisation of each market. If this were applied to the developing world, the result would be a deluge of foreign capital.

Each year the rich world's savers invest something like $1 trillion of new money in equities. The emerging markets represent 5% of world stockmarket capitalisation, so the benchmark would imply an annual transfer of $50 billion. If the savings institutions also began to shift existing funds to reflect that proportion, the transfers could be much bigger still—perhaps amounting to $100 billion a year, suggests David Gill, a former director of the IFC's capital-markets department. That would dwarf the $14 billion that these countries received in 1990 in direct investment by companies, and more than match the annual $80 billion or so that commercial banks were lending to the developing world on the eve of the debt crisis.

Next, consider the scope for issuing international equity. The new rival to the growth of cross-border equity flows is "cross-exchange" trading: investors buy foreign shares traded in their own country, so reducing the worries of currency risk, foreigners' tax rules and so on. Almost half of London's equity turnover is accounted for by SEAQ International, which lists foreign companies. Salomon Brothers calculates that the volume of cross-exchange equity trading jumped from $583 billion in 1989 to $874 billion last year.

Developing countries have recently begun to exploit investors' appetite for international listings. One example is Telmex, Mexico's telephone company, whose listing on the New York Stock Exchange in May raised $2.2 billion; on October 28th Telmex was that exchange's most actively traded stock. South Korean, Indonesian and Thai companies issued $1.6 billion-worth of international equity and convertible bonds among them during the 18 months from January 1990. Indian and Brazilian rivals are tipped to join in next as big issuers.

The growth of international issues brings two big benefits to the top third-world firms, which together should help them to compete with their first-world rivals. The first is cheaper finance. In May Samsung Electronics, South Korea's biggest company, sold a $100m global depository receipt at a 27% premium to its price on the home market; Mexican ADRs also attract premiums over domestic listings. Such premiums do not merely reflect a primitive home market. In the 1980s Japanese firms found it worthwhile to issue billions of dollars of convertible bonds and other securities abroad, even though their home economy was awash with capital.

Second, the move into international markets works wonders for the image. Telmex's successful New York listing makes it easier for the firm to do deals with international partners—and perhaps, one day,

to market its products or services abroad. This advantage is especially important to Asian companies that have grown by making components or products for established partners, but now face the difficult transition to selling under their own names. How many westerners know that Taiwan's CalComp makes four-fifths of the pocket calculators bearing Casio's brand name; or that CalComp is the biggest calculator-maker in the world?

Making it happen

Successful ADRs depend on successful home listings: like the tourist nervously entering a restaurant, the foreign investor likes

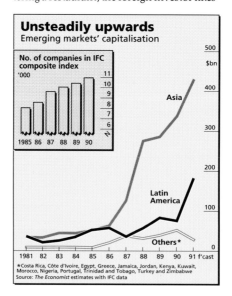

Unsteadily upwards
Emerging markets' capitalisation

to be reassured that the locals share his choice. A healthy home stockmarket is also the precondition for realising those grand projections of foreign portfolio investment. Health depends on three things: opening up markets to foreigners, streamlining their workings, and softening rules that make debt more attractive than equity finance.

This year several countries have moved on the first point. In January Taiwan said it would allow foreigners to invest directly in its stockmarket, though they may still not collectively own more than $2.5 billion-worth of shares. In June Brazil followed, setting no such limit; Peru opened up in September. South Korea has allowed a few foreign brokers to set up shop in Seoul, though it has rejected others and proposes to limit foreign ownership to 10% of the stockmarket. Others lag farther behind. Chile's rules make foreign investments in its market captive for three or more years. India allows no direct investment by outsiders.

Next, the streamlining. Last month Argentina scrapped trading taxes and mandatorily uniform brokers' commissions in the hope of boosting volumes. Foreign investors frequently complain of slow settlement and unreliable custodians; in some cases such troubles cause them to shun a country. In June Manila's stockmarket promised to cut settlement time from three months to ten days. Mexico has been the prince of emerging markets recently, not least because its clearing system is exceptionally efficient.

The bias against equity is less discussed. In part it lies beyond the remit of policymakers: family firms, which dominate many poor economies (and many rich ones), are naturally reluctant to dilute ownership. But governments share responsibility, for their tax systems often make debt cheaper for companies than equity—to a greater extent than is usually the case in developed countries. In South Korea, for example, both corporate and personal tax regimes penalise equity. Moreover, Korea's government has actually subsidised credit to selected companies. It has also insisted that new equity be underpriced: an IFC study of Korean firms going public in 1984-86 put the discount at 40%. Since the average firm in the study sold 26% of its shares, the cost to existing owners was 10.6% of the firm's value. In America the equivalent figure is 0.4%.

The brisk growth of young markets suggests a great success, and one which few would have predicted half a decade ago. If their handicaps can be overcome, however, the existing flow of new equity issues will become a flood. Then the poor world's appetite for equity finance will match rich savers' readiness to provide it.

Share and share unlike

DECEMBER 21ST · PARIS *Minority shareholders in much of Europe get a raw deal. In 1991, they began to demand their rights*

NO LONGER content to be on the outside looking in, minority shareholders in continental Europe are beginning to break down the door. In a recent spate of takeovers they have seen their rights trampled upon, their profits plundered by secretive bosses and their big-shareholder chums. Where once they would have yelped, but little more, disgruntled outsiders are now joining forces and calling their lawyers.

Three cases have sparked shareholder rebellions. The first is a BFr14 billion ($406m) bid in October from Accor, a French hotel company, for Wagons-Lits, a Franco-Belgian travel group. The bid valued Wagons-Lits' shares at BFr8,650 each, a generous 25% above their market price at the time. The price was lower, however, than the BFr12,500 at which Accor valued the company in June 1990, when it bought an option to buy the shares from its ally, Société Générale de Belgique (SGB). Dissatisfied minority shareholders claim that Accor has controlled Wagons-Lits since then, together with the Caisse des Dépôts, a French savings institution that owned 28% of Wagons-Lits.

Accor and the Caisse des Dépôts, which has a 7% stake in the French hotel group, deny co-operating. But on December 4th a judge ordered Accor to increase its bid, and to extend its offer until December 19th. Accor has appealed against the ruling, which could cost it another BFr6 billion. The appeal could drag on for years. Meanwhile, the European Commission froze the bid on December 17th, saying that it had "serious doubts" about the merger's impact on competition in the Community.

Another legal battle involves François Pinault, a French entrepreneur. On November 25th he said that he had paid FFr3.3 billion ($611m) for 41% of Au Printemps, a big retailer which had already attracted the interest of several foreign groups. French law requires anyone owning one-third of a company to bid for at least another third, so Mr Pinault launched an offer for 66%.

Outraged minority shareholders think he should bid for all of Au Printemps. They claim that when Mr Pinault bought his shares, double voting rights on some gave him majority control. Under French law, anyone buying half or more of a company in one go must bid for the remainder. Mr Pinault says that his shares lost their double rights when he bought them. Some claim he controlled over half of the company anyway, because his allies, Crédit Lyonnais and Lazard, also owned part of it. Mr Pinault and the banks deny acting in concert.

The third shareholder spat involves another French company, Exor, which owns a big slice of Source Perrier, the eponymous producer of fizzy water. On November 28th IFINT, a holding company controlled by Italy's Agnelli family, said it held one-third of Exor's shares and would bid for as much again. Investors in Exor immediately said that the bid, which valued Exor at FFr1,320 a share, was too low. To forestall a possible French counterbid led by shareholders including Crédit Agricole and Compagnie de Suez, the Agnellis offered to buy all of Exor. But they refused to raise the price.

Despite protests from minority shareholders of both Au Printemps and Exor, the

Conseil des Bourses de Valeurs (CBV), which oversees the Paris stockmarket, gave the go-ahead to the two bids on December 6th. But the stockmarket's gendarme, the Conseil des Opérations de Bourse (COB), withheld its approval while it investigated transactions in Perrier shares. On December 19th the CBV said that Exor and two other shareholders (both controlled by Société Générale, a bank), had acted together in acquiring more than a third of Perrier's shares, and might have to bid for another third.

Some officials are unhappy with the present takeover regime. Jean Saint-Geours,

COB's president, calls it "perverse". Pierre Bérégovoy, France's finance minister, has said he will consider altering it, if businessmen and the CBV can agree on how.

Minority shareholders in France suffer, but at least they get some protection in law. In Germany a company set on takeover need not make a full or even a partial bid, and buyers must declare only stakes of 25% or more. In practice, hostile takeovers are rare. Most deals are agreed between supervisory boards, and directors are meant to defend investors' interests. Many companies restrict the voting rights of individual shareholders to 5%, making surprise raids harder.

Is this a good thing? Rupert Thistlethwayte of Morgan Grenfell, a British merchant bank that helped Continental, a German tyre maker, defeat a hostile bid from Italy's Pirelli, reckons it is. Without the limit, he says, Conti's minority shareholders would have had to accept a deal that effectively required them to finance the bid. But Continental investors tried to overturn the 5% limit in March, arguing that by hampering a takeover it deprived them of a bid premium for their shares.

For minority shareholders in Italy, even the German system would be an improvement. Italian raiders are not required to disclose any shareholdings in their targets. Nor are they obliged to make even partial bids for companies. A proposed law that would compel anyone acquiring a controlling stake in an Italian firm to bid for the balance of its shares is stuck in the legislative pipeline. It could become law in January, if parliament is not dissolved first.

Governments across Europe are slowly waking up to the plight of minority shareholders. Foreign pressure has helped. A growing number of international unit trusts (mutual funds) and pension funds are investing in European equities. Some have threatened to review their holdings unless minorities get better protection. Norwich Union, a British insurer, is among those taking on Accor. Fidelity, an American investment firm, has challenged the management of Colonia, a German insurer.

The growing discontent is leading some to look to the European Commission for rules. There is a draft directive that would create a pan-European takeover code based loosely on Britain's, requiring a full bid once a one-third stake had been acquired. Another possible directive would enshrine minority rights in other respects. So far, most countries have not cared enough to press those which do to settle their disagreements. That looks like more good news for minority shareholders' lawyers.

Contents

ECONOMICS

The leaders falter

AT THE close of the year the mood in many of the big industrial economies was disappointment mixed with trepidation. Hopes of vigorous recovery from the recessions that began in 1990 were dashed in the closing months of 1991, as output faltered and surveys showed slumping business and consumer confidence. Talk abounded of a "double-dip" recession for the world economy; some even feared that a depression as severe as that of the 1930s was on its way.

The mood had been similar at the start of the year. America's troubled banks and the suspension of the Uruguay round of trade talks in December 1990 recalled the financial collapses and Smoot-Hawley tariffs of the 1930s. War in the Middle East was imminent. Yet the disasters never happened. The Gulf war was over quickly and at little economic cost; the trade talks resumed; America's financial system began to heal itself. It was a year of economic horrors avoided. Few were reassured, however. People remained fearful at the year's end.

One reason was concern over debt—a legacy of the 1980s. During that decade governments changed their priorities in ways that the world economy has yet to come to terms with. First, they turned against inflation. As they won that battle, interest rates fell. Governments also favoured deregulation— which, among other things, released a surge of competition and innovation in banking and finance, especially in Britain and America. Suddenly lenders were keen to lend, and borrowers to borrow. Credit was plentiful and cheap.

Or so it seemed. Low inflation meant that, in real terms, interest rates had gone up, not down: the true cost of debt was higher. So when the economic slowdown of 1990-91 curbed incomes, many found it hard to service their new debts. Creditors felt less secure. Banks became more choosy in their lending (resulting in America's so-called credit crunch); and borrowers began to curb their spending to work off debt. In the second half of 1991 this two-sided contraction in borrowing slowed recovery in Britain and America.

But by the end of the year those faltering recoveries, it was argued, posed the danger of a deepening worldwide recession, driven by further "debt-deflation" in America. That outcome, though possible, was improbable. By December it was clear that America's recovery had paused, but there was no good evidence of a renewed slide into recession. Consumers and companies were learning to live within their means;

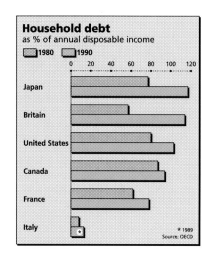

Household debt
as % of annual disposable income

☐ 1980 ☐ 1990

Japan
Britain
United States
Canada
France
Italy

* 1989
Source: OECD

much of that necessary adjustment was complete. And the authorities were, if anything, over-zealous in their determination to avoid a worsening slump. The Fed's easing of monetary policy verged on the reckless in December, when the central bank surprised the markets by cutting its discount rate a full point, to 3.5%. Before long in America, inflation may again be feared as a bigger risk than recession.

In Britain, too, the worst of the recession seemed over by the end of the year—though the government's room for manoeuvre in economic policy had in any case been surrendered (wisely, in the long run) to the disciplines of the European exchange-rate mechanism (ERM). Britain's first full year of ERM membership was a shock twice over. Britain had forsworn devaluation, its customary response to economic difficulties. And it had done so just as Germany's post-1945 halves were reunited, an event that spurred inflation in western Germany and thus in 1991 obliged the Bundesbank to tighten its monetary policy—and hence raise interest rates across Europe.

Perhaps Britain's government hoped that France and other ERM members would call for a full realignment of the system. That would have let Britain devalue, as it were, with honour. But France, which paid its dues for ERM membership in the mid-1980s, was now committed to exchange-rate stability. That commitment was strengthened by all the ERM partners (save Britain) at December's European summit in Maastricht, when the Community pledged itself to create a single European currency by the end of the decade. So the continent offered Britain no way of wriggling off its ERM hook. By the turn of the year, John Major was rejecting calls for a devaluation that would have stripped his government of all economic credibility—demands that came, all too often, from those who had welcomed sterling's entry into the ERM little more than a year before.

Pessimists pointed to slowing growth in Japan as further evidence of the coming global slump. But, as in Germany, the slowdown in Japan was hardly unwelcome. Both economies had been overheating (output grew by 7% in Japan and by 5% in Germany, at an annual rate, in the first half of the year). Again as in Germany, Japan's central bank had raised interest rates to keep inflation in check. During the summer it became clear that demand was cooling, however, and the Bank of Japan began to ease—though much more cautiously than America's Fed. If, as the OECD predicted in December, growth was to slow in the first

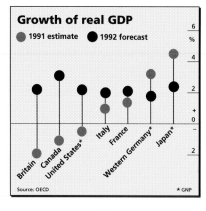

Growth of real GDP

● 1991 estimate ● 1992 forecast

Britain
Canada
United States*
Italy
France
Western Germany*
Japan*

Source: OECD

* GNP

half of 1992 to maintainable rates in Japan and Germany, while recovery gathered pace in Britain and America, the industrial countries were wrong to be so gloomy: they could look forward to moderate expansion and low inflation.

Undeniably, the shocks of the 1980s—disinflation and deregulation—have left the industrial countries with an adjustment problem. But it looks manageable; viewed from Eastern Europe, it looks trivial. No economic shock this century has been more violent in its impact than the collapse of communism—the starkest example there could be of long-term gains at the cost of a painful transition. After falling a long way in 1990, output is guessed to have dropped in 1991 by another 20% in Bulgaria, 12% in Czechoslovakia, 7% in Hungary and 8% in Poland. These ferocious declines were due partly to the collapse of soft-currency COMECON trade (especially with the Soviet Union), to tight macroeconomic policies designed to curb inflation and, above all, to the difficulties of replacing the defunct apparatus of central planning with properly functioning markets.

Throughout Eastern Europe, radical reform continued during the year. Prices have been freed, currencies made convertible and trade barriers eliminated. New commercial laws were written, often from scratch. Foreign investment was not just permitted but eagerly sought. IMF programmes were put in place and official assistance from various national and multinational sources began to flow. This was more progress than many had thought likely. But two worries remained. Ambitious privatisation schemes were slow to appear and were then delayed, so by the end of the year industries remained largely under state control. And signs of exhaustion appeared—not least in Poland, which had hitherto been the boldest reformer. Doubts remained over whether political support for reform could be maintained.

Eastern Europe had the consolation of knowing its sacrifices were not for nothing: its goals were clear. For the Soviet Union, 1991 was, in economic terms, one more wasted year. As the central-planning system failed, output plunged, probably more steeply than in Eastern Europe—but to no purpose. By the summer, Mikhail Gorbachev and his officials had proved themselves incapable of economic reform. In politics, perestroika worked miracles; in economics, it achieved nothing. By accelerating the demise of the union and its central bureaucracies, August's failed coup was a blessing in disguise. In the closing days of 1991, Russia under Boris Yeltsin looked ready to lead the commonwealth of independent states down the hazardous path of economic transformation.

In the 1980s the shock of dear-money disinflation in the in-

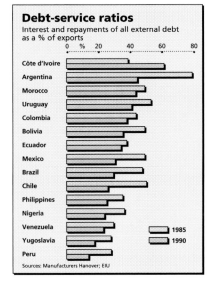

Debt-service ratios
Interest and repayments of all external debt as a % of exports

Côte d'Ivoire
Argentina
Morocco
Uruguay
Colombia
Bolivia
Ecuador
Mexico
Brazil
Chile
Philippines
Nigeria
Venezuela
Yugoslavia
Peru

1985
1990

Sources: Manufacturers Hanover; EIU

dustrial countries touched the third world in the form of the debt crisis. Another blessing in disguise? Many of those distressed debtors have since embarked on reforms of their own. In 1991 the reformers gained confidence from the visible ruin of the socialist alternative. In Latin America, countries such as Chile have been joined by more surprising converts to economic orthodoxy, such as Mexico and Argentina. During the year Mexico moved towards re-establishing normal relations with the international capital markets; other Latin American debtors also tapped the markets for new (voluntary) funds.

Elsewhere in the third world, too, liberal economics gained ground in 1991. Most surprisingly in India, where a new government cast aside 40 years of poverty-creating dogma and called for more trade and foreign investment. Most subtly in China, surrounded as it is by more conspicuous models of East Asian success, but whose southern Guangdong province was possibly the world's fastest-growing region in 1991. That was thanks to economic freedoms and the creation of something close to private property, as the government in Beijing continued to let the province move "one step ahead".

In 1991 the big industrial countries—those champions of liberal capitalism—thus made an odd contrast with the reformers of Eastern Europe and the third world. As the rich countries fastened their eyes on short-term growth, the others attempted structural change with the long-term in view.

That contrast was clearest in the Uruguay round of trade talks—the year's biggest economic disappointment. After the talks resumed early in the year, they made good progress until foundering again on farm trade, with America continuing to insist on stronger reforms to Europe's absurd common agricultural policy than the EC was willing to concede. In December, already a year late, the talks became deadlocked once more. If America and Europe let them fail, it will be a historic triumph of short-term irresponsibility over long-term vision—and a bitter reward for the reforming countries of Eastern Europe and the third world, which will prosper through trade, or not at all.

Dunkel: Mr GATT

Tuesday 1st
The first day of **China**'s new five-year plan. At the meeting of the Communist Party's central committee, just ended in Beijing, the battle between reformers and hard-liners continued. Despite the earlier crackdown, the economy continued to grow (at 7.5% a year during 1986-90), the private sector fastest of all.

Wednesday 2nd
The Bush administration said that parts of the **American economy** were "clearly in recession", claiming that the last quarter of 1990 would have been the worst. The Commerce Department's index of leading economic indicators fell twice as much as expected during November.

Saturday 5th
Poland's new prime minister, Jan Bielecki, promised faster privatisation and appealed for the country's (mainly official) foreign creditors to forgive much of its $50-billion debt. Comecon countries met to agree on dismantling the communist trading block.

Tuesday 8th
Britain detailed its idea of a **hard ecu**, a Euro-currency that would exist alongside national ones, but that could in time replace them, if users wanted it to. Some other European governments restated their preference for more rapid progress towards full monetary union. This would require a single European currency created by government fiat, and a European central bank to issue and control it.

Praising **Czechoslovakia**'s progress as it entered the hardest part of its reforms, the IMF lent it $1.8 billion, the most it has ever granted to an East European country.

Wednesday 9th
John Major, the prime minister, said the recession in **Britain** would not be as bad as people feared. But company profits suffered their steepest quarterly drop since 1981.

Monday 14th
Amid uproar in the Baltics, Mikhail Gorbachev appointed a **new Soviet government**. The new prime minister was Valentin Pavlov, a former finance minister under the discredited Nikolai Ryzhkov, and a member of the damage-limitation school. Bold reformers such as Grigory Yavlinsky (the architect of last year's radical Shatalin plan) and Nikolai Petrakov were left to complain from the sidelines.

Tuesday 15th
Arthur Dunkel, director-general of the **GATT** told trade officials he was "cautiously optimistic" that negotiations on agriculture, which had caused the Uruguay round of trade-liberalisation talks to collapse in December, would soon re- sume. The EC had resisted America's demands for radical reform of its common agricultural policy. Mr Dunkel said he detected new flexibility on both sides.

Explaining why prices in **Brazil** went up 1,400% in 1990, despite ten months of a radical anti-inflation plan, President Fernando Collor blamed Saddam Hussein and the price of oil. In fact, vital parts of the plan (especially privatisation) had been strangled by the bureaucracy. Mr Collor resorted to new wage controls.

Retail sales in America declined by 0.4% in December according to the Commerce Department. As a result, sales grew only 3.6% for all of 1990, the smallest annual rise since 1982, the last time **America's economy** was in recession.

Wednesday 16th
The real war began in the **Gulf**. The price of oil fell sharply on early news that the battle was going well for America and its allies. Over the next two days, stockmarkets soared all over the world but the dollar confounded forecasters by falling sharply. Fears of global recession began to lift.

$ trade-weighted exchange rate 1985=100
Source: Bank of England

Monday 21st
Finance ministers of the **G7** countries met to discuss the recent weakness of the dollar and the outlook for exchange rates. They said they would intervene in the markets if need be. They agreed to reward Egypt for its role in the Gulf war by writing off a third of its foreign official debt. There was talk that Poland might soon win a similar deal.

Tuesday 22nd
Manufacturing output in **Britain** fell more sharply than since 1981. A survey by chambers of commerce pointed to falling orders and deepening pessimism on employment.

Another setback for perestroika. Aiming to curb inflation, the **Soviet Union** "reformed" its currency by cancelling 50-rouble and 100-rouble banknotes (worth roughly $2.50 and $5 at the street exchange rate) and limiting bank withdrawals. Panic followed.

Saturday 26th
A survey of **economic forecasts** in industrial countries showed gathering gloom over the prospects for America, Canada and Britain.

An auctioneer accepted the first bids in the sale of some state-owned enterprises in **Czechoslovakia**. Sixteen small shops were sold for a total of 22m koruna ($800,000). The government declared the sale a great success, but warned of many difficulties to come—not least, opposition to the ambitious privatisation programme from the managers of big state-owned monopolies.

Monday 28th
At the continuing inter-governmental conference on European economic and monetary union, France and Spain offered compromise ideas for slowly adopting a **single European currency**.

Thursday 31st
The **Bundesbank** raised its benchmark Lombard and discount rates by half a percentage point, to 9% and 6.5%, respectively.

February

Friday 1st
The day after the Bundesbank raised German interest rates, the Federal Reserve cut **American interest rates** by half a point. The dollar slid further.

Japan's current-account surplus for 1990 was its smallest for five years, at $36 billion.

With inflation raging, Domingo Cavallo, the new and radically pro-market finance minister of **Argentina**, ordered the country's banks to close and announced a crash package of economic reforms—the eleventh since Carlos Menem became president. The banks were closed in **Brazil**, too: the cruzado had collapsed over the previous few months.

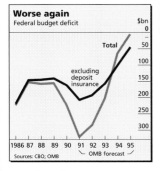

Worse again
Federal budget deficit

$bn

1986 87 88 89 90 91 92 93 94 95
Sources: CBO; OMB   OMB forecast

Monday 4th
The Bush administration unveiled new plans for **America's budget**. They foresaw a deficit of $318 billion in fiscal 1991, falling to less than $50 billion in 1995.

Tuesday 5th
Toshiki Kaifu, Japan's prime minister, continued to face attacks over his plan to contribute $9 billion, raised through taxes, to the allied war effort in the Gulf. The protests reflected the state of the **Japanese economy**. After growing by more than 6% in 1990, it showed new signs of slowing down.

The **GATT** talks were in peril again. EC farm ministers met to discuss proposals from the European Commission for changes in the Community's CAP. These aimed to reduce production and export subsidies, and top up farmers' incomes instead. Europe's ministers were not keen. American senators threatened to remove the administration's fast-track negotiating authority unless Europe changed its tune.

Saturday 9th
Daim Zainuddin, finance minister of **Malaysia** since 1984, resigned. Mr Zainuddin was a principal architect of his country's largely successful economic reforms. His formula was rigour in public spending plus bold deregulation. Malaysia became one of South-East Asia's most successful economies; its GNP grew 10% in 1990.

Tuesday 12th
Amid news of soaring bankruptcies, record mortgage repossessions and rising unemployment, the Bank of England cut **British interest rates** by half a point; base rates fell to 13.5%. The chancellor, Norman Lamont, said that fighting inflation remained his top priority.

The annual presidential report on the **American economy** said that America's recession would be short and mild, that the unemployment rate would rise no higher than 6.7% (from its present 6.2%) and that growth would resume in the early summer. Recession might have been avoided, the report went on to say, had the Federal Reserve not kept interest rates too high

in early 1990.

Alberto Fujimori, president of **Peru**, rebuilt his cabinet and appointed Carlos Bolona as finance minister. Mr Bolona, Oxford-educated, had previously worked with Hernan de Soto (author of "The Other Path") at Peru's Liberty and Democracy Institute. He took charge of an economy in ruins. His first job: to get back on speaking terms with the IMF.

Wednesday 13th
Six **monetarists** (including Sir Alan Walters, formerly an adviser to Margaret Thatcher) wrote to *The Times*; they deplored the government's policies and called for a devaluation of the pound.

Thursday 14th
Finance minister Theo Waigel predicted that **Germany's budget deficit** would be DM69.5 billion ($47.5 billion) in the current year; the broader measure, which includes all parts of the public sector, would reach DM131 billion, or nearly 4.5% of GDP. Anxiety over the costs of unification mounted.

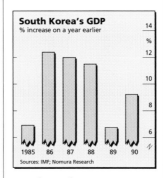

South Korea's GDP
% increase on a year earlier

1985 86 87 88 89 90
Sources: IMF; Nomura Research

Tuesday 19th
Lee Seung Yun, deputy prime minister for economic planning of **South Korea**, lost his job. The economy had grown quickly on his watch (GNP went up 9.2% in 1990), but inflation was approaching 10% a year (on the government's massaged figures) and the trade balance had moved into

the red for the first time in five years. Economists prescribed tighter money, testing a young democracy.

The **GATT** talks resumed in Geneva. The deadlock over farm-trade reform was broken when Europe agreed to talk about cuts in three areas: internal farm supports, border protection and export subsidies.

Wednesday 20th
Federal Reserve chairman Alan Greenspan said that **America's recession** might bottom out soon.

Tuesday 26th
Another compromise plan for European EMU, this time from Germany. **Monetary union** must be based on greater economic "convergence", and be supervised by a fully independent central bank. Such a bank should not be created until 1997 at the earliest. The European Commission was disappointed.

The government announced increases in **Germany's taxes** and social-security payments amounting to DM55 billion ($37.5 billion).

Initial agreement was reached between **Poland** and the IMF on a three-year economic programme. This was expected to pave the way for $2 billion in loans from the IMF and much more besides in official debt-relief. Poland promised to make a first instalment on paying off its arrears to foreign banks.

Wednesday 27th
Britain lowered interest rates by half a point—the second cut this month. Base rates fell to 13%, and banks and building societies cut their mortgage rates. The National Institute of Economic and Social Research said unemployment would rise by 500,000 by the end of the year.

Friday 1st
The parliament of the **Soviet Union** passed a law giving citizens a qualified right to buy and sell foreign currency at uncontrolled exchange rates. The reform took the rouble a step towards convertibility.

Saturday 2nd
Commercial banks agreed a debt-rescheduling and buy-back deal for **Nigeria**, whose external debts of $35 billion were the biggest in sub-Saharan Africa.

Tuesday 5th
A survey of businesses in **Japan** showed that high interest rates and the Gulf crisis had failed to dent confidence in the economy. **America**'s recession appeared to be deepening: figures showed that new orders for manufactured goods fell again, by nearly 2%, in January.

Wednesday 6th
The **GATT** said that it would look into America's complaints that the German government had been illegally subsidising the Airbus, an aircraft built by a consortium of European manufacturers. It was the most recent of many American complaints over the Airbus programme.

Thursday 7th
Representatives of the government of **Kuwait** said the country would need to borrow $20 billion to help rebuild its shattered economy.

Germany announced its first

monthly current-account deficit since the early 1980s, as the slump in eastern Germany continued to prove much worse than expected. Government economists had predicted that recovery would start in the summer; now they said unemployment would more than double, to nearly 2m, by the end of 1991.

Friday 8th
America's **Federal Reserve** signalled a modest easing of monetary policy. Nicholas Brady, America's treasury secretary, said there was "plenty of room in the economy" for the Fed to ease.

Monday 11th
Concerted intervention by the central banks of Germany, America, Britain and some smaller European countries failed to check the **dollar**'s rise. It climbed to DM1.58 and ¥138. Traders attributed the currency's strength to worries about unrest in the Soviet Union (which add to the dollar's attraction as a safe haven).

Thursday 14th
Unemployment in **Britain** rose to more than 2m. February's increase of 85,600 was the biggest since 1980. As the recession deepened, earnings continued to rise at more than 9% a year.

Fernando Collor, president of **Brazil**, marked his first anniversary in office by announc-

ing a new and wide-ranging National Reconstruction Plan. Mr Collor's earlier policies brought inflation down (from 80% a month to 20% a month) but at the cost of a deep recession; promised microeconomic reforms have been slow to materialise.

Friday 15th
The **Spanish peseta** hit its ceiling in the European Monetary System, and the Bank of Spain cut its benchmark interest rate to ease upward pressure on the currency.

Western governments said they would forgive roughly half of **Poland's official debts**.

Monday 18th
Traders reported panic buying of the **dollar**. Fears about the costs of German unification made the D-mark its principal victim. It rose to DM1.63, and to $1.79 against the pound.

Following Poland's debt-relief agreement, the government of **Peru** asked for similar treatment from the Paris Club of creditor governments. Otherwise, the economy minister said, Peru would be forced to stop paying interest. The country's new government had resumed payments only last October.

Tuesday 19th
Norman Lamont, Britain's chancellor of the exchequer, unveiled his first **budget**. He cut the controversial poll tax and made good the loss of government revenue by increasing value-added tax from 15% to 17.5%.

Wednesday 20th
Yasuhi Mieno, governor of the **Bank of Japan**, again rejected demands for lower interest rates.

Thursday 21st
The European Commission started legal action to break

down national monopolies in the **European energy market**. It wanted suppliers to be able to use the network of gas pipelines and electricity grids across the whole Community, allowing users to buy power from the cheapest source.

The Joint Economic Committee of Congress called for measures to spur the **American economy**. It told the Fed to cut interest rates, and the administration to reform unemployment insurance and spend more public money on infrastructure.

Argentina's economy minister, Domingo Cavallo, promised to peg the austral to the dollar and back it with gold and hard currency.

Friday 22nd
Norman Lamont followed his budget by cutting **British interest rates** by half a point to 12.5%. Businessmen had hoped for a bigger cut.

Brazil's government suspended exports of **coffee**, apparently in a new attempt to cartelise the market. The price of coffee futures soared.

Tuesday 26th
The presidents of Brazil, Argentina, Uruguay and Paraguay signed the treaty of Asuncion, which committed them to create a **South American free-trade area** by 1994.

Friday 29th
The **dollar** continued to climb, reaching DM1.70 (up 18% from its low-point in February), ¥141, and $1.71 against the pound. In America, sales of new homes were up and an index of leading indicators showed its first rise since June.

Czechoslovakia sold 70% of Skoda, the state-owned carmaker, to Volkswagen. The government has promised VW protection from imports of new and used cars.

April

Tuesday 2nd
The **Soviet Union** introduced a long-delayed set of price reforms. State-controlled prices for bread and meat trebled; prices of other consumer goods also went up. Prices increased by 60% on average, according to the government. People were promised (less-than-matching) rises in wages and pensions to compensate. The reform was meant to bring demand into line with supply. But the queues stayed long and the shelves stayed empty.

Speculation that the Federal Reserve was about to cut American interest rates and the Bundesbank to raise German ones caused the startling recovery of **the dollar** to pause. The currency eased to DM1.67 and ¥138.

Wednesday 3rd
The foreign ministers of Mexico, Colombia and Venezuela said they planned to create a **Latin American free-trade area** by 1994. This followed a similar announcement from the governments of Brazil, Argentina, Uruguay and Paraguay on March 26th.

Thursday 4th
The German finance ministry said that the **Treuhand**, the agency responsible for restructuring and privatising east German industry, would need to spend roughly DM400 billion over the next ten years. Otherwise, instead of equipping enterprises to survive in the free market, it would be forced to close them.

The "spring offensive"—the annual wage-round in **Japan**—drew to a close. Trade unions accepted employers' arguments that wage increases needed to be smaller this year because of slower economic growth. Despite earlier demands for rises of 8% or more, most unions had been willing to settle for 6% or less.

Wednesday 10th
The government of **Sweden** announced new measures to deal with an unaccustomed problem: rising unemployment. It said it would spend an extra SKr6 billion ($980m) to provide 40,000 more places in training.

Friday 12th
For the fourth time in two months, the Treasury cut **British interest rates** by half a point. Banks and building societies said they would cut their mortgage rates.

Consumer prices fell in **America** in March, the first such drop for five years. The annual rate of inflation was 4.9%, against 5.3% in February. Many expected the Fed to cut interest rates on the news, but it did not. Rumours persisted of a split at the Fed.

Sunday 14th
Finance ministers of the **G7** countries met in London for informal talks. There was friction over burden-sharing and the Gulf. Germany, under American pressure to pay more, believed it had received too little credit for rebuilding

eastern Germany and helping the Soviet Union. Nicholas Brady, America's treasury secretary, asked Japan for faster payment of its promised contribution.

Monday 15th
International action to help **Poland** was interrupted when Japan held up a $500m loan, in protest at the American-led decision to forgive much of the country's debt. The Japanese government said it opposed debt-forgiveness on principle.

Tuesday 16th
Europe's trade policies were attacked by the **GATT**. The harshest criticism was directed at the deals Europe had negotiated with countries such as Japan to limit imports of cars, electronic equipment and other goods.

Thursday 18th
In talks about a new capital increase for the **World Bank**, American officials urged the institution to lend less to governments and state-owned enterprises and more to the private sector.

Friday 19th
According to new figures, output in the **Soviet Union** fell nearly 10% in the first quarter of 1991, and the volume of foreign trade (much of it with the struggling economies of Eastern Europe) fell 34%.

Monday 22nd
The **dollar** rose to a 16-month high at DM1.76, ¥139 and $1.70 against the pound. The D-mark was weakened by the setback for Chancellor Kohl in Germany's state elections.

South Korea took another step towards reforming its conglomerates, or *chaebol*. The government had told each group to choose the three subsidiaries it planned to develop as a core business; other subsidiaries would be then de-

nied investment incentives. The idea was to promote specialisation. But when the Office of Bank Supervision and Exchange published the groups' submissions, it appeared that the *chaebol* wanted to concentrate on the same businesses: petrochemicals, cars and electronics.

Wednesday 24th
New forecasts from the **IMF**, released in advance of a meeting of G7 finance ministers and central-bank governors, were optimistic about the global economic outlook. They predicted growth in world output of 1.2% in 1991, recovering to 2.9% in 1992. Emphasising the growing demands for investment capital worldwide, the Fund told governments to promote savings.

Friday 26th
America threatened to impose **trade sanctions** on Japan unless it agreed within 30 days to improve access for American companies to Japan's construction market. The Bush administration also told China, India and Thailand that they would face sanctions unless they took steps within nine months to improve their protection of intellectual property rights (patents, trademarks and copyrights).

Sunday 28th
The **G7** finance ministers and central-bank governors met in Washington, DC. Nicholas Brady, America's treasury secretary, urged them to cut interest rates and President Bush personally backed his appeal. The response was frosty: Theo Waigel and Karl Otto Pöhl of Germany, supported by officials from Japan and Britain, said their first priority was to reduce inflation.

Tuesday 30th
America's **Federal Reserve** surprised the markets by cutting its discount rate half a percentage point to 5½%.

May

Wednesday 1st
The Bush administration sent Congress an "action plan" on **trade policy** to win support for its fast-track negotiating authority. This was due to expire in June, threatening both the Uruguay round and a proposed free-trade agreement with Mexico. The administration promised to restore tariffs if imports surged; to pay for retraining people who lose their jobs because of freer trade; to appoint environmentalists to trade-policy committees, and so on.

Friday 3rd
An official committee of economists warned that wages in **eastern Germany** were rising too fast. Unemployment, at about 10% of the labour force, had risen much faster than expected in eastern Germany since unification.

Monday 6th
American officials said they would launch a second, and broader, complaint at the GATT about subsidies for the European **Airbus**. America had already brought an action on Germany's exchange-rate support for Daimler-Benz, one of the companies in the Airbus consortium. The new complaint would be about subsidies for development and production costs.

The government of **South Korea**, struggling to reduce inflation, blamed the construction industry for the economy's overheating and said it would allow no new commercial building until the end of Sep-

tember. It also told businesses to sell land that was not directly related to their business interests; those that refused would face new borrowing restrictions.

Tuesday 7th
British officials said that no decision had been taken whether to invite **Mikhail Gorbachev** to July's economic summit in London—an idea first suggested by Margaret Thatcher at the 1990 summit in Houston.

Wednesday 8th
The European Community agreed to impose **anti-dumping duties** on imports of Japanese audio cassettes. It dropped an earlier complaint against imports of tape used to manufacture audio cassettes within the EC.

Thursday 9th
President Fernando Collor of **Brazil** appointed Marcilio Marques Moreira, a banker and diplomat, to replace Zelia Cardoso as economy minister. Many officials resigned along with Ms Cardoso, a fervent supporter of Mr Collor's plans to curb inflation and deregulate the economy. Her reforms had met much opposition and made little headway; her combative style had caused offence at home and abroad. The government promised a more "consensual" approach: it sounded worrying.

Sunday 12th
A meeting of EC finance ministers tentatively agreed on a compromise that might allow **European Monetary Union** to go ahead despite British reservations. Jacques Delors, president of the European Commission, said that Britain could sign a treaty on EMU later this year without committing itself to the final goal of a single currency. But officials said this might oblige Britain to drop, or "modify", its hard-ecu proposal.

Monday 13th
America's industrial production increased by 0.1% in April after six consecutive months of decline. Economists greeted this as the best evidence so far that **America's recession** had bottomed out.

Mikhail Gorbachev signed a decree establishing a "special regime" for some sectors of the **Soviet economy**. Officials said it would improve incentives for workers to raise output. Earlier Valentin Pavlov put the idea in a different light: he said the decree would let the government arrest workers who went on strike, or called for one.

Wednesday 15th
With the country's inflation rate continuing to fall, the Reserve Bank of **Australia** cut its benchmark rediscount rate by one percentage point to 11%.

Thursday 16th
Karl Otto Pöhl, president of the Bundesbank for the past 11 years and one of the most respected economic policy-makers in the world, resigned. He denied falling out with Cahncellor Kohl and said it was for personal reasons.

Edith Cresson, France's new leftist prime minister, fiercely attacked Japanese protectionism. But she reassured financial markets by reappointing **Pierre Bérégevoy**, a conservative, as finance minister.

British inflation

"Headline"
(official retail-price index)
12-month rate

Source: Central Statistical Office

Friday 17th
Britain's inflation fell from

8.2% in March to 6.4% in April, the sharpest drop since the early 1980s. Most of the fall was due to changes in interest rates and taxes.

Wednesday 22nd
Mikhail Gorbachev said he wanted to be invited to the **G7** summit in July, to talk about international co-operation in support of perestroika. He endorsed the efforts of Grigory Yavlinsky to design another plan for reform with academics at Harvard University.

Thursday 23rd
America's House of Representatives voted to extend the administration's **fast-track authority** for trade negotiations. (The Senate passed a similar resolution the next day.) The decision was expected to revive the Uruguay round of GATT talks, stalled since December because of America's disagreement with Europe over farm-trade reform. The administration also hoped for progress towards a free-trade deal with Mexico.

Friday 24th
The Bank of England cut **British interest rates** by half a percentage point, to 11.5%.

Wednesday 29th
Helmut Schlesinger, a career central-banker and a staunch defender of price stability, was named to a two-year term as head of Germany's **Bundesbank**. On his retirement in 1993, the job will go to Hans Tietmeyer, a former finance minister whom many had expected to take over immediately.

Friday 31st
George Bush met Yevgeny Primakov, a close adviser to Mikhail Gorbachev. They discussed **Soviet economic reform**. Mr Bush said the meeting was "very positive" but made no promises about aid or about inviting Mr Gorbachev to the G7 summit in July.

June

Angle of unreality
Foreigners' share of Japanese semiconductor market

Share expected by America following 1986 deal

Actual

1986 87 88 89 90 91

Source: Semiconductor Industry Association

Tuesday 4th
America and Japan signed a new **semiconductor agreement** to cover the next five years. The pact obliges Japan to increase the share of imported semiconductors to 20% of its market by the end of 1992. American computer-makers had criticised a similar, earlier agreement for causing shortages of semiconductors and raising their prices. Carla Hills, America's top trade official, said the agreement "was aimed at enhancing free trade".

Wednesday 5th
Mikhail Gorbachev, accepting the Nobel peace prize in Oslo, pleaded for economic aid from the West, but did not put a figure on the amount needed. At a meeting of the OECD in Paris, officials said the **Soviet Union** could not expect big injections of cash until economic reform was under way.

Thursday 6th
Britain's prime minister, John Major, said Mr Gorbachev should be invited to visit London during the forthcoming **economic summit**. He would not take part in the formal G7 meetings, an official said, but could talk to G7 leaders after the summit had ended.

Friday 7th
New figures showed that **employment in America** went up in May by 59,000. Most analysts had expected a drop. Alan Greenspan, chairman of the Federal Reserve, said that

evidence of economic recovery was mounting.

Monday 10th
The central banks of Europe (led by the Bundesbank) and Japan intervened heavily in the foreign-exchange markets to check the rise of the **dollar**.

Bengt Dennis, chairman of the **Bank for International Settlements** (the central banks' bank) warned the industrial countries not to relax in their fight against inflation.

Germany saw its trade balance move into deficit in April, for the first time in ten years. (Its current account had been in the red since January.) Unification had caused a boom in western Germany, resulting in a surge of imports. Meanwhile fast-rising wage costs had caused a deep slump in the east, and were now jeopardising the whole country's longer-term competitiveness.

Wednesday 12th
Grigory Yavlinsky and a team of economists from Harvard University led by Graham Allison announced that they had drafted a plan for Soviet economic reform—henceforth known as the **Yavlinsky plan**. The authors wanted the West to promise aid of roughly $35 billion a year in exchange for a phased transition to a market economy. Mr Yavlinsky said he spoke for both Mikhail Gorbachev and Boris Yeltsin.

Japan's trade surplus grew sharply in May.

Friday 14th
Sweden said it would apply to join the European Community, aiming to achieve full membership by 1995. A referendum to endorse the terms of entry was planned; it would coincide with the general election after next, due to be held in 1994.

Monday 17th
Britain rejected a draft plan for **European monetary union**, objecting to a new formula that said the EC was a "union with a federal goal". In a speech to the Chicago Council on Foreign Relations, **Margaret Thatcher** attacked the "dangerous illusions" of "little Europeans".

Tuesday 18th
In a new survey of **Greece**, the OECD praised the government's efforts to reform the economy, but doubted whether they would succeed. Targets for lower public borrowing (to fall from nearly 20% of GDP in 1990 to 3% in 1993) were "ambitious", said the report, and estimates of privatisation proceeds might prove optimistic. Reform of the state pension system was urgently needed; at 15% of GNP, Greece's pension bill was the highest in the OECD.

Wednesday 19th
Efforts to curb inflation in **Argentina** were set back when the Congress rejected a bill to defer wage bonuses due to be paid in June and December. The ruling Peronist party remained an unlikely champion of reform; the wage bonuses in question had been introduced by Juan Peron in 1946.

Thursday 20th
In a speech in London, Helmut Schlesinger, president-elect of the Bundesbank, said that Britain would need to free the **Bank of England** from political control before participating in the final stages of EMU.

Friday 21st
The new government of **India** appointed Manmohan Singh as its finance minister. Mr Singh, an economist widely respected outside India, was formerly the governor of the central bank. His daunting task: to contain the government's soaring budget deficit and win further financial support from the International Monetary Fund, without undermining support for the fragile coalition government.

Sunday 22nd
Finance ministers and central-bank governors of the **G7** countries met in London to discuss the dollar's recent rise and aid for the Soviet Union. Their communiqué was non-committal on both points.

Wednesday 26th
Gyorgy Suranyi, the head of the central bank of **Hungary**, said that GNP had not fallen as much as official figures showed. These failed to reflect growth in the booming private sector. Like other East European officials, he cited electricity consumption as a better guide to activity. This showed a rise of 2% in the first four months of 1991, despite a drop of up to 20% in output of steel and other energy-intensive products.

Thursday 27th
New privatisation plans were announced in **Poland**. These aimed to place a first group of 400 enterprises (accounting for 25% of industrial output and 10% of employment) in private hands as soon as possible. Ownership of the enterprises would be divided between a number of closed-end investment funds. These would have Polish chairmen but be run, most likely, by foreign advisers. The plan would give every Polish adult shares in the funds; these would be tradeable from 1993. Many details remained to be worked out.

July

Monday 1st

The Bank of Japan cut its discount rate half a point to 5.5%. The **dollar** rose to ¥138 and DM1.83—its highest level against the D-mark for more than 18 months.

Sweden applied for membership of the European Community. The Community's leaders welcomed the announcement.

A new law in **Russia**: unemployed workers can henceforth register for benefits and for help in finding work. The authorities had previously insisted there was no joblessness in the Soviet Union.

Wednesday 3rd

The semi-annual forecasts of the **OECD** predicted an unspectacular recovery from the economic slowdown. Growth in the industrialised countries in 1992 would average less than 3%, its economists said—too slow a rate to reduce unemployment.

Thursday 4th

New economic reforms were announced in **Romania**. The authorities said they would float the currency (the leu); in 1990 Poland's government, in contrast, had designed its reforms around a fixed zloty. Many more prices were to be liberalised in 1991.

Monday 8th

Mikhail Gorbachev said that he had reached agreement with the **Soviet republics** on a radical economic-reform programme. Officials said the plan would be presented to western leaders at the forthcoming G7 summit in London, when Mr Gorbachev hopes to win moral and financial backing.

Wednesday 10th

George Bush said that he would nominate **Alan Greenspan** for a second four-year term as chairman of America's Federal Reserve.

Germany announced a plan to reduce public spending on subsidies. In a speech aimed partly at the Bundesbank, Theo Waigel, the finance minister, said his budget for 1992 showed his government's budget deficit was under control. The subsidy cuts will amount to roughly DM10 billion a year until 1994.

Friday 12th

The **Bank of England** signalled a cut in interest rates of half a percentage point; bank base rates fell to 11%.

Monday 15th

Hopes of an **American economic recovery** were boosted by new figures for industrial output, which showed a strong and broadly based rise in June.

Tuesday 16th

At the **G7 economic summit** in London, the leaders of the big industrialised economies agreed to offer the Soviet Union a "special relationship" with the International Monetary Fund and the World Bank. Nobody knew what that meant. Beyond repeated pledges of technical support, there were no firm promises of financial support. Privately, western leaders expressed doubts over the prospects for economic reform. The summit partners promised to bring the Uruguay round of trade talks to a successful conclusion.

Thursday 18th

Edith Cresson, France's prime minister, offered further opinions on Japan. She said the Japanese were "ants", living in inhuman conditions. Even her protectionist allies in the Socialist Party seemed embarrassed.

Friday 19th

Ray MacSharry, the European Community's commissioner for agriculture, said that the summit had made no difference to the **Uruguay round**. Europe had offered as much as it could on farming; there was no support for more. Concessions would have to come from other countries.

Tuesday 23rd

It was announced that the **Soviet Union** had formally applied for full membership of the International Monetary Fund, not the (undefined) associate status that had been agreed to at the economic summit. America said it opposed full membership for the moment. The IMF said it was ready to deliver technical assistance immediately.

Wednesday 24th

India announced new economic reforms, including a liberalisation of the licensing system for domestic investment, one of the most oppressive in the non-communist world. Also, foreign investors would henceforth be welcomed. Other changes were promised. If carried through, they would amount to the most radical reform of the Indian economy for decades.

Thursday 25th

The OECD told **Germany** that wages in eastern Germany were rising too quickly. Helmut Schlesinger, due to take over as head of the Bundesbank in August, echoed the warning. He said that inflation was rising in western Germany, too, and hinted that interest rates might have to go up.

Friday 26th

The **European Community** agreed that Japan should be able to sell cars freely in the EC after 2000, but continued to argue about the transition. The European Commission favoured control over "transplants"—Japanese cars made in factories in Europe, notably Britain.

Saturday 27th

Manmohan Singh, the reformist finance minister of **India**, announced that talks with the IMF on new lending would begin immediately. The country was facing a balance-of-payments crisis and remained desperately short of foreign exchange. India wanted the Fund's "stamp of approval" as well as its cash, Mr Singh said.

Alexander Yakovlev, one of the Soviet Union's most committed reformers, said he was leaving Mikhail Gorbachev's team of advisers. It was said he was tired of attacks from the Communist Party, including a recent investigation of his activities. Many regard Mr Yakovlev as the architect of perestroika.

The government of **Ukraine** said it would issue coupons to protect its food and consumer goods, plentiful by Soviet standards, from consumers from other republics. This was seen as a step towards adopting a separate currency.

Tuesday 30th

George Bush, visiting Moscow, said America would give the Soviet union **most-favoured-nation** status as a trade partner. Tariffs against Soviet imports such as furs and vodka would come down. Western trade experts said the change had little value except as a symbol. Mikhail Gorbachev said the West needed to do much more.

August

Thursday 1st
Mexico and Chile said they would sign a **free-trade agreement** soon. Mexico's negotiations to create other free-trade areas (with Venezuela, Colombia, its central American neighbours and the United States) would continue.

Friday 2nd
Payroll **employment in America** fell in July, according to new figures, for the second consecutive month. This, together with the recent slow growth in most measures of the money supply, added to fears that America's recovery was about to fizzle out.

Wednesday 7th
Australia protested to Europe's governments over the European Community's sales of **subsidised wheat** on world markets. Meanwhile Australian farmers complained about America's subsidised wheat sales in Australia's traditional export markets in Asia and the Middle East. America and Australia had previously seen eye-to-eye on farm-trade reform.

Inflation in **Brazil** increased again, to 11.3% in July, equivalent to 260% a year. Further rises looked likely: consumers, anticipating the promised unfreezing of their savings accounts later in the month, were spending eagerly. In a setback to its earlier efforts to deregulate the price system, the government reintroduced price controls on a range of foods.

Thursday 8th
Viktor Geraschenko, the head of **Gosbank**, the Soviet Union's central bank, threatened to starve the Soviet republics of roubles; otherwise, he said, the economy faced hyperinflation. Mr Geraschenko singled out the Russian central bank for refusing to co-operate either in day-to-day operations or in talks to create a new central-bank council, composed of representatives from all the republics.

America's International Trade Commission ruled that Japanese companies were guilty of **dumping** word-processors on the American market.

Friday 9th
Despite recent slumps in share and property values, the **Japanese economy** would keep growing, according to the country's Economic Planning Agency. The fall in share prices had reduced consumer spending through the so-called "wealth effect", said the agency, but cheaper land might spur new investment in housing. Few private economists were so optimistic.

Tuesday 13th
Extending its recent economic reforms, **India** improved its incentives for exporters. Companies in export-processing zones, or entirely devoted to exports, would be allowed to keep 30% of their foreign-currency earnings. The government also shortened the list of goods that private companies are forbidden to import.

Wednesday 14th
To help the country's farmers and fishermen compete with foreign producers after agricultural markets are opened to imports, the government of **South Korea** announced a big new investment programme.

During the Uruguay round of the GATT talks, American trade negotiators had renewed their calls for South Korea to open its rice market.

Thursday 15th
The **Bundesbank** raised its discount rate from 6.5% to 7.5%; it raised the closely watched Lombard rate by only a quarter of a point, to 9¼%. Holland, Belgium and Denmark immediately followed with increases of their own. The bank's new president, Helmut Schlesinger, had earlier expressed concern at the upward trend of German inflation.

America's International Trade Commission ruled against Japanese producers for the second time this month. It said flat-panel displays for personal computers were being sold too cheaply. As a result, **anti-dumping duties** were imposed on two manufacturers. Many American computer-makers complained, saying they used the screens in their own products. IBM called the ruling "an eviction notice to the fastest growing part of the US computer industry".

Friday 16th
Britain's inflation rate fell, from 5.8% in June to 5.5% in July. The underlying rate (excluding mortage-interest costs) fell from 6.9% to 6.8%.

America's industrial output rose 0.5% in July, the fourth monthly increase in a row. Commentators saw it as evidence that the recovery was still under way, after all.

Monday 19th
Mikhail Gorbachev was ousted from power in a **Soviet coup**. Boris Yeltsin, president of Russia, called a general strike. Stockmarkets plunged around the world. The safe-haven dollar climbed from DM2.92 to DM2.96.

German share prices
December 1st 1953=100
Commerzbank index
2,000 / 1,900 / 1,800 / 1,700 / 1,600
A S O N D J F M A M J J A
1990 — 1991

Wednesday 21st
The **Soviet coup** collapsed—a triumph for Mr Yeltsin, who bravely led the resistance. The central Soviet government looked fatally weakened and the task of economic reform, as a result, all the harder. Shares rallied worldwide.

Thursday 22nd
Western commentators called for massive **Soviet aid**, arguing that the failure of the coup had swept away opponents of reform. John Major, chairman of the G7 leaders, said a new aid package should be discussed. America's government remained sceptical.

Monday 26th
Fernando Collor, president of **Brazil**, called for a constitutional amendment that would make it easier for him to raise taxes and cut public spending.

Wednesday 28th
A new four-man committee to take charge of the **Soviet economy** was appointed. Its members were Grigory Yavlinsky (a co-author of the earlier aid-and-reform plan designed by professors at Harvard University), Arkady Volsky (in charge of industry and transport), Ivan Silayev (Russia's prime minister, to take charge of defence and security) and Yuri Luzhkov (food and farming).

Thursday 29th
George Bush and John Major agreed to a six-point plan for **Soviet economic aid**. It offered food aid, other humanitarian help and technical assistance—but little cash.

September

Sunday 1st
Privatisation claimed its newest convert: **Albania**. The government said it had approved new laws to reform the banking system and privatise state enterprises. It also announced plans to peg the lek to the ecu.

Tuesday 3rd
Reflecting the mounting costs of unification, **Germany's fiscal deficit** would be DM50 billion ($29 billion) in 1992, according to the government's new draft budget. Even so, the new estimates allowed for a public-spending rise of only 3% over 1991. The opposition again accused the government of deceiving voters over the true cost of unification.

The central bank of **Australia** cut its benchmark interest rate (the cost to banks of overnight funds) from 10½% to 9½%, the lowest for seven years. (The rate had reached a peak of 18% in early 1990.) Many private economists criticised the move, saying the economy was pulling out of its recent recession in any case.

Thursday 5th
The Congress of People's Deputies, the highest parliament in the **Soviet Union**, dissolved itself and, in effect, handed power to the republics. An Interrepublic Economic Committee, led by Grigory Yavlinsky, was to supervise the economy for the time being. A new economic plan, the most radical yet, was said to be in the making.

Friday 6th
France and other countries objected to a plan to open the EC's steel, textiles and agricultural markets to **trade with Eastern Europe**. Uffe Ellemann-Jensen, Denmark's foreign minister, called the decision "a disgrace".

Monday 9th
Carlos Menem's Peronist party did better than expected in mid-term gubernatorial elections in **Argentina**—a vote of confidence, it seemed, in privatisation, deregulation and the government's other radical economic reforms.

The government of **New Zealand** announced plans to privatise the retail part of its electricity industry by giving shares to every adult.

Wednesday 11th
The **Soviet Union** sent the European Community a request for $7 billion in emergency food aid. In Brussels, Jacques Delors, the commission's president, called on the G7 countries to respond with immediate offers of at least $2 billion.

Japan announced another big rise in its trade surplus, to $6 billion in August. Separately, the French minister for foreign trade and industry said that Japanese car makers plan to drive their EC rivals out of business once Europe's market is fully open after 2000.

Friday 13th
The Federal Reserve cut its discount rate by half a point to 5%. Other **American interest rates** eased as a result. Recent figures for retail sales (sluggish) and inflation (falling) were cited as reasons for the cut.

Tuesday 17th
Nicholas Brady, America's treasury secretary, said that the **International Monetary Fund** had been too slow in sending economic advisers to help the Soviet Union. IMF officials said it was hard to say who they should be dealing with; also, the associate membership of the Fund that had been granted to the Soviet Union in July was still undefined.

Wednesday 18th
Helmut Schlesinger, the head of the **Bundesbank**, said that the worst of Germany's recent spurt of inflation was over.

Thursday 19th
Economic growth in **Japan** slowed to an annual rate of 2% in the second quarter. The figures were worse than expected, and led to renewed calls for the Bank of Japan to cut interest rates.

Yuri Luzhnov, a deputy prime minister of the **Soviet Union**, told EC officials that his country needed $15 billion in food aid, not $7 billion as requested a week earlier.

Friday 20th
The World Bank announced that rich-country donors had promised **India** $7 billion of aid during the current year. In addition, the IMF was likely to reach agreement soon on loans of nearly $2 billion.

Sunday 22nd
At a meeting in Apeldoorn in Holland, Europe's finance ministers agreed to the outline of a new agreement on **economic and monetary union**. The ministers said that the decision to proceed to a single currency must be taken jointly by all 12 members of the Community, though some (including Britain, presumably) might be allowed to join later than others. They claimed this understanding ought to end talk of a "two-speed Europe".

Monday 23rd
Saudi Arabia said it wanted to raise its output of **oil** by about 10% during the third quarter. This would mean an OPEC production ceiling of roughly 24m barrels a day instead of the present 23m barrels. Delegates preparing to attend an OPEC meeting were taken aback but, two days later, agreed to the change.

Thursday 26th
New figures confirmed the depth of America's recent recession. GNP in the second quarter fell by 0.5%; the first official estimates had said that output expanded by nearly that much.

Friday 27th
George Bush met Alan Greenspan, the chairman of the Fed, and, according to the White House, asked him to do something to ease **America's credit crunch**. Mr Bush believed that this was less a matter of cutting interest rates again than of helping banks to be less reluctant to lend. To that end, the Fed was asked to rein back "overly strict bank examiners".

Monday 30th
The European Community reached a compromise agreement to allow East European countries better access to their **agricultural markets**. The aim, in effect, was to balance extra imports from Eastern Europe with an increase in subsidised exports to the Soviet Union, leaving EC farm output roughly unchanged. Some attacked the idea as an attempt to extend the community's ruinous common agricultural policy eastwards.

October

Tuesday 1st
New forecasts from the **IMF** predicted a moderate economic recovery. Growth in the world economy would quicken from a projected 0.9% in 1991 to 2.9% in 1992.

Wednesday 2nd
Germany's cabinet approved a new regional structure for the **Bundesbank**. Helmut Schlesinger, the bank's president, supported it. Unification had brought five new states into the federal republic. Under the old rules this would have increased the number of state central banks from 11 to 16, with an increase from 16 to 21 in the seats on the policy-making council. The new plan creates nine regional banks and shrinks the membership of the council to 14. Some states said it was unconstitutional.

Thursday 3rd
Aiming to protect the region's fragile environment, the **Antarctic Treaty**, signed by 39 countries, banned mining in the continent for 50 years.

Friday 4th
The new prime minister of **Sweden**, Carl Bildt, took office promising to cut taxes, promote competition and efficiency in the country's large public sector, and foster private enterprise. Mr Bildt's right-of-centre Moderate Party led a potentially unstable four-party coalition.

Monday 7th
The International Energy Agency said the global demand for **oil** was rising—a portent of economic recovery?

The EC said it would give 1.3 billion ecus ($1.5 billion) of additional **Soviet aid**, so long as America, Japan and the other industrialised countries contributed another $5.5 billion. The money would be earmarked for food and medical supplies.

Tuesday 8th
Japan said it would contribute $2.5 billion towards the new package of Soviet aid that the EC proposed on October 7th.

Washington announced changes in bank regulations to spur lending and speed the **American economy**. George Bush again blamed the recession on the "credit crunch".

Thursday 10th
Jurgen Möllemann, Germany's economics minister, said that Germany, France and Ireland would not block a deal between the EC and America on farm trade. The fate of the **Uruguay round** still turned on the farm-trade issue. Officials in Geneva were unsure whether Germany's change of mind would break the deadlock.

America began an investigation into **China's trade policies**. China's exports to America had lately soared; Washington's protectionists had therefore made common cause with supporters of sanctions on human-rights grounds.

Ronald Coase won the **Nobel prize** for economics. Mr Coase, emeritus professor of economics at the University of Chicago, was cited for work on the theory of the firm, property rights and transactions costs.

Boris Yeltsin promised to relax state controls on **Russian prices** soon. He warned of a hard winter ahead.

Wednesday 16th
The parliament of **Romania** voted in a new coalition government headed by Teodor Stolojan. The new prime minister said he would press ahead quickly with further economic reforms and call an election "as soon as possible".

Thursday 17th
A batch of disappointing figures dampened optimism about the **American recovery**. George Bush called Congressional leaders to the White House to discuss a possible "growth package" of tax cuts to stimulate demand. Any such deal might cause the earlier pact on the budget deficit to fall apart. Michael Boskin, chairman of the council of economic advisers, said that the Fed might have to cut interest rates again.

At the annual meeting of the **IMF and the World Bank**, this year held in Bangkok, Lewis Preston, the Bank's new boss, said the Bank should not lend more to the private sector; America had been urging such a change. The Soviet delegation, headed by Grigory Yavlinsky, was a shambles; it left G7 officials shaking their heads in dismay. Helmut Schlesinger, president of the Bundesbank, said Mr Yavlinsky's team was a "mirror image of the state of the Soviet Union".

Friday 18th
Eight of the 12 remaining **Soviet republics** signed an economic-union treaty, aiming to create a common market for trade and to co-ordinate efforts at financial stabilisation and economic reform. Ukraine, the second richest republic, did not sign.

Monday 21st
Facing an economic slump and mounting unemployment, **Finnish unions** accepted pay cuts of 7%.

Tuesday 22 1d
The EC and EFTA agreed to create a **European Economic Area** at the beginning of 1993. The aim was to ease the flow of goods and services between the two blocks by lowering all barriers to trade.

Thursday 24th
The **dollar** fell sharply against the D-mark on more disappointing news about the American economy, and further talk of an impending cut in interest rates.

Sunday 27th
The prospects for continued economic reform in **Poland** suffered a blow. In their first free vote for a national legislature in more than 50 years, Poles chose confusion. Six parties linked to Solidarity and backing the reform programme failed to win a majority. It was unclear who would head the new government.

Monday 28th
Alan Greenspan, chairman of the Fed, said that **America's credit crunch** was "utterly unprecedented".

Boris Yeltsin made his clearest and boldest statement yet on **Soviet economic reform**. Prices would be freed, the budget deficit cut, the banking system reformed and most enterprises privatised. He said Russia would go it alone if need be: it might issue its own currency, and would refuse to fund the central bureaucracy. Mr Yeltsin said he would serve as his own prime minister so there would be no doubt about where responsibility lies.

Wednesday 30th
The Fed let a benchmark interest rate ease slightly, signalling a further loosening of monetary policy. The federal funds rate fell from $5\frac{1}{4}$% to 5%.

November

Friday 1st

More evidence of slowing **growth in America**: the unemployment rate rose from 6.7% to 6.8% in October and the index of leading indicators fell for the first time since January. The dollar fell to DM1.64 and ¥130.

Japan's trade surplus widened in September, adding to fears of trade friction between Japan and America. Fujitsu withdrew an offer to give American researchers a supercomputer after complaints on Capitol Hill.

Monday 4th

Vitold Fokin, prime minister of **Ukraine**, said he would sign the Soviet economic-union treaty. Many politicians in Kiev, capital of the republic, were dismayed.

The EC said America must abandon unilateral trade retaliation as part of any **Uruguay round** agreement.

Tuesday 5th

An official of the Soviet Bank for Foreign Economic Affairs raised the spectre of a **Soviet debt default**. The bank did not have enough hard currency to meet its obligations in November, he said.

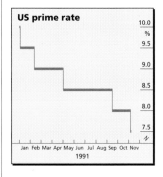

US prime rate

Jan Feb Mar Apr May Jun Jul Aug Sep Oct Nov
1991

Wednesday 6th

The Federal Reserve cut **America's discount rate** from 5% to 4½%. The banks cut their prime lending rates from 8% to 7½%.

Both Ukraine and Moldavia

signed the Soviet **economic-union treaty**. Only Georgia and Azerbaijan remained outside the agreement. Officials from the G7 met to discuss the threat of a Soviet debt default.

Thursday 7th

The prospects for an agreement on **Japanese car imports** into the EC dimmed when France, Italy and Spain blocked a deal on common car standards, needed as part of the single-market programme. The three countries set tight quotas for Japanese cars, fearing a surge in "parallel imports" from Japanese factories in Britain and elsewhere in the EC after 1992.

Workers in **Greece** staged a 24-hour general strike in protest at the government's austerity programme.

Saturday 9th

George Bush, Jacques Delors (president of the European Commission) and Ruud Lubbers (the Dutch prime minister and leader, on rotation, of the EC heads of government) met in the Hague, mainly to discuss the **Uruguay round**. They said they had narrowed differences on farming, financial services and other issues.

John Major, Britain's prime minister, and Helmut Kohl, chancellor of Germany, met in Cologne to discuss European **economic and monetary union**. Britain wanted no mention of a "federal" Europe in the revised Treaty of Rome and an opt-out clause for countries not wanting full EMU; Germany said closer political union was a precondition for EMU.

Monday 11th

In **Sweden**, the new government said it would privatise 35 state-owned companies worth $50 billion.

Officials of the G24 industrial countries met in Brussels to

discuss **aid for Eastern Europe**. The EC's finance commissioner, Henning Christopherson, said America was doing too little.

Wednesday 13th

The **Bank of Japan** cut its discount rate from 5½% to 5%.

America's Senate voted to cap the interest rate that banks charge on **credit cards**. Earlier George Bush had criticised banks for failing to pass cuts in interest rates on to their borrowers; then he attacked the Senate's measure and a similar one before the House of Representatives. Analysts said the new rule would hit banks hard.

Thursday 14th

After a heavy run on the currency, the Finnish authorities said they would unpeg the **markka** from the ecu and let it float.

Friday 15th

Wall Street tumbled, the Dow Jones industrial average falling nearly 4%. Analysts blamed the **mini-crash** on: gloomy economic data; signs of panic in the White House; the proposed cap on credit-card charges; the imminent collapse of the deficit-reduction accord; and so on. The dollar fell. There was talk of another Black Monday.

Monday 18th

It didn't happen. Share-prices bounced back 1% on **Wall Street** after losses in the European markets were smaller than feared. The dollar steadied against the yen at ¥129 but fell further against the D-mark, to DM1.61. The House of Representatives withdrew its bill to cap credit-card interest rates.

The D-mark's rise put the franc under pressure. The **Bank of France** raised its benchmark intervention rate by half a point to 9¼%.

Sterling too came under pressure but, with an election approaching, Britain's government was determined to avoid raising interest rates.

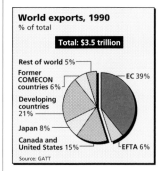

World exports, 1990
% of total

Total: $3.5 trillion

Rest of world 5%
Former COMECON countries 6%
Developing countries 21%
Japan 8%
Canada and United States 15%
EC 39%
EFTA 6%
Source: GATT

A technicality delayed the signing of the EC-EFTA **free-trade pact**, agreed to and initialled on October 22nd.

Thursday 21st

In a deal on official **Soviet debt**, the G7 agreed to defer repayment of principal, extend new credits and set up a $1 billion emergency fund.

Friday 22nd

Russia's parliament voted to bring the former Soviet State Bank and the Bank for Foreign Economic Affairs under the control of the **central bank of Russia**.

Tuesday 26th

Jurgen Möllemann, Germany's economics minister, said **the dollar** was too low. The markets promptly pushed the dollar 1½% higher against the D-mark, to DM1.61.

Wednesday 27th

OPEC ministers meeting in Vienna agreed to keep their wells running at nearly full capacity during the winter. But they said they still wanted to see the **price of oil** rise from its present $19 a barrel to $21.

America said it would put steep tariffs on **imports from China** unless the Chinese government tried harder to protect American patents and copyrights.

Sunday 1st

Russia's government took control of the **Soviet finance ministry** and said it would consolidate its own budget with that of the Soviet Union—its condition for paying the centre's wages and other bills.

Monday 2nd

A survey of corporate purchasing managers showed that manufacturing output in **America** barely rose in November, adding to fears of a faltering recovery.

George Stigler, a professor at the University of Chicago, winner of the Nobel prize for economics in 1982, and one of America's most distinguished economists, died.

Wednesday 4th

Just days after its deal with the G7, the **Soviet Union** suspended repayments of principal to foreign banks, but promised to pay interest.

In their long-running quarrel over **subsidies**, the European Commission accused the American government of indirectly supporting its aircraft makers at a cost of $22 billion since the mid-1970s.

Thursday 5th

Despite fears of rising inflation, the **Bundesbank** decided not to put interest rates up just days before the Maastricht summit. But it hinted that a rise might come soon.

Sweden's central bank astonished financial markets by increasing its benchmark interest rate six percentage points, to 17½%. The bank said it was determined to quash rumours of an impending devaluation.

Bolivia, Colombia, Ecuador, Peru and Venezuela signed the **Andean pact**, which creates a free-trade zone from the start of 1992, with common external tariffs to follow.

Friday 6th

Following news that employers had cut their payrolls in November, the Federal Reserve eased **American monetary policy** further by cutting its federal funds rate a quarter of a point, to 4½%.

Sunday 8th

Russia, Ukraine and Belorussia established a new **commonwealth of independent states**, seen as successor to the fast-vanishing Soviet Union. Leaders of the republics said they would co-ordinate plans for economic reform.

Monday 9th

At the **Maastricht summit**, the EC's leaders reached agreement on their plans for a single European currency. They promised that if a majority of the 12 meet criteria for economic convergence in 1996, they will move to EMU in 1997; if not, any countries that qualify by 1999 will go ahead then, however few they may be. The criteria (on inflation, interest rates, budget deficits and government debt) were demanding: only three of the summit countries currently met them. **Britain** was given an opt-out clause: it would decide later whether to join in.

The **Bank of Japan** said its closely watched survey of business confidence in Japan fell in the previous three months. Financial markets began to anticipate an easing of monetary policy.

Friday 13th

The European Court of Justice ruled that judicial aspects of the recent agreement between the **EC and EFTA** countries to form a single market spanning both groups violated the Treaty of Rome. The European Commission said it would try to answer the court's objections.

Monday 16th

The EC signed new trade agreements with **Czechoslovakia, Hungary and Poland**, giving the ex-communist countries better access to Europe's markets. The agreements also provided for regular consultation and looked ahead to EC membership.

Tuesday 17th

Commercial banks gave officials from Vnesheconombank, the Soviet bank for foreign trade, permission to withhold repayment of principal on **Soviet debt** until 1992. They hoped the new and rapidly enlarging commonwealth of former Soviet states would honour the deal.

Greece was paralysed by a one-day general strike, called in protest at the government's economic policies.

Wednesday 18th

Alan Greenspan, chairman of the Federal Reserve, told Congress that **America's recovery** had "clearly faltered", but he warned it would be a mistake to boost the economy with tax cuts that widened the budget deficit. The markets concluded that a cut in interest rates was not imminent and the dollar edged up, to DM1.57.

Thursday 19th

The **Bundesbank** raised its benchmark discount rate by half a point, to 8%. The move greatly surprised the markets, which, in the days since the Maastricht summit, had come to expect no further tightening of German monetary policy. Bundesbank officials said that the rise was necessary despite slowing economic growth, because German wage settlements continued to be inflationary. The news was especially unwelcome in Britain, where the government feared it might have to raise interest rates to defend the pound within the ERM.

The **OECD**'s new economic forecasts projected average growth of between 2% and 2½% in the industrial countries during 1992.

Friday 20th

The Federal Reserve shocked the financial markets by cutting **America's discount rate** a full percentage point, to 3½%. Many analysts welcomed the move; others accused Alan Greenspan, the Fed's chairman, of panic, inconsistency and buckling to pressure from the White House. The **dollar** closed sharply lower, at DM1.53.

Democrats in America's Congress threatened legislation to curb **Japanese car imports** unless Japan's trade surplus with America narrowed.

Sunday 22nd

Attempts to conclude the **Uruguay round**, already running a year late, by the end of 1991 were abandoned. The negotiators adjourned with Europe seeming to reject last-minute plans from Arthur Dunkel, the GATT's director-general, for farm-trade reforms. Every deadline breached, the talks were due to resume on January 13th.

Sunday 29th

Robert Mosbacher, America's commerce secretary, said that **Japanese trade policies** had been partly responsible for America's recession and slow recovery.

Monday 30th

The **Bank of Japan** cut its discount rate half a point, to 4½%. George Bush, who was shortly due to visit Japan, welcomed the move.

As we reported then

The value-subtractors

JANUARY 5TH *Standard economics assumes that devaluing the currency makes firms competitive. In Eastern Europe, we argued, this may not be true. Many enterprises are so inefficient that they would fail at any exchange rate*

THINKING on economic reform in Eastern Europe has, up to now, drawn heavily on experience from the third world. A reforming government first needs to stabilise its economy—ie, cut its budget deficit and stop printing money in order to finance whatever deficit remains. After that it needs to open its economy to international trade and, most likely, devalue its currency; this will align domestic prices with prices in world markets and force the economy to use resources more efficiently. This advice makes sense for most developing countries, but is it relevant to Eastern Europe?

In one respect, at least, the answer is no. The standard third-world prescription heavily underplays private property. In most developing countries, private ownership is already the rule. Producers are obstructed by governments in all sorts of ways, but enterprises are, by and large, private. In the ex-communist countries almost all enterprises are still owned by the state.

Governments are coming to understand the importance of privatising quickly. However, the past year's changes in eastern Germany and Poland point to another mistake in the standard prescription: its advice on trade policy.

Eastern Germany and Poland opened their economies to the outside world all at once—eastern Germany on July 1st 1990, the day of its monetary union with western Germany; Poland on January 1st 1990, the day of its "Big Bang" of economic reforms. Since then both have seen output fall sharply. Enterprises have sacked workers and are running at much less than their full capacity. Many have shut down.

Eastern Germany and Poland have this in common, even though their exchange-rate policies were quite different. German monetary union converted old East German marks one-for-one into D-marks. At such a rate the East German mark was overvalued. Poland, in contrast, devalued the zloty by 31% on January 1st 1990. This approach, according to the standard thinking, should have made Poland's producers more competitive. Yet the fall in Poland's output since its reforms began has been as severe as in eastern Germany.

In some ways, the comparison is misleading. Unlike Poland, eastern Germany can count on economic support in the form of subsidies and inward investment. Even so, the contraction in Poland's output—despite the fall in the zloty—raises doubts about the efficacy of devaluation.

In a book to be published soon ("The Order of Economic Liberalisation: Financial Control in the Transition to a Market Economy"), Ronald McKinnon of Stanford University suggests a disturbing reason why devaluation may fail in Eastern Europe.

For most purposes it is enough to know that an enterprise makes losses—that its revenues are less than the sum of its wages, its cost of capital and its cost of material inputs

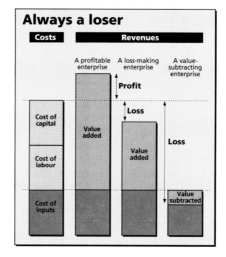

Always a loser

(raw materials, components, energy and so on). But, in principle, an enterprise might be so inefficient that its revenues fail to cover even the cost of materials. Such an enterprise is an absurdity: it uses scarce capital and labour to subtract value from its other inputs (see chart). Valuable metal, plastic, cardboard, rubber, energy go in at one end; Trabant cars worth less than the sum of these parts emerge at the other.

The distinction between making losses and subtracting value is crucial for exchange-rate policy. Devaluation makes an enterprise more competitive by reducing its labour costs measured in foreign currency. Note that devaluation does not affect the cost, measured in foreign currency, of capital or material inputs; in an open economy, these will command their world-market price. A barrel of oil costs Poland so many dollars regardless of the zloty's exchange rate. Even domestically produced coal has a given value in foreign-currency terms.

Because devaluation can cut labour costs, it can make a loss-making enterprise profitable. But a value-subtracting enterprise loses money even if labour (and capital) are free. It is beyond such help.

Value-subtractors have been spotted in many of the worst-run developing countries, but they are rare. In Eastern Europe they are probably much more common. Socialist planners deliberately underpriced energy and other inputs. So what might seem, at local prices, an ordinarily loss-making factory could be a value-subtractor. Poland's price system now works, but even there the true extent of value-subtraction is hard to guess. Many of the enterprises that have survived the first year of reform are still at risk. They are hanging on by refusing to pay suppliers. That cannot last.

In their recent joint report on the Soviet economy, the IMF and other multilateral agencies urged the Soviet Union not to move to free trade overnight, but to set a temporary tariff of 30%. Their reason was that many of the country's enterprises will be uncompetitive at any "realistic" exchange rate. The idea of value-subtraction goes further: it deletes "realistic". But the implication for policy is similar. These countries should move gradually to free trade. All-at-once liberalisation could flatten a large part of the economy overnight.

To give enterprises a chance to adjust and to avoid a crunch that would undermine support for reform, governments might need to start with high tariffs, promising to eliminate them over, say, five years. Adopting initial tariffs of even 100% would still be a bold reform; the implicit tariffs set by the planners approach infinity.

The third-world prescription was clear: liberalise trade immediately and leave privatisation for the longer term. Poland did this. Its reforms have not failed, but they are proving terribly painful. Eastern Germany aside, the rest of Eastern Europe has been economically timid, and the Soviet Union has done next to nothing. When these reluctant reformers are willing to take their chance, they might be wise to do the opposite of what Poland did. They should privatise as fast as possible, and preferably all at once; but then go carefully on trade.

The next 100 years

MARCH 9TH **This article concluded a series on the modern classics of economics, by looking ahead to the next century of economic research. In 2091, confounding its many critics, a recognisable version of the subject will still exist. But its aims and methods will have changed**

WRITERS of science fiction think of economics, if at all, as an evil necessary only for the time being. In their imagined futures, the present arrangements for the production and exchange of goods and services have usually vanished—either because capitalism suffers an environmental or other catastrophe that returns the world to an anarchic dark age, or because the world achieves such material super-abundance that economic choices no longer have to be made. These are entertaining but improbable visions. Scarcity, and economic interaction as a means of dealing with it, may well be inescapable facts of human life.

Like it or not, economists are here to stay. What sort of economists the world will need, and what sort it will get, are harder to predict. The Royal Economic Society has just released the centenary issue of the *Economic Journal*. To mark the occasion, the editor, John Hey, asked some of his most distinguished contributors to speculate on the next 100 years of economics. Anybody who has found this series of briefs interesting would enjoy reading many of those articles in full. But time is scarce. So here are some thoughts gathered from the anniversary issue, together with a few that were not.

Outside looking in

Non-economists unanimously criticise economists on two counts: for lack of "relevance", and for being unable to agree about anything. Will this judgment stand? And if it does, will economics not wither and die?

Consider, first, the charge of irrelevance. Unquestionably, economists are an increasingly isolated tribe. As Milton Friedman points out, the early volumes of the *Economic Journal* were "something of a cross between a strictly professional journal and a journal of broad though specialised coverage, appealing to an audience like that served today by, say, *The Economist*". Today's *Economic Journal* is aimed at a narrow professional audience, few of whom would expect to understand every article.

Businessmen still have a hearty appetite for economic forecasts (perhaps the least useful good that economists produce), but even this appears to be diminishing. Corporate economists have suffered heavy casualties during the present recession in Amer-

ica. The predictions of large-scale macro-econometric models are regarded with ever greater disdain by economists and non-economists alike. Meanwhile, many theorists seem to be engaged in work that will have neither readers nor any conceivable application outside their own circle.

Yet this picture of inward-looking degeneration is inaccurate. As economics grows more sophisticated, it is bound to become more forbidding to outsiders. As a developing social science, economics will

need its corps of specialised technicians and theorists. The question is whether their work will feed through to those engaged in policy advice and other punditry. In due course a good deal of it will.

That leaves the charge of perpetual disagreement. Unlike the natural sciences, economics does not seem to be converging on a fuller, truer account of the processes it examines. Instead it appears to be drifting pointlessly from one debate to the next; nothing is ever settled. Again, however, this is wrong. Economics is concerned with human behaviour, which is unstable in ways that physical events are not. As Lord Robbins said, "The influence of the Reformation made no change in the forces of gravity. But it certainly must have changed the demand for fish on Fridays." Still, economics is making progress; areas of disagreement will narrow and areas of consensus will broaden.

If this trend has not been obvious it is partly because non-economists tend to be more interested in macroeconomics (which is still comparatively weak) than in microeconomics (which can speak with more confidence). It is also because many economists are bad communicators, mischief-makers, or both. They set themselves shamefully low standards in public debate. (In American universities, many economists

commonly refer to the articles they write for popular consumption as "shlock".) Disagreements over substantially non-economic questions are carelessly mixed up with narrower economic issues. Differences are exaggerated, areas of agreement brushed aside. Outsiders see naught but confusion.

In fact, the areas of agreement are already wide. Macroeconomics is at present between paradigms. The neoclassical synthesis of the 1950s and 1960s has broken down and has yet to be replaced. However, the idea of rational expectations (as a working assumption, at least) is no longer controversial; and the crucial role of expectations, rational or otherwise, is universally accepted. The remaining disagreements have spurred New Keynesian research that suggests a new paradigm which will account for market failure instead of merely asserting it. This is progress.

The methodology and central ideas of classical microeconomics are agreed upon. So, by and large, are the prescriptions for policy that flow from those ideas. Across a broad range of questions—from peak-load pricing in transport and utilities, through the case for tariffs over quotas, to the harm done by minimum-wage laws—economists agree. For their own sake, though, they must learn to talk to outsiders.

The new questions that economics will try to answer will, as in the past, be influenced by history. Recently the world has witnessed the collapse of communism in Eastern Europe. In the anniversary issue of the *Economic Journal*, James Buchanan of George Mason University argues that the end of the biggest ideological battle of the 20th century will make economics more fruitful from now on. In the post-socialist century he expects a less polarised debate and a revival of normative argument; that is, less insistence on "objectivity" and a greater willingness to recommend.

Jagdish Bhagwati of Columbia University points to the growing integration of the global economy. Twenty years ago, students (especially in America) were raised on models that assumed the economy to be closed. Now this approach is well on the way to being abandoned. In future, international flows of goods, capital and (increasingly) labour will be the focus of economic research.

A third historical trend, whose significance is harder to judge, is the growing pressure on resources and the environment. Economics has been here before—witness Malthus, witness the Club of Rome (which, in the 1970s, predicted global economic breakdown as energy and other resources ran out). In the past such apocalyptic forecasts have been rubbished by technological progress and, more importantly, by economic forces working through the price mechanism. Scarce resources become dearer; this causes them to be conserved.

Will present anxieties fade, too? Edmond Malinvaud of the College de France thinks they may not. More economists are wondering whether growth is sustainable; and noted mainstream economists such as Yale's William Nordhaus are turning to environmental economics.

Demand side

If economics is a market that is itself subject to economic forces, then events and trends such as the collapse of communism, global integration and environmental degradation are exogenous factors. What of internal market forces? Naturally, this market has a demand side and a supply side. On the demand side, economics has some conspicuous and embarrassing gaps.

The biggest, emphasised by John Kay of the London Business School, is the theory of the firm. Microeconomics knows a lot about groups of firms (ie, industries). But the individual enterprise remains a mystery. So far as mainstream economics is concerned, Ronald Coase's article "The Nature of the Firm" remains the state of the art. It was written in 1937.

"Corporate strategy" has occupied the empty space. "Its tools" says Mr Kay "are jejeune at best, and much of what passes for corporate strategy is platitude or pious exhortation." Here then is an opportunity for economics to recolonise an area that should always have been within its domain. Mr Kay praises Oliver Williamson of the University of California at Berkeley for "almost single-handedly" pursuing a programme of work on the choices that face individual firms. This work looks at the economics of contracts, property rights, information and transaction costs; it aims to explain why firms are as they are, and why they do what they do. This literature is sure to blossom.

A second big gap is growth theory. After pioneering work by Robert Solow and others in the 1950s and early 1960s, this branch of economics went quiet for 20 years. Theorists had been unable to explain how an economy with a stable population could grow in the long term. In these models technical progress, the crux of the matter, was an awkward bystander: an exogenous factor, immune to economic forces. The focus of macroeconomic research was how to raise an economy's actual output to its current potential output (a task which continues to defeat macroeconomists)—not how to raise

both potential and actual output over time.

Recently interest in growth theory has begun to revive. Led by Paul Romer and Robert Lucas of the University of Chicago, economists are developing plausible theories that give technical progress its due weight. Surveying this new literature, Nicholas Stern of the London School of Economics concludes that "we have not yet advanced very far" but now, at least, "some of the right questions are being asked".

A third gap, as noted by Frank Hahn of Cambridge University, is perhaps the most profound; filling it will radically alter the character of economics. Many theorists are increasingly unhappy with the concept of rationality, which is the bedrock of economics. Economic agents evidently do not always behave rationally, at least on the stricter definitions of the term. It is equally obvious, however, that behaviour is, in some looser sense, ordered and sensible.

Economists such as George Akerlof of the University of California at Berkeley have begun to examine the implications of "near-rationality". To do so they are drawing on research in sociology, anthropology and, above all, psychology.

Since economics is a behavioural science, this extension of its research programme is long overdue. The work of Mr Akerlof and his followers has already yielded new and appealing insights (as the earlier brief on labour markets showed), yet the surface has barely been scratched. The price of this much better understanding of economic events—if it is a price—is that such work will make economics softer, more empirical, more experimental; and therefore less theoretical, less analytical.

Supply side

This change in the character of economics will be powerfully reinforced by developments on the supply side. Like many industries, economics is driven by the interests of its producers. Often economists come up with new techniques of analysis, then look for questions that might be susceptible to them. The development of mathematical and statistical methods during the 1950s and 1960s shaped the way economics was done over the following decades.

The next generation of techniques is already in sight. Stephen Turnovsky of the University of Washington sees a bright future for non-linear methods. At present, economic theorists deal mainly in linear relationships—relationships that are, in graphical terms, straight lines. This restriction is actually less limiting than it might seem: non-linear relationships can often be mathematically transformed into linear ones, for ease of handling. But if you use linear equations to build a model that tracks an economy through time (a so-called dynamic model) you always find that this model either settles down at a single point or else explodes. The world, in contrast, tends to move through recurring cycles. These are readily reproduced with non-linear relationships.

Non-linear equations are useful in another way. They capture the fact that small disturbances can have big effects—the simple insight that underlies the study of chaos. Many economic processes appear to be "chaotic", so this new line of research may help economics a lot.

For years economists hoped that game theory would revolutionise their subject. Game theory is concerned with bargaining or "strategic choice"—when Jack's decision depends on Jill's, which depends in turn on Jack's. Until recently the theory was better at highlighting the defects of conventional economics than at offering new answers of its own, but this has changed. Seminal work on industrial economics by Jean Tirole of MIT is built on game theory; so is strategic trade theory. Applications are multiplying. Game theory is not a dead end after all.

These new techniques will come together with the broadening and softening of economics—thanks to the computer. Up until now, economic theory (as opposed to econometric forecasting) has used mainly analytical methods: models are solved for their equilibrium values with brain-power. Non-linear systems and games do not lend themselves to this approach. Lacking analytical solutions they have to be solved by copious number-crunching. (Even uncomplicated dynamic economic models can take days of computing time to crack.)

Computers can also be used to conduct simulations and experiments. In game theory, for example, strategies can be written as computer programs and pitted against others to see which works best.

So in future economists will be more tightly shackled to their computers than ever. With any luck, though, their goal will mainly be to improve their theories and hence their understanding of the world—not, as often in the past, to produce bad forecasts based on weak economics and a steady supply of wildly inaccurate statistics.

Big MacCurrencies

APRIL 13TH *How do you judge whether a currency is undervalued or overvalued? One way is to compare prices in different countries. To do that, we looked once more at a familiar "basket" of commodities*

IT IS time for our annual update of *The Economist*'s Big Mac index, a rough-and-ready guide to whether a currency is under or overvalued. It was launched five years ago in the hope of making economic theory more digestible.

The index is based on the theory of purchasing-power parity (PPP), which argues that in the long run the exchange rate between two currencies should equate the prices of an identical basket of goods and services in the respective countries. Our "basket" is McDonald's Big Mac hamburger, made locally to a rigorous standard in more than 50 countries. Its local prices are less likely to be distorted by international transport and distribution costs than if we used, say, the price of *The Economist* in different countries.

So once again our correspondents have been gorging themselves on Big Macs. In four American cities they paid, on average, $2.25. In Tokyo the Big Mac costs ¥380, equivalent to $2.81. This implies that the dollar is 20% undervalued against the yen: it should, on our Big Mac PPP basis, buy ¥169 on the foreign-exchange market (that is, the yen price of a Big Mac divided by the dollar price) not the ¥135 prevailing when we made our survey. Similarly, the dollar is 13% undervalued against the D-mark; it

should be worth DM1.91.

Indeed, on Big Mac PPP grounds the dollar looks undervalued against most currencies, so its recent rally could have further to run. The exceptions shown in our table are the Australian, Canadian, Hong Kong and Singapore dollars, the Hungarian forint and the Yugoslav dinar, which all look too low in dollar terms.

The cheapest place for a Big Mac (ie, the country whose currency is most undervalued against the dollar) is Hong Kong. The dearest is Russia. In Pushkin Square, Muscovites queue for hours to pay the equivalent of $5.75 at the commercial exchange rate, implying that the dollar is 61% undervalued against the rouble.

One of the biggest Big Mac PPP changes since 1990 has been in the pound. Its PPP has slipped from $1.56 to $1.35; and, more important, from DM3.07 to DM2.58. The reason is that the price of a Big Mac in London has gone through the roof. It is up by 19%—more than twice as fast as prices generally—over the past year, while in Germany it has not changed. Other, more solemn, estimates of

the pound's PPP vary between DM2.50 and DM3.20. But if London's Big Macflation is a pointer to the future, the Treasury is going to get heartburn defending the DM2.95 central rate at which sterling entered Europe's exchange-rate mechanism.

The real test

Hamburger prices

Country	Price* in local currency	Implied PPP† of the dollar	Actual exchange rate 9.4.91	% over(+) or under(–) valuation of the dollar
Australia	A$2.45	1.09	1.27	+17
Belgium	BFr100	44.44	34.50	–22
Britain	£1.67	0.74	0.56	–24
Canada	C$2.35	1.04	1.15	+11
Denmark	DKr26.75	11.89	6.42	–46
France	FFr18.00	8.00	5.65	–29
Germany	DM4.30	1.91	1.67	–13
Holland	Fl5.25	2.33	1.88	–19
Hong Kong	HK$8.90	3.96	7.79	+97
Hungary	Forint115	51.11	75.12	+47
Ireland	I£1.40	0.62	0.62	—
Italy	Lire3600	1600	1239	–23
Japan	¥380	169	135	–35
Singapore	S$2.80	1.24	1.77	+43
S. Korea	Won2100	933	721	–23
Soviet Union	Rouble10	155	103	–34
Sweden	SKr26	11.56	6.04	–48
United States††	$2.25	—	—	—
Yugoslavia	Dinar32	14.22	15.12	+6

* Prices may vary locally. ** Commercial rate. † Purchasing-power parity in local currency; local price divided by dollar price. †† New York, Chicago, San Francisco and Atlanta
Source: McDonald's, Economist correspondents.

Dances with bulls

APRIL 20TH *In the spring, a puzzle: with their economies out of step, why were European stockmarkets moving in line with Wall Street?*

NEW YORK'S stockmarket has risen by 19% from its mid-January low, thanks to a correctly predicted victory in the Gulf and hopes of economic recovery in America. Many economists reckon that America's recession, which began last summer, has now reached its trough; they predict that the economy will soon pick up. Europe, on the other hand, is at a much earlier stage of economic slowdown, perhaps six months behind America.

The chart on the next page makes a crude stab at ranking economies according to their stage in the cycle. Britain and Sweden actually slipped into recession ahead of America, but their recovery is expected to take longer. France, Italy and Switzerland are only now on the brink of recession. Meanwhile, western Germany's economy is

at last starting to look sickly, with growth likely to slow sharply by the end of this year.

If Europe's economic cycle is currently much less synchronised with America's than usual, why do its stockmarkets dance so closely in step with Wall Street? Since mid-January most European bourses have gained 20-30% in local-currency terms.

Even after taking account of the rise in the dollar over that period, European bourses have made strong gains measured in dollars, too. With many European economies just starting to slow, is not Europe's rally premature?

One possible explanation is that the steady globalisation of stockmarkets means that the health of their home economies matters less. There are at least three reasons why national stockmarkets could be ex-

pected to move more closely in line with each other than in the past.

First, the removal of capital controls and the introduction of better communications and trading systems have boosted the cross-border buying and selling of shares. Second, it is increasingly common for big companies to be listed on more than one market. (In 1990 in London the turnover in international—that is, non-British—equities almost matched that in domestic shares.) Third, as multinational companies expand overseas sales, so a firm's share price is increasingly tied to the prospects of other economies. (About half of the profits of British quoted companies come from abroad—either from exports or from sales by overseas subsidiaries.)

A recent OECD study found that share-price movements in different markets have indeed become more linked. One measure of this is the correlation coefficient: a coefficient of zero implies no relationship between any two markets, a coefficient of one means the markets move perfectly in step. The OECD's work suggests that the correlation coefficient between monthly stockmarket returns in New York and London rose from 0.45 before 1973 (in the days when exchange rates were fixed) to 0.59 in the second half of the 1980s.

Put crudely, this implies that price movements in New York "explain" 59% of London's movements. America's correlation with Japan has risen from 0.19 to 0.42, with Germany from 0.39 to 0.45, and with France from 0.28 to 0.44. The highest coefficient in the late 1980s was 0.67, between America and Holland.

Yet closer examination shows that most of the higher correlation between markets is accounted for by times of high price volatility. When there are big price movements, notably during the October 1987 stockmarket crash, international linkages seem to become stronger. During calmer periods the correlation between markets is less and has increased only slightly.

Why should correlations be greatest at

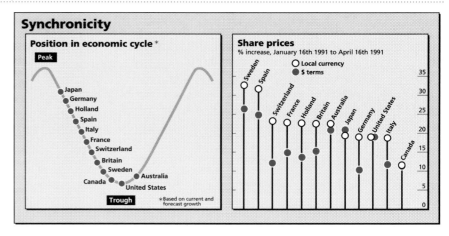

Synchronicity

times of high volatility? One reason may be that in calmer times, when price movements are small, the costs of buying and selling shares exceed the potential gains from international arbitrage, so markets have little effect on each other. In times of big price movements, arbitrage is more profitable, so returns become more synchronised. Transactions costs have fallen over the past two decades, so opportunities for profitable arbitrage—and hence international correlations—should have increased.

Although financial markets are becoming integrated faster than national economies, investors cannot yet toss analysts' research on individual economies into the bin. This year European markets have not simply been lifted up on New York's coat-tails; Europe's recent rally is also underpinned by various local factors.

Many European stockmarkets started the year looking undervalued relative to their own government-bond markets and to American equities. Even after the rally, most, with the exception of Germany, still look a good buy compared with America or Japan.

Inflation is likely to fall by more in Europe than America over the coming year; so, therefore, will bond yields. Some recent analysis by Sushil Wadhwani of the London team of Goldman Sachs shows that economic slowdowns can be good for share prices if they reduce inflation and bond yields. Investors have historically been willing to sacrifice some growth in the economy and corporate profits for lower inflation and, therefore, lower bond yields. That is because investors measure the riskiness of equities by comparing their prospective yields to the guaranteed returns from government bonds.

Looking ahead, France and Spain have the greatest potential for lower interest rates. France, once a high-inflation country, is likely to have the lowest inflation rate among the seven top industrial economies by the second half of this year.

The stronger dollar will lift profits of European firms by boosting exports or by increasing the local-currency value of income from American subsidiaries. In particular, Dutch and Swiss firms will gain. Finally, although Europe is slowing down, "recession" in several continental European countries this year may still mean growth that is no slower than America's "recovery". Despite the problems caused by German unification, many economists are still betting that Europe's economies will outshine America's over the next few years. For once, investors seem to agree with them.

Soviet economic reforms

APRIL 27TH, MOSCOW *Plenty of shock, no therapy: after years of perestroika, the Soviet Union had fallen into ever steeper decline. But at last Mikhail Gorbachev's government was promising action*

THE "anti-crisis programme" of the Soviet prime minister, Valentin Pavlov, is the third tranche of an economic-reform plan that began in January with the confiscation of 50- and 100-rouble notes, and continued in early April with huge price rises. It is likely to be the last chance to rescue the economy from chaos.

Such is the speed of decline (GNP in the

first three months of 1991 was 8% lower than it had been in the same period of 1990, imports were 45% lower) that, if this plan fails, the next one may be either an economic state of emergency imposed under martial law, or a kaleidoscope of programmes started by republics after the Soviet Union breaks up. Unfortunately, the good parts of Mr Pavlov's new plan are likely to be over-

whelmed quickly by the bad.

To work, any Soviet economic plan must do two things. First, stabilise the macroeconomy. This means cutting the budget deficit, freeing prices and trade, and preventing accumulated savings from causing an inflationary expansion of demand. Second, create the microeconomic conditions under which enterprises can thrive. This requires privatisation. But any plan must also meet a third, political, condition: it must settle arguments between centre and republics over who controls policy.

Judged as a plan for macroeconomic stability, the programme is less bad than its many critics claim. It is based on the so-called "main guidelines" adopted by the Soviet parliament last September after it had rejected the widely acclaimed Shatalin plan. However, parts of the radical Shatalin plan reappear in the new programme.

All prices, it says, will be freed by October 1992. If implemented, this would correct the main weakness of early April's price reforms, which left most prices fixed by government fiat. It would also improve upon January's brutal monetary reform, which tried to deal with savings by confiscating some of them: the new plan would raise interest rates to encourage consumers to leave their money in the bank. It would also open the economy to world trade by allowing easier conversion of roubles into hard currency and repatriation of hard-currency profits.

Hyperinflation will still be a threat unless government borrowing (financed by printing money) can be cut. Here, too, the plan borrows from Mr Shatalin. A moratorium is supposed to start next month on all new projects financed by central government. Projects pencilled in for this year which have not yet started will also be postponed. New plans to cut central—and republican—government spending are to be agreed upon for the second half of the year. Worryingly, the plan contains few details on how spending on the army and the bureaucracy will be cut—and it is excessively vague on other points. But it does suggest one reform which, if it went through, would deal with many such doubts.

It proposes setting up a sort of Federal Reserve system of central banks in which all 15 republics would be represented—and which would be told not to lend to the government. This, in effect, would outlaw the inflationary creation of money—a drastic change, if it happens.

All this will benefit the economy only if enterprises respond. That is why privatisation is essential. Mr Pavlov's programme recognises this. One-third of small enterprises—shops, restaurants and so on—are supposed to be privatised by the end of this year, two-thirds by the end of 1992. The plan also says republics should continue their efforts to sell land to peasants.

But this is not nearly enough. Dismayingly, the plan does not explicitly endorse the private ownership of land. It rejects any idea of giving enterprises away (the only way to privatise in a hurry). Instead, a central fund for state property will be set up to sell large and medium-sized companies. The programme talks of selling a piffling 10% of them. Where sales go ahead, workers are to get a stake. Eastern Europe shows that worker-owned factories can be as inefficient as state-owned ones—and a lot harder to shut down. The programme gives absurd powers to the centre. It will have the authority, for example, to block sackings and changes in the pattern of production.

Unless privatisation is delegated to the republics, the microeconomic conditions necessary for reform are most unlikely to be met. But if the republics are to undertake reform for themselves, agreement must be struck between the central and local governments both on the central-bank system and on who owns which factories. Mr Pavlov said that his programme will work only if it is backed by all 15 republics. That will not happen. The six refusnik republics—the Baltic three, Moldavia, Georgia and Armenia—want nothing to do with it.

For the rest, the plan contains two stumbling blocks. The first is a proposal to outlaw "political strikes", use force where the ban is flouted (as it will be) and arrest strike leaders. This is the part of the plan that has attracted most criticism. Though Mr Gorbachev and nine republican leaders signed a declaration broadly supporting the plan on the day the parliament approved it, few republican leaders are likely to agree to use force to break strikes. Second, there is a problem over tax collecting. Republics collect taxes but are refusing to pass them on to the central government. They have contributed only 39% of what the central government requires them to hand over in the first three months of the year.

Rapid agreement on the anti-crisis programme—and bolder measures besides—might forestall disaster. So might the decision to let the republics go it alone on economic reform. Otherwise, it is too easy to imagine what might happen next. If the republican governments pressed for full wage-indexation, the central bank would be unable to keep its promise not to finance budget deficits by printing money. That would mean that the best part of the programme—its price reform—would only cause inflation (already in three digits) to spiral out of control. Meanwhile, thanks to the bad parts, output would fail to recover. Things would get worse, leaving a stark choice between civil war or martial law.

....

The anti-crisis programme was abandoned and the economy continued to deteriorate.

The kindness of chapter 11

MAY 25TH *America's chapter 11 bankruptcy is too kind to a troubled company's existing managers and shareholders, and too harsh on creditors*

AMERICAN firms with serious money troubles have two choices—formal bankruptcy through chapter 11 of the 1978 Bankruptcy Reform Act, or an informal rescheduling of their debts, known as a "workout". Chapter 11 is not cheaper than a workout, so you might think few firms would opt for it. In fact, many do. A study by academics at the London Business School and the University of California at Los Angeles explains why chapter 11 is so popular*.

Chapter 11 works by allowing top management to get the firm out of trouble by drawing up a rescue plan that can involve restructuring the firm and writing down creditors' claims on its assets. After all, reckoned America's lawmakers, these bosses know most about what needs to be done—never mind that they got the firm into trouble in the first place. Workouts do the same, but with much less legal tussle. Chapter 11 is different from British "receivership", where the courts mostly sack existing management and put a finance expert in charge. For managers, the nice thing about chapter 11 is that it protects the firm from its creditors until a rescue deal is sorted out; and the firm can stop paying its interest charges.

This protection seems sensible enough; firms need a breathing space if they are to recover. But it also sets up a fight between a firm's shareholders and its other creditors. Without chapter 11, if a firm were shut down and its assets sold off, the spoils would go first to senior creditors—banks and others that had lent the firm money. Only when senior creditors were paid in full would junior creditors, and after them preference shareholders, get some cash. When all these are paid, ordinary shareholders get what is left, which is usually not much.

This all changes under chapter 11. Shareholders, who know they will get little if the firm is wound up, want the firm to keep trading in the hope that it will come good. Creditors, on the other hand, can be damaged every day that the firm trades without a rescue package. They may lose both because of missed interest payments and because of the legal fees that have to be paid from the firm's shrunken assets. Managers have two good motives to avoid a deal with creditors for as long as they can: they keep their jobs longer, and they work for shareholders, who do not want a deal either.

Senior creditors must battle not only with shareholders, but also with junior

* "How Firms Fare in Workouts and Chapter 11 Reorganisations." By Julian Franks & Walter Torous, London Business School working paper, May 1991.

creditors. Under chapter 11, two-thirds of creditors, of preference shareholders and of equity shareholders must separately back any deal. If junior creditors account for more than a third of the creditors, they can force concessions from their senior partners.

The study looked at 88 big, troubled firms, 41 in chapter 11 and 47 in workouts, between 1983 and 1990. It found that creditors give up some of their seniority rights as a carrot to get management to agree to a deal. The study compared what each type of creditor—holders of debt, preference shares and equity—would have received if strict legal priority had been applied with what they actually got.

The 41 chapter 11 deals gave $878m to claimants that was not due to them (see chart). Shareholders, arguably entitled to nothing, got around a third of the benefit. Junior creditors got just over half, and preference shareholders the rest—all at the expense of senior creditors. This was on top of much bigger write-downs of creditors' claims under chapter 11 deals—on average 47% of pre-deal face value, compared with 23% in workouts.

As chapter 11 is so bad for senior creditors, management and shareholders have a big advantage. If the senior creditors refuse

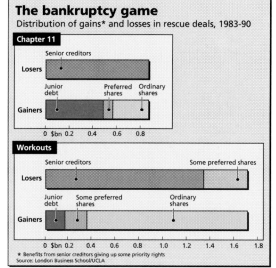

The bankruptcy game
Distribution of gains* and losses in rescue deals, 1983-90

*Benefits from senior creditors giving up some priority rights
Source: London Business School/UCLA

to make a deal it likes, the firm will simply file for chapter 11 protection. So in workouts, too, creditors may be willing to give up their seniority rights. This, the study finds, is the case. In fact, senior creditors give up even more in workouts than in chapter 11 deals, although the write-downs of their claims tend to be a lot less. Of the $1.7 billion shifted from losers to gainers in workouts, senior creditors gave up $1.3 billion. This is less odd than it looks: it pays creditors to

avoid the delays and legal costs of chapter 11.

In effect, then, chapter 11 says it is better to keep a firm running than to honour debt agreements. This is fine for managers and employees, who (or many of whom) keep their jobs, and for shareholders, who would otherwise face large losses. It is also good for politicians, who are spared having to explain job losses, and, as ever, for lawyers. Yet it may be bad for other firms since lenders will become increasingly wary, and may charge higher interest rates overall to make up for their higher risks.

One answer would be for the judges ruling on applications for chapter 11 to get tough in backing creditors' claims against the firm. This may be happening. An earlier study of chapter 11 cases between 1978 and 1984 found that shareholders' gains at the expense of senior creditors were even bigger then than in the more recent cases.

Alternatively America could move towards a system of receivership, which puts creditors before shareholders, but is more likely to end in the firm ceasing to trade. That is not as bad as it sounds. Good parts will be bought by other firms that can make use of them—perhaps better use than the existing management.

A fistful of ecus

JULY 13TH *Might a single European money, planned as part of economic and monetary union, replace the dollar as the world's leading currency? We looked at the prospects for the ecu*

WHEN all the economies of the European Community eventually have a single currency—called the ecu perhaps—how will its international role compare with that of the dollar?

At present the ecu—a weighted basket of the 12 EC currencies—is not legal tender. Yet it has been playing an increasing role in international finance. Adding together private ecu deposits (created by banks holding the appropriate amounts of the component currencies) and official ecus (created when the European Monetary Co-operation Fund swaps 20% of central banks' dollars and gold reserves into ecus), the ecu is already the third-biggest reserve currency, behind the dollar and the D-mark. Ecus are also catching on in international bond markets. In the first six months of this year, 13% of all international bond issues were denominated in ecus, second only to the dollar.

The future replacement of all existing EC currencies by the ecu would boost the ecu share to 46% of all international bonds

(ahead of the dollar's 31%), and 37% of all foreign-exchange reserves (against the dollar's 51%). But these figures probably understate the ecu's future role. As an economic block, the EC is roughly the same size as the United States. But over the next decade it is likely to grow faster and overtake America, thanks partly to the creation of a single market. Moreover, when the ecu becomes a fully-fledged currency, the ecu government-bond market will be the world's biggest financial market: Europe's total government debt, less than America's not long ago, has now overtaken it.

An international currency must perform several functions: as a unit of account for trade invoicing; as a means of payment; and as a store of wealth for governments and private investors.

• **Trade invoicing.** The dollar is still the favourite currency for trade invoicing. Some 42% of big industrial economies' exports were invoiced in dollars in 1987, compared with America's 22% share of those exports. The dollar accounts for an even bigger share

(50%) of imports, because oil and other primary commodities are priced in dollars. The share of European currencies in trade invoicing is smaller than the EC's share in total trade, since about 15% of its exports and 25% of imports are invoiced in dollars.

After EMU the ecu will be the currency of the world's largest exporter and importer. Assuming that oil and raw materials continue to be invoiced in dollars, a study* by the EC Commission reckons that some 10% of EC trade could shift from dollar to ecu invoicing, implying an additional demand for ecus for transaction purposes of $60 billion. The shift could be bigger still if EFTA countries and Eastern Europe also use the ecu for trade. Even OPEC might one day find it more attractive to price its oil in ecus rather than dollars, since it does more than twice as much trade with the EC as with America.

• **Official reserves.** The dollar's dominance as a reserve currency has faded over the past couple of decades. The number of countries that peg their currencies to the dollar has fallen by roughly 50%, and its share of for-

* "One Market, One Money", European Economy no. 44, October 1990.

eign-exchange reserves has fallen from 80% in the mid-1970s to 51% at the end of 1990 (if one treats official ecus as a currency in their own right, rather than just counting the dollars for which they are swapped). Over the same period the share of the D-mark has risen from 7% to 19%, and the share of all EC currencies including ecus from 17% to 37%. The yen still accounts for only 9% of reserves.

EMU will encourage a further shift out of dollars. For one thing, the ecu will provide an alternative anchor for other countries in the rest of Europe, Africa and the Middle East to peg their currencies to, and will thus encourage them to hold more of their reserves in ecus.

Another important aspect is that the creation of a European central bank and the elimination of intra-EC transactions in foreign exchange will make much of EC countries' $400 billion of reserves redundant. Assuming that the EC reduces its reserves by the same percentage as the share of intra-EC transactions in its total foreign-exchange transactions, then the EC Commission estimates that some $230 billion of reserves could be dumped, including a large chunk of dollars.

• **Private wealth.** The commission estimates that in 1988 50% of the world's private-sector wealth that was held in foreign currency (cash, bank deposits and securities) was in dollars, well ahead of America's 34% share of the OECD's total GNP. EC currencies accounted for 27%, as against these countries' 34% share of GNP.

Today's divisions between European financial markets, and the thinness of some of them, discourage foreign investors. But the unification of markets after EMU will make them more liquid, and so trigger new interest in ecu assets.

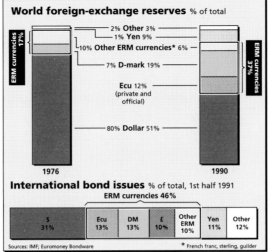

World foreign-exchange reserves % of total

ERM currencies 17% (1976) — ERM currencies 37% (1990)

- 2% Other 3%
- 1% Yen 9%
- 10% Other ERM currencies* 6%
- 7% D-mark 19%
- Ecu 12% (private and official)
- 80% Dollar 51%

International bond issues % of total, 1st half 1991

ERM currencies 46%

| $ 31% | Ecu 13% | DM 13% | £ 10% | Other ERM 10% | Yen 11% | Other 12% |

Sources: IMF; Euromoney Bondware — * French franc, sterling, guilder

This should be reinforced by the promised anti-inflationary stance of the EuroFed, the proposed new European central bank. EC governments have reached broad agreement that it will be independent of them, will have price stability as its prime objective and will be prevented by law from financing budget deficits. In other words its anti-inflationary credibility will be much stronger than that of America's Fed, which by law is meant to worry about employment as well as inflation.

Add in the fact that Europe as a whole is a net foreign creditor, in contrast to America, which is the world's biggest debtor, and the attraction of the ecu as a store of value becomes greater still. The commission suggests that the share of ecus in private portfolios could rise by at least five percentage points after monetary union, to around a third of the total. Some economists reckon the share might rise even further.

So will the ecu knock the dollar off its pedestal? No, it will share it. The ecu will never dominate the world's monetary system as the dollar has or the pound did before it. But EMU will accelerate the shift to a system of multiple reserve currencies, with power shared more evenly between them.

Just when you thought it was safe

AUGUST 17TH *Japan's trade surplus was rising again, confounding many forecasts and arousing new protectionist sentiment in America. We asked why trade flows had shifted once more*

ONLY a year ago Americans and Europeans thought they had slain Japan's mighty trade surplus. Suddenly, the monster has come roaring back. Having fallen from a peak of $96 billion in 1987 to $64 billion last year, Japan's merchandise-trade surplus has jumped to an annual rate of $89 billion in the first half of 1991. The current-account surplus (which measures services and investment income as well as trade in merchandise goods) has jumped from $36 billion in 1990 to an annual rate of $67 billion. Both surpluses may be about to soar even higher.

A new study by Stephen King, an economist at James Capel, a London stockbroker, forecasts that Japan's trade and current-account surpluses will swell to $118 billion and $95 billion respectively next year. These would be record levels in dollar terms. But, because Japan's economy has grown so fast, even at this size neither surplus would be disproportionately large. For example, as a percentage of GNP the current-account surplus would be only about 3% compared with more than 4% in 1986.

That fact, however, is little consolation for Japan's trading partners, for whom Japan's trade surplus seems almost supernatural. In the 1980s Japan did almost everything its trade partners nagged it to do. From its 1985 low, the yen rose in value by almost 50% against the dollar. Japanese firms shifted production overseas, while the Japanese government made efforts to open Japan's markets to foreign firms and stimulated domestic demand, boosting imports. All this did reduce Japan's surplus—but not permanently.

Much of the growth of the trade surplus this year is due to a slowing in import growth, as Japanese domestic demand has slowed. Consumers, in particular, have tightened their belts. Higher interest rates and last year's collapse in the stockmarket have reduced their appetite for up-market goods such as German BMWs or French works of art (art was Japan's second-biggest import from Europe last year after passenger cars). Japan's car imports have fallen this year, for the first time since 1983. Total imports were only 0.2% higher, in dollar terms, in the first half of 1991 than in the the same period of 1990. Import penetration has fallen, for the first time since 1986.

Meanwhile, as domestic sales have slowed, Japanese companies have switched their sights again vigorously toward overseas markets. Japan's share of world markets has started to pick up, after falling steadily for six years. For example, the sales of Sony rose only 10% in Japan last year, but sales in Europe jumped 42% and in America 23%.

As a result, despite recession in America and in parts of Europe, Japan's exports were 12% higher in dollar terms in the first half of 1991 than in the same period of 1990. That rise was helped by a fall in the yen: having risen to ¥120 to the dollar in 1988, the yen has since fallen to around ¥137 today, making Japanese manufacturers more competitive, especially after five years of strong investment in the latest machinery and new products. This investment explains why top exporters are now thought to be competitive at around ¥120 to the dollar. Even more ominous for competitors abroad, many of their latest investment programmes assume a rate of only ¥100 by the mid-1990s.

Recession in America is no small matter for many of Japan's big manufacturers: the American market accounts (including both exports from Japan and "transplant" output in America) for about 20% of Toyota's sales and 50% of Honda's. Although sales in America have slipped this year, they have held up better than those of American companies. In the first six months of 1991, total American car sales fell 16% by volume compared with a year ago; sales of Japanese cars (whether built in Japan or in America) fell by only 8%, boosting the Japanese makers' market share to almost 30%.

Lost sales in America have been more than made up by a rapid increase in exports to Europe, especially Germany, and to South-East Asia. As a result, the proportion of Japan's exports going to America has fallen to 28% this year from 40% in the mid-1980s.

That has helped to ease strained trade relations with America, but has created friction elsewhere. While Japan's trade surplus with America has continued to fall this year, running at an annual rate of $32 billion, barely half its 1986 level, its surpluses with Asian countries and the European Community (EC) have swollen to record levels (see chart). Japan's surplus with the EC has increased by more than half this year. But its surplus with America could soon rise again. As America's economy recovers, consumers there will quickly regain their appetite for Honda cars and Toshiba computers, strengthening demands for more trade protection.

In sum, the measures taken by Japan's government in response to protests from its trade partners seem to have failed. Some basic economics explains why. Japan's current-account surplus reflects the fact that the Japanese save more than they invest. A sustained reduction in the surplus requires a sustained reduction in savings–by individuals, companies or the governmental sector–or an increase in investment.

That has not happened. Japan, urged by America, took the short-term route after 1986 of lowering interest rates to boost domestic demand, discourage personal

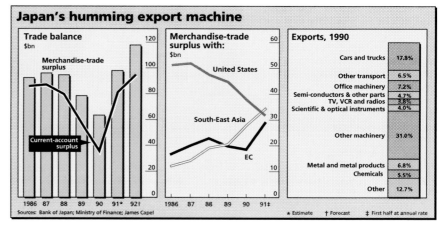

Japan's humming export machine

Sources: Bank of Japan; Ministry of Finance; James Capel

★ Estimate   † Forecast   ‡ First half at annual rate

savings and raise investment. Personal savings did indeed fall, as consumers went on a binge, and investment also surged, sucking in imports. So the surplus was trimmed–for a time. In 1986 Japanese saved 16.1% of their disposable incomes; in the year to March 1990, just 13.8%. But this domestic-demand-led boom was unsustainable. In 1989 mounting inflationary pressures forced the Bank of Japan to push interest rates back up. So domestic spending has been hit, as have imports. There are no official figures yet for personal savings in 1990 or so far this year, but the signs are that they have risen again.

While the Japanese government relied largely on monetary policy to slim the surpluses, its fiscal policy was enlarging them. During the 1980s, the government moved from a big deficit (dis-saving) to a surplus, thanks to tax rises and spending cuts. That increase in government saving helped slow the fall in the current-account surplus and is now helping to push it back up. Moreover, Japanese companies accumulated a big financial surplus in the late 1980s; their do-

mestic investment now looks poised for collapse. If it wants to affect the current account, the government should now either cut its budget surplus, or use microeconomic reforms to lower personal savings.

Surely, though, in the long term Japan's exports should be reduced by rising production in transplant factories overseas? Did not car exports to America fall from 2.4m units in 1986 to 1.7m in 1990, while the output of transplant factories in America rose correspondingly from 500,000 units to 1.3m (and is set to rise to 2.4m by 1995)?

True, but things are not quite what they seem. First, transplant factories import components from Japan. The more cars they build, the bigger those imports. Second, car plants in Japan are not being closed; they are shifting production to luxury cars. So in future an exported "unit" may no longer be a $12,500 Honda Accord but, say, a $61,000 Honda NSX. The number of cars exported may drop, yet their total value still rise.

In the long term, Japan's personal-savings ratio, and probably hence its external surplus, will fall as its population ages. But just when this will happen is anyone's guess. The only certain thing is that the monster trade surplus, though it may move from one export market to another, is not headed for an early demise. Expect more acrimony and more clumsy protectionist ploys from Japan's trading partners.

Making competition take off

OCTOBER 19TH *The key to injecting more competition into the airline business is to free the market for take-off and landing slots*

THERE is little chance of two airlines competing if one operator's aircraft can take off and land and its rival's can do neither. In many of the world's airports, at least during busy times, demand for take-off and landing slots far outstrips supply. In most airports these slots are allocated in ways that stifle competition.

Until recently, this hardly mattered. Airport congestion was rare, and air travel so heavily regulated that slots were the least of the worries of a would-be competitor to established airlines. Today, some airports are operating close to capacity—and they will be even more crowded in future. With plans to let European airlines fly on any route within the Community, and hopes of more liberalisation on other routes, access to slots is at the top of the agenda.

Airlines will pay huge sums to secure good slots. Where they are forbidden to buy them officially, they may pay over the odds for a package of jets and facilities that includes slots in the bargain. That happened this year when Pan Am sold its Heathrow services to United Airlines for $400m, and American Airlines bought TWA's for $445m.

Airlines are willing to pay such sums because of serious flaws in the system for allocating slots. Slots are usually distributed by bureaucratic fiat, not according to how much they are worth to airlines. Worse, this decision is based on "grandfather rights"—if an airline used a slot last year, it has an option on it this year. This ensures the dominance of airports by flag carriers. If a slot is not used over a certain period, it reverts to the allocating body for redistribution. Only at America's four "high-density" airports (Washington National, New York's Kennedy and LaGuardia, and Chicago's O'Hare) can airlines trade slots.

Scarce capacity will be used best if it is allocated to those ready to pay most for it. Also, administrative allocation creates monopoly power. Airport charges for slot-use are usually far too low. That would not matter if the number of slots was unlimited, because new entrants could compete away any resulting excess profit. But slots are scarce. So the lucky winners land a monopoly rent. David Thompson, of the London Business School, calculates that an airline operating from Heathrow collects a rent equal to roughly 10% of the ticket price for flights within Europe.

The best solution is to auction slots to the highest bidder, with the cash going either to the airport, which could use it to build more capacity, or to the government. Slot rights should last for a fixed period, say five years, then be re-auctioned; trading in a secondary market would allow slots to be shifted to the most efficient users.

Implementing such a system would be tricky. The main obstacle is the airline industry. In a recent report* to Britain's Department of Transport, SD-Scicon, a consultancy, notes that "many airlines could scarcely be brought to discuss it rationally." Airlines see slots as their own assets. But stonewalling need not prevent more efficient use of slots. A study of slot trading at America's four high-density airports found that the equivalent of 50% of slots changed hands over the years 1986-88[†]. Most of these trades were between existing slot-holders, as they "fine-tuned" their schedules.

Slot trading, however, does not in itself remove monopoly profits, which still go to airlines (rather than airports). This matters, though not quite as much as you might think. Suppose the airline industry evolves into a market dominated by giants, each

with some monopoly power at home, but at a disadvantage away. In that case, competition among the giants—together with the incentives it creates for greater efficiency—would still be possible. But a market of competing giants is a long way off. In the meantime, to move quickly towards a competitive market, airlines will have to have at least some of their slots taken away.

To avoid endless political battles, airports and competition authorities could barter with the airlines. In exchange for giving up a proportion of slots for auction, airlines could be given ownership rights (preferably for a fixed period) over their remaining slots.

Some critics of auctions reckon that they would make the industry less competitive. Incumbents would block competitors by buying up all the available slots. This is easily avoided. Competition authorities could impose a rule limiting the proportion of slots that a single airline could buy at any one airport. In reality, this should be unnecessary. If an incumbent wants to deter new entrants, it would be far cheaper to do it by increasing service frequency or using predatory pricing than by buying slots.

One last fear is that slot auctions would raise air fares. There is a germ of truth in this. If airlines no longer get monopoly rents from their slots, fares might rise in the first instance—but, since the monopoly profits would instead go to the airport or government, more airport capacity could be provided, eventually driving fares down. A far more important point, though, is this: using slots efficiently will make the market for air travel more competitive. In America and Europe alike, competition among airlines has always meant lower prices.

---

* "Study on Airport Slot Allocation". SD-Scicon. Published by the Department of Transport. [†]"Slot Trading at United States Airports". By David Starkie. To be published by the European Commission.

Roman road to ruin

OCTOBER 5TH *As the EC moved towards economic and monetary union, would Italy's failure to cut its budget deficit consign it to the slow lane?*

FOR years economists have predicted economic and financial disaster for Italy unless its government kept to the fiscal straight and narrow. Unheeding, Italy's economy has continued to thrive, with one of the fastest growth rates in the EC over the past decade. Now, however, massive budget deficits pose a new and embarrassing threat. They could block Italy's participation in EMU. The

draft treaty for EMU proposes to exclude countries with excessive budget deficits. Italy, with a deficit equal to 10.5% of GDP and outstanding debt equivalent to 103%, might therefore find the door slammed in its face.

Italy is the biggest borrower in the EC, though its public deficit as a percentage of GDP is not as big as Greece's. Its ratio of outstanding debt to GDP is roughly double the

average of the other 11 countries. Italy does not have the highest debt-to-GDP ratio of the 12 countries: Belgium and Ireland shoulder bigger burdens. Unlike theirs, however, Italy's debt is growing faster than its economy. The debt was slightly more than GDP at the end of 1990, up from 58% of it in 1980.

The classic "debt trap" has now snared Italy. Spiralling debt boosts interest payments, which leads to more borrowing, and on it goes. Excluding interest payments, Italy's public deficit has actually fallen, from 5.2% of GDP in 1985 to 1.5% in 1990, and should virtually disappear this year. But, because of mounting interest payments, the total deficit has hardly budged.

On September 30th Giulio Andreotti's four-party government agreed to budget cuts of 55 trillion lire ($44 billion) next year. They are intended to keep the 1992 budget deficit to the target agreed earlier this year of 128 trillion lire, or 8.3% of GDP. The goal will almost certainly be missed, as will the government's target of reducing the deficit to 5.5% of GDP by 1994. That is what is needed to stabilise the debt-to-GDP ratio.

With an election due within eight months, politicians are reluctant to propose tough measures, like cracking down on tax evasion, widening the tax base, cutting subsidies or redesigning the national pensions scheme. Indeed, without some reform of the political system itself, to help produce stronger governments, Italian politicians will always be reluctant to take unpopular decisions. Could the prospect of being shut out of EMU give them the kick they need?

European proposals to limit countries' borrowing before they join EMU arise from two fears. One is that profligate governments could push up interest rates throughout the Community. The other is that unsustainable borrowing could trigger financial instability.

At present a big borrower is penalised by the threat of a run on its currency and the higher interest rates needed to curb it. But when Europe has a single currency there is a risk that some governments, free of that fear, will be encouraged to borrow recklessly. That would push up interest rates for all other countries. This threat is exaggerated. Exchange rates have never been reliable fiscal disciplinarians; in the early 1980s, for ex-

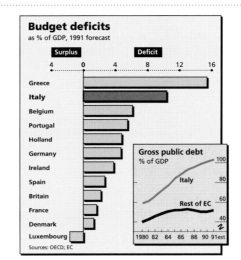

Budget deficits
as % of GDP, 1991 forecast

Sources: OECD; EC

ample, the dollar rose as America's federal government went on a borrowing binge. Another safeguard is that financial markets can discriminate among governments, as among other borrowers: the big borrowers will have to pay more.

The key question is whether, after EMU, the market will differentiate sufficiently to force governments with unsustainable fiscal positions (ie, high and rising debt-to-GDP ratios) into corrective action. Two Italian economists, Alberto Giovannini and Luigi Spaventa, argue in a recent paper* that this will not happen. They say that a fiscally irresponsible government will be under less discipline to trim its borrowing after EMU, and that this could jeopardise the European central bank's goal of price stability.

The treaty on EMU will, it is agreed, for-

* "Fiscal rules in the European Monetary Union: a no-entry clause." Alberto Giovannini and Luigi Spaventa, Centre for Economic Policy Research paper no. 516.

bid the EuroFed, or national central banks, to provide finance to any government. In theory, this ban on bail-outs should force the financial markets to take full account of the relative creditworthiness of government borrowers. But many find it hard to imagine that the European central bank would stand by and allow a member state to go bust. If the threat of default by a government sent the value of its securities tumbling, that could lead to fears for the soundness of the financial institutions holding its debt. In this climate a no-bail-out clause would amount to little: the EuroFed would be forced to inject more liquidity.

Some economists say that New York city suggests the opposite. When the city defaulted on its debt in the mid-1970s, it did not affect the Federal Reserve's monetary policy. But there is a difference. New York city's debt then amounted to only 2.6% of America's federal-government debt. Italy accounts for more than a third of total government debt in the EC. It might be seen as too big to fail. If so, argue Messrs Giovannini and Spaventa, financial markets would fail to impose the necessary fiscal discipline.

Economic and monetary union will not in itself encourage governments to correct their fiscal imbalances. But Messrs Giovannini and Spaventa argue that EMU could nonetheless spur Italian politicians to act. If thresholds similar to those in the draft treaty are adopted, the threat that Italy will be excluded from Europe's next leap forward could have two effects. Italy's prestige would suffer dreadfully, and voters would mind. And, as the risk of a lira devaluation increased, the cost of financing Italy's government debt would rise. What better way to overcome politicians' resistance to unpopular measures?

Memo to Maastricht

NOVEMBER 30TH *On the eve of the Maastricht summit, we asked whether Europe's leaders were about to make three big mistakes on EMU*

AT THEIR meeting in Maastricht on December 9th-10th, the EC's heads of government aim to prepare the way for economic and monetary union (EMU). Their ideas may well change during those talks—and it is to be hoped that they do, according to David Currie of the London Business School.*

Mr Currie draws attention to three defects in the draft proposals:
• **Transitional arrangements.** One worry is the role of the embryonic European central bank in "stage two", which precedes the locking together of EC currencies (due to

* "European Monetary Union: A Rocky Road from Maastricht?" *International Economic Outlook*, to be published in December by London Business School.

happen in stage three, some time after 1997). Until then the bank-to-be will be known as the European Monetary Institute (EMI).

An unfortunate compromise seems to have been reached between those who wanted a long stage two and those who wanted stage two delayed: a long stage two in which nothing really happens. The EMI's job will be to co-ordinate national monetary policies; but its powers are vague. As a result, the locking of currencies in stage three could come as a jolt.

Another difficulty is caused by the popular idea that there will be one last realignment of the exchange-rate mechanism (ERM). Expectations of new parity changes

will drive the EC's interest rates apart—the opposite of the convergence that the leaders want. One way to avoid this would be to promise at Maastricht that there will be no more realignments.
• **Exchange-rate policy.** Once Europe's currencies have been locked together, France, say, will no longer have to worry about the franc's exchange rate against the D-mark. But the EC as a whole will continue to be interested in the exchange rate of the ecu (or whatever) against the dollar and the yen. After EMU there will be exchange-rate policy; the question is, who will be in charge of it?

The current proposals are unclear. It seems that the EC's council of ministers will be responsible for formal exchange-rate agreements; in other cases the council (or commission) might set guidelines. But monetary policy and exchange-rate policy are indivisible. To raise interest rates is, other things equal, to strengthen the currency. It makes no sense to create an "independent" central bank and then talk of exchange-rate guidelines from the council of ministers.

Also, what precisely is a "formal" exchange-rate agreement? Would the Louvre accord of 1987 have qualified? Such deals subordinate the goal of price stability to that of exchange-rate stability. To establish the credibility of the new central bank, governments need to put it in charge of exchange-rate policy, and to give it a veto over future exchange-rate agreements.

• **Fiscal policy.** All of the EC governments except Britain's seem to favour fiscal rules and penalties. Once exchange rates are locked, the argument goes, the market's main sanction against reckless public borrowing—a run on the currency—will disappear. Also, one government's profligacy will force up interest rates for the EC as a whole. Rules to prevent that are necessary. This is debatable. But the main worry just now is not the idea of rules as such, but the form

	Convergence indicators				Criteria satisfied			
	Inflation rate	Long–term govt. bonds	Budget deficit	Public debt	Inflation rate	Long–term govt. bonds	Budget deficit	Public debt
	latest, %		1990, % of GDP					
Germany	3.5	8.1	–1.9	44	yes	yes	yes	yes
France	2.5	8.7	–1.6	47	yes	yes	yes	yes
Italy	6.1	12.6	–10.6	99	no	no	no	no
Britain	3.7	10.0	–0.7	43	yes	yes	yes	yes
Spain	5.5	11.4	–4.0	45	no	no	no	yes
Holland	4.4	8.6	–5.3	78	no	yes	no	no
Belgium	2.2	8.9	–5.6	127	yes	yes	no	no
Denmark	1.8	8.8	–1.5	66	yes	yes	yes	no
Greece	17.9	20.8	–19.8	94	no	no	no	no
Portugal	10.2	14.1	–5.8	68	no	no	no	no
Ireland	3.5	9.3	–3.6	103	yes	yes	no	no
Luxembourg	3.2	8.1	+4.7	7	yes	yes	yes	yes

Convergence criteria are (1) inflation differential between the member and the third best inflation performer in the EC should be no more than 1.5%; (2) long-term interest differential measured in the same way should be no more than 2%; (3) fiscal deficit should not exceed 3% of GDP; (4) debt-to-income ratio should not exceed 60%.
Sources: National statistics; JP Morgan; European Commission

they might take. Another unhappy compromise is in the making. To satisfy those who want strict rules and those who want lax ones, the partners may choose the worst of both: strict rules, weakly enforced.

The current proposal is to limit budget deficits to 3% of GDP and public debt to 60% of GDP. If these ceilings were interpreted as entry requirements for EMU, eight out of the 12 EC countries would be barred on their present performance. The table shows these

figures, together with the other proposed "convergence criteria", or entry requirements, for EMU. The fiscal hurdles stand out: they are implausibly demanding. In practice, if these rules stand, they will have to be waived. Fiscal policy will not be regulated by rules at all, but by discretion.

Even on the view that some sort of fiscal rule will be needed, the proposals are misconceived. After EMU, with no recourse to devaluation as a shock-absorber, governments will need more fiscal flexibility than now, not less. And there is no merit in convergence of debt-to-GDP ratios. By themselves, these tell you nothing about the sustainability of a government's fiscal policy. If there must be a rule, let it not be a ceiling for budget deficits or public debt, but rather a rule that discourages a trend of rapidly growing debt. It is the change in debt over time, not its level, that is the fairest test of a government's creditworthiness.

The summit adopted the main draft proposals. Doubts about future realignments, central-bank independence and the enforceability of the fiscal rules remained.

An economy's best friend

NOVEMBER 16TH *Governments aim for strong growth, low inflation, low unemployment and a "sound" balance-of-payments position. Which were on target?*

ONE rough and ready way to judge how an economy measures up is the "diamond", invented by economists at the OECD, the Paris-based club of rich nations, in the early 1980s. The charts plot each of the four indicators (GDP growth, inflation, unemployment rate, and current-account balance as a percentage of GDP) along an axis with the scale set so that the farther each plot is away from the origin, the better the country's performance. For each country, the four plots are joined up to form a diamond: the bigger the diamond, the better the record.

The charts compare the performance of the six biggest industrial economies in 1980-90 with the "golden age" of 1967-73, before oil prices soared. In the 1960s and early 1970s most economies scored well. But then came the oil shock: growth stalled, inflation and unemployment rose. All countries saw their diamonds shrink during 1974-79, especially Britain and Italy.

Only two of these countries regained their sparkle during the 1980s: Japan and Germany. They bettered their inflation records of 1967-73; this, along with bigger

current-account surpluses, made their diamonds almost as big as before the oil shock—though growth was slower in both countries, as it was for the other four countries as well.

The diamonds of the other four countries all remained smaller in the 1980s than before 1974. America's shrank compared with the 1970s mainly because of the country's huge current-account deficit. Britain, France and Italy all had their diamonds badly dented on the left-hand side by higher unemployment. Shrinking from every direction, Italy's diamond looks as though it might disappear altogether.

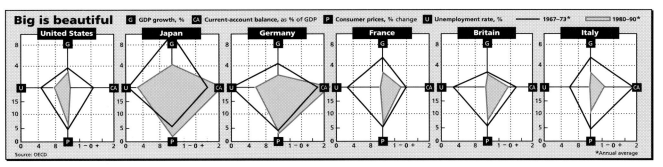

Contents

SCIENCE AND TECHNOLOGY

Time to think small

THE second world war, the war which one physicist described as "won by radar and finished by the atomic bomb", set the stage for modern science just as surely as it did for the cold war and the superpower world. In the shadow of the mushroom cloud, governments decided that science was something they wanted in abundance, and set about paying for it and fostering it. When triumphant Soviet scientific materialism launched Sputnik, scientists and the military industrial complex reaped the benefit of political unease. Money was shovelled into the combustion chambers of the new intercontinental missiles and space rockets—one and the same for the first few years—and into as many sciences as had the gumption to ask for it.

In 1991 some of this investment paid off, as the last remnants of the post-war settlement that gave rise to it fell apart. American technology dominated the Gulf war with precisely guided weapons, communications and surveillance satellites, battle management computers, stealth bombers, electronic warfare and the rest of the high-tech arsenal, keeping allied casualties extraordinarily low. War memorials, it appears, can be miniaturised as well as anything else. But as America's decades of cold-war weapons research proved its mettle, the conditions of its creation were evaporating. The world's other great military industrial complex was coming to grief, as the Soviet Union, founded on the principles of Marxist science, died in the greatest experimental refutation of a theoretical idea ever witnessed.

The turmoil in Russia and the surrounding countries opened up a huge brain drain. Russian scientists, who had seen the cornucopia of equipment easily available in the West, decided to come and partake of it. Many say they are only visiting. Colleagues who have stayed at home look forward to them returning, brimming with new ideas and techniques. But in truth, many of them will stay. The result will not just be more good scientists working in western laboratories. Scientists are creatures of their culture, and different cultures bring with them different interests and outlooks.

Mixing two different groups does not simply bring a doubling of manpower. By bringing together different points of view it can elicit insights that no-one would otherwise have had—though at some risk of deadlock if views that are totally incompatible clash. Such unpredictable, non-linear effects are the domain of chaos theory, which is one of the areas most likely to benefit when Russian brains get weaving on western computers.

The collapse of Russian science and the resulting brain-drain could be as great an opportunity for the West as the flight of scientists from Germany was in the 1930s. But the end of the cold war could well have other effects on the way science is done—salutory ones. Governments will not stop investing in science and technology. But with defence spending falling, countries which spend large amounts of their research money on the military may decide to find new ways to spend it. Those who have looked carefully at what is happening in the scientific world will decide to think small, eschewing megaprojects—for reasons amply demonstrated in 1991.

Governments have a natural tendency to support "big science", which as a result has grown ever larger. The "big" refers to the amount of the investment and the size of the instruments involved. It can also refer to the results. In 1991, one of the first post-war triumphs of big science, the Jodrell Bank radio-observatory near Manchester, was the site of the year's most intriguing scientific discovery. Looking at a pulsar—one of the tiny, fascinating celestial bodies left when a star self-destructs in a supernova—three astronomers found evidence that it was being circled by a planet. It was the first observation of a planet beyond the solar system, and provided lots of excitement for the world's astrophysicists.

No one has ever denied that big science can be good: the more testing question is whether it is good value. Jodrell Bank is, but other great programmes are not. Countries with healthy science budgets, like America, are beginning to notice that they are not getting the outpouring of innovation that they think a burgeoning scientific profession should supply. That is because governments often end up constraining that which they should be liberating—the free progress of the scientific imagination.

One of the problems with big science is that it is so selective. Much investment typically goes into a single huge instrument, to which only a few groups have access, all constrained to look at things in more or less the same way. But the most exciting science, and the quickest to develop, blooms when many groups can tackle the same subject from different directions. That was amply demonstrated by the excitement that surrounded the buckyball in 1991.

A buckyball—a buckminsterfullerene molecule, to the purist—is a group of 60 carbon atoms arranged so as to form a pattern of hexagons and

Big science aloft

pentagons that evokes a soccer ball—a truncated icosahedron. In the past year or so they have been found to be easily made and manipulated, and chemists all over the world are finding them a source of endless amusement. They can form superconductors, they can be linked to create larger structures, they can cage other atoms, they can be used to grow diamonds. They are already moving from university laboratories to industrial ones, and some of their properties will surely be put to use soon. No one expected them, and no big science is used to study them; no one knows what the next chapter in their story might be, but anyone might write it. This is science at its best.

Despite the fast changing nature of the buckyball field, one thing is a sure bet. There will be industrial uses of the buckyball well before the Superconducting Super Collider (SSC) is finished. The SSC is about as big as big science can get, an 80km ring of tunnel under a patch of Texas ranchland, in which subatomic particles will be accelerated to enormous energies and then smashed headlong into each other. It was proposed in the early 1980s with a price tag of about $3 billion. Now it is set to cost over $8 billion, a price quite capable of climbing again before completion—which is meant to come around the turn of the century.

Physics plays a leading role in big science—partly because an outpouring of government money after the second world war encouraged it to develop an insatiable desire for new machines. However, it is still possible to do small physics—and, in so doing, to study the physics of the small. The scanning tunnelling microscope and its various relatives, all developed recently, are allowing physicists to move atoms around surfaces, while relatively cheap lasers allow atoms to be trapped in free space. This leads some to suggest that tiny machines—nanotechnologies, in the jargon—are about to greet the light of day. 1991 saw many steps in that direction. One example was the development of tiny structures called quantun wells which can be used to make lasers and optical sensors, parts crucial to all sorts of potentially tiny machines, not to mention new types of computer. Such progress is incremental, not revolutionary. Its cumulative effect, though, could be enormous.

While physics can be as big as you can imagine, biology, mercifully, is less flexible. Biology works with everyday stuff—living cells, mostly—and though the tools in a biology laboratory are increasingly complex, a few good researchers and a few million dollars of equipment can still produce world class results. That is

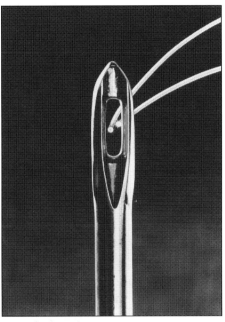

Camel's-eye view

why so much good experimental biology gets done—in 1991 biologists published far more papers than scientists in any other discipline. Such success makes it easy for biologists to resist the dubious blandishments of big science. The nearest biology comes to it is the human genome project, a scheme that aims to list every letter of the DNA code that describes a human being. The genome project is big in its aims, and involves a lot more money than biologists are used to dealing with, but it is not in the same league as the SSC. And it is inherently decentralised. Its work will go on in many existing laboratories, not a vast national centre.

From this, it might appear that the small and vibrant parts of science are the ones close to high-technology industries, such as microelectronics and biotechnology. But the presence of industry does not necessarily help. The greatest political battle over science in 1991 was fought on the floor of the American house of representatives over the fate of the international space station planned by America, Europe, Japan and Canada. This station was originally meant to be a port, a workshop, an observatory, an orbiting garage and more. Of these original justifications, all have now withered, save one: that hardy perennial, scientific research.

There is doubtless some interesting science to be done in such a laboratory. But no scientist could honestly say it was the most important thing in—or off—the world. Space scientists fear that it will eat into the budgets for the orbiting observatories and probes to other planets that are their true loves. Earthbound scientists just wish they could get at the crumbs under the space-going table. When it came to a vote, though, the scientists lobbying against the station were soundly trounced. The aerospace lobby could eat its way through the ranks of space scientists for breakfast and still feel quite peckish by 11 o'clock. So the biggest of big science, and the programme closest to the heart of the aerospace companies that grew up in the cold war and are now looking for new things to do, sailed on.

Devoting immoderate resources to a few high profile projects, the old way of the Soviet Union, is a poor way to serve science. It is like collecting old masters while artistic geniuses starve. It is to mistake the objects that science uses and produces for the spirit of questioning and creating fundamental to the process. It is that spirit that countries should seek to foster. To have great scientists is not enough, as Britain has proved—but, given a choice, it far outshines having the biggest laboratories.

As we reported then

The microchip war

JANUARY 26TH *Military technology is expensive, and during its development often temperamental. For all that, and although subsequent analysis cast doubt on some of the most enthusiastic claims made at the time, the Gulf war showed that it can work terribly well*

"OUR nation has pursued for decades the policy that has substituted machines and technology for human lives. I think especially in this environment we will continue to pursue that policy." His suggestion that America should make Saddam Hussein the target of its attack cost General Michael Dugan his job as air-force chief of staff last September. But what he said about the role technology would play in the war seems to have been as accurate as the laser-guided bombs shown on television.

The technology that has been substituted for human lives on the widest scale is that of the microprocessor. Just as microchips have infiltrated the home and office, so they have invaded the battlefield. The differences between today's weapons and those of the second world war are not unlike those between a 1940s gramophone and a compact-disc player, armed with a laser and stuffed with chips. It does the old job much better and some new jobs too. Although microchips give machines only a smidgen of intelligence, that can go a long way when sensibly applied by human masters.

In some cases, the microchip takes a man's place in facing danger. A Tomahawk cruise missile does the job of a bomber. It is programmed with a flight plan telling it how to get from a nearby "way-point" to its target, and with a set of pictures of how the terrain it will pass over should look to its radar altimeter. It can thus check that it is on course. These map programs take a fair bit of work, and cannot be drawn up on the launching ship; the sailors load a ready-made map into the missile, and tell it how to get to the initial way-point.

When the missile nears its target, it stops relying on radar and turns on a more acute guidance system. This compares what the missile sees through a light-sensitive sensor in its nose to pictures of the target stored in its memory.

As missiles go, a Tomahawk is supremely gifted. But it can carry only one 1,000lb (455kg) warhead, or a set of 166 bomblets which can be dropped in three batches. An F-15E, America's newest fighter-bomber, can carry a weapons load of up to 24,500lb (11,113kg). The Tomahawk also fails fairly often. Of the 104 launched on the first day of the war, it seems, 10-20 fell from the sky. The Tomahawk cannot change course, choose alternative targets, fight off opposition or bring back pictures of the damage done. If a commander thinks it essential to destroy something right away, he will still send bombers. For difficult but less vital tasks, a disposable $1m Tomahawk is a cheap alternative to a bomber and its crew.

No cleverer than it ought to be

Most military chips do not replace men. They protect them and improve their ability to cause damage. The obvious benefits have been seen in videotapes showing missiles and bombs hitting targets with extreme precision. This, in theory, saves lives on the other side—a rare concern in recent wars.

Much of the precision comes from laser guidance. This trick has been used since the last few years of the Vietnam war, and does not rely on any particularly outlandish circuitry. Its success comes from its determination to do one thing as well as it can. Such monomania has been useful to warriors since long before the silicon age.

Laser-guided bombs have a small sensor in their nose, and little fins. The two are linked via a microchip. If the sensor is pointed straight at something reflecting the light of a laser beam—distinctive in its brightness and colour—the bomb's tiny mind is happy. If the laser light wanders off centre, the bomb uses its fins to change its direction and angle of fall until the light is once again centred.

Such simple circuits control many types of missile—radar seekers and heat seekers, for example. The innovation of the laser-guided bomb is that you can aim at anything: just point the laser at it, and the bomb will fall on it if it can. During night missions inside Iraq, the laser shines from the belly of the bomber, and is kept on target by the pilot or the weapons officer, with the help of electronics that compensate for the aircraft's movements. Lasers may later be used by troops to mark out tanks for attack.

Most missiles with pretensions to cleverness are brighter than a laser-guided bomb, but not as clever as a Tomahawk. Some weapons home in on infra-red sources, some on radar, others just go where they are told. Some, like the Stand-off Land Attack

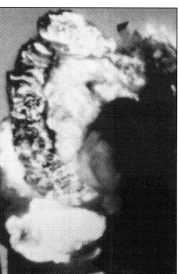

Testing the Tomahawk

Missile, SLAM, or the Israeli-produced Have Nap, can be "flown" by pilots looking through the missile's television eye, while sitting at a safe remove in aircraft.

In getting the bombs to where they can be used, air crews are helped by extensions to their senses—infra-red vision, light amplification and radar for night flight—all of which rely on electronics. "Avionics" circuits help them manoeuvre. They are protected by electronic countermeasures (ECM) which confuse enemy radar by sending out electronic noise and spurious signals. Just as missiles can be guided from aircraft that did not launch them, so jamming can be done by someone else on the bomber's behalf; division of labour pays off in battles, too. The extra range provided to sensors and accurate weapons by modern electronics allows some jammers and bombers to "stand off"—another way in which technology saves lives.

The possibilities of linkage

Microchips also let things happen at inhuman speed. The Patriot missile system is a good example. At its heart is a sophisticated "phased-array" radar, a stationary gridwork of tiny radar transmitters controlled by computer. By putting the elements in the radar out of step with each other to various degrees, the computer uses the array to make a radar beam that can flit across the sky and track a number of targets almost simultaneously.

When the system picks up an enemy, alerted by an early-warning satellite or an AWACS aeroplane, the radar starts tracking it. When it comes into range, the system launches an interceptor. This missile is not particularly clever, but the computers that control it and the radar are. As the interceptor streaks up, the radar tracks it as well as the incoming target. The radar beam which tracks the Patriot missile carries instructions updating it on which way to go to head off the enemy.

When the interceptor gets close to its target, it is used as a second radar receiver. Beams that bounce off the target are received by the interceptor, which passes the information back to the ground. The computers then use it to check the guidance instructions. If the target uses ECM—Scuds do not, but aeroplanes can—then the relatively powerful computers on the ground can have a good crack at sorting out information from disinformation.

The Patriot is a complicated system of launchers, radars, communications and control. The assembly of weapons into systems, spread wide in space but linked by little strings of data, typifies microchip warfare. Machines can keep the disparate parts of such a system co-ordinated much better than men can. An as-yet-unproven system called J-STARS, getting its baptism of fire in the Gulf, illustrates the point. J-STARS uses

A visible improvement

large air-borne synthetic-aperture radars to create images of the terrain 100 miles (160km) or more away, and identify moving objects like tanks and trucks. That information is sent to tactical computers in control stations to produce guidance for artillery and missiles—the American army's new tactical missile system has been designed to operate as part of such a set-up, hitting targets more than 60 miles off.

Not all computers are in the front line. Some are tacticians and some are backroom boys, dealing with logistics and military planning. Desert Storm, with its thousands of sorties a day, could have been planned without computers (the Schlieffen plan launched the first world war with sweat and brainpower, little more); but computers allow the plans to be fine-tuned and to be altered quickly. And some computers find their niche as boffins, designing ever-fancier gadgets.

The F-117A, the "stealth fighter", is a product of computers. Much of its stealth comes from a design that minimises the chance of radar waves bouncing back the way they came. In the 1970s, when it was designed, computers were hard put to work out how to minimise the radar reflected from curved surfaces—so the F-117A is made up of flat ones. The more modern B-2 bomber is more rounded. The F-117A's shape also makes it unstable; without onboard electronics constantly helping the pi-

lot, the stealth fighter would be almost impossible to fly.

Your bill, sir

Microchip warfare is undeniably impressive, but it is clearly not flawless. It is always at the mercy of the people who design and use it. It can have faults in its design, or it can be used incorrectly (correct use needs trained skills). It can also be betrayed. Information from the French, American and Russian experts who helped set up Iraq's air defences will have helped in their defeat or circumvention—a jammer which knows how the enemy radar "thinks" has a great advantage.

The high-technology route is extremely expensive; the sophistication of America's weapons and the plaintiveness of its calls for burden-sharing are directly related. The cost of weapons often means they are in potentially short supply, all the more so because once commanders find that a weapon works, they want to use it for everything.

The weapons are expensive partly because they are made of expensive components, but also because they are time-consuming to develop. The "new" systems being used in the Gulf have all been more than a decade in development. The long gestation comes from the fact that, although mechanical and chemical engineering hold few surprises—if the design looks all right the thing will probably work—electronic engineering carries no such assurances. All programs have bugs, and need endless refinement.

High-tech weaponry has certainly kept down casualties during the air war (it will have less ability to do so on the ground). Whether it allows the exercise of force to be more controlled and effective has yet to be seen. There are still no accurate assessments of damage available. It is clear, and unsurprising, that Patriot missiles sometimes fail. It is easy to deduce that other systems do, too; many targets are being hit again and again. The pictures of precision attacks provide only anecdotal evidence of effectiveness. Smart weapons can clearly produce a dazzling display. Whether they can win wars has yet to be proved.

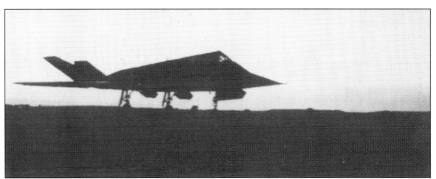

Designed by computer, flown by microchip

The most micro of circuits

FEBRUARY 16TH *In electronics, the move to tininess continues apace. A few months after this article appeared, a report in Nature described the smallest component to date—a switch made from a single atom*

IN THE drive to squeeze more brain-power into a smaller space, the circuitry on microchips is dwindling to the size of atoms. It is a mixed blessing. Effects which are explicable only by quantum theory are beginning to plague designers. Instead of despairing, though, some of them are turning the weirdness to their advantage.

One problem facing atom-sized circuitry is crosstalk: electrons have an annoying habit of leaking through insulating barriers if the barriers are only a few atoms thin. In the days before quantum theory, such behaviour would have been inexplicable. In the quantum world, though, Heisenberg's uncertainty principle applies. Although electrons may initially be on one side of the barrier, their exact whereabouts can never be known. This uncertainty about an electron's position can extend a little beyond the barrier. So it can occasionally pop up on the other side, having "quantum tunnelled" its way through.

Annoying—and, to the layman, baffling—as this can be, interesting things happen when two barriers are placed very close to one another to form a device called a resonant tunnelling diode. The first of these was built by Leo Esaki and his colleagues at IBM's Watson Laboratories in New York in 1974. They deposited alternate layers of aluminium-gallium-arsenide (a poor conductor of electricity) and gallium-arsenide (a better one) on to a gallium-arsenide crystal. Each layer was just a few tens of atoms thick. The electrons in the gallium-arsenide filling of this sandwich are confined to a region one atom or so thick, known as a quantum well.

There is a big difference between electrons confined to such a well and those that are free to roam in a relatively large chunk of gallium-arsenide crystal. The captive electrons can have only certain levels of energy. Imagine that the electrons are books and the energy levels are shelves. All the books in a quantum well are stacked in a bookcase with regularly spaced shelves. In a big crystal, the electrons are scattered in heaps all over the room.

This fact is a consequence of another principle of quantum theory, the Pauli exclusion principle. This states that electrons at a certain energy level will exclude nearby electrons from that level. And the more electrons are confined, the further apart their energy levels must lie. In a chunk of crystal most electrons are confined only to the limits of the crystal; their energy levels can be so closely spaced that they are practically indistinguishable. When electrons are confined in a layer of atomic thickness, the energy levels must become well separated.

As a result, the quantum well has a curious way of conducting electricity. When a

voltage is applied across the well, the heap of electrons at one edge of the well is raised above the heap on the other side. The electrons at the top of the higher heap will tend to slide over to the other side, resulting in an electric current. But they can do this only if there happens to be a shelf (ie, energy level) in the well at just the right height for the electrons to slide across. By increasing the voltage, the position of the top of the heap of electrons can be shifted, making it more difficult for the electrons to cross.

What this adds up to is that increasing the voltage can sometimes reduce the electric current (which is the opposite of what happens in normal materials). This useful property is known as negative differential resistance. In a material with normal resistance, if electrons pile up in one place because of chance fluctuations, they will rapidly disperse. But in a resonant tunnelling diode, such a pile-up will snowball, producing a large pulse of current. When the diode

is tuned to the right voltage such pulses occur in rapid succession, producing an oscillating signal of microwave frequency. Such gadgets outperform conventional microwave diodes at high frequencies; they are also easier to make. Some high-performance astronomical and military equipment already uses them.

As they stand, such diodes cannot be used to build a computer. This is because a diode has only two external connections, an input and an output. Transistors—the building-blocks of computers—need a third connection to control the amount of output for a given input, rather as a tap controls the flow of water. In 1985 Naoki Yokoyama and his group at Fujitsu Laboratories in Tokyo modified the resonant tunnelling diode to get round the problem. One way of doing this is to make a third connection to the quantum well. A small voltage at this connection controls the position of the energy levels in the well and so turns the transistor on or off.

Whereas traditional transistors switch on and off at only one voltage, the resonant tunnelling transistor goes on and off at several different voltages. This happens because, as the voltage is increased, successive energy levels in the well line up with the top of the heap of electrons on the input side, allowing the diode to conduct a current.

This has led some researchers to contemplate revolutionary changes in computer design. The on-off behaviour of normal transistors means that all the information in computers is encoded in binary: sequences of ones and noughts. The possibility of switches with many states means that information could be stored more compactly. A transistor with ten states could represent any of the digits nought to nine. In binary, the number nine has to be represented by four digits (1001), which takes four transistors. One of the first applications of this idea—a device to check for errors in electronic transmissions—was built in 1989 by Federico Capasso, Al Cho and their colleagues at AT&T's Bell Laboratories in New Jersey.

Well, maybe not

Some researchers are not content with quantum wells. They want electrons in even tighter squeezes: "quantum wires" and "quantum dots" are already buzzwords. The electrons in a "dot" of around 100 atoms behave much as though they were in a single large atom. At Texas Instruments in Dallas, Mark Reed, John Randall and their colleagues have already made quantum-dot diodes. But their prototypes have yet to out-perform quantum wells. Nobody has yet managed to make a quantum-dot transistor.

Why bother? By the time somebody wins the race to make one, steady progress in traditional transistors may have whittled away much of the quantum dot's advantage. And binary is so central to computer

design that it may prove impossible to eradicate, even if the replacement is theoretically much better.

Some quantum-dot enthusiasts have bigger ambitions than just making smaller or cleverer transistors. They hope that such devices will be able to exploit one of the most peculiar quantum effects of all: the tendency of particles like electrons to behave as waves. Like ripples on a pond, two electron waves can produce one large one where their crests meet, or they can cancel out if the crest of one meets the trough of

another. Electron waves could provide the ultimate on-off switch.

In large devices, this promise will remain unfulfilled. Before it has travelled far across a traditional transistor, the wave's regular rise and fall will become jumbled by chance collisions with defects in the crystal or because of the jiggling of the crystal's atoms. Make a transistor small enough, though, and the chance of an electron wave being scrambled becomes negligible. On the drawing board, at least, quantum dots fit the bill.

The uses of diversity

MAY 25TH *Scientists love novelty; they also love order. With the fossils of the Burgess shale, they seem to have found the first in abundance. Now they are imposing on it dollops of the second*

ARMED with microscopes, miniature drills and an infinite capacity for taking pains, a few palaeontologists have redrawn their profession's picture of early life. For several decades they have been studying superbly preserved fossils from the rocks of the Burgess shale, found in the Canadian Rockies, which are among the earliest fossils of complicated organisms.

The creatures had previously been forced into convenient taxonomic pigeon-holes, whether they fitted or not. The result was to hide their variety. When the revisionists looked into the pigeon-holes without preconceptions, surprising novelties stared back at them, some with five eyes, some with none. Many of these animals, rather than being simple precursors of sophisticates yet to come, were quite unlike anything ever seen elsewhere.

To some, the huge variety of life in the Burgess shale has been an inspiration. Stephen Jay Gould of Harvard, a friend of the Burgess revisionists, wrote a popular book about their bounty, "Wonderful Life". The history of life, he argued, could have followed all sorts of paths. The weird anomalies of the Burgess shale could have gone on to found evolutionary dynasties while the distant forebears of humanity perished in the ooze.

Others, though not denying Dr Gould's point about the contingent nature of evolution—no true Darwinist can—are less enamoured of the diversity. They feel that there is a danger of being dazzled by it and

thus of missing a unique opportunity to make sense of the early history of animal evolution.

The debate centres on taxonomy, the classification of creatures. A phylum is a group of species which share a basic body plan and thus, presumably, a common ancestor. Today there are 30 phyla around, more or less (some borders are a bit murky). According to work done in the 1970s and 1980s, there could have been up to 32 in the rocks of Burgess shale alone, including many never seen anywhere else. By comparing the number of phyla, one can say, as Dr Gould does, that there was a wider range of life in one little patch of sea floor than in all today's oceans—though that conclusion ignores the fact that today's oceans contain whales, jellyfish, barnacles and octopuses, whereas the Burgess sea contained only little creepy-crawlies.

The Burgess animals have been taken from established phyla in which they did not fit and put into new ones. So new phyla were created to accommodate a few bizarre animals. However the fossils can also be re-interpreted to fit back into old phyla:

• *Wiwaxia* looks like a small Belgian chocolate covered in scales, with some bigger spikes pointing out here and there. Simon Conway Morris of Cambridge University, who played a big part in the first reinterpretation of the Burgess animals, thinks *Wiwaxia* has no living relatives, but is probably related to other fossils he and his colleagues have found in northern Greenland. Nick Butterfield of Harvard, though, thinks *Wiwaxia* is related to a scaly worm, part of a known phylum,

which is also found in the Burgess shale. His view is based on similarities he sees in the scales. The question is not yet decided, one way or the other.

• *Hallucigenia* is one of Dr Conway Morris's greatest finds, an aptly named creature that balances on 14 stilts and waves seven tentacles in the air. However, in last week's *Nature* new fossils found in Burgess-like rocks from China were described by Lars Ramsköld from the Swedish Museum of Natural History and Hou Xianguang from the Nanjing Institute of Geology and Palaeontology. The fossils appear to be relatives of *Hallucigenia*, with flat scaly plates reminiscent of its spines (though not leg-like) and similar tentacles. If they are relatives, then Dr Conway Morris's *Hallucigenia* is the wrong way up: its tentacles, not its spines, were its legs. Dr Conway Morris has always said there could be other ways to make sense of *Hallucigenia*, and agrees that the new interpretation may be better.

Hallucigenia's tentacles appear to be singletons; if they are in fact legs, they should come in pairs. Dr Ramsköld has found traces of extra tentacles on one of the only two really good specimens of the species there are, at the Smithsonian Institution in Washington, DC. He is not allowed to dissect the fossils, though, since they are at present irreplaceable. The new interpretation seems to push *Hallucigenia*, the Chinese fossils, and some other species around at the time (including another of the Burgess oddballs, *Aysheaia*) into the arthropod phylum, with insects, crabs and trilobites. It may be that they are in fact onychophorans, a group of arthropods now represented by caterpillar-like velvet worms that burrow through dead wood in Australia.

• *Anomalocaris* is the biggest predator among the Burgess animals,

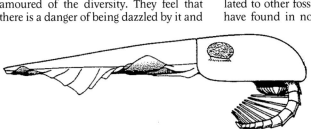

and one of the hardest to interpret. For a long time some of its parts—its mouth and its eating appendages—were classed as separate animals. Once a definitive picture of it was produced, it was given its own phylum. Des Collins, of the Royal Ontario Museum, doubts that it deserves quite such an honour. Dr Collins has the great advantage of being allowed to go out and get new fossils from the Burgess site—everyone else has to make do with what is already in museums. He has found several different types of *Anomalocaris*; from studying the whole lot, he thinks he can make a case for saying that it belongs with the arthropods, not out on its own.

Putting the Burgess weirdoes into more conventional groups whittles away at some of the shale's apparently huge diversity. A more thorough-going approach is to revise the way taxonomy is done. Today's way of grouping things into phyla reflects today's world. It is hardly surprising that it is a poor fit for an-

imals removed from the present by hundreds of millions of years of evolution. Enter Derek Briggs, of the University of Bristol: along with Dr Conway Morris and under the tutelage of Harry Whittington, also of Cambridge, he did much to prise the Burgess fossils from their original mistaken pigeon-holes. Dr Briggs and Richard Fortey (of London's Natural History Museum) have been looking at new ways of classifying the various arthropods in the Burgess.

Their approach, instead of valuing the unique, seeks out the common. Using their shared characteristics, the animals can be arranged into a sensibly small number of groups, joined by the common ancestors with whom the shared features began. The approach allows researchers to see how the diversity came to be, rather than simply marvelling at it. It also shows that, if classed in groups natural to them, rather than in groups based on their re-

mote descendants, the Burgess arthropods are not such a disparate lot. It is possible to do this sort of analysis only within the arthropod phylum, because only that has enough species, with enough measurable features. But what holds true within one phylum may well hold true across them.

In the end, the answers will come as they always do—from the ground. When Burgess revisionism started in the 1960s, the site in Canada was unique. Now Burgess animals and their relatives are found in Greenland, China and elsewhere, as well as at other sites found by Dr Collins near the original one. As more fossils are found, the sense of wonder will no doubt be stirred again, but the systematic research aimed at providing a more complete picture will continue. The message of the Burgess shale—that there has always been variety, and no one can say in what forms it will survive until it has done so—remains. The fascinating details of how it came to be are still waiting to be found.

Killer genes ate my dog

JUNE 1ST *Darwin's thought about natural selection was strongly influenced by the ease with which breeders could amplify traits in varieties of pigeon. Here is a story of similarly unnatural selection, abused*

IF YOU believe Britain's tabloid newspapers, man's best friend has been turned into his worst enemy. The American pit-bull terrier is the most recent in a string of large dogs with big teeth and short tempers which have terrorised the British public. The breed's enemies, including the government ministers who want to wipe it out, say it is worse than all other dogs, and inherently dangerous. Defenders claim that, in the hands of a sensible owner, the pit-bull will cause no more trouble than any other breed.

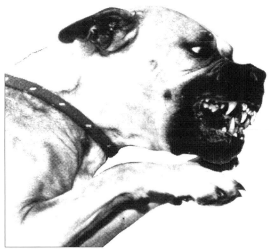

Blame the breeders

There is good reason to doubt this.

The pit-bull has been bred as a fighting dog. German shepherds, Dobermann pinschers and rottweilers are all bred to guard human masters, their livestock and their property. Pit-bulls are designed to kill other dogs. Their large heads and strong jaws make pit-bulls ideal for the fighting life. But it is the unpleasant behaviour bred into the dogs that makes them particularly nasty:

• **Arousability.** Pit-bulls are much more easily aroused than most dogs. Arousal is controlled by a part of the brain called the Reticular Activating System (RAS). The amount of L-tyrosine, a chemical which passes messages from nerve cell to nerve cell, seems to play a role. Since they are genetically controlled, L-tyrosine levels can be changed by selective breeding. More easily aroused breeds have been shown to have lots of L-tyrosine in the RAS. It is a fair bet that pit-bulls do, too.

• Changes in the RAS may also account for the dogs' **perseverance.** Pit-bulls are incredibly tenacious. Once they are fixed on a target, they are all but impossible to distract. The little girl whose recent ordeal pro-

pelled pit-bulls into the headlines suffered a 15-minute attack. The dog's owner and two other adults could not stop the animal, though they beat it until it bled.

• This is due to the dogs' **insensitivity to pain.** To the extent that pain does influence a pit-bull, it may encourage it rather than dissuade it. Most dogs which have been beaten in a fight will cringe submissively when they next meet the victor. A pit-bull will attack. Again, this seems to be a matter of brain chemistry. Endorphins are generated by the body to block pain (morphine and its relatives work by mimicking this effect). Their reactions to anaesthetics suggest that pit-bulls are more than usually sensitive to endorphins. They may also generate higher levels of them. This would enable them to withstand a lot of pain. And endorphins, like morphine, are addictive. The dogs may be junkies, seeking pain so they can get the endorphin buzz they crave.

• The pit-bull's **body signalling** has also been distorted. Most dogs will give notice before they attack. Pit-bulls attack without warning, in order to get the advantage of the first strike. A dog will generally bow to another if it wishes to play. When a pit-bull makes this signal—universal among other breeds—it may follow it with an all-out attack. In effect, it is lying about its intentions.

Not all the traits that have been bred into the pit-bull are bad. They ought, in theory, to be fairly safe to handle, since (at least among those who breed them for fighting) pit-bulls which attack men have usually been killed. But this culling probably tailed off when the dogs became popular as pets. So today's dogs have the temperament for fighting, but little discipline.

So much for nature. How much is nurture? A common feature of allegedly aggressive breeds is that their litters include many potential "alpha" animals. Alphas are likely to try to lead any pack they find themselves in. Although alpha potentiality is probably inherited, dominance depends on the dog's upbringing. Here, the owner's behaviour matters. A dog may come to believe it is dominant without the owner realising that this has happened. Then, when a conflict arises, the dog becomes aggressive, whereas an animal which did not think it was top dog would submit.

In general, if pups are scrutinised for the signs of a tendency to dominance, and then disciplined appropriately, they quickly stop making trouble. But it is unlikely that this would work for the pit-bull, whose behaviour deviates so much from the normal pattern of a dog's life.

The birth of arthritis?

JUNE 29TH, FLORENCE *The seventh international AIDS conference produced little news; in Florence, though, there are always things worth looking at*

WHEN not discussing AIDS in Florence's conference centre, many of the conference-goers found time to tire out their feet and enrich their souls in the city's art galleries. For at least one of them, though, the pictures were not just an uplifting diversion; they were another bit of business. John Morrow, who works for IDEC, a Californian pharmaceuticals company, studies various diseases in which the immune system turns against the body; not only AIDS but also rheumatoid arthritis. And those who study rheumatoid arthritis have a professional interest in the works of Botticelli.

Rheumatoid arthritis has been around longer than AIDS, but it is still a newish disease. The first clear description of a case by a doctor was written in 1827. Nor does it appear in earlier non-medical sources, where other diseases, like gout, are clearly recognisable. The Bible does not mention it, nor does Homer. The emperor Constantine IX Monomachus, who flourished at the turn of the millennium, had a disease that might have been rheumatoid arthritis, but nobody can be sure. The skeletons of Anglo-Saxons and mummified Egyptians show no sign of the disease. However, the bones of American Indians who died 400 years ago in Alabama do.

This prompts the idea that one of the contributory factors to the disease (researchers are sure there are many) might be a microbe that travelled east across the Atlantic from America, thus accounting for the disease's belated appearance in Europe over the past few centuries. It is in testing this hypothesis that the painters come in.

If artists portray the world naturalistically, they may record arthritis. Rubens's second wife, for example, who was one of his models, seems to have had suggestively swollen arthritic wrists. But when is the earliest such record that shows the disease? Botticelli's Venus rose from the waves before Columbus crossed them, so evidence of arthritis in her, or any other paintings of the fifteenth century, would spoil the American-import theory. Some have claimed to see a range of arthritic afflictions in Botticelli's paintings. The little finger on the left hand of Venus is one of their examples.

Dr Morrow, though, was unconvinced by the evidence of the galleries, as others have been before him. Oddities in the hands were common in Botticelli's work and in that of his contemporaries. Either everyone had the disease, or the odd hands are a stylistic quirk or affectation: probably the latter. Alternatively, Botticelli may have had only a few models; all the hands may belong to the same lady. If she had rheumatoid arthritis, a promising theory would be dead—but there might still be a tangential, and medically unimportant, American link. Venus may well have been Simonetta Vespucci, whose brother Amerigo later gave his name to the land over the sea.

Look at the little finger

An accident, or did you planet?

JULY 27TH *The planet around pulsar PSR 1829-10 was arguably the discovery of the year. But before the year was out, it appeared that more planets had been discovered around another pulsar, implying that such planets are fairly common, and thus that they are probably formed after supernovae. Strange and wonderful they may be; earthlike they are not*

PLANETS are not, of themselves, particularly significant. They are just the rubble left over when a star is born from a cloud of gas and dust. To people who live on one, though, the existence of other planets orbiting other stars takes on a disproportionate interest. If there are many planets, the universe may be rich in life. If planets are rare, then life may be rare, too—and even if it is not, life that evolved somewhere other than on a planet might be too alien for humans ever to come to terms with. So astronomers have spent a great deal of time looking for planets around other stars. Now, at last, they seem to have found one—but in a most peculiar place.

Little is known about the new planet except its mass—about ten times that of the earth—and the fact that it orbits its star at a distance of 100m km (63m miles), giving it an orbit like that of Venus around the sun. Nothing odd in that. The strange thing is that the star it orbits is a neutron star, incredibly dense and only about 20 km across. Neutron stars are ghosts, born when a large star dies. They give their progenitor a sort of after-life by preserving some of its attributes—some of its mass, its magnetic field and its spin. These last two make some neutron stars, such as PSR 1829-10, the one around which this planet is orbiting, peculiarly visible. The magnetic field sends out radio waves in a beam, and the star's spin sweeps that beam across the sky, so that from the earth the neutron star appears to flash on and off. Such flashing neutron stars are called pulsars.

It is these radio pulses that reveal the planet. They are normally extraordinarily regular—some pulsars keep time better than the earth's most accurate clocks. But, as Andrew Lyne, Matthew Bailes and Setnam Shemar from Manchester University report in this week's *Nature*, the pulses from PSR 1829-10 oscillate in frequency. If the oscillations are real—and in a field famous for discoveries later withdrawn, the data look very robust—the pulsar is moving to and fro.

The pulsar is wobbling in a little circle, like a hammer-thrower whirling his hammer; by studying the circling, astronomers can work out the basic facts about the hammer, or in this case the planet. Wobble-watchers have long looked at normal stars, where such movements would cause slight changes in the starlight, in hope of finding traces of planets. But the radiation from normal stars does not arrive in nice sharp pulses, so the effect has, as yet, proved hard to pin down—though there are some likely candidates.

A planet orbiting a pulsar is particularly visible; but it is also particularly unlikely. When the core of a giant star collapses to form a neutron star, the star is torn apart. Such a supernova provides great astrophysics for those at a safe distance. It is no fun at all if you happen to be nearby. If the star that goes supernova is a red giant—most of them are—it spends 1m years or so in a state of preparatory bloat, during which planets in close orbits, like the one around PSR 1829-10, would be within the outer reaches of the star. When the core finally collapses, there is a huge burst of radiation, carrying away more than a tenth of the star's mass as pure energy. Hot on its heels comes a shockwave carrying yet more mass.

It is conceivable that a planet might stand up to this without being destroyed (though 1m years being baked in a star would be tough). But there is also the question of its orbit. Imagine a planet orbiting a

star which suddenly loses half its weight. The star's gravity will no longer be strong enough to hold on to the planet; the planet will fly off, like a hammer when the hammer-thrower releases it. Neutron stars weigh 1.4 times as much as the sun: any lighter and they do not form, any heavier and they become black holes. The stars whose deaths bring forth neutron stars have to be between six and 60 times heavier than the sun. So, even without the attendant violence, a supernova explosion still means that the star involved loses most of its weight, and thus

should also lose its planets.

There is a way out of this. Neutron stars are born on the move, because supernovas are not quite symmetric. If a neutron star started off moving in the same direction as one of its lost planets, it could recapture it—the thrower would run and catch his hammer. It sounds unlikely. But then so will all the explanations of this planet's peculiar situation.

Cannibal or kidnapper?

One way to preserve a planet is to soften the supernova. If a star is spinning fast enough, its core might collapse comparatively gently. And you can form a neutron star without a collapsing giant, if you enlist the aid of another star. If matter from another star falls on to a small dense star called a white dwarf, the dwarf can eventually gain enough mass to become a neutron star. PSR 1829-10 has no companion star; but it is possible that a companion did exist, and was destroyed by the pulsar's radiation. A "black widow" pulsar elsewhere has been

seen blowing its partner away. If that was the case, the "planet" might be the last smidgeon of the companion star, though its discoverers doubt it.

There is another way to kill a companion. Imagine two white dwarfs spiralling ever closer to one another. Eventually one will be torn apart. Some of the debris will fall on to its companion, turning it into a neutron star. The rest will form a disc around the new pulsar in which planets could form—just as they are thought to around young sun-like stars.

This notion, put forward by Martin Rees and colleagues at Cambridge University, is one of several that invoke "second-generation" planets—planets that form around the neutron star after the supernova. These ideas all suggest that clouds of muck around the pulsar are what form a new planet or planets, though they differ in their details. If the planet around PSR 1829-10 is a second-generation planet, though, it loses some of its charm. It might reveal lots about the aftermath of supernovas, but little about planets around normal stars, which is what most people want to know.

The planet may have been born with the original star or born after its death; or, Dr Rees points out, it may have been kidnapped. Imagine a neutron star hitting an everyday star like the sun; it would sink to the centre. Matter would rain down on to it. That would give off radiation, which would inflate the remains of the surrounding star until it became a big bright sort-of-star known as a Thorne-Zytkow object. In 100,000 years the pulsar's radiation would blow all the remnants of the other star away, leaving behind a solar system with a neutron star at its centre.

The idea that PSR 1829-10 has become step-sun to another star's family of planets is appealing. If the pulsar's planet comes from a system like the sun's, then such systems may be common; if it was formed in the debris of a supernova, though, it has little in common with the earth. There is no way to prove which of the early hypotheses about the planet is true. The only thing for certain is that many more speculations will follow. The question of whether the fascinating object around PSR 1829-10 reveals much about planets around less outrageous stars will not be answered for a long time.

Little big world

SEPTEMBER 21ST *Eight humans began living in a distant planet, on earth*

THE visitor to Biosphere 2, nestled in the mountains north of Tucson, has a feeling of déjà vu. This could be because he sees so many reminders of things—the 3.15-acre glass palace contains thousands of species of plant and animal, arranged to caricature seven different types of ecosystem, from swamp to desert. In fact, it is because its spectacular artificiality is just like that of a huge film set. The visitor expects one of the red-uniformed inhabitants to turn and address him, revealing a white Siamese in his arms: "So we meet again, Mr Bond."

From September 26th, though, no visitors will be able to entertain such daydreams while strolling in Biosphere 2's rain forest or lying on the shores of its swimming-pool sized "ocean". On that morning, amid a fair bit of razzmatazz and a year or so behind schedule, the biosphere will be sealed for two years, with four men and four women living inside. Biosphere 1, in case you were wondering, is what the other 5.2 billion of us live in.

The idea is to find out whether man can design and live in a self-supporting biosphere in which the environment provides everything needed for life. In principle, Biosphere 2, like the earth, is isolated except for inputs of energy—it needs lots of power, not least to keep itself cool—and information. In practice, its isolation may be less than perfect; many doubt that such a huge structure can be air-tight. They also question whether such a huge uncontrolled experiment can produce any meaningful science. Some make dire predictions—that the hot, moist interior will be heaven for fungal and bacterial diseases, and that the bionauts will find themselves in the sickest of sick buildings.

It is certainly true that Biosphere 2 will be a lot more hectic than Biosphere 1. It has only 70 tonnes of living matter within it, sharing a tiny 60 kilograms of atmospheric carbon dioxide, so things will be in pretty constant flux. Many of the species within are represented by only a handful of specimens. It is hard to believe the "extinction rate" under the glass will be less than 10%—and it might easily be 50%.

Still, the eight bionauts—a slightly spacey, but pleasant, knowledgeable and committed group of people—will probably have fun watching the interactions of their little ecosystems, when not farming in the intensive-agriculture section. They may even learn something. Whether they will make a profit is not clear. The project has been touted as running on a commercial basis. Those in charge—also spacey, but less charming—claim they will make back what they spent through patents on new technologies and tourist revenue. It seems unlikely that this will recoup the costs, which may be $100m. That has come almost entirely, it is said, from Ed Bass, the reclusive heir to a Texan fortune. To show for it, he has one of the most bizarre living spaces in the world—though he will not be in it. Nor will there be any Siamese cats.

One bionaut later had to leave the biosphere due to injury. The others are having to put up with high levels of carbon dioxide, which they hope will decline when plant growth starts in the spring

Out of this world

Fitting the small to the infinite

OCTOBER 12TH, WASHINGTON, DC, AND LOS ALAMOS, NEW MEXICO *After years of getting bigger and more complex, America's spacecraft are beginning to shrink*

WHEN the Space Shuttle *Discovery* launched NASA's Upper Atmosphere Research Satellite (UARS) last month, one researcher rejoiced that it was to previous such satellites as a Rolls-Royce is to an old Volkswagen. He had a point; but the heyday of the space-going Rolls-Royce seems to be past. America's satellites, like its cars before them, are beginning to shrink. The trend is already visible in parts of the military and in some plans for future communications satellites; it is now becoming noticeable within NASA, long the home of big, often excellent and always expensive spacecraft. At a cost of $740m, the 7½-tonne UARS may be the largest thing the space agency puts into orbit round the earth for a long time.

The next champion in the big, expensive and would-be-excellent stakes will be NASA's earth observing system (EOS). It was originally planned as a series of six satellites, of which two would be in orbit at any one time, that would gather data about the earth and its climate for 30 years. NASA planned to spend $17 billion in the 1990s, and well over $30 billion all told. Even in the stratospheric realm of space budgets and the popular cause of environmental research, that looked a bit much; Congress has limited EOS to $11 billion this decade. That has forced some rethinking; so has a report by a panel set up to look into EOS by the National Space Council.

This committee, chaired by Edward Frieman of the Scripps Institute in La Jolla, stated with authority what other outsiders had said before—that the EOS spacecraft were too big. Huge platforms with lots of sensors on board are expensive, and subject to over-runs in cost and time. And launch failures are more disastrous when all the eggs are in one basket. If the rockets used for EOS were to have a failure rate of 10%, then there would be a one-in-two chance that one of the six satellites would be lost at launch.

Grandiose projects have often found favour with NASA; in this case appeal was made to scientific necessity to justify the size. Some questions can be answered only if instruments that pick up different types of information look at the same place at the same time. This can most easily be arranged by having them perched on the same platform. The Frieman panel, composed of scientists and engineers from government, industry and universities, found that most of the required simultaneity could still be achieved if instruments were put on smaller spacecraft flown close together. Small craft would provide more flexibility, since there would be no need to wait for the last instrument to be ready before flying the first. They would also make changing budgets easier to cope with, since delaying a specific launch would not delay half the mission.

NASA is accepting the panel's ideas and rethinking the system so as to have a larger number of smaller satellites, but without actually admitting that it was wrong in the first place. Lennard Fisk, NASA's head of space science, points to changed circumstances: budget constraints and a new launch capability. Until recently, there has been no launch pad suitable for launching medium-sized satellites at Vandenberg Air Force Base in California, the site best suited to the polar orbits the EOS satellites require. Now the air force plans to build such a pad, which NASA can use.

Dr Fisk stresses that the satellites in a reconfigured EOS will still not exactly be small—they will be about the size of UARS. Elsewhere in his empire, though, those planning to explore the solar system are interested in really small spaceships. A set of little lunar probes is being developed to replace a larger lunar orbiter that has been cancelled. Similar small probes might visit a nearby asteroid and travel alongside it. That will be particularly welcome if CRAF, a large spacecraft designed to study asteroids and a comet, goes the way of the lunar mission; this year's budget makes that likely.

Missions to Mars now being planned make use of the same approach. Small simple probes weighing only 150kg (330lb) could be launched three or four at a time. A network of 16 such landers could study

many aspects of Mars, from its sand-dunes to its ice-caps. Through seismology it would learn about the planet's guts. Later variants might carry roving robots. The Jet Propulsion Laboratory, a NASA centre in Pasadena, California, has recently been testing a 25kg rover near Death Valley to see what it might be able to do on Mars.

Pebbles in the sky

One of the advantages of small craft is that if one fails—or even if a few do—the overall mission can still succeed. This appeals to planners who have recently seen too many big expensive projects develop flaws. As well as the Hubble space telescope, there is also the Galileo mission to Jupiter. This big probe, already en route, will send back the only data expected from the outer planets this century—if, that is, its jammed antenna can be persuaded to unfurl. Redundant systems clearly have their charms. So does quick development. Big spacecraft can take decades to get into space. By the time a neophyte researcher has seen a mission through from conception to launch, he can be halfway through his career—and getting data from instruments years out of date. Small craft allow the use of up-to-date technology.

The techniques that make this possible have not been developed at NASA. The space agency has concentrated on engineering projects that cost a lot and keep lots of people busy—the shuttle and the space station—not on the fiddly systems that let spacecraft be small. The champions of that technology have been found on the fringes of the military. Although the air force has yet to be converted to small satellites, the Strategic Defence Initiative Organisation (SDIO), charged with turning "star wars" enthusiasm into some sort of reality, has embraced

them. There was no other option, according to Greg Canavan of Los Alamos National Laboratory. The only way space-based defences can be made remotely feasible is if they are small, numerous and relatively cheap—cheaper to launch than to knock down.

To this end, Dr Canavan, his colleague Lowell Wood at Lawrence Livermore National Laboratory in California, and others came up with "brilliant pebbles". This year SDIO is spending $392m on them—it has asked for $659m to spend in 1992, though it is unlikely to get quite that much. Two aerospace companies, Martin Marietta and TRW, are working on designs. The pebbles—a metre long, less than 100kg—will be equipped with sensors to pick up the rocket plumes of ascending missiles. They are meant to close in on and kill missiles that they see. Some relevant technology has been tested in flight—though no such test has been a complete success. If a missile defence is deployed this decade, some sort of "pebble" will be its space-based component, if it has one.

The sensors in brilliant pebbles, and others that make similar use of recent advances in miniaturisation, will have wider applications. Dr Canavan was a member of the Frieman panel, and suggested ways in which new sensors on small satellites could be used for EOS. He hopes to fly such sensors in the next few years, if he can get money from the defence and commerce departments as well as NASA. If they are shown to work, parts of EOS could end up getting a lot smaller still. A related climate satellite is already under development at Los Alamos—and the laboratory's space team is ready to launch a small astrophysics satellite later this year. ALEXIS will study x-rays. It weighs 100kg, has cost about $15m and will be launched on a Pegasus booster, a new rocket that takes off from under the wing of a B52 bomber, developed by the Orbital Sciences Corporation with military backing.

Various spacecraft manufacturers are now planning to sell small multi-purpose spacecraft. Some have bigger ideas. Last year Motorola announced plans for a constellation of 77 little satellites to provide worldwide mobile communications. Others are aiming to provide the same sort of service with fewer satellites. Motorola is now considering adding sensors derived from SDI work to its constellation, providing images of the earth's surface in which features as little as 5 metres across will be visible. The size of the constellation means that most of the world would be visible most of the time.

Selling data could be a useful second string to Motorola's bow.

The proponents of small satellites have yet to show that they can really deliver working technologies—though there are some simple small spacecraft doing things in orbit right now. They cannot do everything, and only in Dr Canavan's and Dr Wood's more grandiloquent moments does anyone appear to claim they can. But they have the advantage of not costing too much when they fail, and they might greatly enrich existing scientific programmes. NASA can play a part, but it is far from the forefront in this technology—a technology that makes spacecraft available to individual universities and laboratories. Competition may spur its efforts to catch up.

Many lights, long tunnel

OCTOBER 26TH *Molecular biology is beginning to understand Alzheimer's disease. However, finding a pernicious protein is not the same as finding a cure*

FEW biotechnology products have reached the market, but that does not mean the industry just sits and twiddles its well-paid thumbs. Molecular biologists have learnt many clever tricks over the past ten years—tricks which facilitate further learning. This is why the loss-making industry is not despondent. Biotechnologists believe knowledge easily acquired with their new tools will inspire ideas for future commercialisation. This belief has led to broad-based research which takes place in universities as well as companies. Typically, researchers look at a given medical problem at the molecular level, but from many points of view—and with a view to changing things, not merely understanding them. Consider recent work on Alzheimer's disease.

Since the 19th century doctors have known that the brains of those with Alzheimer's disease contain many clumps of protein, called beta amyloid plaques. These are clearly up to no good—but are they a cause or a result of the disease? Today many scientists are becoming convinced they are the cause. A year ago Dr Bruce Yankner and his colleagues at Children's Hospital in Boston showed that if large amounts of the plaque-forming protein,

beta amyloid, are injected into nerve cells from the hippocampus, a part of the brain that plays a crucial role in memory, the cells are destroyed. This year he has demonstrated a similar effect in rats' brains.

Dr Yankner's work was made possible because Konrad Beyreuther, of the University of Cologne, managed to copy the genes of an amyloid protein precursor (APP) in 1987. This is a much larger protein, one small part of which can be snipped off to make beta amyloid. At the same time, Dr Rudolph Tanzi of the Massachusetts General Hospital and others showed that the APP was present in almost every tissue of the body, most notably in the brain and blood. Some researchers hope that work with beta amyloid might lead to treatments for strokes, blockages in the arteries of the brain. It seems that beta amyloid might encourage blood clotting in these arteries. The purpose—as opposed to the unwanted effects—of the protein is unknown.

According to Dr Yankner, beta amyloid bears an uncanny resemblance to a set of protein fragments known as tachykinins. One member of this family is substance P. Conveniently, biotechnologists already knew a lot about substance P, which assists

in the perception of pain; a lot of research has been aimed at dampening its effects. If substance P is injected into rats before injecting damaging beta amyloids, the rats do not suffer nerve degeneration. Substance P or its relatives could thus act as an antidote to beta amyloid and halt the progression of Alzheimer's disease—though many have their doubts. Dr Yankner is now trying to work out precisely how the tachykinins block the action of beta amyloid. The similarity between the two may well be the key.

Meanwhile Dr Tanzi and his team are exploring another therapeutic avenue: how APP breaks down to beta amyloid. Once this is determined it might even be possible to prevent the onset of Alzheimer's disease. Biotechnological tools that are now commonplace, but did not exist a decade ago, have helped determine that APP comes in two forms. One is made of a folded chain of 695 amino acids, the substances that go to make up protein. The other contains 751 amino acids. The brain has both forms: APP 695 and APP 751. The concentration of APP 751, however, increases with age—so it may be associated with Alzheimer's disease.

In 1988 Dr Tanzi discovered that the larger protein, APP 751, carries an extra sequence of amino acids within its coils which inhibits the action of a protease—an enzyme that cuts up proteins. Nobody yet knows whether the protease inhibitor accelerates or hinders the production of beta amyloid from APP. Either is possible. On the one hand the protease inhibitor might block the mechanism that snips the beta amyloid out of the APP. On the other hand, the protease enzyme might be intent on cutting up the beta amyloid itself, and the inhibitor may thwart this.

Further work on this may be helped by the recent development of strains of transgenic mice which carry the gene that describes APP 751. Such mice have been made by California Biotechnology, a company based in Mountainview, and by several other groups. The gene is injected into mouse embryos, together with a "promoter" which switches the genes on in nerve tissue. The mice show signs of nerve degeneration, but the amyloid plaques found in their brains do not resemble those found in people. The relevance of this model is thus unclear. It is possible that these unfortunate mice will prove extremely

useful for work on all sorts of anti-amyloid agents.

In 1987 Dr Tanzi and his team looked at families that carry a genetic disposition for Alzheimer's disease—a rare occurrence. Using a technique similar to the "genetic fingerprinting" used to pick out fathers in paternity suits, they discovered that the gene for APP is located on chromosome-21. The discovery fits well with other evidence. For instance, people with Down's syndrome have an extra copy of chromosome 21; as they age, they show signs of senile dementia similar to those shown by Alzheimer's patients.

At the end of 1990 John Hardy of St Mary's Medical School in London discovered that certain Alzheimer families have a mutation in the APP gene. The mutant gene is called APP 717. In the past few weeks scientists have uncovered yet more mutants among eight Alzheimer families spread around the world. No one has yet shown a clear link between the mutations and the onset of Alzheimer's. Mice with the APP 717 gene may prove the point. Athena Neurosciences, of San Francisco, is now growing some.

If the link is there, work with the 50 or so people who carry APP mutations will reveal more precisely how the synthesis of the APP protein is regulated and why it is produced in excess in Alzheimer's patients. It seems that mutations do not appear to make any difference to the transcription of the APP gene; they may differ at the stage when gene transcripts are "translated" into proteins. If that is the case, a chemical in the cell might be responsible. Dr Tanzi and others are now trying to determine what that chemical might be. Once they know, they may have yet another possible drug.

Much of this sounds academic; but at every stage, the work is done close to the commercial world. Dr Yankner's substance P, for example, is patented; so is Dr Hardy's mutant APP gene. That patent has been bought by Athena Neurosciences, which is working on a diagnostic test with a subsidiary of Eli Lilly. Athena, as well as bigger companies like Upjohn and Bristol-Myers/Squibb, is also working on APP processing. Academics without commercial links are keenly aware of the interest their work arouses. It makes the field exciting. Whether it will make it profitably curative remains to be seen.

Trials and tribulations

MARCH 16TH *In November, the White House suggested that America's Food and Drug Administration should no longer require large clinical trials of a new life-saving drug after its basic safety and efficacy have been proved. So the question of which drug provides the best solution to a medical problem may now be answered by independent trials sponsored by the pharmaceutical industry. Here is a picture of one such trial*

THE International Study of Infarct Survival (ISIS-3) should have been heralded as a triumph. Instead it has been the target of mudslinging ever since it was unveiled at a meeting of American cardiologists in Atlanta at the beginning of March. With 46,000 patients at 1,000 hospitals taking part, ISIS-3 was the world's biggest clinical study. It was designed to determine whether drugs that dissolve blood clots can help people survive heart attacks, and to assess the benefits and risks of three different clot-busting drugs: streptokinase, an old drug, costing $300 a shot, Eminase, a new drug costing $1,700, and TPA, a genetically engineered drug which is available for $2,200.

The study clearly demonstrated that all three "thrombolytic" drugs save lives. The death rate among heart-attack patients given a thrombolytic (plus aspirin and heparin, which prevent the formation of further clots) was 10%. This compares with a rate of 15% for untreated patients (as reported in comparable trials). On the basis of these figures, Rory Collins, one of the ISIS trial's co-ordinators at Oxford University's Nuffield Department of Medicine, hopes thrombolytic treatment will become more widespread. In America only 20% of eligible patients are thought to receive the drugs. Elsewhere the figure is lower.

Two-thirds of that lucky fifth get TPA made by Genentech, a Californian biotechnology firm. The company has convinced cardiologists in America that its TPA, known as alteplase, is the best drug on the

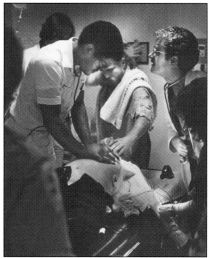

Saving lives

market. Wellcome, a British firm, has also worked on TPA, but while ISIS-3 was going on it abandoned the drug. Genentech's competitors are SmithKline Beecham, the British drugs company which sells Eminase, and three companies which sell streptokinase: Astra and Kabi Pharmacia, two Swedish firms, and Hoechst, a German chemicals giant. Wellcome and SmithKline Beecham paid for ISIS-3 but had no say in its management.

To the joy of some and the consternation of others, ISIS-3 found all three drugs equally effective at keeping people alive.

They differed in their side effects, though: 1.5% of patients getting Eminase and 1.5% of those getting TPA suffered a stroke, compared with just 1.1% of those getting streptokinase.

Genentech was underwhelmed. At a press conference, the company maintained that "most US cardiologists will view the results as inconclusive for US medical practice". It claims the study was of little relevance to its TPA: the TPA used was Wellcome's version of the drug, duteplase, which is slightly different in structure. Genentech has brought a lawsuit against SmithKline Beecham for running an advertisement about ISIS-3, on the basis that it implied alteplase was being used. Genentech cannot deny, though, that the two versions of TPA are extremely similar—so much so that the company has successfully sued Wellcome for infringing its TPA patent in America. According to Genentech, "the fact that the two products are equivalent under the patent laws does not mean that the products are clinically equivalent". According to Dr Collins, other clinical studies have shown that the two versions are equally good at unblocking coronary arteries.

The biotech company also claims that the study was flawed because the heparin used in the trials was injected under the skin, instead of into the vein, which is how it is done in America. This, it said, would show its product up in a bad light. Perhaps. But patients given TPA and under-the-skin heparin had fewer new clots than patients treated with the other two drugs, so clearly TPA was helped by the heparin. Moreover, intravenous heparin can cause more bleeding than the subcutaneous sort.

Genentech's are not the only aspersions being cast. SmithKline Beecham claims that because the trial was "blinded", the charms of Eminase were hidden. Eminase can be given to patients in minutes; streptokinase and alteplase must be infused for several hours. During the trial Eminase was administered under cover of an infusion, so that patients and doctors did not know who was getting it. Dr Collins doubts if more than a few minutes were lost as a result of setting up dummy intravenous infusions. Still, Eminase may sometimes be more convenient.

Furthermore, SmithKline Beecham al-

leges that the strokes were not always diagnosed with a brain scan, so mistakes could have been made—as they point out, ISIS-3 was designed to be a study of death, not sickness. Dr Collins is unimpressed; brain scans are not needed to diagnose strokes. So the company is doing more clinical work to clarify some questions about Eminase and about side-effects that were raised in ISIS-3. Genentech is paying for a new study dubbed GUSTO: a two-year, 33,000-patient trial to measure mortality. It will cost about $40m and compare alteplase with streptoki-

nase and with a combination of the two.

Astra, at its stand at the Atlanta meeting, presented a poster crowing that TPA has at last proven to be as effective as Streptase (its brand name for streptokinase). But this hard-won truth has had little impact on the companies' share prices. That is apparently because it will make little difference to the drugs' success on the market, despite the large difference in their prices. Pharmaceutical analysts say they no longer bother with considering such studies. It is the marketing that counts.

Sunrise

NOVEMBER 30TH *The debate on global warming continued, at a slightly less feverish pitch than the year before, as climatologists refined their forecasts with an eye to advising 1992's UN conference on the environment. There were still surprises— but they were not welcomed*

CLIMATOLOGISTS are keen for everyone to know that the climate is complex, unpredictable and difficult to understand. Now two researchers from the Danish Meteorological Institute, Eigil Friis-Christensen and Knud Lassen, have published data that make it all look rather simple. Their colleagues distrust anything that looks so simple; but, as yet, they cannot show that it is wrong. They should disprove it or learn to live with it if they want politicians to take predictions of global warming seriously.

The Danish paper, published in *Science*, makes the reasonable and widely accepted suggestion that changes in the sun's brightness can affect the temperature on earth; but the article then goes a lot further. Changes in the sun's brightness have been measured accurately only for the past decade, by satellites. They appear to be quite small—a change of around 0.1% in the sun's brightness over the course of the 11-year solar cycle, during which the number of sunspots rises from its minimum (when the sun is dimmest) to its maximum and falls back again. This change of 0.1% is not thought enough to make much of a difference, though there is a theory, widely disputed, that it affects the severity of northern winters.

However, the sun appears also to exhibit an 80- or 90-year cycle, during which the peak intensity of the 11-year cycle varies, as does its length. It is this longer cycle that the Danes have looked at. They think that the sun is brightest when the 11-year cycle is shortest. Putting the solar-cycle length and the surface temperature of the northern continents over the past century on to the same graph, they have found that the two fit together astonishingly well (see chart).

A straightforward interpretation is that the sun's luminosity changes over the 80-year cycle. Most researchers agree that such changes, if they happen, could affect the climate—but not this way. The chart does not show the sun just influencing the climate: it shows it controlling it completely. The vari-

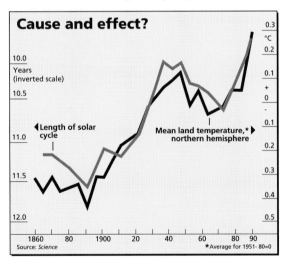

Cause and effect?

10.0
Years
(inverted scale)
10.5

◀ Length of solar cycle

11.0

11.5

12.0

1860   80   1900   20   40   60   80   90
Source: *Science*

Mean land temperature,* northern hemisphere ▶

0.3
°C
0.2
0.1
+
0
-
0.1
0.2
0.3
0.4
0.5

*Average for 1951- 80=0

ability in the climate, particularly that to be expected from the effects of the oceans, is nowhere to be seen—there is no "noise" in the system. Any system as complicated as the climate, depending on the interplay of oceans and atmosphere, should be as messy as the weather is. This result is like finding that the weather can be predicted from the season alone.

There are criticisms to be made. One is that the findings could be a fluke. Although the chances of an accidental fit being this good are slim, other measures of the sun's activity have been tried out against other climate records and have not fitted convincingly. An unlikely achievement becomes

less surprising if people have been making lots of attempts at it. The statistics used to produce the cycle-length data cannot provide data for the present, which have been added using a simpler method. The pre-1905 climate data may not be that good.

More fundamentally, there is the problem of a mechanism. Scientists are loth to discard established theories, even unsatisfactory ones, on the basis of evidence with no theoretical underpinning. How could small changes in the sun's output affect the climate? One answer is that the changes are not as small as a decade's observation makes them seem. Another answer is that small changes are amplified by the climate system in some unknown way—which is hardly likely to satisfy critics.

What, then, of the greenhouse effect caused by man-made gases in the atmosphere? Cautious climatologists—the best sort—have regularly stressed that the increase in global temperature this century could be the result of natural variability, and that the unmistakable signs of man-made warming are yet to come. They will be surprised if all the variability turns out to be solar, but not wrong-footed. They will just have to come to terms with the idea that the climate is not as chaotic as they thought.

Solar effects and greenhouse effects can be told apart, though not easily, by taking the stratosphere's temperature. The greenhouse effect should cool the stratosphere, whereas a brighter sun would warm it. So an enhanced greenhouse effect should still be spottable. But there is no denying that if this link between sun and climate is real, a marked decrease in solar luminosity could counteract greenhouse warming, perhaps to a large degree. If the sun swings the other way, though, it could reinforce greenhouse warming—look at the right-hand side of the chart. Curiosity is called for, doubt is reinforced—but relief is not yet an option.

Contents

BOOKS AND ARTS

The triumph of style

BY THE end of 1991, it was clearer than ever that the artistic movements of the 20th century had run out of steam. In retrospect, the 1960s were the last decade in which men dared to be modern. Since then, art, architecture and music have become timorous and backward-looking. Blessedly so, some might say; but by the 1990s the lack of evident new inspiration in art or in literature was becoming worrying. It was left to cinema, the 20th century's particular child, to keep unashamed pace with the age, its technology and its preoccupations.

In the world of books, as has become habitual, good writing came a poor second to instant journalism. The two overshadowing events of the year were the Gulf war and the break-up of the Soviet Union, and the book trade fell over itself to keep pace. Gulf war books set a new record for time taken between idea and finished volume; in some cases, it was a matter of weeks. The speed was justified, for sales of these books ended abruptly with the victory parades. The collapse of the Soviet Union, however, caught publishers on the hop, and the coup in late summer took them completely by surprise. Aside from Mikhail Gorbachev's own slim account, snatched up for $500,000 by Simon & Schuster in September and rushed to the shops by November, the only other book to catch the wind was Edward Shevardnadze's memoirs, hastily updated by the author to take in August's momentous events.

It was a year of big books—getting bigger all the time, with 800-pagers now quite commonplace–and of large themes. Among the most serious treatises were Christopher Lasch's on progress and Paul Johnson's on the rise of the Modern Age, both of them inherently optimistic. Among the novels, Norman Mailer's "Harlot's Ghost" (October) contained more than 1,000 pages, with another volume to come. Almost as fat, and much more hyped, was "Scarlett", Alexandra Ripley's tepid attempt to write a follow-up to Margaret Mitchell's "Gone with the Wind". Murdered by critics, it sold by the thousand. So too did Kitty Kelley's "Nancy", the biography of Nancy Reagan, which made headlines mostly for insinuations about the ex-First Lady's lunches with Frank Sinatra. For most dirt dished in the shortest space, Julia Phillips's memoir of Hollywood, "You'll Never Eat

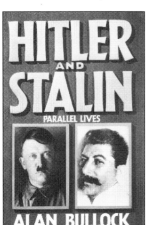

Our chosen monument

Lunch in this Town Again", was the outright winner.

The title of book of the year, if we were to give one, would probably go to Alan Bullock's monumental "Hitler and Stalin", closely followed by John Richardson's biography of Picasso. It was a good year for political memoirs. In Britain, Bernard Ingham, Roy Jenkins and David Owen all produced works full of meat and bite; in France, a strangely narcissistic offering appeared from Valery Giscard D'Estaing; in America, Oliver North, working under deep cover, at last produced his own account of the Iran-contra affair.

Fiction seemed to be in a depressed state. In America the mega-sellers, Stephen King and Amy Tan, brought out books that were received dutifully but not with rapture. New stars were not apparent. Publishers claimed, and bookshops confirmed, that the recession was turning people away from buying books; and although the big publishing amalgamations appeared to be over and the industry settling down, an air of gloom and difficulty pervaded everything.

Cinema started the year sobered by the lessons of 1990, when big-budget films had failed to do well and little movies, without special effects, had seemed to be the recipe for success. They then forgot the lesson with "Terminator II", in which Arnold Schwarzenegger, assisted by multiple special effects, played a metal-fleshed humanoid that saved the world. By the end of October, "Terminator II" had taken in $200m at the box office. The most-talked-about film was "The Silence of the Lambs", a movie that caught not only the fashion for taboo subjects (in this case, cannibalism; in others, death and AIDS), but the vogue for strong, unsexy female characters, a theme underlined in America with the road-movie "Thelma and Louise". This was also the year when black film came of age, notably with "New Jack City" and "Boyz N The Hood". By the end of the year Spike Lee, so recently a pioneer of black film, appeared to be the grand old man of the genre.

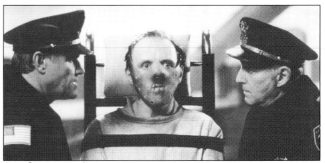

Not for vegetarians

In Britain this was the year of Japan. A massive festival of exhibitions, kabuki, sumo wrestling and origami began in September, but oddly seemed to produce no spinoffs into the general culture, as its predecessor had done a century before. Perhaps the oriental craze could only happen once. In America, this was the year of alternative interpretations of history, with an exhibition debunking the glorious myth of the Frontier and with books aplenty debunking Columbus. It was a quiet year for moral indignation over pieces of art, perhaps because the debacles of 1990 had left everyone exhausted. The hottest topic was not naked men but the de-accessioning and sale of paintings by galleries in order to buy

Seurat in Paris

more (as the Barnes Collection attempted to do in Philadelphia), and the disastrous season in the auction houses, where both Christie's and Sotheby's reported falls in turnover of 50-60% on the year before.

Postmodernism continued to reign, though with increasing catcalls, in architecture, and conceptualism continued to rule in the galleries. On every side works of art were busy making statements, often without much regard for proficiency in the techniques of art itself. Those

Miles Davis missed

who visited the mega-exhibitions of the year—Constable in London, Seurat in Paris, Rembrandt in Amsterdam—could bask in art that was more than image, and contained both depth and life. Visitors to the Pop-Art show at the Royal Academy saw the other, ascendant side of art as message and surface, and could learn where the rot—or the fun—had started.

The year also saw the rise and rise of "new curatorship" in galleries, in which artistic movements have to be set in their international context. In some cases, as in London's National Gallery, this meant a substantial re-juggling of pictures; in others, as in the "Circa 1492" exhibition in Washington's National Gallery of Art, it meant displaying copper heads from Benin alongside Leonardos. In general, the pleasure induced by the opening of many new or refurbished galleries (at the National Gallery and the Royal Academy in London, the Jeu de Paume in Paris and the National Gallery in Dublin) was slightly numbed by a feeling of being lectured at.

The musical world lost pianist Claudio Arrau, and with him a tradition of romantic keyboard playing. It gained a growing crowd of Chinese and Japanese college-age virtuosi, whose compact-disc perfection of playing was the antithesis of the old emotional style. Jazz lost Miles Davis, the king of cool, who was irreplaceable. The western world lost the much-loved vinyl record, now the declared loser to tapes and compact discs. But the musical year was dominated by the 200-year celebrations of the death of Mozart, marked by giant series of concerts throughout Europe.

Much the same divide could be seen in music as in art: there was either pure music, or music that made a Statement. Among the most notorious tributes to Mozart were Peter Sellars's modern-dress versions of Don Giovanni (set in Brooklyn) and the Marriage of Figaro (set in the Trump tower), both of which featured director and designer first and composer second. Thanks largely to the music, the Mozarts worked triumphantly; but Mr Sellars's direction of a new John Adams opera, "The Death of Klinghoffer" showed the full dangers of making music subservient to an idea, in this case the exploration of moral ambivalence towards terrorism in the Middle East. Among performers, British violinist Nigel Kennedy attained notoriety (and wrote a book) on the strength of presenting Brahms and Vivaldi in rock-concert settings.

More than anything, however, this was the year when great things were expected from liberated Eastern Europe; and nothing came. After the decades of exceedingly brave samizdat work, bold graphics and ground-breaking performance art, there was a sudden silence. It was, perhaps, the silence of exhaustion. Soviet painters visited the west in numbers, were shown in galleries, and were treated as heroes; but the artist-heroes of the year were generally to be found elsewhere. One was Salman Rushdie, who published a bravely cheerful children's

Mozart remembered

tale from his continuing exile; one was Nadine Gordimer, the South African winner of the Nobel Prize for Literature; and one was Graham Greene, whose death in April seemed suddenly to leave literature without a moral anchor.

As we reported then

Why the Gulf war?

JANUARY 5TH *The Gulf war and Saddam Hussein were the topics of choice as the year began. Two of the earliest and best books on the subject were "Saddam's War" by John Bulloch and Harvey Morris (Faber) and "Unholy Babylon" by Adel Darwish and Gregory Alexander (Gollancz)*

IT TAKES a special sort of incompetence, if you run a medium-sized third-world country, to manoeuvre the United States into a shooting war with you. It takes at least some incompetence, if you are the United States, to let yourself be so manoeuvred. These two books, one published on the eve of war and one just after, hit both America and Saddam Hussein with some precision-guided recriminations.

Mr Hussein is the easier target. As their title suggests, the authors of "Saddam's War" have no doubt that this one man is chiefly to blame for the present disaster in the Gulf. For a decade and a half, say John Bulloch and Harvey Morris, his ambition had been to create "a strong modern Arab state which would be the equal of other world powers"; and to use violence to do so.

At first, while Mr Hussein was building his power base, the violence stayed at home. In "Unholy Babylon" Adel Darwish and Gregory Alexander describe an all-too-typical example of it: Mr Hussein's purge of his own Baath Party in 1979. The new president summoned several hundred senior party members to a meeting and tearfully read out from a list the names of alleged "traitors". Those whose names were not on the list then formed a firing squad and mowed down their unlucky colleagues. The president was in the firing squad too.

A year later Iraq's president started exporting violence. He invaded Iran and, after eight years, fought it to a standstill. Within days of the ceasefire he turned on his Kurdish population, which he felt had been disloyal. Mr Darwish and Mr Alexander estimate that the Iraqi air force attacked at least 70 Iraqi Kurdish villages with mustard and cyanide gas.

And yet—and this raises the second set of recriminations—he was not only tolerated by the rest of the world but also, to some extent, supported by it. Why? For the Americans he provided a strategic bulwark against Iran. For the Germans and French he was a source of wonderfully lucrative contracts; "Unholy Babylon" is especially excellent in naming the many European firms that helped to build Iraq's arsenal. As for the Arabs, they admired his power. When the Kurds were gassed, and America mildly complained, Arab governments and news media leapt to Mr Hussein's defence. Kuwait was no exception: a little while before the invasion its newspapers were cheerfully praising Mr Hussein's hanging of a journalist from London's *Observer* on trumped-up charges of being an Israeli spy.

So the world got Mr Hussein wrong. What, now, should it do about him? There is little enthusiasm in either of these books for the American-led war in the Gulf. "Saddam's War" hedges its bets. The real test, its authors say, is whether all the problems of the Middle East are addressed in the coming years "in a spirit of dialogue rather than confrontation". The authors of "Unholy Babylon", a less-measured but fizzier read, are more certain that war is a mistake. Their grim conclusion: even if America succeeded in removing Mr Hussein in a destructive war, "a new generation of Arab nationalists would emerge whose anger would eclipse all past experience of Middle Eastern terrorism."

Look on my works, ye mighty

FEBRUARY 2ND *The war had its cultural as well as its human casualties. This piece reflects the anxiety of archaeologists at the height of the fighting*

THE destruction of human life and the destruction of ancient art and architecture are both tragedies, though of different sorts. Bombs raining down on Iraq are producing both. Long before the rise of Greece, the fertile valleys of the Tigris and Euphrates gave birth to one of the first urban civilisations. The peoples of Akkad, Sumer and Babylon built the first temples, forts and palaces. They invented wheeled transport, building bricks, the use of written language (though Egypt disputes that claim) and codified the first laws. Iraq is littered with evidence of their achievements. What will be left once the smoke of battle has cleared?

Sites near airfields and factories seem most at risk. One of the most historic is Ur, the capital city of one of the Sumerian dynasties that ruled southern Mesopotamia for much of the third millennium BC. Sir Leonard Woolley was the first to excavate it in 1922; the exquisite gold and lapis-lazuli ornaments he found in its royal tombs made his reputation. T.E. Lawrence helped on the site, and Agatha Christie paid a visit.

Not far from Ur is the Iraqi military air base of Tell al-Muqayyar. Archaeologists worry that if the base has been bombed, parts of the ancient city might have been destroyed too. That would be a scientific loss as well as an aesthetic one. The site has been out of bounds to civilians for more than ten years, and archaeologists are itching to put recently discovered techniques to work on it. Collecting seeds or animal bones, for instance, would show what animals the Sumerians kept and what crops they grew.

About 650 kms (400 miles) to the north, on the banks of the Tigris, stand the ruins of Nineveh. Rebuilt by Sennacherib, an Assyrian warrior-king, in 700 BC or so, the city still boasts impressive defensive walls and a high citadel mound, called Tell Kuyunjik. Nineveh was superseded by Mosul, an Assyrian foundation on the other side of the river. Modern Mosul is the administrative capital of northern Iraq, and the place from which much of the country's oil industry is run. If allied aircraft attack Mosul, stray bombs might hit Nineveh as well. Unfortunately, Tell Kuyunjik doubles as a site for anti-aircraft guns.

Even if ancient buildings escape being hit by bombs directly, the shock of nearby explosions could shake them to the ground. They are made of mud brick, and are fragile. Just north of Salman Pak, Iraq's biggest biological-weapons plant, stands what is left of Ctesiphon, winter capital of the Persian kings (300-700 AD). Remarkably, the walls of their audience chamber, a graceful arched room 35m high, still stand—or did before the war started. Salman Pak was at-

tacked during the first raids.

War damage would not be a disaster at every archaeological site. Where no standing structures remain, "small, tactfully placed" bombs could even be useful. The holes they created might reveal earlier, buried, buildings. Not much of Babylon remains above ground. The temple thought to have been the original for the Tower of Babel was quarried for its bricks in the 19th century. Even the city's massive outer walls, wide enough, according to Herodotus, to turn a four-horse chariot, have disappeared. Saddam Hussein has rebuilt bits of Babylon, including a triumphal arch and a giant ziggurat, but at half the scale of the original; archaeologists would not grieve if bombs knocked them down again.

Younger Islamic monuments are also at risk. One of Baghdad's finest Islamic building is the 12th-century Abbasid Palace. It stands close to Iraq's defence ministry, an early target of allied raids. Najaf and Kerbala, industrial towns south of Baghdad, are sites of important Shi'a Muslim shrines. But the allied air force has instructions to avoid such holy places; Islamic sites may be safer than older ones like Ur and Nineveh, which hold no religious significance for Arab members of the coalition.

The saddest historical casualties of the Gulf war are likely to be treasures from the splendid Iraq Museum in Baghdad. The museum stands near the television station, and next door to the presidential palace. According to Iraqi radio and to one independent report, air raids have already damaged the building. Smaller pieces have been packed away for safe-keeping, but the museum's large monuments are too heavy to move easily. They include a 5,500-year-old mosaic-covered temple wall, one of the world's earliest example of decorated architecture, and human-headed bulls from Khorsabad, an eighth century BC Assyrian capital. When bombing started, these were still in the museum.

Turning off the celestial freeway

MARCH 16TH *The price of growth and the notion of progress are increasingly fashionable themes. In "The True and Only Heaven" (Norton), Christopher Lasch sets the tone*

IT IS possible to disagree with nearly everything in this disturbing book and yet find it illuminating, even exhilarating. In fact, it is nearly impossible to do otherwise. Christopher Lasch's detailed study of the ideology of progress assaults the cherished assumptions of both the political left and right. His attack is so successful that almost any reader, including the apolitical, will find his book unsettling.

A belief in ever-rising expectations and growing material wealth lies behind political debate and intellectual life everywhere. Mr Lasch, a history professor at the University of Rochester in upstate New York, begins by pointing out how curious that conviction is. In a century full of calamities, during which millions of people have seen war or recession or social changes make their lives worse, how is it that serious thinkers still believe in progress?

For hundreds of pages he traces the history of the idea, as well as noting the many critics and nay-sayers who have been pushed aside by its relentless advance. Until the 18th century the common view of history was cyclical: like humans themselves, nations and civilisations were thought to have a natural span, from the exuberance of youth via a flourishing prime to decline, decay and death. The millenarianism of Christianity, far from contradicting this view, enlarged it to describe a world in perpetual decline until the second coming of Christ.

The philosophers of the Enlightenment provided an alternative to this age-old account by arguing that man and his institutions were perfectible through reason. But the real author of the idea of progress was Adam Smith, who demonstrated how the pursuit of individual self-interest, if left unchecked by the constraints of custom or traditional authority, would increase the general welfare through the "invisible hand" of the market. Together with the advance of science and technology, this idea freed societies from the fate of inevitable decline.

The Victorians thought that moral improvement accompanied material advances. Even Marxists, though quarrelling with the distribution of wealth under capitalism, saw the rising expectations of workers, and their ability to produce ever-greater material wealth, as the driving force of history. War and genocide in the 20th century have stripped the utopianism out of these beliefs; but a view still prevails that prosperity will continue to increase, and life improve, as far as man can see.

Yet ever since the 18th century, says Mr Lasch, a contrary

view of society has been fighting a sort of guerrilla war against the orthodoxy of progress. He carefully pursues this line of thought from Rousseau and Montesquieu on to Thomas Carlyle, Ralph Waldo Emerson, Henry George, Max Weber, Georges Sorel, G.D.H. Cole and dozens of other writers and thinkers. What this disparate group had in common was a belief in natural limits–to human powers and freedom and to the benefits conferred by endless economic expansion.

These men, he argues, were not simple pessimists or victims of nostalgia for a past that never was. They were proposing an alternative view of history that stressed ancient values such as civic virtue, responsibility, family, respect for workmanship, sacrifice and loyalty as the source of the "good" life and the foundation of a healthy society. In today's America Mr Lasch identifies this—in his most startling insight—as the sensibility of the lower middle class.

This class, which in Europe would be called the working class, does not share the educated elite's addiction to consumerism or its belief in the power of medical science to banish tragedy and chance from human existence. Already equipped with the necessities of life, lower middle-class parents do not much care if their children become richer or more successful; they simply want them to become responsible adults. They worry more about preserving their way of life than about acquiring more goods, and have little faith that life will always get better.

Mr Lasch concedes that lower middle-class Americans, like the 19th-century *petite bourgeoisie* from whom they have inherited their views, can also be provincial, racist and narrow-minded. But he feels that politicians should listen to them more than they do, because the philosophy of progress is bankrupt. He gives three reasons for this. First, most people—even in America, the world's richest country—are no longer growing richer and know it. Second, an obsession with material progress has trivialised politics and denied spiritual values by producing a society of individual consumers with little sense of community, duty or responsibility for one another. Third, if the entire population of the world were to be supported at the level of affluence achieved in developed countries, the environment would not stand it; so progress holds out little hope for billions of poor in the third world or even the growing army of poor in America.

This last point is probably the weakest in Mr Lasch's analysis. More compelling is his accusation that an obsession with material progress has led to spiritual impoverishment. Some American reviewers have criticised him for failing to suggest how to govern a modern society without a belief in progress. Though this is true, Mr Lasch still forces readers to question their fundamental convictions: a rare intellectual adventure, and achievement enough for one book.

That Hollywood shuffle

MARCH 30TH, NEW YORK *Black directors in America are moving from the fringe to the mainstream, and have set it alight*

POLICE are at war with a gang of drug dealers; the dealers transform a huge Harlem apartment building into a crack factory that throws the city into a state of Boschian depravity. This is "New Jack City", a film that contains good-looking street-smart cops and villains, violence, sex and even a final triumph of good over evil. In its first weekend it took in $7m. Seats were so scarce that people killed each other to get them. Mortified, producers and director put out a statement insisting that their film, despite its brutality, showed "positive role models". The words are revealing; for this is a black film, not only with a mostly black cast but also with a black director, Mario Van Peebles.

Mr Van Peebles is best known as a film and television actor. Inexperienced as well as black, he would have stood no chance of a studio contract as recently as five years ago. Times have changed. The 1991 season promises at least seven big-studio releases by black directors, more than in the past ten years. Robert Townsend ("Hollywood Shuffle") and Spike Lee ("Do the Right Thing") both have new films coming. Mr Lee, to add to his swagger, has also been hired to lecture on film at Harvard.

Already highly successful in popular music, dance and commercial television, blacks have found the movies a tougher nut to crack. The cost of film-making is only part of it. From the industry's earliest days, blacks in American films were routinely typecast as servants, childlike entertainers or sexual aggressors; in D.W. Griffith's silent classic, "Birth of a Nation", the Ku Klux Klan was presented as the saviour of the postbellum South. Yet as early as this blacks were also making their own films: "race films", shown in all-black theatres during the years of segregation.

Today's new generation of black directors has been spurred on by two particular success stories. One is the popularity of performers such as Richard Pryor and Eddie Murphy, whose films have unprecedented appeal for whites as well as blacks. The other is the story of Melvin Van Peebles, father of Mario. Van Peebles *père* soured on Hollywood after directing the now-classic comedy "Watermelon Man" (1969), about a sub-urban businessman who wakes up one morning to find himself black. He followed that with "Sweet Sweetback's Baadasses Song," the crudely made, picaresque saga of a sexually defiant rebel, starring himself, which he distributed to theatres in black neighbourhoods. It made a fortune and spawned an almost decade-long string of Hollywood imitations, the "blacksploitation" films, built around the exploits of virile leading men.

Following the example of Mr Lee's low-budget hit, "She's Gotta Have It", young black directors began making small independent films, some of which earned national distribution deals only after their directors sweated to get the films made. The stories are familiar enough. Mr Townsend financed "Hollywood Shuffle," about a black actor in Hollywood, on credit-card cash advances. Charles Lane's first feature,

The heavy mob surrounds Van Peebles

"Sidewalk Stories", was a silent black-and-white film shot on the cold streets of New York during two weeks in February, when Mr Lane's actor friends had no other work. Those ordeals, however, taught some young blacks how to make cheap films that looked expensive. Most black directors' budgets are pegged at around $7m, compared with the $25m-40m spent on the average Hollywood film. (Mr Lee's new film "Jungle Fever", an exception, is said to have cost around $19m.)

Black films remain small beer; they are doing little to shape the movie business. A black-owned film studio is still a distant dream, and the Hollywood studios have yet to experience their first black-directed box-office failure, which will test their willingness to entrust big budgets to black directors. The most likely development is that studios will imitate the music business and create separate divisions devoted to films for black audiences, where black producers who know their market best will determine what films are made. The result may transform black American films into a two-tier system, with commercially successful directors on top and independent film-makers at the bottom, scrambling for scarce money. So what's new?

Finis

APRIL 6TH *Graham Greene died on April 3rd. The author of "Brighton Rock", "Our Man in Havana" and "The Quiet American" was mourned both as a writer of thrillers and as the voice of modern man struggling with God. This quotation seemed an apt way to remember him*

"WE HAVE to die sometime," the lieutenant said. "It doesn't seem to matter so much when."

"You're a good man. You've got nothing to be afraid of."

"You have such odd ideas," the lieutenant complained. He said: "Sometimes I feel you're just trying to talk me round."

"Round to what?"

"Oh, to letting you escape perhaps—or to believing in the Holy Catholic Church, the communion of saints . . . how does that stuff go?"

"The forgiveness of sins."

"You don't believe much in that, do you?"

"Oh yes, I believe," the little man said obstinately.

"Then what are you worried about?"

"I'm not ignorant, you see. I've always known what I've been doing. And I can't absolve myself."

The Power and the Glory

End of track

MAY 11TH *Big stores everywhere are abandoning the old vinyl long-playing record for compact disc. Nostalgia seems in order*

FOR many people their stack of vinyl LPs, collected since spotty adolescence, is a potted life history and loved accordingly. Quite a plunge then for Tower Records, which runs some of London's biggest music stores, to decide to clear vinyl from its shelves for good. Demand for the old format is said to be too low—about 15% of total sales—to justify stocking it. Future requests for Sergeant Pepper, Verdi's Requiem or the Bonzo Dog Doo Dah Band will receive a nod towards the cassette stands and those of the great interloper, compact discs. So much for consumer choice.

Although other big record retailers, such as HMV and Virgin, promise to keep stocking vinyl as long as customers buy it, record prices are already creeping towards the CD mark as vinyl production drops. W.H. Smith, which has 300 music stores in Britain, will be phasing vinyl LPs out of half their shops over the next three years.

Retailers admit they can sell only what the record companies want to supply. The latter are falling over themselves to get shot of vinyl; the back catalogue of recordings available on vinyl is shrinking monthly, especially in classical music and jazz. Companies blame customer demand; last year twice as many CDs as vinyl LPs were sold in Britain. Critics of the music industry accuse it of forcing record-buyers to switch to compact discs, which still cost half as much again as the vinyl equivalent in spite of rapidly falling production costs.

For the vast majority of vinylphiles, the marketing patter about perfect sound, unbreakable design and gadgets offering "six hours of pre-programmed music" misses the point. What they would much rather have is the ceremony of Changing the Record. Tedious maybe, but amply rewarded by the 40 minutes subsequently spent poring over the sleeve notes and album cover (an art form that will presumably die out too). For them, owning the album is owning it on vinyl; anything else is just a copy.

Pockets of CD resistance are appearing. One of the most vociferous complainers is John Peel, a veteran BBC radio disc-jockey who would rather hang up his headphones than cue up a compact disc. Writing on the subject in the London *Evening Standard*, he vowed to stick with his "battle-hardened 45s", crackles and all. "What about the surface noise, I hear you whine. Listen mate, life has surface noise and I like it." Mr Peel admits that vinyl is probably doomed. "A society that has already been sold the burger and the vaginal deodorant", he wrote, "is not going to resist something as gaudy as the CD." His only consolation was that the little silver discs with their rainbow glow will probably soon be trumped by yet another "revolutionary innovation"—probably digital tape, which can record off a CD and lose none of that precious sound quality.

Putting out the latest album on CD alone would be unthinkable for many heavy-metal and trendy punk-style bands. After all, how can they expect fans to roll a joint on a CD box? The singles record market, too, is still a bastion of vinyl supremacy; most of them are bought by teenagers with little pocket money. So all is not quite lost. But hip young things should note that grooving will have to go; CDs do not have grooves. They have pits. Not quite the right ring to that, somehow.

The man who never was

MAY 25TH *After the Thatcher coup at the end of 1990, revelatory memoirs from her cabinet ministers were eagerly awaited. Bernard Ingham's "Kill the Messenger" (HarperCollins) got there first, and took the edge off the public appetite. The ferociously loyal press secretary minced no words*

WHEN Margaret Thatcher travelled the world as prime minister, she took a bulldog with her. This jowl-shaking, glowering personification of Britishness was her press secretary, Bernard Ingham—now Sir Bernard. Prizing anonymity in his dealings with the media, he became public property. By the end of a decade in Downing Street, he was as essential to the Thatcher caricature as her steel-framed handbag.

Looking back, almost everything about Mrs Thatcher's 12 years seems touched with gothic melodrama—the political landscape was illuminated not by daylight but by periodic lightning-flashes. Sir Bernard was no exception. He has been likened to Shakespeare's Iago, to the Scottish grave-robbers Burke and Hare, to an ogre, to a rottweiler. He became, in short, a story in his own right, the man who was said to have used his great power as Downing Street's anonymous twice-daily briefer to belittle ministers whom Mrs Thatcher intended to dispose of.

Sir Bernard denies the charge. In two of the best-known cases—his description of John Biffen as a "semi-detached" member of the cabinet and of Francis (now Lord) Pym as the depressive wartime radio character Mona Lott—he goes out of his way to explain what went wrong. But first some background is needed.

The "lobby" is the shorthand term for the club of political journalists who attend off-the-record briefings with the prime minister's press secretary. These occur twice a day and may not, under rules drawn up by the journalists themselves, be mentioned in print. The source of the information and views, which are widely distributed just before evening and morning newspaper deadlines, is therefore hidden. If ministers or others who are attacked by Downing Street at such meetings object, they have no comeback. Officially, the briefings never took place.

Sir Bernard complains that in the case of the Biffen and Pym briefings, his comments "were dragged out of me. They were neither premeditated nor authorised. They came off the top of my head." And, further, "the circumstances in which they came to be made were never reported by journalists." Hardly surprising, this, since they were made at lobby briefings which, of course, never occurred.

Such incidents might have caused Sir Bernard to have second thoughts about the system; but he defends it with passion. In recent years he has set himself up as a cru-

You didn't hear that

sader for higher press and broadcasting standards, regularly harking back to the golden days of his journalistic apprenticeship in Yorkshire, where every fact was triple-checked and every speculation ruthlessly suppressed in the *Hebden Bridge Times*. Yet his criticism has not, by and large, been for the tabloid newspapers whose standards fell to new lows during the 1980s; instead, he has reserved his bile for investigative journalists, particularly if they worked for television, and for those newspaper reporters who decided to boycott his lobby briefings.

Here this reviewer must admit an interest: as political editor of the *Scotsman* in those days, he was one of the latter. The anti-lobby group's tactic, which became a habit, was to report particularly sensational comments made by Sir Bernard or his underlings and to name the source. This was done by comparing the shorthand notes of several senior lobby members who willingly handed them over. The result was predictable: the briefers stopped attacking ministers and others in the old style. To that extent, the lobby revolt was a success.

But Sir Bernard was outraged; and since, throughout this account, he goes on about his rectitude and his impartiality as a civil servant, it is worth quoting him on what happened to journalists who fell out with him. At the time of the lobby revolt, "No one could have been in any doubt that if they went over to [the rebel papers'] side, they would cook their goose with Number Ten." As for Brian Redhead, a BBC radio presenter who had the temerity to call him a conspiracy, "His failure to apologise meant that he never got another interview with Mrs Thatcher as prime minister."

Sir Bernard has nothing but contempt for politically embarrassing journalism. A string of distinguished television current-affairs programmes are dismissed as being soft on criminals and terrorists; television programme-makers turn out to be pretentious, corrupt, cynical and generally "nauseating . . . these saintly people, living off the fat of the land, try to kid you that they are guardians of the common weal!" As for media prizes, "There is only one qualification for a media award these days: the undermining of elected authority."

Despite his sneering tone, Sir Bernard is undoubtedly right that too many journalists, brought up on Watergate, see themselves as saintly crusaders and all government as conspiracy. There is a good, critical book to be written about the limits and excesses of journalistic campaigning. It is not this one.

He had his merits, this strange protector of the Iron Lady; he was courageous, decisive and a punishingly hard worker. But his tenure of the prime minister's press office lowered its reputation and damaged Mrs Thatcher's image. His book has a number of interesting passages about the author's boyhood and his later disenchantment with trade unionism. For the rest, it is distasteful where it is not dull. Sir Bernard's many friends will fear he has not done himself justice. His many enemies will crow that he has.

Terribly sorry, not here really

JUNE 29TH **To a chorus of disapproval, the National Gallery opened its new Sainsbury Wing. It looked better later, when the paintings were hung**

SPOT the odd one out: Masaccio, Fra Angelico, Leonardo, Raphael, Sainsbury. The answer, of course, is Fra Angelico. Why? Because his is the only name not to appear, carved in stone, in the entrance to the new extension to London's National Gallery, the Sainsbury Wing.

If the gallery's future visitors leave with a faint impression that the Sainsburys were painters rather than grocers (the family's supermarket millions paid for the new extension), the fault will be that of the building's American architect, Robert Venturi. The problem with Mr Venturi's creation is that it tries to make no statement of its own, but does so by borrowing shoals of mini-statements from other buildings which are, in its creator's favoured phrase, "analogous". Sometimes, this analogy is spatial. Thus the right side of the Sainsbury Wing's facade, nearest William Wilkins's original National Gallery building, is decked out with Wilkins-like Corinthian pilasters. Further from Wilkins's influence, these pilasters face away, until all that remains is a vaguely Modernist but entirely unobjectionable facade, apparently pining for adjacent commercial architecture in London's West End. Purists will sniff that this chameleon quality is both cowardly and messy, but they are the only ones likely to take offence. The man on the Trafalgar Square omnibus will probably not notice that the Sainsbury Wing is there

at all, which may have been precisely the effect its architect was after.

Inside, Mr Venturi's capacity for analogising continues. Some galleries, like the Tate's Duveen Gallery, commemorate donors by inscribing their names on the

The Sainsburys on site

walls. The Sainsbury Wing follows suit. Others, like the Uffizi, have traditionally inscribed the names of great artists. The Sainsbury Wing also follows suit. Mr Venturi says he likes "to see art in people's houses" (hastily adding, lest confusion arise, that he has "nothing against museums") and has kept the scale of rooms down to that of the Renaissance palazzo. This works well for many of the National's pictures, as do some other period gleanings, like the gallery's sequence of Brunelleschian false-perspective arches.

The overall effect, however, is confusing: ornamental steel trusses paying homage to the National Gallery's 19th-century foundation on the one hand, columns in pietra serena suggesting Medician Florence on the other. "Designing contextually", according to Mr Venturi, "does not mean the same thing as being a slave to context." In this case, however, it looks suspiciously as though it does.

More to the point, Mr Venturi has also been a slave to royal opinion, which may account for his building's eagerness to be both pleasing to everybody and invisible. When the gallery's (admittedly uninspired) initial design for the extension was unveiled in 1984, the Prince of Wales attacked it publicly as "a monstrous carbuncle on the face of a much-loved friend". Hence the unusual reticence of Mr Venturi's building, which will fall under the prince's steely gaze every time he ventures down Pall Mall on his way to much-more-exuberant Charing Cross.

Internal splendour

JULY 6TH **The best exhibition of the year in London, though not the best-attended, was the magnificent Constable show at the Tate Gallery**

IN 1805 Benjamin West, president of the Royal Academy, consoled the young John Constable after the Academy's rejection of one of his paintings. West's advice was prophetic and perceptive: "Don't be disheartened, young man, we shall hear of you again. You must have loved nature very much before you could have painted this. Always remember, sir, that light and shadow never stand still."

The Tate Gallery's magnificent new exhibition of Constable's landscape, sponsored by Barclays Bank, affirms both West's confidence and the special character of Constable's achievement. The show chronicles the painter's life-long vision of natural settings not just as locales to be accurately rendered, but as experiences to be con-

veyed. It establishes him anew as both a great artist and a great romantic, who believed that "painting is but another word for feeling" and whose work translated the constant flux of light and shadow—what he called "the chiaroscuro of nature"—into emotion.

One of Constable's friends aptly observed that his subjects comprised "a history of his affections". The arrangement of the Tate exhibition effectively reproduces it. Chief among these affections, of course, was his native Suffolk, which Constable said "made me a painter", by inspiring him to "a pure and unaffected representation" of the scenes he had been born to. His quest for a kind of painting not covered by standard techniques impelled him to originality. By

1810 he was doing oil sketches out-of-doors, some 60 years before it was Impressionist practice, and by 1814 he was painting full-sized exhibition canvases in the same way.

Even in his early works you can see the distinctive brushwork that is Constable's signature—nervous, varied, jabbing, aiming to reproduce the effects of light and motion in the very quality of the paint. In an age which still prized "finish", critics regularly accused him of "extreme carelessness". Although Constable was aware that "my execution annoys . . . the scholastic ones", it was a sacrifice he had to make for "lightness" and "brightness". Besides, when he wished he could be as finished as the next man. One of the surprises of this exhibition is seeing Constable not infrequently adopt the smoother manner of Claude or Gainsborough according to his mood.

What never changed was his central

commitment to natural subjects. One critic sneered that "Mr Constable appears . . . to have fed his genius, like a tethered horse, within a small circle in the homestead," but Constable sought profundity, not novelty. Like his esteemed fellow-romantic Wordsworth, his concern was not with surface detail or rural anecdote, but with "something far more deeply interfused", which again and again in these paintings emerges in the sweep and energy of texture. Constable once dismissed the question of what subjects were appropriate by declaring "I can find a subject under any stone". For him, what mattered was translating feeling into paint, and he deprecated works that were merely "pictures".

This sense of a painting as something with a life of its own stamps Constable not just as a romantic but as one of the first moderns. It is perhaps not surprising that, while he was receiving mixed notices at home, he caused a sensation at the Paris Salon of 1824, when "The Hay-Wain" was shown there. Seeing it on display, the young Delacroix rushed off to heighten the colours on his own exhibition pieces. Although a Paris dealer offered him a fat fee for his work, Constable wrote that he would "never forsake old England, the land of my happiness". But in terms of influence he had more impact on the immediate history

of French painting than of English, as the Barbizon painters and then the Impressionists pursued his values of light, texture and pure painting.

During his lifetime he had his defenders. One connoisseur spoke of the "internal splendour" of one of his paintings, a telling phrase which often comes to mind at the

Tate. Constable, of course, has long since been acknowledged as a national treasure, the creator of a unique body of English landscapes which are collectively cherished as "Constable country". But the riches gathered in this exhibition also place him in that other, immortal country reserved only for the greatest painters.

Dominatrix of discourse

JULY 27TH *This was the year when Madonna, role model for millions, crossed the line from phenomenon to icon*

TIME was when discussing Madonna was a periodic—if tantalising—distraction. No longer. Academics write dissertations about her; feminist intellectuals deconstruct her image; the middlebrow press celebrates her marketing prowess—or whines about her manipulativeness. Madonna-talk, it seems, is inescapable.

With her new movie, called "Truth or Dare" in America and "In Bed With Madonna" in Europe, Madonna provides pundits with another excuse to pontificate. And, on both sides of the Atlantic, pontificate they have—in reviews, essays, magazine features and on television chat shows. By now, commercial success has little to do with it. The movie has not made much money; her recent record sales (save those of the album compiling her hit singles, "The Immaculate Collection") have been disappointing.

Instead, all the talk is of Madonna as a self-styled icon. That is as it should be. In the ten years since she first registered in the popular mind, she has laboured relentlessly to build for herself a celebrity as potent as that of Garbo, Dean, Presley and (inev-

itably) Monroe. Even though she has succeeded, she is not about to stop now: soon she will have her own multimedia company, courtesy of Time Warner, an entertainment conglomerate. Madonna's mission is plainly nothing less than to embody mass culture itself.

Her detractors—and they are many—split into two groups. One group belittles the notion that what a pop star does is of any consequence. Hence Madonna's provocations (and her admittedly simple-minded defence of them) are mere titillation. This, however, ignores the genuine outrage she causes. In "Truth or Dare" (in which she also carouses in bed with her gay dancers and fellates a bottle of fizzy water), police in Toronto want to arrest her for public indecency; in Italy the Pope condemns her show. And MTV did, after all, censor the video for "Justify My Love". To some at least, Madonna's threat is real.

The second criticism, especially common among "knowing" British writers, rests on a notion of the audience as dupes, taken in by Madonna's shrewd understanding of iconography. Madonna herself says

How long can this go on?

she is "interested in pushing people's buttons." That she does, brilliantly; her fans do not mind. To see that as a failing, either of artist or of audience, is to misunderstand much of pop culture's appeal: the joy of surrender, the guilty pleasure of being willingly taken in. Perhaps more important, it ignores one of the most intriguing questions posed by postmodernism about authenticity and celebrity: what matters more, seeming real or really seeming?

Madonna's detractors, whether conservative or elitist, have long had an unlikely ally: feminists. Madonna's trend-setting wardrobe (underwear as outerwear and "Boy Toy" beltbuckles) and her equivocally anti-abortion song, "Papa Don't Preach", alienated many female intellectuals. Now Madonna's assertiveness has won her a feminist following. As Camille Paglia, an American academic, puts it: "Woman's sexual glamour has bewitched and destroyed men since Delilah. Madonna, role model to mil-

lions of girls worldwide, has cured the ills of feminism by reasserting woman's control over the sexual realm."

But is dominance progress? In a discussion of Madonna on American public television, Lynne Layton, an academic at Harvard, argued that "role reversals don't seem to me to be what feminists have fought for these last 20 years." A fair point. Not so the claims of some British writers that Madonna is somehow less of a feminist because most of her songs have been co-written and co-produced by men. Indeed, as Julie Burchill, a British pop critic, points out, that Madonna uses men in this way is further proof of her final power over them.

In all the ink spilt over Madonna, pundits have been remiss in one respect. They have considered her almost exclusively in visual terms: but it is her music, as much as her command of television, that is essential to her success. Since Elvis, every truly global icon has sprung from the world of music:

the Beatles, Bob Dylan, the Rolling Stones, Bruce Springsteen, Michael Jackson. As Robert Christgau, an American critic who gives Madonna's music its due, has noted, "superstardom has become conspicuously coextensive with rock 'n' roll."

When Madonna's music is discussed at all, it is typically dismissed, in the words of *Time*, as "mere dancefloor fodder". But in the 1980s pop's centre of gravity shifted away from the radio and record shops and toward the clubs and discotheques. In 1990, for the first time in history, not a single traditional, guitar-based rock band topped the singles charts. Increasingly, America's white, middle-class, suburban teenagers no longer emulate rock 'n' rollers. Their styles come from rap—and from disco, which was pronounced dead at the end of the 1970s. Madonna knew better, and her success may owe more to that than to any other gifts for artifice or self-publicity. Above anything else, the girl is a musical opportunist.

Raiders of the lost scrolls

SEPTEMBER 14TH, CINCINNATI *The Dead Sea scrolls, long kept under wraps by a team of scholars, were partly leaked by other scholars using computers*

EVER since their discovery in 1947, the so-called "Dead Sea scrolls" have rightly been considered one of the most momentous scholarly finds of the century, shedding invaluable light on Judaic and early Christian history. At least, it is assumed they do; for the transcripts of the scrolls, in existence since the late 1950s, have been so jealously guarded that only 20% of the text has been released to the public. This wall of academic secrecy has now been breached, and the hoarders flushed blinking into the light.

The breachers were a noted Talmudic scholar at Hebrew Union College in Cincinnati, Ben-Zion Wacholder, 67 and nearly blind, and Martin Abegg, 41, a Baptist doctoral student. Mr Abegg is good at computers, which helped the project considerably. Between them, they have produced a 125-page volume entitled "A Preliminary Edition of the Unpublished Dead Sea Scrolls: The Hebrew and Aramaic Texts from Cave Four, Fascicle One." It is based on a concordance, previously produced by four scholars working in the strictest secrecy at the direction of the Dead Sea scroll editorial team, which was made available in a small edition in 1988. By running the concordance through a computer, it was possible to reconstruct the transcripts.

The book is published by the enterprising Biblical Archaeology Society of Washington, DC. "What is especially galling," writes Hershel Shanks, the editor of the Biblical *Archaeology Review*,

is that the concordance proves that the tran-

scriptions of the text were available as early as 1960. They could easily have been published then, thereby allowing the worldwide community of scholars to study them. It is heartbreaking to realise how much further advanced studies would have been today had this been done.

He added a spirited thrust in the *New York Times*: "We are taking only what is rightfully ours."

Mr Wacholder and Mr Abegg might well be proud not only of their boldness, but also of their technical skill. Their volume apparently represents the first time an ancient text has been reconstructed by computer. But they are disarmingly modest about it. "We can assure the scholarly world", they write, "that, despite its many imperfections, this edition approximates the contents of the unpublished works of the Dead Sea scrolls. It does not presume to present the official edition we all eagerly await."

The new volume has created an international sensation. Members of the current editorial board, their endless delays and secrecy once again exposed, are not amused. One of the editors, Emile Puech, who is based in Jerusalem, has threatened to sue. What Mr Wacholder and Mr Abegg have done, he says, is "a violation of international law".

John Strugnell of Harvard, a British-born authority on Christian origins, went even further. "What can one call it but stealing?" he asked. His angry outburst carried rather less weight when it was noted that he

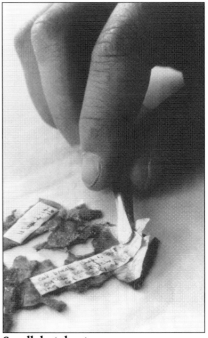

Small, but dangerous

had been dismissed as chief editor of the Dead Sea scrolls after making virulently anti-Jewish remarks to a Tel Aviv newspaper last November.

Important disclosures or findings in the newly published documents may be months or years appearing, although there is now a great impetus to get them out. For example, it is widely believed that the Essenes, the supposed authors of these texts, were a celibate sect. Apparently not so.

"There is a lengthy passage", Mr Wacholder told a news conference in New York city, "that clearly marks what a man had to do to get permission from the rabbi to marry. It makes it clear that monks they were not."

Although most of the Dead Sea scrolls have been under the control of the Israeli government since 1967, it has deliberately exerted little control over the activities of the international editorial board, which came into existence in the 1950s. Some members of the board are known to have passed the unpublished materials in their possession to other favourite scholars, as if the records were their personal property. It is not clear whether the latest turn of events will lead the Israeli Department of Antiquities to take another look at the board.

As for the editorial team, led by Eugene Ulrich, a theologian at Notre Dame University, they are now promising to complete their editorial and publishing duties by the end of the decade. But they are not making any promises about allowing other interested scholars to examine a microfilm or photostats of the unpublished material in the meantime. Meanwhile Messrs Wacholder and Abegg, undeterred by the smoke and flame, are moving ahead as planned, and have promised to complete their extraordinary achievement in four more volumes, to be published over the next several years.

Reality, ritual and crowds

SEPTEMBER 28TH *Japan came to England for three months in a cultural extravaganza mostly remembered for sumo wrestling*

JAPAN'S high profile in the world may seem a relatively new phenomenon, but its relations with Britain go back a long way. In 1885, reviewing the premiere of Gilbert and Sullivan's "The Mikado", a critic observed that "We are all being more or less Japanned." He was referring both to the wave of interest and commerce generated by the 1858 trade agreement between the two countries and, more specifically, to a Japanese exhibition, complete with model village. The term "japanning" was a synonym for imitation lacquer, dating back to the East India Company's first contacts with the Orient in the early 17th century.

Britain is currently being comprehensively japanned by the Japan Festival 1991, a huge affair, with events all over the country, lasting into next January. According to its chairman, Sir Peter Parker, it aims "to demystify and to challenge misconceptions." The demystification got off to a slow start on September 21st with a fair in Hyde Park; thousands of Britons, grumbling in the heat, found in one tiny tent a band of housewives trying origami, in another small piles of Japanese jelly babies on sale for huge sums of cash, and sushi and sashimi stalls so small and undermanned that the squabbling queues stretched for yards. Many were confirmed in their prejudice that the essence of modern Japan is not beauty, but crowds.

Yet the country's traditional arts still cast their ancient spell. At London's Queen Elizabeth Hall, a short season of Noh Theatre was sold out, hypnotising audiences with drama in which the most obviously dramatic elements were suppressed in favour of rigidly stylised gestures of voice, movement and music. Meanwhile, across town, crowds were flocking to the Science Museum to watch state-of-the-art Japanese robots putt golf balls and climb walls. Old and new, both these events might seem to illustrate an attitude central to Japanese culture: a compulsion to control experience, whether by art or technology, and to turn reality into ritual.

It was that sense of ritual which brought about the revolution in 19th-century European design. The elegant beauty of *Japonisme* became all the rage, the most advanced taste in aesthetic circles. Liberty's, a London department store, was founded on its imports of Japanese fabrics and fashions; in 1876 the arrival of a new consignment of fans sparked a near-riot. But the western vogue for things Japanese also became a Japanese vogue for things western. To some Japanese the trend was a corrupting influence, undermining the very practices which made the culture distinctive.

The resulting conflict is the subject of a curiously suggestive show at the Victoria and Albert Museum. "Visions of Japan" is

As Beardsley saw it

not so much concerned with how the West sees Japan but how Japan sees itself. Three young architects have each been given a single room in which to describe an aspect of Japanese experience. The first, called "Cosmos", presents traditional Buddhist practices and beliefs in a self-consciously schematic fashion: one pillar stands for the temple, the walls of a teahouse mechanically fold and unfold. The whole space conveys a decidedly ambivalent, post-modernist view of eternity and belief, an impression confirmed in the second room, "Chaos", which evokes the barrage of conflicting impressions which is life in contemporary Tokyo. Traditional objects jostle with vending machines, comics, traffic robots, *karaoke* boxes, massage machines and computerised fortune tellers. The whole scene sums up the architect's "uncertainty about the way we Japanese can't do more with our cultural inheritance than make it electronic."

The final room, "Dreams", is a vision of the future, in which the entire environment is manipulated electronically. It is a natural outcome of the architect's vision of a world in which "our lives and circumstances become more artificial every day." The room itself has a partly eerie, partly soothing subterranean feeling, with flickering lights and sounds, and 20-feet high video images projected on the length of a wall. In these artificial surroundings life has become another kind of weird ritual, in which the central purpose of the rite has been forgotten.

If these rooms really do offer contemporary visions of Japan, the Japanese are as problematic and mysterious to themselves as they are to outsiders—"worker-bees", as one architect calls them, with an engrained compulsion for highly-organised activity, but uncertain about what lies beyond it. Or perhaps Oscar Wilde was right when, at the height of the Aesthetic craze for Japan, he observed that "In fact the whole of Japan is a pure invention . . . the Japanese people are . . . simply a mode of style, an exquisite fancy of art."

A distant drumming

OCTOBER 12TH   Robert Bly's "Iron John" (Addison Wesley), a book urging men to rediscover themselves, arrived in a sceptical Britain in October

FORGET your hunting rifles, put away those golf clubs. The New American Man has different symbols for his masculinity: the drum and the hankie. No longer does he spend his weekends hitting small white balls or shooting deer. No, the NAM leaves his womenfolk behind and heads for the woods with other NAMs, there to indulge in a spot of communal drumming. That done, the NAMs hug each other for a time, before settling down to some serious crying. Sales of Man-Size Kleenex must be going into orbit.

The man behind all this lachrymation is Robert Bly, whose guidebook, "Iron John", is published in Britain this month after dominating the *New York Times's* best-seller list for a year. Mr Bly's thesis is as follows. Since the Industrial Revolution, fathers have gone out to work, leaving male children without an obvious role model for their emerging maleness. The resultant "father-hunger" (Mr Bly's term) has been compounded in the past 30 years by the emergence of feminism, which has helped to kill off the already ailing "Wild Man" element in American manhood. Far from being a barbaric being, "Wild Man" is rather a benign little soul, much given to sensitivity and "protecting what is his". Without him, American Man has split into two groups, "Savage Man" (personified by Sylvester Stallone) and "Soft Man", Mr Bly's roundabout phrase for a wimp.

As a leader of the "new male consciousness" movement, Mr Bly's mission is to reconcile these two estranged halves of the masculine psyche. Subtitled "A Book About Men", "Iron John" attempts to put the American male back in touch with his lost past by raiding what its author calls the "ancient granary" of male mythology. The book's title is taken from its central myth, courtesy of the Brothers Grimm, about a wild man of the woods who helps young

Wild Man or Savage Man?

princes find their fortunes. But Mr Bly also cites as evidence a paralysingly comprehensive range of mythological tales, from Homer to Navajo shamans via Chrétien de Troyes. His conclusions are that young men need to find themselves platonic mentors (ideally, it seems, Woody Allen or Jimmy Carter, both well-evolved in Bly terms) and

disappear with them into the woods, there to "bond", "feel good about being men", and cry.

Once one has overcome an irrepressible suspicion that Mr Bly may have written an unrecognised comic masterpiece, his tenets seem harmless enough. For all their New Age updating (by blaming the Industrial Revolution and advocating woodland walks, Mr Bly has biodegradability on his side), his ideas join a long poetic tradition. Goethe believed in essences of gender. Mr Bly's fellow American poet, Walt Whitman, was given to sylvan mythologising. The fact that it all seems a little like Baden-Powell for grown-ups, or that Mr Bly's prescription is unlikely to be of much use to the woodless urban poor, is neither here nor there.

What does disturb about "Iron John", however, is its insistently separatist tone. Feminism was good for women, says Mr Bly: now masculism will do the same for men. The fact that American society is already arranged to be good for men does not detain him. More to the point, despite constant protestations that the book is not anti-feminist, Mr Bly portrays women as a race of emasculators. (One female subject is described, memorably, as having "tripod-rage, a desire to kick anything with three legs.") Put in this context, his talk of "wounding" and fondness for drums seems faintly sinister, more "Lord of the Flies" than "Scouting for Boys".

An examination of Mr Bly's own circumstances vis-à-vis American womanhood may help make things clearer. His myth-mash analysis is, after all, lifted from Jung. Mrs Bly is, as it happens, a Jungian analyst. Readers may draw their own conclusions.

The world's worst-kept secret

OCTOBER 26TH   Most-hyped scoop-book of the year was Seymour Hersh's "The Samson Option" (Random House), a story most people felt they knew already

SEYMOUR HERSH won a Pulitzer Prize for exposing the American army's massacre of Vietnamese civilians at My Lai. His latest book is less startling, for an obvious reason: Israel's possession of nuclear weapons is one of the worst-kept secrets in the world. The *New York Times* first splashed Israel's bombs and missiles on its front page 21

years ago. The fullest account of the size of its arsenal was published in 1986 in Britain's *Sunday Times*, and was based on the first-hand testimony of a disaffected Israeli nuclear technician, Mordechai Vanunu.

Israel has not announced having a bomb because doing so would invite political trouble, mainly from the United States.

But since deterrents do not deter if nobody knows about them, Israel has let the general fact of its nuclear status trickle out. The challenge for investigators is to nail down the details. How many Israeli bombs? Where are they? In what circumstances would they be used? Although Mr Hersh, with a reputation to keep polished, has come up with some headline-grabbing answers, not all are new. And few of the new ones are persuasively documented.

How many bombs? About 300, says Mr Hersh, including 100 or so tactical weapons such as artillery shells and nuclear landmines. Apart from the tactical weapons, this is not wholly out of line with the guesses of other authors. But where predecessors have merely speculated that Israel has low-yield neutron warheads, Mr Hersh is positive, apparently because that is what America's own experts decided after seeing the Vanunu evidence.

Where are the bombs? Nobody has bettered Mr Vanunu's description of the Dimona nuclear complex, in the Negev desert. Mr Hersh says that Israel's nuclear-armed missiles are kept at a place called Hirbat Zachariah, west of Jerusalem, and that aircraft equipped with nuclear bombs are located at the Tel Nof fighter base.

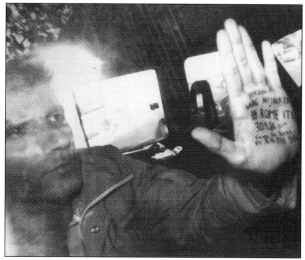
Vanunu knew

Under what circumstances would Israel use its bombs? Mr Hersh believes that, since the 1970s, Israel has included the Soviet Union in its targeting plans. Although this is not a new claim, it is put forward with fresh detail. Mr Hersh argues that the task of Jonathan Pollard, the American Jew who spied for Israel in Washington, was mainly to tell Israel about Soviet targets. It may have seemed reckless for tiny Israel to target the then-mighty Soviet Union, but Mr Hersh says that Israel learnt in 1967 that the Soviet Union had added Tel Aviv, Haifa, Beersheba and Ashdod to its own target list.

On three occasions, according to this book, Israel has gone on nuclear alert. One was during the war of 1973, when the tide of battle threatened to overwhelm Israel's conventional defences (this was reported first by *Time* magazine in 1976). By arming its nukes, Israel persuaded Henry Kissinger to rush in the extra conventional weapons it was pleading for. A new claim is that Israel went on alert again, towards the end of the war, when it thought that the Soviet Union was preparing to intervene. The third occasion, says Mr Hersh, was during the Gulf war. Israel reacted to Iraq's missile attacks by hauling its own nuclear-armed missiles into the open, and pointing them east.

It is noticeable that Mr Hersh offers no evidence whatsoever for this final claim, which is contained in a ragged "epilogue" that has neither sources nor footnotes. Indeed, the persuasive parts of this book tend to be those that deal with ancient history (Israel's decision to go nuclear in the late 1950s, the early help from France) or Washington infighting (on Israel's abuse of satellite intelligence from America, the Pollard affair). The circumstances in which Israel might use its bomb remain as mysterious as Israel presumably intends them to be.

So, in truth, does the size of its arsenal. Mr Hersh says that there were other defectors from Dimona, before Mr Vanunu, who gave American officials photographs of Israeli warheads and revealed that Israel had more than 100 weapons in storage. Israel, American intelligence people concluded, could do "anything we or the Soviets can do." But the defectors, like most of Mr Hersh's informants, are not named. Despite Mr Hersh's hard work, it is difficult to escape the conclusion that the Vanunu evidence remains the best—though some say planted—source on Israel's stockpile.

As for whether Israel was wise to build nuclear weapons at all, Mr Hersh is agnostic, aiming his venom less at the Israeli decision to go nuclear than at America's decision to look the other way. Meanwhile, on the internal evidence of this book, the Israeli policy of building an undeclared nuclear deterrent has served it well. It unblocked the American arms lifeline during the war of 1973, sent a warning to the Russians when they may have been planning to rescue the Egyptian army, and presumably prevented Saddam Hussein from using chemical weapons against Israel during the Gulf war. All this was achieved without Israel incurring the penalties intended for nuclear proliferators. Nice work, while it lasts.

Life's like that

OCTOBER 26TH *Norman Mailer's biggest book yet (Random House/Michael Joseph, 1,200 pages) ran into an appropriately large amount of flak*

NORMAN MAILER was at Brown's hotel in London this week, fighting off accusations that his new novel, "Harlot's Ghost", a sprawling monster that weighs in at 2½ kilos, was perhaps the greatest mistake of his long and controversial career as a commentator on the great themes of post-war America. Hadn't he been a little over-ambitious in trying to cover the whole history of the CIA until 1965 (there is more, much more to come) in 1,200 pages?

Mr Mailer easily brushed that off. It was the reviewers' fault, of course. "You have to stop yourself getting angry with those who are of mediocre

Mailer, god of the intervals

disposition," he said. "The fact is they don't like long novels. It takes maybe six whole days. If they can get through it in an hour and a half, they get their money faster. It's hard work for a reviewer, this book. They can't skip-read it because there are no plot points." And anyway "It could have been twice as long, and then they would have started comparing it with Proust and they know it's only half as good as Proust."

So why were there no plot points? Because the subject was too serious for that. Plot points could be left to the spy novel— "those things are just clocks that are put together. They have nothing to do with life"— and other, lesser genres. Mr Mailer described how it worked: "You see, you blunder forward in this book with a series of potentialities. It's a kind of inner debate. This is not for amusement. If you want to amuse yourself, turn on the TV."

And what did he mean by organising the book in such an odd way—by beginning it in 1983, when Harry Hubbard, the book's central character, is on the plane to Moscow and, after 100 pages, moving back 40 years to his childhood? The problem is, of course, that the book never reaches the point from which it set out. It stops dead at 1965. Before Vietnam. Before Watergate. "I regard this book as a novel with a legitimate architecture—but one with an excluded middle. That's good because it gives the reader some scope. The missing part shapes up in his mind. Life is like that. We're always filling in intervals. I was trying to create an environment that was life-like in this book, one with more questions than answers. We live in a world of fiction—what we think things are, plus a few bits of hard fact."

So there you have it. The more frustrating the book becomes, the more it resembles travelling on the underground at rush hour. Life's just like that.

What? Not Rembrandt?

DECEMBER 7TH *At the year's end, the Rembrandt Research Project put its highly controversial findings on display*

EVERY retrospective of an artist likes to claim that it will inspire a new view of its subject. Few can have done so as sensationally as "Rembrandt: The Master and his Workshop", which has just opened at Amsterdam's Rijksmuseum, midway through a tour that began at the Gemäldegalerie in Berlin in September and will continue to London's National Gallery in March.

The exhibition confronts the public with the practical results of one of the most controversial scholarly investigations ever carried out on an artist's work. Since 1968 the Rembrandt Research Project (RRP), centred in Amsterdam, has been systematically reassessing the authenticity of all the paintings attributed to Rembrandt. Its findings have sent waves of shock through the genteel world of museums and connoisseurs. Famous casualties of the RRP's fearless demoting process have included "The Polish Rider" in New York's Frick Collection, "The Man in the Golden Helmet" in Berlin and "The Girl at the Door" in Chicago. These well-loved "Rembrandts" are now attributed respectively to Willem Drost, Gerrit Dou and Samuel van Hoogstraten, all students of the master.

Although the paintings have not altered a whit, removing them from the Rembrandt canon has had a serious effect on their mystique, not to mention their commercial value. Ordinary art lovers, naturally a conservative lot, demand the evidence for these radical realignments, and the new Rembrandt show provides it in the most straightforward terms. At its heart are some 50 guaranteed and splendid paintings by Rembrandt, plus a selection of drawings and etchings covering the full range of his output. In addition there are 12 demoted Rembrandts, now assigned to various Rembrandt students, beside authenticated works by these same painters, so that viewers may judge the basis of the committee's re-evaluations.

The exhibition is an extremely enlightened example of scholarship taking its public responsibilities seriously. It also challenges art lovers to rethink their conception of what "a Rembrandt" is. He has become synonymous with a certain kind of painting—moody, dimly lit, romantically elusive, the work of a man fighting to follow the gleam of his personal vision against a finally uncomprehending world. This version of the man and his art accords ill with the image underlying this exhibition, of a busy, mostly successful painter who supervised the activities of a large studio and taught aspiring young professionals the tricks of the trade by encouraging them to imitate him—the process which Rembrandt himself had undergone as an apprentice painter.

The result, as summed up by Christopher Brown of the National Gallery (one of the trio of scholars who oversaw the exhibition), is "a leaner, fitter, tougher Rembrandt, with much of the 19th-century accretion taken away." His art is in no way diminished by the revision of his output: but those traits which may have seemed somehow more Rembrandtesque than Rembrandt are now explained. For instance, after the RRP's demotion of "The Polish Rider," one critic admitted "I see weaknesses now I didn't see before." Yet for generations it has been perceived as a great painting, and there is no reason why it should not be so still.

Indeed, the most important effect of the exhibition may be to force viewers to re-examine their reactions, to consider more exactly what they are seeing and what part the mystique of a master's name plays in assessing a work as a masterpiece. All this gives "Rembrandt: The Master and his Workshop" a particular urgency. It also imparts a special value to the exhibition catalogue*, which reproduces the paintings, drawings and etchings and, in a series of thoughtful and comprehensive essays, relates the whole absorbing saga of Rembrandt, his students, his public and the critics. Art lovers may well feel these hefty, handsome volumes are a worthwhile investment for the chance to engage in one of the great debates of today, involving one of the greatest painters who ever lived.

*"Rembrandt: The master and his Workshop; Paintings, Drawings, and Etchings. By Christopher Brown, Jan Keleh and Pieter van Thiel (paintings);Holm Bevers, Peter Schatborn and Barbara Welzel (drawings and etcings). Two volumes. Yale University Press in association with National Gallery Publications. 684 pages; £60 boxed. £29.95 paper

Contents

GOVERNMENT

AFGHANISTAN

Presidential republic. The Watan (Homeland) Party controls a majority of seats in the National Assembly. Presidential elections were last held in November 1987; the next are due in 1994. The last general election was held in April 1988; the next is due in 1993.

President Najibullah Ahmadzai (since 1987)
Prime minister Fazl Haq Khalequiar (since 1990)

ALBANIA

Parliamentary republic. Under an interim constitution adopted on April 29 1991, the 250-member unicameral People's Assembly elects the president and the Council of Ministers. The communist Party of Labour (PLA) has a majority in the People's Assembly, last elected in March-April 1991, but a multi-party government was in place between June and its collapse in December. Elections are scheduled for early 1992.

President Ramiz Alia (since 1982)
Prime minister Vilson Ahmeti (replaced Ylli Bufi in Dec, who replaced Fatos Nano in Jun)

ALGERIA

Presidential republic. The National Liberation Front has had control of the 281-seat National Assembly since 1962. Other parties have been legal since 1989. The last presidential election was in December 1988. A transitional government was appointed in June 1991 to prepare the way for a general election under a multi-party system.

President Col. Chadli Benjedid (since 1979)
Prime minister Sid Ahmed Ghozali (replaced Mouloud Hamrouche in Jun)

PRINCIPAL CABINET MINISTERS
Foreign affairs Lakhdar Brahimi (replaced Sid Ahmed Ghozali in Jun)
Defence Maj. Gen. Khaled Nezzar
Interior Maj.-Gen Larbi Belkheir (replaced in Oct Abdellatif Rahal, who replaced Mohammed Saleh Mohammedi in Jun)
Economy Sid Ahmed Ghozali (replaced in Oct Hocine Benissad, who replaced Ghazi Hidouchi in Jun)

ANDORRA

Parliamentary monarchy, with the president of France and the Bishop of Urgel (in Spain) holding joint suzerainty. These two heads of state are represented in Andorra by the Verguer de Franca and the Verguer Episcopal. A 28-member General Council of the Valleys is elected on a restricted franchise. The last general election was in 1989; the next is due by January 1994.

Co-prince François Mitterrand (since 1981)
Co-prince Joan Marti Alanis, Bishop of Urgel
Permanent French delegate Joan Keller
Permanent episcopal delegate Maj. Ramon Vilardell Mitjaneta
Veguer de Franca Enric Benoît de Coignac
Veguer Episcopal Francesc Badia-Batalla

ANGOLA

Presidential republic. Following independence from Portugal in 1975, the Popular Movement for the Liberation of Angola-Workers' Party (MPLA-PT) was the sole legal political party until a multi-party system came into effect on May 11 1991. The last election to the 289-member National People's Assembly took place in late 1986 (postponed from 1983); a provisional date for multi-party elections, the second half of September 1992, was set in November 1991.

President Jose Eduardo dos Santos (since 1979)
Prime minister Fernando Jose Franca van Dunem (since Jul 1991)

ANTIGUA AND BARBUDA

Parliamentary monarchy. The head of state is the United Kingdom sovereign, represented by a governor-general. The Antiguan Labour Party has controlled the 17-seat House of Representatives since 1976. The last general election was in 1989; the next is due by March 1994.

Governor-general Sir Wilfred Ebenezer Jacobs (since 1981)
Prime minister Vere C. Bird Sr (since 1981)

ARGENTINA

Federal republic. The ruling Justicialist Party (PJ – popularly known as the Peronists), controls the 300-member Congress. The last general election was in 1989; the next is due by May 1995.

President Carlos Saul Menem (since 1989)
Vice-president Eduardo Menem (replaced Eduardo Dunalde in Dec)

CABINET MINISTERS
Defence Antonio Erman Gonzalez (replaced Humberto Romero in Jan)
Economy Domingo Cavallo (replaced Antonio Erman Gonzalez in Jan)
Education and justice Antonio Francisco Salonia
Foreign relations Guido di Tella (replaced Domingo Cavallo in Jan)
Interior Jose Luis Manzano (replaced Julio Mera Figueroa in Aug)
Labour and social security Rodolfo Diaz (replaced Alberto Jorge Triaca in Jan)
Public health and social action Julio Cesar Araoz (replaced Avelino Porto in Nov, who replaced Alberto Kohan in Jan)
Secretary-general of the presidency Eduardo Baua
Justice Leon Carlos Arslanian (replaced Raul Granillo Ocampo in Apr)

ARMENIA

Former republic of the Soviet Union and a founder member of the Commonwealth of Independent States.

President Levon Ter-Petrosyan
Prime minister vacant (Vazguen Manukyan resigned in Sep)

AUSTRALIA

Federalist parliamentary democracy. Head of state is the United Kingdom sovereign, represented by a governor-general. The lower house of the bicameral legislature, the House of Representatives, is elected for three years on the basis of proportional representation. Since 1981 it has been controlled by the Australian Labor Party (ALP) which was elected for a record fourth consecutive term in March 1990, winning 78 of the 148 seats. The next general election is due by March 1993.

Governor-general Bill Hayden (since 1989)
Prime minister Paul Keating (replaced Bob Hawke in Dec 1991)

CABINET MINISTERS
Health, housing and community services Brian Howe
Treasurer John Dawkins (replaced Ralph Willis in late Dec, who replaced earlier in Dec John Kerin, who had replaced Paul Keating in Jun)
Industry, technology and commerce John Button
Foreign affairs and trade Gareth Evans
Finance Ralph Willis (resumed post in late Dec after having been replaced earlier that month by Kim Beazley)
Attorney-general Michael Duffy
Training; employment; education Kim Beazley (replaced John Dawkins in Dec)
Transport and communication Graham Richardson (replaced John Kerin in late Dec, who replaced Kim Beazley earlier in Dec)
Primary industry and energy Simon Crean (replaced John Kerin in Jun)
Social security Neal Blewett (replaced Graham Richardson in Dec)
Defence Robert Ray
Immigration, local government and ethnic affairs Gerry Hand
Arts, sport, environment and territories Ros Kelly
Industrial relations Peter Cook
Administrative services Nick Bolkus
Resources and tourism Alan Griffiths (since Dec)
Shipping and aviation Bob Collins (since Dec)

AUSTRIA

Federal republic with parliamentary democracy. The Socialist Party of Austria (SPÖ) and Austrian People's Party (ÖVP) have ruled in coalition since January 1987. The last general election was in October 1990; the next is due by 1994. Presidential elections are due in April 1992.

Federal president Kurt Waldheim (since 1986)
Federal chancellor Franz Vranitzky (SPÖ) (since 1986)

PRINCIPAL CABINET MINISTERS
Vice-chancellor Erhard Busek (ÖVP) (replaced Josef Riegler in Jul)
Foreign affairs Alois Mock (ÖVP)
Finance Ferdinand Lacina (SPÖ)
Interior Franz Löschnak (SPÖ)
Defence Werner Fasslabend (ÖVP)

AZERBAIJAN

Former republic of the Soviet Union and a founder member of the Commonwealth of Independent States.

President Ayaz Mutalibov
Prime minister Gasan Gasanov

THE BAHAMAS

Parliamentary monarchy. The head of state is the United Kingdom sovereign, represented by a governor-general. The elected 49-seat House of Assembly has been controlled by the Progressive Liberal Party since 1968. The last election was in 1987; the next is due by mid-1992.

Governor-general Sir Henry Taylor (since 1988)
Prime minister Sir Lynden O. Pindling (since Jul 1973)

BAHRAIN

Absolute monarchy ruled by the Emir who appoints a cabinet.

Head of state Sheikh Isa bin Sulman al Khalifa, Emir (succeeded 1961, took title of Emir 1971)
Heir apparent Sheikh Hamed bin Isa al Khalifa
Prime minister Sheikh Khalifa bin Sulman al Khalifa (since 1973)

BANGLADESH

Parliamentary republic. The Bangladesh National Party (BNP) controls an absolute majority in the National Assembly. The last general election was in February 1991; the next is due in 1996. Presidential elections were last held in October 1991.

President Abdur Rahman Biswas (replaced Shehabuddin Ahmed, acting president, in Oct)
Prime minister Khaleda Zia (since Mar 1991)

PRINCIPAL CABINET MINISTERS
Foreign affairs A. S. M. Mustafizur Rahman (replaced Fakhruddin Ahmed in Mar)
Finance and planning Saifur Rahman (replaced Kafiluddin Ahmed in Mar)

BARBADOS

Parliamentary monarchy. The head of state is the United Kingdom sovereign, represented by a governor-general. The Democratic Labour Party has controlled the 28-seat House of Assembly since 1986. The last general election was in 1991; the next is due in 1996.

Governor-general Dame Nita Barrow (since 1990)
Prime minister Erskine Sandiford (since 1987)

BELGIUM

Parliamentary monarchy. Parliament comprises a 212-member Chamber of Representatives and a 181-member Senate. The Flemish Christian People's Party (CVP), the Walloon Social Christian Party (PSC), the Flemish Socialist Party (SP), the Walloon Socialist Party (PS) and the Flemish nationalist People's Union (VU) governed in coalition from May 1988 until the VU withdrew in September 1991. The government resigned in October and a general election was held in November. By the end of 1991 no coalition had been formed. Next election due by 1995.

Head of state Baudouin, King of the Belgians (since 1951)

Prime minister Wilfried Martens (CVP) (since 1981)

PRINCIPAL CABINET MINISTERS
Foreign affairs Mark Eyskens (CVP)
Finance Philippe Maystadt (PSC)
National defence Guy Coëme (PS)
Interior Louis Tobback (SP)

BELIZE
Parliamentary monarchy. The head of state is the United Kingdom sovereign, represented by a governor-general. The People's United Party has controlled the 28-seat House of Representatives since 1989. The last general election was in 1989; the next is due by September 1994.

Governor-general Dame Minita Elmira Gordon (since 1981)
Prime minister George Price (since 1989)

BELORUSSIA
Former republic of the Soviet Union and a founder member of the Commonwealth of Independent States.

President Stanislav Shushkevich (replaced Nikolai Dementei in Sep)
Prime minister Vyacheslav Kebich

BENIN
Presidential republic. In line with decisions made by a policy-making National Conference, presidential elections were held in March 1991 following an 11-month period of transitional government. The next election is due in 1996.

President Nicéphore Soglo (since Apr, replacing Mathieu Kerekou)
Prime minister Nicéphore Soglo (until Mar)

BHUTAN
Constitutional monarchy. Political power is shared between the king (assisted by a Royal Advisory Council), the council of ministers, the National Assembly (the Tsogdu) and the monastic head of the kingdom's Buddhist priesthood. Of the 150 members of the Tsogdu, 100 are directly elected.

Head of state Jigme Singye Wangchuk, Druk Gyalpo (Dragon King); (succeeded in 1972)

BOLIVIA
Presidential republic. A coalition of the centre-left Movement of the Revolutionary Left (MIR) and the right-wing Democratic Nationalist Action Party (ADN) controls the 157-member Congress. The last general election was in May 1989; the next is due by May 1993.

President Jaime Paz Zamora (MIR) (since 1989)
Vice-president Luis Ossio Sanjines

BOTSWANA
Presidential republic. The Botswana Democratic Party has been the ruling party since independence in 1966. It holds 31 of the 34 directly elected seats in the 40-member National Assembly. The last legislative and presidential elections were held in October 1988, the next are scheduled for 1994.

President Quett K. J. Masire (since 1980)

BRAZIL
Federal republic. The National Reconstruction Party (PRN) won the presidential election of December 1989 but does not command a majority in the Congress whose size (487 in 1991) varies in proportion to the population. A plebiscite to determine the future form of government is scheduled for 1994.

President Fernando Collor de Mello (since 1990)
Vice-president Itamar Franco

CABINET MINISTERS
Justice Jarbas Passarinho
External relations Francisco Rezek
Economy Marcilio Marques Moreira (replaced Zelia Cardoso de Mello in May)
Infrastructure Joao Santana (replaced in May Eduardo Teixeira, who replaced Ozires Silva in Mar)
Labour Antonio Rogerio Magri
Social security Margarida Procopio

Education Jose Goldenberg (replaced Carlos Chiarelli in Aug)
Agriculture Antonio Cabrera Filho
Health Alceni Guerra
Navy Adml. Mario Cesar Flores
Army Gen. Carlos Tinoco Ribeiro Gomes
Air force Brig. Socrates da Costa Monteiro

BRUNEI
Absolute monarchy. The sultan has supreme executive authority and presides over an advisory Council of Ministers, a Privy Council and a Religious Council.

Head of state Hassanal Bolkiah, Sultan (since 1968)

BULGARIA
Parliamentary republic. Under the constitution of July 1991 the unicameral 400-member National Assembly is elected for a maximum five-year term by universal adult suffrage and in turn elects the president and the Council of Ministers. A general election in October 1991, brought the Union of Democratic Forces (UDF) to power, replacing the former communist Bulgarian Socialist Party. Presidential elections were scheduled for January 1992.

President Zhelyu Zhelev (UDF) (since 1990)
Vice-president Col.-Gen. Atanas Semerdzhiev

PRINCIPAL MINISTERS
Chairman Filip Dimitrov (replaced Dimitur Popov in Oct)
Deputy chairman; foreign affairs Stoyan Ganev (replaced Viktor Vulkov in Oct)
Finance Ivan Kostov
Defence Dimitur Ludzhev (replaced Col.-Gen. Yordan Mutafchiev in Oct)
Internal affairs Yordan Sokolov (replaced Khristo Danov in Oct)

BURKINA
Presidential republic. Thirteen years of military rule ended in June 1991, following a national referendum on a draft constitution. On June 11th a new constitution allowing for multi-party politics was brought into effect. The last elections were in 1978. The president was re-elected unopposed in December 1991; legislative elections due in January 1992 were then cancelled.

President Capt. Blaise Compaore (since 1987)

BURUNDI
Republic, ruled by a military council. The ruling Military Council for National Salvation took power in a bloodless coup in 1987. The last elections were in 1982.

President Maj. Pierre Buyoya
Prime minister Adrien Sibomana

CAMBODIA
A peace agreement ending the 13-year civil war was signed in October 1991 and provided for a UN Transitional Authority in Cambodia (UNTAC) to oversee the transition to multi-party democracy. Under the previous regime in Phnom Penh, which was recognised by virtually none of the UN member states, elections to a 117-member National Assembly were last held in 1981.

Interim president Prince Norodom Sihanouk (replaced Heng Samrin in Nov)
Chairman of the council of ministers Hun Sen

CAMEROON
Presidential republic. The country is in effect a one-party state, ruled by the Cameroon People's Democratic Movement. Legislative and presidential elections were held simultaneously in April 1988, when the current president obtained 98.75% of the vote. A prime minister was appointed in April 1991 to head an interim government pending promised multi-party elections.

President Paul Biya (since 1982)
Prime minister Sadou Hayatou (since Apr)

CANADA
Federal parliamentary democracy, with the United Kingdom monarch as head of state, represented by a governor-general. It has a bicameral legislature, comprising an elected House of Commons (the lower

chamber) and a Senate appointed by the governor-general. The Progressive Conservative Party (PCP), elected in 1984, was returned to power in 1988 with 170 of the 295 seats in the House; the next election is due by November 1993.

Governor-general Ramon John Hnatyshyn (since 1990)
Prime minister Brian Mulroney (since 1984)

FEDERAL CABINET MINISTERS
Constitutional affairs Joseph (Joe) Clark
Fisheries and oceans John Crosbie (replaced Bernard Valcourt in Apr)
Deputy PM; finance Donald Mazankowski (replaced Michael Wilson as finance minister in Apr)
Public works Elmer MacKay
Energy, mines and resources Jake Epp
Secretary of state Robert de Cotret
Communications Perrin Beatty (replaced Marcel Masse in Apr)
Industry, science and technology; international trade Michael Wilson (replaced Benoît Bouchard for industry science and technology and John Crosbie for international trade in Apr)
Minister of state; government leader in the house Harvie Andre
National revenue Otto Jelinek
Indian affairs and northern development Thomas Siddon
Agriculture William McKnight (replaced Donald Mazankowski in Apr)
National health and welfare Benoît Bouchard (replaced Perrin Beatty in Apr)
Defence Marcel Masse (replaced William McKnight in Apr)
External affairs Barbara McDougall (replaced Joe Clark in Apr)
Veterans' affairs Gerald Merrithew
Forestry Frank Oberle
Government leader in the Senate Lowell Murray
Supply and service Paul Dick
Environment Jean Charest (since Apr)
Employment and immigration Bernard Valcourt (replaced Barbara McDougall in Apr)
Solicitor-general Douglas Lewis (replaced Pierre Cadieux in Apr)
Justice and attorney-general Kim Campbell
Transport Jean Corbeil (replaced Douglas Lewis in Apr)
Minister of state for finance; president of treasury board Gilles Loiselle (replaced Robert de Cotret as president of treasury board in Apr)
Labour Marcel Danis (replaced Jean Corbeil in Apr)

CAPE VERDE
Presidential republic. Until constitutional changes in 1990 the sole legal political party was the African Party for the Independence of Cape Verde (PAICV). In the first multi-party elections, held early in 1991, the opposition Movement for Democracy (MPD) gained 65% of the votes in the elections for the National People's Assembly, and the MPD candidate defeated the incumbent PAICV president.

President Antonio Mascarenhas Monteiro (replaced Aristides Pereira in Feb)
Prime minister Carlos Veiga (replaced Gen. Pedro Verona Rodrigues Pires in Mar)

CENTRAL AFRICAN REPUBLIC
Presidential republic. The present ruler seized power in a bloodless coup in 1981. In November 1986 a referendum approved the establishment of a one-party state, the sole party being the Central African Democratic Rally, set up in February 1987. In April 1991 the President promised the adoption of multi-party democracy.

President Gen. André Kolingba (since 1981)
Prime minister Edouard Frank (replaced Gen. André Kolingba in Mar)

CHAD
Republic, ruled by a military council since December 1990. In February 1991 it was announced that a referendum on a new constitution would be held after a 30-month period. An interim government was appointed in March.

President Idriss Déby (since 1990)

Vice-president Maldoum Bada Abbas (since 1990)
Prime minister Jean Alingue Bawoyeu (since Mar)

CHILE
Presidential republic. The 17-party Coalition for Democracy (CPD) has controlled the 167-member National Congress since March 1990. The last general election was in 1989; the next is due by December 1993.

President Patricio Aylwin (since 1990)

PRINCIPAL CABINET MINISTERS
Interior Enrique Krauss
Foreign affairs Enrique Silva Cimma
Finance Alejandro Foxley
Defence Patricio Rojas

CHINA
People's republic. Effective political control has rested in the hands of the Chinese Communist Party (CCP) since 1949. The last, indirect, elections to the National People's Congress (the unicameral legislature) were held in 1988; the next are due in 1993.

President Yang Shangkun (since 1988)
Vice-president Wang Zhen (since 1988)

STATE COUNCIL
Premier of the state council Li Peng
Vice premiers Yao Yilin, Tian Jiyun, Wu Xueqian, Zhu Rongji, Zou Jiahua
State councillor (minister in charge of the state education commission) Li Tieying
State councillor (national defence) Qin Jiwei
State councillor (finance) Wang Bingqian
State councillor (minister in charge of state scientific and technological commission) Song Jian
State councillor (public security) Tao Siju
State councillor (governor of the People's Bank of China) Li Guixian
State councillor Chen Xitong
State councillor Chen Junsheng
State councillor (foreign affairs) Qian Qichen
Secretary general Luo Gan
Minister in charge of the state commission for restructuring the economy Chen Jinhua
Minister in charge of commission of science technology and industry for national defence Ding Henggao
Minister in charge of state nationalities affairs commission Ismail Amat
State security Jia Chunwang
Supervision Wei Jianxing
Civil affairs Cui Naifu
Justice Cai Cheng
Personnel Zhao Dongwan
Labour Ruan Chongwu
Geology and mineral resources Zhu Xun
Construction Hou Jie
Energy resources Huang Yicheng
Railways Li Senmao
Communications Huang Zhendong
Aeronautics and astronautics industry Lin Zongtang
Metallurgical industry Qi Yuanjing
Machine building and electronics industry He Guangyuan
Chemical industry Gu Xiulian
Light industry Zeng Xianlin
Textile industry Wu Wenying
Posts and telecommunications Yang Taifang
Water resources Yang Zhenhuai
Agriculture Liu Zhangyi
Forestry Gao Dezhan
Commerce Hu Ping
Foreign economic relations and trade Li Lanqing
Materials Liu Suinian
Culture (acting) He Jingzhi
Radio, film and television Ai Zhisheng
Public health Chen Minzhang
State physical culture and sports commission Wu Shaozu
Minister in charge of the state family planning commission Peng Peiyun
Auditor-general Lu Peijian

COLOMBIA
Presidential republic. The Liberal Party (PL), who had controlled the 311-member Congress since 1986, dissolved

it in June 1991 but regained control in legislative elections in October. The last election had been in 1989; the next is due by December 1994.

President Cesar Gaviria Trujillo (since 1990)

PRINCIPAL CABINET MINISTERS
Interior Humberto de la Calle Lombana (replaced Julio Cesar Sanchez in Nov)
Foreign affairs Nohemi Sanin Posada (replaced Luis Fernando Jaramillo Correa in Nov)
Finance and public credit Rudolph Hommes Rodriguez
Defence Rafael Pardo Ruedas (replaced Gen. Oscar Botero Restrepo in Aug)

COMOROS
Federal republic. The last presidential election was in March 1990, the next is due in 1996. Elections to the Federal Assembly were last held in March 1987 when all 42 seats were won by the Union for Comorian Progress. The next Federal Assembly elections are due in 1992.

President Said Mohammed Djohar (since 1990)

CONGO
Presidential republic. The country was dominated by the Marxist Congolese Labour Party from 1970, with the chairman of the party's central committee as the head of state. In February 1991 a national conference began to prepare the country for multi-party elections. On June 8th, the conference elected a prime minister to head a transitional government. The president remained the head of state during the transition period, but with greatly reduced executive powers. Elections were due in 1992.

President Denis Sassou-Nguesso (since 1979)
Prime minister Andre Milongo (replaced Gen. Louis Sylvain Goma in Jun)

COSTA RICA
Presidential republic. The Social Christian Unity Party (PUSC) has controlled the 57-seat Legislative Assembly since 1990. The next general election is due by February 1994.

President Rafael Angel Calderon Fournier (since 1990)
First vice-president German Serrano Pinto

COTE D'IVOIRE
Presidential republic. The Democratic Party of Côte d'Ivoire, under Félix Houphouët-Boigny, has been in power since independence in 1960. The first contested presidential election was held in October 1991, with multi-party elections for the National Assembly the following month. The ruling party retained 163 of the 175 seats.

President Félix Houphouët-Boigny (since 1990)
Prime minister Alassane Ouattara (since 1990)

PRINCIPAL CABINET MINISTERS
Minister-delegate to the prime minister for economy, commerce and plan Daniel Kablan Duncan
Defence Léon Konan Koffi
Foreign affairs Amara Essy
Interior and security Emile Constant Bombet

CUBA
People's republic. Legislative power formally lies with the National Assembly of People's Power, composed of 510 members indirectly elected by popularly elected local assemblies; last elected in 1986 and normally due for re-election in 1991. The sole and ruling party, the Cuban Communist Party (PCC), is the major focus of power.

President Fidel Castro (since 1976)

CYPRUS
The island is de facto divided between two administrations – the (Greek-Cypriot) republic of Cyprus and the (Turkish-Cypriot) Turkish republic of northern Cyprus. The latter was declared in November 1983 and has not received international recognition. The republic of Cyprus is a presidential republic. Of the 80 seats in the House of Representatives, the 24 which are reserved for Turkish Cypriots remain unoccupied. Following the last general election in May 1991 the Democratic Rally continued as the predominant party. The next election is

due by May 1996.

President George Vassiliou (since 1988)
Foreign Minister George Incovou

CZECHOSLOVAKIA
Federal republic consisting of the Czech and Slovak republics, each with its own government. The bicameral Federal Assembly, elected by universal adult suffrage, elects the president who in turn appoints the federal government. Multi-party elections, held in June 1990, were won by Civic Forum in the Czech lands and Public Against Violence (PAV) in Slovakia. A general election is due in June 1992.

President Vaclav Havel (since 1989)
Prime minister Marian Calfa (since 1989)

PRINCIPAL MINISTERS
Deputy premier (economic reform) Pavel Hoffmann (replaced Vaclav Vales in Oct)
Deputy premier (finance minister) Vaclav Klaus
Deputy premier (legislative affairs) Pavel Rychetsky
Deputy premier (human rights) Jozef Miklosko
Deputy premier (foreign affairs) Jiri Dienstbier
National defence Lubos Dobrovsky
Interior Jan Langos
Foreign trade Jozef Baksay
Economy Vladimir Dlouhy
Economic competition Imrich Flassik

PRIME MINISTERS OF THE REPUBLICS
Czech lands Petr Pithart
Slovakia Jan Carnogursky (replaced Vladimir Meciar in Apr)

DENMARK
Parliamentary monarchy. The Conservative People's Party has ruled in a minority coalition with the Liberal Party (Venstre) since December 1990. The last general election was in December 1990; the next is due by the end of 1994.

Head of state Margrethe II, Queen of Denmark (succeeded 1972)
Prime minister Poul Schlüter (Con.) (since Sep 1982)

PRINCIPAL CABINET MINISTERS
Foreign affairs Uffe Ellemann-Jensen (Lib.)
Finance Henning Dyremose (Con.)
Defence Knud Enggaard (Lib.)
Interior; Nordic affairs Thor Pedersen (Lib.)

DJIBOUTI
Presidential republic. The legislature is a 65-member Chamber of Deputies. At the last general election in April 1987 all candidates were elected, by univeral suffrage, from a single list put forward by the Popular Rally for Progress, which since October 1981 has been the sole legal party. The next general election is due in April 1992.

President Hassan Gouled Aptidon (since 1977)
Prime minister Barkat Gourad Hamadou (since 1978)

DOMINICA
Parliamentary republic. The Dominica Freedom Party has controlled the 30-member House of Assembly since July 1980. The last general election was held in 1990; the next is due by May 1995.

President Sir Clarence Henry Augustus Seignoret (since 1983)
Prime minister (Mary) Eugenia Charles (since 1980)

DOMINICAN REPUBLIC
Presidential republic. The Social Christian Reformist Party (PRSC) has controlled the 147-member National Congress since May 1986. The last general election was held in 1990; the next is due by May 1994.

President Joaquin Balaguer (since 1986)

ECUADOR
Presidential republic. The Democratic Left (ID) has controlled the 71-member Congress since August 1988. The last general election was held in 1988 and the next is due by May 1992.

President Rodrigo Borja Cevallos (since Aug 1988)

EGYPT

Presidential republic. The National Democratic Party won 348 of the 444 elected seats in the People's National Assembly in elections (boycotted by the three main opposition parties) in November-December 1990. The president is nominated by the assembly, and by popular referendum for a six-year term. The next general election is due by December 1995.

President Hosni Mubarak (since 1981)
Prime minister Atef Sidki (since 1986)

PRINCIPAL CABINET MINISTERS
Defence and military production Lt. Gen. Mohammed Hussein Tantawi Sulayman (replaced Youssef Sabry Abu Taleb in May)
Foreign affairs Amer Mohammed Mousa (replaced Ahmed Esmat Abdel Meguid in May)
Deputy prime minister; financial and economic affairs; planning Kamal Ahmed Al-Ganzouri
Interior Mohammed Abdel-Halim Moussa
Finance Mohammed Ahmed Al-Razaz

EL SALVADOR

Presidential republic. The ruling National Republican Alliance (ARENA) has no absolute majority in the 84-member Legislative Assembly. The last presidential election was in 1989 and the next is due by March 1994; the last legislative elections were held in 1991; the next are due by 1994.

President Alfredo Felix Cristiani Burkard (since 1989)

EQUATORIAL GUINEA

Presidential republic. The ruling Supreme Military Council (composed of both military and civilians since December 1981) took power in August 1979. Elections to a 41-member House of Representatives last took place in July 1988, when all candidates were elected unopposed for a five-year term. The president was elected unopposed in June 1989 for a seven-year term.

President Brig.-Gen. Teodoro Obiang Nguema (since 1979)
Prime minister Capt. Cristino Seriche Bioko (since 1982)

ESTONIA

Parliamentary republic, which became independent from the Soviet Union in September 1991. The majority of seats in the 104-member parliament, elected in March 1990, were won by the Estonian Popular Front and the Association for a Free Estonia. The President, who is head of state, was elected by parliament.

President Arnold Ruutel
Prime minister Edgar Savisaar

ETHIOPIA

Presidential republic. Following the overthrow of President Mengistu in May 1991 a transitional government was formed under the leadership of the Ethiopian People's Revolutionary Democratic Front (EPRDF). In the 87-member Council of Representatives which was elected by a national conference in July 1991 the EPRDF, with 32 seats, was the best-represented group. A general election is scheduled for 1993.

President Meles Zenawi (since Jun)
Prime minister Tamirat Laynie (since Jun)

FIJI

Parliamentary democracy, prior to the two military coups of 1987 which overthrew a newly elected left-wing government supported by Fijians of Indian extraction. Civilian government was nominally restored in December 1987, but was dominated by Fijians of Melanesian descent, on whose behalf the coups had been staged. A new constitution was promulgated in July 1990, since when fresh elections have been repeatedly promised.

President Ratu Sir Penaia Ganilau (since 1987)
Prime minister Ratu Sir Kamisese Mara (since 1987)

FINLAND

Parliamentary republic. The Centre Party has ruled in coalition with the conservative National Coalition Party, the Swedish People's Party and the Finnish Christian

Union since April 1991. The last general election was in March 1991; the next is due by 1995. The next presidential election is due in 1994.

President Mauno Koivisto (since 1982)
Prime minister Esko Aho (replaced Harri Holkeri in Apr)

FRANCE

Presidential republic. Executive power is vested in a president who is directly elected every seven years, most recently in 1988. The president appoints the prime minister, who is responsible to the bicameral parliament comprising the 321-member Senate and the 577-member National Assembly. The Socialist Party (PS) has governed in a minority coalition with the members of the Union for French Democracy (UDF) or the Left Radical Movement (MRG) (known as the France Unie grouping) since May 1988. The last general election to the National Assembly was in June 1988; the next is due by mid-1993.

President François Mitterrand (since 1981)
Prime minister Edith Cresson (PS) (replaced Michel Rocard (PS) in May)

MINISTERS OF STATE
National education Lionel Jospin (PS)
Economy, finance and budget Pierre Bérégovoy (PS)
Foreign affairs Roland Dumas (PS)
Civil service and administrative modernisation Jean-Pierre Soisson (France Unie) (replaced Michel Durafour (PS) in May)
Cities and regional planning Michel Delebarre (PS)

MINISTERS
Keeper of the seals; justice Henri Nallet (PS)
Defence Pierre Joxe (PS) (replaced Jean-Pierre Chevènement in Jan)
Interior Philippe Marchand (PS)
Equipment and housing; transport; the sea Paul Quilès (PS) (replaced Louis Besson in May)
Labour, employment and vocational training Martine Aubry (replaced Jean-Pierre Soisson (UDF) in May)
Co-operation and development Edwige Avice (PS) (replaced Jacques Pelletier (UDF) in May)
Culture; communication Jack Lang (PS) (since May also government spokesman)
Overseas departments and territories Louis Le Pensec (PS) (until May also government spokesman)
Agriculture and forestry Louis Mermaz (PS)
Relations with parliament Jean Poperen (PS)
Social affairs and integration Jean-Louis Bianco (replaced Claude Evin (PS) in May)
Research and technology Hubert Curien (PS)
Youth and sports Frédérique Bredin (PS)
Environment Brice Lalonde (Ecology Generation)

GABON

Presidential republic. The Gabonese Democratic Party (PDG), formed in 1968, was the only legal party until a national conference in March-April 1990 approved the introduction of multi-party politics. In legislative elections in November 1990 the PDG retained an overall majority in the 120-seat National Assembly, and eight opposition parties gained representation. A government of national union was formed at the end of November 1990, including 24 members of the PDG and eight members of the five largest opposition parties. Presidential elections, last held in November 1986, are due in 1994. Legislative elections are due in 1995.

President Omar Bongo (since 1967)
Prime minister Casimir Oye Mba (since 1990)

GAMBIA

Presidential republic. The Progressive People's Party of President Jawara has 31 seats in the 50-member House of Representatives. Presidential and legislative elections were last held in 1987; the next are due in 1993.

President Sir Dawda Kairaba Jawara (since 1970)

GEORGIA

Former republic of the Soviet Union, not a founder member of the Commonwealth of Independent States.

President Zviad Gamsakhurdia
Prime minister Vissarion Gugushvili (replaced Tengiz

Sigua in Sep)

GERMANY

Parliamentary republic. Under the 1949 Basic Law (constitution) the parliament comprises the Bundestag (lower house), which is directly elected every four years, and the Bundesrat (upper house), in which sit representatives from the *Länder* (states). The president is elected by both houses every five years, most recently in May 1989. The Christian Democratic Union (CDU) together with its Bavarian sister party, the Christian Social Union (CSU), and the Free Democratic Party (FDP) have ruled in coalition in West Germany since 1982 and in the united Germany since 1990. The last general election was in December 1990; the next is due by December 1994.

Federal president Richard von Weizsäcker (since Jul 1984 in West Germany)
Federal chancellor Helmut Kohl (CDU) (since Oct 1982 in West Germany)

MEMBERS OF THE CABINET
Head of chancellery Friedrich Böhl (CDU) (replaced Rudolf Seiters in Nov)
Foreign affairs Hans-Dietrich Genscher (FDP)
Interior Rudolf Seiters (CDU) (replaced Wolfgang Schäuble in Nov)
Justice Klaus Kinkel (independent)
Finance Theo Waigel (CSU)
Economy Jürgen Möllemann (FDP)
Agriculture Ignaz Kiechle (CSU)
Labour Norbert Blüm (CDU)
Defence Gerhard Stoltenberg (CDU)
Health Gerda Hasselfeldt (CSU)
Women and youth Angela Merkel (CDU)
Family; the aged Hannelore Rönsch (CDU)
Transport Günther Krause (CDU)
Environment Klaus Töpfer (CDU)
Post Christian Schwarz-Schilling (CDU)
Construction Irmgard Adam-Schwätzer (FDP)
Research Heinz Riesenhuber (CDU)
Education Rainer Ortleb (FDP)
Development aid Carl-Dieter Spranger (CSU)

PREMIERS OF THE LÄNDER
Baden-Württemberg Erwin Teufel (CDU)
Bavaria Max Streibl (CSU)
Brandenburg Manfred Stolpe (SPD)
Hesse Hans Eichel (SPD)
Lower Saxony Gerhard Schröder (SPD)
Mecklenburg-Western Pomerania Alfred Gomolka (CDU)
North Rhine-Westphalia Johannes Rau (SPD)
Rhineland-Palatinate Rudolf Scharpin (SPD) (replaced Carl-Ludwig Wagner (CDU) in May)
Saarland Oskar Lafontaine (SPD)
Saxony Kurt Biedenkopf (CDU)
Saxony-Anhalt Werner Münch (CDU) (replaced Gerd Gies (CDU) in Jul)
Schleswig-Holstein Björn Engholm (SPD)
Thuringia Josef Duchac (CDU).

MAYORS
Berlin Eberhard Diepgen (CDU)
Bremen Klaus Wedemeier (SPD)
Hamburg Henning Voscherau (SPD).

GHANA

Republic, ruled by military council. The Provisional National Defence Council (PNDC) took power in December 1981. Political parties are banned. Executive power is vested in the PNDC, which rules by decree. There have been no elections at national level since 1981, but presidential elections are promised for the last quarter of 1992. Elections to district assemblies with executive powers were held in 1989.

President Flt-Lt. Jerry Rawlings (since 1981)
Chairman of the committee of secretaries P. V. Obeng (since 1982)

GREECE

Parliamentary republic. The New Democracy Party has held a majority in the 300-member parliament since a general election in April 1990. In July 1990 the ND's single-seat majority was confirmed when a deputy from a smaller party joined the ND. The next general election is due in May 1994.

GOVERNMENT

President Constantine Karamanlis (since 1990)
Prime minister Constantine Mitsotakis (since 1990)

PRINCIPAL CABINET MINISTERS
Foreign affairs Antonis Samaras
National defence Yannis Varvitsiotis
Interior Nicolaos Kleitos (replaced Sotirios Kouvelas in Aug)
Finance Yannis Palaiokrassas

GRENADA
Parliamentary monarchy. The head of state is the United Kingdom sovereign, represented by a governor-general. The National Democratic Congress remains the largest party in the 15-member House of Representatives but does not command a majority. The last general election was held in 1990; the next is due in 1995.

Governor-general Sir Paul Scoon (since 1978)
Prime minister Nicholas Brathwaite (since 1990)

GUATEMALA
Presidential republic. The National Congress has 116 members, 87 elected directly and the rest by proportional representation, for a five-year term; it is dominated by three right-wing parties, the National Centrist Union (UCN), the Christian Democratic Party (PDCG) and the Social Action Movement (MAS). The MAS formed a minority coalition government in January 1991. The last general election was in 1990 (with a second round in January 1991); the next is due by November 1995.

President Jorge Serrano Elias (since January 1991)

PRINCIPAL CABINET MINISTERS
Foreign affairs Gonzalo Menendez Park (replaced Alvaro Arzu Irigoyen in Oct)
Interior Fernando Hurtado Prem (replaced Col. Ricardo Mendez Ruiz in May)
Finance Richard Aitkenhead Castillo (replaced Irma Raquel Zelaya Rosales in May)
Defence Gen. Luis Mendoza Garcia

GUINEA
Republic, ruled by military council. The Military Committee for National Recovery has been in power since 1984 when it suspended the constitution which provided for an elected National Assembly. All political parties are banned. A new constitution, providing for an end to military rule and the creation of a two-party system of government within five years, won overwhelming support in a referendum in December 1990. There have been no recent elections.

President Gen Lansana Conté (since 1984)

GUINEA-BISSAU
Presidential republic. Under the constitution of 1974 the African Party for the Independence of Guinea and Cape Verde defines policy in all fields. The last elections (unopposed) of the president and of the 150-member National People's Assembly were held in June 1989.

President Brig.-Gen. Joao Bernardo Vieira (since 1980)
Prime Minister Carlos Correia (since Dec 1991)

GUYANA
Presidential republic. The People's National Congress (PNC) has controlled the 65-member National Assembly since 1968. The last general election was held in 1985 and the next was to be held in December 1991 but was then postponed until 1992.

President Desmond Hoyte (since 1985)
First vice-president and prime minister Hamilton Green (since 1985)

HAITI
Presidential republic. General elections were annulled in 1988 and 1989 by military coups. The National Front for Democracy and Change (FNCD) formed a minority government in the bicameral 110-member Legislative Assembly, after presidential and legislative elections in December 1990–January 1991. The next election is due by 1992, but is dependent on the surrender of power by the military, who staged a coup in September and drove President Aristide into exile.

President Jean-Bertrand Aristide (replaced Ertha Pascal-Trouillot in Feb)

HOLLAND
Parliamentary monarchy. The Christian Democratic Appeal has governed in coalition with the Labour Party (PVDA) since November 1989. The last general election was in September 1989; the next is due by September 1995.

Head of state Beatrix, Queen of the Netherlands (since 1980)
Prime minister Ruud Lubbers (CDA) (since 1982)

CABINET MINISTERS
Deputy prime minister; finance Wim Kok (PVDA)
Home affairs Ien Dales (PVDA)
Foreign affairs Hans van den Broek (CDA)
Development co-operation Jan Pronk (PVDA)
Defence Relus ter Beek (PVDA)
Economic affairs Koos Andriessen (CDA)
Justice; Netherlands Antilles and Aruba Ernst Hirsch Ballin (CDA)
Agriculture, nature management and fisheries Piet Bukman (CDA)
Education and science Jo Ritzen (PVDA)
Social affairs and employment Bert de Vries (CDA)
Transport and public works Hanja May-Weggen (CDA)
Housing, planning and environment Hans Alders (PVDA)
Welfare, health and culture Hedy d'Acona (PVDA)

HONDURAS
Presidential republic. The National Party (PN) has controlled the 128-seat National Assembly since January 1990. The last general election was in 1989; the next is due by November 1994.

President Rafael Leonardo Callejas (since 1990)

HUNGARY
Parliamentary republic. The highest state body is the 386-seat National Assembly which serves for a five-year term and elects the president. Multi-party elections were held in March-April 1990 and won by the Hungarian Democratic Forum (HDF), which gained 165 seats.

President Arpad Goncz (since 1990)
Prime minister Jozsef Antall (since 1990)

PRINCIPAL CABINET MINISTERS
Defence Lajos Fur
Interior Peter Boross
Foreign affairs Geza Jeszenszky
Finance Mihaly Kupa

ICELAND
Parliamentary republic. The Independence Party (IP) has governed in coalition with the Social Democratic Party (SDP) since the last general election in April 1991. The next election is due by 1995.

President Vigdis Finnbogadottir (since 1980)
Prime minister David Oddsson (IP) (replaced Steingrimur Hermannsson in Apr)

INDIA
Federal republic. The Congress Party was returned to government in June 1991, some 17 months after losing power to a coalition led by the Janata Dal. The last general election to the 545-member Lok Sabha (lower house of parliament) was in June 1991; the next is due by June 1996. The number of pro-government members in the Lok Sabha after June 1991 was 243.

President Ramaswamy Venkataraman (since 1987)
Prime minister Narasimha Rao (replaced Chandra Shekhar in Jun)

COUNCIL OF MINISTERS
Human resources development Arjun Singh (replaced Rajmanfal Pande in Jun)
Finance Manmohan Singh (replaced Yaswant Sinha in Jun)
External affairs Madhavsinh Solanki (post vacant between V. C. Shukla's resignation in Feb and Solanki's appointment in Jun)
Defence Sharad Pawar (replaced Chandra Shekhar in Jun)

Agriculture Bakram Jakhar (replaced Devi Lal in Jun)
Home affairs S. B. Chavan (replaced Chandra Shekhar in Jun)
Health and family welfare M. L. Fotedar (post vacant between Shakul-Ur-Rehman's resignation in Feb and Fotedar's appointment in Jun)
Parliamentary affairs Ghulam Bani Azad (replaced Satya Prakash Malaviya in Jun)
Railways C. K. Jaffer Sharief (replaced Janeshwar Mishra in Jun)
Urban development Sheila Kaul (replaced Daulat Ram Saran in Jun)
Welfare Sitarem Kesri
Law, justice and company affairs K. Vijaya Bhaskara Reddy (replaced Subramanian Swamy in Jun)
Civil aviation and tourism Madhav Rao Scindia (replaced Devi Lal for tourism and Harmohan Dhawan for civil aviation in Jun)
Petroleum and natural gas B. Shankaranand (replaced Satya Prakash Malaviya in Jun)
Water resources V. C. Shukla (replaced Manubhai Koyadia in Jun)

INDONESIA
Presidential republic. The government-sponsored Golkar has won an absolute majority of seats in elections to the House of Representatives since 1971. The last general election was in 1987; the next is due by April 1992. The next presidential election is due in 1993.

President Gen. (retd) Suharto (since 1968)
Vice-president Lt.-Gen. (retd) Sudharmono (since 1988)

PRINCIPAL MINISTERS
Political affairs and security Adml. (retd) Sudomo
Economy, finance, industry and development supervision Radius Prawiro
Public welfare Gen. (retd) Supardjo Rustam
Internal affairs Gen. Rudini
Foreign affairs Ali Alatas
Defence and security Gen. L. B. (Benny) Murdani

IRAN
Religious republic. Overall authority is exercised by the spiritual leader and executive power concentrated in the president. Elections to the majlis (parliament) were held in 1988; the next are due in 1992. The last presidential elections were in 1989; the next are due in 1993.

Spiritual leader Ayatollah Seyed Ali Khamenei (since 1989)
President Ali Akbar Rafsanjani (since 1989)

MEMBERS OF THE COUNCIL OF MINISTERS
Foreign affairs Ali Akbar Velayati Oil Gholamreza Agazadeh
Interior; chairman of state security council Abdollah Nouri
Economic affairs and finance Mohsen Nourbakhsh
Agriculture and rural affairs Isa Katantari
Commerce Abdol-Hossein Vahaji
Energy Namdar Zanganeh
Roads and transport Mohammed Saeedi Kya
Jihad ("crusade") for reconstruction Gholamreza Foruzesh
Heavy industries Mohammad Hadi Nezhad-Hosseinian
Industry Mohammad Reza Nematzadeh
Housing and urban development Sarajuddin Kazeruni
Labour and social affairs Hossein Kamali
Posts, telephones and telegraphs Mohammed Gharazi
Health, treatment and medical education Reza Malekzadeh (replaced Iraj Fazel in Feb 1991)
Education and training Mohammad Ali Najafi
Higher education and culture Mostafa Moin
Justice Hojatolislam Ismail Shostari
Defence and armed forces logistics Akbar Torkan
Intelligence and security Hojatolislam Ali Fallahiyan
Culture and islamic guidance Seyyed Mohammad Khatami
Mines and metals Mohammad Hossein Mahloji

IRAQ
Presidential republic. Governed by a Revolutionary Command Council (RCC) which elects the president. The Arab Baath Socialist Party controls a majority in the 250-seat National Assembly. The last general election was in April 1989; the next is due in 1993.

President Saddam Hussein (since 1979)
Prime minister Mohammad Hamzah al Zubaydi (replaced Saadoun Hammadi in Sep)

PRINCIPAL CABINET MINISTERS
Deputy prime minister Tariq Aziz
Interior Watban Ibrahim al Hasan (replaced Ali Hasan al Majid in Nov, who replaced Samir Muhammad Abdul Wahhab in Mar)
Foreign affairs Ahmad Husayn Khudayyir (replaced Tariq Aziz in Mar)
Defence Ali Hasan al Majid (replaced Gen. Hussein Kamil in Oct, who replaced Lt.-Gen. Saadi Tu'ma Abbas al Jaburi in Jul)
Finance Majid Abd Jafar (replaced Mohammad Mehdi Saleh in Mar)
Oil Usamah Abd al Razzaq Hummadi al Hithi (replaced Brig.-Gen. Hussein Kamil in Mar)

IRELAND
Parliamentary republic. The president is directly elected for a seven-year term, most recently in November 1990. The lower house of parliament is the Dail Éireann with 166 members; the upper house is the Seanad Éireann with 60 members. Fianna Fail has governed in coalition with the Progressive Democrats since June 1989. The last general election was in June 1989; the next is due by 1994.

President Mary Robinson (since 1990)
Prime minister Charles Haughey (since 1987)

PRINCIPAL CABINET MINISTERS
Deputy prime minister John Patrick Wilson
Foreign affairs Gerard Collins
Finance Bertie Ahern (replaced Albert Reynolds in Nov)
Defence Vincent Brady (replaced in Nov Brendan Daly, who replaced Charles Haughey in Feb)

ISRAEL
Parliamentary republic. During the 1980s and 1990s the right-wing Likud has led a series of coalition governments, the latest having been formed in June 1990. The last general election was in 1988; the next is due by November 1992. During 1991 the number of pro-government members in the Knesset (the 120-member legislature) increased from 64 to 66.

President Chaim Herzog (since 1983)
Prime minister Yitzhak Shamir (since 1986)

PRINCIPAL CABINET MINISTERS
Deputy prime minister; foreign affairs David Levi
Defence Moshe Arens
Finance Yitzhak Moda'i
Interior Arie Der'i
Housing and construction Ariel Sharon

ITALY
Parliamentary republic. The Christian Democratic Party has headed the ruling coalition in the 630-member Chamber of Deputies since the last general election in June 1987. The next election has been announced for May 1992.

President Francesco Cossiga (since 1985)
Prime minister Giulio Andreotti (DC) (since 1989)

PRINCIPAL CABINET MINISTERS
Deputy prime minister; justice Claudio Martelli
Foreign affairs Gianni De Michelis
Interior Vincenzo Scotti
Treasury Guido Carli
Budget Paolo Cirino Pomicino
Finance Salvatore (Rino) Formica
Defence Virginio Rognoni
Education Riccardo Misasi (replaced Gerardo Bianco in Apr)
Public works Giovanni Prandini
Agriculture Giovanni Goria (replaced Vito Saccomandi in Apr)
Transport Carlo Bernini
Posts and telecommunications Carlo Vizzini (replaced Oscar Mammi in Apr)
Industry Guido Bodrato (replaced Adolfo Battaglia in Apr)
Labour Franco Marini (replaced Carlo Donat-Cattin in Apr)
Foreign trade Vito Lattanzio (replaced Renato Ruggiero in Apr)

Merchant marine Ferdinando Facchiano (replaced Carlo Vizzini in Apr)
Health Francesco De Lorenzo
Tourism Carlo Tognoli
Environment Giorgio Ruffolo
Mezzogiorno Calogero Mannino (replaced Giovanni Marongiu in Apr)
Civil protection Nicola Capria (replaced Vito Lattanzio in Apr)
Research Antonio Ruberti
Relations with parliament Egidio Sterpa
Institutional reforms Mino Martinazzoli (replaced Antonio Maccanico in Apr)
Co-ordination of EC policy Pierluigi Romita
Urban affairs Carmelo Conte
Social affairs Rosa Russo Jervolino
Public administration Remo Gaspari
Immigration Margherita Boniver (appointed in Apr)

JAMAICA
Parliamentary monarchy. The head of state is the United Kingdom sovereign, represented by a governor-general. The People's National Party (PNP) has controlled the 81-member parliament since February 1989. The last general election was in 1989; the next is due by February 1994.

Governor-general Howard Cooke (replaced Sir Florizel Glasspole in Aug)
Prime minister Michael Manley (since 1989)

JAPAN
Constitutional monarchy with power residing in bicameral legislature (Diet), consisting of 512-member House of Representative (elected for up to four years) and 252-member House of Councillors (elected for six years, with half due for re-election every three years). The Liberal Democratic Party (LDP), which has been in government since its formation in 1955, lost its majority in the upper house in July 1989, but retained its overall majority in the lower house in the election of February 1990, winning 275 seats; the next election is due by February 1994.

Head of state Akihito, Emperor of Japan (succeeded in 1989)
Prime minister Kiichi Miyazawa (replaced Toshiki Kaifu in Nov)

CABINET MINISTERS
Deputy premier Michio Watanabe (since Nov)
Foreign affairs Michio Watanabe (replaced Taro Nakayama in Nov)
Justice Takashi Tawara (replaced Megumu Sato in Nov)
Finance Tsutomu Hata (replaced Ryutaro Hashimoto in Nov)
Education Kunio Hatoyama (replaced Yuaka Inoue in Nov)
Health and welfare Tokuo Yamashita (replaced Shiniichiro Shimojo in Nov)
Agriculture, forestry and fisheries Masami Tanubu (replaced Motoji Kondo in Nov)
International trade and industry Kozo Watanabe (replaced Eiichi Nakao in Nov)
Transport Keiwa Okuda (replaced Kanezo Muraoka in Nov)
Post and telecommunications Hideo Watanabe (replaced Katsutsugu Sekiya in Nov)
Labour Tetsuo Kondo (replaced Sadatoshi Ozato in Nov)
Construction Taku Yamasaki (replaced Yuji Ohtsuka in Nov)
Home affairs Masajuro Shiokawa (replaced Akira Fukida in Nov)
Chief cabinet secretary Misoji Sakamoto
Director-general of management and co-ordination agency Man Sasaki
Director-general of Hokkaido and Okinawa development agencies Yoichi Tani
Director-general of defence agency Yukihiko Ikeda
Director-general of economic planning agency Michio Ochi
Director-general of science and technology agency Akiko Santo
Director-general of environment agency Kazuo Aichi
Director-general of national land agency Mamoru Nishida

JORDAN
Constitutional monarchy. Political parties were effectively legalised in mid-1991. Members of various groups are represented in the 80-member House of Representatives, including broadly pro-government forces, the Muslim Brotherhood and Palestinian and Arab nationalists. The last election to the house was in 1989; the next is due by November 1993.

Head of state Hussein, King of Jordan (succeeded in 1952)
Prime minister Sharif Zaid Ibn Shaker (replaced Taher Masri in Nov, who replaced Mudar Badran in Jun)

KAZAKHSTAN
Former republic of the Soviet Union and a founder member of the Commonwealth of Independent States.

President Nursultan Nazarbaev
Prime minister Sergei Tereshchenko (replaced Uzabakay Karamanov in Oct)

KENYA
Presidential republic. President Moi was returned for a third five-year term in February 1988 without recourse to the electorate, having been proposed as the sole candidate of the Kenya African National Union, itself the sole legal political organisation. Legislative elections for the 202-member National Assembly took place in March 1988.

President Daniel T. arap Moi (since 1978)
Vice-president; minister of finance George Saitoti (vice-president since May 1989)

PRINCIPAL CABINET MINISTERS
Home affairs and natural heritage Davidson Kuguru
Foreign affairs and international co-operation Wilson Ndolo Ayah

KIRGHIZIA
Former republic of the Soviet Union and a founder member of the Commonwealth of Independent States.

President Askar Akaev
Prime minister vacant (Nasirdin Isanov died in Nov)

KIRIBATI
Parliamentary democracy with a 41-member unicameral legislature, 39 members of which are popularly elected for up to four years. The president is elected for a four-year term from within the House of Assembly. The last general election was in May 1991, and presidential elections were held in July; the next election is due by May 1995.

President Teatao Teannaki (since 1991)

NORTH KOREA
Single-party communist state. Nominal constitutional authority is held by the unicameral legislature, the 687-member Supreme People's Assembly (SPA), elected for a four-year term from a single list of candidates approved by the communist Korean Workers' Party, dominated since 1945 by Kim Il Sung. The last legislative elections were in April 1990; the next election is due by April 1994.

President Kim Il Sung (since 1972)
Prime minister Yon Hyong Muk (since 1988)

SOUTH KOREA
Parliamentary democracy with legislative power exercised by 299-member National Assembly elected for four years. Executive power is exercised by an elected president who serves a five-year term. The Democratic Liberal Party was formed in 1990, since when it has controlled two-thirds of the Assembly seats. The last general election was in April 1988; the next is due by April 1992. The president's term of office expires in February 1993.

President Roh Tae Woo (since 1988)
Prime minister Chung Won Shik (replaced Ro Jai Bong in May)

PRINCIPAL MEMBERS OF STATE COUNCIL
Deputy prime minister; head of economic planning board Choi Gak Kyu (replaced Lee Seung Yoon in Feb)
Foreign affairs Lee Sang Ock

Home affairs Lee Sang Yeon (replaced Ahn Eung Mo in Apr)
Finance Rhee Yong Man (replaced Chung Yong Euy in May)
Justice Kim Ki Choon (replaced Lee Chong Nam in May)
Defence Choi Sae Chang (replaced Lee Jong Koo in Dec)
Education Yoon Hyong Sup
Commerce and industry Hang Pong Suh (replaced Lee Bong Suh in Dec)
National unification Choi Ho Joong
Director of agency for national security planning Suh Dong Kwon
Director of environment agency Kwon Hwi Hyuk (replaced Huh Nam Hoon in May)

KUWAIT
Absolute monarchy ruled by the Emir who appoints a cabinet. The National Assembly was dissolved in 1986. Elections to an interim National Council were held in June 1990; a general election has been announced for 1992.

Head of state Jabir al Ahmad al Jabir al Sabah, Emir of Kuwait (succeeded 1978)
Prime minister Crown Prince Sheikh Saad al Abdullah al Salim al Sabah (since 1978)

LAOS
People's republic. Political power rests in the hands of the Lao People's Revolutionary Party. National elections to a Supreme People's Assembly were held in 1989.

President Kaysone Phomvihane (replaced Phoumi Vongvichit in Aug)
Chairman of the council of ministers Gen. Khamtay Siphandon (replaced Kaysone Phomvihane in Aug)

LATVIA
Parliamentary republic, which became independent of the Soviet Union in September 1991. The 201-member Supreme Council, elected in March-April 1990, elects its own chairman, who is de facto president.

President Anatolijs Gorbunovs
Prime minister Ivars Godmanis

LEBANON
Presidential republic. No one political party has a majority in the National Assembly, which, under constitutional amendments introduced in 1991, has equal representation of Muslims and Christians. The last general election was held in 1972. In November 1989 the term of the National Assembly was extended until December 1994.

President Elias Hrawi (since 1989)
Prime minister Omar Karami (since December 1990)

PRINCIPAL CABINET MINISTERS
Deputy prime minister; minister of national defence Michel al Murr
Finance Ali al Khalil
Foreign and expatriate affairs Fares Bouez
Interior Maj.-Gen. Sami al Khatib

LESOTHO
Monarchy, ruled by military council. Political activity was banned in March 1986. The ruling military council took effective power from the king in February 1990, and in November he was replaced by his son. The present chairman of the military council took power in a bloodless coup on April 30 1991. The only contested election since independence in 1966 was in January 1977. A transition to democracy is planned for 1992.

Head of state King Letsie III
Chairman of the military council Col. Elias Ramaema (replaced Maj.-Gen. Justin Lekhanya in Apr)

LIBERIA
Presidential republic. A rebellion in 1990 brought about the collapse of the government and embroiled the country in a protracted civil war. Amos Sawyer was installed in November 1990 as interim president with the backing of a regional peace-keeping force, the Economic Community of West African States (ECOWAS) Monitoring Group (ECOMOG), and re-elected by a national conference in April 1991. The conference also decided that the

transitional government should serve until January 1992, when it would hand over to an elected government.

President (interim) Amos Sawyer (since 1990)
Vice-president Peter Naigow

LIBYA
People's republic since 1969, headed by Col. Moammar Qaddafi as "leader of the revolution". Local people's congresses form an electoral base for the General People's Congress.

Head of state Col. Moammar Qaddafi (since 1970)
Senior adviser Maj. Abdel-Salem Jalloud (since 1970)

LIECHTENSTEIN
Parliamentary principality. The Patriotic Union (VU) and Progressive Citizens' Party (FBP) have governed in coalition since 1938. The last general election was in March 1989; the next is due by March 1993.

Head of state Hans Adam II, Prince of Liechtenstein (succeeded in 1989)
Head of government Hans Brunhart (VU) (since 1978)

LITHUANIA
Parliamentary republic, which became independent of the Soviet Union in September 1991. The 141-member Supreme Council was elected in February 1990, and its chairman, the de facto president, was elected in March.

President Vytautas Landsbergis
Prime minister Gediminas Vagnorius

LUXEMBOURG
Parliamentary grand duchy. The Christian Social Party (PCS) has governed in coalition with the Socialists since July 1984. The last general election was in June 1989; the next is due by June 1994.

Head of state Jean, Grand Duke (succeeded in 1964)
Prime minister Jacques Santer (PCS) (since 1984)

MADAGASCAR
Presidential republic. The Vanguard of the Malagasy Revolution party holds the majority in the 137-seat National People's Assembly, the last elections for which were held in May 1989. The next are due in 1994. Presidential elections, held in March 1989, secured a third seven-year term for the president. Under an agreement reached with the opposition in October 1991, an 18-month state of transition was established prior to the creation of a third republic, and the assembly was dissolved.

President Adml. Didier Ratsiraka (since 1976)
Prime minister Guy Razanamasy (replaced Lt.-Col. Victor Ramahatra in Jul)

MALAWI
Presidential republic. The Malawi Congress Party is the sole legal political party and executive power is vested in its leader, Hastings Kamuzu Banda, who has ruled Malawi since independence in 1966. Legislative power is vested in a National Assembly to which 112 members are elected. The president has the power to appoint an unlimited number of deputies to the assembly. The last general election was in May 1987; the next is due in 1992.

President Hastings Kamuzu Banda (since 1966)

MALAYSIA
Federal monarchy (rotating between nine hereditary sultans). Since the establishment of Malaysia in 1963, the United Malays National Organisation (UMNO) has been the dominant party in a series of National Front coalitions. The last election to the House of Representatives was in 1990; the next is due by October 1995.

Head of state Sultan Azlan Muhibbuddin Shah (since 1989)
Prime minister Mahathir Mohamad (since 1981)

PRINCIPAL CABINET MINISTERS
Deputy prime minister; national and rural development Ghafar Baba
Foreign affairs Abdullah Ahmad Badawi
Defence Najib Tun Razak

Finance Anwar Ibrahim
International trade and industry Rafidah Aziz

MALDIVES
Presidential republic. There are no political parties. Elections to the 48-member Citizen's Assembly (Majlis) were held in 1989. The next are due by November 1994.

President Maumoun Abdul Gayoom (since 1978)

MALI
Republic. In March 1991, the ruling Military Committee for National Liberation was overthrown in a military coup. A 25-member Transition Committee for the Salvation of the People (CTSP), was set up with 10 military and 15 civilian members. A national conference decided in November to extend the transition period to March 1992, when presidential elections were to take place. Presidential elections were last held in June 1985; legislative elections in June 1988.

Chairman Lt.-Col. Amadou Toumani Toure (replaced President Traoré in Mar)
Prime minister Soumana Sacko (since Apr)

MALTA
Parliamentary republic. In a general election in May 1987 the Nationalist Party secured a one-seat majority in the 69-member House of Representatives. The next general election is due in May 1992.

President Vincent Tabone (since 1989)
Prime minister Edward Fenech Adami (since 1987)

MARSHALL ISLANDS
Parliamentary republic, with a compact of free association with the United States implemented in 1986, under which the US is responsible for defence and foreign policy. The 33-member legislature (the Nitijela) is elected for four years and chooses a president from among its members. The last presidential election was in 1987.

President Amata Kabua (since 1987)

MAURITANIA
Presidential republic, ruled since 1978 by a Military Committee of National Salvation. The reintroduction of a National Assembly is decreed by the constitution of July 1991 (to be in place by May 1992). Also in July 1991, legislation was introduced allowing political parties. Presidential elections were scheduled for January 1992.

President Col. Moaouia Ould Sidi Mohammed Taya (since 1984)

MAURITIUS
Parliamentary democracy, with the United Kingdom sovereign as head of state, represented by a governor-general. Elections in September 1991 returned to power the ruling coalition of the Mouvement Socialiste Mauricien, the Mauritius Labour Party and the Organisation du Peuple Rodriguais. The alliance won 59 of the 62 directly elected seats in the 70-seat National Assembly. The next elections are due by September 1997.

Governor-general Sir Veerasamy Ringadoo (since 1986)
Prime minister Aneerood Jugnauth (MSM) (since 1982)

MEXICO
Federal republic. The Institutional Revolutionary Party has controlled the 564-member National Congress since 1929. The last general election was in 1988; the next is due by July 1994.

President Carlos Salinas de Gortari (since 1988)

PRINCIPAL MINISTERS
Government Fernando Gutierrez Barrios
Foreign relations Fernando Solana Morales
Defence Gen. Antonio Riviello Bazan
Navy Adml. Luis Carlos Ruano
Finance and public credit Pedro Aspe Armella
Planning and federal budget Ernesto Cedillo Ponce de Leon

MICRONESIA
Federal republic, with a compact of free association with the United States implemented in 1986, under which the

USA is responsible for defence and foreign policy. The National Congress (which elects the president) has 14 members. The last election was in March 1991.

President Bailey Olter (replaced John Haglegam in May)
Vice-president Jacob Nena (replaced Olter in May)

MOLDAVIA

Former republic of the Soviet Union and a founder member of the Commonwealth of Independent States.

President Mircea Snegur
Prime minister Valeriu Muravsky (replaced Mircea Druk in May)

MONACO

Parliamentary principality, with informal political groupings. The monarch nominates the minister of state from a list of three French diplomats submitted by the French government. The last election, in which the National and Democratic Union won all the 18-member National Council seats, was held in January 1988. The next is due in January 1993.

Head of state Rainier III, Prince (since 1949)
Minister of state Jacques Dupont (replaced Jean Ausseil in Apr)

MONGOLIA

People's Republic, ruled by the standing parliament created in May 1990 and partly filled by popular election. The 430-seat Great People's Hural elects the president. Multi-party elections in July 1990 gave the Mongolian People's Revolutionary Party a majority of seats. A constitution is under discussion.

President Punsalmaagiyn Ochirbat (since 1990)
Prime minister Dashiyn Byambasuren (since 1990)

MOROCCO

Constitutional monarchy, with a government that is a coalition of seven of the ten political parties represented in the 306-member Chamber of Representatives. The last general election was in September 1984; the next is due by September 1992.

Head of state Hassan II, King (since 1961)
Prime minister Azeddine Laraki (since 1986)

PRINCIPAL CABINET MINISTERS
Finance Mohammed Berrada
Foreign affairs and co-operation Abdellatif Filali
Interior and information Driss Basri

MOZAMBIQUE

Presidential republic. A new constitution allowing for multi-party politics came into effect in November 1990. Previously the ruling Front for the Liberation of Mozambique (Frelimo) had been the sole legal political party since independence in 1975. Legislative elections were scheduled for 1991 following the formal registration of political parties, but did not take place.

President Joaquim Alberto Chissano (since 1986)
Prime minister Mario da Graca Machungo (since 1986)

MYANMAR (BURMA)

Republic ruled by military junta. All political power rests with the ruling junta, the State Law and Order Restoration Council (SLORC). The last general election in May 1990 resulted in a landslide victory for the opposition National League for Democracy (NLD). But at the end of 1991 the SLORC had still not transferred power.

Chairman (SLORC) Gen. Saw Maung (since 1988)

NAMIBIA

Presidential republic. On independence in March 1990 the Constituent Assembly, elected in November 1989, was converted into the lower house of a bicameral parliamentary structure by March 1991. The current president, with executive powers, was unanimously elected in February 1990 by the assembly. Legislative elections are due in 1994, presidential elections in 1995.

President Sam Nujoma (since 1990)
Prime minister Hage Geingob (since 1990)

NAURU

Parliamentary democracy, with an 18-member unicameral parliament elected for up to three years. The new parliament elects the president (who serves as both head of government and head of state) from among its members. The last election was in December 1989; the next is due by December 1992.

President Bernard Dowiyogo (since 1989)

NEPAL

Parliamentary monarchy. The Nepali Congress Party (NCP) won a majority in an election held in May 1991 to a newly created House of Representatives. The next election is due by May 1996. The number of NCP members in the 205-member house following the election was 110.

Head of state King Birendra Bir Bikram Shah Deva (crowned in 1975)
Prime minister Girija Prasad Koirala

NEW ZEALAND

Parliamentary democracy, with the United Kingdom sovereign as head of state, represented by a governor-general. The 97-member unicameral House of Representatives, elected for up to three years, is controlled by the conservative National Party which holds 68 seats. The last general election was in October 1990; the next is due by October 1993.

Governor-general Dame Catherine Tizard (since 1990)
Prime minister Jim Bolger (since 1990)

PRINCIPAL CABINET MINISTERS
Deputy prime minister; external relations and trade; foreign affairs Don McKinnon
Finance Ruth Richardson
Attorney-general; leader of the house Paul East
Defence; local government Warren Cooper

NICARAGUA

Presidential republic. The ruling coalition party, the National Opposition Union (UNO) does not command an overall majority in the 90-member National Assembly. The last election was in 1990; the next is due by February 1996.

President Violeta Chamorro (since 1990)

PRINCIPAL CABINET MINISTERS
Foreign affairs Enrique Dreyfus
Interior Carlos Hurtado
Finance Emilio Pereira
Presidency Antonio Lacayo

NIGER

Presidential republic. The current head of state has been in power since November 1987 and was last elected (unopposed) in December 1989. A national conference on the political future of the country, held with a view to the adoption of multi-party politics, began deliberating in July 1991. On Aug 9th, it suspended the constitution, stripping the president of his executive power, although he remains head of state. On Nov 3rd it handed executive power over to Adamou Cheiffou, prime minister during the period of transition to democracy which continues until 1993. Legislative power during the transition is vested in a 15-member Higher Council of the Republic.

President Brig.-Gen. Ali Saibou (since 1987)
Presidium president (national conference) André Salifou (since Sep)
Prime minister Amadou Chieffou (replaced Brig. Ali Salibou in Nov)

NIGERIA

Federal republic, ruled by military council. The present regime took power in a coup in August 1985. The principal decision-making body is the Armed Forces Ruling Council (AFRC), composed of senior officers and members of the police force. The 21 state governors, along with the president, form the National Council of States. The National Council of Ministers, which is responsible for federal administration, is appointed by the AFRC. There have been no elections at a national level since 1983. Local elections were held in 1990.

President Maj.-Gen. Ibrahim Babangida (since 1985)

PRINCIPAL MINISTERS
Vice-president Vice-Adml. (retd) Agustus Aikhomu
Agriculture and natural resources Shetima Mustapha
Budget and planning Chu Okongwu
Education Babs Fafunwa
Employment, labour and productivity Bonu Shariff Musa
External affairs Maj.-Gen. (retd) Ike Nwachukwu
Finance and economic planning Abubakar Alhaji
Health Koye Ransome Kuti
Industry Air Vice-Marshal (retd) Mohammed Yahaya
Internal affairs Maj.-Gen. (retd) A. B. Mamman
Justice; attorney-general Prince Bola Ajibola
Petroleum resources Jibril Aminu

NORWAY

Parliamentary monarchy. A minority Labour government has been in power since November 1990. The last general election was in September 1989 for a fixed four-year-term parliament which cannot be dissolved prematurely.

Head of state Harald V, King of Norway (succeeded Olav V in Jan)
Prime minister Gro Harlem Brundtland (since 1990)

PRINCIPAL CABINET MINISTERS
Foreign affairs Thorvald Stoltenberg
Finance Sigbjorn Johnsen
Defence Johan Jorgen Holst

OMAN

Absolute monarchy. Ruled by the Sultan, who appoints a cabinet. There are no elections and no political parties.

Head of state Sultan Qaboos bin Said (succeeded 1970)
Deputy prime minister Sayyid Fahr bin Taimour al Said (before February 1989)

PAKISTAN

Parliamentary republic. The Islamic Democratic Alliance (IDA) controls an absolute majority in the National Assembly. A general election was held in October 1990; the next is due in 1995. Presidential elections were held in December 1988; the next are due in 1993.

President Ghulam Ishaq Khan (since 1988)
Prime minister; defence, foreign affairs Nawaz Sharif (since 1990)

PRINCIPAL CABINET MINISTERS
Interior Choudhry Shujat Hussain
Finance and economic affairs Sartaj Aziz
Foreign affairs Duties assumed by prime minister after Yaqub Khan resigned in Mar

PANAMA

Presidential republic. The coalition Democratic Civic Opposition Alliance (ADOC) has controlled the 67-member Legislative assembly since December 1989. The last general election was in 1989; the next is expected in 1994.
President Guillermo Endara Galimany (since 1989)
First vice-president Ricardo Arias Calderon

PRINCIPAL CABINET MINISTERS
Treasury and finance Mario Galindo
Foreign affairs Julio E. Linares

PAPUA NEW GUINEA

Parliamentary democracy, with the United Kingdom sovereign as head of state, represented by a governor-general. Traditionally, governments consist of loose and frequently shifting coalitions, based around individuals rather than ideologies. The last election was in June 1987; the next is due by June 1992.

Governor-general Wiwa Korowi (replaced Sir Serei Eri in Nov, who resigned in Oct)
Prime minister Rabbie Namaliu (since July 1988)

PARAGUAY

Presidential republic. The Colorado Party (ANR-PC) has controlled the 102-member National Congress since 1954. The last general election was in 1989 and the next is due by May 1993.

President Gen. Andres Rodriguez (since 1989)

PERU

Presidential republic. The ruling Change 90 (Cambio 90) movement does not command a majority in the 240-member Congress. The last general election was in 1990; the next is due by April 1995.

President Alberto Fujimori (since 1990)
Prime minister; labour Alfonso de los Heros (replaced Carlos Torres y Torres Lara as prime minister in Nov, who had replaced Juan Carlos Hurtado in Feb)

PRINCIPAL CABINET MINISTERS
Foreign affairs Augusto Blacker (replaced Carlos Torres y Torres in Nov who had replaced Vice-Adml. (retd) Raul Sanchez Sotomayor in Feb)
Economy and finance Carlos Bolona (replaced Juan Carlos Hurtado in Feb)
Interior Gen. Juan Briones (replaced Gen. E. P. Victor in Nov, who had replaced Gen. Adolfo Alvarado Fournier in Feb)
Defence Gen. E. P. Victor Malca (replaced Gen. (retd) Jorge Torres Aciego in Nov)

PHILIPPINES

Presidential democracy, with powerful directly elected president whose supporters command a majority in the lower house of the bicameral Congress but not in the Senate. The last presidential elections were in 1986; the next are due in 1992. The last legislative election was in May 1987; the next election is due in 1992.

President Corazon Aquino (since 1986)

PRINCIPAL CABINET MEMBERS
Defence Gen. Renato de Villa (replaced Gen. Fidel Ramos in Jul)
Finance Jesus Estanislao
Foreign affairs Raul Manglapus

POLAND

Parliamentary republic with bicameral national assembly, consisting of the 460-seat Sejm (lower house) and the 100-seat Senate. The president is elected by universal suffrage. A general election in October 1991 resulted in a legislature with no clear party majority. A centre-right coalition government was formed in December.

President Lech Walesa (since 1990)
Prime minister Jan Olszewski (replaced Jan Bielecki in Dec)

PRINCIPAL CABINET MINISTERS
Finance Karol Lutkowski (replaced Leszek Balcerowicz in Dec)
Justice Zbigniew Dyka (replaced Wieslaw Chrzanowski in Dec)
Minister-director of the central planning office Jerzy Eysmontt
National defence Jan Parys (replaced Vice-Adml. Piotr Kolodziejczyk in Dec)
Foreign economic co-operation Adam Glapinski (replaced Dariusz Ledworowski in Dec)
Internal affairs Antoni Macierewicz (replaced Henryk Majewski in Dec)
Foreign affairs Krzyztof Skubiszewski
Agriculture and food economy Gabriel Janowski (replaced Adam Tanski in Dec)

PORTUGAL

Parliamentary republic. The president is elected for a five-year term. A general election to the 250-member Assembly of the Republic (elected for up to four years) was held in October 1991. The ruling Social Democratic Party (PSD) was returned with a majority of 135 seats. The next election is due by October 1995.

President Mario Soares (since 1986)
Prime minister Anibal Cavaco Silva (since 1985)

PRINCIPAL CABINET MINISTERS
Defence Carlos Brito
Finance Jorge Braga de Macedo (replaced Miguel Beleza in Oct)
Interior Manuel Dias Loureiro (replaced Manuel Pereira in Oct)
Foreign affairs Joao de Deus Pinheiro

QATAR

Absolute monarchy ruled by the Emir who appoints a cabinet. There are no political parties; no elections and no legislature.
Head of state Sheikh Khalifa bin Hamad al Thani, Emir; prime minister (since 1972)
Heir apparent Sheikh Hamad bin Khalifa al Thani (since 1989)

ROMANIA

Presidential republic. The bicameral parliament comprises a 396-seat National Assembly and a 119-seat Senate. In a multi-party general election in May 1990, the National Salvation Front, which took power after the overthrow of the Ceausescu regime in 1989 and was dominated by former Romanian Communist Party members, won an outright majority with 263 seats in the assembly and 92 seats in the Senate. The president was directly elected. A referendum in December 1991 approved a new constitution. A general election is expected in spring 1992.

President Ion Iliescu (since 1990)
Prime minister Theodor Stolojan (replaced Petre Roman in Oct)

PRINCIPAL CABINET MINISTERS
Foreign affairs Adrian Nastase
Defence Gen. Constantin Niculae Spiroiu
Finance George Danielescu
Interior Victor Babiuc

RUSSIA

Former republic of the Soviet Union and a founder member of the Commonwealth of Independent States.

President Boris Yeltsin
Prime minister Boris Yeltsin (replaced Ivan Silaev in Oct)

PRINCIPAL MINISTERS
First deputy prime minister Gennady Burbulis
Trade Stanislav Anisimov
Foreign affairs Andrei Kozyrev

RWANDA

Presidential republic. Executive power is vested in the president, who is elected for a five-year term. Legislative power is exercised jointly by the president and the 70-member National Development Council, whose members are also directly elected for five years from a list of candidates put forward by the sole legal party, the National Revolutionary Movement for Development. Presidential and legislative elections were held in December 1988. A new constitution providing for a multi-party system was drawn up in early 1991.

President Maj.-Gen. Juvénal Habyarimana (since 1973)
Prime minister Sylvestre Nsanzima (since Dec)

ST CHRISTOPHER AND NEVIS

Parliamentary monarchy. The head of state is the United Kingdom sovereign, represented by a governor-general. The People's Action Movement has controlled the 23-member National Assembly since June 1984. The last general election was in 1989; the next is due by June 1994.

Governor-general Clement Athelston Arrindell (since 1983)
Prime minister Kennedy A. Simmonds (since 1983)

ST LUCIA

Parliamentary monarchy. The head of state is the United Kingdom sovereign, represented by a governor-general. The United Workers' Party (UWP) has controlled the 17-member House of Assembly since 1982. The last general election was in 1987; the next is due by May 1992.

Governor-general (acting) Stanislaus James (since 1988)
Prime minister John Compton (since 1982)

ST VINCENT AND THE GRENADINES

Parliamentary monarchy. The head of state is the United Kingdom sovereign, represented by a governor-general. The New Democratic Party (NDP) has controlled the 21-member House of Assembly since 1984. The last general election was in 1989 and the next is due by May 1994.

Governor-general David Jack (since 1989)
Prime minister James Mitchell (since 1984)

SAN MARINO

Parliamentary republic, with legislative power vested in a 60-member Grand and General Council. In the 1988 general election, a coalition government of the Communist Party and the Christian Democrat Party was returned to power. The next election is due by May 1993.

Heads of state Edda Ceccoli and Marino Riccardi, Captains-Regent (replaced Domenico Bernadini and Claudio Podeschi in Nov, who replaced Cesare Gasperoni and Roberto Bucci in Apr)

SAO TOME AND PRINCIPE

Presidential republic. In January 1991 the ruling Democratic Convergence Party won the first multi-party elections to the 55-member National Assembly.

President Miguel Trovoada (replaced Manuel Pinto da Costa in Mar)
Prime minister Daniel Lima dos Santos Daio (replaced Celestino Rocha da Costa in Jan)

SAUDI ARABIA

Absolute monarchy ruled by the king who also heads an appointed Council of Ministers. There are no political parties and no elections.

Head of state King Fahd ibn Abdul Aziz (succeeded 1982)

SENEGAL

Presidential republic. The ruling Socialist Party obtained 103 of the 120 seats in the National Assembly in the general election in February 1988. Constitutional changes made in September 1991 limited the presidential mandate to two terms of seven years each and laid down that presidential and legislative elections would not be held simultaneously as before. The next legislative elections are due in 1993 and presidential elections in 1995.

President Abdou Diouf (since 1981)
Prime minister Habib Thiam (since Apr, post hitherto in abeyance since 1983)

SEYCHELLES

Presidential republic. The present head of state seized power in a coup in 1977. Executive power is vested in the president, who is elected for a five-year term by direct suffrage, and appoints the Council of Ministers. There is a unicameral National Assembly of 23 members elected for five years and two members appointed by the president. All candidates in the general election of December 1987 represented the sole party, the Seychelles People's Progressive Front. Multi-party presidential and general elections have been promised by December 1992.

President France Albert René (since 1977)

SIERRA LEONE

Presidential republic. The country was a one-party state under the All-Peoples Party from 1978 until in August 1991 a referendum overwhelming approved a new constitution providing for a multi-party system. In September, the President formed an interim government to preside until a general election in early 1992. Presidential elections were last held in 1985 and legislative elections in 1986.

President Maj.-Gen. Joseph Saidu Momoh (since 1985)
First vice-president Gen. Abdulai Conteh (replaced in Sep Salia Jusu-Sheriff, who replaced Alhaji Abu Bakar Kamara in Mar)

SINGAPORE

Parliamentary republic. The People's Action Party (PAP) has had a majority in the parliament since 1959. The last general election was in 1991; the next is due by August 1996. During 1991 the number of PAP MPs in the 81-member parliament fell from 80 to 77.

President Wee Kim Wee (since 1985)
Prime minister Goh Chok Tong (since 1990)

SOLOMON ISLANDS

Parliamentary democracy, with the United Kingdom sovereign as head of state, represented by a governor-general. In 1989 the People's Alliance Party won control of the 38-member legislature, but in October 1990 the prime minister resigned from the party and formed a government of national unity. The last election was in March 1989; the next is due in March 1993.

Governor-general Sir George Lepping (since 1988)
Prime minister Solomon Mamaloni (since 1989)

SOMALIA
Presidential republic, ruled since January 1991 by a transitional government created under formed under the auspices of the United Somali Congress. According to the constitution readopted in July 1991, a People's Assembly is to be established in due course. In May the north-east of Somalia declared its secession as the Somaliland Republic, with a provisional government (formed under the auspices of the Somali National Movement) and Abdel-Rahman Ahmed Ali as president.

President Ali Mahdi Mohammed (since Jan)
Prime minister Umar Arteh Ghalib (since Feb)

SOUTH AFRICA
Federal republic. Under the constitution of 1984, there is a tricameral parliament, with a House of Assembly (178 members) representing whites, a House of Representatives (85 members) representing people of mixed race ("Coloureds"), and a House of Delegates (45 members) representing Indians, but no representation for the majority black population. Elections were held in September 1989 to all three houses, and F. W. de Klerk was then elected as the new executive state president, by an electoral college composed of 50 members of the House of Assembly, 25 members of the House of Representatives, and 13 from the House of Delegates. The National Party, the party of government since 1948, continues to command a majority in the House of Assembly.

President F. W. de Klerk (since 1989)

PRINCIPAL CABINET MINISTERS
Foreign affairs Roelof F. Botha
Constitutional development Gerrit van Viljoen
Defence Roelf Meyer (replaced Gen. Magnus A. Malan in Aug)
Minerals and energy George Bartlett (replaced D. W. de Villiers in Apr)
Justice Kobie Coetsee
Finance Barend du Plessis
Law and order Hernus Kriel (replaced Adriaan J. Vlok in Aug)
Trade and industry Derek Keys (replaced Org Marais in Dec; Marais had replaced Kent D. S. Durr in Apr)

SOVIET UNION
Formerly comprising 15 republics, the Soviet Union (from which Estonia, Latvia and Lithuania had already split away) ceased to exist at the end of 1991. A new relationship between 11 of the remaining 12 republics (but with Georgia not yet participating) was to take the form of a Commonwealth of Independent States. The former union government, headed by Mikhail Gorbachev as president, had no remaining function and he formally resigned in December.

PRINCIPAL SOVIET OFFICIALS (until Union dissolved)
Head of state Mikhail Gorbachev, President of the USSR
Chairman of Interstate Economic Committee Ivan Silaev (replaced premier Valentin Pavlov in Aug)
Defence Marshal Yevgeny Shaposhnikov (replaced Marshal Dmitry Yazov in Aug)
Finance I. Lazaryev (replaced Vladimir Orlov in Aug)
Foreign affairs Edward Shevardnadze (replaced Boris Pankin in Nov, who replaced Aleksandr Bessmertnykh in Aug)
Internal affairs Viktor Barannikov (replaced Boris Pugo in Aug)
Chairman of Committee for State Security (KGB) Vadim Bakatin (replaced Gen. Vladimir Kryuchkov in Aug)

SPAIN
Parliamentary monarchy. The Spanish Socialist Workers' Party (PSOE) has controlled a majority in the 350-member Congress of Deputies since 1986. The distribution of seats in Congress following a general election in October 1989

was finalised in April 1990, when the PSOE was allocated 175 seats – exactly half. The next general election must be held by October 1993.

Head of state Juan Carlos, King of Spain (since 1975)
Prime minister Felipe Gonzalez (since 1982)

CABINET MINISTERS
Deputy prime minister Narcis Serra (replaced in Mar Alfonso Guerra, who resigned in Jan)
Defence Julian Garcia Vargas (replaced Narcis Serra in Mar)
Interior Jose Luis Corcuera
Foreign affairs Francisco Fernandez Ordonez
Economy and finance Carlos Solchaga
Justice Tomas de la Quadra-Salcedo (replaced Enruque Mugica Herzog in Mar)
Industry, commerce and tourism Claudio Aranzadi Martinez
Labour and social security Luis Martinez Noval
Education and science Javier Solana Madariaga
Public administration Juan Manuel Equiagaray (replaced Joaquin Almunia in Mar)
Agriculture Pedro Solbes Mira (replaced Carlos Romero Herrera in Mar)
Culture Jordi Sole Tura (replaced Jorge Semprun in Mar)
Health Julian Garcia Valverde
Parliamentary relations Virgilio Zapatero
Social welfare Matilde Fernandez
Government spokeswoman Rosa Conde de Espina
Public works and transport Jose Borrell Fontelles (replaced Javier Saenz de Cosculluela in Mar)

SRI LANKA
Presidential democracy. The United National Party has had control of the unicameral parliament since 1977. The last parliamentary election (using proportional representation for the first time) was in February 1989; the next is due by 1995. The president is elected directly; the last election was in December 1988; the next is due by 1994.

President Ranasinghe Premadasa (since 1989)
Prime Minister Dingiri Banda Wijetunge (since 1989)

PRINCIPAL CABINET MINISTERS
Finance and defence D. B. Wijetunge
Foreign affairs Harold Herath

SUDAN
Republic, ruled by a 15-member Revolutionary Command Council, composed of military officers, since June 1989.
Chairman Lt.-Gen. Omar Hassan Ahmad al Bashir (since 1989)

PRINCIPAL CABINET MINISTERS
Deputy prime minister; interior Maj.-Gen Zubir Mohammed Saleh (replaced Maj.-Gen. Faisal Ali Abu Salih as Interior Minister in Apr)
Foreign affairs Ahmed Sahlul
Finance and national economic planning Abdel Rahmim Mahmoud Hamdi

SURINAM
Presidential republic. The New Front coalition has a majority in the 50-member National Assembly. The last general election was in 1991; the next is due by 1996.

President Ronald Venetiaan (replaced Johan Kraag in Sep)
Vice-president; head of government; minister of finance Jules Ajodhia (replaced Jules Wijdenbosch in Sep)

SWAZILAND
Constitutional monarchy. Considerable executive power is vested in the king and is exercised by a cabinet appointed by him. The bicameral legislative body, the Libandla, composed of a Senate and House of Assembly, has limited powers. Elections to both houses are indirect; the last ones were in November 1987. All political parties are banned.

Head of state King Mswati III (succeeded 1986)
Prime minister Obed Dlamini (since 1989)

SWEDEN
Parliamentary monarchy. The conservative Moderate

Unity Party (M) has ruled in coalition with the liberal People's Party (FP), Centre Party (C) and the Christian Democratic Community Party (KDS) since October 1991. The last general election was in September 1991; the next is due by September 1994.
Head of state Carl XVI Gustaf, King of Sweden (succeeded 1973)
Prime minister Carl Bildt (M) (replaced Ingvar Carlsson in Oct)

PRINCIPAL CABINET MINISTERS
Deputy prime minister Bengt Westerberg (FP) (replaced Odd Engstrom in Oct and replaced Ingela Thalen as health and social affairs minister in Oct)
Foreign affairs Margaretha af Ugglas (M) (replaced Sten Andersson in Oct)
Defence Anders Bjorck (M) (replaced Roine Carlsson in Oct)
Finance Anne Wibble (Lib) (replaced Allan Larsson in Oct)
Justice Gun Hellsvik (M) (replaced Laila Freivalds in Oct)
Industry and commerce Per Westerberg (M) (replaced Rune Molin in Oct)
Labour Borje Hornlund (C) (replaced Mona Sahlin in Oct)
Agriculture Karl Erik Olsson (C) (replaced Mats Hellstrom in Oct)
Education Per Unckel (M) (replaced Bengt Goransson in Oct)
Transport and communications Mats Odell (C Dem) (replaced Georg Andersson in Oct)
Public administration Inger Davidsson (KDS) (replaced Bengt Johansson in Oct)
Environment Olof Johansson (C) (replaced Birgitta Dahl in Oct)
Immigration and cultural affairs Birgit Friggebo (Lib) (appointed Oct)

SWITZERLAND
Federal republic. The Christian Democratic People's Party, the Social Democratic Party, the Radical Democratic Party and the Swiss People's Party have ruled in coalition since 1959. The last general election was in October 1991; the next is due in October 1995.

President Flavio Cotti (for 1991)
Vice-president René Felber (for 1991)

MEMBERS OF THE BUNDESRAT
Political (foreign) affairs René Felber (SPS)
Finance and customs Otto Stich (SPS)
Interior Flavio Cotti (CVP)
Military (defence) Kaspar Villiger (FDP)

SYRIA
Presidential republic. The Baath Party has been in power since 1963. Assad was confirmed as President by referendum in December 1991. The last general election to the 250-member People's Council (the legislative organ) was in 1990, the next is due by May 1994. During 1991 the number of Ba'ath Party members in the Assembly was 134.

President Lt.-Gen. Hafez Assad (since 1971)
Vice-presidents Abdel Halim Khaddam; Zuhqir Mashariqa
Prime minister Mahmoud Zubi

TAIWAN
Presidential republic. The government of Taiwan is derived from that which ruled the Chinese mainland prior to the 1949 communist revolution; it maintains its claim to mainland China and continues to designate itself the Republic of China. Under constitutional amendments passed in April 1991, elections were held in December in which the ruling Kuomintang Party won 179 out of 225 elective seats in the new National Assembly; it also took 75 out of 100 allotted seats.

President Lee Teng-hui (since 1988)
Vice-president Lee Yuan-zu
Prime minister Gen. Hau Pei-tsun

TAJIKISTAN
Former republic of the Soviet Union and a founder member of the Commonwealth of Independent States.

President Rakhom Nabiev (replaced in Nov Kadreddin Aslonov, who replaced Kakhar Makhkamov in Sep)

Prime minister Izatullo Khayeyev

TANZANIA

Federal republic. Executive power is vested in the president, who is nominated by the sole legal political party, Chama Cha Mapinduzi (the Revolutionary Party of Tanzania), and is directly elected to a five-year term, renewable once only. The two vice-presidents, one of whom is the president of Zanzibar and the other the prime minister of the Union government, are appointed by the president. Legislative power is vested in the National Assembly, composed of 180 directly elected members and a number of ex-officio, nominated and indirectly elected members. The assembly's term is five years. The current president was elected for a second term in October 1990, when legislative elections were also held.

President Ali Hassan Mwinyi (since 1985)
First vice-president; prime minister John Malecela (since 1990)
Second vice-president; president of Zanzibar Salmin Amour (since 1990)

THAILAND

Monarchy, ruled by military junta. The armed forces toppled the country's elected government in February 1991 and established a ruling junta, the National Peace-Keeping Assembly. A new constitution took effect in December. The last general election was held in July 1988. It was announced in December 1991 that a general election would be held in March 1992.

Head of state Bhumibol Adulyadej (Rama IX) King of Thailand (succeeded 1946)
Prime minister Anand Panyarachun (replaced Chatichai Choonhaven in Mar)
Head of national peace-keeping assembly Gen. Sunthorn Kongsompong

PRINCIPAL CABINET MINISTERS
Defence Adm. Praphat Krisanachan (replaced Chatichai Choonhaven in Mar)
Finance Suthee Singgsaneh (replaced Banharn Silpa-Archa in Mar)
Foreign affairs Arsa Sarasin (replaced Arthit Urairat in Mar)
Interior Gen. Issarapong Noonpackdee (replaced Maj.-Gen. Pramarn Adireksarn in Mar)

TOGO

Presidential republic. A national conference to determine the political future of the country ended in August 1991 with legislative and presidential elections scheduled for 1992. The conference also elected a prime minister, with executive powers, to head a transitional government, and announced the dissolution of the Rally of the Togolese People (RPT), hitherto the ruling and sole legal party. A coup attempt in late 1991 ended with the formation of a national unity government.

President Gen. Gnassingbe Eyadema (since 1967)
Prime minister Koukou Koffigoh (since Aug)

TONGA

Constitutional monarchy, with a unicameral legislature, the majority of whose 29 members are either appointed or serve on a hereditary basis. The last elections were in February 1990; the next are due by February 1993.

Head of state King Taufa'ahau Tupou IV (acceded in 1965)
Prime minister Baron Vaea (replaced Prince Fatafehi Tu'ipelehake in Aug)

TRINIDAD AND TOBAGO

Parliamentary republic. The National Alliance for Reconstruction controlled the 36-member House of Representatives from December 1986 until the general election in December 1991 when the People's National Movement won a clear majority.

President Noor Mohammed Hassanali (since 1987)
Prime minister Patrick Manning (succeeded Arthur Robinson in Dec)

TUNISIA

Presidential republic; the Constitutional Democratic Rally (RCD) controls the National Assembly, although other parties have been legalised since 1981. In the last general election in April 1989 the RCD won all 141 National Assembly seats despite competition from six opposition parties. The next general election is due in held in April 1994.

President Zine el Abidine Ben Ali (since 1987)
Prime minister Hamed Karoui (since 1989)

TURKEY

Presidential republic, with a 500-seat Grand National Assembly elected by universal suffrage. Following the last general election in October 1991 a coalition government was formed by the True Path Party (DYP) and the Social Democratic Populist Party (SHP), which had won 178 and 88 seats respectively in the 500-seat legislature. The next general election is due by October 1996.

President Turgut Ozal (since 1989)
Prime minister Suleyman Demirel (replaced Mesut Yilmaz in Nov, who replaced Yildirim Akbulut in Jun)

PRINCIPAL MINISTERS
Deputy prime minister and minister of state Erdal Inonu (replaced Ekrem Pakdemirli in Nov, post vacant until Jun)
Minister of state Tansu Ciller
Foreign affairs Hikmet Cetin (replaced Safa Giray in Nov, who replaced Ahmet Kurtcebe Alptemocin in Jun)
Justice Seyfi Oktay (replaced Suat Bilge in Nov, who replaced Mahmut Oltan Sungurlu in Jun)
National defence Nevzat Ayaz (replaced Barlas Dogu in Nov, who replaced Mehmet Yazar in Jun)
Interior Ismet Sezgin (replaced Sabahattin Cakmakoglu in Nov, who replaced Abdulkadir Aksu in Jun)
Finance and customs Sumer Oral (replaced Adnan Kahveci in Nov)

TURKMENIA

Former republic of the Soviet Union and a founder member of the Commonwealth of Independent States.

President Saparmurad Niazov
Prime minister Khan Akhmedov

TUVALU

Parliamentary democracy; The United Kingdom sovereign is head of state, represented by a governor-general. A 12-member unicameral legislature, elected for up to four year, chooses the prime minister. The last election was in 1989; the next is due by September 1993.

Governor-general Toaripi Lauti (since 1990)
Prime minister Bikenibeu Paeniu (since 1989)

UGANDA

Presidential republic, ruled by military council. The present ruler came to power in January 1986 at the head of the National Resistance Movement. The president is assisted by a prime minister and cabinet, composed of representatives of a number of political parties; although the parties continue to exist, political activity is banned, and elections held in February 1989 to the National Resistance Council (NRC) were conducted on a non-party basis. The NRC, consisting of 210 elected and 68 presidentially appointed members acts as a legislative body for the interim period until a new constitution has been framed.

President Yoweri Museveni, Minister of Defence (since 1986)
Prime minister George Cosma Adyebo (replaced Samson Kisekka in January)

UKRAINE

Former republic of the Soviet Union and a founder member of the Commonwealth of Independent States.

President Leonid Kravchuk
Prime minister Vitold Fokin

PRINCIPAL MINISTERS
First deputy prime minister Konstantin Masyk
Foreign affairs Anatoly Zlenko

UNITED ARAB EMIRATES

Federation of seven emirates (Abu Dhabi, Dubai, Sharjah, Ras al Khaimah, Fujairah, Umm al Qaiwan and Ajman) represented by a Supreme Council of Rulers which elects the president and vice-president. There are no political parties and no elections.

President Sheikh Zaid bin Sultan al Nahayan (ruler of Abu Dhabi since 1966) (president since 1971)
Vice-president; prime minister Sheikh Maktoum bin Rashid al Maktoum (ruler of Dubai since 1990 – Vice-President of UAE since 1990)

UNITED KINGDOM

Parliamentary monarchy. The Conservative Party has had control of the 650-member House of Commons since May 1979. The last general election was in June 1987; the next is due by July 1992.

Head of state Queen Elizabeth II (succeeded 1952)
Prime minister John Major (since 1990)

CABINET MINISTERS
Lord President of the Council and leader of the House of Commons John MacGregor
Lord Chancellor Lord Mackay of Clashfern
Foreign affairs Douglas Hurd
Chancellor of the Exchequer Norman Lamont
Home secretary Kenneth Baker
Defence Tom King
Education and science Kenneth Clarke
Transport Malcolm Rifkind
Energy John Wakeham
Lord Privy Seal and leader of the House of Lords Lord Waddington
Social security Antony Newton
Chancellor of the Duchy of Lancaster Chris Patten
Northern Ireland Peter Brooke
Agriculture, fisheries and food John Selwyn Gummer
Employment Michael Howard
Wales David Hunt
Trade and industry Peter Lilley
Health William Waldegrave
Environment Michael Heseltine
Scotland Ian Lang
Chief secretary to the Treasury David Mellor

LAW OFFICERS
Attorney-general Sir Patrick Mayhew
Lord Advocate Lord Fraser of Carmyllie
Solicitor-general Sir Nicholas Lyell
Solicitor-general for Scotland Alan Rodger

UNITED STATES

Federal democracy, embodying strict separation of powers between a president (popularly elected for four years), a bicameral legislature, and an independent judiciary. The legislature consists of a 435-member House of Representatives (elected for two years) and a 100-member Senate (elected for six years, with one third being renewed every two years). In legislative elections in November 1990 the Democrats won 267 seats in the House and 56 in the Senate. In presidential elections in November 1988 the Republicans retained control of the presidency. The next legislative and presidential elections are due in November 1992.

President George Bush (since 1989)

CABINET MEMBERS
Vice-president Dan Quayle
State James Baker
Treasury Nicholas Brady
Defence Richard Cheney
Interior Manuel Lujan
Agriculture Edward Madigan (replaced Clayton Yeutter in Jan)
Commerce Barbara Franklin (subject to Senate confirmation; Robert Mosbacher resigned in Dec)
Housing and urban development Jack Kemp
Transportation vacant (post held until Dec by Samuel Skinner)
Health and human services Louis Sullivan
Attorney-general William Barr (since Nov; Richard Thornburgh resigned in June)
Labour Lynn Martin
Energy James Watkins
Education Lamar Alexander
Veterans' affairs Edward Derwinski

OTHER LEADING EXECUTIVE BRANCH OFFICIALS
White house chief of staff Samuel Skinner (replaced

John Sununu in Dec)
Director of office of management and budget (OMB)
Richard Darman
Assistant to the president for national security affairs
Gen. Brent Scowcroft
Representative for trade negotiations Carla Hills
Director, central intelligence agency (CIA) Robert Gates
(replaced William Webster in Nov)
Chairman, president's council of economic advisers
Michael Boskin
Director, office of national drug control policy Bob
Martinez

LEGISLATIVE BRANCH
President of the Senate Dan Quayle (Vice-president)
Senate majority leader George Mitchell
Senate majority whip Wendell Ford
Senate minority leader Robert Dole
Senate minority whip Alan Simpson
Speaker of the House Thomas Foley
House majority leader Richard Gephardt
House majority whip David Bonior (replaced William
Gray in Jul)
House minority leader Robert Michel
House minority whip Newt Gingrich
Chairman Senate Foreign Relations Committee
Claiborne Pell
Chairman Senate Armed Services Committee Sam
Nunn
Chairman Senate Budget Committee Jim Sasser
Chairman Senate Finance Committee Lloyd Bentsen
Chairman Senate Judiciary Committee Joseph Biden
Chairman House Foreign Affairs Committee Dante
Fascell
Chairman House Armed Services Committee Les
Aspin
Chairman House Budget Committee Leon Panetta
Chairman House Ways and Means Committee Dan
Rostenkowski
Chairman House Judiciary Committee Jack Brooks

THE SUPREME COURT
Chief justice William Rehnquist
Associate justices David Souter, Byron White, Harry
Blackmun, John Paul Stevens, Sandra Day O'Connor,
Antonin Scalia, Anthony Kennedy, Clarence Thomas
(replaced Thurgood Marshall in Oct)

URUGUAY
Presidential republic. The ruling National Party (PN or
Blancos) coalition government lacks a majority in the 129-
member National Congress. The last general election was
in 1989; the next is due by November 1995.

President Luis Alberto Laccalle Herrera (since 1990)
Vice-president Gonzalo Aguirre Ramirez (since 1990)

PRINCIPAL CABINET MINISTERS
Home affairs Juan Andres Ramirez
Foreign relations Hector Gros Espiell
Economy and finance Enrique Braga
Defence Mariano Brito

UZBEKISTAN
Former republic of the Soviet Union and a founder
member of the Commonwealth of Independent States.

President Islam Karimov
Prime minister Shukurulla Mirsaidov

VANUATU
Parliamentary democracy, with a 46-member unicameral
legislature controlled by the Vanuaaka Pati, which has
held power since 1983. The last election was in December
1991; the next is due by 1995.

President Fred Timakata (since 1989)
Prime minister Maxime Carlot (replaced in Dec Donald
Kalpokas who had replaced Fr Walter Lini in Sep)

VATICAN CITY
Religious state, with the Pope as head of state. The Pope is
elected for life by the Sacred College of Cardinals. Since
1984 the routine administration of the Vatican has been
delegated to the secretary of state and a Pontifical
Commission, appointed by the Pope.

Head of state His Holiness Pope John Paul II (since 1978)
Secretary of state Cardinal Angelo Sodano

VENEZUELA
Federal republic. The ruling Democratic Action Party (AD)
has no overall absolute majority in the 245-member
National Congress. The last general election was in 1988
and the next is due by December 1993.

President Carlos Andres Perez (since 1989)

PRINCIPAL CABINET MINISTERS
Interior Alejandro Izaguirre
Foreign affairs Armande Duran (replaced Reinaldo
Figueredo Planchart in Apr)
Finance Roberto Pocaterra
Defence Gen. Fernando Ochoa Antich (replaced Adml.
Hector Jurado Toro in Jul)

VIETNAM
Socialist republic. Political power rests in the hands of the
Communist Party of Vietnam. The last general election to
the 496-member National Assembly (Quoc-Hoi) was in
1987; the next is due by April 1992.

President Vo Chi Cong (since June 1987)

PRINCIPAL CABINET MINISTERS
Chairman of the council of ministers Vo Van Kiet
(replaced Do Muoi in Aug)
Vice-chairman of the council of ministers Pham Van
Kai (replaced Gen. Vo Nguyen Giap in Aug)
Chair of the state commission for planning Do Quoc
Sam (replacing Pham Van Kai in Aug)
Foreign affairs Nguyen Manh Cam (replaced Nguyen
Co Thach in Aug)
National defence Gen. Doan Khue (replaced Gen. Le
Duc Anh in Aug)
Interior Lt.-Gen. Bui Thien Ngo (replaced Maj.-Gen. Mai
Chi Tho in Aug)

WESTERN SAMOA
Parliamentary democracy, with elected constitutional
monarch and 47-member unicameral legislature, elected
for up to three years. The Human Rights Protection Party
won 26 seats in the election of April 1991; the next
election is due by April 1994.

Head of state Susuga Malietoa Tanumafili II (since 1963)
Prime minister Tofilau Eti Alesana (since 1988)

YEMEN
Presidential republic resulting from the unification of
North and South Yemen, with a provisional parliament
and a transitional cabinet. A general election is scheduled
for November 1992.

President Gen. Ali Abdullah Saleh (since 1990)
Prime minister Haider Abu Bakr al Attas (since 1990)

YUGOSLAVIA
The civil war since mid-1991 has torn apart the federal
structure, which consisted of the republics of Bosnia-
Hercegovina, Croatia, Macedonia, Montenegro, Serbia
(incorporating Vojvodina, Kosovo and Metohija
provinces), and Slovenia. Slovenia and Croatia declared
independence in June 1991. Since then, fighting has
continued between the Serb-dominated federal army and
Croatian and Serbian separatists. Croat and Slovene
members of federal government bodies have resigned;
Stjepan Mesic, a Croat, was formally recalled from the
presidency of the collective state presidency in December
1991, and federal prime minister Ante Markovic finally
resigned later the same month.

Federal secretary for foreign affairs Milivoje Maksic
(replaced Budimir Loncar in Dec)
Federal secretary for national defence Col.-Gen. Veljko
Kadijevic

PRESIDENTS OF THE REPUBLICS
Bosnia-Hercegovina Alija Izetbegovic
Croatia Franjo Tudjman
Macedonia Kiro Gligorov
Montenegro Momir Bulatovic
Serbia Slobodan Milosevic
Slovenia Milan Kucan

ZAIRE
Presidential republic. The unicameral National Legislative
Council (CNL) is elected for a five-year term, all candidates
being proposed by the Popular Movement for the
Revolution (MPR). Political reforms were announced in
April 1990, envisaging the introduction of a multi-party
system after a one-year transitional period. Mobutu's term
formally expired in December 1991 but a constitutional
amendment allowed him to remain in office pending
elections.

President Marshal Mobutu Sese Seko (since 1965)
Prime Minister Jean Nguza Karl-I-Bond (since Nov,
replaced Bernardin Mungul Diaka, appointed in Oct,
replacing Etienne Tshisekedi, who replaced Mulumba
Lukeji in Sep)

ZAMBIA
Presidential republic. The sole legal political organisation
was the United National Independence Party (UNIP) until
September 1990 when the party agreed to allow multi-
party elections in October 1991. The National Assembly is
elected by direct popular vote for a five-year term. Multi-
party elections in October 1991 resulted in a victory for
Frederick Chiluba and the Movement for Multi-party
Democracy.

President Frederick J. T. Chiluba (replaced Kenneth
Kaunda in Nov)
Vice-president Levy Patrick Mwanawasa (since Nov)

ZIMBABWE
Presidential republic. The Zimbabwe African National
Union-Patriotic Front (ZANU-PF) led by Robert Mugabe
holds 116 of the 120 elective seats in the 160-member
House of Assembly. Presidential and legislative elections
were last held in March 1990 and are due in 1996.

President Robert Gabriel Mugabe (since 1987)

PRINCIPAL CABINET MINISTERS
Vice-presidents Simon Muzenda; Joshua Nkomo
Senior minister, political affairs Didymus Mutasa
Senior minister, finance, economic Bernard Chidzero
Foreign affairs Nathan Shamuyarira
Defence Richard Hove

Contents

ECONOMIC AND FINANCIAL INDICATORS

Income and population

NATIONAL INCOMES Readers often write to ask why our regular economic and financial indicator tables exclude countries such as Ireland or Austria. The reason is simple. The countries featured are the 13 biggest economies in the OECD (the rich countries' club), with a combined GNP that makes up some 95% of the 24-country OECD total. As such, they have by far the greatest impact on the world economy and financial system. Of those 13, by far the most important are the G7, the seven biggest economies, which together account for 84% of total OECD output. America's economy supplies a third of the OECD total and Japan nearly a fifth. In contrast, Iceland, the smallest OECD economy, contributes less than 0.1% of total GNP.

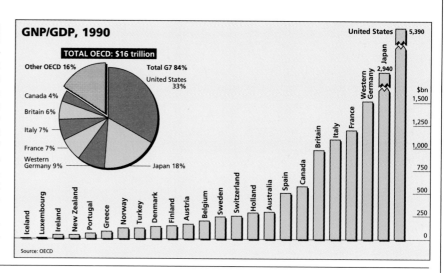

GNP/GDP and population

Looking at the full list of OECD members, the highest income per head in 1990 (the latest year available) was in Switzerland, at $33,550, followed by Scandinavia and Japan. Britain was in only 18th place. In dollar terms the biggest changes in the league table since 1980 were Japan (up from 17th to sixth), Finland (from 13th to second). Holland and Luxembourg fell six places, Belgium five and France four. The poorest in 1990—as in 1980—were Turkey, Portugal and Greece. The best way to compare standards of living in different countries is to use purchasing-power parity (PPP) exchange rates. These equalise the

	Canada	United States	Australia	Japan	New Zealand	Austria	Belgium	Denmark	Finland	France	Germany*	Greece
GNP/GDP, $bn												
1980	263.2	2,686.2	150.0	1,059.3	22.4	76.9	118.0	66.3	51.6	664.6	813.7	40.2
1990	575.9	5,391.3	293.6	2,941.5	43.3	159.3	193.3	130.9	137.4	1,186.0	1,494.7	66.7
GNP/GDP per head, at current prices, $												
1980	10,934	11,794	10,210	9,069	7,108	10,184	11,985	12,940	10,803	12,335	13,216	4,164
1990	21,634	21,446	17,183	23,810	12,814	20,656	19,344	25,467	27,579	21,015	23,698	6,578
GNP/GDP per head, at purchasing-power parities, United States = 100												
1980	93	100	71	68	60	67	69	71	67	74	75	38
1990	93	100	69	80	56	68	68	72	73	72	75	35
Population, 000s												
1990	26,521	249,224	16,873	123,460	3,392	7,583	9,845	5,143	4,975	56,138	77,573	10,047
2000	28,488	266,096	18,855	128,470	3,662	7,613	9,832	5,153	5,077	58,145	76,962	10,193
Population density per sq km												
1990	3	27	2	327	13	90	323	119	15	102	217	76
2000	3	28	2	340	14	91	322	120	15	105	216	77
Population under 15 years, %												
1990	20.9	21.4	22.1	18.4	22.7	17.3	17.9	17.0	19.3	20.1	16.0	19.7
2000	18.7	20.2	20.6	16.9	22.0	16.7	17.3	16.3	17.5	19.4	16.1	17.2
Population 65 years and over, %												
1990	11.4	12.6	10.9	11.7	10.9	15.0	14.9	15.4	13.2	13.8	14.9	13.7
2000	12.7	12.8	11.7	15.9	11.2	15.7	16.5	15.5	14.4	15.4	16.4	16.9

* GNP/GDP – western Germany; population - united Germany

WHO LIVES LONGEST? The average Japanese baby can today look forward to living for 79 years. This is longer than in any other nation, and represents the biggest improvement in life expectancy (from 68 years in 1960) of any rich industrial country. The average American today lives for 76 years. By contrast, because of disease and malnutrition, the average life expectancy at birth in the Sudan is a mere 51 years. Worse still, in Sierra Leone (not shown on the chart) the average person lives for only 42 years. China has had the biggest improvement in life expectancy of any country over the past three decades, up from 47 years in 1960 to 70 years in 1990. The Soviet Union has seen the smallest rise over that period, from 68 years to 71 years.

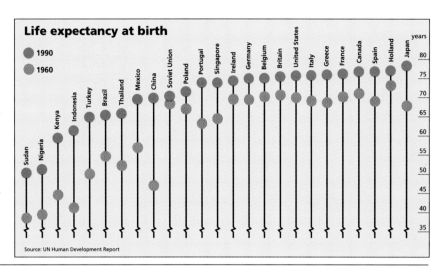

Life expectancy at birth

- 1990
- 1960

Source: UN Human Development Report

cost of a basket of goods and services in different countries. If the OECD's PPP exchange rates are used, the United States has the highest income per head, followed by Switzerland and Canada. Countries with the lowest income per head using current exchange rates are still the lowest on PPP measures.

The United Nations reckons that the world population of 5.3 billion in 1990 will reach 6.3 billion in 2000. The OECD countries account for only 16% of the world's total population, although they contribute almost 80% of total world output. By 2000 the OECD's population will have declined to 14% of the world's total. It will also get older, with 13.9% over 65 (12.5% in 1990) and 18.8% under 15 (20.5% in 1990).

	Holland	Iceland	Ireland	Italy	Luxembourg	Norway	Portugal	Spain	Sweden	Switzerland	Turkey	UK
GNP/GDP, $bn												
1980	169.4	3.2	19.2	452.7	4.6	57.7	25.1	214.5	124.9	101.7	56.9	537.6
1990	278.1	5.7	43.3	1,087.1	8.8	105.3	59.6	491.8	226.5	228.0	107.3	969.8
GNP/GDP per head, at current prices, $												
1980	11,970	14,167	5,654	8,023	12,466	14,120	2,555	5,737	15,028	15,920	1,272	9,546
1990	18,609	22,266	12,361	18,857	23,097	24,823	5,747	12,621	26,441	33,549	1,877	16,893
GNP/GDP per head, at purchasing-power parities, United States = 100												
1980	73	84	42	68	76	80	36	49	77	91	21	67
1990	68	76	46	69	85	81	37	51	75	87	23	70
Population, 000s												
1990	14,952	253	3,720	57,061	373	4,212	10,285	39,187	8,444	6,609	55,868	57,237
2000	15,829	274	4,086	57,195	377	4,331	10,587	40,667	8,560	6,762	66,789	58,393
Population density per sq km												
1990	366	2	53	189	144	13	111	78	19	160	72	234
2000	388	3	58	190	146	13	115	81	19	164	86	239
Population under 15 years, %												
1990	18.3	25.1	27.7	16.7	17.2	18.8	21.3	20.1	17.3	16.4	34.6	19.0
2000	18.4	21.7	24.5	15.5	16.9	18.5	19.3	18.3	18.6	16.8	21.8	19.6
Population 65 years and over, %												
1990	12.7	10.4	10.3	14.3	13.2	16.4	12.9	13.1	18.1	15.0	4.2	15.4
2000	13.6	11.4	9.6	16.9	15.4	15.8	14.4	15.2	17.1	16.3	5.6	15.2

Economic and business forecasts

CONSENSUS ECONOMICS A round-up of economic forecasts in January 1991 was based on the averages of 170 forecasters polled by Consensus Economics. For the first time, it looked at prospects for 1992. The forecasters were gloomy. America, Canada, Britain and Sweden were all expected to see a fall in economic output in 1991; America's GNP was forecast to shrink by 0.4%. The forecasters thought growth would recover in 1992, rising by an average of 2.7% in the 13 countries—an optimism that waned as 1991 wore on. Inflation was forecast to average 5.1% in 1991, falling to 4.1% in 1992. Sweden was expected to stay bottom of *The Economist's* overall ranking in 1991 and 1992—though its growth was forecast to resume, and its inflation to fall, in 1992.

Forecasts for 1991 & 1992 (previous month's, if changed)

	Real GNP/GDP % increase		Consumer prices % increase		Current-account balance, % of GNP/GDP		The Economist's ranking*	
	1991	1992	1991	1992	1991	1992	1991	1992
Australia	1.0 (1.2)	2.7	5.7 (6.0)	5.4	-4.3(-4.6)	-4.2	11	11
Belgium	2.6	2.7	3.7 (3.6)	3.4	+1.5(+1.4)	+1.6	4	4
Canada	-0.4 (0.2)	2.9	6.1 (6.2)	3.8	-1.9(-1.8)	-1.6	12 (10)	7
France	2.4	2.6	3.4 (3.8)	3.0	-0.8	-0.7	5 (6)	5
Germany†	3.0 (2.9)	2.9	3.5 (3.7)	3.2	+1.6(+1.5)	+1.0	3	3
Holland	2.4	2.7	2.9 (3.1)	2.5	+3.0(+3.1)	+3.0	1 (=1)	2
Italy	1.8 (2.1)	2.6	6.6 (6.4)	5.9	-1.4(-1.5)	-1.3	9 (=7)	10
Japan	3.6 (3.7)	3.8	3.0 (3.1)	2.4	+1.0(+0.9)	+0.9	2 (=1)	1
Spain	2.7 (2.8)	3.4	6.5 (6.6)	5.5	-3.6(-3.5)	-3.4	7 (=7)	=8
Sweden	-0.2 (0.1)	1.3	9.4 (9.3)	6.3	-3.6(-3.8)	-2.9	13	13
Switzerland	2.1 (2.2)	2.3	4.6 (4.4)	3.5	+2.9(+2.7)	+3.5	6 (5)	6
UK	-0.2 (0.4)	2.1	6.4 (6.7)	5.0	-1.8(-2.0)	-1.8	10 (12)	12
USA	-0.4 (0.1)	2.5	4.6 (5.0)	4.0	-1.5(-1.6)	-1.3	8 (9)	=8

Source: Consensus Economics Inc, London   †Current-account figures now on all-German basis; others western Germany only.
*Based on sum of three measures.

THE ECONOMIST In July 1991 *The Economist* started to poll a group of forecasters, then calculate the average of their predictions for 13 industrial countries. The previous month's figure (if changed) is shown in brackets. In December our seers were feeling gloomier about the American economy; they cut their average forecast for GDP growth in 1992 to 2.0%, down from 2.5% in November. Growth forecasts for 1992 were trimmed in nine other economies. Since July, only two countries– Canada and Britain–had not had their 1992 growth forecasts shaved. Sweden continued to suffer a deep recession, but at least its inflation rate was dropping. The average forecast for Swedish inflation in 1992 was 5.4% in July; in December it was 3.9%. Japan was ranked top overall again.

The Economist poll of forecasters, December averages (previous month's, if changed)

	Real GNP/GDP % change		Consumer prices % increase		Current-account balance, % of GNP/GDP		The Economist's ranking*	
	1991	1992	1991	1992	1991	1992	1991	1992
Australia	-1.0(-0.7)	2.8 (3.0)	3.4	3.8 (3.9)	-3.6(-3.7)	-3.7	9	7=(9=)
Belgium	1.7	2.0 (2.1)	3.3	3.1	2.1	2.2	2	2
Canada	-1.0	2.7 (3.0)	5.8	3.1 (3.3)	-3.0(-2.6)	-2.8(-2.6)	11=	4= (5=)
France	1.3	1.9	3.1	2.9	-0.6	-0.6	4 (5)	3
Germany†	3.3	1.8 (1.9)	3.6	3.8	-1.0(-0.4)	-0.4(-0.1)	5 (4)	7=
Holland	2.1	1.7 (1.9)	3.7	3.8 (3.7)	3.6	3.6 (3.8)	3	6 (5=)
Italy	1.1	1.9	6.4	5.7	-1.4	-1.4(-1.0)	10	12
Japan	4.3 (4.2)	2.8 (3.0)	3.2 (3.3)	2.2 (2.3)	1.9	2.0 (1.9)	1	1
Spain	2.6	2.9 (3.0)	6.0	6.0 (5.9)	-3.2(-2.8)	-3.1(-3.2)	8	11
Sweden	-1.1(-1.0)	0.5 (0.7)	9.3 (9.5)	3.9 (4.4)	-1.8	-1.6(-1.8)	13	13
Switzerland	-0.1(0.1)	1.3 (1.6)	5.9 (5.8)	4.4	4.2 (4.1)	4.1 (4.0)	6	10 (8)
UK	-2.1	2.1	5.8	4.1	-1.2	-1.3(-1.4)	11=	9
USA	-0.5(-0.4)	2.0 (2.5)	4.2 (4.3)	3.5 (3.6)	-0.4(-0.3)	-1.0(-1.1)	7	4=

Participants: BZW, EIU, Goldman Sachs, Hoare Govett, James Capel, Kredietbank, Lehman Brothers, Long-Term Credit Bank, Merrill Lynch, JP Morgan, Morgan Stanley, Nomura, Nordbanken, Paribas, Salomon Brothers, Scotiabank, Toronto Dominion Bank, UBS Phillips & Drew, S. G. Warburg, Williams de Broe. *Based on sum of rankings for the three measures. †Current-account figures now on all-German basis; others western Germany only.

ASIA In April 1991, the slowdown of South-East Asia's miracle economies looked set to continue. Worst hit, reckoned Business International, would be Singapore, with real GDP growth down from 8.3% in 1990 to 5.2% in 1991. Thailand, 1990's top performer, could expect growth to slow from 10% to 7.4%. Malaysia looked set to snare first place in 1991: its GDP was forecast to grow by 8.3%, down from 9.4% in 1990. Higher oil prices at the start of the Gulf saga did not help; nor did recession in America and Western Europe. There were also signs that some Asian economies had hit capacity limits after five years of rapid growth. But with 2.0% growth forecast for OECD countries in 1991, Asia still looked healthy. Only the Philippines, expected to grow by 1.8%, was badly below par.

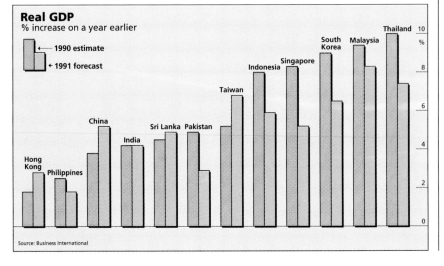

Real GDP
% increase on a year earlier

← 1990 estimate
← 1991 forecast

Hong Kong, Philippines, China, India, Sri Lanka, Pakistan, Taiwan, Indonesia, Singapore, South Korea, Malaysia, Thailand

Source: Business International

OECD Prospects for recovery in the world's industrial economies were good, reported the Organisation for Economic Co-operation and Development (OECD) in July 1991. The Paris-based rich-man's club issued bullish projections, in contrast to the gloomier views of many other forecasters. The end of the Gulf war, reckoned OECD officials, boosted business confidence, and this was expected to produce 2.4% annualised growth in OECD countries in the second half of 1991—up from a paltry 0.3% in the first six months. 1992 should be even better, with 2.9% growth. America's GNP, though likely to fall by 0.2% in 1991, was forecast to grow by 3.1% in 1992. Its inflation rate (as measured by the GNP deflator) was expected to fall to 3.6% in 1992.

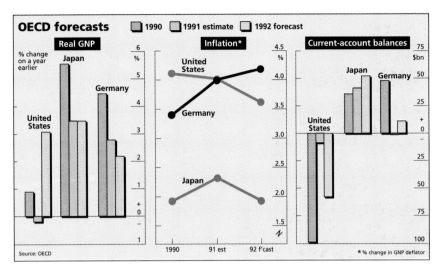

COMPETITIVENESS Each year IMD, a Swiss business school, and the World Economic Forum jointly publish a survey on international competitiveness, as measured by such factors as economic strength, degree of state interference and quality of management. In 1991 Japan held on to first place, for the sixth year. IMD reckons Japan's competitive edge is built on its manufacturing ability, quality and technological know-how. America's climb from fourth to second place is partly explained by the relative competitive weakness of a unifying Germany and by Switzerland's poorer performance. Austria saw the biggest rise in competitiveness in 1991, surging from 11th to sixth place, because businessmen see the country as a gateway to Eastern Europe.

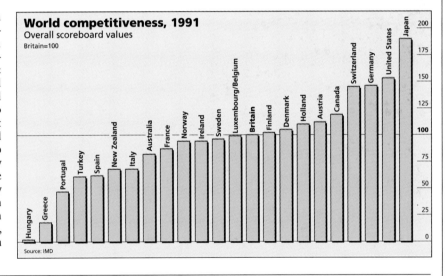

BUSINESS CONFIDENCE According to Dun & Bradstreet's survey of sales expectations in November 1991, businessmen's moods were changing in different ways in the world's big economies. The most dramatic switch of expectations was in Britain, where optimists outweighed pessimists by 11%, up from a negative 13% in the previous quarter. By contrast, the Swiss became gloomier, with a net 19% of those polled expecting sales to fall during 1991's fourth quarter, up from 7% in the third quarter. Japanese confidence slipped for the fifth quarter in succession, still leaving 40% of businessmen optimistic, but down from a peak of 84%. Americans were slightly less sure of revival than three months earlier, but Germans perked up: nearly 50% expected sales to rise.

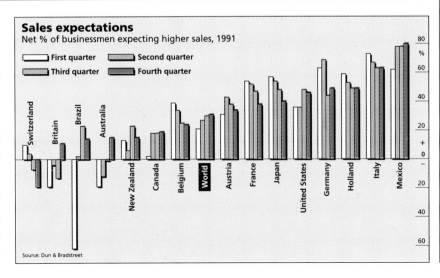

Economic growth

OECD FORECASTS At the end of 1990 the OECD forecast growth for industrial economies of an average of 2.0% in 1991, down from an estimated 2.8% in 1990. However, the OECD expected seven countries to have real GNP growth of 3% or more. Two economies were tipped to grow significantly faster than in 1990: Iceland (3.4%, compared with a decline of 0.1% in 1990) and New Zealand, where GNP was forecast to "surge" by 1.5%, after a dismal annual average of 0.3% during the past five years. Only one country was expected to see its GNP decline between the two years: Sweden, with a 0.5% drop. At the other extreme, Japan was predicted to be the OECD's fastest grower in 1991 (3.7%), followed closely by Turkey (3.5%).

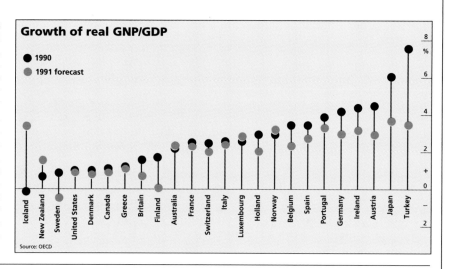

Growth of real GNP/GDP

● 1990
● 1991 forecast

Iceland, New Zealand, Sweden, United States, Denmark, Canada, Greece, Britain, Finland, Australia, France, Switzerland, Italy, Luxembourg, Holland, Norway, Belgium, Spain, Portugal, Germany, Ireland, Austria, Japan, Turkey

Source: OECD

Real GNP/GDP*

Gross domestic product (GDP) is the total value of a country's annual output of goods and services. Gross national product (GNP) also includes net factor income from abroad, for example profits and investment income. Most countries use the GDP measure–the United States switched to GDP from the third quarter 1991–leaving Japan and western Germany as the only GNPs in our table. Growth rates are measured at constant prices, so exclude inflation. The OECD's prediction that Japan would grow fastest in 1991 looked right when preliminary estimates were published at the end of 1991.

% change on a year earlier

		Australia	Belgium†	Canada	France	Germany‡	Holland	Italy	Japan	Spain	Sweden	Switzerland	United Kingdom	United States
1990	1st qtr	3.6	na	1.4	3.7	3.5	3.6	3.1	4.5	4.8	1.3	2.5	1.7	1.5
	2nd qtr	2.6	na	1.0	2.9	4.4	3.5	1.9	6.7	4.0	2.0	2.3	2.4	1.4
	3rd qtr	0.2	na	0.5	3.1	5.5	4.4	1.5	5.1	3.1	0.5	2.2	0.5	1.2
	4th qtr	0.6	na	-1.1	1.7	5.3	4.4	1.4	4.7	2.8	-0.4	1.8	-0.7	-0.1
1991	1st qtr	-2.0	na	-2.8	0.5	5.2	2.1	0.7	5.9	2.7	-0.8	0.2	-2.2	-1.2
	2nd qtr	-2.9	na	-1.3	1.1	4.3	2.4	1.4	4.5	2.5	-2.0	-0.6	-3.6	-1.2
	3rd qtr	-1.9	na	-0.8	1.2	1.9	2.2	–	4.1	2.5	-1.9	-0.7	-2.2	-0.9
	4th qtr	–	na	–	–	–	–	–	–	–	–	–	–	–

OECD estimates and forecasts, December 1991 % change on previous period at annual rate

		Australia	Belgium†	Canada	France	Germany‡	Holland	Italy	Japan	Spain	Sweden	Switzerland	United Kingdom	United States
1991		-0.6	1.4	-1.1	1.4	3.2	2.2	1.0	4.5	2.5	-1.2	-0.2	-1.9	-0.5
	1st half			-2.4	0.9	5.2		0.9	6.6				-2.8	-1.9
	2nd half			2.5	2.2	-2.0		1.1	0.8				1.1	1.4
1992		2.6	2.0	3.1	2.1	1.8	1.8	2.0	2.4	2.9	0.2	1.2	2.2	2.2
	1st half			3.1	1.9	3.3		2.3	2.7				2.4	1.8
	2nd half			3.8	2.4	2.6		2.4	3.3				3.1	3.7
1993		3.2	2.7	4.1	2.7	2.5	2.3	2.5	3.5	3.2	1.5	1.8	3.2	3.8
	1st half			4.2	2.7	2.5		2.5	3.5				3.2	3.9
	2nd half			4.1	2.8	2.5		2.5	3.7				3.1	3.8

Nominal GNP/GDP*

		Australia	Belgium†	Canada	France	Germany‡	Holland	Italy	Japan	Spain	Sweden	Switzerland	United Kingdom	United States
1991		0.7	4.9	2.5	4.2	7.8	5.4	8.1	6.8	9.2	5.7	6.0	4.2	3.2
	1st half			1.3	3.8	10.0		9.2	9.2				3.1	2.3
	2nd half			6.3	5.3	3.2		6.5	3.1				6.3	4.3
1992		5.8	5.4	6.1	5.1	6.4	5.0	7.9	4.5	9.0	3.3	5.7	6.5	5.2
	1st half			5.9	5.0	8.0		8.4	4.9				6.4	4.8
	2nd half			6.2	5.2	6.5		8.2	5.3				7.0	6.9
1993		7.2	5.9	6.4	5.4	6.5	5.7	7.8	5.5	8.4	5.6	5.3	7.0	6.8
	1st half			6.6	5.5	7.0		7.7	5.5				7.0	6.9
	2nd half			6.3	5.5	5.8		7.5	5.7				6.7	6.6

*GDP except for Germany and Japan, and United States OECD data, GNP. †Annual rates only. 1990 GNP:3.4% ‡western Germany: consolidated figures for Germany not yet available.

Industrial output

TRENDS Since the start of 1985, industrial output has grown faster in Japan than in any other of the seven biggest economies of the OECD. In 1991 Japan's industrial output has slipped slightly from its high point in the fourth quarter of 1990, but it is still 28% bigger than in 1985. Output in western Germany—the second-best performer over the whole period—has also fallen from its high (in the first quarter of 1991), thanks to post-unification economic troubles. Having had similar growth paths between 1985 and 1988, the Group of Seven's fortunes since have been strikingly mixed. The worst performer is Canada; despite a recovery during 1991, its industrial output is only 3.5% higher than in the first quarter of 1985.

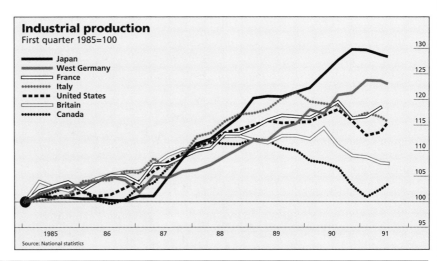

Industrial production
First quarter 1985=100

- Japan
- West Germany
- France
- Italy
- United States
- Britain
- Canada

Source: National statistics

Industrial production

Industrial production indices measure movements in the output of the production industries. These generally include manufacturing, energy and utilities and, in some countries, construction. Output is measured in constant prices to give an indication of volume movements, excluding inflation effects. Industrial production accounts for as much as 30% of gross domestic product in the United States and 40% in Japan. The 12-month percentage changes in our table are based on statistics from national sources, so definitions vary slightly. Switzerland's indices are calculated only quarterly.

% change on a year earlier

		Australia	Belgium	Canada	France	Germany*	Holland	Italy	Japan	Spain	Sweden	Switzerland	United Kingdom	United States
1990	Jan	9.6	2.6	-3.8	2.2	5.0	7.9	0.9	1.7	3.6	-2.6		-0.1	-0.2
	Feb	1.6	2.5	-4.2	0.5	5.1	-0.6	1.4	3.4	0.4	-2.3		0.6	0.8
	Mar	7.5	3.2	-3.3	2.0	5.9	1.3	3.8	0.2	5.0	-2.8	6.0	1.3	1.1
	Apr	-1.4	3.1	-4.9	nil	1.1	0.4	1.4	3.8	-6.5	-3.5		0.4	0.2
	May	1.3	3.4	-3.9	1.8	8.7	0.4	2.1	4.0	2.1	0.2		2.9	1.0
	Jun	2.2	4.0	-2.9	1.0	4.4	4.5	-0.7	3.1	-0.6	-1.8	nil	4.3	1.6
	Jul	0.5	3.5	-1.9	2.4	5.1	3.7	-1.3	7.1	-0.2	1.2		-0.4	2.4
	Aug	-2.8	3.3	-3.3	2.4	5.6	3.8	-0.7	5.1	-0.7	-1.8		-2.2	2.1
	Sep	-5.1	3.5	-5.1	2.3	6.2	7.7	-1.2	5.5	-2.4	-2.0	3.5	-2.1	2.2
	Oct	-0.8	3.8	-4.1	1.4	6.2	2.5	-2.8	8.0	-1.1	-5.0		-2.2	2.0
	Nov	-2.3	4.0	-6.8	-0.6	5.3	2.6	-3.9	6.6	0.1	-6.0		-3.4	0.2
	Dec	-1.4	3.7	-8.0	-1.6	3.8	4.7	-5.4	6.1	nil	-5.5	1.8	-4.1	-1.3
1991	Jan	-2.0	3.8	-5.5	1.3	5.9	4.8	0.1	7.8	-1.6	-6.7		-3.7	-0.8
	Feb	-1.9	3.2	-6.9	1.9	4.0	19.0	-2.4	6.8	0.3	-6.7		-2.1	-2.6
	Mar	1.2	1.3	-7.5	-1.8	4.6	2.5	-2.8	3.5	-10.5	-5.3	-1.6	-3.2	-3.6
	Apr	-2.4	0.8	-5.5	0.4	5.7	2.0	-4.0	3.8	6.8	-8.3		-6.6	-3.1
	May	-2.4	0.1	-5.2	0.4	3.9	8.4	-2.8	4.3	-2.7	-9.4		-6.0	-2.7
	Jun	-2.5	-1.3	-4.3	0.4	5.4	4.5	0.3	1.1	-3.9	-8.6	nil	-5.0	-2.5
	Jul	-5.1	–	-4.5	-1.1	3.8	2.4	-2.0	2.5	0.4	0.9		-2.0	-2.1
	Aug	2.5	–	-3.5	-1.1	2.0	1.5	-7.7	0.1	-1.6	-9.6		-1.7	-2.3
	Sep	0.5	–	-1.2	-0.8	-0.3	-5.6	-3.1	0.9	1.3	-12.2	–	-2.2	-2.2
	Oct	–	–	-1.9	0.4	-0.5	–	–	-1.8	–	-12.7		-1.2	-1.5
	Nov	–	–	–	–	–	–	–	–	–	–		–	-0.5
	Dec	–	–	–	–	–	–	–	–	–	–		–	–

*western Germany: consolidated figures for Germany not yet available.

Unemployment rates

Recessionary factors throughout the world took their toll as the unemployment rates of most of the countries in our table rose markedly during 1991. The exceptions were Holland, the only country where unemployment fell and Japan, western Germany and Spain, whose rates stayed fairly constant throughout the year. Switzerland was the unlikely worst performer as its unemployment rate virtually doubled, but that was from a starting point of only 0.9% of its workforce in January 1991. Britain's jobless rate had risen to 8.8% by November, up by a third since January. In June, America's hit a five-year high of 7.0%. The rates quoted are those reported nationally. The OECD makes a stab at standardising the figures (see chart opposite), which has the effect of raising the rates for Holland by over two percentage points and for Britain by over one point, but lowering Germany's by about two points and Belgium's by half a point.

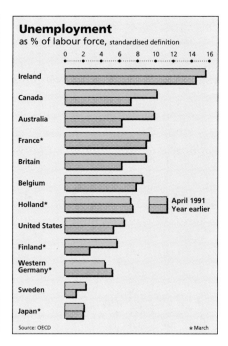

Unemployment
as % of labour force, standardised definition

Source: OECD ∗March

STANDARDISED COMPARISONS In May 1991 the Paris-based Organisation for Economic Co-operation and Development published international comparisons of the jobless as a proportion of the total workforce, which made gloomy reading. The figures use a standardised definition of unemployment (which differs from the national definitions used in the table below). In April 1991, as 12 months before, Ireland had the highest rate of unemployment of the countries in the chart, at 15.5%. Compared with April 1990, only two of the countries had shown any improvement: Holland, where unemployment had fallen from 7.5% to 7.2%, and western Germany, where it fell from 5.2% to 4.4%. Britain's unemployment rate rose from 6.2% to 8.9%. Australia had the highest increase in jobless rates, surging 3.6 percentage points to 9.8% in April 1991. Japan's already low unemployment rate crept up by a mere 0.1% to 2.1 % in April 1991.

Unemployment

% of labour force

		Australia	Belgium	Canada	France	Germany	Holland	Italy	Japan	Spain	Sweden	Switzerland	United Kingdom	United States
1990	Jan	6.1	7.8	7.7	9.1	7.6	5.5	10.0	2.2	15.8	1.6	0.6	5.7	5.3
	Feb	6.4	7.7	7.6	9.0	7.5	5.3	9.8	2.1	15.8	1.4	0.6	5.7	5.3
	Mar	6.2	7.6	7.2	9.0	7.4	5.3	9.8	2.0	15.7	1.3	0.6	5.6	5.3
	Apr	6.3	7.5	7.3	8.9	7.4	5.1	9.7	2.1	15.7	1.1	0.5	5.6	5.4
	May	6.5	7.5	7.7	8.9	7.3	4.9	9.9	2.1	15.6	1.3	0.5	5.7	5.3
	Jun	6.7	7.5	7.6	8.9	7.3	4.9	9.8	2.2	15.6	1.1	0.5	5.7	5.3
	Jul	7.0	7.7	8.0	8.9	7.2	4.8	9.8	2.1	15.5	1.5	0.5	5.7	5.5
	Aug	7.3	7.7	8.4	8.9	7.1	4.9	9.9	2.1	15.6	1.6	0.5	5.8	5.6
	Sep	7.4	7.7	8.5	8.9	7.0	4.9	10.0	2.2	15.7	1.8	0.5	5.9	5.7
	Oct	7.7	7.7	8.9	8.9	6.8	5.0	9.8	2.2	15.7	1.8	0.6	6.0	5.7
	Nov	8.2	7.8	9.1	8.9	6.6	4.7	9.6	2.1	15.5	1.9	0.7	6.2	5.9
	Dec	8.1	7.8	9.3	8.9	6.6	4.7	10.1	2.1	15.4	1.8	0.8	6.5	6.1
1991	Jan	8.3	7.9	9.7	8.9	6.3	4.8	10.1	2.0	15.2	2.3	0.9	6.7	6.2
	Feb	8.7	8.0	10.2	9.0	6.3	4.9	10.1	2.0	15.3	2.3	1.0	7.0	6.5
	Mar	9.2	8.0	10.5	9.1	6.2	4.9	9.8	2.2	15.3	2.2	1.0	7.4	6.8
	Apr	9.9	8.0	10.2	9.2	6.2	4.7	9.8	2.1	15.2	2.1	1.1	7.6	6.6
	May	9.4	8.0	10.3	9.3	6.3	4.6	9.9	2.0	15.1	2.1	1.1	7.9	6.9
	Jun	9.3	8.1	10.5	9.4	6.3	4.4	10.0	2.1	15.1	2.2	1.1	8.1	7.0
	Jul	9.8	8.1	10.5	9.6	6.4	4.3	10.0	2.2	15.0	2.8	1.2	8.3	6.8
	Aug	9.8	8.2	10.6	9.5	6.4	4.3	10.0	2.2	15.0	3.1	1.3	8.5	6.8
	Sep	10.2	8.3	10.2	9.6	6.3	4.4	10.0	2.2	15.2	3.1	1.3	8.6	6.7
	Oct	10.1	8.3	10.3	9.7	6.3	4.3	10.3	2.0	15.4	3.1	1.5	8.7	6.8
	Nov	10.5	8.4	10.3	9.8	6.3	4.4	10.2	2.1	15.3	3.2	1.7	8.8	6.8
	Dec	–	–	–	–	–	–	–	–	–	–	–	–	–

Retailing

SHOP RENTS In 1991 in Hong Kong's Pedder Street it cost $7,421 to rent a square metre of shopping space for a year, the most expensive anywhere in the world. Tokyo's bustling Ginza, which in 1990 topped Healey & Baker's league table of shop rents, came a close second, with a rent of $7,319 per square metre. A long way behind in third place was America's most expensive shopping area, Manhattan's East 57th Street, with a rent per square metre of $4,842. The most expensive street in Europe was Munich's fashionable Kaufingerstrasse ($2,606 per square metre), only just ahead of London's Oxford Street, where a square metre cost $2,552 per year. The cheapest rents, just $801 a square metre, were in Lisbon's Amoreiras.

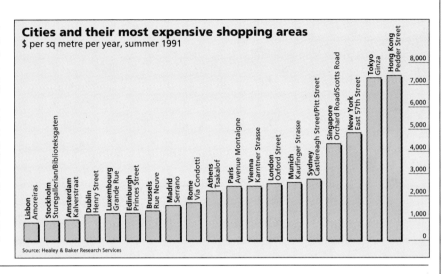

Cities and their most expensive shopping areas
$ per sq metre per year, summer 1991

Source: Healey & Baker Research Services

Retail sales, volume

Retail sales provide an indicator of consumer demand, measuring the volume of sales in the shops. A growth rate of 3% a year is considered healthy. A lower rate suggests that the economy is slowing down, while one of more than 4-5% indicates overheating. In all countries in our table except Japan retail sales were either flat or falling in 1991. The 12-month percentage changes in our table are based on statistics from national sources and from the OECD. Definitions vary, covering different ranges of retailers. Where necessary, the OECD has deflated the sales values by the appropriate consumer-price indices.

% change on a year earlier

		Australia	Belgium	Canada*	France	Germany†	Holland	Italy	Japan	Spain	Sweden	Switzerland	United Kingdom	United States
1990	Jan		7.5	-1.2	2.7	3.3	5.3	0.5	9.7	6.2	-3.1	1.8	1.8	1.0
	Feb		6.5	-1.5	0.3	5.0	4.0	6.4	8.4	5.5	-0.4	-0.7	1.9	1.4
	Mar	5.5	5.3	0.9	-1.4	6.3	4.6	-5.3	-6.9	7.9	-1.0	-1.8	-0.2	1.1
	Apr		4.9	-3.8	1.8	5.6	4.2	-7.0	19.9	3.0	0.7	8.5	2.2	-0.5
	May		5.4	-2.7	1.4	8.5	5.7	-4.2	11.0	8.6	-0.3	-2.5	0.7	-0.8
	Jun	5.4	2.7	-2.7	1.6	4.1	3.9	-2.3	12.8	8.8	-1.2	2.3	0.8	nil
	Jul		5.3	-1.0	0.7	14.8	2.5	-3.6	8.6	6.4	-2.0	1.3	2.3	-0.2
	Aug		3.3	-1.4	-1.2	12.0	5.3	-4.3	6.8	5.3	-3.0	-0.2	-0.4	-2.0
	Sep	4.4	0.9	-2.4	-1.1	12.9	2.3	-7.0	7.7	1.6	-6.9	-0.5	-0.1	-2.2
	Oct		1.9	-2.8	4.2	8.8	4.5	-4.3	2.9	17.3	-3.5	-1.6	-1.0	-1.1
	Nov		-0.9	-4.0	-2.8	9.8	3.6	-2.1	3.4	11.4	-5.4	-3.0	-1.4	-1.6
	Dec	2.4	-0.9	-3.9	0.6	7.3	3.3	-1.6	3.2	8.7	-6.6	-0.1	-1.2	-3.1
1991	Jan		–	-15.7	-0.3	14.5	5.8	3.4	3.7	8.7	0.4	0.3	-1.5	-5.8
	Feb		–	-11.4	-1.6	10.1	1.9	-5.9	2.9	7.6	-2.3	-2.1	-2.6	-3.4
	Mar	-1.5	–	-12.2	0.5	11.4	1.5	6.4	2.4	4.4	-5.3	-1.0	1.9	-2.3
	Apr		–	-10.9	0.4	9.0	2.0	-8.3	2.5	13.5	-3.5	-7.8	-2.1	-1.8
	May		–	-9.5	-2.0	6.9	1.6	-7.0	1.9	3.2	-3.0	0.5	-3.2	-0.8
	Jun	-2.2	–	-10.1	-2.5	13.3	-1.1	–	3.4	5.5	-5.2	-4.1	-0.4	-1.7
	Jul		–	-10.4	3.2	2.9	4.1	–	–	1.7	-0.3	-0.4	-0.5	-1.6
	Aug		–	-11.9	-0.8	-2.2	2.5	–	–	2.0	-1.6	-2.3	-0.1	-1.7
	Sep	0.2	–	-10.3	-2.4	-0.7	-4.6	–	–	-0.4	-3.0	-3.6	-0.5	-1.1
	Oct		–	–	–	1.8	–	–	–	1.1	–	–	-0.1	-0.5
	Nov		–	–	–	–	–	–	–	–	–	–	1.6	-0.7
	Dec	–	–	–	–	–	–	–	–	–	–	–	–	–

*From January 1991 indices exclude goods and services tax; previously included federal sales tax. † western Germany: consolidated figures for Germany not yet available.

Prices

LIVING COSTS According to Business International's April survey, Tehran remained the world's most expensive city for expatriates: the cost of living there was 39% higher than in second-placed Tokyo. The survey compares the cost of maintaining a western standard of living in various cities, based on general living expenses such as groceries, household goods, transport and so on. Most West European cities were dearer than New York, America's most expensive city. But the recent rise in the dollar had tarnished America's reputation as a bargain location. Eastern Europe and India were the least costly places to live. In late 1990, Warsaw was the cheapest major city in Eastern Europe, but by 1991 inflation had pushed it above Prague.

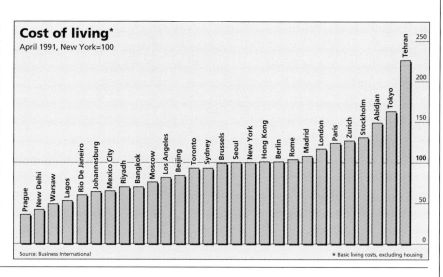

Cost of living*
April 1991, New York=100

Source: Business International   * Basic living costs, excluding housing

Consumer prices

The level of consumer-price inflation is one of the economic indicators which western governments are most sensitive about, as it is the benchmark against which most people measure the value of the currency in their pockets. The trends in the table below show a general decline in inflation from a high at the beginning of the year. The main exception was western Germany where big wage rises and an increase in indirect taxes, to help pay for the cost of unification, lifted its inflation rate from 2.8% in January to 4.2% in November. The highest 12-month rate during 1991 was Sweden's 12.6% in February.

% increase on a year earlier

		Australia	Belgium	Canada	France	Germany	Holland	Italy	Japan	Spain	Sweden	Switzerland	United Kingdom	United States
1990	Jan		3.6	5.5	3.4	2.7	2.2	6.4	3.4	6.7	8.7	5.0	7.7	5.2
	Feb		3.4	5.5	3.4	2.7	2.3	6.2	3.9	7.3	8.6	4.9	7.5	5.2
	Mar	8.6	3.3	5.3	3.7	2.7	2.3	6.1	3.7	7.0	11.2	5.0	8.1	5.2
	Apr		3.2	5.0	3.2	2.3	2.2	5.9	2.7	7.0	10.0	4.7	9.4	4.7
	May		3.1	4.4	3.0	2.3	2.3	5.7	2.6	6.8	10.2	5.0	9.7	4.4
	Jun	7.7	3.0	4.3	3.0	2.3	2.3	5.6	2.3	6.5	9.7	5.0	9.8	4.8
	Jul		3.0	4.2	3.0	2.5	2.4	5.7	2.3	6.3	10.8	5.3	9.8	4.8
	Aug		3.3	4.2	3.5	2.8	2.4	6.3	2.8	6.5	11.1	6.1	10.6	5.6
	Sep	6.1	3.7	4.2	3.8	3.0	2.7	6.3	2.8	6.5	11.5	6.0	10.9	6.2
	Oct		4.4	4.8	3.9	3.3	2.9	6.2	3.0	7.0	11.3	6.4	10.9	6.4
	Nov		4.0	5.0	3.6	3.0	2.8	6.5	3.9	6.7	11.4	6.0	9.7	6.3
	Dec	6.5	3.5	5.0	3.4	2.8	2.6	6.3	3.8	6.5	10.9	5.3	9.3	6.2
1991	Jan		3.9	6.8	3.5	2.8	3.2	6.5	4.0	6.7	10.0	5.5	9.0	5.6
	Feb		4.0	6.2	3.5	2.7	2.9	6.7	3.6	5.9	12.6	6.2	8.9	5.4
	Mar	4.8	3.3	6.3	3.2	2.5	3.1	6.6	3.6	5.9	9.9	5.8	8.2	4.9
	Apr		2.9	6.3	3.2	2.8	3.1	6.7	3.4	5.9	10.7	5.8	6.4	4.9
	May		3.2	6.2	3.2	3.0	3.3	6.8	3.4	6.2	10.1	5.8	5.8	5.0
	Jun	3.4	3.6	6.3	3.3	3.5	3.3	6.9	3.4	6.2	10.1	6.5	5.8	4.6
	Jul		3.8	5.8	3.4	4.4	4.5	6.7	3.5	6.0	9.1	6.5	5.5	4.4
	Aug		3.5	5.8	3.0	4.1	4.6	6.3	3.3	6.0	8.2	6.0	4.7	3.8
	Sep	3.2	2.5	5.4	2.6	3.9	4.4	6.2	2.7	5.7	8.1	5.7	4.1	3.4
	Oct		2.2	4.4	2.5	3.5	4.5	6.1	2.7	5.5	7.8	5.1	3.7	2.8
	Nov		2.8	4.2	3.0	4.2	4.8	6.2	3.1	5.7	7.9	5.5	4.3	3.0
	Dec	–	2.8	–	–	–	–	–	–	–	–	–	–	–

Wholesale, or producer prices, as they are often known, measure the prices of home-produced goods at the factory gate. Movements in the index (which in most countries covers only manufacturing) provides a useful indicator of domestic cost pressures. Wholesale prices tend to fluctuate more than consumer prices (eg, prices often fall over 12-month periods because they are more sensitive to changes in the prices of raw materials). In most countries in the table wholesale-price inflation fell during 1991. In America, for example, prices fell 0.2% in the year to November, compared with a 12-month rise of 7.0% a year earlier. Britain had the highest rate of wholesale-price inflation: 5.1% in the 12 months to November, though down from 6.3% in January. Belgium's 12-month rate of wholesale-price inflation was negative for virtually the whole of 1991. On the information available at the end of 1991 seven countries had negative rates.

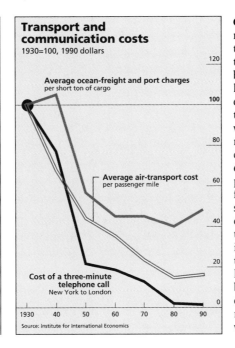

Transport and communication costs
1930=100, 1990 dollars

Average ocean-freight and port charges
per short ton of cargo

Average air-transport cost
per passenger mile

Cost of a three-minute
telephone call
New York to London

1930 40 50 60 70 80 90

Source: Institute for International Economics

GOING CHEAP According to a 1991 report, the world may soon be your oyster, as it gets smaller and cheaper. Over the past 60 years the cost of sending cargo by sea has more than halved in 1990 dollars. Flying has, in relative terms, become even cheaper: the average cost of air transport is now only a sixth of what it was in 1930. But telephone calls are the real bargain. A three-minute transatlantic call in 1990 cost barely 1.5% of what it did 60 years ago, though its most dramatic price fall occurred in a 20-year period from 1930, when calls plummeted a massive 78%. But while the price of telephone calls continued to fall during the 1980s, the cost of air transport increased by 21% in the past ten years and the cost of sea transport crept up as equipment and labour became dearer. That trend would be bad news if it continued: the past few decades of tumbling transport and communication costs have helped to boost world trade.

Wholesale prices

% change on year earlier

		Australia	Belgium	Canada	France	Germany	Holland	Italy	Japan	Spain	Sweden	Switzerland	United Kingdom	United States
1990	Jan	7.0	2.0	-0.7		1.9	-3.2	8.1	3.7	3.3	5.8	2.3	5.2	5.9
	Feb	6.3	1.4	0.1		1.7	-2.8	6.0	3.5	2.8	5.3	2.3	5.3	5.1
	Mar	6.6	1.6	-0.5	-1.7	1.5	-1.8	5.2	3.9	2.3	4.5	2.0	5.6	4.5
	Apr	6.6	0.5	-0.6		1.5	-0.8	4.4	2.7	2.2	3.5	1.5	6.2	3.7
	May	5.3	-0.1	-0.2		1.5	-1.1	4.0	1.7	2.2	3.3	1.0	6.3	3.0
	Jun	4.5	-0.4	-0.5	-2.3	1.6	-1.1	5.5	0.9	1.9	3.6	1.1	6.3	3.1
	Jul	4.1	-0.4	-0.5		1.4	-0.8	5.5	0.8	1.0	3.4	1.6	6.0	3.7
	Aug	5.0	0.8	-0.2		1.9	-0.4	9.5	1.1	1.3	3.9	1.9	6.0	5.1
	Sep	6.1	1.0	0.9	-1.4	2.1	1.5	11.0	0.9	2.0	4.8	1.8	5.8	5.9
	Oct	6.7	1.0	1.5		2.0	3.5	12.0	1.5	2.5	4.6	1.1	5.9	6.5
	Nov	7.2	0.4	1.9		1.8	4.6	9.5	2.0	2.2	4.4	0.7	5.9	7.0
	Dec	6.3	-0.6	2.3	0.7	1.5	2.8	8.1	2.2	2.3	4.1	0.2	5.9	5.9
1991	Jan	5.1	-0.1	2.2		2.3	0.7	7.8	2.1	2.3	3.7	0.8	6.3	4.2
	Feb	4.0	-1.3	1.0		2.2	0.9	9.7	1.6	1.7	3.2	0.8	6.3	3.5
	Mar	2.3	-2.1	0.5	0.7	1.8	1.1	8.2	1.0	1.6	3.1	-0.1	6.3	3.3
	Apr	1.6	-1.2	nil		2.2	1.1	7.3	0.1	1.7	3.0	-0.1	6.2	3.5
	May	1.8	-0.5	-0.9		2.2	1.4	7.9	0.6	1.7	2.6	0.2	6.0	3.7
	Jun	2.7	0.2	-0.8	-0.7	2.3	1.8	7.2	0.6	1.9	2.3	0.5	5.8	3.2
	Jul	2.6	0.1	-0.7		3.3	2.7	6.9	0.4	2.2	2.2	0.6	5.9	2.6
	Aug	1.5	-1.5	-1.3		2.7	2.5	3.1	0.1	1.7	1.4	0.3	5.7	1.8
	Sep	–	-2.2	-2.4	-1.6	2.6	2.0	2.1	-0.4	1.1	0.4	-0.2	5.6	0.6
	Oct	–	–	-2.7		2.4	–	-0.3	-0.8	0.6	-0.1	0.6	5.2	nil
	Nov	–	–	–		2.5	–	–	-1.3	–	–	–	5.1	-0.2
	Dec	–	–	–	–	–	–	–	–	–	–	–	–	–

Wages and earnings

LABOUR COSTS For most firms the cost of labour includes much more than merely wages. Non-wage costs—pension plans, social-security taxes, free meals, extra holidays and a host of other perks—can be hefty. Of the 20 countries in the chart, only in Italy did manufacturing firms' non-wage expenses exceed wage costs, accounting for 50.7% of total labour costs in 1990. Austria, where non-wage costs account for 49% of total labour costs, came close. Denmark had the lowest relative non-wage costs, accounting for only 19.7% of total labour costs; but its overall labour costs were the fifth highest in the chart. The cheapest labour was to be found in Portugal, where overall costs were only a fifth of Germany's, the country with the highest overall costs.

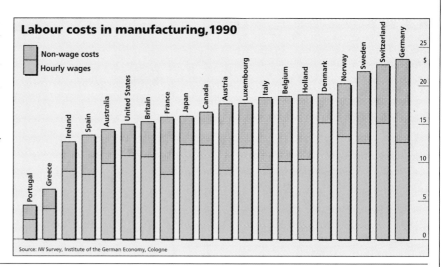

Labour costs in manufacturing, 1990

- Non-wage costs
- Hourly wages

Source: IW Survey, Institute of the German Economy, Cologne

Wages and earnings

The figures for more than half the countries in our table represent wage increases for all workers. Those for Belgium, Canada, Italy, Japan, Sweden and Switzerland refer to industry or manufacturing only.

Switzerland publishes wage figures only once a year. Britain started 1991 with the fatest 12-month rate of increase in earnings (9.5%). But as unemployment rose and inflation fell, wage growth slowed to 7.5%

in October. The fastest decline in the rate of wage increases occurred in Australia, to less than half the rate of a year ago. Sweden's rate also fell sharply, to 4.7% in October.

% increase on a year earlier*

		Australia	Belgium	Canada	France	Germany	Holland	Italy	Japan	Spain	Sweden	Switzerland	United Kingdom	United States
1990	Jan			5.0	4.4	5.1	2.7	7.5	6.2		10.2		9.5	3.5
	Feb	6.5		5.1		5.1	2.8	7.6	3.8		9.7		9.5	3.8
	Mar		3.7	5.6		5.2	2.8	7.1	3.7	8.6	9.3		9.5	4.1
	Apr			5.7	4.8	5.7	3.3	6.9	4.3		11.2		9.8	3.6
	May	6.3		6.6		5.7	3.2	7.2	5.0		9.3		9.8	3.8
	Jun		5.5	6.3		5.7	3.2	7.2	7.4	9.1	11.0		10.0	4.2
	Jul			5.9	5.2	5.7	3.6	7.5	6.3		9.2		10.3	3.9
	Aug	6.3		5.1		5.9	3.6	7.4	0.7		9.2		10.0	4.1
	Sep		4.5	4.9		5.8	3.5	7.2	4.8	9.3	9.2		10.3	4.0
	Oct			5.5	5.1	6.1	3.5	7.2	4.7		8.0	5.2	9.8	3.3
	Nov	7.3		5.5		6.1	3.5	7.4	5.1		8.3		9.8	3.6
	Dec		3.4	6.0		6.2	3.5	7.1	6.3	8.7	9.0		9.8	3.5
1991	Jan			5.8	5.1	5.9	3.2	7.8	1.8		7.9		9.5	3.7
	Feb	6.9		6.9		5.9	3.2	7.8	5.5		4.5		9.3	3.2
	Mar		5.3	6.4		6.6	3.2	8.0	4.2	8.2	4.8		9.0	3.1
	Apr			6.3	4.4	6.7	3.4	8.4	3.9		2.8		8.8	3.2
	May	3.0		5.2		7.1	3.5	–	4.0		4.8		8.5	3.6
	Jun		3.5	5.5		7.2	3.7	–	4.5	9.0	3.3		8.0	3.5
	Jul			5.3	4.7	7.2	3.8	–	1.9		4.1		7.8	2.9
	Aug	3.0		5.3		7.0	3.8	–	6.5		4.9		7.8	3.1
	Sep		–	5.6		7.1	3.9	–	2.8	8.4	4.4		7.8	2.8
	Oct		–	–	–	6.9	3.9	–	–		4.7	–	7.5	3.1
	Nov	–		–		–	–	–	–		–		–	3.1
	Dec		–	–	–	–	–	–	–	–	–		–	–

*Hourly earnings for all employees except Australia, weekly earnings; Spain, quarterly earnings; UK, monthly earnings; USA, hourly earnings; Japan and Switzerland, manufacturing monthly earnings; Belgium, Sweden, industrial hourly earnings; Canada, Italy, manufacturing hourly earnings.

BIG BANKS At the end of 1990 there were no American banks among the world's 20 biggest (as measured by assets), for the first time in 50 years. Citicorp, tenth in March 1990 and once the world's number one, ended the year languishing in 21st place. Despite problems with their capital ratios, Japanese banks filled the top six places in the league, and ten of the top 15. The biggest was Dai-Ichi Kangyo, with assets of $428 billion, just ahead of Sumitomo and Mitsui Taiyo Kobe (now Sakura Bank), each of which had about $409 billion. Europe's three biggest banks were all French. Top was Crédit Agricole, seventh largest in the world, with assets of $305 billion, just ahead of Banque Nationale de Paris and Crédit Lyonnais, both of which are state-owned.

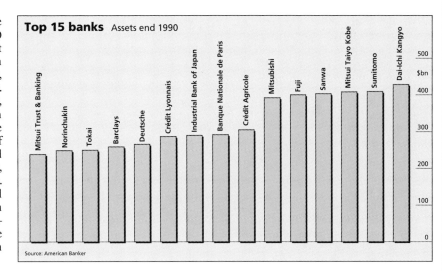

Top 15 banks Assets end 1990

Source: American Banker

BIG FIRMS The Gulf war helped to push oil companies up the league table of the world's biggest firms by market capitalisation. Exxon, fourth in 1990, was second in May 1991, with its market value up to $74 billion from $57 billion. Royal Dutch/Shell, worth just $500m less than Exxon, was third. The world's most valuable firm, by far, was still Nippon Telegraph and Telephone (NTT), Japan's telecoms giant. Worth $105 billion in 1990, NTT's capitalisation had risen to $108 billion. Philip Morris, eighth in 1990, had climbed to fourth. Buying Suchard, a Swiss confectioner, helped the American cigarette-maker's value rise from $39 billion to $62 billion in one year. 1990's second-biggest firm, IBM, slipped to sixth; its capitalisation fell from $62.5 billion in 1990 to $59 billion.

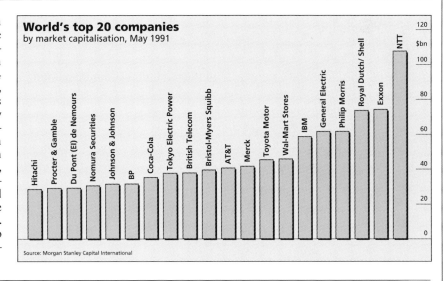

World's top 20 companies
by market capitalisation, May 1991

Source: Morgan Stanley Capital International

ENVIRONMENTAL SPENDING Comparing environmental virtue in different countries is tricky. Current and capital spending are one guide, though imperfect. Some countries may spend more efficiently than others. A dirty country needs to spend more on cleaning up than a clean one. Of the ten countries in the chart, western Germany and America spent the most on pollution control as a proportion of their GDPS in the mid-1980s (the most recent figures). Germany's environmental investment was three times bigger in real terms in 1988 than a decade earlier. The Japanese government spends much more on pollution than other countries, but Japanese industry's spending is tiny: by 1987 its investment had fallen to a fifth of its 1975 level.

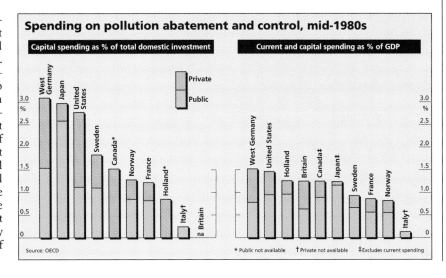

Spending on pollution abatement and control, mid-1980s

Capital spending as % of total domestic investment

Current and capital spending as % of GDP

Source: OECD

* Public not available   † Private not available   ‡ Excludes current spending

The Economist commodity-price index

Each week *The Economist* publishes a set of commodity-price indices. Our indices are based on 1985=100 and weighted by the value of imports into OECD countries in 1984-86, net of intra-EC trade in commodities affected by the common agricultural policy. Judging from movements in our indices, a feeble rally in the second quarter of the year was followed by another long slump in prices, taking them to the lowest level in real terms since *The Economist* began calculating an all-items commodity-price index in 1845. Over 1991 as a whole, the all-items index, measured in terms of SDRs, a basket of currencies, fell 10% and was 38% below its peak at the beginning of 1989. In dollar terms, the index lost 9% in 1991. Metal prices fared worst; by the end of the year the SDR metals index had dropped 20% from its 1991 peak in April. Producers postponed costly cuts in output in the hope of riding out the recession,

flooding the market with extra metal. The collapse of domestic demand in the former Soviet Union and the country's desperate attempts to raise foreign exchange by increasing metal exports to the West depressed prices further. Base-metal stocks in London Metal Exchange warehouses rocketed to a record 1.6m tonnes. Other industrial materials also suffered. The slump in the tyre industry dragged rubber prices to a five-year low. The Australian Wool Corporation, saddled with a massive stockpile, ended 17 years of price support in February. As a result, wool prices plunged by a third before recovering somewhat near the end of the year. Cotton prices fell 26% in the second half of 1991, to a 2½-year low. Food prices, in SDR terms, declined by only 2% in 1991, avoiding a steeper fall largely because of a rise in grain prices, which were sustained by a 6% fall in output after 1990's record harvests.

Weights in the index

Industrials, %		Foods, %	
Metals		Beef	6.7
Copper	28.4	Lamb	2.1
Lead	4.4	Wheat	4.9
Zinc	9.9	Maize	8.5
Tin	6.3	Coffee	33.3
Aluminium	41.8	Cocoa	10.7
Nickel	9.2	Tea	3.0
Nfas*		Sugar	8.1
Wool 64s	10.5	Soyabean meal	7.6
Wool 48s	10.5	Soyabeans	10.3
Cotton	20.2	Soyabean oil	1.1
Jute	0.2	Groundnut oil	0.7
Sisal	0.3	Coconut oil	1.4
Hides	11.2	Palm oil	1.6
Rubber	14.2		
Timber	26.8	**Foods**	49.8
Soyabeans	4.4	**Industrials**	50.2
Soyabean oil	0.4	**Metals**	29.3
Coconut oil	0.6	**Nfas***	20.9
Palm oil	0.7	**All items**	100.0

*Non-food agriculturals

Averages,1985=100		Dollar index					Sterling index					SDR index				
		All items	Food	Industrial materials			All items	Food	Industrial materials			All items	Food	Industrial materials		
				All	Nfas	Metals			All	Nfas	Metals			All	Nfas	Metals
1986		103.7	106.6	100.9	103.9	98.7	90.6	93.1	88.1	90.8	86.2	89.8	92.4	87.3	89.9	85.4
1987		111.5	93.1	129.9	131.7	128.6	87.1	72.8	101.3	102.9	100.0	87.4	73.0	101.7	103.3	100.6
1988		147.4	113.2	181.4	144.9	207.2	106.2	81.6	130.6	104.4	149.1	111.4	85.6	137.0	109.5	156.5
1989		139.5	108.0	170.7	137.3	194.4	109.0	84.4	133.3	107.5	151.6	110.4	85.6	135.2	108.8	153.8
1990		126.4	98.4	154.2	135.6	167.4	91.3	71.2	111.3	98.1	120.6	94.7	73.8	115.5	101.7	125.3
1991		110.5	89.2	131.6	122.7	137.8	80.3	64.9	95.6	89.4	100.1	82.0	66.2	97.7	91.2	102.3
1990	Jan	121.0	97.8	144.1	136.1	149.6	94.0	75.9	111.9	105.7	116.3	93.1	75.3	110.9	104.8	115.2
	Feb	121.7	98.7	144.5	138.5	148.8	91.9	74.5	109.2	104.6	112.4	93.1	75.5	110.6	106.0	113.8
	Mar	129.5	102.7	156.1	138.5	168.5	102.4	81.2	123.4	109.5	133.2	101.0	80.1	121.7	108.0	131.4
	Apr	129.9	104.3	155.3	140.2	165.9	101.8	81.8	121.7	109.9	130.0	101.5	81.5	121.3	109.6	129.6
	May	131.8	105.6	157.9	142.8	168.5	100.9	80.8	120.8	109.3	129.0	101.6	81.4	121.7	110.0	129.8
	Jun	127.6	99.8	155.1	140.5	165.4	95.6	74.8	116.3	105.3	124.0	98.5	77.1	119.8	108.6	127.8
	Jul	127.6	97.3	157.7	140.2	170.2	90.0	68.6	111.2	98.8	119.9	96.2	73.4	119.9	105.6	128.2
	Aug	130.4	95.9	164.7	134.9	185.9	87.5	64.4	110.5	90.5	124.7	96.0	70.6	121.3	99.3	136.8
	Sep	133.2	96.8	169.4	134.0	194.5	90.8	66.0	115.5	91.3	132.6	97.4	70.8	123.8	97.9	142.2
	Oct	126.9	94.7	158.9	129.7	179.5	83.8	62.5	104.9	85.6	118.5	92.4	67.4	113.2	92.4	127.9
	Nov	119.4	93.2	145.5	125.6	159.6	77.7	60.6	94.7	81.7	103.8	83.8	65.3	102.1	88.1	111.9
	Dec	117.2	93.2	141.0	125.0	152.4	78.3	62.3	94.3	83.5	101.8	83.5	66.4	100.5	89.0	108.6
1991	Jan	115.1	89.6	140.5	124.5	151.8	76.4	59.4	93.3	82.6	100.8	82.1	63.9	100.3	88.8	108.3
	Feb	114.2	88.8	139.4	122.8	151.2	74.6	58.0	91.1	80.2	98.8	80.5	62.4	98.3	86.6	106.4
	Mar	114.6	90.9	138.1	120.7	150.3	80.6	64.0	97.2	85.0	105.8	83.9	66.6	101.1	88.4	110.1
	Apr	114.1	89.8	138.2	123.9	148.2	83.3	65.5	100.9	90.5	108.2	85.7	67.5	103.9	93.1	111.4
	May	110.8	86.3	135.2	132.4	137.0	81.8	63.7	99.8	97.8	101.2	83.7	65.2	102.1	100.0	103.5
	Jun	111.4	87.3	135.4	136.4	134.6	86.5	67.8	105.1	105.9	104.5	85.7	67.2	104.1	104.9	103.5
	Jul	111.1	89.1	132.9	128.8	135.7	86.5	69.3	103.5	100.3	105.7	85.3	68.4	102.1	99.0	104.2
	Aug	107.8	88.1	127.5	119.8	132.9	82.2	67.1	97.2	91.4	101.3	82.0	66.9	96.9	91.1	101.0
	Sep	108.0	90.3	125.5	116.7	131.8	80.2	67.0	93.2	86.6	97.8	80.9	67.7	94.1	87.5	98.8
	Oct	106.7	90.0	123.4	115.8	128.8	79.5	67.0	92.0	86.3	96.0	79.7	67.2	92.1	86.4	96.2
	Nov	107.4	89.8	124.9	118.3	129.5	77.2	64.5	89.7	85.0	93.0	78.6	65.7	91.4	86.6	94.7
	Dec	106.0	90.2	121.7	115.3	126.2	74.3	63.2	85.3	80.8	88.5	76.3	64.9	87.6	82.9	90.8

1985=100	Dollar index					Sterling index					SDR index				
	All items	Food	Industrial materials			All items	Food	Industrial materials			All items	Food	Industrial materials		
			All	Nfas	Metals			All	Nfas	Metals			All	Nfas	Metals
1991 Jan 1	116.7	90.2	143.2	127.0	154.6	77.5	59.9	95.1	84.4	102.7	83.3	64.3	102.1	90.6	110.3
8	116.9	90.4	143.2	124.7	156.2	78.6	60.8	96.3	83.9	105.1	84.3	65.2	103.3	90.0	112.7
15	114.3	88.9	139.6	124.2	150.5	76.9	59.8	94.0	83.6	101.3	82.4	64.1	100.7	89.5	108.5
22	114.7	89.8	139.6	123.4	151.0	75.5	59.0	91.8	81.2	99.3	81.1	63.4	98.6	87.2	106.7
29	112.8	88.5	136.9	123.0	146.7	73.4	57.6	89.1	80.1	95.5	79.6	62.4	96.6	86.8	103.5
Feb 5	113.4	88.8	137.9	125.0	147.0	73.3	57.4	89.1	80.8	95.0	79.5	62.3	96.7	87.6	103.1
12	114.5	88.0	140.9	125.2	151.9	73.7	56.6	90.6	80.6	97.8	79.9	61.4	98.2	87.3	106.0
19	114.7	89.1	140.2	122.8	152.6	75.3	58.5	92.1	80.6	100.2	81.2	63.1	99.2	86.9	107.9
26	114.1	89.3	138.7	118.2	153.2	76.1	59.6	92.6	78.9	102.3	81.6	63.9	99.2	84.5	109.6
Mar 5	115.9	92.0	139.7	121.7	152.4	78.1	62.0	94.1	82.0	102.7	83.3	66.1	100.3	87.4	109.5
12	114.7	91.2	138.0	119.8	150.8	79.1	62.9	95.2	82.7	104.0	83.3	66.3	100.3	87.1	109.6
19	113.6	90.1	136.9	120.4	148.7	82.5	65.4	99.4	87.4	107.9	83.8	66.5	101.1	88.8	109.7
26	113.7	90.3	137.0	121.0	148.3	83.1	66.0	100.1	88.4	108.4	85.5	67.9	103.0	91.0	111.5
Apr 2	115.0	91.7	138.2	121.9	149.7	83.4	66.5	100.2	88.3	108.5	86.4	68.9	103.8	91.5	112.4
9	114.7	90.9	138.4	124.2	148.4	82.1	65.1	99.1	88.9	106.2	85.7	67.9	103.3	92.8	110.8
16	114.7	90.7	138.6	124.1	148.8	82.2	65.0	99.3	88.9	106.7	85.1	67.3	102.8	92.1	110.4
23	113.8	89.1	138.4	124.6	148.2	85.2	66.7	103.7	93.3	111.0	86.7	67.8	105.4	94.8	112.8
30	112.0	86.5	137.3	124.8	146.1	83.3	64.3	102.1	92.8	108.6	84.8	65.5	103.9	94.4	110.6
May 7	111.4	86.7	136.0	128.3	141.4	83.0	64.6	101.3	95.6	105.3	84.4	65.6	103.0	97.1	107.1
14	110.6	86.2	134.9	131.7	137.0	81.6	63.6	99.4	97.1	101.0	83.6	65.1	101.9	99.5	103.5
21	110.5	86.2	134.7	133.1	135.7	81.6	63.6	99.4	98.2	100.2	83.4	65.0	101.6	100.4	102.4
28	110.6	86.0	135.1	136.6	133.9	81.3	63.2	99.2	100.4	98.4	83.4	64.9	101.8	103.0	101.0
Jun 4	110.7	87.3	134.0	137.2	131.6	83.3	65.7	100.8	103.3	99.0	84.4	66.5	102.1	104.6	100.3
11	111.6	86.6	136.5	137.2	136.0	86.1	66.8	105.3	105.8	104.9	85.8	66.5	104.9	105.4	104.5
18	111.8	87.5	135.9	135.9	135.8	88.9	69.6	108.0	108.1	107.9	86.8	68.0	105.5	105.6	105.4
25	111.5	87.8	135.1	135.2	134.9	87.8	69.2	106.4	106.5	106.2	85.9	67.7	104.0	104.2	103.9
Jul 2	110.6	86.4	134.6	130.6	137.5	88.5	69.1	107.7	104.5	110.0	85.8	67.0	104.4	101.3	106.6
9	111.3	87.8	134.7	130.5	137.7	87.9	69.4	106.4	103.1	108.7	86.1	67.9	104.1	100.9	106.4
16	111.0	88.7	133.1	129.3	135.7	86.4	69.1	103.7	100.7	105.7	85.2	68.1	102.2	99.2	104.2
23	110.7	89.8	131.5	127.3	134.4	84.2	68.3	100.1	96.9	102.3	84.5	68.5	100.4	97.2	102.6
30	111.7	92.8	130.5	126.4	133.3	85.2	70.8	99.5	96.4	101.7	85.0	70.6	99.3	96.2	101.4
Aug 6	110.5	91.9	129.0	122.4	133.5	82.7	68.8	96.5	91.7	100.0	83.2	69.3	97.2	92.2	100.6
13	107.7	86.8	128.5	121.3	133.5	81.5	65.7	97.3	91.8	101.1	81.5	65.7	97.2	91.8	101.0
20	105.3	84.2	126.4	118.7	131.8	82.4	65.9	98.9	92.8	103.1	81.0	64.7	97.2	91.2	101.3
27	107.8	89.3	126.2	117.0	132.7	82.2	68.1	96.2	89.2	101.2	82.1	68.0	96.1	89.0	101.0
Sep 3	107.6	89.0	126.1	116.4	133.0	81.5	67.5	95.6	88.2	100.7	81.7	67.6	95.8	88.4	100.9
10	108.8	90.5	127.0	116.4	134.4	80.6	67.1	94.1	86.2	99.6	81.5	67.8	95.1	87.2	100.7
17	108.2	91.1	125.1	117.8	130.3	79.6	67.0	92.0	86.7	95.8	80.5	67.8	93.1	87.7	97.0
24	107.4	90.7	123.9	116.2	129.4	78.9	66.6	91.0	85.4	95.0	80.0	67.6	92.4	86.6	96.4
Oct 1	106.9	90.8	122.9	115.0	128.5	78.4	66.6	90.1	84.3	94.2	79.5	67.5	91.4	85.5	95.5
8	106.0	89.8	122.2	113.9	128.1	79.3	67.1	91.4	85.1	95.7	78.9	66.8	90.9	84.7	95.2
15	105.3	88.6	121.9	114.8	126.8	79.3	66.7	91.8	86.5	95.5	78.7	66.2	91.0	85.8	94.7
22	108.1	90.5	125.7	118.2	130.9	80.9	67.7	93.9	88.4	97.9	80.8	67.6	93.9	88.3	97.8
29	107.3	90.1	124.5	117.0	129.8	79.9	67.0	92.6	87.0	96.6	80.6	67.6	93.5	87.8	97.4
Nov 5	107.9	90.2	125.5	119.5	129.6	78.1	65.3	90.9	86.5	93.9	79.4	66.3	92.3	87.9	95.4
12	106.7	89.0	124.3	118.2	128.6	77.1	64.3	89.9	85.5	93.0	78.4	65.4	91.3	86.8	94.4
19	107.1	89.7	124.4	117.2	129.5	76.4	64.0	88.8	83.6	92.4	78.1	65.4	90.8	85.5	94.4
26	107.9	90.4	125.3	118.2	130.2	76.9	64.5	89.3	84.3	92.9	78.4	65.7	91.1	86.0	94.6
Dec 3	107.1	90.2	123.9	117.4	128.5	77.5	65.3	89.7	85.0	93.0	78.3	66.0	90.6	85.9	93.9
10	105.6	89.9	121.2	115.4	125.2	74.8	63.7	85.9	81.8	88.8	76.3	65.0	87.6	83.4	90.5
17	105.2	89.7	120.5	113.8	125.3	74.1	63.2	84.9	80.1	88.2	76.0	64.9	87.1	82.2	90.5
24	106.0	90.9	121.0	114.2	125.8	72.4	62.1	82.7	78.0	86.0	75.4	64.7	86.1	81.2	89.5
31	106.1	90.3	121.9	115.5	126.4	72.7	61.8	83.5	79.1	86.6	75.3	64.0	86.5	81.9	89.7

Focus on commodities

METALS *The Economist* dollar metals index fell by 27% in the year to October 1991 and was more than 50% below its June 1988 peak. The base-metal market was glutted. Producers were riding out the current recession without reducing output, while the Soviet Union increased shipments of metals to the West in 1991. Combined stocks of base metals on the London Metal Exchange (LME) stood at a record 1.3m tonnes in October, twice the level at the end of 1990. The aluminium industry fared worst. Producers claimed that prices were the lowest ever in real terms, and that 60% of primary capacity was operating at a loss. Zinc stocks on the LME almost doubled in April during a technical squeeze and remained high over the following six months.

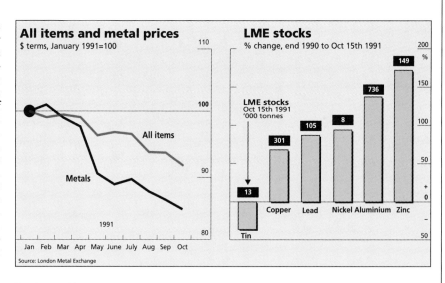

All items and metal prices
$ terms, January 1991=100

LME stocks
% change, end 1990 to Oct 15th 1991

Source: London Metal Exchange

FOODS *The Economist* dollar food index was at a four-year low in July 1991, 30% below the peak it reached during the American drought in 1988. World grain output was expected to be 2% lower and stocks close to a ten-year low, yet prices remained depressed. The Soviet grain harvest was expected to be only 190m tonnes in 1991, a fall of 13% on 1990. America's wheat output was forecast to be 26% lower, but it expected bumper maize and soyabean harvests. Soyabean prices fell by 20% in the year to July 1991. World cocoa stocks were a massive 1.6m tonnes; prices touched an 18-year low in New York in July. Coffee prices were the lowest for 15 years, with stocks a little below 1990's record level. Bucking the trend were sugar prices, which surged in June.

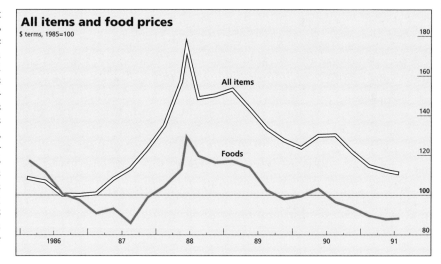

All items and food prices
$ terms, 1985=100

OTHER AGRICULTURALS *The Economist* dollar index of non-food agricultural commodities gained 8% between the beginning of 1991 and its peak in mid-June. This was thanks to soaring timber prices, up by more than 40% since mid-February. Slack demand closed many of America's timber mills in February; by June production was still less than normal, and supplies short. Cotton prices fell 26% in the second half of the year to a 2½-year low after the United States had its biggest crop in 50 years. Wool prices bounced back in May after collapsing by a third in February, when the Australian Wool Corporation ended 17 years of price support, only to fall away again in the third quarter. Rubber prices languished at a five-year low because of the slump in the mould-tyre industry.

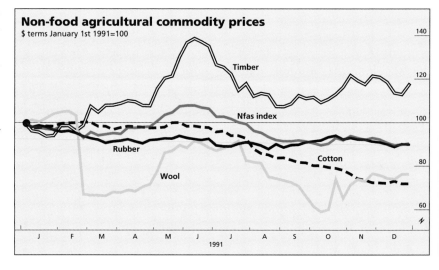

Non-food agricultural commodity prices
$ terms January 1st 1991=100

GOLD The gold price edged above $370 an ounce—a six-month high—during December. Even so, it remained low by the standards of the late 1980s. Bulls hoping for strong demand for jewels and falling mine output in 1992 may be disappointed. Jewellery sales could fall due to depressed demand in some markets. Much of 1992's gold production has been pre-sold on the futures market, and Australia and South Africa are mining more gold than expected. Yet Andy Smith of UBS, a merchant bank, believes that gold can still glister: stocks held by the crumbling Soviet Union are tiny; its 1992 exports may fall by half, to just 7% of total western supply. If this is not matched by central banks selling from reserves, prices could soar—especially if gloom deepens in other financial markets.

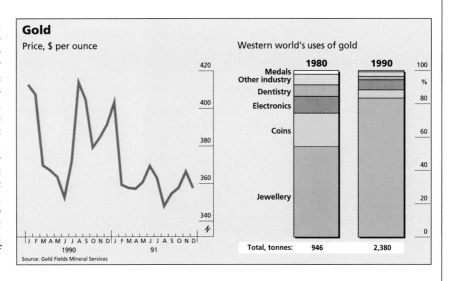

Gold

Price, $ per ounce

Source: Gold Fields Mineral Services

Western world's uses of gold

1980   1990

Medals
Other industry
Dentistry
Electronics
Coins
Jewellery

Total, tonnes: 946   2,380

UNLEADED PETROL Even green western Germany has been put to shame by Japan's and America's commitment to lead-free petrol. Japanese refiners stopped producing leaded petrol in December 1987. Americans have almost worked through the gas- and lead-guzzling Cadillacs of the 1970s. Yet Europe is growing greener. Lead emissions from British vehicles fell by more than half between 1975 and 1988. From 1993, all new cars in the EC must be fitted with catalytic converters, which cannot tolerate lead. By 2000 the great majority of cars will run on unleaded fuel. Spain has plenty of catching up to do. But the real villains are the Luxembourgers and Italians who stubbornly continue to buy leaded petrol, even though many of their petrol stations offer the cleaner alternative.

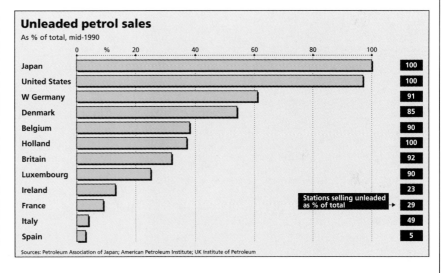

Unleaded petrol sales

As % of total, mid-1990

	Stations selling unleaded as % of total
Japan	100
United States	100
W Germany	91
Denmark	85
Belgium	90
Holland	100
Britain	92
Luxembourg	90
Ireland	23
France	29
Italy	49
Spain	5

Sources: Petroleum Association of Japan; American Petroleum Institute; UK Institute of Petroleum

YELLOW AND BLACK GOLD Prices of gold and oil followed similar trends in 1991. They both peaked just before the start of the Gulf war and fell steeply until the war ended. In September gold struck a five-year low of $345 an ounce. There were fears that the break up of the Soviet Union would lead to a flood of gold coming on to the market. Prices rallied when it became apparent that Soviet gold reserves were probably under 1,000 tonnes. By the end of the war at the end of February, oil prices had fallen to the year's low of $16.75 a barrel. With no oil exports from Iraq and Kuwait, other producers were able to pump oil flat out without flooding the market—prices climbed to $22 a barrel in October. But they were below $18 a barrel by the end of the year.

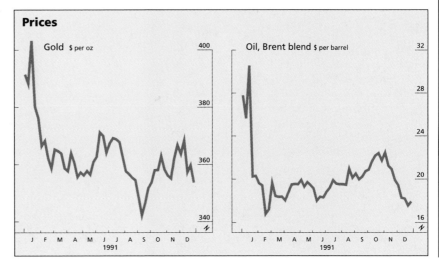

Prices

Gold $ per oz

Oil, Brent blend $ per barrel

1991   1991

World stockmarkets

Stockmarkets began the year in a jittery mood due to the Gulf crisis. The world index fell 4.9% between the end of 1990 and the day the Gulf war started on January 17th. However, triumph brought euphoria to London and Wall Street, with hopes that economic recovery must be on its way. London hit an all-time high in July of 2679.6. Wall Street was spurred on by signs that the United States was climbing out of recession and hit a record in October of 3077.2. Tokyo had a bumpy ride, hit by many financial scandals. Between mid March and August the Nikkei dropped by 21%. Renewed worries over the world econ-

Share-price indices

End month

		Australia	Belgium	Canada	France	Germany	Holland	Hong Kong	Italy	Japan
		All ordinaries index 1/1/80=500	Brussels SE index 1/1/80=1000	Toronto composite index 1/1/75=1000	CAC general index 31/12/82=100	Commerzbank index 1/12/53=100	CBS All Share index 31/12/83=100	Hang Seng Bank index 31/7/64=100	Banca Commercial index 1972=100	Nikkei 225 average
1990	Jan	1677.0	6259.8	3704.4	519.2	2237.5	193.8	2751.6	682.8	37186
	Feb	1575.1	5679.3	3686.7	497.5	2206.8	187.8	2952.0	655.7	34592
	Mar	1535.8	6134.7	3639.6	521.2	2403.1	197.8	2998.0	683.9	29981
	Apr	1434.5	6064.9	3341.0	547.1	2221.5	191.8	2950.1	689.6	29585
	May	1512.0	6281.7	3582.0	562.2	2254.3	199.6	3132.3	746.7	33131
	Jun	1500.7	6263.0	3544.0	545.1	2297.3	198.5	3278.2	753.8	31940
	Jul	1573.8	6292.0	3561.1	526.8	2353.2	198.6	3438.5	731.0	31036
	Aug	1507.6	5608.1	3346.3	464.4	1987.7	179.7	3087.5	626.9	25978
	Sep	1398.3	5007.1	3159.4	415.3	1628.7	167.6	2760.8	557.6	20984
	Oct	1327.2	5205.8	3081.3	428.1	1765.8	170.7	2991.0	560.5	25194
	Nov	1319.7	4994.8	3151.0	425.7	1767.9	169.1	2965.1	503.2	22455
	Dec	1279.8	4963.8	3256.8	413.0	1701.2	168.3	3024.6	516.6	23849
1991	Jan	1321.5	4924.8	3272.9	419.2	1724.6	167.3	3243.3	496.2	23293
	Feb	1405.6	5613.8	3462.4	465.6	1892.2	182.5	3552.1	572.5	26409
	Mar	1444.2	5774.7	3495.7	479.8	1833.6	195.7	3746.0	581.2	26207
	Apr	1534.2	5770.7	3468.8	479.6	1930.1	200.7	3588.4	575.8	26111
	May	1510.0	5782.7	3546.1	488.5	2035.2	201.7	3707.0	609.6	25790
	Jun	1506.2	5761.4	3465.8	470.8	1923.2	197.5	3668.6	586.2	23291
	Jul	1572.4	5706.4	3539.6	464.5	1909.5	200.8	4009.6	573.4	24121
	Aug	1540.4	5640.7	3517.9	486.7	1928.9	199.3	3998.3	555.4	22336
	Sep	1562.1	5407.9	3387.9	496.4	1869.5	193.9	3956.7	539.1	23916
	Oct	1683.0	5512.5	3515.8	494.7	1836.9	195.5	4038.7	515.7	25222
	Nov	1605.7	5375.4	3448.5	477.4	1814.6	191.9	4149.8	518.5	22687
	Dec	1651.4	5481.4	3512.3	476.7	1804.5	191.4	4297.3	507.8	22984
1990 high		1713.7	6599.4	4009.5	564.6	2414.0	206.3	3559.9	763.5	38713
1991 high		1696.3	5892.7	3604.1	503.5	2035.2	203.1	4297.3	619.4	27147

Market capitalisation, $bn

	Australia	Belgium	Canada	France	Germany	Holland	Hong Kong	Italy	Japan
End 1990	106	65	222	297	342	114	84	148	2,806
End 1991	141	67	246	319	342	121	119	145	2,945

Top five companies by market capitalisation, November 1991

Australia	Belgium	Canada	France	Germany	Holland	Hong Kong	Italy	Japan
BHP	Petrofina	BCE	Elf Aquitaine	Allianz	Royal Dutch	Hong Kong Telecom	Generali	NTT
National Australia Bank	Electrabel	Northern Telecom	Alcatel	Daimler-Benz	Unilever	HSBC	Fiat	Dai-Ichi Kangyo Bank
CRA	Générale de Belgique	Seagram	LVMH	Siemens	ABN-AMRO	Hutchison Whampoa	STET	IBJ
Coles Myer	Solvay	Imperial Oil	BSN	Deutsche Bank	International Nederlanden	Cheung Kong	SIP	Mitsubishi Bank
BTR Nylex	Tractebel	Thompson	Total	Bayer	Philips	Hang Seng Bank	Mediobanca	Sumitomo Bank

Source: MSCI

omy were reflected in stock-market performance in the final quarter. Hopes that America and Britain would recover briskly from recession were dampened by a string of poor economic statistics. London fin-ished 7.0% down on its record high and echoes of October 1987 were heard as Wall Street fell 3.9% on November 15th. Tokyo had to cope with its own slowing economy and was 41% down on its all-time high. Johannesburg was our best performer rising 49% in dollar terms since the start of the year. All bourses rallied at the end of 1991. Wall Street hit an all-time high on December 31st.

		Singapore	South Africa	Spain	Sweden	Switzerland	United Kingdom	United States	World
		Straits Times Industrials 30/12/66=100	JSE Industrials 28/9/78=264.3	Madrid SE index 30/12/85=100	Affarsvarlden General 1/2/37=100	Swiss Bank Industrials 31/12/58=100	FT-SE 100 30/12/83=1000	Dow Jones Industrials	Morgan Stanley Capital Int index* 1/1/70=100
1990	Jan	1515.0	2923.0	278.9	1238.8	750.5	2337.3	2590.4	539.9
	Feb	1550.1	3010.0	273.4	1175.1	756.0	2255.4	2627.3	515.9
	Mar	1581.1	2976.0	254.0	1142.2	747.2	2247.9	2707.2	488.8
	Apr	1458.4	2802.0	272.2	1161.6	740.3	2103.4	2656.8	475.9
	May	1553.6	2943.0	284.9	1265.7	811.5	2345.1	2876.7	525.1
	Jun	1527.0	2963.0	295.8	1309.7	830.0	2374.6	2880.7	520.4
	Jul	1554.8	3037.0	294.2	1314.7	805.9	2326.2	2905.5	524.2
	Aug	1277.9	2901.0	257.7	1159.6	699.2	2162.8	2614.4	474.1
	Sep	1098.7	2660.0	209.4	910.0	613.4	1990.2	2452.5	423.1
	Oct	1154.0	2710.0	232.1	900.4	648.5	2050.3	2442.3	461.6
	Nov	1106.6	2792.0	228.8	842.3	625.0	2194.4	2559.7	453.1
	Dec	1154.5	3018.4	223.3	870.0	628.5	2143.5	2633.7	461.5
1991	Jan	1267.3	2882.0	231.2	970.6	635.8	2170.3	2736.4	477.4
	Feb	1459.6	3218.0	264.1	1070.1	700.2	2380.9	2882.2	520.6
	Mar	1465.9	3389.0	284.3	1093.7	734.5	2456.5	2913.9	504.3
	Apr	1553.9	3542.0	274.1	1152.9	734.0	2486.2	2887.9	507.2
	May	1554.2	3608.0	284.2	1108.8	766.1	2499.5	3027.5	517.8
	Jun	1489.9	3817.0	277.0	1130.9	740.9	2414.8	2906.8	484.8
	Jul	1482.9	4085.0	269.5	1116.6	761.6	2588.8	3024.8	506.8
	Aug	1432.2	4114.0	273.2	1097.5	768.9	2645.7	3043.6	504.2
	Sep	1360.6	3974.0	274.4	1035.3	738.7	2621.7	3016.8	516.4
	Oct	1407.1	4263.0	263.8	1015.7	753.9	2566.0	3069.1	524.1
	Nov	1453.2	4220.0	246.4	954.8	719.7	2420.2	2894.7	500.0
	Dec	1490.7	4169.6	246.2	917.6	734.5	2493.1	3168.8	533.4
1990 high		1607.1	3211.0	309.7	1329.9	845.5	2463.7	2999.8	571.0
1991 high		1565.6	4364.0	289.2	1149.8	769.3	2679.6	3077.2	529.2

Market capitalisation, $bn

	Singapore	South Africa	Spain	Sweden	Switzerland	United Kingdom	United States	World
End 1990	68	113	105	93	163	882	2,814	8,444
End 1991	79	160	113	95	187	908	3,168	9,832

Top five companies by market capitalisation, November 1991

Singapore	South Africa	Spain	Sweden	Switzerland	United Kingdom	United States	World
Singapore Airlines	De Beers	Telefonica	Procordia	Nestlé	Glaxo	Exxon	NTT
Development Bank of Singapore	Anglo American	Repsol	Astra	Roche	BT	Philip Morris	Exxon
OCBC	Richmond Sec	Endesa	Ericsson	Sandoz	BP	Wal-Mart	Royal Dutch Shell
United Overseas Bank	S.A. Breweries	Banco Bilbao Vizcaya	Asea	Ciba-Geigy	Shell T&T	General Electric	Philip Morris
Sime Darby†	Gencor	Iberduero	Sandvik	Schweiz Bankgesell	British Gas	Merck	Wal-Mart

Source: MSCI   *$ terms   †Malaysia

WORLD Morgan Stanley Capital International's World Index is weighted according to the market value of 1,504 companies in 20 countries. In January 1990 Tokyo-listed companies accounted for the largest share of the index, with a collective weight of 39%. By the end of July 1991, thanks to tight monetary policy, a (slightly) weaker yen and some startling financial scandals, this had fallen to 30%. American firms' share of the global equity market rose from 31% to 37%, helped in recent months by better company results and signs of economic recovery. Europe's share of the market increased from 24% to 28% (Britain's share increased from 8.0% to 10.7%). Despite falling early in 1991, by September 3rd 1991 the world index stood 8.2% higher in dollar terms than a year before.

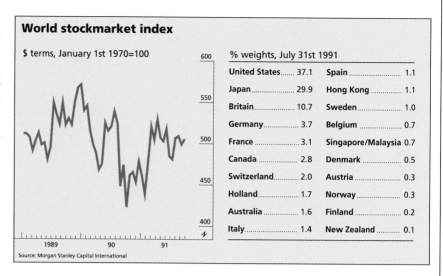

World stockmarket index

$ terms, January 1st 1970=100

% weights, July 31st 1991			
United States	37.1	Spain	1.1
Japan	29.9	Hong Kong	1.1
Britain	10.7	Sweden	1.0
Germany	3.7	Belgium	0.7
France	3.1	Singapore/Malaysia	0.7
Canada	2.8	Denmark	0.5
Switzerland	2.0	Austria	0.3
Holland	1.7	Norway	0.3
Australia	1.6	Finland	0.2
Italy	1.4	New Zealand	0.1

Source: Morgan Stanley Capital International

NEW YORK The Dow Jones industrial average, New York's main share-price benchmark, was first calculated in 1884, when it was based on just 11 shares. By 1928 it had grown to cover 30 shares, its present size. Strictly, the Dow is not an average (nor even an index), though it began as a simple average of the prices of the shares it covered. As more companies were included and others dropped out, this average value had to be "adjusted" to provide continuity; an adjustment of this sort is now done every day. Although service firms form a growing slice of the American economy, the Dow continues to include mostly industrial shares. Food and financial companies account for just 15.2% of the index; chemicals and drugs firms represent 16.7%.

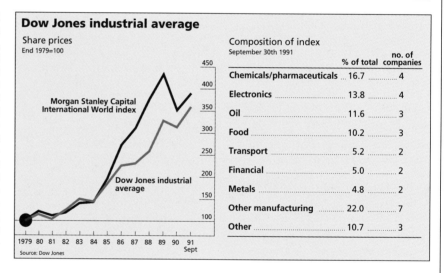

Dow Jones industrial average

Share prices
End 1979=100

Morgan Stanley Capital International World index

Dow Jones industrial average

Composition of index September 30th 1991	% of total	no. of companies
Chemicals/pharmaceuticals	16.7	4
Electronics	13.8	4
Oil	11.6	3
Food	10.2	3
Transport	5.2	2
Financial	5.0	2
Metals	4.8	2
Other manufacturing	22.0	7
Other	10.7	3

Source: Dow Jones

LONDON Britain has the world's third-largest stockmarket by value (behind New York and Tokyo). It has several share-price indices, but the best known is the Financial Times-Stock Exchange 100 Share Index (FT-SE 100). It is a capitalisation-weighted, arithmetic index of the share prices of the 100 largest British companies, which account for about 70% of London's total market capitalisation. The FT-SE 100 can be calculated more rapidly and hence more frequently (every minute) than can wider indices, such as the FT-Actuaries All-Share Index which covers 661 companies. The index started with a base of 1,000 on December 30th 1983, and its constituents are reviewed every three months. In the eight years since 1983, the FT-SE 100 has increased by 196% in dollar terms.

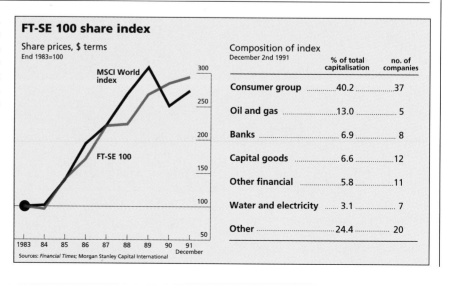

FT-SE 100 share index

Share prices, $ terms
End 1983=100

MSCI World index

FT-SE 100

Composition of index December 2nd 1991	% of total capitalisation	no. of companies
Consumer group	40.2	37
Oil and gas	13.0	5
Banks	6.9	8
Capital goods	6.6	12
Other financial	5.8	11
Water and electricity	3.1	7
Other	24.4	20

Sources: *Financial Times*; Morgan Stanley Capital International

INVESTMENT RETURNS Where would investors have enjoyed the best return on their money over the past decade? Of the markets shown in the chart, the answer is Dutch equities. If somebody had invested $100 in Dutch shares in 1981 it would have been worth a princely $599 (assuming reinvestment of dividends) in 1990. In real dollar terms (deflating by America's consumer-price index) Dutch equities yielded an annual average return of 14.2% over the period, just a whisker ahead of the 13.9% average real return on Japanese shares. In all but three countries, equities performed better than government bonds or cash (bank deposits). The exceptions—Italy, Canada and Australia—all had high interest rates which tended to favour bonds and cash.

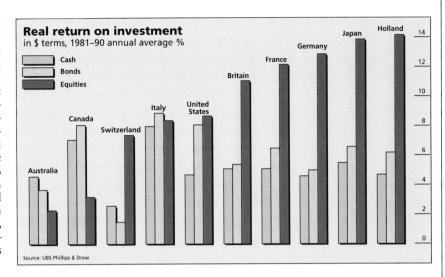

Real return on investment
in $ terms, 1981–90 annual average %

Cash
Bonds
Equities

Source: UBS Phillips & Drew

WAR In the three months after the start of the Gulf war on January 17th 1991, stockmarkets boomed. New York and Tokyo both gained 19% in local-currency terms; London rose 23%. But the biggest rises were in the small, emerging markets. Best of all was Argentina, up by 208% in the three months, thanks to tougher economic policies. The government had make the austral, the country's currency, fully convertible and promised to prevent it falling below a given rate. All the other emerging markets in the chart rose by more than half, with the exception of South Korea, where economic woes and a bribery scandal held back prices. Tight fiscal policy and an IMF loan helped the Philippines' market rise by 81%, more than making up for its sharp fall in 1990.

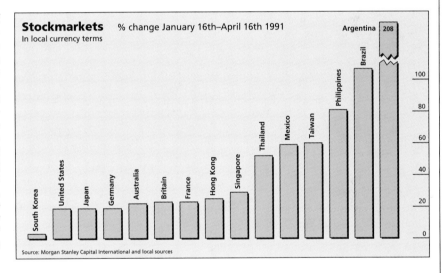

Stockmarkets   % change January 16th–April 16th 1991
In local currency terms

Source: Morgan Stanley Capital International and local sources

COMPANY DIVIDENDS Why do some firms pay bigger dividends to their shareholders than others? According to a study by Kleinwort Benson there are striking national differences in dividend pay-out rates. In November 1991, Japanese and German firms paid shareholders, on average, less than 35% of their profits, American firms paid out 53%, and British ones a huge 70%. These national differences widened during the 1980s; in 1975 the rates were closer—47%, 41%, 48% and 51% respectively. It was in the mid-1970s that America liberalised its financial system; and Britain, where dividend controls had applied in the 1970s, did the same in the mid-1980s: so the rising trend is not surprising. The bigger oddity is why German and Japanese pay-out ratios have fallen so sharply.

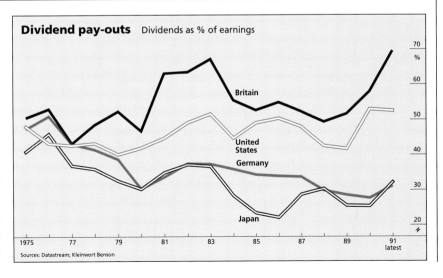

Dividend pay-outs   Dividends as % of earnings

Sources: Datastream; Kleinwort Benson

ECONOMIC AND FINANCIAL INDICATORS
Money supply

Narrow*, % change on year earlier

		Australia	Belgium	Canada	France	Germany	Holland	Italy	Japan	Spain	Sweden	Switzerland	United Kingdom	United States
1990	Jan	-0.9		1.1	7.8	3.1	6.3	11.3	0.5	14.4	na	-5.6	5.7	1.2
	Feb	-1.0		2.5	6.7	3.7	1.1	10.4	0.7	14.6	na	-6.3	6.6	2.0
	Mar	0.6	8.7	-2.1	7.1	2.2	1.6	9.8	0.8	16.3	na	-7.1	6.5	2.6
	Apr	3.4		-0.4	4.7	4.3	4.1	9.6	2.2	21.7	na	-6.4	7.2	3.4
	May	2.3		-2.8	5.7	4.0	nil	8.9	-0.6	23.2	na	-4.2	6.8	4.0
	Jun	3.9	7.8	-2.0	7.3	3.2	2.6	8.4	1.9	25.4	na	-2.6	6.2	4.8
	Jul	5.1		-5.0	3.2	4.0	3.5	7.6	4.9	23.1	na	-4.0	5.6	4.0
	Aug	4.4		-4.0	2.9	5.1	3.2	7.3	2.6	25.2	na	-5.1	4.9	4.7
	Sep	7.3	4.3	-3.9	3.8	5.1	6.7	9.0	3.3	27.1	na	-4.6	4.7	5.0
	Oct	6.2		-3.7	0.8	5.8	5.3	9.2	4.2	26.1	na	-2.9	4.0	4.2
	Nov	6.9		-0.6	0.6	6.0	6.0	8.7	4.4	25.7	na	-3.3	3.2	4.4
	Dec	7.3	2.2	-1.2	3.8	7.0	2.5	7.9	6.2	27.4	na	1.3	2.8	4.0
1991	Jan	9.6		-0.7	-0.4	na	7.1	6.6	5.1	27.8	na	1.3	3.4	3.9
	Feb	7.7		-1.5	1.5	na	11.0	7.5	1.0	29.5	na	2.1	2.6	4.4
	Mar	8.0	4.5	3.5	0.5	na	10.7	8.6	1.2	28.1	na	nil	2.5	4.8
	Apr	5.7		3.3	2.3	na	7.2	6.6	0.3	22.8	na	2.8	1.5	4.3
	May	7.0		4.6	1.2	na	9.9	8.0	3.2	20.8	na	3.4	1.6	5.5
	Jun	6.9	6.3	5.0	-0.3	na	4.6	8.5	6.6	20.0	na	1.0	1.9	5.8
	Jul	8.0		9.6	-0.6	na	4.9	7.4	6.1	18.8	na	3.3	2.1	6.0
	Aug	11.3		7.8	2.7	na	7.4	7.9	7.2	17.9	na	3.8	1.6	6.1
	Sep	8.2	–	8.0	-2.3	na	nil	8.6	7.1	16.3	na	1.0	2.3	5.9
	Oct	9.7		2.5	-2.8	na	1.1	8.5	7.5	16.2	na	–	2.6	7.1
	Nov	–		6.1	–	na	–	–	8.5	16.3	na	–	2.9	8.1
	Dec	–	–	–	–	na	–	–	–	–	na	–	–	–

Broad†, % change on year earlier

		Australia	Belgium	Canada	France	Germany	Holland	Italy	Japan	Spain	Sweden	Switzerland	United Kingdom	United States
1990	Jan	21.3		12.6	10.5	4.4	14.9	10.4	11.5	9.5	10.9	5.0	18.2	3.4
	Feb	20.1		12.1	9.4	4.4	11.8	10.9	11.8	8.9	9.6	4.0	17.9	3.5
	Mar	19.4	12.7	10.3	9.0	4.2	13.1	10.0	11.6	8.9	9.2	3.0	17.7	3.1
	Apr	18.2		10.8	8.4	4.0	13.8	9.9	13.2	9.1	8.1	2.6	17.5	3.0
	May	16.9		10.2	8.2	3.8	8.9	9.4	13.2	9.0	8.6	1.7	17.0	2.9
	Jun	14.3	9.2	9.8	9.3	4.2	9.2	8.8	12.6	9.1	8.2	1.3	16.9	2.6
	Jul	11.1		9.4	8.1	3.9	8.9	8.6	12.2	8.6	8.0	1.1	16.6	2.1
	Aug	10.7		9.0	7.9	3.9	8.7	8.3	11.9	8.9	7.4	1.3	15.6	2.3
	Sep	12.3	6.8	8.9	8.0	4.7	10.9	9.1	12.0	8.8	8.0	2.2	14.8	2.3
	Oct	11.7		9.0	7.7	5.2	9.3	10.0	11.8	9.0	5.8	1.9	14.2	2.0
	Nov	12.2		8.1	7.7	5.6	9.1	9.8	9.9	9.7	6.1	1.9	14.4	1.7
	Dec	12.0	4.5	8.0	9.2	5.3	6.4	9.9	8.5	11.7	10.5	2.8	12.3	1.4
1991	Jan	9.9		8.2	7.5	1.6**	7.1	8.2	7.4	12.5	6.2	2.7	11.2	1.5
	Feb	8.3		8.6	8.0	3.5	8.5	8.5	5.5	13.5	6.8	2.9	10.7	2.1
	Mar	8.0	3.1	8.9	7.9	4.3	7.6	8.9	5.1	14.0	9.5	3.2	9.8	2.2
	Apr	6.6		8.0	7.8	3.4	4.8	8.1	3.8	13.3	8.2	3.6	9.7	2.1
	May	7.1		7.9	7.2	3.5	9.0	8.1	3.6	12.7	10.2	4.0	9.3	2.2
	Jun	6.4	5.4	7.5	6.4	3.3	3.1	8.9	3.7	11.9	11.2	3.9	7.8	2.0
	Jul	6.1		7.3	6.5	3.7	4.5	8.7	3.4	11.9	12.0	4.3	7.8	1.5
	Aug	4.9		6.0	6.9	4.2	7.0	8.5	2.7	11.5	10.7	3.7	7.2	1.1
	Sep	4.0	–	5.8	5.8	4.5	1.0	7.8	2.2	12.3	12.0	2.6	6.5	0.8
	Oct	3.6		6.1	4.7	4.7	2.8	7.9	2.1	12.7	13.2	–	6.3	0.9
	Nov	–		6.3	–	5.1	–	–	2.5	13.0	11.4	–	5.6	1.0
	Dec	–	–	–	–	–	–	–	–	–	–	–	–	–

* M1 except UK M0   † M3 except Belgium, Holland, Italy M2, Japan M2 plus CDs, Spain M3 plus other liquid assets, UK M4   **Western Germany up to December 1990. Total Germany from January 1991: monthly figures show % change from 4th quarter 1990 at annual rate.

Interest rates: money market

Overnight, %, last Tuesday of month

		Australia	Belgium	Canada	France	Germany	Holland	Italy	Japan	Spain	Sweden	Switzerland	United Kingdom	United States
1990	Jan	18.00	10.38	13.88	10.69	7.55	8.63	12.75	6.47	15.02	12.40	9.25	12.50	8.19
	Feb	16.45	10.38	14.00	10.25	7.80	8.75	13.00	6.56	15.17	15.25	9.00	13.73	8.25
	Mar	16.50	10.25	13.13	10.19	7.50	7.94	13.13	6.88	14.52	14.35	9.50	13.88	8.25
	Apr	15.15	10.00	13.50	9.63	7.85	7.63	12.38	7.09	14.53	13.35	9.75	14.94	8.19
	May	15.00	10.13	14.00	9.88	7.90	7.81	11.75	7.19	14.67	12.25	8.75	15.50	8.25
	Jun	15.05	9.75	13.50	9.88	7.85	7.56	11.63	7.34	14.73	12.00	8.78	14.88	8.31
	Jul	15.15	9.50	13.50	9.69	8.05	8.33	11.50	7.41	14.38	12.15	8.88	14.94	8.00
	Aug	14.05	9.00	13.13	9.88	8.00	8.13	11.38	7.41	14.74	12.40	7.75	15.19	8.00
	Sep	14.15	9.25	12.88	9.81	8.00	8.00	10.13	7.63	14.66	12.40	8.00	14.69	8.25
	Oct	13.10	8.00	12.25	9.75	8.05	8.15	10.13	7.81	14.68	16.30	8.00	14.06	7.25
	Nov	13.05	8.88	12.88	9.81	8.15	8.53	11.25	7.94	14.71	14.35	8.25	12.31	7.91
	Dec	12.00	9.88	12.00	9.88	8.50	9.56	12.75	8.12	14.80	14.50	8.75	13.62	7.25
1991	Jan	12.10	9.75	11.75	10.06	8.50	9.00	12.75	8.06	14.42	13.35	8.00	14.00	6.00
	Feb	12.00	9.10	10.25	9.19	8.70	8.84	13.13	8.19	14.57	12.25	7.44	14.00	5.50
	Mar	12.10	8.70	9.75	9.75	8.95	9.19	12.13	8.19	13.63	12.25	9.00	13.38	6.13
	Apr	11.50	8.30	9.44	9.25	8.85	9.16	11.75	8.16	13.21	12.10	8.38	8.63	5.94
	May	10.40	8.75	9.25	10.00	8.95	8.94	10.88	7.88	12.80	11.25	8.00	11.50	5.88
	Jun	10.50	8.75	8.75	10.13	8.85	8.72	10.88	7.94	12.81	10.15	7.75	10.31	5.81
	Jul	10.50	8.75	8.88	9.56	9.00	8.81	11.50	7.41	12.65	10.10	7.63	11.13	5.69
	Aug	10.55	8.90	8.50	9.06	9.15	9.06	11.13	7.44	12.59	10.10	8.00	10.63	5.50
	Sep	9.50	9.00	9.00	9.25	9.10	9.06	11.00	6.81	12.59	9.90	8.00	10.38	5.25
	Oct	9.20	9.10	9.00	8.93	9.10	9.19	10.75	6.69	12.39	10.60	8.13	9.00	5.11
	Nov	8.55	9.10	7.38	9.81	9.10	9.06	11.13	6.25	12.58	10.55	7.75	11.00	4.94
	Dec	8.50	9.30	7.75	10.50	9.50	9.88	12.63	5.72	12.73	14.25	8.50	10.00	4.09

Three-month, %, last Tuesday of month

		Australia	Belgium	Canada	France	Germany	Holland	Italy	Japan	Spain	Sweden	Switzerland	United Kingdom	United States
1990	Jan	17.33	10.40	12.55	10.75	8.20	8.80	14.00	6.17	15.42	12.95	9.63	15.06	8.13
	Feb	16.23	10.40	13.30	10.63	8.30	8.95	13.75	6.25	15.56	15.25	9.19	15.09	8.16
	Mar	15.36	10.30	13.30	10.31	8.30	8.55	13.25	6.43	15.22	14.95	9.13	15.25	8.30
	Apr	15.08	10.20	13.65	9.63	8.15	8.65	12.50	6.67	14.97	13.90	9.50	15.22	8.33
	May	15.00	9.85	13.90	9.69	8.30	8.20	12.63	6.87	14.98	13.25	8.75	15.09	8.16
	Jun	15.11	9.40	13.70	9.88	8.20	8.22	11.50	6.86	15.00	12.65	8.81	14.94	8.15
	Jul	14.76	9.25	13.30	9.56	8.15	8.20	12.00	7.06	14.97	12.90	8.88	15.00	7.88
	Aug	13.73	9.15	13.04	10.15	8.38	8.50	11.75	7.20	15.05	13.70	8.63	14.94	8.03
	Sep	13.61	8.95	12.48	10.05	8.31	8.44	11.13	7.47	15.12	13.30	8.19	14.91	8.09
	Oct	12.75	9.06	12.47	9.81	8.50	8.46	11.75	7.55	14.95	17.00	8.19	13.81	7.85
	Nov	12.45	8.95	12.19	9.88	8.75	8.84	13.88	7.58	14.99	15.55	8.75	13.41	7.91
	Dec	12.00	10.05	12.00	10.00	9.25	9.48	13.88	7.61	15.29	14.90	9.13	14.03	8.14
1991	Jan	11.85	9.86	10.70	10.06	9.13	9.18	13.63	7.64	15.04	14.20	8.13	13.88	6.92
	Feb	11.70	9.32	9.95	9.38	8.94	8.96	13.50	7.62	14.59	13.00	8.00	13.00	6.60
	Mar	11.60	9.41	9.78	9.38	9.13	9.12	12.50	7.65	13.28	13.55	8.56	12.50	6.29
	Apr	11.20	9.25	9.32	9.15	9.06	9.17	12.13	7.57	13.45	12.42	8.44	11.69	5.92
	May	10.00	8.92	8.90	9.25	8.88	9.03	11.63	7.46	12.46	11.35	8.13	11.44	5.91
	Jun	10.50	9.25	8.70	9.94	8.94	9.11	11.75	7.41	12.55	10.65	7.88	11.25	6.11
	Jul	9.90	9.31	8.90	9.58	9.25	9.22	12.00	7.08	12.91	10.67	7.88	11.13	6.00
	Aug	10.25	9.20	8.00	9.69	9.20	9.27	12.13	7.00	12.62	10.82	8.00	10.81	5.74
	Sep	9.50	9.26	8.42	9.44	9.20	9.26	11.88	6.47	12.35	10.28	8.06	10.31	5.52
	Oct	8.50	9.40	7.88	9.06	9.35	9.34	11.50	6.15	12.64	10.77	8.44	10.47	5.31
	Nov	8.10	9.50	7.44	9.68	9.40	9.41	10.15	6.19*	12.82	11.42	8.06	10.69	4.94
	Dec	7.35	9.75	7.25	10.25	9.55	9.68	13.19	5.75*	13.02	13.38	8.31	10.94	4.45

*New series. Sources: Banco Bilbao Vizcaya, Chase Manhattan, Banque de Commerce (Belgium), Credit Lyonnais, Bank Nederland, Royal Bank of Canada, Svenska Handelsbanken, Westpac Banking Corp, CSFB, The WEFA Group. These rates cannot be construed as offers by these banks.

Interest rates: prime

The prime rate is charged by banks for short-term loans to their best business customers. It is the key commercial borrowing rate in America, making headlines when altered, usually because of changes in the discount rate the Federal Reserve charges for lending to banks. In other countries it is more an indicative rate for business loans. In Belgium, Germany, Holland, Italy and Switzerland it is the rate charged to prime business customers for overdrafts. Britain's is banks' base rate plus 1%. During 1990 rates for most of the countries in the table changed little. Many fell in 1991, particularly in countries affected by recession. At the end of January 1990, America's rate was 10%; by the end of December 1991, it had fallen to 6.5%, the lowest since 1987. Over the same period, Australia's drop ped from 20% to 12.5%, Canada's from 13.5% to 8.0%, Britain's from 16% to 11.5%, and Italy's from 14.0% to 12.6%. Buoyant Germany's rate rose from 10.5% to 11.3%

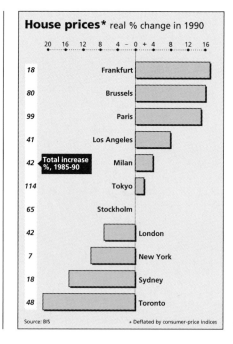

House prices* real % change in 1990

18	Frankfurt
80	Brussels
99	Paris
41	Los Angeles
42	Milan (Total increase %, 1985-90)
114	Tokyo
65	Stockholm
42	London
7	New York
18	Sydney
48	Toronto

Source: BIS   * Deflated by consumer-price indices

HOUSE PRICES Real property prices boomed in most of the world's rich cities during the second half of the 1980s, led by Tokyo with a cumulative gain of 114%, according to the BIS's 1991 annual report. Cities in continental Europe fared well too, with prices in Paris almost doubling over the five years to 1990, and in Brussels rising by 80%. New York saw a cumul   a tive gain of only 7%. Households in the four English-speaking economies–America, Australia, Britain and Canada–should be feeling poorer; average prices for 1990 dropped 21% in real terms in Toronto, 15% in Sydney, 10% in New York, and 7% in London. On the other hand, house prices remained buoyant in Los Angeles, rising in real terms by 8% on top of a 30% increase in 1985-89, a reminder that the United States is still a collection of regional economies, not a single national one. In Frankfurt, demand created by east German workers encouraged a leap

Commercial banks' prime-lending rates, %

Last Tuesday of month

		Australia	Belgium	Canada	France	Germany	Holland	Italy	Japan	Spain	Sweden	Switzerland	United Kingdom	United States
1990	Jan	20.00	12.75	13.50	11.00	10.50	10.75	14.00	6.25	16.25	13.00	11.25	16.00	10.00
	Feb	19.50	13.25	14.25	11.00	10.50	10.75	14.00	6.25	16.25	13.00	11.00	16.00	10.00
	Mar	19.50	13.25	14.25	11.00	10.50	10.75	14.00	6.25	16.25	15.50	11.25	16.00	10.00
	Apr	18.75	13.25	14.75	10.80	10.50	10.75	14.00	6.25	16.25	15.50	12.25	16.00	10.00
	May	18.75	13.25	14.75	10.50	10.50	10.25	14.00	7.13	16.25	14.00	10.75	16.00	10.00
	Jun	18.75	13.25	14.25	10.50	10.50	10.25	13.00	7.13	16.25	14.00	11.00	16.00	10.00
	Jul	18.25	13.25	14.75	10.50	10.50	10.25	13.00	7.13	16.25	13.50	11.00	16.00	10.00
	Aug	17.75	12.75	14.25	10.50	10.50	10.25	13.00	7.38	16.25	13.50	9.38	16.00	10.00
	Sep	17.00	12.75	13.75	10.50	10.50	10.25	13.00	8.00	16.25	13.50	9.88	16.00	10.00
	Oct	16.00	12.75	13.75	10.35	10.50	10.25	13.00	8.00	16.25	13.50	9.88	15.00	10.00
	Nov	16.00	12.75	13.25	10.15	10.50	10.50	13.00	8.00	16.25	15.00	10.25	15.00	10.00
	Dec	15.50	13.25	13.00	10.15	10.50	10.50	13.00	8.00	16.25	15.00	10.50	15.00	10.00
1991	Jan	15.50	13.25	12.25	10.15	10.50	10.50	13.00	8.25	16.50	14.00	10.25	15.00	9.50
	Feb	15.50	13.25	11.25	10.15	10.50	11.00	13.50	8.25	16.50	13.50	10.13	14.00	9.00
	Mar	15.50	12.75	11.25	10.15	10.50	11.00	13.50	8.25	16.50	13.00	10.88	13.50	9.00
	Apr	15.00	12.50	10.25	10.15	10.50	11.00	13.50	7.88	16.50	13.00	10.63	13.00	8.50
	May	14.25	12.75	9.75	10.15	10.50	11.00	12.88	7.88	16.50	13.00	10.13	12.50	8.50
	Jun	14.25	12.75	9.75	10.15	10.50	11.00	12.50	7.88	16.00	12.00	9.75	12.50	8.50
	Jul	14.25	12.75	9.75	10.15	10.50	11.00	12.50	7.63	16.00	12.00	9.38	12.00	8.50
	Aug	14.25	12.75	9.75	10.15	11.50	11.25	12.50	7.63	16.00	12.00	10.63	12.00	8.50
	Sep	14.25	12.75	9.50	10.15	11.50	11.25	12.50	16.00	12.00	10.13	11.50	8.00	8.00
	Oct	13.50	12.75	8.75	10.00	11.50	11.25	12.50	7.00	16.00	12.00	10.00	11.50	8.00
	Nov	12.50	12.75	8.50	10.00	11.00	11.25	12.50	6.63	16.00	12.00	9.88	11.50	7.50
	Dec	12.50	12.75	8.00	10.35	11.25	11.75	12.63	6.63	16.00	14.50	10.13	11.50	6.50

Interest rates: bank deposits

The table below lists indicative interest rates which commercial banks offer customers for deposits of large sums for three months' duration. Unlike regular deposits, the money is not available on demand; the customer must wait until maturity or pay a penalty for early withdrawal. In compensation the banks offer rates close to money-market interest rates. The Australian, Swedish, British and American rates are for certificates of deposit (CDs), an investment instrument which started in New York in the 1960s and is popular with commercial customers because it can be traded in secondary markets run by the banks themselves and, discount houses. Because they are too large to be covered by deposit insurance, CDs are viewed as a slightly riskier investment than government-guaranteed Treasury bills and consequently offer higher rates of interest. In December 1991 Japan had the lowest deposit rates, Sweden the highest.

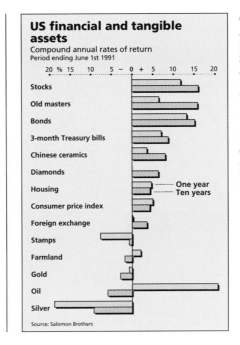

US financial and tangible assets
Compound annual rates of return
Period ending June 1st 1991

Stocks
Old masters
Bonds
3-month Treasury bills
Chinese ceramics
Diamonds
Housing — One year / Ten years
Consumer price index
Foreign exchange
Stamps
Farmland
Gold
Oil
Silver

Source: Salomon Brothers

CAPITAL RETURNS Oil and bonds were a better investment than equities in the 12 months to June 1st 1991, according to Salomon Brothers' league table of American investments. Oil, helped by events in the Gulf, jumped by 20.7% in the year and bonds yielded a total return of 13.2%. But precious metals and collectibles like paintings and ceramics did badly compared with their ten-year performances. Old masters were up by just 6.5% on a year earlier, diamonds were unchanged, and the value of stamps fell by 7.7%. The worst investment was silver, down by 18.9% during the year, while gold fell by 0.7%. Over the past decade, shares topped the league, with a compound annual return of 16%, a whisker ahead of old masters (15.8%) and bonds (15.2%). Housing barely outperformed inflation with an annual average return of 4.4%. The worst investments of the past ten years were silver and oil, offering negative annual returns of 9.3% and 5.9%.

Three-month commercial-bank deposits, %

Last Tuesday of month

		Australia	Belgium	Canada	France	Germany	Holland	Italy	Japan	Spain	Sweden	Switzerland	United Kingdom	United States
1990	Jan	17.00	10.25	12.50	10.94	7.46	8.80	na	2.04	7.25	12.90	9.00	15.06	8.19
	Feb	16.23	10.25	13.25	10.81	7.55	8.95	na	2.04	7.25	14.95	8.25	15.09	8.24
	Mar	15.36	10.05	13.30	10.44	7.55	8.55	na	2.04	7.25	14.70	8.38	15.25	8.35
	Apr	15.08	10.10	13.65	9.81	7.42	8.65	na	2.04	7.25	13.70	8.75	15.19	8.50
	May	15.00	9.65	13.85	9.88	7.55	8.20	na	3.63	7.25	13.15	8.25	15.06	8.28
	Jun	15.11	9.20	13.70	10.06	7.46	8.22	na	3.63	7.25	12.50	8.06	14.88	8.28
	Jul	14.76	9.15	13.30	9.94	7.42	8.20	na	3.63	7.25	12.65	8.06	15.00	7.83
	Aug	13.73	9.05	12.90	10.31	7.62	8.50	na	3.63	7.25	13.60	8.13	14.88	8.04
	Sep	13.61	8.70	12.48	10.38	7.56	8.44	na	4.08	7.25	13.25	7.56	14.88	8.25
	Oct	12.75	8.94	12.47	9.94	7.74	8.46	na	4.08	7.25	15.75	7.06	13.81	7.96
	Nov	12.45	8.90	12.19	10.00	7.96	8.84	na	4.08	7.25	14.99	8.00	13.38	8.31
	Dec	12.00	9.75	11.75	10.19	8.42	9.48	na	4.08	7.25	14.10	8.38	14.00	8.13
1991	Jan	12.00	9.60	10.70	10.19	8.30	9.18	na	4.08	7.25	12.79	7.50	13.88	6.95
	Feb	11.70	9.05	9.95	9.56	8.14	8.96	na	4.08	9.50	11.74	7.25	12.97	6.67
	Mar	11.60	9.50	9.78	9.50	8.31	9.12	na	4.08	9.50	12.43	7.69	12.41	6.33
	Apr	11.20	9.15	9.30	9.28	8.30	9.17	na	4.08	9.50	12.40	7.69	11.69	5.90
	May	10.00	8.75	8.90	9.38	8.08	9.03	na	4.08	9.50	11.25	7.63	11.38	5.88
	Jun	10.50	9.25	8.70	9.81	8.13	9.11	na	4.08	9.00	10.65	7.13	11.25	6.04
	Jul	9.90	9.38	9.00	9.75	8.42	9.22	na	4.08	8.50	10.60	7.88	11.06	5.90
	Aug	10.25	9.05	8.56	9.44	8.37	9.27	na	3.75	8.50	10.70	7.50	10.81	5.66
	Sep	9.50	9.31	7.25	9.31	8.37	9.26	na	3.75	8.50	10.35	7.31	10.28	5.39
	Oct	8.50	9.20	7.00	9.16	8.51	9.34	na	3.75	8.50	11.10	7.69	10.44	5.28
	Nov	8.10	9.40	7.00	9.68	8.55	9.41	na	3.25	8.50	11.40	7.31	10.50	4.88
	Dec	7.35	9.50	7.37	10.07	8.69	9.68	na	2.75	8.50	13.55	7.56	10.88	4.30

Interest rates: government bonds

Government bonds are a popular investment with the conservative investor because of their guarantee of minimal exposure to the risk of insolvency and a steady income not affected by stockmarket fluctuations. Yields shown in this table are for long-term bonds with maturities ranging from 5 years for Sweden to 30 years for the United States. In Belgium, Canada, Japan and Spain yields are for a single bond; all others are the average of yields for bonds of similar maturity. According to the New York merchant bank Salomon Brothers, the total of central government bonds outstanding for the countries listed below was $4.7 trillion at the end of 1990, just over 40% of all publicly-issued bonds outstanding. In Britain, government bonds comprise 60% of the total bond market. America's government bond market is the world's largest, with $1.7 trillion outstanding at the end of 1990. Japan is second with a total of $1.2 trillion.

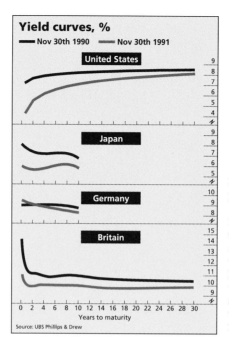

Yield curves, %
— Nov 30th 1990   — Nov 30th 1991
United States
Japan
Germany
Britain
Years to maturity
Source: UBS Phillips & Drew

BOND YIELDS The yield curve compares yields on bonds with different maturities. Long-term yields are usually higher than short rates–ie, the curve is positively sloped–to allow for the risk of holding long-term bonds. But when monetary policy is tightened and short-term interest rates rise, the yield curve inverts. America's yield curve is sloping upwards much more steeply than a year ago, reflecting a loose monetary policy: three-month interest rates are only 4.2%, 30-year bond-yields are 8.1%. Britain's yield curve, by contrast, is still slightly inverted; three-month interest rates are 11.0%, while 30-year bond yields are 9.8%. Germany is the only country where policy is tighter (ie, its curve is more inverted) than a year ago. Long-term bond yields have fallen in all the big economies over the past year, signalling lower inflationary expectations. In the United States, they stood at 7.8% at the end of November 1991, compared with 8.4% in 1990.

Government-bond yields, %

Last Tuesday of month

		Australia	Belgium	Canada	France	Germany	Holland	Italy	Japan	Spain	Sweden	Switzerland	United Kingdom	United States
1990	Jan	12.00	10.35	10.06	9.57	8.05	8.26	12.35	6.55	13.43	13.55	6.10	10.61	8.55
	Feb	13.34	10.97	10.45	10.11	8.95	8.89	12.41	6.94	13.23	14.54	6.45	10.95	8.56
	Mar	13.39	9.93	10.72	9.91	8.80	8.79	12.46	7.34	13.20	14.54	6.50	11.91	8.48
	Apr	14.34	10.09	11.33	9.77	9.00	9.02	12.20	7.38	13.09	14.10	6.63	12.08	8.84
	May	13.45	9.86	10.88	9.68	8.95	8.94	11.67	7.00	12.92	13.55	6.39	11.55	8.67
	Jun	13.57	9.93	10.89	9.80	8.90	8.91	11.23	7.19	13.17	13.05	6.23	11.05	8.49
	Jul	13.18	8.50	10.67	9.58	8.70	8.70	11.24	7.58	13.23	13.20	6.07	11.13	8.48
	Aug	13.56	10.12	10.71	10.18	8.95	9.04	12.23	8.17	13.37	14.09	6.59	11.79	9.17
	Sep	13.73	10.40	11.23	10.49	9.05	9.28	11.53	8.68	13.27	13.86	6.60	11.49	9.13
	Oct	13.35	10.05	11.14	10.27	9.03	9.18	11.47	7.70	13.04	13.85	6.54	11.25	8.76
	Nov	12.18	10.01	10.49	10.05	9.00	9.08	11.88	7.41	12.98	13.29	6.57	10.75	8.42
	Dec	12.06	10.05	10.25	10.00	8.94	9.16	11.86	7.08	14.03	12.58	6.61	10.68	8.25
1991	Jan	11.61	9.82	10.04	9.55	8.94	8.97	12.06	6.75	14.30	11.71	6.42	10.16	8.24
	Feb	11.47	9.21	9.67	9.04	8.40	8.57	11.90	6.43*	13.63	11.19	6.25	9.98	8.04
	Mar	11.38	9.40	9.75	9.13	8.55	8.74	11.64	6.55	12.68	11.69	6.14	10.18	8.31
	Apr	10.97	9.28	9.71	8.70	8.50	8.65	11.18	6.73	12.27	11.30	6.06	10.13	8.18
	May	10.45	9.16	9.89	8.87	8.40	8.55	11.15	6.66	11.54	10.49	5.89	10.22	8.28
	Jun	11.31	9.51	10.28	9.23	8.65	8.67	11.55	6.83	12.06	10.71	5.96	10.44	8.51
	Jul	11.00	9.61	10.13	9.25	8.90	8.89	11.93	6.59	12.44	10.71	6.01	10.06	8.40
	Aug	10.65	9.52	10.00	9.10	8.76	8.84	11.58	6.46	11.79	10.54	6.53	9.86	8.12
	Sep	10.41	9.38	9.63	8.89	8.68	8.80	11.20	5.99	11.32	10.03	6.12	9.44	7.88
	Oct	9.78	9.36	9.25	8.79	8.66	8.80	11.07	5.87	11.65	10.10	6.77	9.59	7.89
	Nov	9.81	9.40	9.29	8.94	8.58	8.76	11.03	6.40	11.97	9.88	6.67	9.83	7.95
	Dec	9.50	9.18	8.98	8.72	8.47	8.60	11.23	5.38	11.74	9.94	6.40	9.60	7.45

* New series

Interest rates: corporate bonds

Corporations issue bonds to borrow money on terms which are often more favourable than those offered by banks. Unlike shareholders, investors buying the bonds do not have voting rights; however, corporate bonds do offer the guarantee of a steady stream of income, or should the corporation go bankrupt, a place in the queue of creditors. Corporations can issue bonds in both the domestic and overseas markets. Yields in this table are for domestic bonds, and for most countries represent the average for a sample of bonds of similar maturity. But in Belgium, Canada and Spain a single bond's yield is quoted. Maturities range from six years for Germany to 25 for Britain. Corporate bond yields are usually higher in countries with high inflation rates. Investors also usually demand higher yields on corporate bonds than on government bonds because of the greater perceived risk of default.

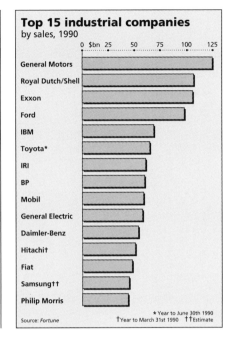

Top 15 industrial companies
by sales, 1990

General Motors
Royal Dutch/Shell
Exxon
Ford
IBM
Toyota*
IRI
BP
Mobil
General Electric
Daimler-Benz
Hitachi†
Fiat
Samsung††
Philip Morris

Source: Fortune

* Year to June 30th 1990
†Year to March 31st 1990 ††Estimate

INDUSTRIAL COMPANIES In 1990 General Motors (GM) remained the world's largest industrial company, with sales of $125 billion. GM's turnover rose by nearly a third from 1985—when GM was also placed first. According to the annual survey published by America's *Fortune* magazine in July 1991, the Anglo-Dutch Royal Dutch/Shell group climbed from fourth to second place, with sales up by a quarter since 1989. But America's Exxon was breathing down its neck. Ford, in fourth place, was not far behind, with sales of $98 billion. America's IBM, in fifth place, was still lagging well behind the top four industrial companies: its sales were little more than half GM's. Seven of the world's 15 biggest industrial companies were American, five are European, and the remaining three Asian. The largest Japanese firm, Toyota, was ranked only sixth in the league. South Korea's Samsung moved from 20th place in 1989 to 14th in 1990.

Corporate-bond yields, %

Last Tuesday of month

		Australia	Belgium	Canada	France	Germany	Holland	Italy	Japan	Spain	Sweden	Switzerland	United Kingdom	United States
1990	Jan	13.00	10.35	10.83	10.37	8.10	8.85	11.81	6.79	14.45	14.28	6.85	12.63	9.23
	Feb	14.46	10.81	11.25	10.99	8.95	9.67	12.06	6.94	14.30	15.35	7.04	12.97	9.33
	Mar	14.52	9.91	11.50	10.70	8.80	9.61	12.15	7.44	14.18	15.45	7.11	13.70	9.43
	Apr	14.91	10.12	12.27	10.41	9.60	9.54	12.09	7.56	14.08	15.13	7.07	13.95	9.50
	May	14.68	9.91	11.63	10.25	8.95	9.56	12.17	7.23	13.12	14.54	6.99	13.07	9.50
	Jun	14.62	9.97	11.63	10.39	8.90	9.40	12.05	7.01	13.57	14.38	6.77	12.80	9.39
	Jul	14.27	9.63	11.46	10.23	8.70	9.24	11.71	7.48	14.30	14.22	6.69	12.50	9.29
	Aug	14.52	10.09	11.70	10.56	8.95	9.41	12.43	8.14	14.25	15.08	7.02	12.92	9.65
	Sep	14.55	10.31	11.99	11.25	9.05	9.74	12.00	8.59	14.35	14.87	7.13	12.73	9.68
	Oct	14.13	10.05	12.00	10.99	9.03	10.02	11.92	7.88	14.17	14.97	7.11	12.51	9.72
	Nov	13.25	10.02	11.46	10.80	9.00	9.94	12.01	7.85	13.98	14.10	7.22	12.54	9.53
	Dec	13.72	10.14	11.19	10.84	8.95	10.06	12.35	7.60	14.46	14.12	7.26	12.15	9.31
1991	Jan	12.25	9.85	11.02	10.34	8.96	9.98	12.33	7.29	14.46	12.75	7.14	11.89	9.36
	Feb	13.15	9.28	10.69	9.80	8.50	9.51	12.29	7.36	13.73	12.52	6.83	11.42	9.07
	Mar	13.15	9.42	10.62	9.80	8.60	9.48	12.23	7.51	13.36	13.00	6.80	11.44	9.22
	Apr	12.70	9.27	10.64	9.65	8.57	9.37	11.78	7.64	13.91	12.89	6.78	11.43	9.04
	May	12.10	9.13	10.64	9.66	8.42	9.43	11.23	7.60	13.76	11.73	6.62	11.45	9.16
	Jun	13.00	9.52	11.02	9.86	8.75	9.14	11.31	7.77	13.50	11.88	6.60	11.50	9.29
	Jul	12.70	9.63	10.83	9.87	9.05	9.47	11.42	7.44	14.19	11.83	6.66	11.44	9.17
	Aug	12.20	9.53	10.93	9.60	8.91	9.51	11.48	7.26	13.91	11.99	7.08	11.19	8.89
	Sep	11.83	9.45	10.69	9.55	8.79	9.49	11.55	6.56	13.91	11.57	6.77	10.76	8.69
	Oct	11.14	9.43	10.46	9.31	8.76	9.51	11.24	6.17	13.61	11.78	7.04	10.97	8.73
	Nov	11.01	9.49	10.19	9.51	8.71	9.49	11.27	7.86	13.41	11.73	7.08	11.21	8.70
	Dec	10.45	9.35	10.18	9.47	8.61	9.75	11.33	6.12	11.96	12.47	7.03	10.93	8.32

Interest rates: Eurocurrency deposits

A Eurocurrency is any currency deposited and lent ouside its country of origin, for example, D-marks deposited in London are Euromarks. Eurodeposits are always lent for a fixed term, which can vary from overnight to five years. For each currency the rate taken is the mid-point between the bid and offer rates. Since January 1990, the Eurocurrency deposit rates have fallen for all the currencies in our table, except for the Euromark and the Euroguilder. The Eurodollar rate has dropped to almost half its level at the beginning of 1990, reflecting the weakening dollar over the period. The Euroyen rate rose to 8.4% at the end of 1990, but since then has lost more than two percentage points, to 5.6%. Since joining the Exchange Rate Mechanism of the European Monetary System, in October 1990, Eurosterling rates have tumbled by four percentage points. The Euromark rate has risen more than one percentage point since German monetary union, in July 1990.

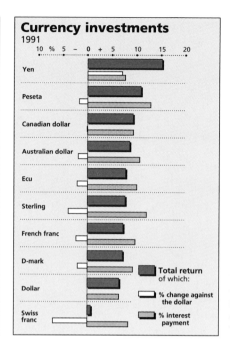

Currency investments
1991

INVESTMENTS An international investor's total return on a currency deposit depends upon both the rate of interest and exchange-rate movements. Armed with a crystal ball, the canny investor would have put his money into yen in 1991. Taking account of the yen's 7% rise against the dollar during the year, together with interest earned (7.6%), $1,000 placed in a three-month Euro-yen deposit account at the start of 1991, then reinvested each quarter, would have been worth $1,151 at the end of December, a 15.1% return. Although the dollar rose against all the other main currencies in 1991, it yielded the second-lowest total return of the currencies in the chart because dollar interest rates were so low, averaging just 6.4%. At the other extreme, cash placed in a Spanish peseta deposit earned 12.8% interest in 1991, to give a total return of 10.8% after taking account of the peseta's slight drop against the dollar.

Three-month Eurocurrency deposit rate, %

Last Tuesday of month

		Australia	Belgium	Canada	France	Germany	Holland	Italy	Japan	Spain	Sweden	Switzerland	United Kingdom	United States
1990	Jan	16.13	10.63	12.63	10.94	8.25	8.56	12.75	7.00	14.75	12.75	9.56	15.06	8.31
	Feb	15.78	10.56	13.13	10.25	8.38	8.94	12.75	7.38	15.70	14.94	9.13	15.13	8.31
	Mar	14.88	10.38	12.88	10.38	8.25	8.50	12.50	7.38	15.56	15.19	9.13	15.28	8.44
	Apr	14.63	10.31	13.25	9.81	8.38	8.50	11.88	7.38	14.50	13.50	9.69	15.22	8.56
	May	14.56	10.81	13.38	9.94	8.44	8.31	11.81	7.38	14.20	12.88	8.75	15.06	8.44
	Jun	14.63	9.81	13.38	9.94	8.13	8.19	11.13	7.44	14.58	12.25	8.81	14.72	8.31
	Jul	14.75	9.38	13.00	9.88	8.25	8.25	11.13	7.75	14.25	12.25	8.88	15.00	7.88
	Aug	13.44	9.25	12.56	10.25	8.38	8.50	11.38	8.06	14.44	13.13	8.56	14.88	8.13
	Sep	13.16	9.00	12.19	10.31	8.38	8.44	10.38	8.31	14.45	13.13	8.19	14.91	8.38
	Oct	12.38	8.00	12.13	10.00	8.63	8.38	10.88	8.25	14.09	14.75	8.13	13.81	8.00
	Nov	12.19	9.13	11.88	9.94	8.94	8.84	12.63	8.38	14.37	14.56	8.75	13.50	8.19
	Dec	11.59	10.13	11.25	10.13	9.25	9.56	12.06	8.38	14.40	14.19	8.69	14.03	7.50
1991	Jan	11.56	9.81	10.44	10.13	9.13	9.06	12.25	8.19	14.25	13.00	8.25	13.91	7.06
	Feb	11.25	9.88	10.56	10.06	9.06	9.13	12.31	8.13	14.20	12.63	8.06	13.63	6.56
	Mar	11.53	9.38	9.44	9.38	9.13	9.13	11.63	8.16	12.95	12.30	8.50	12.44	6.38
	Apr	10.88	9.25	9.00	9.19	9.06	9.19	11.50	8.03	12.81	12.35	8.50	11.84	6.00
	May	10.00	8.88	8.63	9.31	8.94	9.00	11.00	7.72	12.00	11.25	8.13	11.34	6.00
	Jun	10.03	9.25	8.50	9.88	9.00	9.13	11.13	7.84	11.70	10.75	8.00	11.25	6.13
	Jul	10.13	9.25	8.69	9.63	9.31	9.19	11.38	7.41	12.56	10.62	7.88	11.10	6.00
	Aug	10.00	9.25	8.38	9.25	9.13	9.25	11.50	7.28	12.25	10.63	8.13	10.81	5.75
	Sep	9.44	9.19	8.13	9.38	9.19	9.19	11.25	6.50	12.06	10.30	8.13	10.31	5.50
	Oct	8.50	9.25	7.75	9.13	9.44	9.44	11.00	6.28	12.25	10.63	8.44	10.50	5.38
	Nov	7.75	9.44	7.38	9.81	9.38	9.44	11.75	6.19	12.22	11.38	8.13	10.69	4.94
	Dec	7.38	9.56	6.88	10.25	9.56	9.56	12.25	5.63	11.67	13.23	8.13	10.94	4.19

Interest rates: Eurobond yields

A Eurobond is issued by a company, or government, in a market outside that of its currency of denomination and is issued internationally, on the Euromarket, rather than in just one domestic market. The advantage of the Eurobond is that it escapes any national financial regulations. The rates in the table are collated by Crédit Suisse First Boston to represent an average, except for Spain, which is from the Ministry of Economics. Over the past two years bond yields have fallen for most of the countries in the table, as economies slipped into recession. Since January 1990 the yield on Eurodollar bonds has dropped by two percentage points, to 6.22%; most of this fall was in the last six months of 1991 as a result of the deepening recession in the America. Euromark bond yields have remained steady at around 8.5% throughout the year. There are no longer enough issues of Australian dollar Eurobonds to calculate an average.

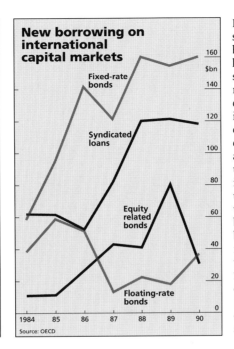

New borrowing on international capital markets

Fixed-rate bonds

Syndicated loans

Equity related bonds

Floating-rate bonds

$bn

160 · 140 · 120 · 100 · 80 · 60 · 40 · 20 · 0

1984 85 86 87 88 89 90

Source: OECD

INTERNATIONAL BORROWING After six years of vigorous expansion, total new borrowing on international capital markets (ie, international bonds and shares, syndicated credits and other instruments) fell sharply in 1990 to $425 billion, down from $467 billion in 1989. Borrowing conditions became increasingly difficult during 1990 as a result of the slowdown in the world economy, concerns about the fragility of the financial systems in America and Japan and the creditworthiness of companies, as well as uncertainty over events in the Gulf and the Soviet Union. The decline in total borrowing was more than accounted for by a sharp drop in new issues of equity-related bonds, the driving force behind the market in 1989. Figures up to August 1991 showed a rebound following the resolution of the Gulf crisis. Fixed-rate bond issues were also looking stronger; syndicated loans and floating-rate bonds were still in the doldrums.

Eurocurrency-bond yields, %

Last Tuesday of month

		Australia	Belgium	Canada	France	Germany	Holland	Italy	Japan	Spain	Sweden	Switzerland	United Kingdom	United States
1990	Jan	14.03	10.43	10.56	10.74	8.22	8.58	11.73	6.53	na	13.58	7.47	12.08	8.65
	Feb	13.75	10.68	11.45	11.09	9.13	9.10	12.17	7.04	na	14.65	7.28	12.46	8.75
	Mar	14.24	10.05	12.19	10.09	8.84	9.19	12.34	7.41	na	14.75	7.41	13.94	9.26
	Apr	14.28	10.06	13.03	9.84	8.86	9.23	12.23	7.33	13.60	14.35	7.28	14.03	9.66
	May	14.71	9.85	11.76	9.58	9.03	9.26	12.04	6.98	13.96	13.78	7.05	12.62	9.42
	Jun	14.62	9.97	12.56	9.88	9.02	9.16	11.68	6.98	13.48	13.27	6.70	12.38	9.13
	Jul	14.66	9.97	12.30	9.71	8.40	8.89	12.37	7.27	13.40	13.34	6.84	12.59	8.69
	Aug	14.73	10.10	12.09	10.42	8.90	9.30	11.77	7.99	14.45	14.02	6.98	12.65	9.15
	Sep	14.01	10.46	12.13	10.57	9.09	9.39	11.72	8.42	14.25	13.43	7.14	12.65	9.24
	Oct	13.90	10.01	12.25	10.53	8.98	9.43	11.46	7.54	14.13	15.12	6.95	11.78	9.01
	Nov	14.20	10.00	11.63	10.25	8.84	9.30	11.26	7.22	13.75	13.60	6.97	11.25	8.25
	Dec	14.42	10.11	11.71	10.21	8.54	9.37	11.19	7.03	13.80	13.20	6.89	11.50	8.34
1991	Jan	11.97	9.87	10.59	9.95	8.88	9.38	11.31	6.80	13.73	12.07	6.96	11.20	8.32
	Feb	11.73	9.22	10.09	9.24	8.34	8.91	11.34	6.56	13.15	11.63	6.35	10.66	7.89
	Mar	12.17	9.42	10.21	9.21	8.26	8.88	11.29	6.87	12.55	11.82	6.67	10.67	8.09
	Apr	na	9.28	10.04	9.06	8.41	8.90	11.25	6.89	12.17	11.82	6.55	10.70	8.14
	May	na	9.21	9.99	8.97	8.31	8.85	10.38	6.86	11.70	10.89	6.36	10.80	8.13
	Jun	na	9.38	10.47	10.80	8.22	8.82	10.92	7.11	12.00	13.98	6.41	10.84	8.80
	Jul	na	9.48	10.28	9.10	8.68	8.91	10.26	6.85	12.06	10.92	6.54	10.59	8.13
	Aug	na	9.34	10.10	9.03	8.71	8.98	10.23	6.54	11.73	10.73	6.54	10.44	7.76
	Sep	na	9.22	9.64	8.83	8.40	8.90	10.25	6.07	11.61	10.61	6.72	10.01	7.40
	Oct	na	9.14	9.01	8.70	8.10	8.90	10.15	5.88	11.36	10.48	7.11	10.05	7.07
	Nov	na	9.22	9.16	8.85	8.08	8.87	10.25	5.92	11.77	10.28	6.86	10.43	6.81
	Dec	na	9.01	8.81	8.79	8.19	8.74	10.23	5.75	11.96	11.48	6.79	10.40	6.22

BANK LENDING Learning from their costly generosity in the 1980s, banks have become cautious. New syndicated loans (those involving a group of banks) totalled just $63 billion in the first eight months of 1991, down by 16% on the same period in 1990. Concern with matching risks to returns led to a sharp increase in spreads. Interest charges to borrowers rose from an average of 59 basis points (hundredths of a percentage point) above LIBOR in January–August 1990 to 79 points in the same period in 1991; average maturities shortened to five years and three months. Despite Eastern Europe's reforms, lenders see the region as an increasingly risky place to do business. Spreads there rose 88 basis points between the first eight months of 1990 and the same period of 1991.

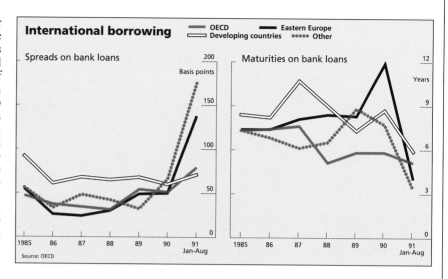

HOME BORROWING According to a Bank of England study published in May 1991, total mortgage debt in Britain rose from 32% of GDP in 1982 to 58% in 1989, by far the highest ratio in the big economies. It is no coincidence that house prices rose faster in Britain in the 1980s (by an average of 5.9% a year in real terms) than elsewhere. America was not far behind, with total mortgage debt equivalent to 45% of GDP in 1989. In the more restricted financial climates of Japan, France, Germany and Italy, mortgage debt ranges between 7% of GDP in Italy and 25% in Japan. In Germany, where mortgage interest payments are not tax-deductible and mortgage loans rarely exceed 60% of the value of a house (compared with 100% in Britain), home prices fell in real terms in the past decade.

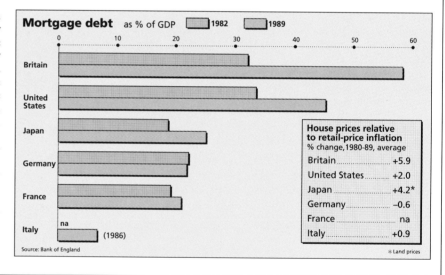

BONDS Government bond markets offered excellent returns for investors in 1991, spurred by weak economic growth, and falling inflation and short-term interest rates. All the markets in the table showed double-digit returns (yield plus capital gains) during the 12 months to December, and, even after adjusting for currency movements, all had dollar returns of more than 9%. The world government bond index compiled by JP Morgan showed a total return of 15.5%. Australia topped the league, with a return of 24.3% in dollar terms; Japan and Canada also posted gains of more than 20%. The European markets lagged behind, as the German Bundesbank tightened its monetary policy. Spanish bonds were Europe's top performer, with a total dollar return of 16.6%.

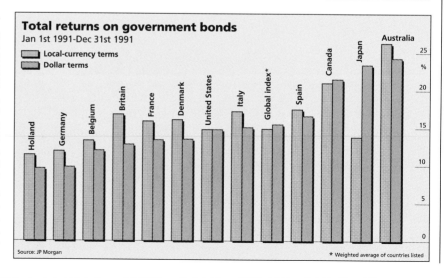

BUDGET DEFICITS America's government has the biggest budget deficit in the world in dollar terms, but its general government deficit (the total of central, state and local government budgets plus social-security balances) is a modest 2.8% of GNP. By contrast, Greece has a deficit of 15.9% of GNP, and Italy's is 10% of GNP. Four countries were expected to have a budget surplus in 1991 (up from three in 1986): Japan, Australia, Sweden and Norway. Japan's, at 2.7% of its GNP, would be the biggest. Norway's budget surplus has fallen from 5.9% in 1986 to an expected 0.1% in 1991. Ireland has seen the biggest improvement in its fiscal position since 1986: its deficit has narrowed from 11.6% of GNP to 2.3%. By contrast, western Germany's deficit has grown from 1.3% of GNP to 5.2%.

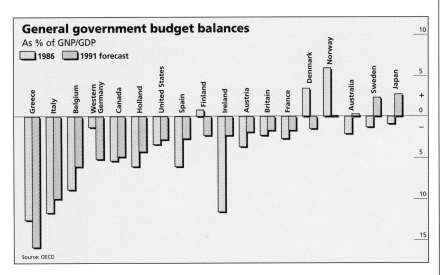

VALUE-ADDED TAX Ireland has the highest standard rate of VAT (23%), while Denmark, whose tax is broader-based, takes the largest slice (22%) of consumer spending. The Japanese are the lowest taxed, with a standard rate of 3%. America has no national sales tax, but some cities and states levy their own. Standard and effective VAT rates vary widely because some countries apply their standard rates to almost all goods, whereas others make wide use of exemptions and reduced rates. Britain "zero-rates" basic goods (such as food), which, all told, account for a quarter of consumer spending—so with a highish standard rate, 17.5%, its effective sales tax is only 10%. Several countries have higher VAT bands, too. Italians pay a tax of 38% on "luxury goods".

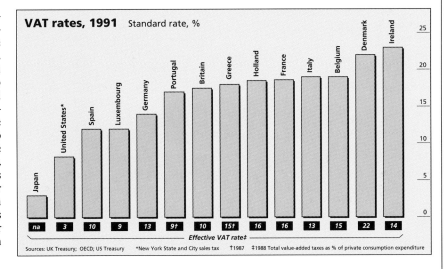

TAX REVENUES The ratio of total tax revenues to GDP is a measure of a country's tax burden. On that basis, Scandinavian countries top the tax league. Sweden has the highest taxes, equivalent to 57.7% of GDP in 1990, up from 49.1% in 1980. A long way behind, in second and third places, are Denmark (48.1% in 1990) and Norway, which was the only country to reduce its tax burden significantly, from 47.1% in 1980 to 46.2% in 1990. Despite the much trumpeted "tax cuts" in the 1980s in America and Britain, the tax burdens of both countries actually increased. Britain's taxes rose from 35.3% of its GDP in 1980 to 36.8% in 1990; America's edged up from 29.5% to 30.1%. America and Australia have the lowest tax burdens among the OECD economies.

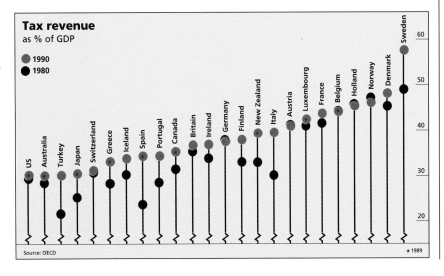

Trade

Australia, France, Canada, Japan, Britain and America measure their visible-trade balance using exports free on board (fob) less imports fob, which means that goods are valued only up to the point of embarkation. Other countries in the table use cost-insurance-freight (cif) for imports; in these countries the valuation of goods imported includes all transport costs and insurance to their destination. Since July 1990, when western and eastern Germany joined to form a monetary union, the visible-trade figures have been for the whole of Germany; its 12-month trade surplus has fallen by more than 80%, to $12.4 billion in October 1991. America's 12-month trade deficit has narrowed to $72.0 billion in October 1991 from $110.4 billion in January 1990. Australia has witnessed the biggest turnaround, from a 12-month visible-trade deficit of $4.3 billion at the beginning of 1990 to a surplus of $3.0 billion in October 1991.

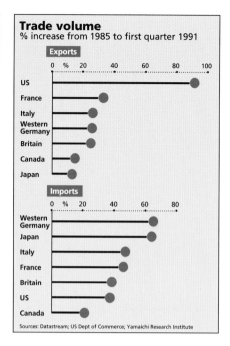

Trade volume
% increase from 1985 to first quarter 1991

Sources: Datastream; US Dept of Commerce; Yamaichi Research Institute

TRADE Which big industrial country had the fastest export growth in the past six years? Neither Japan (which actually had the slowest export growth, at 12%, of the G7 economies) nor western Germany, but America. The volume of its exports surged by 91% between 1985 and the first quarter of 1991, thanks mainly to the 40% fall in the dollar's trade-weighted exchange rate over that period. The second-fastest export growth was in France, up by 32%. Americans complain loudly that Japan does not import enough. Yet the volume of Japan's imports jumped by 63% from 1985 levels —admittedly a low base—as its domestic demand boomed. Of the big economies, only western Germany had faster import growth (64%) over the same period, partly due to a surge in consumer demand in 1990 in the former East Germany. In Britain, imports grew by 38% over the period, whereas exports increased by only 24%.

Trade balances, $bn

12 months to date

		Australia	Belgium	Canada	France	Germany	Holland	Italy	Japan	Spain	Sweden	Switzerland	United Kingdom	United States
1990	Jan	-4.3	1.5	3.5	-6.6	72.9	3.5	-12.3	73.1	-28.5	2.4	-6.9	-40.2	-110.4
	Feb	-3.9	0.8	2.9	-6.9	73.3	3.3	-12.4	69.9	-29.2	2.1	-7.0	-38.9	-107.6
	Mar	-3.8	0.5	3.1	-7.1	73.7	3.4	-12.6	70.0	-29.2	2.1	-6.9	-39.3	-107.3
	Apr	-3.5	-0.7	3.6	-7.2	73.5	3.6	-12.0	65.9	-29.7	2.1	-7.0	-38.9	-106.8
	May	-2.9	-0.4	4.2	-7.1	74.6	2.6	-12.6	63.3	-29.9	2.2	-7.0	-38.0	-104.8
	Jun	-2.5	-0.6	5.4	-7.0	73.3	3.4	-11.0	63.8	-30.6	2.3	-6.8	-37.6	-102.6
	Jul	-2.2	-0.6	5.9	-6.6	73.3	4.1	-10.7	62.1	-31.1	2.2	-6.7	-37.9	-102.8
	Aug	-1.6	-0.6	6.4	-6.2	72.0	4.2	-10.1	61.3	-30.8	2.3	-6.6	-36.7	-102.2
	Sep	-1.1	-0.7	7.5	-8.3	71.0	3.9	-10.3	61.2	-30.9	2.1	-6.6	-34.7	-102.5
	Oct	-0.6	-1.4	8.6	-8.0	71.7	5.4	-11.3	61.6	-31.8	2.1	-6.4	-34.1	-102.6
	Nov	-0.3	-1.6	8.8	-7.9	68.2	5.5	-13.1	61.9	-32.3	2.6	-6.0	-32.6	-102.2
	Dec	-0.1	-1.8	9.4	-9.3	64.6	5.6	-11.7	63.5	-32.1	2.7	-5.9	-32.7	-101.7
1991	Jan	0.5	-2.1	9.5	-10.4	57.7	6.0	-13.0	65.6	-33.2	2.7	-5.5	-31.8	-99.0
	Feb	0.5	-2.1	10.4	-10.8	52.8	6.0	-12.2	67.3	-32.6	3.1	-5.5	-30.7	-97.0
	Mar	1.3	-2.1	10.8	-11.4	47.7	6.6	-10.1	69.9	-32.2	3.3	-5.7	-28.4	-92.5
	Apr	1.2	-1.3	11.1	-11.0	42.2	6.2	-11.2	74.1	-32.6	3.7	-5.7	-26.4	-89.4
	May	1.7	-1.3	11.2	-10.5	35.0	7.3	-11.7	77.0	-32.7	3.6	-5.5	-25.4	-86.0
	Jun	2.0	-1.7	11.0	-10.8	30.0	7.2	-12.4	79.2	-32.1	4.0	-5.7	-23.0	-83.5
	Jul	2.2	-2.2	10.5	-10.7	24.1	6.8	-13.8	82.6	-32.6	4.3	-5.8	-20.6	-80.2
	Aug	3.0	-2.4	10.9	-10.4	21.1	7.2	-13.8	86.8	-32.8	4.4	-5.5	-19.4	-77.4
	Sep	3.1	–	9.7	-9.1	16.2	–	-14.6	89.9	-33.1	4.6	–	-19.5	-75.2
	Oct	3.0	–	8.8	-6.8	12.4	–	-14.4	94.2	-32.6	5.0	–	-18.6	-72.0
	Nov	–	–	–	–	–	–	–	–	–	5.1	–	-18.2	–
	Dec	–	–	–	–	–	–	–	–	–	–	–	–	–

Current account

A country's current-account balance measures both visible and invisible (eg, services such as banking, insurance, tourism and shipping) trade. Since monetary union in July 1990, Germany's figures relate to the whole country. It moved from the widest 12-month current-account surplus in our table, of $57.2 billion at the beginning of 1990, to a $16.0 billion deficit in October 1991. Contributions towards the cost of the Gulf war helped America to record its first current-account surplus since 1982 in the first quarter of 1991. Japan's current-account surplus fell during 1990, but since then rose to $60.5 billion in the 12-months to October, almost twice as big as at the end of 1990. As the recession took hold, Britain's 12-month current-account deficit narrowed to $10.9 billion in November 1991, because dampened consumer demand curbed imports. Switzerland, Holland and Belgium remained in surplus.

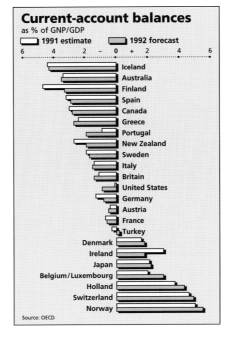

Current-account balances
as % of GNP/GDP
□ 1991 estimate   ▨ 1992 forecast

Iceland, Australia, Finland, Spain, Canada, Greece, Portugal, New Zealand, Sweden, Italy, Britain, United States, Germany, Austria, France, Turkey, Denmark, Ireland, Japan, Belgium/Luxembourg, Holland, Switzerland, Norway

Source: OECD

EXTERNAL BALANCES For years economists had nightmares over America's current-account deficit, but it has been shrinking fast. Indeed, in 1991 it is estimated to have been in rough balance, partly thanks to the transfers from foreign governments to help pay for the Gulf war. The OECD forecast in December 1991 that America's deficit would widen in 1992 to 0.9% of its GDP, but that would still be a fraction of its 1987 peak of 3.5% of GDP. In 1991 Germany had the biggest current-account deficit of any industrial economy, at $21 billion (1.3% of GDP). After doubling in 1991, Japan's current-account surplus is forecast to widen further in 1992, to $82 billion, or 2.2% of GDP. As a percentage of GDP, Norway is forecast to have the biggest current-account surplus (5.5%) in 1992, Iceland the biggest deficit (4.3%). Britain's current-account deficit is forecast to widen in 1992, to 1.4% of its GDP, but that is still well below its peak of 3.9% in 1989.

Current-account balances, $bn

12 months to date

		Australia	Belgium	Canada	France	Germany	Holland	Italy	Japan	Spain	Sweden	Switzerland	United Kingdom	United States
1990	Jan	-18.1				57.2			54.1	-11.7	-3.5		-34.0	
	Feb	-18.0				57.4			51.7	-11.6	-3.7		-33.1	
	Mar	-18.2	3.1	-19.5	-5.0	59.3	8.6	-10.7	53.4	-11.6	-4.3	6.8	-33.9	-101.4
	Apr	-17.8				58.2			48.8	-12.4	-4.3		-34.2	
	May	-17.3				59.0			46.7	-12.7	-4.4		-34.0	
	Jun	-17.0	3.4	-19.2	-6.0	55.4	7.7	-12.7	47.0	-13.4	-4.4	7.2	-34.1	-95.8
	Jul	-16.8				55.0			43.4	-14.0	-5.0		-33.4	
	Aug	-16.3				53.7			40.9	-14.1	-5.2		-31.5	
	Sep	-16.0	3.7	-18.8	-8.1	53.1	9.7	-12.0	39.5	-14.9	-5.9	7.6	-28.7	-93.4
	Oct	-15.5				53.2			38.4	-14.8	-6.3		-27.5	
	Nov	-15.2				48.7			36.0	-14.5	-6.1		-25.6	
	Dec	-15.1	3.7	-18.9	-8.5	47.4	10.4	-14.2	35.8	-15.7	-5.9	8.6	-25.3	-92.1
1991	Jan	-14.4				39.7			36.4	-15.7	-5.9		-24.6	
	Feb	-14.2				33.6			37.6	-16.3	-5.6		-23.7	
	Mar	-13.2	3.6	-18.4	-12.2	22.6	10.2	-12.7	33.7	-16.9	-5.0	9.4	-21.7	-59.0
	Apr	-13.4				17.6			39.5	-16.8	-4.8		-18.7	
	May	-13.0				9.6			42.4	-17.0	-4.9		-16.8	
	Jun	-12.6	3.7	-18.5	-9.9	5.8	11.1	-15.2	44.5	-17.5	-4.7	9.3	-13.6	-33.8
	Jul	-12.4				-0.3			47.6	-17.0	-4.6		-11.8	
	Aug	-11.6				-4.6			52.2	-16.6	-4.3		-11.1	
	Sep	-11.4	–	-20.4	–	-9.7	–	–	56.4	-16.7	-3.6	9.0	-11.8	-20.4
	Oct	-11.4				-16.0			60.5	-16.3	–		-11.3	
	Nov	–				–			–	–	–		-10.9	
	Dec	–	–	–	–	–	–	–	–	–	–		–	

OPEC The aggregate visible-trade surplus of OPEC, the oil producers' cartel, crashed from $171 billion in 1980 to a low of $13 billion in 1986, the result of oil prices slumping from $36 to $13 a barrel. Saudi Arabia, the cartel's biggest producer, saw its trade surplus plunge from a high of $81.9 billion in 1981 to a meagre $3.1 billion in 1986. In August 1990, the Gulf crisis pushed prices back up to $40 a barrel but prices had fallen back to around $19 a barrel a year later. That cut OPEC's trade balance to a forecast $46 billion for 1991. These lower revenues have tipped OPEC's current-account balance (ie, including invisible trade) back into deficit, after a $14 billion surplus in 1990. Saudi Arabia's trade surplus was forecast to be 22.6% of the OPEC total in 1991.

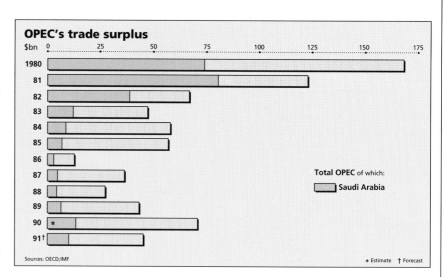

OPEC's trade surplus

Sources: OECD; IMF

Total OPEC of which: Saudi Arabia

* Estimate † Forecast

AID In 1990 the world's rich countries increased their official aid to the third world, by 4% in real terms. In dollar terms it rose to $54.1 billion, from $46.7 billion in 1989. America, Japan and France all increased their aid substantially. Ireland, Britain, Italy, Australia and Sweden all gave less in 1990 than the year before. Compared with 1980, however, America's aid fell, from an already niggardly 0.27% of GDP to 0.21%. Japan, too, gave developing countries a slightly smaller share of its national income in 1990 than in 1980: 0.31% compared with 0.32%. On this measure, the governments of Sweden, Denmark, Holland and Norway have long been the most generous donors. In 1990 Norway topped the list; it gave just over $1 billion, or 1.17% of its GDP.

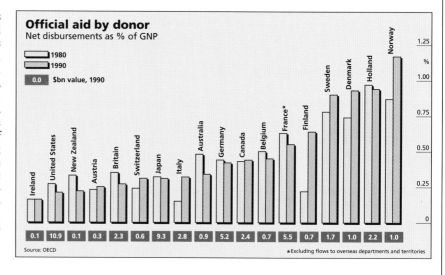

Official aid by donor
Net disbursements as % of GNP

1980
1990
0.0 $bn value, 1990

Source: OECD

Ireland 0.1 | United States 10.9 | New Zealand 0.1 | Austria 0.3 | Britain 2.3 | Switzerland 0.6 | Japan 9.3 | Italy 2.8 | Australia 0.9 | Germany 5.2 | Canada 2.4 | Belgium 0.7 | France* 5.5 | Finland 0.7 | Sweden 1.7 | Denmark 1.0 | Holland 2.2 | Norway 1.0

*Excluding flows to overseas departments and territories

EXPORTS In 1990 the value of world trade in merchandise was $3.5 trillion, according to the GATT. That was a rise of 13% over 1989. In volume terms trade expanded in 1990 by 5%, slower than the 7% in 1989; the GATT expected growth to slow again in 1991. The champion exporter of 1990 was Germany, with foreign sales of $421 billion, or 12.1% of the world total. America, number one in 1989, came second in 1990, with exports of $394 billion (11.4%). America yielded first place despite its exports rising 8.5% in volume terms, compared with a rise of only 1.5% for Germany; and it would still have done so even if unification, which added $22.5 billion to the exports of the former Federal Republic, had never happened. The reason was 1990's 16.5% rise in the D-mark against the dollar.

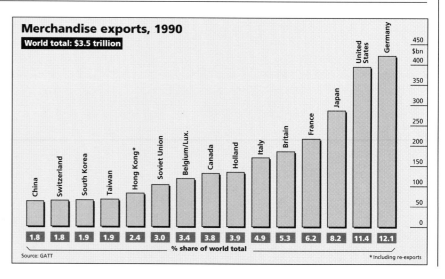

Merchandise exports, 1990
World total: $3.5 trillion

Source: GATT

China 1.8 | Switzerland 1.8 | South Korea 1.9 | Taiwan 1.9 | Hong Kong* 2.4 | Soviet Union 3.0 | Belgium/Lux. 3.4 | Canada 3.8 | Holland 3.9 | Italy 4.9 | Britain 5.3 | France 6.2 | Japan 8.2 | United States 11.4 | Germany 12.1

% share of world total

* Including re-exports

Exchange rates: trade-weighted

At the end of 1991, currencies in general were little changed from a year earlier. The members of the European exchange-rate mechanism (ERM) were particularly stable. During the year, however, the non-ERM currencies showed considerable movement. The dollar's trade-weighted index went from a low of 59.3 in February 1991 to a high of 68.7 in July 1991, thanks to post-Gulf war confidence and optimism about the end of the recession. Against the D-mark, the dollar hit a new all-time low in February 1991. The yen index strengthened sharply in the middle of the year and then stayed around 140, much the biggest increase of the currencies in the table from the base year of 1985. The sterling index ended the year down 3% from its level before ERM entry on October 8th 1990. The exchange-rate indices used are those calculated by the Bank of England and the Reserve Bank of Australia.

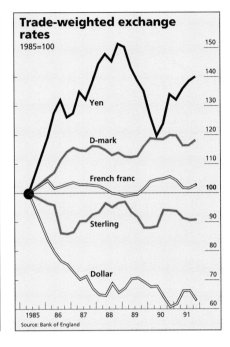

Trade-weighted exchange rates
1985=100

Source: Bank of England

CURRENCIES The best way to measure shifts in a country's exchange rate is to use its trade-weighted (or "effective") exchange rate. This is an index of the average of all its bilateral rates, weighted by the pattern of trade with other countries. For instance, other ERM currencies account for 72% of the French franc's trade-weighted basket, and the dollar accounts for 44% of the yen's. As ERM currencies are pegged to each other and account for a big part of each other's baskets, the stability of the trade-weighted values of the French franc and the D-mark compared with the dollar and the yen is no surprise. Despite its rally, the dollar's trade-weighted exchange rate ended 1991 still 40% lower than in 1985. The yen has been the strongest currency over the past six years: its trade-weighted index was 40% up on 1985 in December 1991. After a 20% fall in the 18 months to mid-1990 the yen's index recovered most of it in the next 18.

Trade-weighted exchange-rate indices, 1985=100

End month

		Australia	Belgium	Canada	France	Germany	Holland	Italy	Japan	Spain	Sweden	Switzerland	United Kingdom	United States
1990	Jan	88.3	109.9	102.4	103.6	118.7	114.5	100.3	129.3	104.8	94.0	108.8	89.0	67.0
	Feb	87.7	110.0	102.1	103.8	118.3	114.4	100.6	125.5	105.3	94.8	109.7	89.9	67.6
	Mar	88.9	111.1	104.5	105.0	119.1	114.8	101.4	118.5	105.9	95.3	109.6	87.9	68.6
	Apr	88.6	111.6	104.9	105.3	119.2	115.1	102.1	117.1	108.1	95.2	112.5	86.6	68.4
	May	89.5	111.1	103.8	103.7	118.0	114.1	100.7	122.3	109.0	94.6	114.5	89.0	67.8
	Jun	91.5	111.2	104.1	104.3	118.1	114.1	101.0	121.1	110.1	94.4	113.2	91.4	66.8
	Jul	89.7	111.5	104.8	104.9	118.7	114.4	101.7	122.7	110.5	93.8	113.8	94.1	64.3
	Aug	91.2	111.6	103.4	105.0	118.7	114.5	100.3	124.1	109.3	93.6	116.8	95.0	63.6
	Sep	91.5	111.5	103.0	105.4	118.9	114.6	99.5	129.1	108.8	93.4	116.9	93.3	62.9
	Oct	85.0	111.8	100.8	105.7	119.2	114.8	99.6	135.5	109.0	92.9	114.2	94.5	60.9
	Nov	84.5	112.1	101.3	105.5	120.2	115.5	100.1	131.0	108.5	92.8	114.8	94.0	61.2
	Dec	85.1	112.6	101.8	105.1	121.0	116.0	100.2	129.0	108.2	92.9	115.2	93.7	61.4
1991	Jan	85.4	112.7	101.1	104.9	120.7	115.9	100.4	132.0	110.1	93.1	115.2	94.2	60.6
	Feb	86.0	112.4	102.8	104.3	120.0	115.3	100.6	132.7	110.3	93.2	112.3	93.8	61.5
	Mar	88.7	110.4	104.6	102.3	116.9	113.1	98.7	132.0	108.1	93.7	112.1	92.4	66.3
	Apr	89.5	110.0	105.1	102.1	116.0	112.7	98.9	137.0	107.8	94.1	112.5	91.4	65.9
	May	86.9	110.1	106.0	101.9	116.2	112.8	98.7	135.9	107.7	94.2	111.5	91.2	66.4
	Jun	88.7	109.5	107.2	101.2	115.3	112.1	97.8	139.9	105.2	92.6	109.7	89.5	68.0
	Jul	89.3	110.2	105.4	101.8	116.5	112.9	98.2	137.6	106.5	93.1	108.8	90.9	66.8
	Aug	89.9	110.2	106.4	101.8	116.3	112.9	98.2	138.4	107.0	93.0	108.6	90.5	66.7
	Sep	90.0	111.0	106.2	102.4	117.7	113.8	98.9	138.9	106.4	93.5	110.0	91.1	64.3
	Oct	88.1	111.0	107.0	101.9	117.5	113.7	98.5	141.7	106.8	93.5	109.0	90.8	64.2
	Nov	87.7	111.6	105.6	102.9	118.7	114.5	98.9	140.8	106.6	94.5	109.4	90.6	63.5
	Dec	83.1	112.8	102.0	104.3	120.5	115.9	99.5	141.9	107.9	95.9	109.3	91.4	60.8

Currency units per $
End month

		Australia	Belgium	Canada	France	Germany	Holland	Italy	Japan	Spain	Sweden	Switzerland	United Kingdom	United States
1990	Jan	1.30	35.3	1.19	5.73	1.69	1.90	1253	145	109.0	6.14	1.50	0.59	na
	Feb	1.31	35.3	1.19	5.74	1.70	1.91	1253	149	109.0	6.11	1.49	0.59	na
	Mar	1.33	35.1	1.17	5.68	1.69	1.90	1243	157	109.0	6.12	1.49	0.61	na
	Apr	1.32	34.7	1.17	5.63	1.68	1.89	1230	159	106.0	6.10	1.45	0.61	na
	May	1.30	34.9	1.17	5.73	1.70	1.91	1250	153	105.0	6.13	1.43	0.59	na
	Jun	1.26	34.2	1.17	5.60	1.67	1.87	1223	152	102.0	6.03	1.42	0.57	na
	Jul	1.26	32.7	1.15	5.32	1.59	1.79	1162	146	97.6	5.81	1.35	0.53	na
	Aug	1.23	32.4	1.16	5.28	1.58	1.78	1169	144	98.2	5.79	1.31	0.53	na
	Sep	1.21	32.3	1.16	5.24	1.57	1.77	1172	138	98.0	5.76	1.30	0.53	na
	Oct	1.27	31.2	1.17	5.08	1.52	1.71	1136	130	95.0	5.63	1.29	0.51	na
	Nov	1.29	31.1	1.17	5.07	1.50	1.69	1127	133	95.4	5.60	1.28	0.51	na
	Dec	1.30	31.0	1.16	5.09	1.50	1.69	1128	136	95.6	5.63	1.28	0.52	na
1991	Jan	1.28	30.5	1.16	5.03	1.48	1.67	1112	131	92.8	5.54	1.26	0.51	na
	Feb	1.27	31.4	1.15	5.20	1.53	1.72	1140	133	95.1	5.66	1.33	0.52	na
	Mar	1.29	35.2	1.16	5.78	1.71	1.92	1269	141	106.0	6.17	1.46	0.57	na
	Apr	1.28	35.3	1.15	5.80	1.72	1.93	1270	136	106.0	6.20	1.45	0.58	na
	May	1.32	35.7	1.15	5.90	1.74	1.96	1291	138	107.0	6.23	1.48	0.59	na
	Jun	1.30	37.3	1.14	6.15	1.81	2.04	1348	138	114.0	6.55	1.56	0.61	na
	Jul	1.28	36.0	1.15	5.94	1.75	1.97	1302	137	109.0	6.34	1.53	0.59	na
	Aug	1.27	36.0	1.14	5.94	1.75	1.97	1304	137	109.0	6.34	1.53	0.59	na
	Sep	1.25	34.3	1.13	5.66	1.66	1.87	1244	133	105.0	6.07	1.45	0.57	na
	Oct	1.29	34.4	1.12	5.70	1.69	1.88	1250	131	105.0	6.10	1.47	0.57	na
	Nov	1.28	33.6	1.14	5.55	1.63	1.83	1225	130	103.0	5.96	1.44	0.56	na
	Dec	1.32	31.3	1.17	5.18	1.52	1.71	1149	125	96.7	5.54	1.36	0.53	na

Currency units per £ End month

		Australia	Belgium	Canada	France	Germany	Holland	Italy	Japan	Spain	Sweden	Switzerland	United Kingdom	United States
1990	Jan	2.19	59.3	1.99	9.63	2.83	3.19	2105	243	183	10.3	2.52	na	1.68
	Feb	2.21	59.7	2.01	9.70	2.87	3.22	2118	252	184	10.3	2.52	na	1.69
	Mar	2.18	57.8	1.93	9.35	2.78	3.13	2047	259	178	10.1	2.46	na	1.65
	Apr	2.18	56.8	1.91	9.23	2.75	2.09	2016	260	173	10.0	2.38	na	1.64
	May	2.18	58.5	1.97	9.61	2.85	3.21	2095	256	176	10.3	2.40	na	1.68
	Jun	2.20	59.7	2.03	9.76	2.90	3.27	2133	266	178	10.5	2.47	na	1.74
	Jul	2.35	60.8	2.15	9.90	2.95	3.33	2162	272	181	10.8	2.51	na	1.86
	Aug	2.32	61.3	2.18	10.00	2.98	3.36	2212	272	185	11.0	2.47	na	1.89
	Sep	2.26	60.4	2.16	9.82	2.93	3.31	2196	259	183	10.8	2.43	na	1.87
	Oct	2.48	60.7	2.27	9.86	2.94	3.32	2208	253	184	10.9	2.50	na	1.94
	Nov	2.50	60.3	2.26	9.83	2.91	3.28	2186	258	185	10.9	2.48	na	1.94
	Dec	2.50	59.8	2.24	9.82	2.88	3.25	2177	262	184	10.9	2.46	na	1.93
1991	Jan	2.51	60.0	2.29	9.88	2.90	3.27	2185	258	182	10.9	2.47	na	1.96
	Feb	2.44	59.9	2.20	9.92	2.92	3.28	2177	254	181	10.8	2.53	na	1.91
	Mar	2.24	61.2	2.01	10.00	2.96	3.34	2207	246	183	10.7	2.53	na	1.74
	Apr	2.20	60.9	1.99	10.00	2.96	3.33	2190	235	183	10.7	2.50	na	1.72
	May	2.25	60.6	1.95	10.00	2.95	3.33	2193	235	182	10.6	2.52	na	1.70
	Jun	2.11	60.4	1.85	9.95	2.94	3.31	2183	223	184	10.6	2.52	na	1.62
	Jul	2.17	60.6	1.94	10.00	2.94	3.31	2194	232	184	10.7	2.57	na	1.68
	Aug	2.14	60.5	1.92	9.98	2.94	3.31	2192	230	183	10.7	2.57	na	1.68
	Sep	2.19	60.0	1.98	9.92	2.91	3.28	2180	233	184	10.6	2.54	na	1.75
	Oct	2.24	60.0	1.96	9.94	2.90	3.27	2178	228	183	10.6	2.55	na	1.74
	Nov	2.25	59.3	2.00	9.80	2.87	3.23	2162	230	183	10.5	2.53	na	1.76
	Dec	2.46	58.5	2.16	9.70	2.84	3.20	2149	234	181	10.4	2.54	na	1.87

Exchange rates: SDR and ecu

Currency units per SDR End month

		Australia	Belgium	Canada	France	Germany	Holland	Italy	Japan	Spain	Sweden	Switzerland	United Kingdom	United States
1990	Jan	1.72	45.7	1.57	7.58	2.23	2.52	1661	191	144	8.16	1.98	0.79	1.33
	Feb	1.73	46.4	1.57	7.54	2.23	2.51	1646	195	143	8.06	1.96	0.78	1.32
	Mar	1.73	45.6	1.52	7.41	2.20	2.48	1625	204	141	7.97	1.95	0.79	1.30
	Apr	1.64	45.2	1.52	7.34	2.19	2.47	1604	208	138	7.95	1.9	0.80	1.30
	May	1.71	45.7	1.54	7.48	2.22	2.50	1632	199	138	8.00	1.87	0.78	1.31
	Jun	1.68	45.5	1.54	7.43	2.21	2.49	1623	202	136	8.00	1.88	0.76	1.32
	Jul	1.73	44.8	1.57	7.33	2.18	2.45	1594	201	134	8.00	1.85	0.74	1.37
	Aug	1.70	44.5	1.60	7.27	2.17	2.44	1607	200	135	7.98	1.79	0.73	1.39
	Sep	1.69	44.9	1.61	7.29	2.18	2.46	1630	192	136	8.03	1.81	0.74	1.39
	Oct	1.82	44.7	1.67	7.28	2.17	2.45	1629	185	136	8.07	1.84	0.74	1.43
	Nov	1.84	44.4	1.66	7.25	2.15	2.42	1612	190	136	8.04	1.83	0.74	1.43
	Dec	1.84	44.1	1.65	7.30	2.13	2.40	1608	191	138	8.11	1.84	0.74	1.42
1991	Jan	1.83	43.8	1.67	7.24	2.14	2.40	1604	188	134	7.97	1.82	0.73	1.43
	Feb	1.81	44.4	1.63	7.35	2.16	2.43	1615	188	135	8.01	1.87	0.74	1.42
	Mar	1.74	47.5	1.56	7.83	2.31	2.60	1706	190	143	8.20	1.97	0.78	1.35
	Apr	1.72	47.8	1.54	7.85	2.32	2.68	1717	184	143	8.31	1.96	0.79	1.34
	May	1.76	47.6	1.54	7.84	2.31	2.61	1718	185	143	8.29	1.97	0.78	1.34
	Jun	1.71	49.1	1.50	8.08	2.38	2.68	1772	181	149	8.60	2.05	0.81	1.31
	Jul	1.72	48.0	1.54	7.92	2.33	2.63	1740	184	146	8.45	2.03	0.79	1.33
	Aug	1.70	46.9	1.53	7.91	2.33	2.62	1738	183	145	8.45	2.04	0.79	1.34
	Sep	1.71	46.9	1.55	7.75	2.28	2.56	1704	182	144	8.30	1.98	0.78	1.37
	Oct	1.74	47.2	1.54	7.82	2.29	2.58	1713	179	144	8.34	2.01	0.78	1.37
	Nov	1.77	46.0	1.58	7.64	2.23	2.52	1686	180	142	8.18	1.98	0.78	1.39
	Dec	1.88	44.7	1.65	7.41	2.17	2.45	1647	179	138	7.91	1.93	0.76	1.43

Currency units per ecu End month

		Australia	Belgium	Canada	France	Germany	Holland	Italy	Japan	Spain	Sweden	Switzerland	United Kingdom	United States
1990	Jan	1.58	42.7	1.44	6.93	2.04	2.30	1515	175	132	7.44	1.82	0.72	1.21
	Feb	1.59	42.6	1.44	6.92	2.05	2.30	1512	180	132	7.40	1.80	0.72	1.21
	Mar	1.60	42.3	1.41	6.88	2.05	2.30	1505	190	131	7.39	1.80	0.73	1.21
	Apr	1.61	42.2	1.42	6.87	2.06	2.30	1500	193	129	7.42	1.77	0.74	1.22
	May	1.58	42.3	1.43	6.92	2.05	2.32	1511	185	128	7.44	1.74	0.72	1.21
	Jun	1.56	42.4	1.44	6.93	2.06	2.32	1514	188	126	7.45	1.75	0.71	1.23
	Jul	1.64	42.5	1.50	6.93	2.07	2.34	1514	189	127	7.53	1.75	0.70	1.30
	Aug	1.62	42.5	1.52	6.92	2.06	2.33	1531	190	129	7.62	1.72	0.70	1.32
	Sep	1.59	42.4	1.52	6.89	2.06	2.33	1541	182	129	7.58	1.71	0.70	1.32
	Oct	1.73	42.4	1.58	6.90	2.06	2.34	1544	176	129	7.64	1.75	0.70	1.36
	Nov	1.76	42.4	1.59	6.92	2.05	2.32	1540	182	130	7.64	1.74	0.70	1.36
	Dec	1.77	42.2	1.58	6.95	2.04	2.31	1540	185	130	7.67	1.74	0.71	1.36
1991	Jan	1.77	42.2	1.61	6.96	2.05	2.32	1539	182	128	7.66	1.74	0.70	1.38
	Feb	1.72	42.2	1.55	6.98	2.05	2.32	1538	180	128	7.64	1.79	0.70	1.35
	Mar	1.55	42.4	1.39	6.98	2.06	2.32	1532	181	127	7.40	1.75	0.69	1.20
	Apr	1.53	42.4	1.37	6.96	2.06	2.32	1524	162	126	7.37	1.72	0.70	1.19
	May	1.57	42.3	1.37	6.98	2.06	2.32	1527	165	128	7.42	1.77	0.70	1.19
	Jun	1.48	42.3	1.30	6.96	2.05	2.32	1529	156	129	7.43	1.77	0.70	1.13
	Jul	1.51	42.3	1.36	6.98	2.05	2.32	1532	162	129	7.46	1.80	0.70	1.18
	Aug	1.50	42.3	1.34	6.98	2.05	2.31	1533	161	128	7.45	1.80	0.70	1.18
	Sep	1.54	42.2	1.39	6.98	2.05	2.31	1531	164	130	7.48	1.78	0.70	1.23
	Oct	1.57	42.1	1.37	6.99	2.05	2.31	1533	159	129	7.45	1.79	0.70	1.22
	Nov	1.60	42.0	1.42	6.99	2.03	2.29	1530	162	130	7.44	1.79	0.71	1.25
	Dec	1.76	41.9	1.55	6.95	2.04	2.29	1542	169	130	7.45	1.82	0.72	1.34

NORWAY Oil is still the key to Norway's economy, despite attempts to reduce its dependence. Higher oil prices pushed Norway's current-account surplus to $2.8 billion in 1990, from rough balance in 1989 and a deficit of $3.7 billion in 1988. GDP growth slowed in 1990, to 3.0% from 5.0% in 1989. In its February 1991 survey of Norway, the OECD forecast growth of 3.2% in 1991, above the OECD average for the third successive year. Despite strong growth, unemployment rose from 2.0% of the workforce in 1986 to 5.3% in 1990, but stayed below the OECD average. A looser fiscal policy should help to reduce the jobless total. Inflation, at 4.1%, dipped beneath the OECD average in 1990 for the first time in ten years. But if domestic demand remains strong, inflation may rise again.

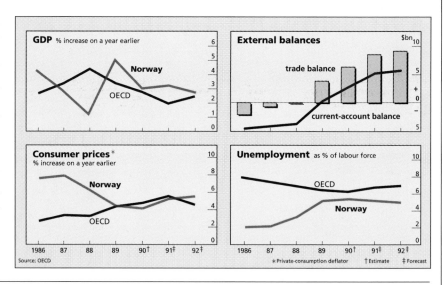

TURKEY The adverse effects of the Gulf crisis gave Turkey's economic reforms a severe test in 1990, as its budget and external deficits worsened. In March 1991 the OECD's report on Turkey said that reducing its huge public-sector deficit (nearly 10% of GNP) should be the government's priority. A fiscal boost in mid-1989 pushed real GNP growth to 7.6% in 1990, up from 1.7% in 1989, but it was forecast to slow to 3.5% in 1991. Inflation slowed to 60% in 1990, from 72% in 1989, but this was still by far the highest rate in the OECD. After two years of surplus, the Gulf crisis and a stronger lira pushed the current account into a deficit of $2 billion in 1990. The OECD expects the deficit to remain large. Turkish unemployment (10.2% in 1990) was also well above the OECD average.

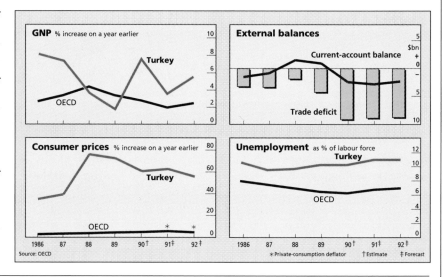

AUSTRIA In recent years the Austrian economy has outperformed most other industrial economies. In 1989 and 1990 its real GDP growth of 4-4.5% a year was well ahead of the OECD average and its unemployment rate was only 3.3%, yet its inflation rate remained lower than the industrial countries' average and the current account of its balance of payments moved into surplus. In March 1991 the OECD forecast that Austria's growth would slow to 2.9% in 1991 and 1992, still ahead of most other countries—thanks mainly to strong import demand from Germany, its biggest trade partner. Austria has been successful despite having one of the most regulated OECD economies. Nevertheless, the Austrian government is urged to hasten deregulation to help sustain success.

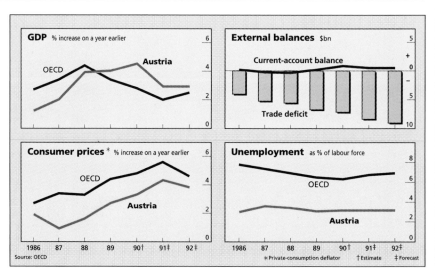

PORTUGAL Despite relatively tight fiscal and monetary policies, Portugal's economy is still overheated. In 1990 GDP growth eased back to 3.9%, still well above the OECD average of 2.8%. In January 1991 the OECD's seers predicted that growth would remain buoyant in both 1991 and 1992. Inflation had soared: in 1990 consumer prices rose by 13.3%; in 1991 they were expected to moderate a little but still remain roughly double the OECD average. Unemployment, at 5.1% of the workforce in 1990, is likely to remain below the OECD average. The OECD's forecasters expect Portugal's visible-trade deficit to increase from $7 billion in 1990 to $10 billion in 1992. Its current-account deficit is also forecast to rise, from 2% of its GDP in 1990 to 3.1% in 1991.

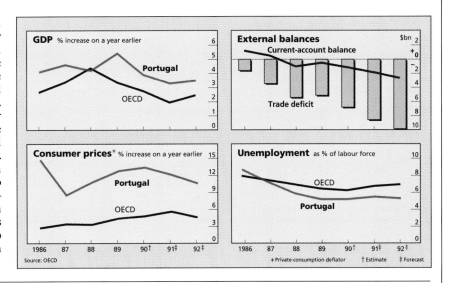

IRELAND The Irish economy has achieved an impressive hat-trick in recent years: strong growth (real GDP grew by an average of 5% in 1989 and 1990); low inflation (less than 3%); and a current-account surplus. The black spot is its unemployment rate of 14%, which is more than double the OECD average. The Irish government has reduced its borrowing requirement from 19% of GDP in 1980-84 to 3% of GDP in 1990. Its public debt has fallen to 111% of GDP from a peak of 131% in 1987, but this is still the second highest (behind Belgium) of any industrial economy. The OECD, in its review of Ireland in May 1991, forecast that growth would fall by more than half in 1991, to 2.2%; and it worried that the government's hard-headed policies were going soft.

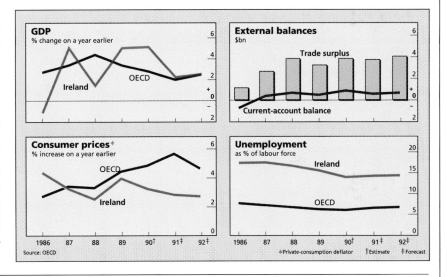

GREECE After years of political and economic troubles, Greece has started to recover, the OECD reported in June 1991. The election of a single-party New Democracy government in April 1990, after three general elections and a period of weak coalition government, made possible a serious anti-inflationary policy. Inflation, at worrying levels throughout the 1980s, reached 20% in 1990 (the OECD's average was 4.8%); it was forecast to fall to 17.8% in 1991 and 13.2% in 1992. Greece's visible-trade deficit, which rose to $12.3 billion in 1990, was also expected to shrink, to $10 billion in 1991. GDP growth, which averaged less than 0.5% in 1990 and 1991, should pick up to 1.4% in 1992—still below the OECD average. But unemployment will rise, from 7.7% in 1990 to 10% in 1992.

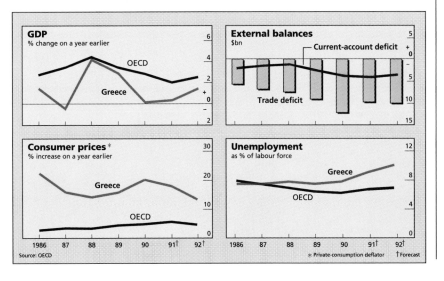

Foreign reserves

Official foreign reserves are roughly equivalent to a nation's bank balance. They consist of foreign currencies, special drawing rights (SDRS) and the country's reserve position in the International Monetary Fund. The source for the figures in the table is the IMF, so the basis of calculation for each country is the same. Gold is not included: holdings often remain unchanged for years though the market value will vary with the price of gold. The United States, for example, has a massive 262m ounces of gold. Changes in reserves can reflect a country's underlying trading problems or the amount of official intervention in the currency markets. Japan's huge lead of $17 billion over the United States at the beginning of 1990 shrank to less than $7 billion in October 1991. Sweden's reserves showed one of the biggest increases: from $10 billion in January 1990 to $18 billion in September 1991. Spain's reserves rose to 49%.

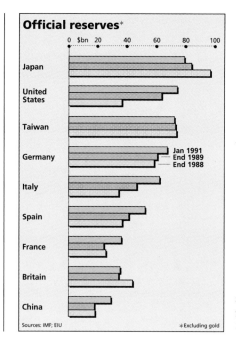

Official reserves*

Japan
United States
Taiwan
Germany
Italy
Spain
France
Britain
China

Jan 1991
End 1989
End 1988

Sources: IMF; EIU   *Excluding gold

FOREIGN RESERVES Japan boasted the world's biggest official foreign reserves at the end of January 1991, with some $79 billion-worth (including foreign currency, SDRS and its reserve position at the IMF, but excluding gold). But Japan's reserves had fallen by almost a fifth since the end of 1988 as the Bank of Japan tried to support the yen. Over the same period America's reserves doubled to $74 billion, putting it in second place; back in 1988 it was in only sixth place with $36.7 billion, barely a third of Japan's reserves then. All the European countries in the chart except Britain had fatter official reserves in January 1991 than in 1988; their growth did not match America's but Italy managed a strong 80% increase. In third place was Taiwan, the developing country with the largest foreign reserves, though they had shrunk slightly since the end of 1988. China's reserves grew strongly during 1990, pulling it into ninth place.

Official foreign reserves, $bn

End month

		Australia	Belgium	Canada	France	Germany	Holland	Italy	Japan	Spain	Sweden	Switzerland	United Kingdom	United States
1990	Jan	13.5	10.9	14.9	24.3	60.8	16.5	48.4	81.8	41.1	10.1	22.0	34.6	64.4
	Feb	13.3	10.9	12.9	24.8	61.9	17.0	48.2	80.4	41.2	9.8	21.8	34.6	63.1
	Mar	12.8	10.9	13.8	25.4	61.5	16.8	51.4	73.5	41.0	10.7	22.6	34.1	65.2
	Apr	12.5	10.8	14.2	28.1	61.6	17.0	53.0	73.3	41.6	13.0	22.2	34.0	65.2
	May	14.3	10.9	13.2	28.0	62.6	17.2	58.4	73.8	42.3	12.7	23.0	33.8	66.0
	Jun	14.5	11.8	13.9	28.6	63.5	17.0	64.0	74.1	43.0	12.7	24.0	34.2	66.2
	Jul	14.7	11.3	15.3	28.4	62.5	16.9	67.7	75.3	47.4	12.9	23.7	35.0	66.8
	Aug	14.7	11.6	17.7	28.6	63.7	17.2	69.5	76.1	47.8	12.1	24.9	35.7	67.8
	Sep	15.2	11.6	17.5	31.9	64.4	17.3	69.0	76.3	48.4	12.6	25.0	35.7	69.0
	Oct	15.6	12.1	17.4	34.3	66.0	17.7	68.7	77.3	50.0	15.7	24.6	35.9	71.8
	Nov	15.5	12.2	17.7	36.3	67.1	17.6	64.3	77.7	51.0	18.4	25.6	35.7	72.0
	Dec	16.3	12.2	17.8	36.8	67.9	17.5	62.9	78.5	51.2	18.0	29.2	35.9	72.3
1991	Jan	16.1	12.0	18.1	35.8	68.2	17.9	62.4	79.1	53.0	20.8	26.0	36.1	74.0
	Feb	16.2	12.0	16.8	36.3	66.4	17.6	62.8	79.5	53.0	20.3	26.0	39.1	71.7
	Mar	15.5	10.5	17.0	36.1	59.1	17.0	61.1	72.8	51.6	18.2	26.6	37.3	66.9
	Apr	15.6	10.5	15.8	35.2	59.7	16.0	59.5	70.8	54.5	17.6	25.3	38.5	67.2
	May	16.3	10.6	17.2	34.2	60.5	16.3	57.3	71.1	58.3	20.9	25.4	38.5	67.2
	Jun	15.5	10.1	16.5	32.0	57.7	15.8	54.4	70.7	57.4	21.0	25.1	38.2	63.9
	Jul	15.7	10.6	16.7	33.3	59.5	16.5	55.4	70.4	59.8	20.2	24.3	39.3	63.8
	Aug	15.7	10.7	16.1	33.5	60.2	16.3	54.7	69.8	60.6	18.3	24.9	39.3	62.5
	Sep	16.2	11.2	18.1	34.5	61.2	16.8	57.0	69.9	61.9	18.1	25.5	40.4	63.7
	Oct	16.2	–	16.9	–	60.4	16.6	53.9	70.1	61.3	–	25.6	39.9	63.5
	Nov	–	–	–	–	–	–	–	–	–	–	–	–	–
	Dec	–	–	–	–	–	–	–	–	–	–	–	–	–

THE ECONOMIST'S EDITORIAL STAFF

Susannah Amoore, *managing editor*

John Andrews, *Asia editor*

Amanda Attersley, *editorial assistant*

Robert Banbury, *reprographic manager*

Carol Banks, *editorial assistant*

Graham Bayfield, *editorial systems supervisor*

Jenny Bielenberg, *assistant to the editor*

Matthew Bishop, *economics journalist*

David Bradshaw, *foreign affairs journalist*

Andrew Bristow, *pre-press technician*

John Browning, *computers correspondent*

Ian Cable, *pre-press technician*

Frances Cairncross, *environment editor*

Duncan Campbell-Smith, *Britain editor*

Edward Carr, *resources/trade correspondent*

Geoffrey Carr, *science journalist*

Jonathan Carr, *Bonn correspondent*

Nicholas Colchester, *deputy editor*

Liz Conway, *cartographer*

Fiona Cooper, *researcher*

Una Corrigan, *senior designer*

Chris Coulman, *statistician*

Andrew Cowley, *South-East Asia correspondent*

Clive Crook, *economics editor*

Roland Dallas, *foreign affairs journalist*

Peter David, *international editor*

Muriel Davis, *New York office manager*

Graham Douglas, *cartographer*

Marsh Dunbar, *editorial assistant*

Emma Duncan, *Britain journalist*

Celina Dunlop, *picture editor*

Michael Elliott, *Washington bureau chief*

Miranda Ellis, *editorial assistant*

Bill Emmott, *business affairs editor*

Peter Farren, *head of publishing systems*

Edmund Fawcett, *foreign affairs journalist*

Daniel Franklin, *Europe editor*

Penny Garrett, *head of design department*

Martin Giles, *European business correspondent*

Anthony Gottlieb, *surveys editor*

Charles Grant, *Brussels correspondent*

Jean Greaves, *telex room supervisor*

John Grimond, *foreign editor*

Peter Haynes, *management correspondent*

John Heilemann, *media/entertainment correspondent*

Peter Holden, *deputy head of research*

Carol Howard, *head of research*

Stephen Hugh-Jones, *special features editor*

Ian Jones, *pre-press supervisor*

Anita Lawrence, *pagination co-ordinator*

Judith Liverman, *editorial assistant*

Suzy Lyttle, *graphic designer*

Paul Maidment, *New York finance correspondent*

Sebastian Mallaby, *finance journalist*

David Manasian, *business editor*

Liz Mann, *statistician*

Paul Markillie, *transport correspondent*

Andrew Marr, *political editor*

Carol Mawer, *letters editor*

David McKelvey, *research assistant*

John Micklethwait, *Los Angeles correspondent*

Andrew Mitchell, *pre-press technician*

Pauline Molyneux, *editorial systems manager*

Edwina Moreton, *diplomatic editor*

Oliver Morton, *science editor*

Virginia O'Riordan, *deputy editorial systems manager*

Hiroko Ofuchi, *Tokyo office manager*

John Parker, *Moscow correspondent*

Sophie Pedder, *Britain journalist*

John Peet, *finance journalist*

Rupert Pennant-Rea, *editor*

Keith Potter, *researcher*

Sara Pritchard, *senior statistician*

Gideon Rachman, *America journalist*

Anna Reid, *telecoms correspondent*

Krysia Rejt, *senior designer*

Matt Ridley, *America editor*

Caroline Robinson, *editorial assistant*

Jim Rohwer, *Asia correspondent*

Chris Rowles, *pre-press technician*

Yvonne Ryan, *picture researcher*

Craig Santus, *cartographer*

Roy Saunders, *publishing systems manager*

Tom Scott, *pre-press production manager*

Barbara Smith, *foreign affairs journalist*

Peter Sonderskov, *cartographer*

Merril Stevenson, *finance editor*

Ruth Taylor, *cartographer*

Tony Thomas, *American business correspondent*

Ian Troy, *process technician*

Brooke Unger, *banking correspondent*

Nick Valery, *Tokyo bureau chief*

Avril Walker, *Washington office manager*

Anna Wolek, *researcher*

Chris Wood, *Tokyo finance correspondent*

Pam Woodall, *economics journalist*

Adrian Wooldridge, *Britain journalist*

Ann Wroe, *books & arts editor*

Alex Wyke, *drugs/chemicals correspondent*

Dominic Ziegler, *Washington correspondent*